Gravesite of Sarah, the mother of Israel ben Eliezer, the Ba'al Shem Tov.
Photo courtesy of Douglas Hykle, Tluste/Tovste, www.tovste.info.

Translator's footnote: The original headstone was erected by the Ba'al Shem Tov's grandson. This replica was erected in 2009 (5769) by the council of "Ohalei Tzadikim" ("Tents of the Righteous") led by the Hasidic rabbi Meir Gabay.

Memorial Book of Tluste
(Tovste, Ukraine)

Translation from *Sefer Tluste*

Original Yizkor Book edited by: Gavriel Lindenberg
Published in Tel Aviv, 1965
By the Tluste Association of Former Residents in Israel and the
United States
(Hebrew and Yiddish, 520 pages).

Postcard view of Tluste Marketplace, c. 1901, showing old St. Anne Catholic Church at right and Spitzer building materials store at left. Photo courtesy of Douglas Hykle, Tluste/Tovste, www.tovste.info.

Published by JewishGen

**An Affiliate of the Museum of Jewish Heritage—A Living Memorial to the Holocaust
New York**

Ogólny widok Tłustego — Totalansicht von Tluste

Postcard view of Tluste showing the Marketplace. Postcard printed by K. Langholz, 1910. Image courtesy of Douglas Hykle, Tluste/Tovste, www.tovste.info.

Memorial Book of Tluste
Translation from *Sefer Tluste*

First Printing: January 2020, Tevet 5780

Translators: Sara Mages, Yael Chaver, David Horowitz-Larochette
Editor of the English Version: Douglas Hykle
Layout: Donni Magid
Cover Design: Nina Schwartz, artstop@impulsegraphics.com

Published by JewishGen, Inc.
An Affiliate of the Museum of Jewish Heritage
A Living Memorial to the Holocaust
36 Battery Place, New York, NY 10280

JewishGen, Inc. is not responsible for inaccuracies or omissions in the original work and makes no representations regarding the accuracy of this translation. Digital images of the original book's contents can be seen online at the New York Public Library website.

The mission of the JewishGen organization is to produce a translation of the original work, and we cannot verify the accuracy of statements or alter facts cited.

Printed in the United States of America by Lightning Source, Inc.

Library of Congress Control Number (LCCN): 2019948430
ISBN: 978-1-939561-86-2 (hard cover: 586 pages, alk. paper)

Front cover photo: The Jewish cemetery in Tovste, 2017.
Photo courtesy of Douglas Hykle, Tluste/Tovste, www.tovste.info.
Back cover photo: Aerial view of Tovste, 2016. Courtesy of Iryna Pustynnikova, Castles and Temples of Ukraine, www.castles.com.ua.

JewishGen and the Yizkor Books in Print Project

This book has been published by the **Yizkor Books in Print Project**, as part of the **Yizkor Book Project** of JewishGen, Inc.

JewishGen, Inc. is a non-profit organization founded in 1987 as a resource for Jewish genealogy. Its website [www.jewishgen.org] serves as an international clearinghouse and resource center to assist individuals who are researching the history of their Jewish families and the places where they lived. JewishGen provides databases, facilitates discussion groups, and coordinates projects relating to Jewish genealogy and the history of the Jewish people. In 2003, JewishGen became an affiliate of the **Museum of Jewish Heritage—A Living Memorial to the Holocaust** in New York.

The **JewishGen Yizkor Book Project** was organized to make more widely known the existence of Yizkor (Memorial) Books written by survivors and former residents of various Jewish communities throughout the world. Later, volunteers connected to the different destroyed communities began cooperating to have these books translated from the original language—usually Hebrew or Yiddish—into English, thus enabling a wider audience to have access to the valuable information contained within them. As each chapter of these books was translated, it was posted on the JewishGen website and made available to the general public.

The **Yizkor Books in Print Project** began in 2011 as an initiative to print and publish Yizkor Books that had been fully translated, so that hard copies would be available for purchase by the descendants of these communities and also by scholars, universities, synagogues, libraries, and museums.

These Yizkor books have been produced almost entirely through the volunteer effort of researchers from around the world, assisted by donations from private individuals. The books are printed and sold at near cost, so as to make them as affordable as possible. Our goal is to make this important genre of Jewish literature and history available in English in book form, so that people can have the personal histories of their ancestral towns on their bookshelves for themselves and for their children and grandchildren.

A list of all published translated Yizkor Books in the project with prices and ordering information can be found at:
http://www.jewishgen.org/Yizkor/ybip.html

Binny Lewis, Yizkor Book Project Manager
Joel Alpert, Yizkor-Book-in-Print Project Coordinator

JewishGen
Yizkor Book Project

This book is presented by the
Yizkor Books in Print Project
Project Coordinator: Joel Alpert

Part of the
Yizkor Books Project of JewishGen, Inc.
Project Manager: Lance Ackerfeld

These books have been produced solely through volunteer effort
of individuals from around the world. The books are printed and
sold at near cost, so as to make them as affordable as possible.

Our goal is to make this history and important genre of Jewish
literature available in English in book form so that people can have
the near-personal histories of their ancestral towns on their bookshelves for themselves and for their children and grandchildren.

Any donations to the Yizkor Books Project are appreciated.

Please send donations to:
Yizkor Book Project
JewishGen
36 Battery Place
New York, NY 10280

JewishGen, Inc. is an affiliate of the
Museum of Jewish Heritage
A Living Memorial to the Holocaust

Acknowledgements

Many thanks to Sara Mages for voluntarily translating all the Hebrew articles in this book and to Douglas Hykle for his meticulous editing of these translations.

History of Tluste

Prior to World War II, Tluste (now Tovste, Ukraine) was a flourishing Polish market town with a Jewish presence dating back to the 1700s. Over the next two centuries, Jews came to comprise two-thirds of the population. Tluste is famously associated with the Ba'al Shem Tov, the spiritual founder of Hassidism, who grew up here.

A relatively peaceful co-existence among the Jewish, Ukrainian and Polish communities was disrupted, first by the Soviet occupation of 1939, then by the Nazi German invasion of 1941. During the war years, Tluste and   its vicinity became an important transit point and congregation center for Jews fleeing persecution from other towns and villages. While thousands of Jews perished in the town, particularly in targeted mass killings, many survived in nearby agricultural labor camps and in hiding. The original Hebrew and Yiddish contributions to *Sefer Tluste* shed light on the destruction of the Jewish community, and tell the stories of those who survived it. The 1965 book also documented in rich detail the Jewish way of life in former Tluste, with its cultural traditions and social institutions. The recent testimony of former residents and survivors complements these precious historical accounts.

Notes to the Reader:

We apologize ahead of time for the poor quality of images in the book. Often these images had been scanned from the original Yizkor books which were of poor quality to begin with, being copies of old photographs. Each transfer results in loss of quality. We have done the best we could, given the original material and the resources and technology at hand. Even though images often appear of higher quality on computer screens, that does not transfer to high quality images in print. A reader can view the original scans on the web sites listed below.

Within the text the reader will note "{34}" standing ahead of a paragraph. This indicates that the material translated below was on page 34 of the original book. However, when a paragraph was split between two pages in the original book, the marker is placed in this book after the end of the paragraph for ease of reading.

Also please note that all references within the text of the book to page numbers, refer to the page numbers of the original Yizkor Book.

The original book can be seen online at the New York Public Library site:
https://digitalcollections.nypl.org/items/014d6ae0-2fea-0133-c8c0-58d385a7b928

or at the Yiddish Book Center web site:
https://www.yiddishbookcenter.org/search/collection?search_api_views_fulltext=tluste&Submit+search=&restrict=

In order to obtain a list of all Shoah victims from the town, the reader should access the Yad Vashem web site listed below; one can also search for specific family names using family name option. These lists are continually updated by Yad Vashem, so it is worthwhile to periodically search these lists.

There is much valuable information available on this web site, including the Pages of Testimony, etc.
http://yvng.yadvashem.org

A list of this book and all books available in the Yizkor-Book-In-Print Project along with prices is available at:
http://www.jewishgen.org/Yizkor/ybip.html

1913 Polish map "Jagielnica und Czernelica" showing Tluste City (Miasto) and Village (Wies). Courtesy of Topographic Maps of Eastern Europe, easteuropetopo.org.

Geopolitical Information:

Located at 48°51' N 25°44' E

Situated 240 miles WSW of Kyyiv, 50 miles S of Ternopil (Tarnopol),
46 miles E of Ivano-Frankivsk (Stanislawów).

Alternate names for the town are: Tovste [Ukr], Tluste [Pol], Toist [Yid], Tolstoye [Rus], Tlusta [Yid], Tluste Miasto, Tluste Myasto, Toyst, Tolste, Tolstoya

	Town	District	Province	Country
Before WWI (c. 1900):	Tluste	Zaleszczyki	Galicia	Austrian Empire
Between the wars (c. 1930):	Tluste Miasto	Zaleszczyki	Tarnopol	Poland
After WWII (c. 1950):	Tolstoye			Soviet Union
Today (c. 2000):	Tovste			Ukraine

Notes: Ukrainian: Товсте. Yiddish: טלוסטא / טויסט. Russian: Толстое.
Hebrew: טלוסטה

Jewish Population 2,157 (in 1880), 1,196 (in 1921)

Nearby Jewish Communities:

- Bil'che-Zolote 8 miles SE
- Ustechko 8 miles SW
- Potochyshche 10 miles SW
- Ozeryany 10 miles ENE
- Palashëvka 11 miles NW
- Chortkiv 12 miles NNE
- Lanivtsi 12 miles E
- Horishnya Vyhnanka 13 miles NNE
- Zalishchyky 14 miles S
- Chernelytsya 14 miles W
- Oliyevo-Koralivka 14 miles SE
- Borshchiv 15 miles ESE
- Yazlovets 16 miles WNW
- Horodenka 17 miles SW
- Losyach 17 miles ENE
- Tsyhany 17 miles E
- Probezhna 17 miles NE
- Vasyliv 18 miles SSE
- Yaseniv-Pilnyy 18 miles SSW
- Zolotyy Potik 18 miles WNW
- Chernyatyn 18 miles SW
- Sokolov 19 miles WNW
- Kopychyntsi 20 miles NNE
- Tyshkivtsi 20 miles WSW
- Doroshivtsi 20 miles SSE
- Verkhneye Krivche 20 miles ESE
- Sukhostav 20 miles NNE
- Tovtry 20 miles SSE
- Skala-Podilska 21 miles E
- Yabloniv 22 miles NNE
- Budaniv 22 miles N
- Buchach 22 miles NW
- Vasyl'kivtsi 22 miles NE
- Vikno 22 miles SSE
- Chortovets 23 miles WSW
- Ustya 23 miles SE
- Zastavna 24 miles SSE

POLAND

BELARUS

RUSSIA

SLOVAKIA

Tovste

● KIEV

DNIEPER RIVER

HUNGARY

● DNIPRO

MOLDOVA

ROMANIA

ODESSA

MARIUPOL ●

MAP OF UKRAINE IN 2014

SEVASTOPOL ●

xii

Hebrew Title Page of Original Yizkor Book

ספר טלוסטה

חערוך : גבריאל לינדנברג
הוצאת אירגון יוצאי טלוסטה והסביבה
בישראל ובארצות הברית
תשכ"ו • 1965

Translation of the Title Page of Original Hebrew Book

Book of Tluste

Editor: Gavriel Lindenberg
Published by the organization of former residents of Tluste and surrounding areas
In Israel and the United States
1965 * 5726

Table of Contents

xvi

Personalities and Figures

Introduction to the Book

[Page 7 - Hebrew] [Page 12 - Yiddish]

Oh, Tluste my tiny little town
(*From a ballad by Shimshon Meltzer: "Meir the musician became a commissar"*)

by Shimshon Meltzer

Woe Tluste, my tiny little town
Woe, that you fell at the hand of a conqueror,
without a crying telegram, without
knowing if you were sentenced to fire or bombs.

Kotov and Kitev were mentioned a lot,
Śniatyn–Założce a city among cities;
and even Zaleszczyki – it is so close!
and only you, only you were left in the dark.

And also the printer forgot to include
you in the big map, to point you with a dot;
like you were a little enclave,
like you never existed in the world!

You exist and you live in my heart,
and sometimes my heart escapes to you;
and in you my father, brother, sister–in–law, sister,
and brother–in–law, waiting for a letter.

And in you my father's ramshackle house is standing,
and the acacia tree is turning green in the garden,
a bucket is lowered to a well in the yard,
and the spinning wheel is whistling and creaking....

I will remember to the day that I die
the creaking coming from the well!
and if the truth is allowed to be told,

it woke up the child (me).

Awaken, he can see the green acacia tree
through the wide eastern window,
and a soft morning sun is looking
between the branches at the smiling baby ....

Childhood is homeland! And there is no difference
if we saw her, here or there;
and she is the kernel of the wide open space
and she is the center of the world.

So, it is no wonder, and why should we deny?
We can candidly say that all of us
keep the town of our childhood
in a secret room in our heart. Always and always!

Always and always, for she is the station
from which we left for our first journey,
and her name will be displayed at the last stop,
on the day that we finish our last journey...

Everyone to his town – and I'm to my town!
Even if she is not Vilna, nor Brody,
I dedicated a place for her at the beginning of this poem
and I shall not betray her memory at the end.

 Why should I deny you and why should I be ashamed
of you, Tluste my tiny little town,
and the acacia tree in your garden is roaring,
and a bucket is lowered to a well in the garden ...

———

[Page 8 - Hebrew] [Page 13 - Yiddish]

Tluste My Little Town

by Leah Ilani–Sternlieb

A long street continuing to the entrance of town, orchards loaded with fruit on both of its sides. A Polish school that summoned its students to class or to a break with its big bell – this is how I remember my town.

Streets full with people dressed in their Sabbath clothes, the preparations on Passover eve by the doorstep. The Purim actors dressed in their colorful customs at their grandfather's home, the train station platform waiting for its passengers and always concealing a surprise, the clatter of wheels transporting a person's hope far away from town, to the big world. Modest small houses, some of them new and some leaning to fall, and inside them the busy daily life with its joy and worries.

I was a girl at the time when my parents decided that their children should receive their Hebrew education in Eretz–Yisrael. And they said, and they did. Close to my graduation from elementary school I separated from my small town and we sailed to our homeland, to Eretz–Yisrael.

On that day no one thought that the day would arrive and a hidden corner in a remote part of Poland, the one that we left, would be slaughtered by fire.

We lived among the gentiles, but my little town had a Jewish identity. Each holiday and Jewish festival sunk their mark on her. Not once it looked to me that the gentiles who lived among us were happy when our holidays arrived, and enjoyed the atmosphere of the Jewish holidays together with us. I remember the "Sabbath gentile woman" who knew how to "give judgment" in Kashrut laws, and I remember the gentile who answered Amen to my grandfather's "Hamotzi," knew the exact hour to light the Sabbath candles, and the date of a certain holiday.

And I remember that spacious hut, the "Gordonia" club house that was too narrow to accommodate the tens of teenagers who met there for pioneer Zionist activities, all of them looking forward to the happy moment, the moment when their turn would arrive to emigrate. The sparks of love and friendship penetrated through its windows on the long winter nights, while we weaved through conversation, song and dance for our future in the wonderland, in Eretz–Yisrael.

And, in one of the alleyways, in a one story building, we nursed the first nectar of our Hebrew awareness. There, our Halutz [pioneer] teacher, Mordechai Spector of blessed memory, taught us our first Hebrew words. There we met for the first time, almost face to face, our patriarch Abraham who was standing next to the three angels waiting to serve them. There we witnessed the sacrifice of Yitzchak that shook our little hearts, not knowing that the day would come and thousands of martyrs, the purest sons and daughters of Abraham, Yitzchak and Yakov, would be sacrificed in this place.

And there, in the corner of the small room, stood a bookcase loaded with Hebrew books, children's books that I craved and swallowed like a firstborn before summer. I retained from them my first admiration to Zionism – the love for my nation and my homeland.

A small town, a typical Jewish town, with its joy and sadness, masters and beggars, a beloved corner that encircled the days of my childhood with a halo of holiness.

Voices will no longer penetrate from its synagogues, the melody of the Heder boys will no longer be heard, and the stories of Avraham Avinu and his children will no longer be told in a lively Hebrew...

She is empty... empty from her Jews, empty from her Jewish character. Only the headstones in the abandoned Jewish cemetery, only the floor tiles and the walls of the silent homes will shout the cry of a grieving orphan, of a deep–rooted Jewish town that lost the sons who built her.

**The Hebrew School with the teacher Mordechai Spector
(The writer of the article – second to the teacher's left)**

[Page 9]

The Organization of former residents of Tluste in Israel

by Shmuel Fiderer (son of Moshe)

The "Organization of former residents of Tluste and the vicinity in Israel" started its activities in 1952. Its goal was: giving assistance to new immigrants from our town, the few survivors who managed to save their lives during the Holocaust or those who came from Soviet Russia through Poland.

The founding committee included the following members: Yosef Shechner (son of Yitzchak) z"l, Yosef Shechner (son of Antshel) and Shmuel Fiderer. We prepared our bylaws and presented them to the authorities in order to obtain a legal status for the organization.

Our first general meeting was also the first memorial service for the martyrs of our town. All the members of our town, who were in the Israel at that time, participated in it. A committee of seven members, from Tel–Aviv and

Haifa, was elected: Yosef (son of Yitzchak) Shechner, Meir Sternlieb, Dov Pfeffer, Dov Hernes, Yisrael Gertner, Yosef Schechter, and Shmuel Fiderer. Yosef Shechner z"l was unanimously elected as chairman of the committee and he began fruitful work, which has brought great benefit to the members of our town in Israel.

We founded a charitable fund to provide financial aid to new immigrants and the veterans of our town. For the establishment of the fund we were only helped by the members of our town in Israel. Their participation was active and most generous. The amount of money that was collected enabled us to give a loan to each person who needed it. The committee members who were the most active in the establishing of the fund were: Misha Shadmi–Goldhaber and Natan Maymon.

Since the first memorial service in 1952 we hold a yearly memorial service for the martyrs of our town. The date of the memorial day was determined by the date of the "Great *Aktzya*" in Tluste, 22 Iyar 5703 (27 May 1943). The yearly memorial service is held in Tel–Aviv or Haifa. Only once we held the memorial in Jerusalem during the dedication of the memorial plaque for the martyrs of our town in "*Martef Hashoah*" [the Holocaust cellar Museum in Jerusalem].

Among the other activities of our organization we especially need to note the planting of a grove in *Yaar HaKedoshim* [the martyrs' forest in Jerusalem] in memory of the martyrs of our town. The grove was planted by the "Pioneer Women" organization in the United States in honor of the public activist Mrs. Miriam Rosenbaum–Miler (daughter of R' Shneur Rosenbaum), and according to her request it was dedicated to the memory of Tluste's martyrs.

For our many accomplishments we thank our friend, Yosef (son of Yitzchak) Shechner z"l, who served as chairman of our organization until his death. He was devoted with all his heart to the matters of the organization and was always ready to help to the best of his ability. We will always remember him as a symbol of dedication and a model to those who continue the cultural activities of our organization.

A few years ago, a plan to publish a memorial book for our community that has been destroyed was brought up. We presented our plan before our landsmen in the United States in order to include them in this project. Luckily a number of them came to visit our country. Among them were: Sabetai

Gelband and his wife, Leo Valdman and his wife and Yoel Feldman and his wife. They showed great affection for this plan and thanks to the efforts of the Landsmannschaft chairman in the United States, the member Walter (Vave) Hausfeld, we received the amount of two thousand dollars for the publication of the book and a promise for additional funds. In addition to that we organized a successful fundraising campaign among our members in Israel. In this way we have achieved the goal we set for ourselves – the publication of a memorial book for our town Tluste.

A group of members from the book committee with the guest from the United States, Mrs. Popa Eidelsberg

[Page 10]

The "Landsmannschaft" of former residents of Tluste in the United States

by Walter (Vave) Hausfeld)

The day after my arrival to the United States, in the last months of 1939, I turned to the former residents of our town, Tluste, and signed up as a member in their association. I participated in all their meetings and saw their great activity in all areas on behalf of the residents of our town. I remembered how they helped the members of our town before the war and knew to appreciate their help. They donated thousands of dollars to *"Gemilut Hasadim"* in Tluste and every year, before Passover, they sent two thousand dollars to support the town's poor.

Finally we reach the end of the Second World War. At that time a letter arrived from Yosef Shechter and in it was a list of survivors. We convened a meeting of all the members of our town and I would never forget the moment in which the list was read and my brother's name was not mentioned in it. Later I learnt the details of his death.

At that time we established the aid fund of the former residents of Tluste and started to work vigorously. To our great sorrow there were only a few who needed our help. We collected large sums of money and sent many packages to the survivors. Our landsmen, Mr. Hirsh, excelled with his dedication to this work and Yoel Feldman, son of Gedalia Feldman from Vorolintza [Worworlince], helped us financially.

Later, a number of survivors arrived to the United States and a new chapter was opened in the activities our organization. Among others we decided to build a memorial for Tluste's martyrs in the cemetery so we can visit it the way we visit the graves of our ancestors. Lately we accepted the duty to help with the publication of "Sefer Tluste" so our sons would be able to read about the beautiful life of our town in the past and about her destruction in the hands of the Nazi gangs who inflicted destruction on all the Polish and Western European Jewry.

I want to mention that there are two associations of "*Tlusteim*" in the United States: "the veteran association" and the "young association" (that's how they are called). The veteran "*Tlusteim*" already lost their attachment to their birthplace. Their association is based more on the financial aspect and they do not participate in any of the activities for the benefit of the members of their town. When I received the "control" of the "young" group, I tried to unite the two groups, or at least tried to include the "veterans" in the aid activities, but I was not able to do so. They did not participate in the building of the memorial or help to finance the memorial book. They had one claim in their mouth – there is no need for this or for that.

With the publication of "Sefer Tluste" I want to express my hope that all the former residents of our town around the world will read it, learn about their origin and remember and know that we all came from the same place, from the town of Tluste, and we should not forget her all the days of our lives. May the word "Tluste" be a symbol of unity and dedication, brotherhood and deep friendship among the members of our town around the world.

A group of members from the "Landsmannschaft" book committee in the United States

[Page 11 - Hebrew] [Page 14 - Yiddish]

Preface by the Editor

Good and sad neighboring between Tluste and Horodenka

by G. Lindenberg

In the past twenty years the concept of "twin cities" took root in the world. Cities and towns, which were far from each other as east is far from the west, signed a friendship treaty and declared themselves "twin cities" with all that is involved in the matter: frequent visits, gifts when the occasion arises, and financial aid in time of need. This is a new custom for us, but we can assume that it has a foundation in the history of nations. Indeed, there were always towns that historical events bound inextricably, even though it was not always a connection of unity and friendship.

It appears that the towns of Tluste and Horodenka in Eastern Galicia were also twin towns. Fate tied them together during the last stages of their existence in the world. The saying that Horodenka and Tluste were like "a room and a small bedchamber" was popular in Horodenka. In the Horodenka book, Shimshon Meltzer is telling how Tluste's Jews escaped across the Dniester to Horodenka from the Russian invaders during the First World War. In the same book, Yitzchak Shapira is telling how Tluste's Jews helped the Jews of Horodenka to fulfill the deed of waving the *lulav* during the Russian occupation. First, they loaned them an *ethrog* for only twenty–four hours and later, the town of Tluste was able to obtain a second *ethrog* for its "sister" Horodenka from Chortkov [Czortkow]. When the tragic end of the two communities arrived, the community of Tluste was "rewarded" to be the last in line for a total destruction. Many of Horodenka's Jews found shelter in Tluste, and a number of them were also able to save their lives there. According to the book in front of us, the people of Tluste learnt about the "*Aktzya*" in Horodenka on the same Thursday at the beginning of December 1941. Afterwards, one of the killing pit survivors arrived to Tluste, the slaughterer's daughter who was lucky to remain alive. She commemorated her experience and hardship in a poem that was published in the Horodenka book.

When time arrived to place a memorial for the community of Horodenka, and a qualified editor was needed, the committee members were not able to find a better editor than Shimshon Meltzer, Tluste's poet, who was not just a man from the area but in a way also a Horodenka man. The editor kindly thanks him in the introduction to the book, and mentioned that during the year that he worked as a teacher in Horodenka, before his immigration to Israel, he had sufficient time to "love the town, its landscape and its people," and thus he earned a citizenship, or at least half a citizenship, of that town.

I was lucky to be Shimshon Meltzer's helper and right hand with the preparation of the material for the Horodenka book. Thus, I was rewarded, when time arrived, to be elected as the editor of the book before us. In my work I did not have the personal knowledge of the town and her people that the editor of the Horodenka book had, and surely not his talent, knowledge and experience. But, I can say at the end of the work that, like him, I have done my work with trust and dedication, not less from what I have done in the Horodenka book. I want to express my gratitude to Meltzer, the poet and editor, for his advice and for standing by me during the entire period of editing this book. He also read all the material, corrected my mistakes, my facts, my language and style, in order to bring this book to a perfect and corrected form.

I must mention the detailed description of Dr. Avraham Stupp. It provides us with a full picture of the Jewish existence in the towns of Eastern Galicia and the special Jewish way of life in Tluste. This is one of the fundamental articles of the book before us, not only for its wide scope, but also for the important description of the way of life of the last generation before the holocaust. It is fitting to praise and honor the comprehensive testimony of R' Dov Glick that includes the entire history of the holocaust and the destruction of Tluste, with exact details and dates. This work is a testimony that was given to the Jewish committee for the research of the holocaust in Łódź, and the fruit of the dedication and excellent memory of the oldest former resident of Tluste who now lives in Israel.

I must mention with kindness the members of the publishing committee who worked hard collecting material and preparing the lists of holocaust victims. I must mention Mr. Shmuel Fiderer, who stood on his guard and made sure that the stories about the holocaust would not include shocking details that might hurt someone, and also the publisher, Mr. Natan Maymon, who collected all this extensive work. They, and all the members of the committee, should be blessed at the end of the project and they have a large part in its success.

And I will end with a quote from Meltzer's words in his introduction to the Horodenka book. These words should to be written in each memorial book:

"It is a sad task to write, edit and publish a book that is not a book but a headstone on a grave of a thriving Jewish community that no longer exists. It is a depressing and draining work that eats her workers, but as the Jewish proverb goes: "There's luck in unlucky." Not every town was lucky that her descendents and survivors liked her so much and were eager to build her a written memorial and create a name for her in the history of the Jewish nation. And Horodenka won"

And now, also Tluste won.

The Town and Its People

[Pages 17-31]

Life in Jewish Tluste

by Dr. Abraham Stupp

Tluste was a town like all other Jewish towns in Galicia. Out of a population of three thousand there were about two thousand Jews. For many years the mayor, Eli Albin, was Jewish. Eli Albin was a rich Jew and the owner of many estates, some that he owned and some that he leased. His face was adorned with a handsome beard, and he built the most beautiful and the most expensive house in Tluste.

The town's clerk, Kanper, was also a Jew and he served in his position for many years. Two or three non– Jewish policemen ruled the town on behalf of the municipality. Each one of them wore a uniform and carried a sword by his thigh. The most recognized by the public was the old policeman Bodnarski, the owner of the drum – one of the town's most important accessories. Equipped with his drum, Bodnarski went out to announce and inform all kinds of information on behalf of the town: when the young people must enlist to military service, when to register the children for school, when to bring the babies for a smallpox inoculation, the closing of roads and bridges for traffic due to repair work, and other important information of that sort. Bodnarski had an extra merit, as he announced his announcements in the spoken languages, in Yiddish, and all the members of the town from the young to the old were able to understand his words.

Until the days of our generation, the Jews who lived in those towns were subjected to a difficult lifestyle within the walls of customs and habits that had ruled their lives for hundreds of years. These lifestyles, and the customs that were created out of them, ruled the lives of the Jews day after day, from morning to night. And so it continued from generation to generation for hundreds of years. When we come today to write something about the life of a Jewish town in Galicia, two different kinds of Jews who belong to two different periods of time, are standing before our eyes: the first period lasted from the first days of the Jewish settlement until the days of the First World War; and the second period, from the end of the First World War until the days of holocaust and destruction. For that reason, a Jew who was born in 1897, at the end of the 19th century, can try to describe the two different kinds of Jews who are mentioned above, because he himself lived and acted during those periods which are different from each other.

In a town like Tluste, a Jewish child started to feel his Judaism when he reached the age of three. At that age, he was sent to the "Heder" [religious elementary school] to learn the alphabet. It was not required by law or influenced by any kind of organization. Every Jew knew that it was his duty to make sure that his son received a traditional Jewish education.

I studied at Aba "Melamed" [teacher]. He started to educate me according to the system that was customary in those days, with the help of his assistant Leybush. The system was very old. A large number of schoolchildren spent all the hours of the day in the "Heder," immersed in their games. Twice a day, the rabbi and his helper brought the children in and taught them the letters of the alphabet. To do that the rabbi held two instruments in his hands: a "Teitel" [a pointer] made out of wood – to point to the letters in the Siddur, and a "Kantshik" – a kind of a whip that was used to punish disobedient students. Without these two instruments he did not earn the title "the primary teacher." There was a third educational instrument that was used very seldom. It was an old "Shtayrml" [a fur–edged hat, worn by rabbis and Hasidic Jews on the Sabbath and holidays], that he put on the head of the delinquent child who stood in the corner for an hour as a punishment for his crimes. Outside of school hours, children spent their time playing games. Beside the game of "horses" and other children's games, we had a unique "job" in Rabbi Aba's "Heder". In front of the house there was a round stone, and bricks of different colors were scattered around it. So, the "Heder" boys started to produce flour in different colors by crushing the bricks on the stone. We came home from this "job" with an eye infection, and our mothers had to put cold towels on our eyes to cure the results of the strange flour–grinding work at our rabbi's home.

And so we continued our "studies" and advanced from month to month. I remember when I was already a "young man" of five and went to pray with my own prayer book. A respected old Jewish man, Aytzik Fiderer of blessed memory, approached my father and said in this language: Reb Moshe, your young man is "showing off his Judaism and turning it into a heap of......." All of my life I was not able to forgive this old Jewish man, although with my many sins he was right in his judgment...

When a boy reached the age of five he started to study the "Chomash" [one of the five books of Pentateuch]. It was the highest possible step in the primary teacher class. Two other steps preceded it and they were called: "half a step" and a "full step." After that, they started to study the "Chomash." This matter entailed a full ceremony for which they practiced for many weeks. First they started to study the book of "Vayikra" [the book of Leviticus], which was explained in a very simple way: since the book dealt with the rules of "Holiness" and the Jewish children who started the "Chomash" were the holy flock that would study it. This reason was expressed by the "One who asked" and by the "One who blessed" in the "Chomash" ceremony, and the two duties were given to two of the "Chomash boys'" friends. The three of them climbed on a table and the ceremony took place in front of all the participants. For the duration of the ceremony a number of watches, which were borrowed from the guests, were hung on the chest of the "hero of the day." I remember that I did not finish the whole ceremony. When it was my time to climb on the table with two of my friends, my father's friends changed their mind and did not let me climb up for fear of the evil eye.... and so, the three of us were left with our words inside us and we not given the opportunity to say them. But the matter did not bother me later on in my studies, and did not prevent me from studying in the "Heder" until I reached the age of 17, as it is going to be told hereinafter.

Since I saw myself as one of the "last Mohicans" of the typical Heder boys, I want to note how unprepared and unqualified our teachers were. Not once they repeated words that they learned in their youth, without thinking about the meaning of the words or understanding what they were saying. Their interpretation of the "Chomash" expression "Shesh Moshzar"[twined linen] was "twisted and spun," believe me, even today I don't know what was spun and what was twisted. Another example: the Rabbi translated the word "Nad" [skin bottle] to "raw skin". I am sure that the rabbi himself, may he forgive me, never saw the shape of "raw skin" in his life, and did not know what it looked like. Some years later, when I lived in Israel, I saw an Arab carrying cold water in a black skin–bottle, and I knew that that's what the rabbi was talking about. Or for example, the rabbi translated the word "Tiger" to "Lempert" [a lion cheetah]. Many years later, after I left for the big world, I visited one of the big city's zoos. When I saw the word "Leopard" posted next to one of the animals, I thought to myself that this is the animal that our rabbi called by the name "Lempert." I am still wondering today where our rabbi found the explanation of Rashi's words: "The Lord created the sun and it shone hotly from her case," the rabbi translated the words "from her case" to "from her ring". Even today, I can't imagine the shape of the ring that the sun is incased in. I also remember another incident. I was maybe eight years old when we studied "Mesechet Ketuvot," I think it was written on page seven or eight, "I am a virgin deflowered by accident," and Rashi interpreted it as: "In the same place." My friend Yodele' Meimen wanted to know the meaning of "In the same place" and, instead of an answer he received two slaps on his cheek that are still ringing in my ears.

My first public appearance during the period of my studies in the "Heder" happened eight years after I started to study the "Chomash", when I read my sermon before a large audience on my "Bar–Mitzvha". My mother of blessed memory prepared the meal for my "Bar–Mitzvah" as though she was getting ready for a large wedding. She cooked and baked all night. At noon, all the worshipers from Chortkov's Hassidim synagogue gathered, and during the meal I read my long sermon which my teacher and rabbi of that time, Rabbi Zalman Kelman, wrote for me. This time they let me say my words, and a number of guests argued with me. For the event, they dressed me in a new black silk coat with pockets in the back. My father also wanted to buy me a fur hat, but I refused. I did not want to be the only boy in town whose head was covered with such a hat.

From my years of study in Aba Melamed's Heder, I remember the three "holidays" that only we, the "Heder" students, celebrated. From time to time, we went together with the rabbi's helper to recite the "Shema" by the bed of a woman who had just given birth. It was done to protect the newborn from evil spirits and demons. Surely, the child's father did not trust us, and he pasted all kind of swear words against demons and evil spirits on the walls. Once a year, on Lag Ba'Omer, all the students went out of town – "to Mount Sinai." Each one of us was equipped with a stick – in memory of the destruction – and we staged a war to commemorate the heroism of Rabbi Akiva's students during the revolt days of Bar–Kokhba. The third holiday was Tu B'shvat, when we ate the fruits of Eretz Yisrael.

Of the importance of protecting a mother and her infant from evil spirits, I can tell from my own personal experience. Surely, for the sake of the truth, my personality at that time was not highly measured, since I was only a baby of three or four days. The words that I am telling here were given to me by my mother – may she rest in peace – during my childhood around sixty years ago and, according to her words, the story was as follows: A few days after my birth, when she was still confined to her bed, the members of the family went out and left her alone in the room. Suddenly, the door opened and a tiny "Ashkenazi" with a hard hat on his head entered. In a loud and scolding voice he demanded my mother to give him the baby. It turned out that my mother did not give him the boy but screamed with all her might and called for help. The neighbors gathered to the sound of her screaming, among them Jews dressed with the "Four Fringes." When they saw that my mother was as pale as chalk, holding her baby as tight as she could (meaning me), they all started to call"Shema Yisrael!" and the tiny "Ashkenazi" disappeared, not through the door, just vanished in the air – vanished and was no longer there. The neighbors understood that it was not just a matter of so what, but the situation was very serious... And now you need to arrive at your own conclusion, what could have happened if the Jews with the fringes had not come to call "Shema Yisrael!" – I am afraid that someone else would need to bother himself and describe our town on the pages of this book...

*

And so, the first three years passed in the company of the infant teacher. In the sixth year of his life, the boy was given to the first Gemara teacher. There were a number of teachers of that kind in our town: my teacher was called Rabbi Kehet, a Jew with a handsome beard and eyes the color of copper. On the same day there was a small party in our house, and I was given my first Gemara, the " Baba Mezia" tractate in white fabric binding. And so, I sailed and went swimming in the great and wonderful Talmud sea, sailing that lasted from the first Mishna "Two are holding on to a garment..." to the seventeenth year of my life.

But not only the study of the Gemara was a new "trade", there was a difference between the studies with R' Kehet and the studies with the primary teacher. Also the study of the "Chomash", which we started with the primary teacher, received a new structure and a new meaning. We were not forced to explain and translate the words in the known version, but we had to show that we fully understood the meaning of the subject. Whoever studied in the "Heder" would never forget the special melody in which the rabbi explained the contents and the meaning of the written words in parashat "Vayechi&3148; – "And as for me, when I came from Padan, Rachel died by me," and it seems to me, that the words should be written in the book as clear and interrupted as it came from the mouth of our rabbi, R' Kehet.

"And – I – and I am Yakov, when I came – came from Paddan – it is Paddan–Aram – died – passed away, unto me – because of me, Rachel – Rachel Imenu... Although, that I trouble you to take me to be buried in the land of Canaan, though, I did not do so for your mother... and I know that there are hard feelings in your heart against me, but you should know that by the words I buried her there so that she should be of aid to her children"... and so, we went and interpreted the wonderful interpretation of Rashi: "... and when Nebuzaradan would exile them and they would pass through by way of her tomb, Rachel would go out onto her grave and weep and seek mercy for them", as it is said (Jeremiah 31) "A voice is heard in Ramah"... and the Almighty answered her: "for there is reward for your work, says the Lord – and the children shall return to their own border."

And the rabbi explained and we learned to interpret the words. And, in this way, the difficult feelings of enslavement in the Diaspora and the hope for a brilliant future – "And thy sons shall return to their borders" – entered our tender hearts. In the winter, as we walked home in the evening to the light of the flickering lamp – and we were only seven–year–old boys then – we saw in our imagination Yakov Avinu [our Patriarch] walking from Fadan–Aram, we saw Rachel's tombs by the road side, and a beautiful tall woman with long black hair was standing next to it (that's how the image of our Mother Rachel was pictured in my imagination), and she stretched her arms pleading before G–d, as written – "A voice is heard in Ramah, Lamentation bitter weeping. Rachel is weeping for her children..." and the young boy's heart was full of pride and happiness for all that he studied in the "Heder", for the wonderful feelings and images, in which none of the gentile boys who lived around him took part.

Our Rabbi R' Kehet thought that, in addition to teaching us a page in the Gemara, he also needed to teach us the art of writing. First, he taught us to write the Aleph–Bet and, later on, he prepared a weekly "written sample" that we had to copy every day of the week. At the top of the page our rabbi wrote â€˜With G–d Help' in handsome curly letters, but none of us was able to write it that way. So, we only copied the contents of the script and, while doing so, we managed to stain our clothes with ink to such degree that our mothers were forced to prepare a new washed and ironed suit every morning. Also our fingers were black after this work.

At the end of our studies with the teacher R' Kehet, we started to study with R' Shmuel Naman. It was a higher level of study, and we "ploughed deeper" into the "Talmud for the beginners," R' Shmuel's apartment was next to the Rabbi's apartment, and I remember how our Rabbi entered almost every day to check the details of the subject of study. R' Shmeul's mother–in–law was called "Sara, a daughter of a good family" by the townspeople, because all her days she was looking for the opportunity to perform a mitzvah. Her husband did not belong to the town's rich, but she always remembered where a hungry sick person was lying, and brought him a little cholent, and where to give a few "coins" for food. In the room of R' Shmuel Naman there were many young men – and it was necessary to make sure that they washed their hands before the meal and said their prayer, and for that she brought them the water and poured it on their hands. And the "Mishnayoth" in Beit Ha'Midrash needed to be replaced – and it was her duty to make sure that a new one would be purchased. In short, she was the real image of "Sara, a daughter from a good family."

After I finished my studies with R' Shmuel Naman, my father tried to bring teachers for me from other towns. They were highly educated Jews who tried to give us some of their knowledge, although it was not done in an organized system and without an explanation to the historical facts that were connected to the subject. The class was very small, only four or five students, and there were two problems: we had to provide "food" for the rabbi and also find an apartment for him. Since my father was interested in "buying" a good study friend for me, sometimes he had to provide my friend's share of the rabbi's food if my friend was unable to pay. Finding a room for the rabbi was also not easy. I remember how I walked with my friend – both of us were eight or nine – to find an apartment for the rabbi. We also spent all hours of the day studying in that apartment until the late hours of the evening. I remember the names of two Jews who used to rent apartments to teachers from out of town: Yosel Haim Glezer and R' Mendale Dulig. This "Heder" did not have a legal license, and we were always under the fear that perhaps a policeman would surprise us while we studied. If we saw a policeman through the window, the Gemaras were closed and the students went out for a walk. For us, the students, it was very good and comfortable if we found a policeman at least once a week, and to our bad luck it happened only once every two months.

My education was illegal to a certain point. Every year, my father received a notice from the authorities to send me to the general school that was established by Baron Hirsh. But every year he paid a fine of Ten Crowns and never thought of sending me to that school. He was firm in his decision that he had to find a teacher to teach me the art of writing and mathematics, and that the rest of my time should be dedicated to the studies of the Gemara and Posekim. With the teachers, who came from other towns, we went through a good portion of the six orders of the Mishna. In addition, we studied "Meginim" and "Yoreh De'ah" [one of the four parts of Sulhan Aruch]. As I found out, not many youngsters studied that way or were rewarded to study with such excellent teachers, but a good portion of the town's Jews educated their sons in that manner. Young men, who finished their studies with the town's teachers, always sat in groups in Beit Ha'Midrash and also in the synagogues of the Chortkov Hassidim and the Vishnitz Hassidim and studied on their own.

All these young men, when they reached the age of twenty–one, had to present themselves for a test before a military drafting board, not only once, but three times in a period of three years. Since no one wanted to spend three years as a soldier in the Kaiser's army, they used to "suffer" a few weeks before the test. At night the "sufferers" walked around in groups, singing and shouting in order to stay wake. Out of mischief, they stopped at their relatives' homes in order to wake them up from their sleep. Others went farther in order to be exempt from military service. Some mutilated their bodies and lived all of their lives blind in one eye or with two fingers attached to their palm.

The teaching in the "Heder" was mostly dedicated to the study of the Gemara, and there was no understanding of other studies. In all my years in the "Heder" I did not study grammar, and chapters from the Bible were hastily taught before the rabbi went to pray Mincha and Maariv [afternoon and evening prayers]. It was customary that the rabbi prayed with the public, and we boys were left in the "Heder". After the rabbi returned from his prayers we sat down to study. In the winter we studied until eight in the evening. In order to walk home in the dark winter nights, the parents purchased lanterns for their children. There were different kinds of lanterns: a simple one with a candle for light, and a better quality one with a small oil lamp and a small fixed mirror behind it. Not once, when the "older" boys "dealt" with the small oil lamp, the kerosene caught on fire and the fire spread to lantern owner's coat. Then, they had to remove it from the child's hand and immediately save his life. And so the studies continued year after year in the winter season.

Also at home the air was saturated with the smell of the Torah, but in a different way than the "Heder". After the evening meal was finished, and the family members went to bed, my father of blessed memory pulled the lamp down, opened the Gemara and sat down to study his "lesson" in an enthusiastic melody. Every evening I fell asleep to the sound of his singing, and the taste of that melody stayed with me all the days of my life.

This was the substance of the life of a "Heder" boy, and there was nothing else beside it. I remember my father's attitude towards one of my "pranks" that brought me a lot of pleasure. In the winter evenings, when we sat and waited for the rabbi to come back from the synagogue, the boys went out to the nearest hill and sled downhill. And it happened that one of my father's friends saw me in my "corrupt behavior" and told my father. In my father's eyes, it was a terrible and dreadful crime, and he explained at length that the practice of "sliding on my buttocks" was not proper. I had to promise him with a handshake that I would never do it again. And surely, since then, I abstained from this pleasure and did not touch a sled.

*

Not all the town's Jews were Hassidim. There were also simple Jews, who usually prayed in the Great Synagogue and in Beit Ha'Midrash. But many of Tluste's Jews gathered in the Hassidic synagogues that were called "kloizen" [the "kloiz" often represented the professions and the association of its worshippers]. The largest "kloiz" belonged to the Hassidim from Chortkov [Czortków]. The Great Synagogue and Beit Ha'Midrash stood to its right and to its left. A little farther up, next to the road, stood the Zaleszczyki Hassidim "kloiz". The "Kleizel" [small "kloiz"] of the Vizhnitz Hassidim was located inside Beit Ha'Midrash.

I still remember the building of the old Beit Ha'Midrash, with its cracked walls and low roof that the town's goat walked on with great pleasure. Later on, our townswoman, Rivke Braksmier, woke up and donated ten thousand Crowns for the construction of a new building. A sign with golden letters was posted on the facade, and it said: for eternal memory, Rivke Braksmier donated the money for the building of the new Beit Midrash. There was also a sign on the Chortkov Hassidim "kloiz", but the letters were not golden but painted in black, and it was written: Chortkov's "kloiz", its glory was renewed in the year..." for many years the sign hung on the wall for all to see, and the "kloiz"'s worshipers, most of them great scholars, did not realize that the inscription was not according to the correct grammar.

The town's Jews gathered in Beit Ha'Midrash and in the "kloizen" twice a day. There were three days a year when the synagogue looked different: First on Yom–Kippur – on that day the floor was covered with a layer of straw because the worshipers took their shoes off and walked only in their socks. The second, on Tisha BeAv [the Ninth of Av] first of all – the benches were turned, and the worshipers sat on the turned benches, as low as they possibly could. The chandeliers were not lit, and by the dull light of a few candles they sat and lamented the destruction of the holy temple. There were Jews who cried, and there were Yeshiva boys who threw thorns on the worshipers, inside their beards and side curls in order to add misery to their sorrow. The third time was during the holiday of Shavuot. Then, the synagogue was decorated with greens, green branches and flowers, in remembrance of Mount Sinai where the Jews received their Torah.

And when we stand on the affairs of Yom–Kippur, it is worth mentioning the tradition of the lighting of the "Yom–Kippur candles." It was a law, and every Jewish family had to prepare two big wax candles – one for the living and the second for the dead who reside in the next world. The candle making ceremony started by the "inserting the wicks." The expert was an elderly woman, and the wicks were inserted in her house while the proper "pleas" were said during the act. A few days before Yom–Kippur, my mother went to her house and when she returned her eyes were red from crying. One of the two candles was lit at home on Yom–Kippur eve, and the second was taken to the synagogue and was lit over there. Boxes full of sand stood on the tables and the candles were inserted in it. It is easy to assume that hundreds of burning candles did not do good to the quality of the air in the synagogue, but everyone came to the same agreement – that we must light the candles in memory of the dead. Viktor, the gentile cemetery keeper, walked all day in the synagogue and straightened the bent candles. On the conclusion of Yom–Kippur we took what was left of the candles home. We tried to take the candles while they were still burning. The candle stub was used during the year as a Havdalah candle on the conclusion of the Sabbath.

On Yom-Kippur eve, during the morning hours, we waved the "Kaparot." A white rooster or a white hen was prepared for each member of the family. During the waving of the "Kaparot" we said a special prayer "People who sit in darkness and deep shadows" – at the end of the prayer, the fowl was waved above our heads while we said: "This is my exchange, this is my substitute." During the event, the chicken looked at the large letters in the prayer book without understanding the meaning of the matter. From here came the slogan: "He is looking like a rooster who is looking at people".

Before Rosh-Hashanah and before Yom-Kippur, we woke up early and went to "Selichot" [prayers of repentance], and sometimes we went to "Selichot" at midnight. Then, the young "crowd" lit candles that were glued to planks of wood and sent them afloat in the river – in honor of the "Selichot" There were other holidays, each holiday had its own character, its own flavor and a special influence on the lives of the town's Jews.

The holiday of Passover required many preparations at home, more than any other holiday. We started before Hanukkah when the geese were purchased, and the fat for Passover was made out of them. About two weeks before Passover we pickled the red beets in a small wooden barrel in order to prepare beet root soup for the holiday. A few days before the holiday we cleaned the kitchen and the oven. It was not an easy thing to do. For that, we put a large barrel covered with a clean white sheet in our home, and we had to follow the "shiktze" [a non-Jewish girl] who brought water from the well and watch her carefully that, G-d forbid, she would throw a little Chametz into the pails.

We were "Shmura eaters," meaning that during the seven days of Passover we only ate "Matzha Shmura" [guarded matzha], and it was forbidden to bring a simple matzha to the table. Only on the last day of Passover my father agreed to use regular matzha. When I was small, they let me eat matzha on Passover but not at the table, only on a small table that stood in the corner of the kitchen. We had special dishes for Passover that we brought down from the attic before Passover, year after year. Each one of us searched and found his small glass and all the special plates and bowls for Passover. Today, no one is able to taste and understand the special flavor. Up to this point is the matter of Passover.

A totally different matter was the holiday of Succoth. Immediately after Yom–Kippur, we started to build the Sukkah. In most cases the Sukkah was built outside, next to the house. In the newer homes the Sukkah was inside the house, on the balcony with a small rotating awning that was opened for the period of Succoth. This Sukkah had a special advantage, you were able to close the awning when it rained and keep the Sukkah and the people inside from getting wet.

In addition to the Jewish synagogues and the religious schools, there were also two churches in town, one for the Poles, and the other for the "gentiles," meaning the Ukrainians. My foot never stepped on the threshold of their house of worship. I only knew that every Jew who passed next to their house of worship had to say: "You shall not bring an abomination into your house, and like it come under the ban". Another matter that they committed to my memory was: if a priest crossed my way I had to find a straw reed and throw it behind him. The reason for that is: in ancient times, when our forefathers were forced to make bricks for the pharos in Egypt, they were not given straw (as it is said – your servants are given no straw, yet we are told, make bricks!). The priests helped our forefathers and gave them straw for the bricks, and for that reason we must pay our forefathers' debt.

I must mention the two different kinds of "Eruvim" [a boundary for the Jewish Sabbath that allows observant Jews to carry needed items in public on the Sabbath] that were customary in our town, as in many other Jewish settlements. One was "Eruv Hazerot" [the mixing of domains], that encircled the whole town and created one "yard", enabling us to carry our belongings within its boundaries during the Sabbath. The "Eruv" was created by tying a string between two high wood posts that were stationed in different locations. The second "Eruv" was "Eruv Tavshilim" [mixture of foods]. Thanks to it, we were allowed to prepare food on a holiday for the Sabbath that followed it (according to the law it was allowed to cook on a holiday, but only for that particular day). A general "Eruv Tavshilim" was created with a matzha that was framed and covered with glass, and it was hung in a visible place in the synagogue. By doing so, anyone who forgot to create "Eruv Tavshilim" in his home according to the law, was exempt from this duty. It was one of the compromises that the Jews had with G–d, like "Heter 'Iska" [transaction permit] and the selling of the Hametz that were strictly observed. If it was discovered that the Eruv broke in one of the locations on the Sabbath, it was announced in all the synagogues, and then the worshipers were careful not to fold their tallit and carry it in their hands, but instead they wrapped it on their shoulders as though they were wearing it for their pleasure. It was also not allowed to transfer a handkerchief in their pocket, and they had to tie it to the palm of their hand.

And so the Jews of our town lived and acted. Even the members of the young generation, who did not believe in all of that, tried to the best of their ability to keep their unconventional ideas to themselves. In Tluste there was one and only Jew, Dr. Krasutski, who allowed himself to smoke in public in the street on the Sabbath.

The influence of the Admorim [Hassidic rabbis] from Chortkov and Vishnitz was felt the most in our town. There was always an argument between the Hassidim and their supporters. The matters that they argued about were not among the most important ones, but the arguments were hard and without a compromise. Once, it was the matter of hiring a second Shochet [ritual slaughterer] in town. The victory was with the Vishnitz Hassidim, and the community leaders decided to accept Rabbi Shlomo Shochet. Immediately, the opponents started with a cruel war against the Shochet from Vizhnitz. In our home his slaughtering was strictly forbidden, as if it was pork meat, only the slaughtering of Feybush the Shochet was considered to be Kosher. The same thing was repeated later with the matter of the community leader position. This position was given the old way before the practice of elections arrived to the world.

I remember that Manie Gertner held in his possession the community's copper seal. It was heated by a candle flame and the documents were sealed with red wax. Later on, when Haim Nagler became the community leader, the Chortkov's Hassidim organized a difficult campaign against him until he resigned. After him, the position was transferred to the hands of Baruch–Itsha Vitashka, a rich Jew and a man of property who belonged to the Chortkov Hassidim. He held this position until the First World War and some years after it.

The town's Jews were not only divided between Hassidim and non-Hassidim, but also according to their trade and their occupation. Most of them were merchants, big merchants or smaller ones – but merchants. All of them earned their livelihood mostly on Thursday, the day of the weekly market. Thousands of farmers gathered in the market. They came from thirty farms and they were recognized from a distance with their special customs and mostly by their hats, since each village had its own unique hat. They brought the agricultural products to sell in the market: fruits and vegetables, butter, eggs, chickens, and also animals and grain. When they sold their merchandise, they came to the stores to buy the necessities for their homes. In the whole town there was almost no home without a store. In some places there were warehouses for grain, eggs or wood. Whoever came out to the streets on market day was terrified from the sea of thousands of people's heads, who were walking in the market or standing next to the different stalls. Pants, dresses, shoes, boots, and other merchandise were hung on display. Some of the stalls sold soda water and other kinds of drinks. A gentile beggar always sat on the side of the road, singing melancholic songs and playing the violin that he was holding in his hand. Tears poured from the peasant women's eyes to the sound of his songs, and they dropped a few small coins into his hat. Not far from there, a Jew stood with a music box and a parrot stood on top of it. The parrot pulled a piece of paper with its beak – a fortune paper – which the gentiles bought for a few coins with a complete trust that their entire future was written on it...

The Jews were not only merchants but also tradesmen. The selling of meat – with the exception of pork – was in the hands of the Jews. Many gentiles came to the butcher shop to buy the back parts that were not kosher.

Only later, during the days of New Poland, the anti–Semites started a campaign against kosher butchery in order to take the meat trade from Jewish hands. Also the selling of spirits in the government stores and in the inns were all in the hands of Jews. Most of their income was also earned on Thursday. Market day brought income to almost all the Jewish population in town and provided the needed provisions for the whole week. Even if there was a great noise and chaos during that day, it passed without any incidents. It was a very difficult day for the Austrian policemen who had to keep the order in town, and most of the time they succeeded in doing so.

And now, when I tell about Tluste, and mostly about Tluste's market day, it is difficult to avoid telling about the nearby town of Lashkovitz [Lisowce]. This town was located around seven kilometers from our town and excelled with two things. First, every year around 7 July the great Lashkovitz market took place. Merchants from all over the world came to it. Second, the rabbi who knew how to evict evil spirits sat there... Different stories circulated about this matter, but we don't have the space here to repeat them. I just wanted mention the fact.

It is also important to mention that all the Jews, no matter their occupation or trade, looked the same and dressed the same. Even Shemya Ashre's, who was the owner of a large wagon for heavy loads – stood by his cart with the reins in his hands, dressed in a black "caftan" [a full length coat] and a black sash. Only once, he allowed himself to tuck the edge of his caftan into his sash so it wouldn't interfere with his work. He never thought of wearing a short coat – more appropriate for his work – because it was known and customary that every Jew must wear a long caftan.

Market–square during a fair. In the background – the Polish Church

A special division in the Jewish population was the hagglers – or to be more precise – the women hagglers – who resided in the market square on both sides of the road, and their main occupation was the selling of all kinds of fruit.

They had their own language, kind of "correct answer" language, that none of Tluste's Jews was blessed with. If one of the customers dared to say something that the haggler did not like, he got such an immediate answer from her that he did not know where to run to. And in an instant, you were able hear the echo coming from the other hagglers, like a piano that had one of its keys touched. None of the town's residents had such a treasure of foul language and curses in his mouth as the haggler's "lexicon." They sat by their stalls in the heat of the summer and the chill of the winter, warming themselves by the "hot kettle" that was standing next to their feet. In the summer, they sold apples, pears and other kinds of fruit, and in the winter they sold goose meat. In our town, there were certain young men, who walked around holding a long stick with a nail fixed on its end. And so, they were able to "buy by pulling" an apple or a pear from the stands. One of them was Rochale's son, who became the chief of police during the Bolsheviks days thanks to his "ancestral merits." At that time the town's commissioner was Meir Margalit, the musician. These two "community leaders" sent me one Saturday morning, together with other young men from our town, accompanied by a band, to the village of Lashkovitz to fix a bridge.

You were not able to get a divorce in Tluste, since the river that flowed in town did not have a name. Nevertheless, there was a scribe in town who dealt with the writing of *Tefilin* and *Mezuzut*. Reb Moshe Sofer [the scribe], was a chubby Jew with a very long beard. It is not necessary to say that he was a pious Jew, but he had something that was "not so": he simply did not like to work. There was a popular story on that subject: A Jew started to build a house immediately after Passover so he would be able to finish it by Rosh–Hashanah and before the rainy season. The same Jew came together with the builder to R' Moshe Sofer to order two *Mezuzut* for his house. The Jew was busy all summer building his house, and forgot to worry about the *Mezuzut* that he had ordered. At the end of the summer he met R' Moshe Sofer in the street and asked: "R' Moshe, what about the *Mezuzut* that I ordered?" R' Moshe answered him: "I am going to write the second *Mezuzah*."All was in order, and they continued to build the house throughout the month of Elul. On Rosh Hashanah eve, the homeowner moved, with good luck, to his new home. Before evening, after he finished arranging the furniture, the Jew remembered that the most important items were missing in his new house: the *Mezuzut* were not there! And how could a Jew enter a house on Rosh Hashanah eve without *Mezuzut*? He rushed to R' Moshe Sofer to collect the *Mezuzut* that he had ordered at the beginning of the summer. R' Moshe had just returned from the *Mikve* [bath house], and on his table was an unfinished Mezuzah.

"You see" he said, apologizing to the homeowner, "I did not have the time to finish the *Mezuzah*." With tears in his eyes the homeowner faced him and said: "if so, could you at least give me the first *Mezuzah* so my home will not be without a *Mezuzah*." R' Moshe answered him: "you have to understand, this time I started to write the second *Mezuzah* before the first one"...... Nevertheless, Reb Moshe the scribe was a respected learned man, and if he wrote a lot or wrote very little – he was called by all: Reb Moshe the scribe.

In cultural understandings, the Jews tried very hard to draw from the nation's ancient springs. If some of them had a little time after they finished with their negotiations, they dedicated it to their studies. The one who was an expert – studied a page from the *Gemara*, the one who was not able to do so – studied and read "*Ein–Yakov*", "*Midrash Raba*" or "*Chok L'Yisrael*" and the one who was not well versed in all of them – simply read from the book of Psalms. Their private life gave them enough satisfaction and they were not eager to connect with the outside world. In those days, there were maybe two or three Jews who read the newspaper.

Most of the Jews lived with the opinion that all these matters did not have any value. And so, their lives were set in the traditional iron mold and no one wanted to become acquainted with the new.

This traditional way of life ordered them to pray for the "rain" and to pray for the "dew" at the time and place when such a prayer was not needed. It ordered them not to obey the law of the country where they lived. For example: as we know, the life of the Jewish family was very very pure, but none of them thought of registering their marriages as the law required. So it happened that all the children, myself included, were written as illegitimate in their birth certificates, meaning that their parents were not legally married...... Everyone who knew my father, Moshe Stupp, and my mother of blessed memory, knew for sure that a situation of that sort was far from their hearts and their character – but this was the situation in regards to the rule of the country. They lived within themselves and without contact with the world around them. One time a cardinal came to town for a visit. The Jews showed him respect like all the other residents, they walked towards him holding a Torah in their hands, the rabbi stood next to the cardinal and tried to smile at him, but he was not able to exchange two or three words with him. And so, the matter continued from generation to generation. They sunk their head in the past and asked for "amendment" for the whole world. Once a month they blessed the moon and the entire Jewish community, most of whom were not able to supported their families, stood and prayed from the bottom of their heart: "May the light of the moon be like the light of the sun..." – as though it was their one and only worry. They made sure that, G–d forbid, they would not fail to fulfill a mitzvah. For example: it was forbidden to study the Torah on "Christmas Eve" so the soul of "that man" would not enjoy the "sparks of holiness" that were created from the breath of the *Heder* students when they dealt with the Torah. Therefore, they spent the evening playing the "notes" game. Also, during Hanukah, we used to play this game. The making of the "notes" was a job in itself. We sat and carefully drew the letters of the alphabet. My father did not think that it was right for me to play this game with children my age, therefore he sat and played the "notes" game with me every evening during Hanukah.

The same Jews, who were knowledgeable in the Torah and spent all their time studying the *Gemara*, adapted the Talmudic terminology to themselves, even during the time when they spoke Yiddish to each other.

Amusing stories were told in this matter, and here are two of them:

The father of Feybush the slaughterer was a learned Jew. One Friday afternoon he sat in his home and studied the Torah. A gentile woman entered his home and offered to sell him yellow sand to spread on the smooth plaster floor for the Sabbath (at that time most of the homes did not have wooden floors). The gentile woman asked him in the Ukrainian language: Who wants to buy sand? Feybush' father answered her in the *Gemara* language: Who will buy – will buy, and who will not buy – will not buy.

And here is a second story: Once, during the reading of the Torah, two homeowners started a quarrel that ended in blows. The matter reached the authorities, and the rabbi was also invited to testify before the judge. The judge asked the rabbi if he was able to answer in Polish. The rabbi answered: No. In Ukrainian? No Maybe German? The rabbi answered: I know a little German. The judge asked the rabbi to give his opinion about the incident. The rabbi answered him in "German" in this way: At the beginning, I was angry at him — to destroy, to kill and to lose. Such a *Chutzpah* [insolence], a disgrace to the Torah during the reading! But after the fact, I fully forgave him, and I am asking the judge not to punish him. We can easily assume what the judge was able to understand from the rabbi's words which were spoken in "flowery German."

The Jews' social life was strictly among themselves, mostly among the Hassidim. I remember that every Sabbath, after services and after, so to speak, "pleasant singing," the "*kloiz*"'s worshipers made arrangements to meet at the "*kloiz*" in the afternoon. When they gathered, they sent two young men to the "tavern" with a note in their hands (in place of money), and the two young men rolled a small keg of beer back from there. And so, they sat, drank and sang Hassidic songs, and at the end they got up and danced around the table singing "with a pure heart we will faithfully serve you," and by doing so they came with the expression "*Neshama Yetira*" [the extra soul that every Jew acquires on the Sabbath according to legend] and the feeling of "Oneg Sabbath" [enjoyment of the Sabbath] that every Jew must feel on the Holy Sabbath. The simple folks also gathered and spent their time cracking seeds. When we returned home from the synagogue we met Gavriel the water–drawer and his friends in the street, leaning against the railing by the water canal and cracking seeds. It was already "after the event," meaning after the prayer and after the meal. In the afternoon most of them went for a walk in the direction of Swidowa, and for that it is worth to tell the following incident – an event that really happened.

On 1 August 1914, the First World War erupted. It was on *Tisha BeAv* [the Ninth of Av] that fell on the Sabbath. There were many reservists in town, and each man answered Kaiser Franz Joseph's public statement "to all the people of my country," that was announced on Saturday morning. They left their homes the next day and reported to their units. The reservists were mostly Jews over the age of forty who had served in the army in their youth. One of them was Antshel Pfeffer "a cavalry man" in his time – they took him and put him on a horse. A second Jew was Haskel (Yechezkel) "Olnick," the owner of the oil–press, a Jew with a long beard who pumped oil all of his life. They dressed him with new blue uniform and stationed him with a gun in his hand to guard the mail box. His friend (I can't remember his name) and companion in the reading of a chapter in "*Ein Yakov*" [teaching of the Talmud], walked alone lonely and dejected. When he arrived at the mail box he saw his friend Haskel dressed in his uniform. He called him from the other side of the street: Haskel, you became a "member of the kingdom," tell me please, that is happening in the political world? And Haskel answered him instantly: "And if I knew, would I tell you?...

As I already mentioned, the town's Jews lived in their own world, withdrawn and separated from everything around them, but the Hassidic way of life contributed to the expansion of their narrow way of life. They traveled to their rabbi, and there in the rabbi's court, they met Jews from other locations. They talked to them about politics, about matters of trade, and of course about "Jewish" matters, the bitter life in the Diaspora and the arrival of the Messiah.

Generally, the trip to the rabbi's court was not so special. I still remember the great impression that the court in Chortkov left on me, when my father of blessed memory took me with him when he traveled to his rabbi. The Great Synagogue with the garden that surrounded it, the quiet pond with the swans that swam in it, Munish the cantor, and Hershil Rapoport the *Gabai* [synagogue manager]. I was mostly impressed with the respect that the Hassid showed his rabbi when he met him and gave him his note that listed all of his heart's wishes, and then he stood and waited for the rabbi's blessing. I remember one of our visits to the rabbi (R' Yisrael'nio, May the memory of the righteous be for a blessing). The rabbi faced my father, pointed at me with his finger, and said: "Moshe, is this your only son? What will I bless him with? – May it be the wish that he will follow the righteous ways and his soul desires the Torah!" And surely, both blessings came true, and if the rabbi had added and said "may he also be very rich" – perhaps, and without a doubt, it might have come true. But the rabbi did not add that, and I'm unable to forgive him all of the days of my life.......

The connection between the Hassidim and the rabbi's court was very tight. On every happy occasion, or G–d forbid during a tragedy, they approached the rabbi and informed him about it. It seems to me, that there was not a single Hassid in town without a "charm" from his rabbi. The "charm" was in the form of a coin that the rabbi gave as a "remedy," a protection from evil spirits. When I was a teenager, I also carried a "charm" on my neck that the rabbi from

Chortkov gave me. It was inside a small bag, and was tied with a white string. My father collected many "charms" until he gave them to a silversmith to make a box for his smelling tobacco that he used only on the Sabbath and the holidays. The Hassidim loved their rabbi and his court. On the day when the rabbi from Rizshi, May the memory of the righteous be for a blessing, died, they prepared a community meal and the Hassidim wives saw the preparations for the meal as a great mitzvah. On *Hohsana Raba* [the last intermediate day of Sukkoth], the day Rabbi Duvid–Moshe'nio died, there was a great celebration in the Chortkov Hassidim "*kloiz*". We, the " *Heder*" boys, walked between the town's stores and collected colorful paper that we used to make colorful lanterns that we hung for display, so every person in the world would know how the Hassidim were keeping the memory of their rabbi in their hearts.

Those Jews who were not Hassidim, who did not travel often to their rabbi, received greetings from the great world through a "preacher" who came to town every once in a while and preached to the crowds on Saturday afternoon. We also had our own preacher in town, R' Pinchas Lapiner. Every once in a while a wandering Jew arrived in town with a cart full of books. When he arrived in our town, he displayed his books on a table in the "*kloiz*" or in *Beit Ha'Midrash*, and Jews, who read books, came and bought one or two books from him, each person with his needs and understanding. Also, once or twice a year, a "Jew from Eretz–Yisrael" came to our town to collect money for charitable organizations in Israel, for a "Yeshiva" or for "*Bikur Cholim*" [visiting the sick]. This Jew was warmly welcomed in *Beit Ha'Midrash*. Everyone listened, with fear and love, to every word that came out of his mouth about the situation of our Jewish brothers in the Holy Land. I remember to this day, how impressed I was from the words of that "emissary" who told us that in Israel it was customary to cook borsht out of oranges. Another continuing connection with Israel was the boxes of Rabbi Meir Baal HaNess that every woman dropped a few coins into on Sabbath eve, or just at the time when she requested something special from G–d. The slaughterers emptied the boxes twice a year and, at the same time, gave a receipt for the money that they took out from the previous box. There were pictures of different organizations in the Holy Land on the receipts and we, the "*Heder*" boys, were very impressed by them.

*

Each town, without exception, had its own public organizations. First of all
– the rabbi: I still remember the old rabbi, R' Pinchas Chodorov, who
associated with the Vizhnitz Hassidim. He was a great scholar, but he
stuttered when he preached in front of a large crowd. He died in 1915 during
the days of the First World War, as one of the first victims of the cholera
epidemic that raged in the towns that were close to Austrian and Russian
front lines. The entire town accompanied him with respect to his resting place
in Tluste's cemetery. And this is the place to mention that there are ancient
tombstones in Tluste's cemetery, from three hundred years ago and more.
Among them is the tombstone of Ba'al Shem Tov's mother, with the
inscription: "Here lies buried Sara the mother of Yisrael Ba'al Shem." In the
1920s, my friend and I repainted the stone, took a picture and sent it to
Jerusalem.

After the death of R' Pinchas Chodorov, his widow, the Rebbetzin
Sheindale', remained in town. She was a wise woman and a very important
Rebbetzin. His two sons also stayed – Shmuel Aba and Yehusua Heshil. The
oldest son, R' Shmuel Aba, was nominated as Tluste's Rabbi. He was still
young, but he had the "right of claim" to the rabbinical chair in our town. I
studied with his brother Yehusua in the Heder, and our friendship lasted for
many years after that. Each time I came home from Lwów [Lemberg] (after I
became unworthy....) I visited the rabbi's home. During the Second World War,
Yehusua wandered to Tashkent where he lives today with his wife and his two
daughters. Yehusua's son arrived in Israel a few years ago, and he works as a
postal clerk in Tel–Aviv.

Besides the rabbi there were three other Jews in town who knew how to
"give judgment to a question." The three Jews were: R' Hershil Meir, R' Zalman
Kelman, one of my teachers who taught me Torah, and R' Yankel Schorr, who
was called by the name "Yankel the tinsmith's son." When the rabbi left town,
and a woman needed an answer to a "question" about a chicken, or about a
cooking–pot, she rushed to one of the three to ask her "question."

The second Jewish organization that was extremely important was the
community committee, which I already talked about above. Its main duty was
to provide the salaries to the rabbi and the slaughterers. One of its main
incomes came from the selling of slaughtering notes. Also the cemetery was
under its care. Besides all of that it was not very active. There was not a
"Talmud–Torah" or "Bikur Cholim" and not even a home for the elderly in town.

The care for the sick was limited to one thing: providing enough ice to the town's residents. In winter the ice was brought to an underground warehouse and covered with straw. When summer arrived, it was possible to get ice for cooling drinks during a party, or G–d forbid, to cool the fever of the sick.

The second organization in town was the Baron Hirsh School. I remember two of its principals, one by the name Prochtman, and the second was Yakov Fel. The school's principals and its teachers were Jews who had moved away from Judaism and, for that reason the school did not have a Jewish educational value. All of its value was in the fact that it was possible to go to a general school without the danger of desecrating the Sabbath. There, the children studied the art of writing and arithmetic, they learned a little of the languages of the country, Polish and German, and by doing so they got closer to the non–Jewish environment. Among the teachers there was also a teacher for Jewish studies by the name of Kurzer, but the students learned very little about Judaism from him. After the world war he served as a teacher and a cantor, and was rewarded to see one of his sons settle in Israel. Evening classes for older teens were also organized at the school, and the sons of the simple folks received elementary education there. Yakov Fel also took care of the birth books, and was the director of a lending fund that gave easy payment loans to hagglers and craftsmen.

As in every town, there was also "Hevrat Kadisha" [burial society] in our town. The two caretakers Shemaya and Michael, and a third by the name of Haim Schwarzbart who prayed at the Chortkov's Hassidim "kloiz", took care of burial matters. The cemetery caretaker was Tovye, a Jew who enjoyed his "intoxicating liquor". He was helped by a gentile by the name of Viktor, who dug the graves.

I remember the two cantors of Tluste. One was R' Alter Wasser, who prayed in the Great Synagogue and had a little knowledge in reading music notes. Some years later he left Tluste and moved to Chortkov [Czortków]. In his free time, he was painting and drawing. He also drew needlepoint samples for women and girls who needed them. I remember when we created a needlepoint picture of Kaiser Franz Joseph – the cantor finished the picture by drawing the Kaiser's head. After R' Alter Wasser left our town he was replaced by R' Yitschak Velphberg who, in addition to being a cantor, was also a scribe. My father was very satisfied with this "change of personnel." He said that it was better that a Jew who knew how to write a mezuzah walked by the ark than a

Jew who just talked to a "gentile woman" in regard to a painting that he painted for her.........

The cantors who passed by the Holy Ark during the High Holidays, on Rosh Hashanah and Yom Kippur, had a great influence on the young generation. In our "*kloiz*", the Chortkov Hassidim "*kloiz*", Motya Spitzer passed before the Holy Ark during the *Shacharit* [morning] service, and Hershel Kopel during the *Musaf* service [additional morning prayers during the Sabbath and holidays]. From the days of my childhood until the First World War, I used to listen to their prayers year after year, meaning fifteen times during my lifetime, and their melodies remained in my heart for eternity. If I was asked today to repeat one of their prayers, I would be able to repeat every detail of it. Not once during my old age, with the heart of full of sadness, I see Hershel Kopel Rozenkratz before my eyes, standing and praying the Yom Kippur *Musaf* service and, as though on its own, a silent melody leaves my mouth."

The public prayer during Rosh Hashanah and Yom Kippur contained a large portion of our "Jewish awareness." It seems to me, that every person who heard Hershel Kopel Rozenkratz prayers fifteen times in his life – would not be able to release himself from his Judaism and would remain a Jew for the rest of his life. It is pity that today we cannot bring life to prayers said in synagogues, so the young generation can draw inspiration from them for the rest of their lives.

The melodies that a Jewish man absorbed during his adolescence in the synagogue and in *Beit Ha'Midrash* followed him all of his life. Every tailor apprentice had an inner need to entertain himself with a melody hunched over his work. He never heard arias from "Tosca" in his life, never saw "Madam Butterfly" in his life, but he heard the cantor's melodies and the prayers from the *Mahazor* were sunk deep in his heart. And that tailor apprentice sat, singing to himself while pulling the needle with the white tread, and the singing and the work wrapped into each other and, by the time he finished stitching a pair of pans, he finished the prayer in fullest detail.

The influence of the melodies was felt mostly on the Sabbath and during the holidays. On the Sabbath, when the city's streets were empty from people, before the residents left their homes after the Sabbath nap, the sound of the melodies was heard from each home.

The best and well known cantor in our town was R' Yankel Schorr who was mentioned above among the scholars. Moshe Katz, Abali Pfeffer and other cantors traveled to the nearby villages as representatives of the local synagogues.

To be fair, I cannot skip the public bath. There were two *Mikvahot* [baths] in our public bath – a cold one and a hot one. The last one was called the "Ba'al Shem Tov *Mikveh*." It is said that one winter night Ba'al Shem Tov went to the Mikveh without a candle. He asked the caretaker, who was walking behind him, to go and bring an icicle from the building's roof, and he carried it like a candle in his hand to light the baht house. You are allowed to believe this story or not believe it, but in each "Hassidic community" book, you will find it printed in black on white: Shimshon Meltzer, our town's poet, dedicated his poem "One winter night" to this legend.

*

At the end of my short story about the life of Tluste's Jews at the beginning of the twentieth century, I would like to describe in a few words the clothing and the food of the town's Jews, even though our town was not different than any other town. We will start with the Sabbath clothing. First of all, each Jew wore a "*Streimal*" [fur hat] on the Sabbath. It was kind of a headdress with a velvet top that was wrapped with thirteen reddish color "fox tails". I never knew from where this costume came to us. Years later, I happened to be in Zurich during a folk festival in which the locals were dressed in traditional middle age clothing. To my great surprise, I saw them wearing almost the same "*Streimalach*" that our forefathers wore. So we can assume that we kept this practice since ancient times, and a headdress of that kind was customary as a holiday dress by the local population of central Europe.

The Sabbath's outer garment was a "frock" that was sewn out of black silk with a velvet collar, and at times also with velvet cuffs. Under the "frock" they wore a silk "caftan." Those were also the wedding clothes that were given to the groom and, on those days, no one imagined to himself that it was possible to walk under the *Chuppah* without them. No one was willing to give up the right to wear a silk "caftan." A Jew who was not able to afford a new one – continued to wear the old caftan without paying attention to the fact that it was torn and the internal fabric was coming out of it. In the winter months, rich Jews wore a fur coat that was made out of silk.

During the weekdays they wore a coat. Underneath it they wore a "caftan" sewn out of a regular fabric or a light coat and, at home, they wore a "house coat." All their clothes were long and you were not able to see a "decent" Jew walking in the street wearing a short coat. Boys who passed the age of Bar–Mitzvah wore a "caftan," not a suit and a jacket. The Hassidim and other orthodox Jews wore a velvet hat also during the weekdays, and under it they wore a yarmulke. People who were not Hassidim wore a black hat. Very seldom were you able to see a colorful hat in town. The few "Ashkenazim" in town – like doctors and lawyers – wore "hard" hats.

There were two doctors in Tluste: the first was Jewish – Dr. Yeger, and the second a Pole – Dr. Gilnrayner. Most of the Jews called on Dr. Yeger. Once a year on 18 August, Dr. Yeger gave a speech at the synagogue in honor of Emperor Franz Joseph's birthday. Dr. Gilnrayner was anti–Semitic by nature, but he took care of his Jewish patients with dedication and devotion. The name of the pharmacist was Emil Titinger. Also the veterinarian was Jewish – Dr. Shperitser. His daughter arrived in Israel and lives in Tel–Aviv. Dr. Yeger's son – Moshe Tzayad – is an engineer by profession and today he works as a high ranking clerk in Haifa's city hall. Yeger and his wife left our town in 1941 and moved to Lwów where Dr. Yeger continued to work as a doctor. His wife became an important Zionist activist in the "Zionists Jewish Women" organization. As far as I know, both of them were killed during the days of the holocaust in the total destruction of the Polish Jewry.

Besides the two doctors there was also "Moshe the Doctor" in town. He was crowned with this title despite the fact that it was not his main occupation. He was a barber by profession and was busy all day long shaving people's beards and fixing their hair. His "medical" business provided him an additional source of income. When he pulled a tooth from the mouth of one of the gentile farmers, his shouts reached the center of the heavens. It was always possible to obtain a number of leeches, and in time of need he knew how put suction cups on a sick person who needed them. Apart from that, he did not know much but it was customary among the town's Jews that in case of sickness not to call the doctor, but to call "Moshe the Doctor" first. And "Moshe the Doctor" came to the patient equipped with two "instruments": he brought his small thermometer and his big head. The thermometer was used to read the patient's temperature, and Moshe attached his head with the big cold ear to the patient's stomach in order to hear what was happening inside it. In truth, many were of the opinion that Moshe's hearing was not very good, but he did not give up his listening. And only after he listened to something, or did not listen to what he wanted to listen, he ordered to put a bandage or to wash with salt water. Two days later it was necessary to call the doctor, but without the care of "Moshe the doctor" it was not possible to cure an illness.

In regards to the "tradition of eating," there was a significant difference between the rich families and those with minimum income. Not everyone was able to provide generosity to his family and properly feed his family. And the truth was that there were many Jews who tried to spend very little during the week. Only a few were able to allow themselves to eat meat every day, and the others were only able to eat potato soup, a small measure of grits in milk and other cheap food. All their worries were centered in one area – from where they would bring the needed food for the Sabbath. There were many Jews, who blessed their hearts if they were able to provide bread for the whole week because also a slice of bread seasoned with onion or garlic was not a bad meal. There was a saying among the poor: "the one who eats bread and garlic – his cheeks are red," and if it was possible to "slaughter" a salt herring for dinner – it was life of "affluence.". In fact, the greatest part of the Jewish population lived in poverty, except for a few Jews whose situation was better.

A totally different matter was the Sabbath's food. In preparation for the Sabbath they polished the silver candlesticks, or the brass candlesticks, and each housewife tried to put many good dishes on the table. When I bring to my memory all the different dishes that were served on our table on the Sabbath, it is impossible for me to understand how we were able to eat and feed everyone. For example, on Saturday afternoon when we returned from the synagogue we blessed with whiskey (on Friday evening we blessed with raisin wine), and to wash it down we ate thick sandwiches, a little boiled beans and "calf's foot jelly." After that, the members of the family washed their hands before the meal, and the affair of eggs with fried onions, fish and a joint of calf's leg that was seasoned with garlic, and all of that was just an appetizer before the meal. Later, grits soup and meat "kugel" (kind of a pie) were served. All of that was put in the oven on Friday evening and taken out on Saturday afternoon. If it was a special Sabbath, like *Rosh Hodesh,* or if a holiday fell on the Sabbath, it was necessary to serve two pies. It is understood that between dishes we sang "melodies." This was a Sabbath meal in the home of a rich Jew. They made sure that the young boys wouldn't eat part of a heart or a brain because, as we know, it can bring bad influence on the memory.

The town's Jews did not eat a lot of vegetables except for potatoes. In general, we only knew a few kinds of vegetables: onion and garlic, big radish and small radish, cucumbers, beet, carrot and cabbage, parsley to season the soup, dill to pickle the cucumbers and horseradish for the meat. We did not eat any other vegetables and we did not even know about their existence. Bread and *Halla* were prepared on Thursday or on Friday for the whole week, and for that they started to bake early Friday morning, twice, one after the other. At first they filled the whole oven with all kinds of "trifles" – ring–shaped rolls baked in pans and without pans, pastry stuffed with mashed potatoes or cooked buckwheat, "malai" (a pastry made out of corn meal) or "mandeburtshink" (a pastry made from mashed potatoes). In the summer during the fruit season, they also baked blueberry doughnuts. In the second "oven" they baked pretty twisted *Hallot*. On Friday night mother put a wide untwisted Halla and a twisted Halla on the table, both covered with a pure white cloth, so they wouldn't feel unworthy because the homeowner blessed the wine and not the Hallot... In the second "oven" they also baked beautiful rye bread. In the last years before I left town, a Jewish baker came to settle in town. His name was Leon (Leyb) Stein but we used to call him the "Ashkenazi baker." The bread that he baked was very tasty when it was fresh and people said that he used a special powder. His small loaf of bread, which cost ten Agorot, lasted for only one meal therefore it was said that buying bread from him was like bankruptcy... During the week we ate the round bread that our mother baked on Friday, which stayed fresh all week long thanks to the climate conditions.

Up to here is the matter of eating. The matter of "drinking" did not cause special problems because the Jews were not heavy drinkers. For the Sabbath they cooked raisins and made raisin wine for Kiddush, besides that, there was half a liter of whiskey at home that we drank after eating fish. We gave our guests tea from the kettle and on special occasions we put the "samovar" on the table so everyone was able to pour his own tea and drink as much as he wanted.

*

And this is how the life of the Jews in Eastern Galicia was carried out at the beginning of the twentieth century. Of course, it is not a detailed description because it is given in a book of a completely different interest – the description of the destruction of this life during the first 40 years of this century. Up to now I only described the traditional way of life, all that is left for me is to describe the changes that took place in the life of the Jews of our town during the first 40 years of the twentieth century. We need to list the many changes that took place in the last generation, my generation, and when I look and try to reach the source of these changes I remember a well–known Jewish tale:

In one of the places the Rabbi gave the tailor a piece of fabric to make him a pair of pants. A long time passed – and the pants were nowhere to be found. The rabbi came to the tailor and complained: look and see, my teacher and rabbi the tailor. For a number of weeks, you are holding my fabric in your hands and you have done nothing with it, and during this time I gave many sermons and I have many more to give. The tailor answered him and said: "Let's see what is the difference between us."

What is the connection? Until the beginning of the twentieth century, Jewish life in Eastern Galicia was conducted the way the holy books dictated them. They did not wish for more and did not ask for more. But, when the Zionist movement was born, new winds started to blow in the Jewish street and, only then, part of the members of our nation started to search for new solutions for their troubles, and new possibilities for contact with Jews around the world in order to find together the desired answers and resolutions. From that time, the emphasis was not of what Rashi said and what the Rambam said hundreds of years before, but what was said and done during that time.

It started with the formation of small groups in each town and city, one from the city and two from the family. Most of them were young men from good families who received their education in the "*Heder*" and *Beit Ha'Midrash*. It was the minority of the minority of the Jewish population, but it was a very active minority. Most of the Jews continued to see the center of their lives within the walls of the "*kloiz*" and *Beit Ha'Midrash* but, even there, arguments erupted between those in favor and those who objected. Those small groups did not remain in their isolation, so they started to connect with the Jewish world, and took part in committees and conferences. Each activity of that kind found an echo within the community, in the synagogues and in *Beit Ha'Midrash*. Later on, they started to establish Zionists groups that directed their activities in two directions: first of all – the deepening the awareness that Israel was the future home of the Jewish nation, and the second – organizing cultural activities in the Diaspora in order to take the Jews out of the ghetto where they had lived for hundreds of years. In Lwów, "The Yiddish Journal," a daily newspaper was published and Jews started to read newspapers that greatly influenced Jewish public opinion. I still remember the shocking headline in the same newspaper: "your brothers' blood is shouting," after the military shot a number of young Jewish voters in the city of Drohobycz during the 1911 election to the Austrian "Reichstag" [parliament]. The background to that matter was the Polish struggle in Galicia against the central power that the Jews were dragged into. During the census each person had to declare his nationality, and the Poles wanted to influence the Jews to declare their loyalty to the Polish nation. It is worth mentioning that the rabbis and the *Admorim* [Hassidic rabbis] helped the Poles with their scheme and influenced their Hassidim to declare their loyalty to Poland, and the song "the Rabbi ordered to write Poland" was sung in the synagogues. The following joke circulated at that time: A Hassid entered the registration office together with his escort who was instructed to direct him what to say. The Polish clerk asked the Hassid questions about his education, about the language that he spoke at home, and about the books that he was reading. But the Hassid did not understand him, and after each question he asked his "guide": "What is the master saying?" Finally, the Polish clerk faced the Hassid and asked him to declare his nationality. The escort answered him spontaneously: Your eyes see that he is Polish, so please write Polish nationality..."

Certainly the Zionists rebelled against this denial of the Jewish nation and invested all their youthful enthusiasm in this war. Those years, when the Jewish national movement walked its first steps on the world's stage, were the most beautiful years of the new period. The small Zionist groups, which were scattered in the cities and in the small towns, saw themselves as the pioneer army of a big movement that was given the duty to wake the world from its deep sleep. Their first duty was to shake the Jewish world from its complacency, and turn the Jews' attention to the solution that the Zionist movement offered in the countries where they lived. This process lasted many years. Zionist activists by the thousands and tens of thousands started to organize themselves in an international Zionist movement, and their intensive activities resulted in the revival of the country of Israel only fifty years after the establishment of the Zionist Union.

Today the scope of the Zionist movement weakened, but on those days, the first years after the establishment of the Zionist movement, its followers were full of excitement with the duty that was given to them – to be the messengers of the new period in the life of the Jewish nation. As far as I remember, the first Zionists in our town were Motya Mozer (who now lives in Israel and with G–d's blessing passed the age of eighty), Melech Freid, and Ben–Zion Libman. They established the first Zionist group "Tikvat Zion" [Hope of Zion] and started to acquire souls to the Zionist concept. I remember when I returned home from the "*kloiz*" on the Sabbath together with my father, the member Gutman, Natan Hikand's son–in–law, shoved into my hand the new newsletter that had just arrived from Lwów. This newsletter was a new greeting from Israel, more important than the greetings that we were getting from the butchers when they emptied Rabbi Meir Bal Hanes' charity boxes. *Keren Hakayemet* collection boxes appeared in some homes and were hung next to Rabbi Meir Bal Hanes' box. Surely, these boxes did not reach my father's home, and no one thought during those days that a *Keren Hakayemet* box could be hung in a Hassid home. Despite all of that, a certain movement was felt – a *Keren Hakayemet* collection "bowl" was placed on Yom Kippur Eve even in the Chortkov Hassidim "*kloiz*". I still remember how R' Moshe Vilner, a "*kloiz*" member and a friend of my father, faced me and said "you have to understand Avramele,' we don't need it, we are only doing it for you since you are Avramele' the son of Moshe Monya..." Many years later, after the great holocaust, I've been told that the same R' Moshe Vilner shouted in a great voice "God is great, G–d is the Lord" when he was led to his death at the cemetery. At the same time I remembered his words to me, "Avramele', we don't need it...." I don't have any complaints against him – everyone was like him and that's how they led their lives. Only a minority, the few exceptional ones, tried to establish a Hebrew school, a Hebrew nursery school, and from time to time they also organized a talent show. Of course, the members of the Chortkov Hassidim "*kloiz*" did not come to watch a "comedy", but the "simple audience," the ordinary Jews, came and enjoyed themselves and learned what theater was all about. Even today, I still remember the great impression the show "The Slaughter" left on me. Miriam Rozenboim, the daughter of Shneior Melamed, and her friend Abrahamtzi Laster excelled in this show. At that time Miriam was the director of the Hebrew nursery school in our town (today she lives in New York). I was only a young "*Heder*" boy at that time.

There were a number of Yeshiva students who received the Hebrew newspaper "*Hazfira*" or the weekly magazine "The World" (the Zionists' union weekly magazine), and there was only one *Yeshiva* student who tried to establish a private library. That one is our friend Yisrael Shechner who now lives in Israel. I was younger than him by a few years, but I was able to borrow from him all the books that he purchased, and so I became familiar with what was called then "Hebrew literature." Yisrael Shechner studied the *Gemara* in his youth and even today he did not forget his studies. But he was one of those *Yeshiva* students who was dedicated to the Zionists' idealism. The flour shop that belonged to his father served as a meeting place for his friends and they let me join their meetings despite the fact I was a lot younger than all of them. His father, R' Itsha Finies, was not happy with the many "customers" who negotiated with his son each time he came to the store.

In general, there was always a struggle between the old and the new generations. Also, years later, when I left to study in Lwów and it was known that I "became unworthy," R' Fishel Goldig, one of my father's friends, met me when I returned home and asked me jokingly: "tell me Avrahmele' – are you still circumcised...?"

During the days of the First World War a total change occurred in the situation. At first, the town was emptied of its young Jews, and eventually most of the town's Jews were forced to take their wandering stick in their hands and all of them became "refugees." In 1915, close to their first retreat, the Russians set the whole town on fire. Our house stood out of town, I climbed on a tree in our yard and from there I saw the town engulfed in flames. Later on it was found out that the town's liberation from the Russian invaders lasted only a few days, and again the Austrians were forced to retreat. It was then that I left town with my mother of blessed memory, and we became refugees. We returned only in 1918 and found the town in poor condition – it was completely burnt and half empty. We went through all the revolutions and changes in power that occurred in the days after the First World War: the Ukrainian republic, the "invasion" of Petlura's people, and six weeks of Bolshevik rule during the Polish–Russian war in 1920. At the end of the war against the Bolsheviks, life started to return to normal. Those were the years after the Balfour Declaration. It was then that we organized a Zionist movement on a large scale. There were a number of Jewish estate owners who gave us a helping hand, such as the Stekel family who for many years leased a farm in the village of Rozshanovka [Różanówka], the father of Professor Martin Buber, and also Pohorilles who owned an estate in the village of Hinkevitz [Hińkowce], and a number of others. All of them accepted *Haluzim* for pioneer training and by doing so they helped us with our activities.

The General Zionists committee: in the center – Dr. A. Stupp

Our activities to organize work for the members of the Halutz movement gave the Poles the impression that the leaders of the Halutzim groups were in fact their leaders, and assumed that they were Socialists and Bolsheviks. The matters reached the point where, before their retreat from the Bolsheviks, they decided to take with them two Zionist leaders as hostages. One of them was, Ludvig Stekel (who died in Israel in 1961), he discovered it in time and moved from Tluste to Lwów. I was the second hostage. I was a young man then. In the morning the Poles invited me to their office, which was located in our home, and advised me not to leave home since I was going to join them that night. The news spread throughout the town and caused a lot of commotion: "The Poles are taking Avrahmele' with them!" I remember that R' Dovide Fiderer came to me on the same day and gave me a sizeable amount of money so I would not travel empty handed. None of the young Zionists dared to walk in the street. At that time the young group included the members Yisrael Shechner, Moshe Pfeffer, Yisrael Fiderer and others.

When the time arrived to leave town, the Poles changed their mind and did not take me with them, but during the six weeks of the Bolshevik occupation I only left the house during the night from the fear that they would come back and take me with them.

The Zionists' activities increased after the country calmed down from the Polish–Russian war. After the historic conference in San Remo, when England was given the mandate for Israel in order to create a home for the Jewish nation, we made sure that the declaration would be read in public in all the synagogues. Also the Halutz movement grew larger and a number of students who gave up their studies joined it in order to arrive quickly to Israel and help in the building of the country.

In 1922 the Ukrainians in Galicia decided to boycott the elections to the Polish parliament. According to the election results the Jews received the seats in the parliament that the Ukrainians relinquished. And so we had more than twenty Jewish delegates in the Polish parliament. The whole town was decorated when Dr. Bernard Hausner, one of the new delegates, came to visit Tluste. Almost all the town's Jews came to welcome him at the train station. He gave a speech at the great synagogue about "Keren Hayesod" [United Israel Appeal] and I don't think that there was one person in town who did not join the fund–drive. I remember how Slome'le the cart owner, whose only possessions were his horse and his flat cart, came to me complaining that I did not come to him to receive his donation to Israel.

We were also very active in other fields. We established a Zionist library and, since we did not have a room for it, we kept the books on the balcony of Yakel Pfeffer, Moshe Pfeffer's father–in–law. I stood there every Friday afternoon, also on the freezing winter days, and handed out books to read. The simple girls had one claim: "May his master give me the thickest book..." and the smart ones choose a book according to its contents and subject. There was another kind of reader – I used to bring books to the Chortkov Hassidim "kloiz", and people who were pious in their heart and their soul received them from me in secret under the table so they could read them in their homes. Among them were: R'Baruch Itsha Vitaska, one of the richest men in our town, and R' Yisrael Glick, the father of Berzie [Berel] Glick, a wise man and one of the greatest scholars of our town. I still remember the great impression that the book "Herzl's diary," which was published in those days, left on them.

Not once arguments erupted in the "kloiz" as a result of reading these books, and we felt the cultural benefit that these books brought to our town.

Every once in a while the different Zionists Unions that were located in Lwów sent delegates to our town. Despite the fact that our town was small and the Zionist groups were small, they had a great influence on the town's Jewish population and many came to hear the delegates' lectures. The "good old days" before 1914, when the community leaders closed the synagogue or Beit Ha'Midrash before a Zionist lecturer were gone. Many from each sector of the Jewish population attended each conference and each party that the Zionists organized. A new kind of "millionaire" was created – people who calculated how many millions of Dunams were in the hands of the Jews, and how many Jews were needed to complete the first half a million Jews in Israel.

*

At the beginning of my article, I talked about the two different kinds of Jews who lived and worked during the two different periods of Jewish life in the Diaspora. However, also during the second period after all the changes in the Jewish community, this community was composed of two different kinds of Jews. In anti–Semite Poland, where the life of the Jews grew worse day after day, everyone wished and waited for a change. However, while the Zionist section was awake and active and wished to bring changes, the other section was completely passive and accepted their life the way they were. And so the situation lasted until the tragic hour that threw the Polish Jewry into Hitler's rule, the greatest and most dangerous enemy of the Jews in all the generations.

And only in this period, which is both tragic and full of glory – the period when one–third of the Jewish nation was killed in such a cruel way, in which the independent sovereign nation of Israel was established – I came to the correct understanding of the Gemara words: – May the Messiah arrive – but my soul will not see him coming. Our generation was witness to the destruction of two different kinds of Polish Jews. It was destined to live in a sea of troubles, blood and tears, in a way that no other generation had experienced before. But all of that will be written and told by those who saw it with their own eyes, those who miraculously saved their souls from the hell of total extermination.

Translated from Yiddish by Gabriel L.

[Pages 31-32]

Early History and Memories
Told by the town's elders and from what I have seen

by Y. Sternlieb

The town of Tluste, which was located by the main Lwow–Czernowitz road, was established in the 18th century during the period of Baal Shem Tov, who lived in our town before his revelation. Baal Shem Tov's mother also lived in Tluste and she also died and was buried there. During the partition of Poland the town became part of the Austrian Empire and since then belonged to the District of Ternopol.

Before the railway was constructed all the goods were transported by wagons on the Lwow– Chernovitz main road through the town of Tluste and every second house in town served at as an inn and a tavern. Like all the towns in Poland the town belonged to a Polish landowner – to Prince Poninski. At the entrance to his castle stood a two story building which was built in the form of a fortress and called "*Brama*" (the gate). It was told in town that, at that time, it was used as a convent for Polish nuns. Later, the fortress served as a center for Polish underground fighters and their weapons were kept in the large cellar. In recent years the Poles opened a cooperative store named "*Kolko Rolinitza*" (agricultural department) on the first floor.

The fortress served as sort of a core and the town's first institutions were built around it. The Polish Church was built next to the castle and the council building, which was called "the council house" by the town's Jews, was built about hundred meters from it. The council building was built with big and strong stones and there was also an inn and a tavern inside it. Small stores, in which the Jewish shopkeepers sold their merchandise, were built around the council building. Every Thursday was a market day in town, the local farmers brought their products to sell and with the proceeds they purchased all the needed merchandise for their homes. The weekly market days and the special fairs, which took place from time to time, provided the main source of income for the town's Jews. During the last years, before the Second World War, Yehoshua Halpern's tavern served as a meeting place for the estate owners who came to town every Thursday and in this way a "stock exchange" for grain was created there.

At the beginning, during the days of the Kingdom of Poland, there were five big stables in town that were built at various points on the edge of town. After the town was passed to the hands of the Austrian rule, these buildings served as stables for the Emperor's cavalry. Later, they were transferred to the hands of the local authorities and given to local public organizations or sold to the town's residents. The stable on the road to Zalishchyky [Zaleszczyki] was given to the Ukrainians who turned it into a community center. The building on the way to Chortkov [Czortkow] was purchased by R' Binyamin Kamerling and became his family's home. The building on the way to Borshtshov [Borszczow] was given to the Jewish community, which turned it into the town's Great Synagogue. The fourth building housed the Polish community center, the "Star", and the fifth stable, which was located on the road to Buczacz, was purchased by a court clerk named Paslavski.

In 1848, the Austrian Emperor, Franz Josef the first, came to visit our town. The town's Jewish residents welcomed him with salt and bread, holding a Torah in their hands, as it was customary to welcome a distinguished guest. When the Emperor asked the Jews what is their question and what they desire, the community leaders asked the Emperor to give the Jews the exclusive right to all the inns and taverns in town. The emperor obliged to their request and gave the order. For many years my grandfather, R' Yehoshua Nagler z"l, kept the certificate in a silver case.

In 1899 the railroad was inaugurated in town and this matter completely changed its appearance. Stores were built in place of the inns and the export of agricultural products to Germany began. According to the regulations this merchandise was exempt from taxes. Estate owners started to fatten the bulls which were also intended for shipment to Germany.

With the expansion of the trade the town's Jewish population also grew. Besides the Great Synagogue there were also a number of religious schools and three Hassidic synagogues: the "Chortkov Kloiz," "Vizhnitz Kloiz" and "Kopyczynce Kloiz." There were also social associations and organizations: the society of "Bikur Cholim" [visiting the sick], the association "'Yad Harutzim" [hand of the diligent men] and the school that was established by Baron Hirsh.

The members of "Bikur Cholim" helped the sick by giving them financial aid, sleeping at their homes and helping those who needed their dedicated help. One Sabbath a year, the Sabbath of Parashat Mishpatim, was dedicated to this organization. On that Sabbath the town's Jews gathered at the Great Synagogue and all the vows of that Saturday were devoted to "*Bikur Cholim*."

The association "*Yad Harutzim*" was founded by the craftsmen to provide help to poor and needy craftsmen. They also had their own synagogue in the cellar of *Beit Ha'Midrash*.

Jewish boys from all walks of life were educated at the Baron Hirsh School. The sons of the poor received a hot lunch at school during the winter months and clothes for all seasons of the year. The institution sent outstanding students, at its own expense, to the agricultural school in "Slobodka Leshna." The graduates of the agricultural school were sent, with the institution's help, to J.C.A. [Jewish Colonization Association] farms in Argentina and Israel. Our townsman, Chaim Gabai, who lives today in Haifa, was one of the "Slobodka Leshna" students who were sent to Israel. The school officials also helped in organizing the cottage industry in town, especially the industry of hair nets that the town's needy girls specialized in. Next to the school was also a bank for loans and "*Kupat Gemilut Hasadim*" ["Interest–Free Loan Fund"] which was founded by the Baron.

A few years before the First World War, a Zionists association named "*Tikvat Zion*" [Hope of Zion] was established in town. Its leaders were Ben–Zion Libman and Melech Freyd. The secretariat of "*Keren Kayenet Le'Yisrael*" [JNF] was established by the association and its secretary was Aba Gutman. He was rewarded to immigrate to Israel and died here a few years ago in Kiryat Haim near Haifa. At the same time a Hebrew School was opened in town. The first Hebrew teacher was Mr. Zilberharber. The teaching, of course, was done in the Ashkenazy accent. A nursery school was also opened under the directorship of Miriam Rosenbaum, daughter of the intelligent teacher, R' Shneor Rosenbaum, who taught the bible to his student with Mendelson's "interpretation." They said that he knew all of Shiller's poems and works by heart. It turned out that all the Hassidim boycotted him and none of them gave his son to his hands. Miriam Rosenbaum lives in the United States and a year ago visited Israel as a tourist.

In 5666 (1906), the town was overrun by a mass of Jewish refugees from Czarist Russia who escaped across the border for the fear of the pogroms. Some of the refugees remained in town but most of them continued their journey across the ocean.

In the same year the new *Beit Ha'Midrash* building was dedicated. It was built with the money that was donated by my aunt, Rivke Braksmier z"l (Rivke the "philanthropist"). A sizable sum was invested in the building of *Beit Ha'Midrash* – ten thousand Florin, but *Beit Ha'Midrash* was opened with a disagreement. According to the plan, the "places" should have been given to regular worshipers, the "veterans," but, in fact, the places were sold to the highest bidders. As a result, the argument divided the town and the matter reached to a desecration of God's name – every Saturday, during prayer time, a number of policemen stood next to *Beit Ha'Midrash* and kept the order...

At the same period a controversy also erupted over the control of the community committee. For many years the community committee was in the hands of the "*Amcha*" [ordinary Jews] and the head of the committee – the community leader – was my grandfather, R' Chaim Nagler z"l. The estate owners – Eliyahu Albin, Meir Kleiner and Yitzchak Vitashka – eyed this position and wanted to take the reins of power into their hands and with the help of the "squire" and the help of the authorities they even succeeded. The argument in this matter ended only in 1914 when the Russians invaded the town and burnt it.

At the end of my article I want to mention two distinguished personalities from among the residents of our town.

R' Pinchas Chodorov zt"l. He was the rabbi of the community of Tluste for many years and one of the greatest rabbis of his generation. He died in the cholera epidemic that broke in our town during the First World War and killed many of its residents.

The second figure was Sara, daughter of Mordechai–Hirsh. She was called "Sara daughter of a well–established family" by many. She was a modest woman who dedicated all her life to the needs of others. Every Friday she walked around town collecting Hallot for town's poor. She cared for the sick and took care of their needs. She also took care of the Jewish prisoners, supported and encouraged them.

Such was the image of our town that was destroyed together with all other Jewish communities in the European Diaspora.

A group of General Zionists with Yehoshua Sternlieb and his family prior to their immigration to Eretz–Yisrael

[Pages 33-34 - Hebrew] [Pages 80-82 - Yididsh]

From the Distant and Recent Past of Our Town

by Shmuel Fiderer–Margulies

It is fitting to begin my words about the distant and recent past of our town with the popular saying: "When we leaf through the history book of our town..." However, is there any written history, printed or handwritten, for our town, which was destroyed, from which we can draw information about the existence of our community in previous centuries? Indeed, a rumor reached my ears on the existence of a history booklet named "Tluste on the Dupa River" that was written by a Polish writer and published in Lwów eighty years ago. However, as hard as I tried to get this booklet, I was not able to acquire it. On the other hand, the handwritten collection "Pinkas Tluste," which was found at the home of R' Zeida, the rabbi's son, included a lot of information about various religious issues, the *Gabaim* [synagogue's treasurers], the slaughterers, the order of prayers, the cemetery and almshouse, but there is almost no historical value to it. Therefore, we need to find the answers to the following questions: since when was there a settlement in Tluste; who were the first families in our town; what was their lifestyle, their source of income, and so on....?

R' Zelig Kramer, May he rest in peace, who was an educated man and knowledgeable in history, told that at the beginning of the 16th century Tluste was only a district market place, a place where local farmers came to sell their products. One clear day, two Jewish families, who came from Russian–Ukraine or from Podolia, settled there and opened small taverns to sell spirits and mead to the farmers who came to the fair. Those were the forefathers of R' Aizik Sternlib (from our time) and they settled on the hill above the water well, not far from the cattle market. Later, several other families arrived from the same area and built houses and opened stores. At the beginning of the 18th century, during the days of Ba'al Shem Tov, there were already several hundred Jewish families in Tluste who were mostly engaged in buying and selling. The Baroness Poninska, whose rule extended through the whole area, had a lot of interest in the development of the town. Therefore, she amended a decree that any Jew who wanted to build himself a house or a store in town would get the land and the garden for his house for free. For the building of the house, he was allowed to use the trees from the local forests for free, his cattle were allowed to graze for free in the town's meadows and he was rewarded with many other benefits. According to a special decree, which was signed at the Baroness' house, Tluste was declared a "free town" and received a special status in the whole area. It is said about the same Baroness, that, during her later years, she happened to be in town during one of the market days. When she saw the first store that sold fabrics, she was so impressed that she bought herself a few meters of "*tzitz*" [fringe] for a dress and paid a great fortune for them – ten gold Ducats!

And so it went year after year. Tluste remained a free town while the rest of the towns and villages had to pay taxes to the Baroness for everything small and large. This situation continued also after the Baroness' death since she included an order to her heirs in her will not to change the status of the town. Once upon a time, a Tluste Jew arrived to the Baroness court and asked to see the late Baroness' son. When he was brought before the Baron, he told a tale that never happened. He said, that he came as a delegate of the Jewish community of Tluste to ask him – in the name of all the Jews – to cancel all the special benefits that were given to the town by his late mother since the Jews did not want to have better living conditions than their neighbors... they wanted to pay the same taxes that all the other towns were paying. The same Jew also presented a forged document that was supposedly written by the management of the Jewish community and sealed with its seal. In it they wrote, black on white, that they do not want a "free town." The Baron thought for a while, and later said: "If this is the will of the Jews, I will fulfill their wish..." From then on, matters rolled according to protocol: the Baron called his director and ordered to change all the "procedures," meaning, to take back all the extra rights of Tluste's Jews and remove the town's "duty free" status! It turns out that, from that day on, the Jew became a regular guest at the home of the Baron and his business manager, and instructed him on the practical work of "skinning" the Jews of Tluste. And, in doing so, he made sure that some of the new taxes that were imposed on town's Jews would enter his pocket.

Therefore, the chapter of payments and extortion of taxes, by all kinds of tricks and excuses, from the rich and the poor alike, started. Anyone who was not able to pay was sent to "*Chad Gadia*" [prison] or was seated at the home of the "*zakitznik*" [executor]. The "*zakitznik*" appeared in the form of a "*dragoon*" (cavalry soldier) from Zalishchyky [Zaleszczyki] who came riding his on horse, sat in the home of the person who owed tax, and lived on his account until the debt was paid in full. And so, the "*zakitznikim*" became regular guests at the homes of Tluste's Jews. I've heard this story, and other stories, from our friendly neighbor, M.Z. Kramer.

Not less interesting is the story about the war of Tluste's Jews against the rioters who were called by the name "*Baraber*", a war that they won.

And who were the "*Barabers*"? And how did they arrive in Tluste and for what? The story was as follows:

In 1898, during the reign of Emperor Franz Joseph I, the Austrian government laid a railroad track throughout Galicia, and the execution of this gigantic enterprise was very difficult. The workers who laid the section of the track near our place were called "*Baraber*" by the Jews. They were tall gentiles with broad shoulders who frightened everyone who came around them with their wild behavior and extreme drunkenness. They spoke with kind of a Polish dialect that was not understood in our locale, and were always happy to start an argument and a fight. And why were they given the nickname "*Baraber*"? For that you cannot come with questions to our Tluste Jews. Who is wise and can investigate the source of the different and strange nicknames that were circulating in our town. It is possible that they were called by that name because they looked a bit like Arabs... There's reason to believe that they were Polish "*Masurians*," but no matter what the origin of the "*Barabers*" was, the fact is that they decided to carry out a small "pogrom" on Tluste's Jews exactly on the first day of the holiday of Shavuot in the year 1898. The excuse for that: the bartenders exploited them, charging higher prices for the drinks, while the shot glasses in which they served the "alcoholic beverage" were too small. The Jews did not know of the danger awaiting them. At that time, they were in the synagogues and the houses of prayer enjoying the sound of the holiday melodies. But, as we say, "Behold, the guardian of Israel neither slumbers nor sleeps." Franz Joseph's gendarmes knew what was going on and burst into the synagogues, in the middle of the prayer services, shouting: "Jews, save your lives!" In the blink of the eye everyone ran to their homes, grabbed anything in sight – axes, "balances" for the carts, and other weapons – and stood behind the gendarmes and marched to face the enemy on the road to Swidowa. The strong and the brave marched in the first rows: the horse traders, the butchers and teenagers, with the determination in their heart to teach the "*Barabers*" a lesson – "for they can hear and see"... The meeting between the two camps took place out of town, on the main road. The gendarmes' leader shouted at them: Stop or I will shoot you! But his shout did not help. They started to throw stones at us and rushed towards us with their weapons: shovels, picks and iron poles. The gendarmes answered with real fire and a number of them were instantly killed. The "*Barabers*" turned their backs and fled. Our people ran after them to the camp where they lived and beat them up. The attack lasted only a few minutes, but brought great disaster on the attackers. A number of them were killed but only a few Jews were injured. No one talked loudly about the results of the attack, they only whispered for fear of "what will the gentiles say," because the authorities were going to investigate the loss of life... But, in the end, the matter calmed down and, since then, the "*Barabers*" quieted down and did not hurt anyone. A few weeks after the event they finished their work and left town. Since then the local gentiles treated us with "respect" and this attitude lasted for a number of years. This was the compensation for the turmoil and for the holiday that was disrupted on Shavuot of 1898.

These events and others like them – sad, interesting and also soul lifting – took place in the town where we were born and grew up. Where our loved ones lived their lives in days of joy, days of mourning and sadness, and in which they perished together with six million holy and pure martyrs from our nation. We will never forget them, we will tell about them and about our town, which is engraved deep in our hearts, to our sons and the sons of their sons, to the end of all generations.

The main street and the main road from Zalishchyky [Zaleszczyki] to Chortkov [Czortków] during the Russian occupation (1915)

[Pages 35-36]

Rabbis, Homeowners, Hasidim, and Scholars

by Y.H. Chodorov

It was customary and acceptable in the Jewish Diaspora that, when an important man came to one of the places and wanted to know the nature of the Jewish community and its spiritual essence, he made the effort to introduce himself to the community's rabbi and, according to the nature of the rabbi, he expressed his opinion on the whole community. For that reason, it is fitting to examine and investigate who sat on the rabbinical chair in Tluste in recent generations, a period of approximately two hundred years.

Like other small communities which became famous in the entire Jewish world thanks only to great sages and Torah scholars who lived there, the name of the community of Tluste was known afar thanks to Rabbi Yisrael Baal Shem Tov who lived and worked in our town for a long period of time. To my sorrow, I don't have the exact details about that period, and I am afraid that these data don't exist: only a few letters, in which Baal Shem Tov added the notation, "from Tluste," next to his signature, and also the tombstone of his mother, Sara, in our town cemetery. From all the calculations we can assume that Ba'al Shem Tov lived in Tluste for ten years, from 5490–5500 (1730–1740). At that time, there was already a Beit Midrash in town, and also a bath house with a Mikveh. That Mikveh was still in existence during the latter period, and was called by all "the Mikveh of Baal Shem Tov."

At that time, there was a rabbi in Tluste by the name of R' Yitzchak. His son, R' Eliyahu–Arye, sat after him on the rabbinical chair. I don't have any additional information about the two rabbis, I only have a few details about the rabbis who came after them and sat on the rabbinical chair during the last one hundred and ten years. I will not attempt to describe the nature and qualities of these rabbis, I will just settle for stating their names and their attributions – each generation and its preachers.

The first was R' Dov–Ber (Bertsi) z"l from the renowned Shapira family. He was the son of the Holy Rabbi, R' Yehudah Meir z"l of Shepetivka and grandson of the holy rabbi, R Pinchas of Korets, May his virtue stand us in good stead. He died in Tluste in the year 5610 (1850). The famous rabbi, R'

Meir Shapira z"l, and the rabbi from Vikno, R' Alter, were the grandsons of Dov–Ber.

The second rabbi was the famous rabbi, R' Avraham Yehoshua–Heshel z"l, a descendent of the famous rabbinical family, Katzenelbogen. He was the son of the Holy Rabbi, R' Mordechai of Korets, May his virtue stand us in good stead. R' Avraham Yehoshua–Heshel z"l, died in Tluste on 9 Nisan 5654 (1894).

The third rabbi was the son–in–law of R' Katzenelbogen, my father my teacher, the famous R' Pinchas z"l, a descendent of the famous Chodorov family from Berdychiv. He was the son of the famous rabbi, R' Duvid z"l from Ros–Banila Romania, grandson of the Holy Rabbi, R' Haim of Kosov and the Holy Rabbi R' Pinchas of Korets, May his virtue stand us in good stead. He died in Tluste on 26 Menachem Av 5675 (1915).

The fourth rabbi was the son of R' Pinchas, my brother, HaRav, R' Avraham Shmuel Aba Chodorov, May the Lord avenge his blood. The murderers, may their names be blotted out, sent him to Belzec together with his family during the "Aktzya" on Isru Chag of Sukkoth 5702 (October 1941). My honorable mother, the Rebbetzin Sheindele, May the Lord avenge her blood, was shot and killed there.

This short list of Tluste's rabbis does not need additional explanation. There aren't many small communities that were rewarded with several consecutive generations of famous rabbis, who sat on the rabbinical chair not only for their merit, but they were also the sons of great and famous rabbis who were educated on the knees of the Torah and piety. This greatly contributed to the fact that the community of Tluste was also an important and well–known. And here, I only want to add one additional detail to the image of my father z"l, who, all his life, fulfilled "You shall meditate on it day and night," and stopped his studies only on the second watch, an hour or two after midnight.

Most of the families in our town originated from Ukraine; many Jews crossed the border and settled in Tluste during the decrees of 5408 and 5409 [1648–9], and also during the prosecutions and pogroms at the end of the 19th century. One of the families, whose attribution continued from the period of the Holy Ba'al Shem Tov, was, according to my best knowledge, the Hornig family. I still remember how R' Alter Hornig walked, at the age of eighty, from house to house on Sabbath eve to collect challot for the town's poor.

The large majority of Hassidim gathered at the Chortkov Kloiz [synagogue] and the Vishnitz Kloiz. The leaders of the Chortkov Hassidim were: R' Aharon-Wolf Brecher, R' Mendel Fiderer, R' Simsho Klein, R' Monye Stupp and R' Motye Shpitser. The dignitaries of the Vishnitz Kloiz were R' Yosi (Yosef) Epstein who was R' Duvid Fiderer's brother–in–law, R' Aharon Drimer, R' Hirsh Bremer and R' Shlomo the ritual slaughterer. All as one were modest G–d fearing Jews, and all of them wished that their sons would be Torah scholars. Besides that, there were the Hassidim of the rabbi of Kopyczynce, the rabbi of Zalishchyky [Zaleszczyki] and other rabbis. It should be noted, that the name "Hassid" was a very wide concept and covered many people who were very different from each other. There were Hassidim who clung to their rabbi and really wanted to follow his ways and study the Torah from him. With my own eyes I saw what one of the rabbis wrote in his notebook: "someone asked me to pray for him, that G–d will give him the heart to understand the Torah." However, Hassidim of this type were already scarce in our days. There were Hassidim who traveled to their rabbi as though he was a "miracle–maker" in order to seek salvation and comfort from his words, because they believed wholeheartedly in the saying "The righteous decides and the Lord fulfills", and all as one believed that "Everything that is connected to purity – is pure."

There was an old Beit Midrash in town, and there was a new Beit Midrash that was built from the money of Mrs. Rivke Braksmier, daughter of R' Yehoshua Nagler z"l, who invested twelve thousand Reynish in its construction. Beit Ha'Midrash was a center for Torah and prayer, and its doors were open almost all day and all night. At the hour of three or four in the morning, the Shamash [caretaker] walked from house to house and woke those who were asleep with his song: "Wake up, rise to work for the creator!" and in the middle of the night, the young and the elderly sat there and studied the Torah with great dedication and diligence.

From among the important homeowners who prayed on the Sabbath at the Great Synagogue, I remember R' Chaim Langholz, who was an important man with a distinguished character. He was not one of the Hassidim, but he "respected their rabbi." In general, I don't member Jewish "Mitnagdim" [opponents of the Hasidic movement] in our town. Even the homeowners who weren't Hasidim appreciated the rabbi and honored him, and everyone paid respect to Torah students. I remember, that Yitzchak Shechner z"l used to come to my father z"l almost every evening, except on Sabbath eve, and for a long hour stood on his feet – in respect of the Torah – and refused to sit in the presence of my father.

A number of Jews excelled as prominent scholars during the last generation: R' Yakov Schor z"l (son of Reb Yitzchak the tinsmith), R' Hirsh Meir z"l and R' Zalman Melamed z"l. They were "learned men," and so they were called by the people. Dr. Berel Wachstein [Bernhard Wachstein] z"l, one of the students of Beit HaMidrash in Tluste, was a known scholar with a world–wide reputation. He became the director of the Jewish library in Vienna, and his compositions in the field of deciphering tombstones in ancient cemeteries left a great impression among the circles who engaged in the new Jewish wisdom.

After many years of separation from my town and my birthplace, it is difficult for me to remember and to list all the respected and important homeowners who wanted, with all of their hearts, to lead their sons in the righteous way, raise them according to the Torah and good deeds. Even so, I will mention a few of them: R' Haim Nagler, R' Monye Gertner, R' Yitzchak Shternlib and R' Haim–Monye Hirsh.

At the beginning of the Jewish settlement in town, during the days of the Polish Kingdom, most of the Jews earned their living producing spirits and selling it during market days. The same was the situation in the early years of the Austrian rule, until the opening of the government stores when the selling of spirits was under the government monopoly. After the railroad from Ternopol to Chernovitz was laid, the grain trade was developed and provided jobs and livelihood to many of the town's Jews. There were also those who engaged in selling agricultural products to Germany.

Yet, many of the townspeople immigrated to the United States in the period before the First World War, and there was hardly a family in town who did not have a relative in America. Many young people, who couldn't find a base for their future in town, left and settled in Vienna or Germany. With the help of the financial aid organization of Baron Hirsh, a number of young people studied in the agricultural school in Slovodka [Słobódka], to be able to settle in the Jewish villages in Argentina. With the initiative of this fund many girls worked in the production of hairnets.

The second event happened during the days of the First World War. Almost all the Jewish homes were set on fire and a great panic broke out. All night long the sound of those who were "burning" reached the center of heavens. After that, a typhus epidemic broke out and in a number of days several hundred Jews perished. As a result, the town's entire Jewish population, except for a very few, joined the Austrian army in its second retreat on Rosh Hashanah 5676 (September 1915), and many never returned to our town. The deportation of Snyatyn Jews by the Russians, which happened on the Holiday of Shavuot 5675, left a difficult and depressing impression in the hearts of Tluste's Jews. When they arrived to Tluste, the town's people have done their best to help them.

This is, in short, what I was able to remember about the life in our hometown, Tluste, and its Jewish community until the period of the holocaust, when this community was annihilated and wiped from under the sky.

May the souls of the pure and sacred be bound in the bond of life, and may the Lord avenge their blood.

———

[Page 36]

The Defeat of Frank in Tluste

by Menachem Teiber

It is known that the Hassidim of Yakov Frank in Galicia succeeded to attract many and sound from the towns around Tluste, such as Chortkov [Czortków], Borszczów, Kopychintsy [Kopyczyńce], Ozieran [Jezierzany] and others. But it was not so in Tluste. And in this matter, a story that I heard from my father of blessed memory, remained in my memory.

Frank's visit to our town happened on a Friday during the winter. Heavy snow covered the town and the roads leading to it, and the townspeople went out to shovel the snow and clear the road for the guest who declared that he was the reincarnation of the "Messiah" Shabbetai Tzvi. Frank arrived in a magnificent carriage, accompanied by a convoy of horsemen dressed in Cossacks uniforms. The guest stayed at the rabbi's house, as it was appropriate for a distinguished man like him.

On Sabbath eve, when the guest opened his mouth to bless the wine, the rabbi immediately felt that he was a complete ignorant, but he did not dare to say so. On the next day, the Sabbath, something happened that exaggerated it and caused the rabbi to lose his temper. One of the town's women came to Frank bitterly crying and asking him for medicine for her sick child. Frank advised her to go to the pharmacy and buy a specific medicine for which one needed to pay a full price. The rabbi, who saw it as a desecration of the Sabbath, approached Frank and called with anger: "You ignorant, get out of my home immediately!" Frank got scared and on the same day he escaped with his entourage to Chortkov.

It was the beginning of Frank's downfall, who pretended to be the "Messiah" of the Jewish people. He and his entire congregation moved farther and farther from Judaism and, in the end, converted and assimilated among the Poles.

[Page 37]

In the Old Cemetery

by Shimshon Meltzer

Translated by Dave Horowitz-Larochette

In the old cemetery the fence is breached all around
And a goat or a cow, and also a horse enters the breach and passes,
Treading on gravestones and skipping and jumping on graves
To graze the good green grass fresh for the unborn.

In the old cemetery the graves are crowded–crowded,
Scattered like wild flowers hunched–hunched gravestones.
Weeds rose on the cheek of every weeping stone and monument,
Moss covered almost every inscription.[1]

In the old cemetery only one gravestone is
Standing upright, not bent over from old age;
The grass around it green and a cow doesn't approach to graze it,
Because it is the gravestone of Sara the righteous mother of the Baal
Shem Tov.

The mother of the Baal Shem Tov died poor and exhausted
And a grave was dug for her among the graves at the end of the row.
A year joined a year until the day came and arrived
To place a tombstone on her grave – but the location was not known.

They traveled to the *tzadik* of the generation – and there's no generation
that doesn't have its *tzadik* –
The *tzadik* heard and held his beard in his palm and smoothed it,
And said: take two young cows that have never been yoked
And they will carry Sara's gravestone and it shall stand wherever it falls.

The cows carried the stone on their backs and it was not tied,
Straight between the graves and dropped it at the end of the row.
Everyone who saw knew and saw that the place was found and known,
And here is the grave of Sara, of blessed memory, to this day.

(From "*Keter*" [Crown] by Shimshon Meltzer)

Translator's Footnote:

1. The examples ק"לפ (referring to the date) and נ"פ (here lies) are used by the author

————

[Pages 37-39]

The Baal Shem Tov in Tluste

by G. Lindenberg

In his short introduction to the history of Baal Shem Tov in his book, "The Hassidut and the Hassidim" (Davir Publications 5688), Dr. Shemuel Aba Horodtzki writes: "We do not have in our hands a reliable source on the history of Baal Shem Tov because it does not exist. I had to get all the material about the history of Baal Shem Tov from various societies that were mentioned in the book "The praises of Baal Shem Tov," and other books that were written by his students and their students."

In view of the admission of one of the first researchers of the Hassidut, it is very difficult to clarify the facts regarding the time that Baal Shem Tov spent in Tluste. At most, it is possible to compare the different versions in this matter and to clarify which one is the most logical. According to prevailing tradition, Tluste itself was, by all accounts, one of the main stops in the walk of life of the founder of the Hassidut.

The lack of clarity and accuracy regarding the walk of life of Baal Shem Tov starts with his birth date. Shimon Dubnov writes (The History of the World, volume 7, page 128): "Yisrael Baal Shem Tov was born in the year 1700 on the border of Wallachia and Podolia in the town of Okop." Dr. S.A. Horodtzki writes in his book "The Hassidut and the Hassidim" (page 1): "Baal Shem Tov was born around the year 5460 [1699] in a small town, on the border of Poland and Wallachia, that was known at that time by its name Okop." A more exact date was written in M. Shrantski's book "Images of the great Hassidim" published by "Beit Yakov" in the year 5705 [1944]. Based on the book "18 Elul" by the Lubavitch Admor, the writer states that Baal Shem Tov "was born on 18 Elul in the year 5458 [1689], on the second day after the Sabbath in the town of Okop in Wallachia."

There is no difference of opinion as to the location of Baal Shem Tov's birth place. Everyone agrees that he was born in the town of Okop, in Podolia, on the border of Wallachia. All the writers of his history also mention that, as a boy, he was orphaned from his father and his mother and was raised by the members of his town. From their words, it is possible to understand that both his father Eliezer and his mother Sara died in Okop, but, as it is known to the people from Tluste, his mother's grave is located in Tluste. Most of the writers of his history silently skip this detail. Indeed, Dr. S.A. Horodtzki knew that Baal Shem Tov's mother is not buried in Okop, but for some reason he moved her burial site to the town of Kutow [Kuty]. And so he wrote in his book "The Hassidut and the Hassidim" (page 2): "immediately after he weaned his son Yisrael, his father, R' Eliezer, died. Days later his mother also died and, to this day, her grave is located in the town of Okop." h It is difficult to understand how a veteran researcher like him was caught in such an error.

Based on the undisputed fact that Baal Shem Tov was orphaned from his father at the dawn of his life, it is possible that he arrived in Tluste with his mother during his childhood, and after her death he was taken to his birthplace where he was raised by the townspeople. It is possible, that his mother had relatives in Tluste who were as poor as she was. According to legend that was common in Tluste, the stone on his mother's grave was erected many years after her death and nobody knew or remembered the place of her burial. One of Baal Shem Tov's grandsons ordered that the stone be carried to the cemetery, and when it fell from the hands of those who carried it – that place was chosen as her burial place. And so they did, and there they erected it. The fact, that Baal Shem Tov's mother was buried in Tluste, proves that he had a special connection to this town where he probably stayed twice during his wanderings between the towns and villages of Podolia.

A partner to this theory is, Eliezer Steinman, who wrote the book "Rabbi Yisrael Baal Shem Tov" (Jerusalem 5708). In the chapter in which he briefly describes the history of Baal Shem Tov (page 100), he writes: "We do not know how many years he served in this craft (of teacher's assistant) and where he went after he left Okop. We only know that he got married when he was around the age of 18, and his wife died some time later. According to tradition, he worked for a period of time as a primary school teacher in the town of Tluste. There is also a theory that at the same time he worked as a forest watchman and, at times, as a caretaker in a synagogue. Once he was invited to be an arbitrator in a trial together with R' Efraim from Kutow. The rabbi, who examined him carefully, realized that he worshiped God with a great mind, and expressed his wish that he marry his divorced daughter, Chana. They came to an agreement and composed an engagement contract. A few days later the Rabbi of Kutow died. His son, R' Gershon, a popular scholar, objected to the matchmaking because he saw that the groom was a simple man and was considered to be a complete ignorant. At the end, he changed his mind after his sister demanded that he keep their dead father's wishes. R' Gershon agreed to his sister's marriage to the man who, according to all signs, did not know how to read or study, under the stipulation that he find himself a craft in order to provide for his wife."

The above–mentioned story is also told in Dr. S.A. Horodtzki's book: "The Hassidut and the Hassidim" (page 5) with a few changes. According to his story, R' Yisrael got married in Okop at the age of 17 and became a widower shortly thereafter. Later, he left his town and moved to a small town near Brody and there he became a teacher. He was an arbitrator in a dispute that happened to R' Efraim of Kutow who offered him his divorced daughter as a wife. R' Efraim traveled and died midway.

The continuation of the story is known. Shortly after the marriage the couple moved to a small village between the towns of Kosow and Kutow, and R' Yisrael earned his livelihood digging clay from the mountain side. His wife delivered the clay in a cart to the town and sold it as floor mortar to Jewish homeowners. R' Yisrael sought solitude in the Carpathian Mountains and prepared himself for his future destination. According to tradition, he lived that way for seven consecutive years, and at the end of these seven years Baal Shem Tov returned and settled in the town of Tluste. His "revelation" took place in this town or perhaps in the village of Koschilovtza [Koszyłowce] near Tluste when he was 36 years old. All the sources are in complete agreement in this matter, and it is fitting to bring here a number of them.

The main source is the book "The praise of Baal Shem Tov" which was written by R' Dov Ber, son of R' Shmuel a slaughterer in Linz, son–in–law of R' Alexander Shohet who was a student and an author of Baal Shem Tov. The book was printed for the first time in Kopys Lita in the year 5575. The words that are brought here were taken from the addition that was published by Dr. S.A. Horodtzki (Davir, 5707, page 53):

"Later, he settled in the holy community of Tluste and was also a teacher there. He was not able to have a Minyan at his home, so he collected people and prayed with them. He was only dressed in Tuzlik of Komey [traditional peasant clothing], and his toes penetrated from the holes in his shoes because he was very poor. Before prayer he went to the mikveh, even during the month of Tevet, and, while praying, drops of sweat dripped from him... and at night, they told him that he turned thirty–six ... and he left the teachings, and they traveled to him from all places."

Dr. Horodtzki, with great caution, also refers to these things as words of legend. In his book, "The Hassidut and the Hassidim," he writes about Baal Shem Tov's return to society in general and to Tluste in particular: "Despite the great patience of Baal Shem Tov and his wife, they were not able to cope with the great poverty in the village, but he also did not wish to beg before his brother–in–law and, again, held to his first work as a teacher's assistant. Another source is telling that some time before his revelation, R' Yisrael was an assistant to a teacher in Horodonca [Horodenka] (according to "Kvutzat Yaakov" page 52). Later, he became a teacher to a customs official. Meanwhile, he studied the craft of slaughtering and he and his family settled in the village of Koschilovtza [Koszyłowce] near the town of Yazlivitz [Jazłowiec]" (there page 7).

And on page 10 he writes: "His time to be revealed has arrived, the thirty-six years that he had to be hidden and concealed ended... and if this legend doesn't indicate the place where Baal Shem Tov was discovered, here is another legend which calls the name of the place of his revelation: it is the town of Tluste in Galicia." This legend can be relied on because he was called by all "Baal Shem Tov from Tluste." And in a comment there: "In a letter from Baal Shem Tov to the Rabbi of Kutow (his brother–in–law, R' Avraham-Gershon) he is not signing himself in the name Baal Shem Tov, as he always does, but he is writing from the community of Tluste to the community of Kutow, May G–d protect and preserve him (the great scholar)."

**The gravestone of Baal Shem Tov's mother in
Tluste's old cemetery**

After the First World War the stone was found
leaning and in danger of falling and was re-erected
by Zionist youth. Under the year 5500 there were
two additional blurred letters. The picture was
published for the first time in "*Menora*" in Vienna (in
German). The picture was brought to Israel in 5693
[1933] and was given to the collection of the national
library in Jerusalem.

Shimon Dubnov writes with more certainty and detail about this matter in his book "History of the Hassidut" (Davir, 5708). Here are a few quotations from this book: "Close to the year 5490 (1730), R' Yisrael settled in the town of Tluste in Galicia, and started to work there as a teacher. At times, he traveled to nearby villages and taught the Torah to the tax collectors' sons. But, despite this, his income was insufficient. A legend tells, that he was dressed as an ignorant peasant and his toes came out through the holes in his shoes because he was very poor" (there, page 46). "In the first years, after the revelation of Baal Shem Tov, Tluste was probably the center of his activities. He lived there permanently, but from time to time he walked around the nearby communities in Galicia and Podolia, such as Horodnica, Kutow, Nemirov [Niemirów], Shargorod [Szarogród]... he mostly traveled to the villages and engaged in the healing of customs officials and Jewish leaseholders. At times, even Polish "land owners" invited him as a doctor" (there, page 48). Approximately between the years 5500 and 5505 (1740–1745), a change came to the life of Baal Shem Tov. He moved from his permanent home, from the Galician town of Tluste, to the town of Medzibozh where he stayed to the day of his death." In a remark there: "It is possible to assume that after his "revelation," about the year 5495 (1735), he stayed for a few years in Tluste, where he previously worked as a teacher, and around the year 5499 (1740), he moved to Medzibozh (there, page 51)." We find that Baal Shem Tov lived in Tluste for fifteen years, from 5490 to 5505, and at least from 5490 to 5500 – ten years!

Also Y. Alfasi, in his book: "Sefer HaAdmorim" (Tel–Aviv, 5721, page 9), briefly mentions the matter of Baal Shem Tov's stay in Tluste: "Rabbi Yisrael Baal Shem Tov was raised by the people of his town Akuf (of course, it should be Okop). He served as a teacher assistant and at night he studied the Torah and the Kabala. From Okop he moved to Tluste... at the age of 36 he was discovered with all of his greatness. He returned to Tluste where he became famous." (According to this, his revelation took place outside Tluste, maybe in a village near Brody. He returned to Tluste in which he became famous!)

As opposed to the detailed testimony of the above–mentioned researchers about the affinity of Baal Shem Tov to Tluste, there were many who did not find it necessary to specify the location of Baal Shem Tov's revelation. Professor Martin Buber brings in his book, "Hidden light" (Schocken Publishing, 5718), only the simple facts about the revelation of Baal Shem Tov, but he does not list Tluste as the location of his revelation: "A student of

R' Gershon from Kotow" (Baal Shem Tov's brother–in–law) traveled to his rabbi and against his will stopped at Baal Shem Tov's for the Sabbath. On Sabbath eve he saw a fire burning above the oven etc. On Sunday he came to Brody, and before he turned to his rabbi he turned to the "great Hassidim sect" in town, told them what had happened to him and added: "A great light is living nearby, go and bring him to the city. They went, met Baal Shem Tov near the village at the edge of the forest, made a throne out of tree branches, sat him on it and he preached the Torah to them."

Also the Hassidut book of Yitzchak Refael (Verfel) does not mention at all the name Tluste in the history of Baal Shem Tov. More than that, a picture appears in the book: "the grave of Baal Shem Tov's mother", but there is no mention where it is located...

*

In this book, which is dedicated to the community of Tluste that was destroyed and no longer exists, we found it necessary to clarify the affinity between Baal Shem Tov and the town of Tluste, and bring the words of the best historians in this matter. These words are especially important for the "next generation" who will know the town only from the descriptions in the book in front of us. The townspeople, who lived there most of their lives, must know to what extent the city was saturated with the "awareness of Baal Shem Tov" which was always renewed by the existence of his mother's grave in the old cemetery, Baal Shem Tov's Mikveh, and especially in the many legends about Baal Shem Tov that passed from person to person. Tluste was rewarded that one of her sons, the poet Shimshon Melzer, has done a lot to deepen the connection between the town and the founder of the Hassidut, with his many poems about the Hassidut in general and Baal Shem Tov in particular that became the inheritance of the Jewish nation.

According to the words of S. Anski, who visited Tluste in 1915 and stayed there for one confusing night during the Russian occupation, in his book "The destruction of Galicia." "The town of Tluste has its own "sacred places." Some say that Baal Shem Tov was born here. In any case, his mother lived here, and here he spent his childhood years. We can see his mother's grave at the cemetery, and at the edge of the town they point to the location of Baal Shem Tov's Mikveh. Baal Shem Tov's mother was a midwife, and he himself was called in youth Yisraelik the midwife's son."

"They told me here many amazing stories about Baal Shem Tov. One of the important homeowners in town dared to oppose Baal Ha'Shem. Baal Ha'Shem said: "this man will remember me"... and surely, a curse stuck to this man for ten generations, his family and his home suffered from many tragedies, and there was not a Zaddik [Hassidic rabbi] who was able to save them."

"Once, on Passover eve, the gentiles brought a murdered Christian boy to Baal Shem Tov's home in order to falsely accuse him of a blood libel. During the Seder, the house was surrounded by gangs of gentiles and soldiers. At the last moment, Baal Shem Tov discovered the murdered boy. What did he do? He dressed him in a Jewish boy's clothing, put a skullcap on his head and sat him next to the table. The dead boy sat together with everyone as though he was alive and well. Baal Shem Tov raised his voice on him: "You bastard! I order you to sway!" and then, the dead boy started to sway like everyone else as if he was reading the Haggadah. The gentiles broke into the house and searched for the dead boy all over the house, but they were not able to find him. None of them thought that the boy, who was sitting and swaying over the Haggadah, was the dead boy that they were looking for. After they left, the boy's soul was taken again and Baal Shem Tov buried him in his yard."

As we know, this blood libel story also served as a subject for Shimshon Meltzer's ballad, "The Guest," and in his way he only took the core out of the legend and changed many details for artistic necessity. In one edition of his books ("The seven strings") he attributed the miracle to Eliyahu HaNavi [Eliyahu the prophet], but, in other editions, he returned and attributed it to Baal Shem Tov.

[Page 40]

Between Tluste the Town and Tluste the Village

by Shimshon Meltzer

Translated by Dave Horowitz-Larochette

Between Tluste the town and Tluste the village,
From the dead afar, on the mountainside,
In a house poor, low and narrow
Lived the Baal Shem Tov, *zatz"l*[1]

The Baal Shem Tov *zatz"l*, was – grief! –
Clothed in a *bruslak*, the attire of a Gentile,
Old and worn, without charm,
And patch on patch and wear on wear.

Wear on wear the body wrapped,
But on the inside love all through
To every crow on the *eruv*[2] [wire]
In repose from weary flight.

The falling snow white and pure
Through the window shone its light...
His lucent eyes had he but opened
"*Modeh ani*"[3] he spoke with awe.

He donned a boot and another boot
And in the *bruslak* he wrapped himself.
Out he went – and at the door
The mezuzah kissed with his palm.

Out he went in light awash –
Into the body dripped the light;
And only one sullen crow
Called "rak ra"[4] from the *eruv*.

The Baal Shem Tov stood, looked around:
"White world, world so bright –

And only a crow calls to fight..."
"*Rak ra, rak ra*" answered the crow.

The Baal Shem hurried to a stream –
A stream that night had made to ice;
The Baal Shem struck the ice and struck again –
In the ice he made a bath

He shed a boot, a boot took off,
And the *bruslak* also was cast;
To the water down he *zatz"l* went,
Submerged himself with great intent.

He dipped, arose and dried himself
And wrapped himself in the *bruslak*.
A world renewed, a festive world,
A world so pure to it he laughed.

He stood and looked around, around...
Barefoot he walked, trod the path.
And from his soles a drizzle
Red on the shining white did spread.

A drizzle of blood on the pure snow –
But he forgot all, forgot.
A splendid world, so beautiful –
And he strode, strode, strode...

Then came one, old and aged,
And straw he carried on his back,
He spread and lay before his feet –
The bleeding ceased and did not flow.

The bleeding ceased and did not drip.
On the *eruv* a crow did beat
A black wing on its black back:
"*Kara'a, kara'a*"[5] – and flew away.

The Baal Shem Tov knew: the decree was torn.
And to his poor house he returned,
From the dead afar, on the mountainside,
Between Tluste the town and Tluste the village.

Translator's Footnotes:

1. *Tzadik* of blessed memory

2. A ritual enclosure that Orthodox Jewish communities construct in their neighborhoods as a way to permit Jewish residents or visitors to carry certain objects outside their own homes on Sabbath and Yom Kippur.

3. "I give thanks" is a Jewish prayer that observant Jews recite daily upon waking, while still in bed.

4. "Only evil" in Hebrew.

5. "He tore, he tore", in Hebrew.

[Page 41]

Hasidut in Tluste at the Outset of the Century

by Meir Sternlieb

The years 5663–5674 (1903–1914) were the years of growth for the Hasidic movement in our town. Most of the town's Jews belonged to one of the three Hasidic rabbis that were popular in our town: the Chortkover Rebbe, the Vizhnitzer Rebbe and the Kapishnitzer Rebbe. Each Hasidic sect had its own synagogue. The Chortkov Hasidim congregated at the "Chortkover Kloiz," the Vizhnitz Hasidim had their own synagogue the "Vizhnitzer Kliezel" in one of the rooms in old Beit Ha'Midrash, and the Kapishnitz Hasidim prayed at the "Kloiz" that was rented from Elik Platzker. All three synagogues were located on the road to the village of Lisowitz [Lisowce].

The three Hasidic groups belonged to three different social classes. The Chortkov Hasidim were wealthy people – estate owners, bankers and money lenders, lumber merchants and forest lessees, leather and fabric merchants and others. The Vizhnitz Hasidim belonged to the middle class – grain merchants, store owners, teachers and brokers. The Kapishnitzer Rebbe was the rabbi of the simple folks. Also, most of the women followed the Kapishnitzer Rebbe. There were Jews in town who did not belong to any Hasidic sect. They prayed at the old "Beit Ha'Midrash" and were close to the Vizhnitz Hasidim.

From time to time the Vizhnitzer Rebbe and the Kapishnitzer Rebbe came to town for a visit, but the Chortkover Rebbe did not come, and his Hassidim traveled to him.

The rabbis used to come to town on Thursdays and stayed for seven days. That week was a holiday week in town. When the Kapishnitzer Rebbe came, the horse merchants decorated their horses and left to welcome him. They brought him to town in a multicolor procession with songs and dances.

On Sabbath eve they "set the table" in "old Beit Ha'Midrash" which was full to capacity. On the same Sabbath eve the square next the synagogue also changed its appearance and was crowded with people, men, women and children who came to enjoy the radiant face of the holy rabbi. After the prayer and the meal, when each Hasid tried to grab a little "leftover" from the rabbi's food, the Hasidim escorted their rabbi to the hostel with song and dance, full of devotion and enthusiasm. At that hour the entire "gentile" street was conquered by Hasidim dressed in kapotas [black coats] and "streimlachs" on their heads. All the townspeople, from the young to the old, joined in the singing and clapping and their voices erupted to the Heavens.

On Saturday night they ate the third meal at the rabbi's hostel and the sound of their melodies sounded from there late into the night. Also the little ones mixed among the older Hasidim. They sat and listened to the amazing stories of the Hasidim about the miracles and wonders that the rabbis and the tzadikim have done as their eyes shone from excitement and happiness. At the end of the meal, about an hour before midnight, the various "request seekers" started to arrive, each holding a "note" with a request in his hand. Hundreds stood in line to hand the rabbi the "note" with "redemption" on its side.

The bustle and joy continued throughout the week that the rabbi stayed in town. Evening after evening, the Hasidim gathered at the rabbi's lodging and sat and talked to him to the late hour of the night. And all that time the landlady served them the best delicacies: stuffed dumplings, "Knishes" [stuffed dough] with fragrant roast and different types of beverages. The rabbi's Hasidim also came from the nearby villages to see their rabbi and receive his blessing.

At that period, in first years of the 20th century, the committee of the Jewish community of Tluste was mostly composed of Vizhnitz Hasidim. The community leader was Chaim Nagler. The Chortkov Hasidim did not accept this situation. In the elections to the community council, which took place in 1908 and 1913, a difficult struggle took place between the Chortkov Hasidim and the Vizhnitz Hasidim. The leader of the Vizhnitz Hasidim was an old rabbi, R' Pinchas Chodorov, and his helper was Yitzchak Shechner. Leading the fight on the Chortkov Hasidim side were the estate owners Eli Albin and Baruch–Itsi Vitashka. In the 1913 elections, the Chortkov Hasidim won but the departing community leader, Chaim Nagler, refused to hand over the community legers and only with the help of the police were they able to take them from him. Since then, and until the First World War, the community leader was R' Baruch–Isti Vitashka from the Chortkov Hasidim. After the triumph of the Chortkov Hasidim both sides reconciled and the opponents made peace with each other. Since then, the matters of the community ran peacefully and quietly until the outbreak of the First World War in August 1914.

[Page 42]

One winter night

by S. Meltzer

Translated by Sara Mages

One winter night HaBal Shem Tov went
for a dip in the *Mikveh* named after him,
surely, it is the *Mikveh* in our town, the town of Tluste,
that maybe today its location is known...

The winter night was a dark cold night,
not a shining moon not a hinting star,
only the snow was white and slightly blue
showing the path to the treading boot...

And HaBal Shem walked fast,
walked straight, no hesitation, no fear,
and after him walked with fear and trembling
and trepidation, the man servant....

But when they entered the bathhouse
it was pitch dark, like never before –
and the servant started to tremble more,
and suddenly he raised his voice with a cry:

"Woe, our rabbi, I do not see a thing...
the darkness is sealed... hurting me a lot...
scratching and scraping... needles in my flesh...
as if skewers are stuck in my head!"

"Don't be afraid! Don't be afraid!" HaBal Shem answered him,
and a smile sounded clearly in his voice:
"These are only icicles not skewers...
God's beautiful wonder and work ...

Raise your hand upwards, hold the tail
of one of the hanging icicles and say:

"Candle of frost, candle of frost, please light up
please shine and glow, Let there be light, Let there be light!"

Though there was cheer in the voice
of a man who was mocking and ridiculing a fool,
the servant, not knowing, repeats
the words of HaBal Shems and says:

"Frost candle, frost candle catch on fire and alight
please light up and glow, Let there be light, Let there be light!"
and immediately fire gripped the icicle,
the simple icicle of ice and frost.

And here it is burning, and here it is shining,
splashing sparks, sparks on sparks,
glittering toward him like crystals
the rest of the icicles that are hanging around

And the servant is standing wondering and looking
staring with wide open eyes,
wonder of wonders, precious stones
wherever the eye rests....

And again he raises his hand up
and he wants to touch, to examine and to inspect...
but HaBal Shem says (in the meantime he dipped,
wrapped, and climbed) to the servant in a laughing voice:

"If you were allowed to light and look,
you were not allowed to touch, to examine and to inspect..."
and he puts one hand on the servant's eyes –
and immediately the sight and the light disappeared...

And he puts his second hand on the hand
that is raised to examine and to inspect,
and holds it gently, with compassion, with love,
like a father holding a baby's hand in his hand...

And HaBal Shem is walking outside
walking straight, no hesitation, no fear,
and follows him like an embarrassed child,
and with trepidation the man the servant...

But it is a winter night outside – a bright illuminated night,
the moon is shining, the star is hinting,
and the snow is bluish and very white,
and answers with a whistle to the treading boot...

[Page 43]

Reb Velvel Melamed

by Yisrael Shechner

As one of the students of R' Velvel Melamed, I see it as my duty to write a memorial for him in Tluste's Yizkor Book. I am afraid, that none of the townspeople who closely knew him is left, and therefore it is my duty to describe the image of the teacher who taught the Torah in our town. Many students studied the Torah from him, before and after me, and everyone came out of his school armed with the great knowledge that was taught according to the customary system of those days, fifty to sixty years ago.

As we know, the educational methods at that time were very far from the methods of today, and there were many flaws in the expression and the explanation. The teacher did not even find it necessary to properly explain the expression "Come and hear" that appears in the Talmud every so often. He never imagined that his students didn't know how to distinguish between the two different kinds of "Come and hear," that one is in the form of a question while the other solves the problem. For a long time I did not even know the simple thing, that the literal meaning of "Come and hear" is "Come and listen" until the book "Introduction to the Talmud" came to my hands. At that time, I was not able to forgive the teachers who did not provide those regulations to their students and did not try to make it easier for them to understand the special way of the Talmud by bringing the problems and the solutions in the lectures.

Velvel's knowledge of the Torah, in the first five books on the Old Testament, was quiet good. Without a doubt, his duty as a "reader" in the synagogue helped him with that. However, his knowledge of the Prophets and the Writings was very weak. He did not know how to explain a verse without reading the explanation to it first, and also after he did so, his explanation was weak and faulty. I remember that once he was asked to explain the verse "Al yithalel hoger kimfate'ah" [he who goes into battle should not boast as much as the one who has won it] – he translated the word Hoger [soldier] to lame. It can be said, that the verses of the Bible were mostly known to him from the references of "Torah Or" in the "Gemara" and not from the source in the Bible. In general, at that time they did not value the study of the Bible and knowing a "passage" was not considered "acquiring knowledge." A "scholar" was only the one who was well versed in the Gemara, "erudite and powerful debater," while knowing the Prophets and the Writings and grammar was considered to be the beginning of an "education" which ended with mischief and agnosticism. For that reason, the teachers did not see the reason for investing time in the studies of the Bible, including my rabbi, R' Velvel Melamed.

In the intervals between studies he read us words from the Torah according to his method. He used to say: "The Torah, Moses' Torah, is compared to wheat. Can a man eat grains of wheat as they are? First, you have to grind the grain into flour, sift the flour, knead it to dough and bake the bread. Only after all of that, a man can eat the bread and digest it. The same is with the words of the Torah. First came the Tannaim [Rabbinic sages] who clarified the theories according to the thirteen measures that the Torah requires, after them came the Amoraim [Jewish scholars], and after them the various commentators. Without all of them we were not able to understand the laws of the Torah."

On the side of his occupation as a "Melamed" [teacher], R' Velvel Melamed set himself time for the study of the Torah. By the time he reached the age of eighty, he managed to "get through" the six orders of the Mishna eight times. R' Velvel was the typical "wise student," but he did not have any concepts in world matters. We can see his philosophy and approach to world matters from the expression that he used to say: "It is written: the Lord said, I have the silver and I have the gold, but do I need to safeguard his money? Mendel Fiderer can do it, not me...", and by the way, Mendel Fiderer's three sons, Alter, Leibtsi and Moni studied with R' Velvel. The Hasidim in town did not send their sons to him, because he was known as a "Mitnagged" [opponent to the Hasidut].

R' Velvel had difficulties making a living and lived in poverty all of his life. He had one son who was a scholar like him, but, unlike his father he was a Hassid. He also had three daughters who came of age but never got married. However, R' Velvel accepted everything with love and, God forbid, he did not resent the creator and the way that he had treated his worshipers. As he used to say: "Everything God does is for the best." All of his life he behaved like a pious God–fearing Jew and performed all the deeds – the easy and the severe alike. He was an extreme "Mitnagged," so much so that he hated the Hasidut, the Admorim and the Hasidim alike. Once I was a witness to this event: R'

Velvel sat in the Chortkov Hasidim Kloiz, diligently studying his lesson in the Gemara. A group of Hasidim, who sat next to him, told stories about the marvels that their rabbis preformed and drank "LeChayim" for the spiritual exaltation of one of their rabbis who passed away on that date. Later, they studied a chapter of "Mishnayot" [the smallest unit in the Mishnah] in memory of that righteous, and after their studies they stood and recited "the Rabbi's Kaddish." As a pious Jew, R' Velvel was forced to stop his studies and repeat "Amen, may the Lord be blessed…" However, he was furious and angry that he was forced to "stop his studies." I also learned from him for the first time about the scandal that took place at the court of the rabbi of Luh. The son of the Ruzhiner Rebbe locked himself in his room on Yom Kippur eve and refused to receive his Hasidim with their "notes" and their "presents." In this, the matter of opposition to the Hasidut R' Velvel was in agreement with the "Maskilim" of that generation even though in all other matters there was a polar contrast between his opinions and their opinions.

This is how the image of my teacher and rabbi, R' Velvel, remained in my memory. He was a Jew who has devoted himself all his life to serving the Creator, fulfilled the Torah from poverty without enjoying the "vanities of this world." He firmly believed that this world is only a corridor to the parlor – to life in the next world.

[Pages 44-45 Hebrew] [Pages 86-87 Yididsh]

The Beginning of the Zionist and the Socialist Movements in Our Town

by Shmuel Fiderer–Margulies

During the first decade of the 20th century, when the different streams of Zionism already succeeded to arouse and stir the emotions of the Jewish population around the world, Tluste's Jews were immersed in a deep sleep. Surely, there were few individuals, mostly people who traveled to the big cities of the Austrian Empire for their business, who were touched by the sparks of Zionism, but when they came to spend the Sabbath or celebrate the holidays at the bosom of the families, they did not have the time or the will to establish a Zionist association in our town. Even a passionate Zionist like Aba Gutman (Natan Hikand's son–in–law), who expressed his Zionism with a handsome and well kept "Herzl beard," also stayed away from the public and has done almost nothing to create a Zionist group in our town. The writer of these lines does not know about the existence of a Zionist association before 1921. For a short period of time, a tea house was opened at R' Yosele' Sternlieb's new home. A few Yeshiva students with Zionist inclinations gathered there to read the Hebrew newspaper "Hazefira" and other nationalist newspapers and conduct conversations and discussions over a cup of tea. But also this "club" did not last long. R' Yosele' Sternlieb came to the conclusion that keeping a tea house in order to sell a few cups of tea was not a profitable business and after a short period of time liquidated his business.

Approximately at the same period of time (in 1912), a Hanukah party was organized by Meir Platzker (son of R' Leybus). The party took place at "Goviarda" hall and the program was both nationalist and Zionist. The speech that was given by the Zionist preacher who was brought from Lvov left a great impression. The program, which included the reading of poems by Haim Nachman Bialik and the singing of "Hatikvah," aroused the public interest.

Since then, the Jewish public gathered from time to time at the town's Great Synagogue and a Zionist speaker from one of the big cities preached before them about Zionism and various national problems. But, all of that did not reach the founding of a Zionist association with regular members who would establish the movement in town and help with its programs and finance.

One of the strong opponents of the Zionist movement was Tluste's rabbi, R' Pinchas Chodorov z"l, who was a wise and great Torah scholar. He was afraid that the new movement would bring atheism to the community of Tluste which was considered to be the fortress of Hasidut. I remember an event that took place: Once, a famous lecturer came from Lvov, entered the rabbi's house in order to talk to him about Zionism. He opened in this language: "Our teacher and master the rabbi! All of us are the sons of the same father, so why are we divided into two different camps! We should unite and work shoulder to shoulder for Zion and Jerusalem! The rabbi answered him with his great wisdom: "The matter is true and correct! We are the sons of one father and one mother, but what is not allowed for us – is allowed for you...!"

In comparison to the lack of national activities among the Jewish population, there was an active national activity among the non–Jewish population. There were three national Polish associations and a Ukrainian association named "Sitesh." These associations, with their active and noisy activities, brought jealousy to the hearts of the young Jews and increased their will to work and act for the Jewish nation. However, only at the end of 1912, a few weeks after the Jewish socialist movement was established in town, the young adults who leaned towards Zionism woke up and established a Zionist association. This association fulfilled its duty with great success and stood at the head of the Jewish National activities until the days of holocaust and destruction. In the light of the difficulties and the stumbling blocks that stood before the Union, like the great opposition of the rabbi and the Hassidic organizations, we see in the establishment of the Zionist Union an important accomplishment in Tluste of those days.

*

The fact is, there was not a substantial basis for the existence of a Socialist movement in our town. We did not have "proletarians" (although we had more than enough beggars....) and the craftsmen didn't differ in their social status from the small merchants, nor were they inferior to them. For example, R' Zeida the tailor, the owner of a long beard who sewed cloths for the Polish landowners around Tluste, had a big house (next to the river close to the Bathhouse Street), as well as the carpenters, two or three in number, who worked together with their sons. Even the bookbinder had his own house. Therefore, it is no wonder that the socialist teaching of Marx and Engels found no echo in the hearts of most of the townspeople.

At the beginning of the summer of 1912 a doctor from Ternopol with socialist ideas happened to be in our town. During his vacation he came to visit his relative and, with nothing to do, he gathered on Saturday eve several dozen boys and girls at the Babtzi's home and laid before them the international socialist program. He was not content with just the Marxism theory, but brought evidence from the Torah on the social character of Jewish morality. In this way he excited the hearts and minds of the youth to the socialist idea and after a short discussion it was decided to establish a socialist association in town and a planning committee has been elected on the spot. One of its members was Berale' Weisman who was an apprentice in a cobbling upholstery shop. When he was in Chernovitz he was a member of the socialist association there and knew all the songs that they used to sing by heart. Berale' Weisman taught us various revolutionary songs and two months later, during the first association meeting, we already knew how to sing the songs of "storm and struggle" and repeated them before the crowd in the thin voice of young boys. This time the lecturer was the socialist Hirsh Bratholz from Zalishchyky [Zaleszczyki], who delivered a long speech in which he excited the young audience. Our choir sang songs by Adelshtat and Bovshovar,

and ended with the anthem of the Bund movement "Brothers and sisters from work and hardship." With a lot of enthusiasm, the assembled decided to establish the Jewish social association "Z.P.S" [Jewish Social Party]. The leadership was elected in place but the registration of members to the association and the collection of money for financing the activities were postponed to Saturday night. We returned home late at night from the meeting where we formed an alliance with the "doctrine" of Marx and Engels. Our spirits were high and our eyes were raised to our town's pure sky, to the glowing moon that hung and stood over the summit of "Mount Moriah" and felt in our hearts the meaning of the verse: "And the Jews experienced light and happiness..."

With great energy and excitement, we started to work. We rented a hall, handed a request to the district governor to approve our by-laws and called the "Jewish Social Party" (Z.P.S) center in Krakow. With that we ordered newspapers and books, opened a library and started to organize an amateur theater. The director of the theater was a young talented woman named Ginandel who was also a dance teacher in Tluste. After that we tried to organize an eight–hour work day for the boys who worked as shop–assistants, but we failed due to our lack of experience in this kind of a struggle.

On the other hand, our second activity, the May Day celebration, was only partially successful. At noon we gathered at the association club house and from there we marched in the town's streets holding sticks covered with red paper (so we wouldn't look like the "Heder" boys on Lag Ba'omer). We sang songs and shouted: "Hurray to May first!" until the town's one and only policeman arrived and scattered the "demonstration."

After that we continued to bring speakers from Zalishchyky, Chernovitz, and Stanisławów. Those speakers widened our education and lit the "source of our souls" until the outbreak of the First World War in 1914 which destroyed all of our socialist dreams. Without a doubt, at the end of the war the young generation continued to weave the golden yarn of the political and social activities as a continuation to our modest start in the Zionist and socialist activities.

[Pages 45-46 Hebrew] [Pages 80-89 Yididsh]

The Period of the War
Between Poland and the Ukraine

by Ben–Shlomo

The First World War lasted for more than four years. At the beginning of 1919, after the military collapse of Germany and Austria, Tluste's Jews started to return to their half– destroyed town. In most cases they did not find their homes or their businesses standing. Each one of them wanted to find a roof over his head, to find a shelter wherever possible. Those who came back carried the meager belongings that were left in their hands and crowded into the few houses that were left standing after the destruction. They seized and filled the building of Baron Hirsh School, Beit Ha'Midrash, the courthouse, the jail cells, and even settled in the homes of those who arrived late from their wanderings. Slowly, slowly they began to strengthen their bodies and straighten their tired backs, and after four years of wandering each one of them wanted to enjoy the years of calm and relief that started to appear in the political horizon.

And now, suddenly, amid of all this preparation a new war broke out! This time between the Ukrainians and the Poles.

At the beginning, the front was far away from us, somewhere in Przemyśl [Poland]. But a battle also took place in Lwów where the two sides fought each other using canons from the Great War and other tools of destruction. The whole matter was unrealistic, how? The great world diplomats were sitting in Paris, negotiating peace and arguing about the fourteen principals of President Wilson that were designed to secure the freedom and safety to all mankind and to all nations – and here, two small nations found a window of opportunity to fight each other. Two nations, which were enslaved to other nations for hundreds of years, were spreading death and destruction among their own people and the Jews who lived among them.

The story was as follows: The Poles prepared themselves during the days of the World War for the time when their national independence would be returned to them. They prepared an administrative government, trained their army and also marked the borders of their kingdom. In contrast to that, the

Ukrainians approached the matter only at the end of the war. In great haste, a small Ukrainian country was established in Stanisławów under the leadership of the lawyer, Petroshevitz, and immediately started a war against the Poles. For us, Jews, a "delicate" and dangerous situation was created, and our leaders tried to adopt a natural position in the conflict between the two nations. In the meantime, "The Jewish National Committee," which was organized in Stanisławów, demanded equal rights and a social–national autonomy from the Ukrainians. In truth, the Ukrainian leaders promised to fulfill all the demands, and the cultured and civilized among them repeated and expressed their support and sympathy to our demands. However, at the same time, the mobs, who were carrying weapons, shouted: Jews, get ready, now we are the masters!" and started to persecute the Jews. In spite of that, at the beginning there were Jews who claimed that it was not correct and fitting to take a neutral standing toward a country that we lived in and found shelter on its land. In this case we have to take a positive stand to support it and help it... The main spokesman of this kind of "positivism" was the lawyer, Dr. Yisrael Waldman, brother of the Zionist leader Moshe Waldman. Under his influence a Jewish brigade was organized in Ternopol and was given a double duty: providing protection to the Jews from Ukrainian gangs and, on the other hand, to fight with them against the Poles. But this strange political outlook blew up very fast, like a soap bubble, immediately after the pogrom that was carried out by Petliura's gangs in the cities of Ukrainian Russia. At the same time when we were all in grief and anger over the acts of the Ukrainian gangs, we did not see any expression of sympathy from our "friends," the Ukrainians of Eastern Galicia.

*

It is a wonder in my eyes how, at that time, Tluste's Jews managed to maintain peace of mind. They did not lose control and didn't get caught in panic. During that period, which was filled with tension and great danger, their sense of responsibility to maintain their unique Jewish existence awakened in them and they made every effort to protect it. The youth, the socialists and the Zionists started to work diligently in order to strengthen their ranks. They organized meetings, established committees to help the needy, and organized cultural parties and classes in Hebrew. In general, they managed their social and cultural activities with energy and dedication, as though the days were normal days, as though nothing had happened. The ground burned under our feet and various gangs and armies passed by our town. Once, they arrived from Chortkov [Czortków] and once from Zalishchyky [Zaleszczyki]. They terrorized women and children, and here and there even tried to loot and scorn. At the same time, the young met in the evenings in the union hall to hear a lecture, to organize a political debate, or practice for a show. There was not even the slightest feeling of depression or despair (we were probably sworn optimists).

For the sake of truth, it should be noted that the Ukrainian dignitaries in our town prevented, to the best of their ability, any riot or violent attack on their Jewish neighbors. The mayor, Avrila Bunder, used to warn the Jewish grain merchants each time the Ukrainian authorities wanted to confiscate their merchandise. The teacher, Badluk, an educated man with a musical talent, used to come to our parties and sing "Ha'Tikvah" or the "Marseilles" with the audience. At that time he was the commissar in charge of political interest and prevented, as much as he was able to, any discrimination and any injustice towards the Jews. There were also a number educated Ukrainians who eased our sufferings during that difficult period, the period of the "Petrosvitz scandal." There have been cases when the military headquarters in our town confiscated grain or other kind of merchandise from the Jews, who were going to transport it to another town where there was shortage of food, and distribute these products free of charge among the needy gentiles. A delegation of Jewish socialists went to lobby before Badluk and obtained his agreement that the merchandise that was confiscated from the Jews would be given to the socialist group who would distribute it among the needy Jews. The merchants, who suffered from these confiscations, attacked the socialist group with shouts and "ethical" claims. They claimed, that Jewish property cannot be confiscated and given for free, and other claims of the sort. They demanded that the confiscated merchandise be returned to them, or at least half of it. But the socialists did not respond to their demand, kept their agreement with Badluk and divided everything among the poor people in town. Among the members of the socialist group were young energetic men, who went to the forests of R' Meir Kleyner and Baruch Itizik Vitashka in winter carts, and brought from there (with the agreement of the forests' owners) wood for the poor, and even chopped the wood with their own hands. Those activities were welcomed with joy and satisfaction by the town's poor, and aroused anger among the wealthy persons in town.

At the same time, an amateur group from the socialist association practiced the production of the play "G–d, Man and the Devil" by Yakov

Gordin, and also performed it in Chortkov for the benefit the town's orphanage.

An enthusiastic activity also took place among the Zionists in town, especially in light of the hopes and the possibility that a Jewish state would be established. The awakening started after the publication of the "Balfour Declaration," Our town's landsman, Avraham Stupp, who was a talented speaker, spoke on different occasions in the synagogues and, with the power of his words, he gained souls to the Zionist movement. Miriam, daughter of Shenior Melamed, organized a group of girls and taught them Hebrew. Preparations were made to establish a pioneer center in order to train and educate young people for their immigration to Israel. The activities of the Zionist sector did not lag behind the activities of the socialist group. They also had an amateur group with talented members, and also organized parties that brought excitement to the hearts of the teens. In this manner, we were able to pass the difficult period of the Polish–Ukrainian war without halting or minimizing our social and national activities.

*

Meanwhile, the Polish army was getting closer to our region and our locations, and the Ukrainians were losing the positions they held in their hands. Now, we found out that the Poles were already in Ternopol and a week later they already captured Chortkov. One summer morning the Polish army arrived in Tluste and put an end to Petrosvitz's power.

In the midst of those days, the writer of this article was able to get out of Eastern Galicia, which, at that time, resembled a barrelful of gun powder, and never had the chance to visit his beloved birth place. Since then, for a period of more than forty years, his strong longing for the town where he was born, Tluste in the Zalishchyky district, never ceased.

[Pages 47-49]

The San Remo Celebration and the Zionist Activity

by Shmuel Fiderer (son of Moshe)

After the approval of the Balfour Declaration at the San Remo Conference and presentation of the mandate on Eretz–Yisrael to the British government, a great celebration was also to take place in our town, to mark the event which sparked a wave of joy in the heart of every Jew in the Diaspora, especially in the hearts of our Zionist friends. As is customary in such cases, a committee was elected for the preparation of the celebration and, besides the Zionists, it also included homeowners who were not organized in the Zionist federation.

First and foremost, the committee turned to the state authorities and requested a license to hold the celebration and a demonstration–parade in the town's streets, and received permission to hold a celebration and a parade. The district governor gave the committee members a letter addressed to the commander of the state police in which the police were asked to keep the order on the day of the party. On its side, the police also promised to help us.

After we received the permit in our hands, together with the promise from the police, we started to plan the celebration so we could hold it with great glory and splendor. There were two Hebrew schools in town, one under the management of Mordechai Spector whose fame was known all over the area, and the second under the management of Yosef Lechter who also had a large number of students. In both schools the students started to study songs and poems with Zionist content – to sing and to recite, and they were trained to march in a procession. A uniform was chosen for the students: white dresses for the girls, dark pants and a white shirt for the boys.

The preparation towards the celebration left its mark in town and within a few days all the stocks of blue and white ribbons, which were purchased for the purpose of decoration, were sold out. Michael Hesing, a former horseman in the Austrian Cavalry, organized a company of riders and Jewish estate owners promised to send the best riding horses in their stables for that purpose. Everything was organized to perfection. The youngest among the marchers in the procession were going to wear blue and white silk ribbons, and hundreds of button loops, in the national colors, were prepared for distribution among the rest of the marchers and the spectators. And the most important of all – we prepared a large number of blue and white flags to hoist in the procession. All the townspeople, Jews of all walks of life, also got ready for the celebration. They mended their clothes towards the celebration and decorated the facade of their houses with national flags and other decorations. The balcony of Dr. Emil Bleicher was decorated with a magnificent Persian carpet, the picture of Dr. Theodor Herzl was displayed in its center and two long blue and white flags adorned it on both sides.

The whole town was filled with life and movement and the sound of happy people came from all sides. However, we were not the only ones who were busy with preparations for the day of the parade – also the anti–Semite rioters, from among the Poles, were getting ready. They organized their battle troops in order to disturb us and stop our celebration. To do so they gathered in town all their friends from the entire area.

*

The day of the celebration arrived. It was a warm and pleasant spring day. The wind did not blow and even a small cloud did not darken the blue sky. From early morning there was vigorous activity in the town: Young and old, men, women and infants, everyone rushed to the gathering point on the town's border, to a place that was called the "valley" by the townspeople. It was a grass–covered valley with enough space for the townspeople who came to participate in the procession. Last minute preparations took place there, little girls came in their sparkling white dresses and their chests were decorated with blue and white ribbons. The older teens came dressed in dark pants, white shirts and blue and white ribbons tied to their hands. The elderly Zionists also came to join the procession. The Jewish estate owners, who lived around Tluste, kept their promise and sent handsome riding horses which were also decorated with blue and white ribbons. Michael Hesing, the riders' commander, stood before his unit for a training exercise.

Meanwhile, news arrived from the town that masses of farmers from the entire area started to gather in it and their number was growing by the minute. This news spread concern among the assembled crowd, but the organizers of the festivities believed that they had someone to rely on: after all, they had a written permit signed by the provincial minister and a promise from the police to keep peace and order in town. And if so – what is the concern and what is the fear? Therefore, we continued to organize the procession according to plan, and started to march in perfect order towards the town's streets.

When the procession got closer to the building of Baron Hirsh School, thugs emerged from the adjacent alleys and attacked the small children first. The children panicked and began to flee in tears and shouts to their homes. The leader of the thugs, Peranishek Blumicz, stormed Dr. Emil Bleicher's house, tore the expensive Persian carpet in two, broke Dr. Herzl's picture and furiously tore apart the national flags that were hung on both sides of the picture. At the same time the thugs, under the leadership of Antosko Dodekei who at that time was the commander of the municipal police, broke into the ranks of youth, tore off their ribbons and loops and at the same time ripped their clothes and underwear with great pleasure. When the young people who rode the horses tried to resist them and deter them from their actions, a dangerous situation was created and almost ended in a "pogrom." However, the events did not reach a dangerous stage and there were no casualties, only a few among us were slightly wounded and two have been seriously wounded: Yisrael Gertner, brother–in–law of David Nuremberg, and Mesholam Eger.

When the commotion began we tried to turn to the state police for help, but there was not a living soul in the police station. Throughout the day, and until the late hours of the evening, a policeman hasn't been seen in the town. They deliberately disappeared and abandoned the Jews to the mercy of the rampaging thugs, and they even did not see the need to apologize for it.

The panic subsided shortly after the dispersal of the procession and people calmed down. The streets were filled with crowds of people and everyone was getting ready for the festive meeting which was to take place in the evening. During the evening hours, people came from all corners of the town to Beit-Ha'Midrash where the impressive meeting took place. Several speakers took the stage, spoke in honor of the festive occasion and even brought practical ideas for the continuation of the Zionist activities among the adults and the youth. The festive meeting for the San Remo resolution was closed in a festive mood and the singing of "Techezakna" and "Hatikvah."

"Macabi" soccer team

Keren Hakayemet committee of "Gordonia"

The attack of the thugs, which greatly prevented the joy of the holiday, also caused some positive effects. It enhanced the sense of unity among the town's residents resulting in increased participation in the festive meeting in Beit-Ha'Midrash to the point that it was too small to accommodate those who came and many were forced to stand outside, and also gave the speakers a lot of material for Zionist propaganda. The speakers rightfully pointed at the behavior of the people of the new regime, who had just entered their new positions after they were enslaved to a foreign regime, the Austrian regime. Now they were seen in all of their ugliness and demonstrated that they hadn't learned anything from the lessons of the past. The speakers approached the town's Jews of all works of life, and asked them to join the ranks of active Zionists, to buy the Shekel [membership in a Zionist organization] and take part in the elections to the Zionist Congress, and turned to the young people with a call to join the ranks of those who fulfilled their Zionist dream. He asked them to give up their education and dedicate themselves to constructive work within the Zionist youth organizations and the "Halutz" movement.

There was a lot of echo to the things that were said at the meeting. The next day, people who usually stayed away from Zionism and "politics" now gathered in groups, argued passionately and took a stand on statements made at the meetings. With that, an enormous push was given to the Zionist movement and to the political activity in town. Each political party strengthened its connection with the party's headquarters in Lvov in order to increase their activities during this window of opportunity. The general secretary of the Zionist Socialist party, "Hitachdut," the member Fishel Verber z"l, came at that time to our town. He gathered the party members and lectured before them. We immediately started to reorganize the "Hitachdut" chapter in town and also elected a new management ("presidency") which included the following members: Yehoshua Schechter – chairman; Meir Sternlieb – vice chairman; Chaim Naglar, Yeshayahu Rosenthal, Lion Brandes and Dov Pfeffer – board members, and Shmuel Fiderer – secretary.

Immediately after that we rented an apartment that served as our club. It was a three–room apartment in Lion Brandes' building, on the floor above his apartment. There, we were able to develop our wide and varied activities. We arranged our special library, a drama club and a non–political soccer team under the leadership of Dr. Greenberg. And most importantly – the first "Halutz" group was established within the ranks of our party. At the same time we received an order from the "Halutz" headquarters in Lvov to establish an aid fund for the Halutzim, and to start with our activities to train the Halutzim in the agricultural farms in our area.

And here began a bitter struggle with the estate owners and the Jewish tenants near our town. When we turned to them with the offer to accept a group of Halutzim to work and train on their farms, each one of them tried to evade us with different excuses and pretexts. One simply said that he did not believe in the ability of young Jewish men to work such a difficult work. The second pretended to be "merciful" and claimed that his heart did not allow him see young Jewish men working in such exhausting work that they are not used to. Everyone rejected our offer with different excuses, and it is better not to mention and list them.

And now, salvation came to us from one place. Near us was a village by the name of Hinkovza [Hińkowce] where the quality of its land was the worst of the worst, the worst land in our area. The Hinkovza farm owner was a pious Jew, R' Avraham Pohoriles z"l. He was a generous man when it came to giving to charity, and loved Israel with all of his heart. Twice a year he gave his products to our town's poor: he sent potatoes for Passover, firewood for heating upon the arrival of winter in addition to other charitable acts that he performed. So we decided to leave for R' Avraham Pohoriles' farm and try to talk to him about the possibility of accepting a number of Halutzim for "Hakhshara" [pioneer training].

When I came to him and presented my request before him, he burst out laughing and said: "who knows better than you, my friend, my fields are poor and meager, are you playing a joke on me with this offer?" I explained to him that all the farm owners were afraid to receive Jewish workers, and I wanted to prove to them that R' Avrahamzi Pohoriles was not afraid and willing to sign a contract to employ a group of Halutzim in order to influence them and move them from their stubborn stand. R' Avrahamzi pondered a bit and said: "if so, send me ten Halutzim." I asked him to add two young women, but to that R' Avrahamzi did not want to agree. Only after I explained to him that in the absence of Jewish girls to "Koshering" the meat, the young men were likely to fail and eat non–kosher meat – R' Avrahamtzi agreed to add two young women to the contract.

In this manner we arrived at the first contract of employment of twelve Halutzim, and we knew very well that they wouldn't be able to cope with the conditions in Hinkovza because of the poor quality of its land. A short time after the Halutzim left for Hachshara, I came to visit them and asked R' Avrahamzi if he was satisfied with their work. R' Avrahamsi answered me and said: "the children, God bless, are very well, they dance..." and, as it is known, that with the dancing of the "Hora" a pioneer soul is being formed.

When I turned to the estate owners and showed them the contract with R' Avrahamzi Pohoriles, they also started to relate differently towards the matter of employing groups of Halutzim. I left, together with Isko Viesglas, to one of his relatives who owned an estate in Chersheniowce [Szerszeniowce]. In his home we met his father-in-law, Guthertz from Chernovitz, who was a known Zionist public figure in Bukovina (at that time it belonged to Romania). After negotiation the estate owner, Viesglas, signed a contract to employ sixty Halutzim. His main property was the Zastavna estate, but there was plenty of space in Jezierzany for the many workers who arrived from Tluste, Jezierzany, and Lvov. Today, most of them live in Kibbutz Schiler near Rehovot, and a number of them are scattered around the country, in cities and in farms. After that, we were able to send Halutzim to almost all the Jewish–owned farms, and I am able to say with confidence that everyone was satisfied with their work.

We also established a troop of "Hakhshara" in town that was housed at the home of Sheindl Rottenstreich, and also this troop succeeded in its work. The Halutzim success in the farms was so great, that non–Jewish workers started to see them as serious competition. The matter reached the point that the non–Jewish workers in Rozhanovka [Różanówka] and Hinkovza organized a strike against the employment of Jewish workers. The police interfered in Rozhanovka, and a Polish policeman named Zakshevski was beaten and wounded. In spite of all that, the Halutzim continued to work onthe farms because the estate owners were satisfied with their work. Only the farm in Hinkovza was deserted because of the difficult condition of its land.

The "Hitachdut" branch in Tluste was in constant contact with the Halutzim in all the Hakhshara locations and sent them lecturers for Sabbath social gatherings and other cultural events. At the same time, the Zionist youth movement, "Gordonia," was established in town under the patronage and with help of the "Hitachdut" party. "Gordonia" youth association accepted the best of the youth in town. Most of them were able to reach Israel before the Holocaust and they live there today.

The activity of the branch of "Hitachdut – Socialist Zionism" stood on a high level. All the Jewish newspapers, in Yiddish and Polish, were available in our club. On the Sabbath it was possible to find there about fifteen newspapers of all kinds, and many of the worshipers stopped at the club on their way home from the synagogues to peek at a Jewish newspaper. On Saturday nights, lectures on different subjects took place at the club and drew a large number of listeners. Our town was a town of Zionists and intellectuals, and many of its residents showed great understanding and interest in the theater, from local productions to visiting theaters.

In 1933 I emigrated to Israel with a "personal certificate." Unfortunately, I was forced to return to Poland in 1938 and suffered, together with all of

Tluste's Jews, in the horrible years of war, 1939–1945. In spite of that I was lucky that able to return to Israel after the war. I remember that in one of the "aktzyot" my wife urged me to hurry up and hide, I answered her and said: I ridicule Hitler and his killers together because I ate meat in Eretz–Yisrael, as the tradition says, the one who eats meat in Eretz–Yisrael must lay his bones there...

A group of members of _Gordonia_

[Page 50]

The Hebrew School

by Klara Spector

After the First World War, the teacher, Mordechai Spector, arrived in our town and started to establish the first Hebrew School in town. He earned his Jewish education in a "Yeshiva" where he dedicated himself to his religious and Jewish studies and, in addition, received a quick training to teach Hebrew. The first class was opened in his private apartment without any special furnishing. The benches and the tables were made of simple wood planks, and the school lacked the facilities that were customary in institutions of that sort. However, it was very successful and many students flocked to him to learn conversational Hebrew.

The people of "Agudat Yisrael" did not approve of the establishment of a Hebrew school in town. Immediately, they established a religious school by the name "Beit Yakov," and, in addition, started to spread rumors and slander against the Hebrew School. Then, an incident happened that gave them the opportunity to bash the new school. During one of the school's trips to visit the Halutzim, who were in the Hakhshara [pioneer training camp] in Szerszeniowce, one of the students was inflicted with stupidity and went, without his teacher's knowledge, to buy pork meat. The matter became known in the city and the teacher was invited to the city's rabbi. The rabbi rebuked him that he was feeding his students with pork meat and using S.L. Gordon's inappropriate interpretation in his teachings. The teacher was able to dismiss the first claim, and as for Gordon's commentary, the teacher proved to the rabbi that the interpretation is clear and comprehensive, and there's nothing inappropriate with it. As a result, the rabbi was asked to announce in public, at the synagogues, that all the words of slander against the school were unfounded and baseless.

After this argument there was a short pause until the men of "Aguda" found a new subject with which to torture the school. They started to claim that the students were ignorant in matters of Judaism, and didn't even know how to wrap their Tefillin. Also this claim was immediately refuted. One of the parents, Izyo Herman, asked the teacher to teach the laws of Tefillin to his son, and the boy was so successful that everyone saw the lack of taste and logic of this claim. Since then, the school started to prosper and students who first studied in "Beit Yakov" also moved there.

It was Spector's great joy to see the school in bloom, to hear his students speaking the Hebrew language in the city's streets, and to receive the admiration of the city's residents. The school prospered and about ninety students studied there, in addition to the students who received special private classes.

One of Spector's exceptional students was Shimshon Meltzer, and the teacher dedicated special attention to him. When he was asked why he was so dedicated to this student, he said: a student who shows a strong will to study needs to be encouraged, and this student deserves all the encouragement that he is given.

The Hebrew School with the teacher Mordechai Spector

———

[Pages 51-52]

The Hebrew Language in our Town

by Atalia Segev (Ettel Teiber)

A Hebrew school, and also a Hebrew kindergarten, existed in our little town, Tluste, even before the First World War. The teacher, Miriam Rosenbaum, daughter of the teacher Shneor, was a resident of our town. She's currently in the United States. The school was not just intended for a handful of educated people, but for the broad sectors of the town. Ordinary Jews – store keepers, small merchants and craftsmen – sent their children to the kindergarten and to the Hebrew school.

The Hebrew school, which consisted of three classrooms, and the kindergarten next to it, resided in a private home, the Guttesman home. The Hebrew language was taught in the Ashkenazy accent and efforts were made to speak Hebrew within the school premises. Even today I still remember the song, "We are Hebrews – we will speak in Hebrew," that I learnt at the first Hebrew school. I remember with kindness the teacher Zilberhaber, who taught us the language in the "Hebrew in Hebrew" method with reading and music, and with the Hebrew songs that we became fond of. The kindergarten and the first grade constituted one class. It was decorated with pictures and maps which illustrated to the children the meaning of the Hebrew words with the help of pictures, just as is the case in today's schools. The curriculum and the songs that were sung – all of them were related to the Land of Israel and planted in the hearts of the young students the love to Zion and the longing to the Eretz–Yisrael, to immigrate and to live in it.

I remember the memorial service for Dr. Herzl that took place in our town, and I got to participate in it. The great preparation for the service was felt at school and in the kindergarten and we, the children, were taught to sing a Hebrew song which started with the words "Cry Yisrael!" On the day of the memorial service we were led to the Great Synagogue where eulogies have been read. At the end of the eulogies three children from our school, me included, climbed on the stage and recited the poem "Cry Yisrael!" in memory of the great leader.

I remember this experience from my days in the kindergarten, but because of my young age I was not able to go to school. Meanwhile, the First World War broke out. We were exiled from our town and wandered in the countries of the Austrian Empire. At the end of the war we returned to Tluste. The town, most of whose homes were destroyed or burnt, was rebuilt and life started to flow in their usual course.

As a result of the Bolshevik Revolution in Russia, many Russian refugees arrived to Poland. In this way the teacher, Spector, arrived in our town. He settled in Tluste and started to give lessons in Hebrew in the Sephardic accent. Among the first students of Spector the teacher were my friends: Michael Mesing z"l (died in Hulda), Beno Pfeffer z"l, Munia Haspel z"l and May he live – the poet, Shimshon Meltzer. (Of course, there were many others whose names I no longer remember). In time, my sister Zirel and I joined the Hebrew class that was taught by the modest and noble teacher, Spector. We were among the first girls who studied Hebrew in our town and the push to join the circle of students was given to us by our friends in the following circumstances:

The teacher Spector and his students decided to produce and present a Hebrew play named "The selling of Yosef." When the roles were assigned it turned out that they were lacking the proper "sources" who knew Hebrew. Then, a few friends came to me, invited me to their teacher's apartment and presented me with the fact: they started with the rehearsal and gave me the part of Levi, Yosef's brother. My excuses that I can't speak the language, that I forgot the little that I've learnt before the war, did not help. At the end, I caved in to the teacher's pressure and my friends' insistent pleading and took the part. I repeated the teacher's words that he read to us without understanding the meaning of most of them. Indeed, the play was held and received many cheers from the audience most of whom did not know Hebrew and were satisfied to know the content of the play.

My participation in the play brought me closer to the teacher Spector and the group of his students and I joined the class together with my sister. The members of the class spoke only Hebrew among themselves.

Over time Mr. Spector opened a private Hebrew school (at the home of Rochtsi Manis Gartner). The interest to study Hebrew grew among the young people. Youth movements, such as "Acheva" and "Gordonia, " were established and gathered the best Jewish youth in town. All of them strived to provide their members with the knowledge of the Hebrew language before they left for "Hakhshara" [pioneer training] and the emigration to Eretz–Yisrael. My sister and I also joined the "Halutz" movement.

In 1927 I emigrated to Eretz–Yisrael speaking the language and turned to agriculture. Today, I am active in teaching the Hebrew language and the value of Judaism to Jewish children who came from various countries in the Diaspora. In this manner I continued the thread that my teacher and rabbi, Spector z"l, started to weave. He also got to emigrate to Israel, but passed away a short time after he arrived here.

The seed that was sown in my hometown, Tluste, was not planted for nothing. It sprouted and grew, its stalks ripened and they are harvested in joy in the independent country of Israel, our liberated homeland.

The Hebrew School with the teacher Meidman

[Page 52]

The "*Gordonia*" Branch in our Town

by Menachem Teiber

I do not know the exact date on which the branch of the "Gordonia" movement was established in our town. I only know that the preparation for the establishment of the branch started in 1926. The initiator was Bernard (Dov) Peffer, among the active members of the "Hitachdut" movement in our town and one of loyal and dedicated Zionists. In fact, his brother, Beno (Baruch) Pfeffer, was the organizer but for some reason he was disappointed with the movement and left it. Over time he grew closer to the extreme right and established a chapter of the Beitar movement in our town.

The activities of the branch were the same as the activities of other youth Zionist movements. We organized trips out of town and sang the songs that we studied at the Hebrew School from our teacher Mordechai Spector z"l. In 1927, I left for a Gordonia summer camp in Biltsha–Zlota [Bilcze Zolote] and brought from there the famous "Hora" of Bistritski. I was the only member from our town who participated in that summer camp.

The chapter received a great push when Michael Mesing joined its leadership. Michael was already a graduated Halutz, spent a number of years in the "Hakhshara" [pioneer training] and was a candidate for emigration to Israel. During that time there was a split in the Halutz movement and Michael joined "Gordonia" He directed our branch until the day of his emigration to Israel.

In 1929, when I was seventeen years old, I left for "Hakhshara" training in Lvov. My friend, Tevel Reinish (Arazi), who was the same age as me, left with me. I did not have any difficulties with my parents because our home was a Zionist home, but my friend left his home against his parents' wishes and after a difficult argument. A year later, in 1930, I emigrated to Israel.

When I visited our town in 1935 I found a magnificent "Gordonia" branch. A number of my friends finished their "Hakhshara" training and were getting ready to emigrate to Israel, but only a few of them succeeded in doing so.

A group of members of *Gordonia*

[Pages 53-55]

The "*Beitar*" chapter in our town

by Natan Maimon

The Revisionist Zionist Movement, which was founded and started its activities in the 1920s, immediately found supporters in our town. That same year a chapter of "Brit HaTzionim HaRevizionisti" ["Union of Revisionist Zionists"], under the leadership of the lawyer Roth, was established in our town. The members of this new political party were mostly young people who were very enthusiastic about the Zionist idea. They also managed to excite many others, especially from circles that until the arrival of the revisionist faction were very far from the Zionist idea.

The plan of action of the branch of the Revisionist Zionists was not much different from the rest of the Zionist parties. Like the members of other parties, the members of "Brit HaTzohar" [acronym for HaTzionim HaRevizionistim] also engaged in cultural activities, distribution of the "Zionist Shekel" in preparation for the congresses, fundraising for various Zionist funds and stormy arguments on Zionist matters. At that time, the fulfillment of the Zionist idealism was only a distant dream because none of the members thought about immigration to Eretz–Yisrael in the near future. Therefore, they weren't different from the members of other Zionist parties of which only a few of them dared to immigrate to Eretz–Yisrael at that time.

The turning point came much later when the youngest members of "Brit HaTzohar" became impatient and started to ask questions along the lines of "Ma Nishtana?" [what has changed?] – "How is "Brit Hatzohar" different from other Zionist parties? Can we just preach others to immigrate to Eretz–Yisrael? How long can we admire the achievements of a few immigrants and at the same time sit idle in the Diaspora?" In this manner these members continued to grumble and be difficult until they drew the logical conclusion from their different stance. They got up, left "Brit Hatzohar," and founded a chapter of "Beitar" (the alliance of Yosef Trumpeldor) in our town. The leader of the chapter was Herman Steinig z"l, who at that time was a law student. However, it was quickly discovered that he wasn't the right person for the position of the commander of "Beitar." Indeed, he was a good and serious young man, but in his soul he was a "Brit Hatzohar" man. He dreamt of a legal career in the

Diaspora and had no intention to immigrate to Eretz–Yisrael in the near future. Maybe we were wrong in our assessment of this man but, the fact is, we decided to replace him. We elected Beno Pfeffer z"l, who continued in this duty until the Holocaust period. This is the place to mention that there were no ideological differences between "Brit Hatzohar" and "Beitar." and both worked in full collaboration.

A Hebrew class was founded in the period when Beno Pfeffer was the commander of the chapter of "Beitar." The Hebrew teacher was Yosef Lechter z"l who dedicated a lot of time, effort, and unlimited love for this goal. "Beitar" rented a separate clubhouse (the first clubhouse was located at the home of Fishel Schor z"l). There, the members started their activities in order to prepare themselves for emigration. They "invaded" the large plot of land where R' Fishel Pfeffer's lumber yard stood and organized military exercises and sports games to the discontent of the "host. " R' Fishel Pfeffer, Beno's father, always claimed that he was ready to give up his son's "customers" who disturbed his customers from buying lumber and coal. However, R' Fishel Pfeffer was a good Jew with a compassionate heart and never thought of banishing his unwanted guests. I'm afraid to say, that he even enjoyed watching the boys playing with "guns" and that his son was the "commandant• who commanded them. The exercises usually took place in the afternoon and on Saturday.

Beno Pfeffer – the commander of
"Beitar."

Immediately after its founding, the chapter of "Beitar" started to search for places in "Hakhshara" kibbutzim for its members, and a short time later three members left for a "Hakhshara" kibbutz in Klesów, Wolyn. The first three were: Yeshayahu Mozer z"l, and May they live a long life – Yakov Schechter and Natan Maimon. They were followed by Shlomo Heler, Ben–Zion Fink and many others. Several members of "Beitar," who didn't want to wait until they were able to immigrate the usual way, skipped all the stages of pioneer training and emigrated illegally to Israel in various ways.

As far as I remember, the members of "Beitar" were the first to distribute products made in Israel among the town's Jews. They left in pairs in the evenings carrying fruits and products from Israel: oranges and grapefruits, wine and juices, halva and sweets. It is fitting to note that the chapter of "Beitar" in our town was not built on the account of other political parties, and only a few members from other parties joined it when it was established. Most of the members came from circles that were far from Zionism, and even did not dream of joining a Zionist party. The members of "Beitar" gained the respect of the town's people with their level–headed behavior and their good deeds. I wish to mention here two events that won a special respect from the residents of our town:

In 1933, "Beitar's" clubhouse received the news that Ze'ev Jabotinsky, the leader of the Zionist–Revisionists alliance and "Beitar," would arrive in Chortkov for a visit and give a lecture on Saturday afternoon. It is understood that the young Beitarim, the students and the admirers of Jabotinsky, longed to hear the words of their leader, and more than that, they were craving to see him face to face. But how could you travel on a Sabbath from Tluste to Chortkov, a distance of twenty–five kilometers? Surely, the members of "Beitar" were taught to respect the holy values of our nation, and it is known that you can't desecrate the Sabbath in public and hurt the feelings of the town's Jews who were mostly pious. And on the other side – it is not describable, that the Beitarim wouldn't see, or hear, their teacher and master when he was so close to them. What did they do? They decided that whoever wanted to reach Chortkov and listen to Jabotinsky's lecture needed to walk to Chortkov. And who among the members of "Beitar" did not want to arrive?

And so, all the members of the "Beitar" chapter, dozens of teenage boys and girls, left on Saturday morning by foot for Chortkov. Unfortunately, it was a rainy day and a downpour accompanied them all the way. The heart was aching to the sight of these beloved teens who walked in the rain and got wet to their bones. But, they were happy, they sang and were joyful and their faces radiated from happiness.

This deed of strictly observing the holiness of the Sabbath (to be more precise – preventing the desecration of the Sabbath) by "those unruly teens", found an echo in the hearts of all the town's residents, and increased their respect. Even those who treated the activities of "Beitar" as "childrens" games", changed their minds and started to treat the "Beitar" chapter and its activities with great admiration.

The second event took place a few months before the 17th Zionist congress, when all the political parties in town started to get ready for the election war. First of all, they started to raise money for this target. It was customary to organize a fundraising campaign among the members and the supporters, and in that manner balance the election budget. The "Beitar" headquarters decided to take care of the matter its own way. They decided to raise the required money for the election fund not from the members and the supporters, but from the labor of their members.

But how can you make a living in Tluste which has no factories, clerical work is not known at all because nobody needs clerks, and all the agricultural work is done by Ukrainian farmers who do not stand and wait for Jewish teens to come and help them with their work. And if so – from where will salvation come? But, there is no need to worry. As we know, nothing is standing before the will, all the more so when it is guided by the desire for a lofty goal. And if those two join together – work would be found also in Tluste for Jewish teens.

There were many wheat merchants in our town who bought, among other things, ripened corncobs and stored them in their attics, or in special barns that were called in a foreign language "Koshnitzes."

Members of "*Beitar*" in a festive demonstration

There, the corn dried very well during the winter months and in the spring the kernels were "peeled" off the cobs and packed in sacks for shipment. Since the preparations for the election war started in the spring months, "Beitar's" headquarters eyed the job of "peeling" corn, a work that could be done by the Beitarim and the income would be dedicated to the election fund. It is understood, that on one side the Beitarim were ready to take the job offer wholeheartedly, but on the other side the merchants, who were giving the job, thought that the idea was very strange. Who saw and who heard that young Jewish children from "good homes" would take upon themselves such a hard work? And which merchant, who respected himself, would give such a job to Jewish teens? It is clear and known that they were not able to do the work properly. For sure they would play with the work for an hour or two, bring disorder to the warehouse, and leave. No, good boys, I can't give you such a work" – the Beitarim heard from each of the merchants that they approached for the job. Also R' Fishel Pfeffer, father of the chapter's commander, was one of the wheat merchants. Without a choice, Beno Pfeffer approached his father and asked him to give the job of peeling the corn to the Beitarim. Also Fishel Pfeffer did not want to hear about handing the job to the Beitarim. The matters reach the point that Beno threatened to go on a "hunger strike" if his father would not obey his wishes. The father was not influenced by the threat and excused his son with a forgiving smile. But, Mrs. Leah Pfeffer z"l, the mother of the chapter's commander, gave her husband a serious "ultimatum" and tipped the scale in favor of her son. In the end, Fishel Pfeffer gave the job of peeling the corn to the members of "Beitar."

The peeling work was not done by empty hands. Fishel Pfeffer had a hand operated machine that helped with the work and the machine was made available for the Beitarim to use. And these young teens worked diligently and performed the work seriously and with full responsibility. R' Fishel Pfeffer was greatly influenced by the positive attitude and the dedication that the teens showed, and he himself started to lobby for them. He walked from merchant to merchant and told each one of them about the "miracle" that the Beitarim instigated with their work, and so he influenced them to agree to hire them. After the work was done for R' Fishel Pfeffer, it was not difficult to get work from other wheat merchants. Everyone treated the Beitarim with trust and fondness, and willingly gave them the work of peeling the corn. The Beitarim's dedicated work, and the way they chose to collect the money for the election fund, granted them the admiration of the residents. Later it was expressed with the larger numbers of votes that were given to the Revisionist Zionist list, and it was greater than the optimist prediction of the Revisionists.

Such were the members of "Beitar" in Tluste, beloved teenage boys and girls. It's a pity that not all of them managed to reach their desired target – Israel. May this article be their memorial.

May their souls be bound in the bond of life.

A group of members of "*Brit Hatzohar*" (Revisionist Zionists)

[Page 56]

Zionist activity and pioneer training

by Eliyaho Albin

Translated by Sara Mages

When I think about the Zionist activity in our town, I recall the days of the blood riots in Eretz–Yisrael in 1929. The Jewish press in the Diaspora announced them in bold letters and called the Diaspora Jewry to mobilize aid for the Jewish settlements in Israel. This news touched the heart of each of us. Every day a list of the settlements that were attacked, and the names of the victims, appeared in the newspapers. Also our town, Tłuste, which was one of the small towns in Poland, came to the rescue and greatly increased its contributions to Keren HaKayemet and Keren Hayesod. To this day I remember the meeting that took place then at the Great Synagogue. All the townspeople, from the youngest to the oldest, participated in it. HaRav, R' Shmuel Aba Chodorov, Tłuste's rabbi, spoke from the synagogue's Bimah and after him spoke director Pel and Dr. Albin. All of them called the town's Jews to help their brothers in Eretz–Yisrael and enable them to acquire the necessary weapons for self–defense. After the meeting, the town's dignitaries went from house to house and collected the contributions of the Jewish residents. At that time, director Pel, Dr. Albin, Mrs. Krasutski and Yakov Stekel participated in the collection of donations.

Seven years later, in the days of the riots of 1936, there were already a number of Zionist youth organizations in our town. They helped the adults to collect funds for the benefit of the national funds. The most common form was organizing a "flower day." Usually, this activity took place on a Sunday when most of the residents were free from their business. That day various merchants and agents came to visit our town and the chances of success have increased considerably.

There were also two "points" for pioneer training in our town. One was on the Rozanowka [Różanówka] estate, with Stekel, where the pioneers engaged in agricultural work. The second was the Betar center in the town itself. There, they engaged in various "unskilled" jobs such as chopping wood, loading sacks of grain at the train station, and other such jobs. It turned out that it was very difficult to exist from these jobs. I remember that Fischel Pfeffer saw it his duty to invite the members of Betar to work: in the winter – unloading coal, in the summer – preparing wood crates, and in the spring – the work of "peeling" corn cobs. Also during the "dead" season, when they weren't able to find work, Fischel Pfeffer cared for them, gave them a few loaves of bread, a little flour, a little meat and wood for cooking the Sabbath meal. He always said to them: "take children, I am giving it to you as an advance payment for your work"... he was a kindhearted man and showed extreme devotion towards the young people who longed to emigrate to Israel. Also his youngest son, Baruch, behaved in the same way. The son gave without his father's knowledge, and the father gave without his son's knowledge. In this way, the training center of the Revisionists movement existed in Tluste.

The town's girls in a knitting class prior to their emigration to Israel

[Page 57]

A last visit to Tluste

by Dov Hendel

In 1937, I came from Eretz–Yisrael to visit my mother at her home in Bodzanów and also came for a few days to my brother David z"l, who got married and built his home in Tluste. I arrived in Chortkov [Czortków] from Bodzanów, and on top of the mountain in Chortkov I stopped a gentile with a calm expression. I climbed on his cart and came together with him to the town center, in the market place of Tluste, at the height of market day.

The shop of my brother David, which sold leather and shoes, stood in the market square. There, stood my brother with his wife, Feiga z"l, who came to help him for only a "short time." She was in a hurry to return home to her two children, Yitzchak, age four, and Shlomo, age two, who were left under the care of their grandfather, Shmuel Meltzer z"l.

The loud voices of the "negotiators," the sellers and the gentile buyers, filled the store. The selling was as difficult as parting the Red Sea because there was a great competition between the stores. There were also rumors that the Ukrainians were planning to open their own cooperative stores that, for sure, would deprive the livelihood of the Jewish merchants. In brief – it was difficult for the Jews to earn a living. My brother, who always felt it on his flesh and skin, muttered occasionally: God, if only I can get rid of all of this I would be able to reach Eretz–Yisrael.

Yes, everyone wanted to emigrate to Eretz–Yisrael. Many would have emigrated to Israel at that time if they were given the opportunity to do so. Before evening, on the way home from the store, I met a number of Jews who greeted me with a warmhearted, "Shalom Aleichem." As a Jew who came from Eretz–Yisrael I was dear to them and my presence excited them and reinforced their longing. Most of the young people showed interest and many lowered their eyes with shame that they were still in the Diaspora, that they were not able to gather their courage to emigrate to Eretz–Yisrael.

[Page 58]

Tluste's Public Goat

by Shimshon Meltzer

Translated by Dave Horowitz-Larochette

Come, my yearning heart, let us dip our pen and sing,
About the public goat of Tluste, the firstling goat of Chana–Mira!

A goat had Chana–Mirl, first–born of a young nanny goat;
His horns both tall and frightening, and a beard of ornament and splendor!

Mornings, on your way to *cheider*, and going back home in the afternoon,
Remember and beware for your soul of meeting those horns!

A boy injuring the goat, this is desecration of a holy sacrificial animal!
If the goat gores the boy – only he, the injured, will be found guilty!

What is the commotion there at the market? What happened to that lady stall owner?
Why is she so tearfully weeping and her hands clasping?

Woe to her, the goat turned her fruit stand over!
He knows: he's not to be touched, in peace and quiet he left!

Who ripped Reb Itzik's kaftan from top to bottom?
The white lining peeks from the tear – never has an eye seen such a rip!

The goat's horn did this, for it is a complete and experienced ripper!
The man injuring it – sins, but were it to gore a man – exempt he is!

Why is the goat so angry and only destroys and brings havoc?
Because of his character in his [former] life – now he is just a reincarnation!

Do not speak of him in the morning, and please do not dwell on him at night!
Instead of speaking badly of him – better you shut your mouth...The sword [beware]!

Consecrated he is, consecrated is the goat, and sin all those who even touch him!
And none shall be absolved of those who disrespect him!

Throw to him bread from afar, so he bites and he chews to his fill!

Sway will the splendorous beard, the horns tall and frightening!

Obituary the same morning, as soon as the town heard the rumor,
That the horned one was dead, the one with a splendorous beard.

It was in the morning of a winter day, the frost tightly packed,
New and glowing the snow, and white the world, all alabaster.

Who has seen the goat? Chana Mira is looking for him.
He hasn't slept in his manger tonight, yesterday evening he left for the town.

So Chana Mirl said, and she took it a step further;
Into the study–hall she stumbled, to the women's section there upstairs.

Every day she prayed, this was her custom for ages...
Where has he disappeared to, this goat woe–to–me, Father, Oh merciful Father!

Thus groaned Chana Mira having made her climb up there.
Slowly she opened the door and – behold, oh, woe and alas to her!

Here he is! The goat is here! He's dumped with splayed legs,
And a wave of *shemos* [1] covers him from tail to head and horns!

He has no soul nor spirit, his eyes are closed shut!
She touched him – he is cold and frozen, his hoofs still and bloody!

The very same day they buried him, wrapped in a sheet and all as by custom.
And an appropriate grave was dug in the snowy gleaming earth.

Thus he was buried, this goat, respectfully although near the fence,
Springtime – and the buds scrambled up the tomb and blossomed grandly.

Thus he was buried, this goat, as is custom, by the Chevre Kadisha.
Not one eye wept for him, not one tear for him was dropped.

Not thus was our brother buried – Woe, my heart, woe my pen, do not remind!
This is a poem about Tluste's firstborn, the firstling goat of Chana Mira!

Translator's Footnote:

1. Discarded holy scripts which are kept for burial, in or near synagogues

[Page 77]

A Short Walk through the Streets of Tiuste:
Our Town before the First World War

by Sosha Margules

Translated by Yael Chaver

There were no great, imposing buildings in our town. Nor could we boast of natural wonders that would delight the eye and arouse ecstasy in strangers or passing tourists. But even so, our town was blessed with thousands of charms and idyllic sights that would inspire even an artist like Chagall to create pictures of sloping alleys and small houses – a town so tiny you would miss it if you yawned. Other lovely sights were a small stream that flowed noisily along its route from faraway Svydova [Świdowa] and alongside the mill on its way to Tłuste village, Vorvolenets [Worwolińce] and other villages far away; the part of town that was known as "under the trees," where the young men of Tłuste would go walking on Saturday afternoons in summer, and meet up with girls. The stream ran by the Polish church, where frogs croaked, and near "Malye's hill," as well as other mounds and valleys... But let's walk slowly and methodically, the length and breadth of the town, as is proper, and describe the town's appearance.

"Kaiser's Road"

One should start, I believe, from the iron milepost marker located at the police post, on the road to Zalishtshyka [Zaleszczyki]. The spick–and–span Kaiser's Road leads downhill from there, through small houses, to the courthouse, the tax office, and then right into the city. The Tłuste village side street runs parallel to Kaiser's Road, near the houses of Reb Nusen Hikand, Shapse Lang, the Zaleszczyki kloyz, and turned towards the sloping house of Reb Meir Shuster and Reb Ahrn Boimayster, and reconnected with the main street. A wooden bridge across the road leads to a courtyard, which at that time belonged to the richest person in town, Reb Eli Albin. The courtyard included a large structure with beautiful rooms, nicely painted. It also contained small houses for the servants and stables for the horses and other farm animals. Every Simchas Toyre and Purim young folks and pranksters would come in to wish Reb Eli a good holiday, entertain him with joyous songs and tunes, and be rewarded with wonderful food and drink.

When we go back on the bridge to Glavno Street, we see another bridge across from the house of Reb Leyb Platzker (young girls hid under the bridge during the First World War, for fear of the rampaging Cossacks). Near the stream, on the left, was the fine house that the town rabbi, Reb Pinkhes Khodorover [Pinchas Chodorov], built, and whose completion he celebrated with great pomp. Opposite, across the water, the baker Reb Avrom (or Note) had a house that was almost sunken into the earth. Not only his own children, but goats and a ram belonging to Yevanitske [ed. Yevan or yovn was a derogatory term for a Russian soldier, and often extended to non-Jews in general] would climb the roof and rip it to shreds. They say that when the baker went to the police to complain, he told them, in Polish: "He has three goats, which rip strips off my roof, and when I complain to him he laughs at me." Naturally, we children sided with Yevanitske and mocked the baker. We liked the non-Jew because of his ram, which we rode all across town. Sheva, the baker, lived two houses further along. She made the finest baked goods, but only for the wealthy; she spoke Polish hektus-perfektus (in Tluste folklore, according to all the rules of grammar). Across the way, Reb Yosele Shternlib [Sternlieb] had built a two-floor brick building, and rented out the top floor to a female French teacher (the only one in town), who also gave piano lessons. When the Frenchwoman moved in, they had to drag her heavy piano up through the first-floor windows with heavy ropes and iron rods (for technical reasons), and everyone rushed to take a look at the "weird hauling," and watch the strong goyim drag the colossal instrument as they yelled "God forbid" to make sure that the ropes would not tear or the iron rods break under the heavy load... Further along was the pub run by Rivke, Zaynvel's wife. The pig-merchants would go there after the Thursday market to get drunk and yell, "Rivke, give us grief (horivke)!" [ed. In this context, it likely refers to alcoholic drink.]

On the right was the Polish church, which was very full on Sundays or during their holidays, when they celebrated their rituals. Nearby was the large house of Malke Fiderer and the wholesale fabric store. Further along, there is a whole row of shops, up to the street where the school is located. In front of the shops, on the large square, the female market vendors sit, seeking customers or quarreling among themselves to pass the time. On the opposite side, there are shops around the town hall and a large square, where fairs are held every Thursday. The town hall itself was abandoned, with a dark interior, and surrounded by buildings. These buildings, with their shops, gave the town hall an imposing appearance.

[Page 78]

Near Synagogue Street, across from Reb Yehoshua Halpern's hotel, there was another mile marker. This was followed by the trafika, the government tobacco shop, in Reb Khayim [Chaim] Langholz's house. Opposite that is the municipality building, where the deputy mayor, Avrile [Haryło] Bodnar, served, along with his Jewish secretary Yisro'el Krampf. Further along are the houses of Baruch–Itzik Vitashka, Mordkhe [Mordechai] Fiderer, and Itzik Fiderer. Here, you could already hear the terrible sounds made by animals waiting their turn at the ritual slaughterhouse. Apparently, at one time this marked the end of the Jewish part of Tłuste. Any Jewish home on the Svydova road was outside the community. This was as far as our town extended, along Kaiser Road. Now it's time to take a look at the narrow side streets and see what goes on there.

The side streets

Let's start with Rozanowka [Różanówka] road, which runs near the bridge to Reb Leybish Platzker's house. Immediately to the right, next to the Rabbi's house, there was a small house where the melamed Reb Shmuel Ne'eman [Neuman] lived with his family. He was a strange person: besides teaching, he tinkered day and night, mending furniture, hammering nails like a professional, and manufactured his own snuff tobacco from dried orange peels combined with chicory. He beat his pupils savagely, even the good ones, on the pretext that "good horses should be whipped more." His in–laws Reb Mordkhe and righteous wife Sore (the daughter of Mordkhe–Hirsh) also lived there. Every Friday afternoon they would lug a heavy bag through the town, with challahs, rolls, and buns, collected from the wealthy folks for the poor people of Tłuste, for Shabbes. (My God! Did we really have that many poor people? The sight of that enormous sack of challahs was frightening...). Reb Mordkhe [Mordechai] Hirsh was the only Jew in Tłuste who had never ridden the train, either out of fear or principle. Who knows? Climbing further up, on the opposite side, was the spacious building housing the "Baron Hirsch School", with a residence for Fel [Pel], the director – but that's a topic for a separate article. It's worth mentioning that one of the school's teachers, named Shayner, converted to Christianity with his family in a country church, shortly before the First World War. This was the only instance of conversion in our town. Further on, one street runs through the Rogatke [toll–gate] towards Rozanowka. Another street leads to the Targovitse [marketplace] (another topic in its own right), where a side street branches off to the home of Reb Itze, Pinye's son. This house had tall trees and an orchard full of sweet fruit. When we were children, sneaking into that yard on a beautiful summer's day was one of our greatest pleasures.

This was another boundary of Tluste's Jewish territory. We need to return to Kaiser's Road, just before the Polish church. We walk downhill to Bathhouse Street. In winter, the hill was lively with sleds going up and down. Cheyder assistants accompanied small children to Reb Aba Melamed's cheyder, to learn the alphabet. In the summer the age–old tones of komets–alef–o floated sweetly through the open windows. The house of Reb Yosye Shuster rang with delightful folksongs from the shoemakers' apprentices and Reb Yosye's charming, blond–haired daughter. All these sounds, together with the murmur of the nearby stream, combined (according to the Baal Shem Tov's style) and sent a song of praise to the heavenly Father. Every day, the two water carriers would meet on their way to the spring. One (the "aristocrat," as it were) had his own horse and a two–wheeled barrel, and thrived. The other, unlucky man, owned only two cans, which he carried on a kromisl [ed. Likely a shoulder–yoke], and thus barely made a living by his hard labor. This was also the site of the bath–house, with the Baal–Shem's mikveh, and the stone steps where people whipped their sweating bodies every Friday.

Returning to the hill and crossing over to the other side of the stream, we see below the Polish church the calm little river that the Poles comically called Tupa. People would catch fish in summer, and skate over the ice in winter on ice–skates, or wearing boots with iron horseshoes nailed on. The mill with its great wheel was on the right bank of the river; on hot summer days, people would splash in the wheel's miniature waterfalls. (Young folks would walk as far as Svydova to bathe and swim in the river there, but the river reeked from Moshe–Yankel's tannery and the foul–smelling animal pelts that he would wash in it.)

[Page 79]

It wasn't far from the mill to the green meadow, known as "under the trees." Young men and girls would walk there on Shabbat in summer (usually with a book under one arm, to appear more "intellectual") and make love. This is also where the German–Jewish writer Karl–Emil Franzos took walks and was inspired to write his novels, which were very popular at the time and were translated into many European languages. Apparently, his best novel, "The Jews of Baranovic [Barnow]," is based on characters from Tluste.

We walk back to the small alley below the church, starting with the house of Shneyer the melamed, and come straight to Synagogue Street, location of almost all the prayer–houses in our town. The synagogue, the bes–medresh, the Hasidic kloyz, and even the cemetery itself, all deserve longer descriptions. From here, we make our way to the Ukrainian church, opposite Town Hall. Compared with the Polish church, it appears shabby and neglected. Now we turn towards the butcher shops, where butchers rendered the meat kosher. Further left there was the large "Star" [Gwiazda] building, where theatrical performances and meetings were held. Next was Railroad Street, where you would meet the local carriage drivers and their horses, decorated with bells, growling like lions. We find ourselves again on Kaiser Road, near the tobacco shop, and catch a glimpse of Reb Khayim Langholz, sitting in the shade and stroking his silken beard, while his wife (a heavy–set woman) reads a Polish newspaper and smokes a cigarette.

Here we end our short walk through Tluste. That is enough for now. My memory is failing and my feet will not carry me further to rummage for reminiscences of all the narrow streets and houses of prayer where we spent our youth, dreamed our dreams, and where, finally, during the reign of Hitler (may his name be blotted out) the innocent blood of our nearest and dearest souls was spilled. May their memories be bound in the bond of everlasting life.

[Page 82]

Legends and Events

by Shmuel Fiderer-Margulies

Translated by Yael Chaver

"One leafs through the history of our town" – this is how a written memoir of the Tłuste Jewish community should begin, in flowery language. But does there already exist a printed, or written, history of our destroyed town, to provide information about the previous hundred years of its existence? There are rumors of a small historic booklet, by a Polish writer, titled "Tłuste on the Dupa" [ed. "Tłuste nad Dębną"] published about 80 years ago [ed. actually 1923] in Lemberg. Unfortunately, I could not obtain this small book, in spite of all my efforts. On the other hand, the handwritten Pinkes Tluste, which was housed in the house of my grandfather, the rabbi, contained much information about religious issues, synagogue managers and ritual slaughterers, prayer style, the cemetery, and houses of prayer, but almost no historical information. Thus, the question remains: How long has the town of Tłuste existed? Who were the first Jewish families in our town? What was their lifestyle? How did they make a living?

Reb Moyshe Zelig Kremer, may he rest in peace (an intelligent person, a history expert), said that at the beginning of the 16th century Tłuste was a market spot, a place for fairs, where the villagers from the region would gather to sell their products. One fine day, two Jewish families that had moved from Russian Ukraine or Podolia settled there and opened two small taverns to sell the villagers brandy and mead. These were the ancestors of Reb Itzik Shternlib of our time. They settled on the hill above the well, not far from the market. More families arrived later from the same region, built houses and opened shops. Thus, at the start of the 18th century, when the Ba'al Shem Tov was born, several hundred Jewish families were living in Tłuste and had developed a commercial life. The ruler of the entire area, Countess Poninska, was very interested in the commercial development of the town and decreed that Jews who wanted to build houses or storehouses would receive free plots for these buildings and gardens. They were allowed to get wood from the surrounding forests and graze their livestock without charge in the pastures. They enjoyed additional privileges. A written proclamation, sealed with the crest of the

Count, elevated Tluste to the status of a "free city"; it was the only such town in the entire area. According to legend, when the now elderly Countess came to Tluste and saw the first manufactured textile shop in the town, she marveled, and went in to buy a few yards of calico for a dress, for which she paid a fortune of ten gold ducats.

This continued for years. Tluste remained a "free city," while other towns and villages in the area had to pay the Countess taxes for everything and everyone. This continued even after the death of the Countess, because her will stated, for the benefit of her heirs, that Tluste should remain a "free city."

One fine day, a Jew from Tluste arrived at the palace of the noble family, requesting an audience with the son of the deceased Countess. Once he entered the Count's presence, he bowed submissively, and told a strange tale: he had come as a messenger from the entire Tluste Jewish community, and requested – on behalf of all the town's Jews – that all the privileges granted previously should be revoked, because the Jews of Tluste did not want to be an exception. They wanted to bear the same responsibilities as the residents of other towns. The young man also placed a forged document on the table, signed by the consent of the Jewish community council and sealed with wax. The document stated explicitly that they did not want to be a "free city." The Count considered for a while, and then said, "Well, if that's what the Jews want, I'll do it for them..." The rest went as smoothly as a chapter of Psalms: the Count called in his office manager and instructed him to change the entire procedure, in other words – to revoke all the privileges of the Jews of Tluste, ending the "free city." Of course, that young man became a constant visitor in the manager's office, advising him on how to go about the practical work of cheating the Jews of Tluste. He manipulated it so that he would benefit from the new taxes the Jews had to pay.

[Page 83]

As a result of this cunning scheme, they started extorting money from everyone, rich and poor alike. Anyone who could not pay was jailed, or an enforcer was sent to his home. An armed cavalryman from Zaleszczyki would ride in on horseback and take up residence in the debtor's house (including bed and board) until he got the tax payment. Our friendly neighbor, Mr. M. Z. Kremer, told us this story and others.

No less interesting is the episode of the battle, and victory, of the Jews of Tluste against the perpetrators of a pogrom by a band called the barabbers. Who were these barabbers? What were they doing in Tluste? The incident was as follows:

In 1898, the Austrian state, under Emperor Franz Joseph, had not yet completed laying the rail line into Galitzia. The workers in our part of this gigantic project were called barabbers: tall, powerful non-Jews with wide shoulders, who spread fear with their wild behavior and constant drunkenness. They spoke an incomprehensible Polish dialect and provoked fights. Why were they tagged with the nickname barabbers? You never know, with our Tluste Jews! The source of other nicknames is also hard to pinpoint. Were they tagged as barabbers because some likened them to Arabs? More reasonable is the opinion of others, who claimed that these were Polish Masurians. However, whatever their origin, these barabbers decided to attack the Jews of Tluste, on the first day of Shevues, 1898, with a pogrom. The pretext was that our tavern-keepers had supposedly cheated them by charging high prices for brandy and serving small glasses of the alcoholic drink.

Our Jews did not know of the impending catastrophe. The town was at prayers, enjoying the holiday chants. However, the guardian of Israel never rests or sleeps. Franz Joseph's gendarmes knew what was coming. They entered the synagogue and bes medres in the middle of the service and sounded the alarm to the entire community, yelling, "Jews, save yourselves!" Everyone ran home, grabbed iron bars, axes, and other means of battle, placed themselves behind the gendarmes, and marched against the enemies. The strongest ones marched in the first rows: horse-traders, butchers, and the young people. With courage and decisiveness, they wanted to teach the barabbers a lesson, as an example. The first encounter was in Kaiser Street, outside town. The chief gendarme yelled out to the marauders, but with no result. They started throwing stones and stood facing us with their weapons: spades, picks, crowbars. The gendarmes responded with fire, immediately felling several of them. The barabbers started running back, and our guys followed them, gave them a good beating, and drove them back into their own neighborhoods. The entire attack only lasted several minutes, but the results for the barabbers were catastrophic: they had several fatalities. We, on the other hand, suffered only a few wounded. No one spoke openly about the outcome of the intended pogrom, only in whispers. People were afraid of what the gentiles would say, because the authorities wanted to investigate the deaths. However, everything calmed down eventually, and the barabbers never bothered anyone again. A few weeks later they left the town, after they had finished their work.

But from then on, the local non-Jews and those in the surroundings had respect for the Jews of Tluste. This reputation lasted for many years. It was the only bit of satisfaction derived from the barabber adventure and the disrupted Shevues holiday of 1898.

Such were the events, these and others, sad, odd, as well as inspiring, that unfolded in our town, in which we were born and grew up, and where our nearest and dearest lived through joy and sorrow. They were later cruelly murdered, along with six million other innocent martyrs of our nation. We will never forget them. We will tell our children and their descendants down the generations about them and about the town that is so dear to our hearts.

[Page 84]

Tluste during the First World War
(a chapter from *The Destruction of Jewish Galicia* (1920))

by S. An–sky *

Translated by Yael Chaver

Jagielnica is the southernmost point in Galicia that remained in Russian possession until their final retreat, and was therefore undamaged. The area farther off had been deserted by the Russian army during their first retreat, in 1915, and was recaptured in June or July 1916 by Brusilov's army. This led to dreadful destruction.

Once you leave Jagielnica, the landscape changes abruptly. Every step yields fresh traces of military trenches, ripped barbed–wire fences, charred villages, and ruins, endless ruins.

I found the town of Tluste, several dozen versts from Jagielnica, in terrible condition (ed. "verst" is a unit of length, slightly over one kilometer; the actual distance between the two towns is only 12 km). Of its pre–war 516 houses, barely 32 remained, and even those were half–ruined. Those few structures served as packed quarters to the 134 families remaining of the previous 2000 households (numbering about 5000 people). One can only imagine their crowded living conditions!

The Russians entered the town for the first time in September 1914, at the outset of the war. Only 60 or 70 households left with the Austrian authorities. The town did not suffer from the battles, but a pogrom, forced labor, requisitions, and isolation created terrible famine. At the end of Tammuz [referring to the Jewish month occurring in June–July], a cholera epidemic broke out; 300 souls perished over six or seven weeks, among them the rabbi. The terrified populace started fleeing in all directions. Disregarding the severe prohibition against leaving the town, more than 100 households moved away. About a year later, just before Rosh Hashone [September 1915], the Russians left town, but not before they set it on fire. The Austrians arrived, stayed for one week, and withdrew. Almost all the Jews left with them. No more than ten families remained. When the Russians returned, they set fire to the town again. They tore down about fifty houses and carried away the wood.

A week after the Russians returned, 200 hundred Jewish families passed through, exiled from the town of Ustichka [Uścieczko] to Zbarazh. Fifty or sixty families stayed here, in the abandoned Jewish houses. Thirty or forty more families exiled from the surrounding villages also arrived. At the same time, about fifty of the households who had fled because of the cholera epidemic returned. Thus, about half of the population were new arrivals, unemployed, and suffered from hunger.

I arrived in Tluste in the evening, and stayed with a member of the Committee (ed. the Jewish Committee for the Relief of War Victims). I held the meeting in his house; the meeting went on until midnight, as an argument had broken out among us. The Committee requested additional funds for wood, and Homelski had told me that there would be no additional funds. When the meeting was over, I realized that I had nowhere to spend the night. It was bitterly cold and windy, and it would have been dangerous to set out on the road in such weather. The driver, who was already asleep, would certainly not have voted to travel. There was absolutely nowhere to stay here, in such crowded conditions. The Committee chairman, a local householder, who was considered wealthy, invited me to spend the night at his place, and I agreed. But when I got there I saw that he and his family of seven were living in one small room. The husband and wife talked quietly for a while, and she then began to prepare a bed for me on the one couch in the room.

"And where will you sleep?" I asked. "What do you care, what do you care, everything is in order," the husband calmed me down.

When I got up the next morning, I found out that at midnight the husband had sent his wife and three daughters to stay with neighbors. He, his son, and his elderly father had spent the night on the floor. I was extremely uncomfortable, but there was nothing I could do, and I stayed the night.

The moment I lay down, I sensed very cold air coming from a window above the couch. I got up and saw that the window frame was much smaller than the window opening, and there were large gaps above and around the frame. Apparently, someone had inserted a window frame from a different, smaller building.

[Page 85]

I was barely able to stuff my cushion into the gaps, and lay down again. At dawn, I woke up with a terrible, bitter taste in my mouth and a dry tongue. I noticed that the walls and ceiling were covered with a thick layer of mold. The awful taste stayed in my mouth for several days. This is how even the richer people lived.

Before I left, I offered the wife money for the night's lodging. She refused. But the old man, the householder's father, looking greedily at the few rubles in my hand, shouted angrily at her, "Take it, take it! If they offer it - take it! Take it! Take it!"

Tluste has its relics. They say that this is where the Ba'al Shem Tov was revealed. In any case, his mother lived here and he spent his early years in this town. His mother's grave is pointed out in the cemetery. The location of the Ba'al Shem Tov's mikveh is shown at the edge of town. His mother was a wet–nurse, and he himself was nicknamed "Grandmother's Yisroel."

I was told many stories about the Ba'al Shem Tov. In one of these tales, a local householder, Reb Hersh, opposed the Ba'al Shem Tov. The latter said, "He will remember me." Reb Hersh was then cursed for ten generations. To this day, his descendants continue to suffer from misfortunes, and no spiritual leader can help them.

Once, the day before Passover, non–Jews "planted" a dead non–Jewish child at the Ba'al Shem Tov's house, as a blood libel. While the Seder was being celebrated, non–Jews and soldiers surrounded the house. The Ba'al Shem Tov saw the dead child, quickly dressed him in Jewish clothes and cap, and seated him at the table. The dead child sat there as though alive. The Ba'al Shem scolded him loudly, "You good–for–nothing! Sway during the service!" The dead child began to sway over the Haggada. When the non–Jews burst into the house, they searched everywhere but found nothing. They had no idea that the child sitting at the table and swaying over the Haggada was the one they were searching for. Later, after they left, the child reverted to a state of death, and the Ba'al Shem buried him in the yard.

I heard more stories, among them how the Ba'al Shem set fire to the river. But I have forgotten them.

* ed. Shloyme–Zanvl Rapoport (1863–1920), better known by his pseudonym S. Ansky (or An–sky), was a Belarusian Jewish author, researcher of Jewish folklore, polemicist, and cultural and political activist. He is best known for his play The Dybbuk or Between Two Worlds, of 1914.

[Page 90]

The *Bet–Ha'am* [Meeting House] that was never built

by Shmuel Fiderer (Ben–Moshe)

Translated by Yael Chaver

In 1930, Reb Nusen Hikand invited me to meet with him, and let me know that he was ready to donate a construction site if a meeting house would be built on it. I immediately asked him what compensation he required in return. He asked for only one thing: once the building was complete, he wanted a plaque with an inscription stating that Reb Nusen Hikand had donated the building site for a meeting house.

I soon convened the representatives of all the Zionist organizations: Union, General Zionists, Beitar, and "Grossmanites." They all joyfully adopted the plan. Shortly afterwards, Reb Nusen Hikand officially registered the plot's ownership to the local Zionist parties, and we took physical possession of it. There is a photograph of the representatives on the occasion of taking over the property. Clearing, and preparations for construction, soon began.

However, it seems that we did not take into account the difficulties posed by the municipal authorities. As soon as we filed a request to build a meeting house – a "national house" – an uproar started up in the town. The Poles felt it would be competition for the Polish national house, the "Star," and they began agitating against granting us a construction permit. After all, Poland was a democracy, and Jews were the majority of the town's population while Poles were a small minority – yet they had leverage against the Jews. Under Mayor Marcin Kobiernik, who was also a Sejm delegate on behalf of the non–affiliated bloc for cooperating with the government (throughout his term he made only one speech, consisting of two words: a friend of his sneezed during session, and he called out loudly "your health"), the matter dragged on for three and a half years. He finally decided that he was not authorized to issue a construction permit, as it was a social building; only the head of the local district could make that decision. Accordingly, he soon forwarded the documents to Zalyshchyki [Zaleszczyki]. The district head, Krzyszanawski, was strongly anti–Semitic, and procrastinated until the outbreak of World War Two. In this way, the construction of a meeting house in our town came to nothing.

Preparations to build the meeting house.
Center – Reb Nusen Hikand, who contributed the construction site

[Page 91]

How we performed *hazzan*

by Shloyme Trembovelski [Shlomo Trembowelski]

Translated by Yael Chaver

On Rosh HaShone, right after the afternoon prayer in the synagogue, the house of prayer, and the kloizen, the congregation members set out to go to hazzan. They waited outside the house of prayer's door, and the moment Yitzkhok the hazzan took his place at the head of the group, people started out. It was a short, straight route to the small river, directly to the bridge. Everyone walked heavily, as if carrying a heavy burden, each person with his own thoughts. We children used the opportunity to escape from the close supervision of our fathers. We had an important job ahead of us: preparing the "flotilla" that we launched on the river every year, where the town Jews "drowned" the sins of an entire year, unburdened themselves, and shook everything off their coattails.

In order to prepare the "flotilla," we first had to gather all the candles we had pilfered, not only from our house of prayer but from the smaller locations and tiny synagogues... For several days after Rosh HaShone, Shmaya the sexton would roam the house of prayer looking for the candles; when he couldn't find them, he would sound angrily off about our fathers, and curse them to the fourth generation...However, we gave as good as we got, and "honored" him with a nickname that fitted him well: "bull." We invented this nickname because at Hanukah, when the sexton lit the Hanukh candles and said the blessing, instead of chanting the last phrase of the blessing, we all yelled out in chorus, "Boo, Shmaya, boo!" We had to run away immediately to the tiny Vizhnitz kloiz and bar its door with several prayer stands...

In addition to bringing the candles, we had another important task: stealing wood from Leyb Shteyn's fenced wood storehouse. The storehouse was on the riverbank, and Leyb Shteyn [Leib Stein] kept dry wood there for his bakery. We would swipe dry boards, glue several candles to each, and let them float on the stream. The candles would float while people performed hazzan, until they reached the mill, where they dropped into the mill wheel's waterfall and were lost. Our childish joy was especially great when we noticed a satisfied smile on our fathers' faces. They must have been secure, knowing that they had gotten rid of an entire year's serious sins by throwing them into the water, where they would reach the mill wheel along with our candles, and be shredded until every trace was gone...

Their heads raised high, striding resolutely with shtraymls cocked to one side, they left the river's bank, accompanied by the joyful song of Yitzkhok the hazzan.

The main street before World War One
In the background – the Polish church

[Page 92]

Memories of a bygone home

by Walter Hoyzfeld [Hausfeld] (New York)

Translated by Yael Chaver

As a person who was born and grew up in Tłuste, I'd like to contribute to this memorial book some memories of my youthful days in the town. I want to mention a few of the events that caused me – as well as all young boys and girls – to mature quickly, compared with children of our age that I see here in America. These events turned us into adults, who have to forget their youth and start to work, strive, and ensure their existence and their future.

Our premature adulthood was the result of the general situation in which we lived, as well as fear of the future, which we understood so well and took into account. At the same time, we also reached full political maturity. Each of us belonged to a political organization, one of those that promised to move us out of Poland and bring us to the Land of Israel. Whether we were General Zionists, Revisionists, or Po'alei Zion and members of the Labor Federation, the goal was identical: get out of here!

We knew very well that we had no future in this town, and assessed the situation correctly.

There were constant conflicts between the party branches in our town, intrigues and "maneuvers," mainly before elections to the World Zionist Congress. I remember the following incident: In advance of the Congress, I secured the votes of some people who were unaffiliated with my party, but wanted to support me. I bought "shekels" (ed. membership dues) for them and awaited the election results. However, it appeared that they had not voted for us at all. My comrades Borekh Kritzer [Baruch Kritzer] and Shtaynig [Steinig] confronted me, saying, "Well, Vove, where are the votes you were supposed to bring in?" I had no answer. I inquired of those people who they had voted for, and they na?vely explained: "Your brother Mendl (may he rest in Paradise) brought us a note and said that Vove wanted us to put this note in the ballot box, and return the note he gave you." They thought that Mendl's instructions were sacred, because he was more important than me... This is how I found out what had happened to my votes. But I wasn't angry with him over it – I was even prouder of him. I knew we were all on the front line against a common enemy, who wanted to gobble us all down, regardless of party affiliation...

This is how we lived, and had no idea what youth was. Only now, living in America, do I see for the first time what a beautiful and good life young people have under normal conditions, conditions that none of us ever knew. It would have been worth it, if we would all have at least lived to see the great miracle of the State of Israel, of our own Jewish state, for which, unfortunately, we paid so dearly. To our great regret, only a few of us lived to see it.

I still remember our town Tluste, and my experiences there, very well. I remember my good friend Shimshon Meltzer, from whom I learned a great deal – the bit of Hebrew that I remember. He would often explain something to me, and may have thought that what he was telling me was like "a voice in the wilderness," but I saved it all in my memory. He also taught me how to draw monograms and paint signs. I shall be forever grateful to him for this, because when I came to America I had a "trade" in hand. When they asked me what I could do, I proudly replied that I was a sign–painter. When I was further asked in which school I had studied and who the director was, I said that I didn't remember the director's name, but that my teacher was Shimshon Meltzer. Actually, I didn't continue in this profession, because sign–painting is quite different here. But I had a trade when I came, thanks solely to Shimshon Meltzer who had taught me.

**The Hoyzfeld family donates a Torah
scroll to the synagogue**

[Page 93]

I did not travel to America so much as flee. I had had an American visa for three months before the war, but did not go because I didn't want to leave my dear mother (may she rest in peace). I tried to get a visa for her as well. I might have succeeded if the war had broken out two months later. But it wasn't meant to be...

I will never forget that day. It was a Wednesday morning, two days before the war that that person, may his name be blotted out (ed. the Yiddish phrase der yimakhshmoynik here refers to Hitler), brought upon the world. My dear mother came up to me and said, "My child, I swear by my life and beg you – flee! When, with God's help, things will calm down, I will follow you..." With broken hearts, my brother Meir (who is here in America with me) and I went to the railroad station, to travel to Lemberg on the express train. I met many young people at the station, among them some of my friends who were on their way to be drafted into the Polish army in order to defend the "fatherland." Gedalia Gertner, may he rest in peace, travelled with us as far as Lemberg; he was a very sweet and sincere fellow. We parted there, a very tragic parting. My brother and I went to Warsaw, and from there to the Latvian border. I could write a book about our experiences until we saw the Statue of Liberty in New York.

Once I got to New York, I immediately wrote my mother, my brother, and my friends. I was able to write to them and receive answers until 1941. But all connections were cut off following the German invasion. During 1940 I got several letters from Hershele Gertner (Gedalia Gertner's brother), who was in a German prison. I mailed him many packages, but heard nothing more from him. I have kept his letters to this day.

A group of Tluste natives in America

[Pages 99-120]

The Destruction of the Town

Five years of war and destruction

by Berl Glick

Translated by Sara Mages

1. Before the Second World War

The town of Tłuste resides (maybe it is correct to say – resided) in Eastern Galicia near the main road leading from Lvov [Lwów] to Chernovitz [Czernowitz]. Also, the Lvov-Chernovitz railway, passed by our town. The town belonged to the Zaleszczyki region and the Chortkov [Czortków] district. The number of residents in the period before the Second World War was around seven thousand, among them around two thousand Jews, two thousand Poles and three thousand Ukrainians. In the elections to the city council, which took place once every six years, the Jews received a greater representation than they should have. Usually, the relationship between the Jewish and the non-Jewish population was quite good. A small portion of the town's Jews, around 20%, were engaged in different businesses, and the remaining 80% were engaged in commerce and peddling. The grain trade was extremely developed in our town. Tłuste was the most important grain trading center in all of Podolia, and the rates that were set on market days were published in the commercial press. In general, the financial state of the town's Jews was satisfactory. There was a credit union in town (*Zvenyanzek Creditavi*), that gave loans to merchants and tradesmen. There was also a charitable fund *"Gemilut Hasadim"* that gave interest-free loans in easy payments. Every year, before the holiday of Pesach, Tłuste's "Landsmannschaft" organization in New York sent a few hundred dollars to our town's poor. That money was divided, together with the amounts that were collected in town for *"Meot Hittim"* [Pesach foods for the needy], to satisfy the holiday needs of the local poor.

Politically, the town's residents belonged to different movements. There were Zionist organizations of all streams, *"Bund"* [federation] and *"Agudath Yisrael"* [Union of Israel]. Jewish children studied in a general school and also in a *"Heder."* The girls didn't study in the *"Heder,"* but in *"Beit Yakov"* a well-organized girl's school. There was a public library with a reading room in town. There were also a number of people with higher education: four doctors, six lawyers and one Jewish judge.

During the last years, the community was headed by R' Meir Kleiner who was a wealthy estate owner, a pious Jew and a follower of the Chortkov Rabbi. Tluste's last rabbi was R' Shmuel Aba Chodorov, the son of the famous Genius Rabbi, R' Pinchas Chodorov, an offspring of the *Admorim* [Hassidic rabbis] from Kosov.

There was a Great Synagogue in Tluste of historical value, a number of small synagogues (*Kloizen*) and *"Beit Midsrash."* *"Beit Ha'Midrash"* was a new building named after Dvora Braksmier who built it with her own money and without public participation. The important synagogues were: the Chortkov Hassidim *Kloiz*, the Vizhnitz Hassidim *Kloiz*, and the Kopyczynitz Hassidim *Kloiz*. The synagogues and *"Beit Ha'Midrash"* were always full of worshipers, and the sound of prayer and the words of the Torah always ascended from them.

One of the most important periods in the history of Tluste is the "revelation" of Ba'al Shem Tov which took place when he lived in Tluste and vicinity. A few legends were left in our hands from that period, and here is one of them:

In the period of his revelation, Ba'al Shem Tov was an infant teacher in the village of Koszyłowce, a distance of around twelve kilometers from town. Every day, in the summer and in the winter, he left at dawn to swim in the river. During the great freeze, when the river was covered with a layer of ice, Ba'al Shem Tov dug himself an "opening" in the ice and lowered himself into the river. A gentile who saw the behavior of the "rabbi," preceded him and laid a small amount of straw on the ice. Ba'al Shem Tov was immersed in the "superior world" and did not feel that his feet were not touching the ice. One day, Ba'al Shem Tov came earlier to the river and caught the gentile "performing the deed" of scattering a bundle of straw on the ice. The rabbi asked the gentile to choose one of the three blessings that he was offering him:

wealth, long life, or decent sons. The gentile answered innocently: "Rabbi I am choosing all three together". Ba'al Shem Tov responded and blessed him. Ba'al Shem Tov's blessing came true. The farmer's family was known in the whole area as a wealthy honest family, and all the members of the family lived a long life on the face of the earth.

After he left Koszyłowce, Ba'al Shem Tov was an infant teacher in Tłuste. His mother also lived in Tłuste, died there and was buried in the Jewish cemetery. The following story about her gravestone was told in our town. The gravestone was erected by one of Ba'al Shem Tov's grandsons. When the grandson arrived in Tłuste to erect the stone over his grandmother's grave, nobody knew the location of her burial. What did they do? They placed the gravestone in the hands of a number of Jews and told them to carry it to the cemetery. The Jews carried the tombstone to the cemetery, and when they got tired the stone fell off their hands. The matter turned into a miracle because the place was the correct location of her burial. The gravestone was erected in that place, and it is standing there "even today."

Besides the gravestone of the mother of Ba'al Shem Tov, another substantial reminder was left from the time that Ba'al Shem Tov lived in our town. Until the days of the Holocaust there was a special *Mikveh* [bath house] where Ba'al Shem Tov immersed himself, and it was called by all: "the *Mikveh* of Ba'al Shem Tov."

2. The beginning of the Second World War

On 1 September 1939, immediately after Poland was attacked by Germany, panic broke out in town. Masses of refugees, Poles and Jews alike, started to stream towards the Romanian border. Everyone passed by our town which was located only 24 kilometers from the border town of Zaleszczyki. The Germans' advance was swift. A number of days later, people started to flee from Tłuste, mostly young adults and the town's intelligentsia. There were also many refugees in town from Stanisławów, and everyone wanted to leave town as fast as possible and reach Romania. Many succeeded to reach their target by different routes.

On Sunday, 17 September 1939, a message arrived from Berezdów that the Red Army crossed the border at two o'clock at night. No one trusted this report but it was confirmed on the same day. At 11 o'clock in the morning the town was occupied by the Soviet army. Immediately, the army closed the border and blew up the bridge crossing over the Dniester. Refugees who did not have sufficient time to cross the border were left on this side of the border under the Soviet regime.

During the Soviet regime a great change occurred in the life of the Jewish population, mostly in the life of the merchants who were forced to liquidate their businesses. The big merchants left town and settled in larger cities such as Chortkov and Kołomyja. Some of the small merchants received "permits" and were allowed to keep their business. The transition was not easy, but slowly matters settled down, life returned to its usual course and in some areas the situation even got better. The Soviets improved the sanitary conditions, established a big hospital with a special maternity ward, and the Jewish bathhouse was renovated and given for the use of the whole town. And so matters continued for close to two years, until 22 June 1941.

3. The Germans attack the Soviet Union

On Sunday, 23 June 1941, at six o'clock in the evening, at the time when the streets were full of people, a German airplane suddenly appeared and opened fire on the people who were walking in the street. There were not many victims but the matter caused great panic in town. The radio announced that the Germans were advancing and getting closer to our area. On 29 June, Romanian refugees, who had escaped towards the Soviet border, arrived in our town. Again, the refugees' arrival caused panic in town and many young people were getting ready to escape to the Soviet Union. The refugees' movement increased and lasted three days. On Tuesday, late in the afternoon of 1 July 1941, the Soviet's institutions also left town.

On the same day, Tuesday, 6 Tamuz 5701, my father-in-law, R' Shmuel Meltzer z"l, passed away in Tłuste. He died at the age of seventy-two and left an extensive family – four sons (the youngest son Shimshon Meltzer was already in Israel), three daughters and many grandchildren. Before the funeral many people gathered next to his home – family members, neighbors, friends and acquaintances. As it was customary and known, the deceased's daughters and daughters-in-law mourned and cried for him. The matter became known at the office of the NKVD [*Narodny Komissariat Vnutrennikh Del* – the Soviet secret police], and the commander himself came in his car to see the reason for the gathering. He did not trust the words of the mourners, that their only intention was to accompany the deceased to his resting place, pushed his way

through the crowd to the coffin, and asked to expose the deceased's face ....
After that, he turned to the crowd and said: "I think that if a man lived,
completed his life and died in his bed, there is no need to mourn and cry for
him. You must be comforted with the fact that it is possible to accompany him
to his eternal rest with so much respect. For us, military men, a funeral like
that is not proper..." Later on he said farewell to the crowd and, a few hours
later, all of them left town.

4. The bombing

The Red Army retreat lasted until Friday, 4 July 1941. On Friday, the
military movement stopped and the town remained without a regime. The
residents hid, each person in his own home, and the streets emptied. A young
man around the age of twenty, who dared to appear in the street, aroused
panic and almost caused a disaster: one of the last Soviet soldiers suspected
that he was a spy and started to chase him. The young man hid in one of the
homes and disappeared from his sight. The soldier thought that he was hiding
in the home of Marcus (Manie) Schwartz. He got closer to the house, looked
through the window and threw a hand grenade. Fortunately, the Schwartz
family had enough time to hide in the bunker, also taking their old mother
who was lying on her sick-bed. And so the incident passed without casualties.

On Friday evening, the last train from Chernovitz passed towards the
Soviet border. It was a very long train. In order to allow it to move faster the
Russians disconnected eight railcars and left them in Tłuste. Early morning
Saturday, a number of residents, Jews, Poles and Ukrainians, approached the
train to see what was left inside the cars. They opened one of them and saw
that it was full of expensive fabrics, gold and jewelry. Immediately they started
to empty the car and the other three that were also full of valuables. The
remaining four cars were full of bombs.

In the afternoon there were rumors that the Soviets were planning to blow
up the bombs in the cars. All the townspeople were frightened but no one
knew where to run to, so they all stayed at home. And indeed, the cars were
set on fire at about four. There was a tremendous explosion that shocked all
the buildings, and all the windows within a ten-kilometer radius were
shattered by the blast. A Ukrainian was killed, but otherwise there were no
other casualties in this explosion.

Sunday passed in peace and the soldiers were not seen in town. Only a few refugees returned, Jews from Kołomyja, Horodenka and Śniatyn, who had tried to escape towards the Soviet border but were forced to return.

Early morning, 7 July, on the holiday of "Saint Ivan," Ukrainians who lived in the twenty-two villages around Tluste attacked the Jews who resided there and killed almost all of them. Over two hundred people were killed in these attacks. The attackers used axes and other deadly weapons for those killings. Only in one village, in Worwolince, the Jews were not harmed. Forty Jews were also killed in the town of Ułaszkowce (Lashkewitz). A number of Jewish residents from that town were able to escape and arrived in our town.

In Tluste, the Ukrainian murderers were not able to carry out their plot thanks to the intervention of the Ukrainian priest Izbulskie [Anton Navolskyy – ed.]. He posted loyal and honest Ukrainians on all the roads leading to town, and prevented the murderers from entering. Early Monday morning, 7 July, a group of thugs armed with axes and sacks tried to enter the town in order to perform a massacre and loot it. But the local Ukrainians fought them and did not let them enter the town. The priest walked all day in the town's streets and calmed the frightened Jews. Also, during the German occupation, he comforted and supported Jews who were in trouble. He did not wish to be a partner to the enthusiasm that the members of his nation expressed towards the Germans. In the nearby towns and villages the Ukrainians raised monuments – "*Mogila*" in their language – in honor of the Germans' arrival. The Germans promised the Ukrainians that they would establish an independent Ukrainian nation after they won the war. In each location a priest went out with the residents to "sanctify" the monument. Only Izbulskie [Navolskyy – ed.] refused to do so, and the monument in Tluste was the only one that was not blessed by a priest.

The Polish priest warned his congregation and influenced them not to contaminate their hands with Jewish blood. In one of his sermons he mentioned a passage from "*Parashat Vayelech*": "And I will surely hide my face on that day...." and said: "At the present time, G-d is hiding his face from the Jews and giving them to the hands of their killers. But we should not hurt them, so G-d will not be angry with us and will not do to us what he has done to the Jews." The priest's words were not for nothing. The fact is that Tluste's Jews suffered very little at the hands of their Polish and Ukrainian neighbors.

5. Under the shadow of the Magyar's rule

A few days after the withdrawal of the Russian army, a Magyar [Hungarian] advanced guard unit appeared in the early morning hours. They did not stop in town, and only passed through it. As they left, they split and went in different directions. Towards evening, a reinforced Magyar squadron arrived with a military command unit and settled in town. All this went very peacefully but the Jews were afraid to go out to the streets and lived in fear. A few days later, a cavalry company arrived and immediately put their horses in *Beit Ha'Midrash* and in the corridors of the Great Synagogue. They started to dismantle the fences around Jewish homes and used the wood for heating. Later on, they started to dismantle the vacant Jewish homes and also the reader's desk in the synagogue. The Ukrainian priest pleaded before the military commander to stop these acts of destruction, but he was unsuccessful.

Shortly afterwards came an order requiring Jews to deliver their radios to the headquarters within three days. But the Jews were wiser and hid their radios with their non-Jewish friends. Immediately after this, the Magyars started to recruit Jews for different jobs such as cleaning and community service. All that happened in the period before the Germans were seen in our town.

On Sabbath eve, 9 Av 5701 – 1 August 1941, about two thousand Hungarian Jews from the Carpathian region were brought to our town in trucks. Most of them were pious Jews and there were many rabbis among them. They brought all their possessions with them, their clothes and even their bedding. Immediately a committee of twelve members, with Yakov Pel [Fel] as a leader, was established to help the exiled and ease their difficult situation. Thanks to the pleading of the Hungarian Jews, the horses were removed from *Beit Ha'Midrash* and from the synagogue and the Hungarian Jews were housed there. During the week, four thousand additional Hungarian exiles arrived; the Hungarian headquarters refused to accept more than that. The transports that arrived later were directed to Borszczów or to Skałat. In the town of Jazłowiec, Ukrainians attacked a group of Hungarian Jews and chased them to the *Yeshiva*. Many of them were shot and killed and their bodies were thrown into the Stripa River. There were also cases in which people were thrown into the river alive. In most cases the bodies of the victims were tied to each other with barbed wire. Jews from the town of Uścieczko and the city of Zaleszczyki pulled many of the bodies out of the water and brought them to a Jewish grave.

Compared to other towns, the situation in our town was quiet and orderly. With the arrival of the Hungarian Jews the whole town turned into a big market. Those Jews sold most of the belongings that they brought with them. Some were forced to, in order to survive, and some sold them willingly since they did not know where they were going and what was waiting for them. Farmers from the surrounding areas bought most of the items. The aid committee for Hungarian refugees worked diligently and with great dedication. Different committees were established: a financial committee, a housing committee, a supply committee that I was active in, together with Yisrael Yorist, May he rest in peace. The work was difficult and responsible, therefore we added three more people: the two sons of Reuven Albin and a refugee by the name Motale' Viner. Our duty was to collect flour from homeowners, two to three kilograms from each family. The baker, Marim Funk, baked the bread for us for free, and we distributed it among the refugees - 500 gram per person every day. On Sabbath eve we also baked *Hallot*, and each refugee received one *Halla*.

All that lasted for about three weeks. Later on, the headquarters forced the refugees to continue their way to Russia. Many were transported by trucks and others were led on foot. The refugees took their bundles and moved to Kamieniec-Podolski. Twenty-two thousand Jewish refugees from Buczacz and other towns were exiled there. In Kamieniec, the refugees were taken out of town and shot to death.

When the news of the murder in Kamieniec became known, many refugees tried to stay in Tłuste. Some hid and some paid money for their freedom. The Ukrainians were not satisfied and wanted to get rid of the Jews. And so, they started to complain before the authorities that the refugees caused diseases, hunger and shortage and that they needed to send all of them away. On the other hand, the Jews did all that was possible to prevent the deportation because they knew very well that it was a life-saving issue. And indeed, they succeeded to cancel the deportation order.

The Ukrainian priest, Izbulskie [Navolskyy – *ed.*], helped them a lot in this matter. He calmed the Ukrainians and also supported the refugees with his own money, as much as he was able to afford. And so, around two thousand

Hungarian refugees remained in town. The aid committee made an accurate list of the refugees, moved them to vacant Jewish homes, or housed them in the apartments of the town's Jews.

After the deportation of the four thousand Jews to Kamieniec-Podolski, both *Beit Ha'Midrash* and the Great Synagogue were emptied. The Hungarian army refused to return those buildings to the town's Jews and removed the doors, the windows and all the wooden parts for firewood. And so the army started the destruction of the holy places; later on the Christian population continued the work until it was completed.

6. Horrible days under the swastika regime

On Rosh Hashanah eve [Monday, 22 September 1941], four Gestapo men arrived in Tluste from Chortkov. Fear and terror fell on the town's Jews because we already knew the meaning of the matter. All the Jews hid, myself included. The Gestapo men came with a demand, they wanted us to select the highest quality furniture and transfer it to Chortkov in order to furnish 15 rooms for the Gestapo. Without delay they went with the Jewish lawyer, Dr. Krasutski, entered Jewish homes, and made a list of the best furniture. They confiscated all the furniture in Dr. Bernard Meltzer's apartment. The confiscation continued also on the next day. On the first day of Rosh Hashanah the Jews were panic-stricken. They prayed in public but not in the synagogues. They held short prayer services in private homes. Later they tried to stay at home and stayed away from the streets.

After Rosh Hashanah, during the "Ten Days of Repentance," the city council started to recruit Jewish workers for all kind of jobs. The refugees' aid committee also helped the municipality to collect the required workers. Each worker received one kilogram of bread per day, and for that reason many people registered to work on their own accord.

The Gestapo men arrived from Chortkov on Yom Kippur [Wednesday, 1 October 1941]. They took Jews out of the synagogues, and under a shower of blows forced them to remove the confiscated furniture from the homes and load it on vehicles in order to transfer it to Chortkov. Since they were not able to take all the registered furniture with them, the council was forced to deliver the rest of the furniture by wagons to Chortkov on the conclusion of Yom Kippur.

7. The establishment of the "Judenrat"

A few days after Yom Kippur, a number of Gestapo men arrived from Chortkov. They approached the leader of the refugees' committee, Yakov Pel, nominated him as the "Jews elder" and ordered him to assemble a "*Judenrat*" [Jewish council]. The duty of the "*Judenrat*" was to supply Jewish workers, to fulfill the Germans' demands, and be responsible for all that was happening between the town's Jews. They demanded that a council representative come to Chortkov in order to receive additional instructions. Dr. Krasutski and two other council members traveled to Chortkov.

The Gestapo men in Chortkov did not talk to the council representatives face to face, but through a closed hatch. Again, they emphasized the need to establish a "*Judenrat*" that would fulfill all of the Gestapo's demands, and the orders of the local commander and the city council. Jews would do all the work in the town. They were instructed to organize a kitchen "for Jewish laborers" and promised to supply the necessary food for that kitchen. Together with that, they informed them that only the workers would get food. They emphasized that whoever disobeyed any of these orders and instructions would be sentenced to death. The representatives returned to Tluste shocked and confused from all that they had heard.

On the next day, a Gestapo representative arrived from Chortkov and ordered the council to collect gold, silver, jewelry, fine fabrics and other valuables from the town's Jews and deliver them to the Gestapo. On the intermediate days of Sukkot, representatives of the refugees' aid committee scattered throughout the town. They walked from home to home and encouraged the residents to give their share towards the "ransom" that was cast on the town. On *Hoshana Rabba* [The seventh day of Sukkot – Sunday, 12 October 1941], the collection of valuables started in the council office. Three council members received the items: Yakov Pel, Yisrael Yorist and myself. The items were registered with the help of an experienced jeweler and the donors received a detailed receipt.

Midpoint through this activity a Jew from Stanisławów, by the name of Flesher, who was the mediator between the Jews and the Gestapo in Chortkov district, arrived to town. We asked him to release us from our duty as members of the "*Judenrat.*" He agreed to release me and Yorist, but refused to release Pel since he had a lot of influence in town. On the same day a meeting was arranged with Flesher, and a new "*Judenrat*" was chosen with Yakov Pel as the leader.

Immediately after the holidays the Hungarian headquarters left town and power was transferred to the hands of the Germans. The district's government was located in Zaleszczyki, and the regional authorities and the Gestapo were located in Chortkov. The mayor was a Ukrainian, and a Ukrainian police force was established with a German commander. The conditions of the Jews worsened. Every once in a while, the "*Judenrat*" received instructions and new orders that they had to fulfill with great precision. A Jewish police was established next to the "*Judenrat*" and included 15-20 policemen who terrorized the Jews. A "prison" was organized, and Jews who dared to disobey the "*Judenrat*" orders were locked up there. The offices of the "*Judenrat*" and the Jewish police were located in the "credit union" building. The policemen were mostly young men from Tłuste, but there were also a number of young men from Zaleszczyki and the surrounding area.

8. The kitchen

"The kitchen for Jewish workers" was the continuation of the Hungarian refugees' kitchen that was established in our town at that time. The German authorities gave us enough supplies for only 150 workers, but the kitchen continued to care for the refugees and the needy, roughly one thousand people. In order to obtain all the supplies, a tax of between one to five Zlotys a week was enforced on the town's rich and we, the kitchen organizers, also took care of collecting this tax. We added Yosel Shechter and David Bronstein as workers. Also a number of women worked in the kitchen. The kitchen was well organized and was strictly kosher. It operated during the winter of 1941-1942. It was closed during the days of Passover and reopened after the holiday. We distributed potatoes and cash among the families who ate in the kitchen. The children of those families were housed in the homes of families with means and ate at their table during the eight days of Passover.

The budget for the kitchen was not only based on the taxes that we collected from people with means. We also received an allowance from the "*Judenrat*." It was not an easy duty to take money out of their hands. The person in charge of social aid was Yehoshua Shechner, and we always had to argue and bargain with him until we got what we wanted.

9. During the German rule

Close to their arrival, the Germans received ownership of the farms in the area, and merged them under one administrative unit that was called *"Liegenschaft"* [real estate or immovable property] in German. The administrator of the farms in Zaleszczyki and Berezdów was a Gestapo man by the name of Zocher. In September 1941, this Zocher settled in Tłuste and started to acquire ownership of these fields. He employed a large number of Jewish workers and tradesmen from Tłuste. Those who worked on the farms that were far from town were forced to settle there. Zocher was evil-hearted and cruel. He hit his Jewish workers with cruelty, and at times he even hit Jews who did not work for him. He robbed Jewish property and was extremely dangerous when he was drunk, a condition that he was in most of the time.

In November 1941, another German joined the *"Liegenschaft"* management, an S.S. man by the name of Stoll. After a short period of time, the *"Liegenschaft"* was divided. Stoll remained in Tłuste while Zocher received the management of *"Liegenschaft"* in Zaleszczyki. They also divided the Jewish managers between them. The two who remained on the farm in Tłuste were: Hillel Kenigsberg and his nephew Martzeli Kenigsberg. Stoll was a decent man and treated his Jewish workers with kindness. Approximately at the same period of time, at the end of 1941, an order arrived from the Gestapo in Chortkov that all Jews, including children from the age of ten, must wear a special mark on their left shoulder that would indicate their Judaism – a white ribbon with a blue Star of David. All those orders were passed to us through the regional *"Judenrat"* in Chortkov.

At the end of January 1942, rumors spread in town that in the near future the management of the farms would be transferred to the hands of the "Wehrmacht" [German armed forces]. These rumors became true. In February 1942, the "Wehrmacht" received ownership of 23 farms on the road between Chortkov and Tłuste. The farms were given to a company by the name of "G.G. Caoutchouc" that was engaged in growing a special kind of plant that they tried to produce rubber from. The seeds for growing the plant were brought from Russia. The main office of that factory was in Jagielnica and the managers were two agronomists: Major Dr. Hanf from Berlin and his helper Lauterbach.

Dr. Hanf demanded that he be supplied with 6000 Jewish laborers to work in the rubber farms. He promised the *"Judenrat"* that he would employ the Jewish workers in fair conditions, and their situation would improve. But

Tłuste's Jews were under the rule of the Gestapo in Chortkov, and it was impossible to receive a permit from them to employ the Jews on the farms. Hanf made many efforts in this subject, and Tłuste's Jews sent lobbyists to Lvov and spent a great amount of money to obtain the necessary permit. Hanf received 300 to 400 workers from the "*Judenrat*" every day, but he wanted to employ all of the Jews in town. The Jews who worked for him received enough food during their work in the fields, no one was tormenting them, and they were even allowed to walk around without an arm band.

The management of the "G.G. Caoutchouc" company brought Jewish workers from the Tarnopol area, including about one hundred young Jewish women. These workers were housed in huts on the Kozia-Gora farm, and so a labor camp was created. The laborers worked there temporarily and they were to be released at the end of the season. The rubber plantation did not develop properly and the few Jewish workers were released and sent home.

On 12 August 1942, Dr. Hanf informed the regional labor office in Chortkov that he was going to release the last workers from the Kozia-Gora camp, and demanded train tickets for them. Only around seventy women and teenage girls remained in the farm. The labor office informed him that those workers were to be handed to the Gestapo. Three days later, Gestapo men arrived in Tłuste from Chortkov and demanded that the "*Judenrat*" hand them 10% of the Jewish population, mostly those who were not able to work, in order to "take them" out of town. They threatened that if the "*Judenrat*" did not deliver the people – they would "take care" of removing them from their homes. The "*Judenrat*" gathered for a long meeting but it was very difficult to come to a decision. In the end it was decided, without any other choice, to deliver to their hands old men and women and sick children – a total of one hundred and seventy people. Since the Gestapo's demand of 10% of the Jewish population was not met, the Germans added the seventy young women from the Kozia-Gora farm to the quota. The Jewish police, with the help of the Ukrainian police, brought them to Tłuste. On the way, the girls were ordered to sing "*Hatikvah.*" In Tłuste, the 240 Jews were put in rail cars and transported to Belz concentration camp. Three young women were able to jump from the moving train and returned to Tłuste the following day. With that, the first "*aktzya*" ended in our town.

The "*Caoutchouc*" plants, from which the Germans were hoping to produce synthetic rubber, were not as successful as they hoped for. Therefore they decreased the size of the plantations and the land was mostly used for wheat.

As a result of this change, the German administrators who managed the farms also were changed. A new "work manager" arrived to our town. He was a German from the city of Dargun in Mecklenburg, and his name was Patti [Vathje]. Thanks to him, all of Tluste's surviving Jews were saved from liquidation. He was a real friend to the Jews and he risked his life for them a number of times. He always tried to get information in advance about the "*aktzyot*" that were going to take place in Tluste, and always alerted the Jews before the arrival of the Gestapo.

In October 1941, the "*Judenrat*" received a demand from the regional "*Judenrat*" in Chortkov. They wanted dozens of healthy Jews in order to send them to the labor camps in Kamionka and Glembotzk [Hluboczek]. Thirty people, most of them refugees who lived in town, were sent. We were promised that the workers would receive plenty of food in their place of work, and they would be replaced with another group of workers in three weeks. A short time later, bitter and bad news started to arrive from the people who were sent to the camps: the work was very difficult, most of it was in road repairs and in the paving of new roads and railroad tracks. In addition to that, they were severely beaten and they were not given any food. After the arrival of this news, no one wanted to work in those camps in place of the first group of thirty. When the "*Judenrat*" demanded that they come to register, no one came and everyone hid wherever they could.

10. The "aktzyot" in Tluste and in nearby towns

At the beginning of December 1941, on a Thursday [4 December], we received a message from Horodenka across the Dniester River about the "*aktzya*" that took place there on that day. At first, we found out that a large number of Jews, around two thousand five hundred, were taken out of their homes and locked in the building of the Great Synagogue. On the next day we received a report that those Jews were transferred by trucks and by foot to a forest near the Dniester, almost across from the town of Uścieczko. There, they were shot to death and buried in a big mass grave that was prepared in advance. Farmers, who arrived from the area, told us that the Jews were ordered to remove their clothes before the killing. The sound of the victims' shouts was carried and heard several kilometers away in the town of Uścieczko on this side of the Dniester.

I heard a detailed description of the "*aktzya*" from the daughter of Horodenka's slaughterer, who miraculously survived and pulled herself out of the killing pit. The Jews were ordered to take their clothes off and put them in a designated location. After that they were forced to climb on a plank of wood that was put across the burial pit, then, they were shot and fell into the pit. Most of those who fell into the pit were dead or seriously wounded. She also stood on the wood plank with her son in her arms. Her son was hit and she fell together with him into the pit. She remained in the pit until late at night, and then she pulled herself out of it without a cover on her skin. One of the farmers from the village of Siemakowce, which was near the killing location, gave her a dress to wear and a sweater to cover herself, and so she arrived to our town.

At dusk, on the same Thursday [*sic*], we were informed that a similar action also took place in the city of Zaleszczyki. There, an order was given to the "*Judenrat*" that all Jews must report on Friday morning to a number of locations in the city: The craftsmen were told to report to the police station, and the other residents were ordered to come to the military base out of the city equipped with cleaning tools: shovels, brooms and pails. On Friday, we found out that the craftsmen, who gathered at the police station, were let go, but the rest of the residents, around 700 people, were taken from the base to an unknown location and disappeared [This *aktzya* actually occurred on 14 November 1941 – *ed.*]. No one knows what happed to these Jews.

On the same Friday [5 December 1941], in the morning, a number of Gestapo men arrived from Chortkov. With the help of the Jewish police they went out to the streets to catch Jews, as if they were planning to replace the Jews who had been sent to the labor camps. By chance, I stood at the same time across from the "*Judenrat*" office together with the slaughterer, R' Shalom Lam. Suddenly, two Germans and two Jewish policemen appeared. One of them was Zushe Shporn [Zishe Sparen] who started to shout: "Stop!" Also the Germans ordered us to stop. An aqueduct separated us and a small crossing bridge was not far from us. The policemen and the Germans turned to the bridge in order to catch us, but I was able to escape and hid in Berel Eringer's home. The slaughterer was not able to escape and was caught. On the same day, around seventy or eighty Jews were caught and led on foot to the

"*Judenrat*" in Chortkov. A few of them were able to pay ransom and free themselves, and the others were sent to labor camps, together with one thousand Jews who were caught in the area on the same day. The first group of thirty Jews, who were sent to camps earlier, was not released and continued to suffer there. Their relatives sent them food parcels every two weeks in order to ease their suffering. The "*Judenrat*" also sent food parcels every once in a while.

On 20 December 1941, another roundup took place. This time about one hundred and twenty Jews were sent to camps. Among them there were three "*Judenrat*" members: Dr. Krasutski, Moshe Pfeffer and Yisrael Krampf. Some time later, a few of them were able to release themselves from the camp after paying a lot of money and with the intervention of the "*Judenrat*" in Skalat. The members of the Meiman family were also released. After this big round-up similar smaller actions took place. In these actions the Gestapo was helped by the Ukrainian police and also by the people of the Jewish police. The abductees were usually sent to the regional "*Judenrat*" in Chortkov, and from there the Germans transferred them to labor camps.

11. The "fur aktzya"

In December 1941, an order arrived that within a period of 14 days all of the town's Jews must give their furs to the "*Judenrat*" who would transfer the furs to the Gestapo. Those who refused to obey the order would be sentenced to death. As the Gestapo had done in each town, they also arrested a number of Jews in our town and held them as hostages until the order was fulfilled. Among others they arrested R' Ahron Meiman, z"l, and R' Gavriel Hessing, May he rest in peace. Most of the residents obeyed the order and brought their furs to the "*Judenrat*." Only a few endangered themselves and gave their furs to their non-Jewish friends or sold them for a cheap price. A number of people hid their furs in the ground, and there were others who burnt them. Among those who hid their furs was Berel Oringer, who hid them in the ground together with other valuables. Someone informed on him, Ukrainian and Jewish policemen searched his home and found the pit where the articles were buried. He was arrested, sent to Chortkov and received a death sentence. For a large sum of money, the "*Judenrat*" was able to exchange the death sentence for a hard labor sentence in the Kamionka labor camp. So, they sent a seventy-year old man to a labor camp, and a few months later they liberated him with a lot of money. When the "fur *aktzya*" ended, it was necessary to care for the release of the hostages. Also this matter was not easy. They were released together with other hostages who were arrested in nearby towns, only after their families paid ransom for them.

Besides the robbery of the furs which was organized like an "*aktzya,*" the Gestapo men came to town every once in a while, and made "orders" in the value of thousands of Zlotys. The orders included goods and valuables such as: leather coats, boots, fabrics, jewelry and such. In order to supply those orders, the "*Judenrat*" was forced to enforce a tax on Jews, and the Jews became poorer from day to day. The Jewish police was ordered to collect and extort the tax by any means, by conducting searches, torture and imprisonment. At times the police found a few hundred dollars and expensive jewelry, mostly among the refugees, and confiscated it. It is no wonder that the town's Jews were afraid of the Jewish police and showed very little sympathy towards it, if I want to express myself in a soft language.

The "*Judenrat*" members carried out the Germans' demands. One of the duties that was forced on them was to supply Jewish workers. The workers were sent to work according to their place in the queue. There were Jews who were able to release themselves from work duty by paying 20 Zlotys for each day of work.

At the end of the winter of 1941-1942, Yakov Pel resigned from his duty as the "Jews elder" and Dr. Averman took his place. He came from Mykulińce near Tarnopol. He was a very decent man and his only wish was to protect the town and its Jews.

12. The events of the summer of 1942

The spring months and the beginning of the summer of 1942 passed without any special events. In June there was a shortage of food supplies because the Germans confiscated all the grain and transferred it to their country. Everything became more expensive, and people ate only potatoes and potato skins. The kitchen had to increase the number of meals that were given to the needy at midday, and was not able to satisfy the hunger of the many Jews who came and asked for help. Many gathered by the kitchen's doors at all times, and not once the police had to intervene and introduce order. Due to the difficult situation, the kitchen gave tea "to everyone" between five in the afternoon until eight. Those with means paid 10 Grushin, but most of the people who came received it for free.

There were a number of Jews in town whose situation was not that difficult since they had something to sell to the farmers and get food in exchange. I was one of those lucky ones: I still had a few haberdashery items and bottles of perfume that I was able to hide. There were also those who endangered their lives, snuck out of town and went to work for the farmers in exchange for food.

The condition of the Jews in Kolomyja, Stanisławów and Lvov was worse. There, they were actually dying from hunger in city streets. I, and other Jews, sent small packages of grain to our families in those cities. Every once in a while, it was possible to mail a one-kilogram package and the grain was ground in coffee grinders. The matter of grinding grain in coffee grinders was very common in those days, because the Jews were not allowed to use the flour mills. Each Jewish home had a grinder like that. They turned it all day long, and they were able to grind around four kilograms of wheat during the day. This work was done in secret, and the same was done with the baking of the bread and eating it.

In the summer of 1942, a number of decrees and limitations were enforced on our Jewish brothers: (1) They were forbidden to walk in the town's main street. Only two passageways, which connected the two sections of town, were allocated to them. A notice board was located next to each passage and the inscription "Jewish passageway" was written on it. (2) Jews were forbidden to draw water from the central well that always supplied water to the residents. (3) They were forbidden to communicate with the non-Jewish population, such as having a conversation with them, saying hello and such. (4) An order was given that all Jews who still lived in the villages, and also Jews who lived in the suburbs, must move to the town center and live among the Jewish population. The homeowners whose homes stood on the main street were forced to lock their front door and only use the back door. Jewish shops were liquidated and everything was transferred to the hands of the Ukrainians. (5) Jews were allowed to send or receive packages in the mail as long as they didn't exceed the weight of one kilogram. There were not any limitations in this matter to the non-Jewish population.

In the summer of 1942, there was an event that agitated the whole town. During the occupation, nearly one hundred Jews worked in Tluste train station. They filled and leveled the pits that had been created by the bombs, and other jobs. The "*Judenrat*" came to an agreement with the station manager and he agreed, for a certain monthly payment, not to be strict with the number of people who worked there, or with the quality of their work. At one time, the "*Judenrat*" was late with its "bonus" and did not give it on time. The station manager called the Gestapo in Chortkov, and informed them that the Jews were on "strike" and did not show up for work. At four o'clock in the afternoon, two cars full of Gestapo men arrived to the "*Judenrat*" office, and demanded to bring all of the train station workers to their place of work. The "*Judenrat*" scattered all over town and recruited each person who crossed their path, and even took the kitchen workers with them (they did not take me because of my beard). After all of them were brought to the train station, the Gestapo men ordered to bring two freight cars, loaded the Jews on them and locked them in. The common opinion was that the Gestapo was waiting for a train to arrive in order to send those Jews to an "unknown destination." A great panic broke in town and the "*Judenrat*" went into action. They bribed the station manager with a large sum of money, and also gave "ransom money" to the Gestapo. And so, the "*Judenrat*" succeeded to cancel the decree of transporting the Jews. They were released and given to Dr. Averman, who was ordered to detain the workers until morning and send them from there to their work place. This event left a difficult impression in town; the whole town was confused and the train station workers did not allow themselves to skip work again.

During the last summer months, an order arrived from the regional "*Judenrat*" to assemble a group of six "strong men" to purchase old metal from the whole area and collect it at the train station. It was clear and understood that it would be difficult work, but many Jews wanted it since it would provide them with the possibility to move freely in town and outside it. Immediately there were Jews who agreed to pay a large sum of money for the right to be a member of this working group. The lucky ones who were chosen for this duty received a special identity card from the Gestapo, and they had to carry the letter A on their chest meaning: "Jewish laborer." It became clear that they used their freedom to buy food out of town and bring it to the ghetto.

In July 1942, the Germans issued an order that all Jews from the cities of Zaleszczyki, Chortkov and Kopyczyńce who did not belong to the "Jewish laborers" class would be transferred to Tłuste. Immediately Jewish families started to arrive in our town from those cities, and the housing situation became extremely grave. The wealthy exiled families rented apartments with their own money and the "*Judenrat*" was forced to pay for the housing of poor families.

13. The second "aktzya" in Tłuste

During the "High Holidays" rumors spread in town about the massacres that took place in other cities, and depression took over immediately. During the holiday of Sukkot [end of September / beginning October] we found out that two thousand Jews were captured in the nearby town of Borszczów, and sent to Belzec concentration camp. The report caused panic and fear in town, and anyone, who had the opportunity started to install a "bunker" in his home for times of trouble. I also installed a hiding place in the attic of my home.

On Simchat Torah [3 October 1942], we received a warning from the regional "*Judenrat*" in Chortkov that the Gestapo was planning an "*aktzya*" in Tłuste. On the next day, around five in the morning, Gestapo men, escorted by Ukrainian policemen, scattered around town and started to abduct Jews. My family, myself and a number of other Jews, all together eleven people, sat in the hiding place in the attic. Through a small window I saw how they were leading a group of around one hundred Jews to a central location. Besides the Ukrainian police, groups of rioters armed with axes and sticks also participated in the search. They walked from house to house, and when they found Jews hiding in a bunker they led them to the central location. Many of the abducted Jews were killed in that place. The murderers also arrived at our "bunker" and started to break the wall with axes. Fortunately, one of them mentioned that the wall was very old, and he did not think that there was a "bunker" behind it. Then, they all left and went on their way.

The "*aktzya*" lasted until three o'clock in the afternoon. At three, a siren indicated that the "*aktzya*" was over. I looked through the small window and saw a number of Jews walking freely in the streets, so I also went down from the attic. The "*aktzya*" was directed by a Gestapo man from Chortkov by the name of Palre [Pal – *ed.*]. A number of Jews, who were hiding in the post office, heard Palre informing Chortkov by phone "the operation was successful, the result – 128 dead and 900 prisoners..."

The "prisoners" were loaded on rail cars and transferred to Belzec. Among them was also Tłuste's rabbi, R' Shmuel-Aba Chodorov, with his wife, son and daughter. The rabbi's mother, who was around seventy years old, informed the Gestapo men that she refused to walk to the gathering place, and if they wanted to kill her they had better shoot her right there. The murderers fulfilled her wish and killed her where she was standing. A few Jews who jumped from the moving train were saved. R' Chodorov also had the opportunity to jump from the car, but he did not wish to do so. His sixteen-year-old daughter jumped from the death-car near Lvov, but she perished later on.

The victims of this "*aktzya*" were mostly refugees who did not live in town and did not have suitable "bunkers" to hide in. On the same day, the "*Judenrat*" cared for the burial of the victims in the local cemetery. According to the Gestapo order, the "*Judenrat*" collected the belongings of the "transferred" with the assistance of the Ukrainian police, and put them in a special warehouse. The Gestapo men left after the "*aktzya*" was over, and the Jews came out of their hiding places to observe and see the evil act that was done to them.

14. Tluste becoming a central location for Jewish survivors from fifteen towns

On the day after the "*aktzya*" we found out that the same massacres and "transfers" also took place in most of the towns around Tluste. We learnt from different circles in the regional "*Judenrat*" in Chortkov that the Germans were planning to liquidate the Jewish population in most of the towns except in the cities of Chortkov, Borszczów and Kopyczyńce, where they were planning to leave a small Jewish settlement. They were also thinking of saving one more city: Jezierzany (Uziran) or Tluste. The councils of the two towns started to lobby vigorously before the regional "*Judenrat*," each one in favor of its own town, and each one of them was willing to pay large sums of money for the right to be a "city of refuge." Meanwhile, the Jews in the two towns sat on their belongings, ready to leave for the road in case they would be forced to move to another town.

In the end, Tluste's "*Judenrat*" won. The day after the "victory" – on a rainy Sabbath – Jews from the nearby towns started to arrive to Tluste. Most of them came in wagons and brought their belongings with them. The matter lasted all week, and at the end of the week the number of Jews in town reached about eight thousand. In the message that was sent to the Gestapo, the number of Jews was reduced by one-third from the correct number, since they were afraid to admit that "so many Jews" settled here... This scheme seriously hurt the nutritional system since the Germans provided food rations according to the number of residents. The overcrowding condition in town grew above all measures. Also before that there was a shortage of apartments and the transfer of thousands of Jews "to an unknown destination" did not lower the overcrowding conditions. The Germans sold the transferees' apartments to the municipality, who gave them to the farmers for a very cheap price so they could take them apart and reuse the building materials. The kitchen continued to operate, but it was not able to provide enough food to the hungry. Out of the Hungarian refugees almost no one was left in town. During the summer of 1942 each one of them tried to reach his home in Hungary.

At the beginning of December 1942, the Gestapo established a camp in Swidowa [Świdowa], a distance of nine kilometers from Tluste. The camp belonged to the "*Wehrmacht*" and the camp workers were marked by the letter W. Only healthy people without children were accepted to work in that camp. The Jews believed that the workers of this camp would be protected from future "*aktzyot*". Some paid ten thousand and even fifteen thousand Zlotys for the privilege to be included among the camp's workers. Most of the people, who were accepted there, were Jews from Chortkov who had connections with the Gestapo. They were allowed to bring their valuables with them and a number of them even brought their carpets.

Jews who were able to register and be accepted to the Swidowa camp were considered to be blessed. Meanwhile, a number of Jews also started to look for a way to return to their towns. Some of them were able to arrange jobs for themselves, like collecting metal or similar jobs. It became evident that each success of that kind was involved with a large payment to the Gestapo or to the local commander.

15. The bitter end of Dr. Bernard Meltzer and his family

Fifty, or sixty years ago, an important learned Chortkov Hassid, R' Kalman-Matye Meltzer, lived in Tluste. One of his grandsons, Dr. Bernard Meltzer, married the daughter of R' Berel Kotner, May he rest in peace, and settled in Tluste. He was a good doctor and excelled in diagnostic medicine. During the Soviet regime, he was appointed director of the regional hospital where he worked with five doctors and a large medical team. After the Germans occupied the town, he left his position and saw patients at his home. Very quickly he earned a good reputation, even among the Germans who also came from Chortkov to seek medical treatment from him.

In November 1942, a Ukrainian doctor entered his apartment accompanied by two Gestapo men, and ordered him to evacuate his apartment without taking anything out of it. He left his apartment and moved to his brother's apartment which was located nearby. Since then he was afraid to spend the night in town and, every day after dark, a farmer who was one of his friends came and took his whole family to sleep on his farm.

On 20 December 1942, the farmer did not come to take him as he did day after day, and he spent the night together with his wife and two daughters in his brother's apartment. At six o'clock the Ukrainian police commander came and took the whole family to the police station. The "*Judenrat*" started to appeal for their release, but it came to nothing. An hour later all of them were transferred to Chortkov. Early the next morning, Dr. Averman and two other "*Judenrat*" members left for Chortkov as they always did when it was necessary to cancel one of the decrees. But this time they were too late. Before they arrived in Chortkov, Dr. Meltzer, his wife and two daughters were taken to Rożyszcze forest and were executed there.

16. The "Roundup" in Tluste

At twilight, on Monday, 21 December, a sudden panic took over the town. The Ukrainian police invaded the streets and started to catch Jews - men and women, old people and young people. And so, thirty people were caught and locked in the police station cellar. During the night, the "*Judenrat*" managed to release a number of them, but on the next evening the hunt continued. After a lot of pleading we learnt from the police commander that the roundup was executed according to a command given by the Gestapo in Chortkov. They ordered them to catch and arrest the "wanderers" (who do not work). On the evening of the fourth day Jews were not seen in the streets, everyone was hiding in his home or in his hiding place. Again, the police invaded the town, broke doors and demolished "bunker" walls, and arrested around thirty Jews. And so, around eighty Jews were captured over a period of three days. On Thursday, 24 December 1942, in a snow storm and frigid weather, they were loaded on sleds and transferred to Chortkov. On the last night, Yosel Grill's wife was arrested for the second time after she was released the night before, against payment of one thousand Zlotys.

Under the pressure of the detainees' relatives, the members of the "*Judenrat*" traveled to Chortkov and tried to release them or pay ransom for them, but all their efforts came to nothing. They remained in prison together with many other Jews from different towns. They were released only on January 1st, and a few days later they returned to their homes. They told us that they had been beaten with great cruelty when they arrived at the prison in Chortkov, their shoes were taken from them and they were not allowed to receive packages from their families or from their friends. A few days later, forty strong men were taken out, given digging shovels and transferred by trucks to a forest in Rożyszcze. It was clear to them that they were going to dig their own grave and the graves for the rest of the prisoners. But the snow was very deep, the truck turned over on the way and they were not able to reach the forest. All of them returned to Chortkov and later on all the detainees were released. During their release they were beaten and tortured and their shoes were given back to them. No one received his own pair of shoes and the shoes did not match. There were some who were given two right shoes or two left shoes. Chortkov's Jews took the liberated prisoners to their homes, gave them food and a place to sleep until they were able to return to their towns.

Shortly after the Jews returned from prison they became ill with typhus. It was clear that it was a German plot to release the Jewish prisoners so they would infect the town's Jews and spread this dangerous illness among them.

*

During the entire time, the Gestapo men never stopped coming to our town to give an "order," and the "*Judenrat*" was forced to give them what they wanted so they wouldn't have an excuse to take advantage of the town's Jews. The kitchen operation stopped on 15 January 1943, and the last remnant of Jewish mutual aid was put to an end. Only the Jewish police continued to exist and continued to extort the last possessions from the Jews. Epidemics and illness spread and caused casualties among the Jewish population, and the number of dead was 25 to 30 people every day.

We also received bad and bitter news from the Jews who worked in the camps. After the Germans suffered from great defeats on the battlefront, the conditions in the camps worsened and many Jews were shot to death.

The "*Judenrat*" in Skalat managed to release a number of men from the neighboring camps, but most of the camp's workers remained there, and were tortured to death by the difficult work and the unbearable living conditions.

On Friday, 12 February 1943, a number of Gestapo men arrived from Chortkov to give an "order" to the "*Judenrat*." Before evening we suddenly heard the sound of gunfire. Jews escaped for the lives and hid in their bunkers all night. Only in the morning we learnt the reason for the shooting and the result: On the way from the "*Judenrat*" building, the Gestapo men turned to the Jewish homes in Targowica, and shot the Jews whom they met by chance. Forty Jews died on the same Friday. On Saturday morning the martyrs were led to the cemetery and were buried according to Jewish tradition.

17. Passover 5703 – 1943

Tluste's Jews lived under horrible conditions throughout the winter. But on the eve of the holiday of Passover [20 April 1943] they baked matzha and got ready to celebrate Passover properly. About three days before Passover, a message arrived that an "*aktzya*" had taken place in a nearby town. Eight thousand Jews were taken out of town in addition to the many Jews who were killed on the spot. On Passover eve, we found out that an "*aktzya*" was raging in the nearby town of Borszczów. When the Jews heard the news, they left all that they prepared for the holiday and hurried to their hiding places. Around half of them escaped to the fields and to the forests. There were incidents when local Ukrainians, who served in the "Kripa" [criminal police], tried to stop the escaping Jews. So it happened to two families - Trembovelski and Hendel, who tried to reach Olchowa forest through a side road. The Ukrainians blocked their way, they resisted and a scuffle started between them. The Jews were beaten and injured, but they also beat their opponents and escaped to the forest. An eight-year-old boy, Shlomo Hendel, lost contact with his family and returned to the town on his own.

On the first day of Passover [Tuesday, 21 April 1943], in the morning hours, everyone remained in his hiding place. It was quiet in town and the tension calmed down a little. Panic broke again in the afternoon hours. The Borszczów "*Judenrat*" called to inform us that the "*aktzya*" was finished in their town, the "Angels of Destruction" had left town and they were traveling in the direction of Tluste. Immediately, the "*Judenrat*" sent the Jewish police to urge the residents to go to their hiding places. My wife and I hid in a "bunker" that was located in the attic of Fishel Pfeffer's home. Three hours later, the "*Judenrat*" called Borszczów for the second time and we found out that the murderers had returned to Chortkov. They calmed Tluste's Jews, and said that they didn't think that the Germans would arrange additional "*aktzyot*" in the next few days because of the holiday of Easter. After hearing this news everyone came out of hiding. Only the Jews who escaped out of town did not hurry to return and remained in their hiding places in the fields and in the forests. And so, a relative calm prevailed in town and lasted during the days of Passover.

18. The great massacre in Tluste

In spite of the peace that prevailed during Passover, all of us were full of fear. We knew and we felt that our town would not be different from its close neighbors. Even before Passover the Germans ordered us to mark the Jewish homes with a blue Star of David, and the homes where Jews and Christians lived together with a red Star of David. It was clear to everyone that it was ordered in preparation for "*aktzya*" day so the murderers would be able to tell the different between the Jewish and the Christian homes. With fear and terror we waited for the terrible Day of Judgment. And the dreadful day, the day of trouble and destruction of Tluste's Jews arrived.

At midnight on Tuesday, 25 May 1943, 32 days to the counting of the Omer, I heard the voice of the "Jews elder" Dr. Averman passing by my window. He was walking to his brother [in-law], Ahron Gertner, who lived in the next building. I waited for him and when he returned I asked him the reason for his late visit. He told me that delegates of the "*Judenrat*" were in Chortkov. There, they found out that the situation had reached a very dangerous stage and we needed to hide. Immediately after, Ahron Gertner came to me and we decided to escape from the town in the early morning hours.

At three o'clock in the morning we all left town, my wife and myself, Gertner with his wife and their baby. We arrived in the village of Holovtshinza [Hołowczyńce] which was located around two or three kilometers from Tluste. There, I entered the yard of a Polish friend by the name of Wlodya Ostropolski. The whole family was asleep so we entered his stable and stayed there until morning. In the morning Ostropolski let us into his home. His daughter vacated her room for us, and he calmed us all down and promised to hide us if we were in danger. Later on he locked us in his home and went to see what was happening in town.

The same day of the week, Wednesday, passed peacefully. In the evening I wanted to return to town, sleep in my home and return to the farm early the next morning. Ostropolski did not allow us to return. He advised us to ask our family members who remained in town for their opinion. I gave him letters addressed to my sister Rachel Meiman, my brother-in-law Chaim Bronshtayn, and to my aunt Malcha Sternklar. My sister and my aunt said that it was possible to return to town since it was quiet there. On the other hand, my brother-in-law advised me to wait and see. We took his advice and spent the night in Holovtshinza.

Early in the morning of Thursday, 27 May 1943, Ostropolski's son-in-law came to tell us that the "aktzya" had started. Ostropolski and his son-in-law went out to the streets and there they saw Jewish people running full of fear and panic with their bundles and their children. They ran on side roads towards the fields. Among the escapees they also saw my wife's sister, Feiga Hendel, with her husband and three children. The sound of gunfire and other weapons of destruction were heard from all directions.

Around ten o'clock an armed Ukrainian policeman arrived in the village. Ostropolski's daughter got very scared, entered our room and asked us to leave the house. Immediately her father entered and sent her away from the room. He arranged a secret corner for us and left us in his home. In order to remove any suspicion from his home he opened the windows, locked his door and went to town. A short time later he came back and told us that the "aktzya" was in full strength. Many Germans, and many more Ukrainians, were abducting Jews, taking them out of their homes and leading them to the market square where they were strictly guarded by armed Ukrainians. The matter lasted until three o'clock in the afternoon. Then, the abductions stopped and the murderers selected forty strong Jews and led them to the cemetery to dig pits. The Germans promised them that if they would work well – they would let them go. A few farmers, who lived in town and in the nearby villages, helped to discover Jews who were hiding. In return for their help they received all the Jewish property as gifts. Before evening, an armed Gestapo brigade arrived from Chortkov. The Ukrainian policemen led the Jews from the market square to the cemetery, and there the Nazis shot and killed them.

During the day Ostropolski visited town a number of times, and from him I found out what was happening there. Late in the afternoon, at the end of the "aktzya," we did not know what tomorrow would bring. There were those who assumed that the murders would continue on the next day, and there were those who assumed that for now the "aktzya" was over.

On Friday morning, Ostropolski went to town. We agreed that if he did not return in an hour, it meant that the "aktzya" was over and it was possible for us to leave our hiding place. To be safe we decided to wait more than an hour; and when he did not return three hours later my wife and I left Ostropolski's house and started to walk to town. On the way farmers loaded with Jewish property were walking towards us, and we also met a few miserable and frightened Jews who returned to town from their hiding places.

When we were close to town, we turned to a side road and approached the home of my sister Rachel Meiman who lived at the entrance to the town. A wagon harnessed to horses stood in the yard and a number of Jews, Reuven Albin's two sons included, were loading the victims' bodies on the cart. I was sure that my sister and my brother-in-law were among the murdered, and because of it I became dizzy and fainted. My brother-in-law, who was standing nearby, ran to me and calmed me down. I found out that all of my family members remained alive, and the murdered were a rabbi from Pinsk who lived with my brother-in-law, Reuven Albin's third son, and a number of other Jews.

I found out that most of the members of the Jewish police and the Jewish workers who carried the letter A or W, were able to escape and hide. If one of them was caught the murderers treated him differently from the way they treated the rest of the Jews: they did not shoot him but forced him to help with the "aktzya." The same happened to Berish Hessing. He was in the W work section and was forced to escort the captured Jews from the town square to the cemetery. I heard following story from him: Walking in one of the groups to the cemetery was the well-known town resident, R' Moshe Vilner, who shouted in a great voice: "*Shema' Yisrael Adonai ekiheinu Adoni ehad*" ["Hear, O Israel, the Lord is our God, the Lord is one"]. One of the Germans asked Hessing: "What is this Jew shouting?" Hessing explained to him that he was calling God. To that the German answered: "but this is the God who rejected you and cursed you..."

As it is told above, the Germans promised the forty Jews, who were selected to dig the pits that their lives would be spared in exchange for their work and they would not be killed. And indeed, the Germans kept what they promised... They were not murdered together with everyone else. After the graves of the thousands of Jews were sealed, these Jews were ordered to dig a small pit, they were shot to death next to it and buried in it.

At the home of Yoshe Grill there was a "bunker" where his family and the Trembovelski family hid. All together 15 people hid there. Trembovelski's four-year-old son started to cry, and all the efforts to calm him down were in vain. The murderers were running around the house searching for Jews, and the boy's cry could have given them away and endanger the lives of the people who were sitting there. Out of desperation, one of them took a pillow, covered the boy's body with it, and sat on the pillow in order to silence the boy's cries. Indeed the boy became silent – for eternity. The people who were hiding in the "bunker" survived, and they live and exist to this day.

The streets were full with the bodies of those who were shot trying to escape from their murderers. The body of Dr. Langholz, son of Akiva Langholz, was lying next to my house. The bodies were collected by the members of the Jewish police and other Jews who were selected for this duty by the "*Judenrat*." They were taken to the cemetery and buried there in a "common grave."

The slaughter in Tłuste was executed under the command of the Gestapo commander in Chortkov. Around two hundred Germans, four hundred Ukrainian policemen and the people of the special "Shupo" [security police] and "Kripo" [criminal police] police units took part in this action. On Friday, the "*Judenrat*" received a bill in the amount of 2,500 Zlotys for the bullets that were used in the "*aktzya*." The "*Judenrat*" paid the amount and received a valid receipt.....

On the same Friday, the day after the "*aktzya*," all the furniture and valuable items were taken out of the homes of the murdered Jews. All the furniture was stored in the "credit union" building, and the rest of the items in Berish Hessing's home. The "Jewish laborers" helped in this operation.

3,500 Jews perished in this blood massacre. By chance none of the members of my family, which was one of the largest and extended families in town, was among them. Besides a twelve-year-old girl, the daughter of a family member by the name Hernes, the rest of my relatives were not hurt in this "*aktzya*."

After the Jews came out of their hiding places, in the town or outside it, the total number of Jews in Tluste was around three thousand people.

19. The strange case of a Jew from Horodenka

In 1938 I entered a partnership with a Jew from Horodenka by the name of Herman Shteynkol [Steinkohl]. Together we became the representatives of the "Bata" company. In the course of working together we got close to each other. In July 1931, the "Bata" company canceled the agreement because of our Judaism and Shteynkol returned to his town of Horodenka. In 1940, when I was on my way to Kolomja, I visited Shteynkol's home in Horodenka and had the opportunity to meet his family.

At the end of 1942, I received a letter from Shteynkol from the town of Stary or Sambor. He informed me that his wife and his little daughter disappeared from his sight when they tried to sneak across the border to Romania. He and his small son wandered to Kolomja, and from there they were sent by train to Belzec. On the way he managed to jump from the car, and so he was left alone in the world without any financial means. He asked me to try and send him some money to live on. I sent him 100 Zlotys and asked the "*Judenrat*" to send him a larger amount.

On the same day, in the evening, a woman came to my home with her girl and asked me if I still remembered her. She was Herman Shteynkol's wife. She managed to reach Chernovitz but was returned from there and was given to the Ukrainian police. In Kosov she met a Jewish relative who paid the police 100 Dollars as ransom for her and her daughter. She returned to Horodenka but when she did not find any Jews there she tried to reach Tluste. She came to me since I was her friend. I carefully told her that her husband was alive and that I had a letter from him. The next morning she wrote a letter to her husband and some time later she received an answer from him. Now a problem arose on how to reunite the family. Meanwhile Shteynkol became ill with typhus. Also it was very difficult to send letters because Jews were not allowed to use the postal service. The only way to exchange letters was with the help of non-Jewish friends. In time, Shteynkol recovered from his illness, started to work, and was even able to send money to his wife through the "*Judenrat*". His main wish was to reach his family, but he was afraid to endanger himself in "such a long journey" due to the conditions of those days.

On the last days of the month of May, a letter arrived from Shteynkol saying that he had decided to travel to Tluste dressed as a gentile. And indeed, he kept his word and arrived in Tluste but did not find his wife and daughter among the living. Both had been killed in the great massacre together with 3,500 Jews. Again, Shteynkol remained lonely and depressed. He stayed in Tluste and was tormented in different camps until the town was liberated by the Red Army in March of 1944.

20. After the massacre

The handful of Jewish survivors in Tluste were not even given time to cry for their relatives and friends who perished in the great massacre. Three days after the massacre, on 30 May 1943, rumors spread that the Germans were planning to declare the whole area "*Judenfrei*", meaning, to kill all the surviving Jews in the whole area. The rumor cast great confusion among the Jewish survivors in town, and no one knew how to face the upcoming trouble.

On Monday, 31 May, we became aware of a new decree. The "*Judenrat*" and the municipality received an order to transfer all the Jews who remained in town to one street by 5 June 1943. The "*Judenrat*" did not see the possibility of crowding the survivors in one street. Therefore they traveled to Chortkov to appeal in the matter and to get permission to add another narrow alleyway to the "ghetto". Early Wednesday evening it was clear to everyone that all the efforts failed, and there was no escape from being locked in a "ghetto". In order to secure a place for myself in the "ghetto", I approached my friend Moshe Shulman and he agreed to provide me a corner in his apartment. But I was not the only one who came to him, and very quickly his apartment was completely full and there was no place for us and our belongings. The confusion grew from moment to moment. Jews were willing to sell their belongings for a few coins, but they were not able to find a buyer. There were those who gave their belongings to their Christian friends in order to get them back if they survived. I and my brother-in-law Bronshtayn also did the same.

On Thursday 5 (*sic*) June [Thursday would have been 3 June – *ed.*], Dr. Averman returned to Tluste with the news that there was a spark of hope to survive the liquidation. There were six farms around Tluste under the management of a German by the name Paul Friedrich Patti [Vathje]. He had a good heart and actually liked the Jews. He became friendly with many Jews in Tluste, had good connections with the "*Judenrat*", and every so often helped the Jews to the best of his power. After the great "*aktzya*", Patti approached the agricultural administration in Jagielnitza [Jagielnica] and received permission from the Gestapo to take out one thousand Jewish workers from Tłuste, and settle them on the six farms that were under his management. The "*Judenrat*" used the opportunity and received permission from Patti to select the workers and to provide the work cards that were signed by him. More than that, Patti agreed to provide cards to two thousand people despite the fact that he received permission to provide cards to only one thousand people. According to the instruction the cards were only destined for healthy workers, but Patti gave an order not to be strict and also to give cards to the elderly and children. He also gave permission to bring children without any cards. The Jews treated those cards as a permit to stay alive, and they were ready to give everything they had in exchange for a work card.

On Friday, 4 June, Tłuste's surviving Jews had to leave their apartments and move to the "ghetto". Those who were able to get a work card left for the farms. There were Jews who escaped to the forests, and a number of Jews were able to find shelter with their Christian friends. Every person plotted and searched for a way to avoid being locked in the "ghetto". Early on Friday morning, the "*Judenrat*" also moved to the "ghetto" and settled in the home of Antshel Pfeffer. On Saturday, 5 June, at 12 noon, the ghetto was locked. The members of the Jewish police were posted to guard its entrance, and no one was allowed to enter or exit it.

Patti was not satisfied in saving only the lives of the Jews whom he managed to take to the farms under his control. On Saturday evening he invited Hilel Kenigsberg, who worked for him as an agronomist, and told him to order 120 able Jews from the "*Judenrat*" for Sunday morning (usually no one worked in the farms on Sundays). He was planning to engage these workers in a very strange work: pulling weeds from a plot of land that was far away from town. The work had to be done by hand since he was not able to provide them with the tools needed for this work. He also instructed that all Jews must work on that Sunday on the farms, and no one would be exempt from work. At the end, the "*Judenrat*" sent him only 85 Jewish workers because nobody wanted to do it.

At dawn on Sunday, Patti traveled from farm to farm, and repeated the order to keep the Jews busy in their work and under no circumstances to let them leave. He also convinced the Jews whom he met in town to return to the farms and join the workers. There were those who did not listen to him and later paid with their lives. Among them was the wife of David Wasser. Despite Patti's warning, she hurried to town but she was not able to return and lost her life together with the rest of the Jews who were locked in the ghetto.

On the same Sunday, approximately at eleven, a number of cars full of Gestapo men suddenly arrived. Among them was Major Simon, the commander of "Sipo" [*Sicherheitspolizei* - security police], and the S.S. Nazi oppressor Thomanek. They stopped by the "ghetto" and blocked the entrance. A church stood next to the "ghetto" and it was full of Ukrainians. The murderers told them not to be alarmed from the sound of the gunfire in the "ghetto", because it was only intended to exterminate the Jews and they were not going to hurt them. Immediately after this message was given, they entered the "ghetto" and started to shoot in all directions. They searched and found the "bunkers" where some of the Jews were hiding and did not let anyone escape. And so in a matter of 2-3 hours they liquidated over one thousand Jews.

Late in the afternoon, after the massacre was over, the few Jews who had been able to hide came out of their hiding places. Some of them found work on the farms and the rest, around 120 Jews, remained in town and settled in a few buildings in the "ghetto". On Wednesday, 9 June 1943, (the first day of Shavuot 5703) the town received an order from Chortkov to transfer the surviving Jews over there. It was explained that the whole area had become "*Judenrein*" and therefore Jews were not allowed to remain in town. The municipality fulfilled the order and sent the Jews to Chortkov in wagons, but they were not allowed to enter Chortkov. They were taken to the air force base in the Rosochots [Rożyszcze] forest, and shot to death. Among the last Jews was R' Mordechai the slaughterer and his family, and Shmuel Gertner, an elderly Jew around the age of seventy, and his wife. And so the history of the community of Tluste had come to its end.

Thanks to the actions of the "Oberleiter," Patti, all Jews who were accepted to work on the agricultural farms were saved from the slaughter and, in addition to that, over eighty Jews who worked pulling weeds. Several Jews, who were on their way to town and brought back by Patti, were also saved. About the course of the last "*aktzya*," on Sunday, 6 June 1943, and about the transfer of the last Jews to Chortkov and their elimination on the way, we learned later from Hillel Konigsberg who remained in Tluste until its libration by the Red Army. After the war, Konigsberg moved to Łódź where he was appointed director of Zundelovitch-Shtekel's pharmacy.

21. How I survived the last "aktzya"

Immediately after I learnt about the plan to transfer one thousand Jews to work on the farms around Tłuste, I approached Dr. Averman and received his agreement to give me six work cards – for me, my wife and four family members: my brother-in-law Chaim Bronshtayn and his son, and Zalman Sternklar and his wife. We paid the "*Judenrat*" 20 dollars for each card. At first, Dr. Averman did not want to give so many work cards to one family, but he took into consideration the fact that Broyshtayn's wife, who was under his medical care, died from typhus only a few days earlier. Therefore, his heart did not allow him to send Broyshtayn away empty handed. According to the work cards, we had to work in the Shershenyovtza [Szerszeniowce] farm, and we were given permission to bring all of our belongings. I invited my Polish friend, Ostropolski, and two of his neighbors to come with their wagons. On Friday, early in the morning, we loaded the belongings of the three families on the three wagons and traveled to Szerszeniowce. When we arrived, the camp was full to capacity and we did not have a choice but to return. On the way we turned to the farm in Kozia-Gora. The farm manager, a Pole by the name Hrabczuk, was one of my acquaintances. In addition, Reuven Albin's two sons were there and they had a certain influence on the manager. The manager was promised many gifts until he agreed to accept six more people in addition to the one hundred and fifty who were already there, but he demanded a referral to work in Kozia-Gora instead of the referral to Shershenyovtza that we had in our hands. There was no room for our belongings on the farm, so we returned them in the wagons to Ostropolski's farm and to two other farms. We spent the night in Kozia-Gora. A farmer by the name of Ramarshtok, who was one of our acquaintances, let us to spend the night in his barn that was located in his yard.

The next day, Saturday morning, a few hours before the ghetto was locked, the town's Jews were running around not knowing what to do. Whoever had the possibility to leave town, and was not locked in the "ghetto," hurried to escape from it.

At eleven o'clock, before noon, I walked to town with my wife in order to exchange our work cards. The Jewish policeman (his name was Letz), who stood at the entrance to the "ghetto," warned us that the gates to the ghetto would be locked exactly at noon and then we would not be able to leave it. The home of my friend, Yisrael Yorist, stood near the entrance. He saw me when I entered and tried to convince me to stay at his home. He had a well-concealed hiding place, and he hoped that this hiding place would not be discovered. Also my sister, her husband and their children were staying at his home. His offer confused me because I did not know what was better. In the end I decided to take my chance changing our work cards, and only if the matter failed would we take his offer.

I arrived at the "*Judenrat*" building with my wife, but we were not able to enter it because of the large crowd that gathered outside. From an open window I saw Dr. Averman (he was taller than everyone). He also saw me and started to shout towards me: "Glick, what happened?" I managed to push my way in and reached him. I told him what I needed. Immediately he corrected my work cards and ordered two policemen to take me out of the ghetto. On our way to the farm we saw Jews running in all directions without any clear purpose, some were loaded with bundles and some carried their children in their arms.

We arrived at Kozia-Gora farm with the correct work cards and the manager accepted us without objection. We were among the lucky ones. Jews stood around the farm begging to be let in, but they were not allowed to enter. The farm buildings were overcrowded and there was not even a space for six additional people. The farm manager promised to build another hut, but for the time being we had to sleep in Ramarshtok's home.

On Sunday morning we went to the farm to join the rest of the workers. Everyone sat idly on the farm and did not go to work, so we returned to Ramarshtok's house in order to eat our meal. Suddenly we heard the sound of gunfire coming from town. The local farmers who were in the church for their Sunday prayers, started to run to their homes in a great panic. No one knew the reason for the confusion or for the shooting. Some assumed that they were abducting Christians in order to send them to work in Germany, others said that there were killing Jews. To our sorrow the second version came true. It was the total and final liquidation of Tłuste's Jews.

The one hundred and fifty Jews who found refuge in Kozia-Gora were afraid to stay on the farm. They escaped to the nearby fields and hid in the standing corn that was already very tall. Also our small group of six people did the same. We escaped from Ramarshtok's home and hid in the field next to his house. An hour later, Ramarshtok was told by one of his workers that the Germans were planning to arrive at his farm and we must leave his field. Immediately we ran to the forest near Shershenyovza [Szerszeniowce] where a number of Jews, who escaped from the town, were already hiding.

At five o'clock in the evening, residents of the village of Oleksińce attacked the Jews who were hiding in the forest, beat them and robbed their possessions. From a distance we heard the cries of the beaten Jews and started to run to the fields. But the hooligans saw us and started to chase us. They caught Zalman Sternklar and his wife, beat and wounded them and stole their suitcase that contained expensive valuables. They hit my brother-in-law, Chaim Bronshtayn, on the head with an iron post and seriously injured him. Only my wife and I were able to escape unharmed. After the hooligans left, we bandaged Bronshtayn's head and returned to Ramarshtok. There, we found out that all the Jews in Tluste had been shot and killed to the last of them. We remained in Ramarshtok's home and waited until the situation would be clear.

A few days passed and the work on Kozia-Gora farm, and also on the rest of the farms, returned to its regular course. Besides the 170 Jews who lived there, 50-70 Jews worked for local farmers. A Jew by the name Vaks was nominated as the "commander" of the labor camp. He was the son of the pharmacist from Zaleszczyki and lived on the farm together with his wife.

Many of the inhabitants of Kozia-Gora camp were afraid to spend the night there, and were able to find places to sleep in the homes of the local farmers. The farm manager, Hrabczuk, did not like this idea. He approached the farmers and strictly forbade them to house "his" Jews. He walked from house to house and raised his whip on the Jews he found there. After that, he plotted with a number of former "*Judenrat*" members, and they tried to extort money from the Jewish survivors in the camp. They collected all the Jews in the camp and separated the healthy young people from the elderly and the children. The first group was sent to work, and the rest were sent to a special hut. At the same time a message was given, that a German committee was coming to perform a "selection" in the camp in order to "take out" a portion of the Jews who found refuge there. After that, the two former "*Judenrat*" members came and announced the creation of a ransom fund for the Jews who would be selected for eviction. Vaks, the camp commander, "smelled" that the whole matter was an act of extortion and refused to take part in the proposed "fund". He started an argument with the former "*Judenrat*" members and beat one of them. In the end the two of them disappeared without achieving anything. Later on it was discovered that the rumors about an upcoming "selection" were also spread in the other camps, but nothing of that kind ever happened.

I was not in the camp during that incident; at that time I was working in the field. A few days later, in the morning hours, the manager assembled all of the people who lived in the camp, stood them in two rows and flogged each Jew who was not standing straight. After that, he gave us a lecture in which he informed and emphasized that he was anti-Semitic from birth, and in the past he broke many windows in Jewish homes. Now he found a good opportunity to take revenge against Jews, and he would do so to the best of his power. Jews would be forced to work sixteen hours a day for him, from sunrise to the late evening hours, but on the other hand lawlessness was not permitted. Ukrainian policemen would not be allowed to come and shoot Jews the way they were allowed to do in other camps. In summary – anyone who could hold on, and cope with the hard work and the beating that he would receive from his hands, was guaranteed to remain alive until the end of the war. After this speech we were sent to work.

Also the quality of the food in the camp was very bad. The Germans provided food for the workers, but the farm manager took it for himself and gave us only dry bread. Vaks collected money to buy food supplies, but the "buyer" was the farm manager who took the money for himself and did not buy anything. We also did not get wood for cooking and we had to go and steal logs or bundles of straw for cooking.

On 21, or 22 June, we were working in a field that was far from the camp. It was impossible to work since it was raining very hard, but we were not allowed to return to the camp. At noon a wagon passed by and in it was a farmer from Swidowa who was one of my acquaintances. He called me to the side and told me that on the same morning Gestapo men attacked the camp in Swidowa and killed five hundred Jews who were healthy and able to work. He told me that he came to warn me because rumors were circulating that the Germans were planning to do the same in other camps. Sternklar's wife was not with us at that time; she went to the camp to bring our lunch. She came back a short time later, and told us that the news about the massacre in

Swidowa had already reached the camp and caused great confusion and panic. Therefore, we decided not to return to the camp but to escape to the forest, all of us together, the six people in our group.

Olchowa forest was located around six kilometers from Kozia-Gora. At one time it belonged to me and to my partner, Gertner. The forest watchman was a man by the name Kibzoy, who stood on his guard also during the German occupation and after they confiscated the forest. A short time before the event that I mentioned earlier, I came to him to purchase wood for the camp's kitchen (of course out of "favoritism" since he was not allowed to give wood without the Germans' permission). He received me nicely and told me a secret that a number of Jews were hiding in the forest, and he was taking care of them and their needs. He encouraged me to turn to him for help in time of trouble, but first I would have to talk to his friend "Maxim" (it was his assumed name, not his real name) whose house was located near the edge of the forest. Therefore, our first thought was to approach Kibzoy and ask for his help.

My wife and I traveled to the forest with the farmer from Swidowa, and our relatives were planning to get there by foot. We waited for them until evening and, in the meantime, we dried our clothes that had become wet in the rain, but they did not arrive. Without a choice we went alone to Kibzoy's house. On the way we met a gentile dressed in a strange outfit. We got scared, but he was not interested in us and continued on his way. We arrived at Kibzoy's home around ten o'clock at night. His dogs greeted us and did not let us to get closer to the house. And so we waited for half an hour. In the end, the same gentile that we met on our way came out and asked for our wish. I replied to him that I could only talk to Kibzoy about it and not to anyone else. Ten minutes later, Kibzoy came out armed from his foot to his head, and put us temporally in the stable that was located next to his home. An hour later he took us out of there and walked us to a hiding place deep in the forest. On the way we found out that our relatives had also reached him, and he hid them in one of the buildings next to his home. My wife pleaded with him to take us to them so we could be together. He agreed to her request and again we returned to his home. There, Kibzoy took us to the same place where our family was hiding. Before he left he warned us that it was only a temporary hiding place, and we needed to leave it early in the morning and walk to another hiding place deep in the heart of the forest. He promised to come for us at seven o'clock in the morning. We agreed that when he would get closer to our hiding place, he would start singing so we would know that he was the one approaching us and we would not be frightened from the sound of his steps.

We did as we were told and left before morning for the forest. We waited impatiently for his arrival at seven o'clock in the morning, but he only arrived at eleven. He apologized for his late arrival and told us the reason: he had just come from a meeting with the Germans that lasted all night. The Germans knew that a number of Jews were hiding in the forests and they were planning to discover their hiding places and kill them. In addition, he told us that he was taking care of a number of Jews who were hiding in the forest, and he did not know what their future would be. Seven members of the Kleiner family from the Teklówka farm, and fifteen members of the Manheim family from the Myszków farm were hiding in the forest. He was very worried and concerned about the fate of the persecuted Jews, and suggested to divide us between his friends: my wife and I on the Hinkovza [Hińkowce] farm and our relatives in a different location.

I did not like his plan because I was afraid to be in a village among people. I told him that we were not ready to trust anyone but him, and asked him to find us a secure hiding place in the center of the forest. He hesitated a bit, and later on led us to a dense grove of young trees. The trees were tangled among each other, and we were only able to crawl through them in order to reach the center of the forest. There, we found an opening with a large thick tree. Kibzoy asked us with a smile if this apartment was to our liking. We were satisfied since we felt secure in this place that was separated from the world around us. Kibzoy went on his way, but before he left he promised to send us enough food for our needs. I gave him ten Dollars. At first he refused to take it saying that he did not need money since he had more than he needed, but in the end he agreed to take it from me.

An hour later, the same farmer whom we met the evening before on our way to Kibzoy, arrived with a basket full of food. Later on he came again and brought us a big piece of waterproof fabric to use as a tent. He brought bedding for all of us and clothes for my wife and myself. A downpour started after he left and we all got wet under the shelter of our so-called tent. And so we sat in our hiding place for a few days, and Kibzoy's messenger brought us food twice a day. On Sunday morning he brought us less food than usual and I was able to see that his facial expression was different than the previous days. I asked him to send Kibzoy to us. He did not answer me and left.

At five before evening, we suddenly heard light whispers nearby and, in an instant, a number of Ukrainian urchins appeared. The two who stood on the side recognized me and were a bit embarrassed. The other two approached us, told us that Ukrainian policemen had come to take us and they were waiting for us in Kibzoy's house. According to them they were sent by the policemen to bring us there. I understood that the whole matter was fabricated. If the policemen knew about our existence in this place, they would have come to take us out of there. In addition, there was no reason to stay in a hiding place that was already discovered. Therefore, we agreed to go with them in the direction of the village of Olchowa. On the way I loudly scolded the urchins that they were bothering us, they got scared and took off. I understood that their only intention was to bring us to a remote corner and rob us.

We returned to the forest, sat down and started to consider our options. Not far from there stood "Maxim's" house so we decided to approach him. He knew about our existence in the forest, but he did not know about the event that just happened. According to his advice our relatives remained at his home, but my wife and I went together with him to the home of the forest watchman. He was not at home and the house was locked. "Maxim" waited with us until two in the morning, but at the end he was forced to return to his home. He hid us in the forest among the bushes and promised to send Kibzoy at the crack of dawn. At eleven before noon we heard the sound of Kibzoy's singing. He approached us with a basket full of good food and revived our souls with it. At ten at night he came to us for the second time, dressed in his official head forester uniform, armed from head to toe. He told us that our relatives were staying in his attic, and he was going to take us to the home of one of his friends until he would find a better and more secure place for us. We walked together for an hour along secret routes until we arrived at the farmer's home and spent the night in his barn. In the morning the farmer's son and daughter came to us and I gave ten Zlotys to each one of them. They looked satisfied with that, gave us a tall ladder and helped us to climb on top of the hayloft where we were able to look around. We also felt a lot safer up there than down in the barn.

On the next day, the farmer came and asked that I give him a few articles of clothing for his son and his daughter. I gave him a letter to my sister-in-law who was staying on the Holovtshinza [Hołowczyńce] farm. I told her about our location and asked her to use her judgment and give the farmer a few articles of clothing. My sister-in-law gave him clothes and shoes and also sent clothes for my wife and me, but the farmer took everything for himself. From a letter that he brought back from my sister-in-law, we found out that our relatives had left Kibzoy's home and returned to Kozia-Gora camp. They worked there as before, but they lived in fear and were not able to rest during the day or sleep at night. It was Tuesday, 6 July 1943.

Two days later, the farmer climbed up to us at two o'clock in the morning. He told us that the police would arrive in the village around noon in order to confiscate furs from the farmers, and because of that he was afraid to let us stay at his home. He advised us to return to the forest for a short period of time and wait there until the danger had passed. We did not take his advice because we were afraid that the shepherds would find us in the forest. The farmer took us into his field and hid us in the standing wheat. The smell of the wheat intoxicated our senses, my wife fell asleep and I was also close to doing the same. Suddenly we heard the order "Halt!" (Stop!) followed by two shots. We got very frightened but no one came to us. A few hours later the farmer's daughter came and brought us food. We found out from her that the police had stopped two Jews, a man and a woman from Zaleszczyki and led them to the police station in Verbolinza [Worwolińce]. Later on we found out who they were. One of them was Vaks, the Kozia-Gora commander, who had walked together with his fiancée to find a hiding place for their parents. The police stole their watches, money and all of their valuables, and in the end shot and killed them in Verbolinza.

We continued to sit in the field and the farmer brought us food every day. Sunday 11 July was a rainy day, we got wet and froze. In the late evening we left our hiding place in order to reach Kibzoy's home. The rain continued to fall and we lost our way. I tripped and fell and I was not able to get up. My wife stood next to me crying. Suddenly we heard footsteps; it was the farmer's son. He took us to his father's house where we warmed up and ate the meal that was given to us. Without waiting long, the farmer informed me that he wanted me to give him one thousand Zlotys, and that he needed the money by the next day. Without a choice I gave him a letter to Ostropolski and asked him to give him the demanded money. In exchange, the farmer built us a hiding place in his yard above the pigpen. Our hiding place was next to the road and we were able to see what was happening in the area, and all the vehicles that passed in the road.

Two days later, the farmer came to us and told us that for unknown reasons the Germans were frightened and packing their equipment. The Jews' work on the farms stopped, and there was hope that the Germans would leave in two days. But the panic did not last long. We found out that the panic started after a sudden attack by Soviet partisans. A few days later, the Germans calmed down and the Gestapo men continued to liquidate the remaining Jews on the agricultural farms with a lot more energy and a lot more cruelty.

On Monday, 19 July 1943, Gestapo men arrived at Shershenovtz [Szerszeniowce] camp, surrounded it on all sides, and killed all the Jews who were there. Out of 150 people who were in the camp only three were able to escape. The news about the killings quickly spread to the nearby camps. My brother-in-law, who was in Kozia-Gora at that time, told me later that all day Monday, and on the following night, the people in the camps stood on their guard fully dressed. Early Tuesday morning, 17 Tamuz [20 July], at three o'clock in the morning, Gestapo men and Ukrainian policemen were seen traveling towards the camp. Immediately a warning was sounded and all the camp residents started to run to the fields. The murderers noticed them and opened machine gunfire at the escapees. My brother-in-law managed to escape to the field and hid behind the bushes, from there he saw how the murderers were running around in the fields on their horses, searching for the escaped Jews. Out of the 170 Jews who escaped, 67 were brought back. They were forced to sit and wait until the pits were dug. Later a special Gestapo unit arrived from Chortkov and shot all of them to death. Among the members of my family who perished there were: Moshe, the second son of Chaim Bronshtayn, my relative Malcha Sternklar and her husband. At the same time and in the same way the remaining Jews were liquidated on all the farms, except for those who were able to slip away and escape. There was only one extraordinary farm – the Lisowce farm. The Lisowce farm manager was an elderly German by the name of Frank, a family member of the famous General Frank who was the governor of the district of Krakow during the days of the German occupation. On the same Tuesday, 17 Tamuz, Gestapo men and policemen arrived early in the morning to execute an "Aktzya". At first, they turned to the field where the Jews were working. The Jews escaped from them but the murderers chased them and killed 17 Jews. Later on, they approached the farm manager and asked him to deliver all the Jews to their hands. Frank refused their request and declared that he was not giving even one of his

Jewish workers, because without them the farm work could not be done. If they exterminated the Jews against his judgment – he would leave the farm and abandon it, and the responsibility would fall on them. After a long negotiation, the Gestapo men were forced to leave the farm without executing their plot. Fortunately, most of the Lisowce Jews lived in the village in the farmers' homes, and were not concentrated in huts on the farm's grounds. If all of them were concentrated in one location – I doubt if Frank's interference could have saved them from the hands of the Gestapo. In any case, around two hundred and fifty Jewish men and women were saved thanks to Frank's intense interference.

After this event the massacre survivors started to gather in Lisowce. A few days later there were around five hundred Jews there. At that time around twenty Jews worked on the farm in Tłuste, but they were not hurt during the massacre since it was not an official Jewish labor camp. The details told above about the 17 Tamuz 5703 [20 July 1943] massacre, were given to me by my brother-in-law Chaim Bronshtayn and by other Jews who were there during the event.

I also want to tell a miraculous surviving story of a Jewish boy that happened on the same 17 Tamuz day. During the pogrom in Tłuste, before the arrival of the Germans, the baker Kimelman, his wife and three children hid in the attic of his home. When the rioters broke the house door, they all jumped into the garden and escaped for their lives. Kimelman and his wife managed to escape but the three children were caught and killed. Later on, the couple came back to Tłuste and a son was born to them during the occupation. They were very happy with him, and found consolation in him for the loss of their three other children. When the ghetto was established in Tłuste, Kimelman and his family moved to Roshanovka [Różanówka] and received work on the farm. On "*aktzya*" day, 17 Tamuz, the family escaped from the farm and hid with ten other Jews in the field. While they were in the field the boy started to cry and it was impossible to silence him. Ukrainian policemen from the village were running around searching for hiding Jews and the boy's cry could have endangered the lives of the ten Jews. Without a choice, the mother threw a pillow on his face and suffocated his cry. When the murderers left, the mother uncovered the boy's face; it was blue without a breath of life. The mother started to pull her hair out from pain and despair. At the same moment, a strong wind blew and revived the half- suffocated boy. The boy opened his eyes and started to cry. The parents were very happy. The whole family remained alive at the end of the war.

22. The day of the "aktzya" and the day after

On the same day, 17 Tamuz, my wife and I sat in our hiding place above the farmer's pigpen. During the day I heard the farmers, who were standing next to the well, talking to each other about the killing of Jews and about the one hundred dollars that were found in a pocket of a murdered Jew. Only in the evening we heard from one of our friends about the liquidation of all the Jews in the area's farms. In addition, the farmer informed us that he could no longer keep us in his home and we must leave. With great difficulties he agreed to let us find shelter in one of his distant fields, but he emphasized that he would not bring us food. We left for the field before sunrise and sat in the blazing sun until eleven o'clock in the afternoon. Then, the farmer came and brought us bread and a bottle of water. He also told us that my brother-in-law Bronshtayn had survived the massacre and he was staying at his home. He invited us to come to his home in the evening in order to find us a hiding place together with my brother-in-law. I asked him to invite my friend Kibzoy to the meeting; maybe he would be able to find a sensible solution.

In the evening, I met my brother-in-law at the farmer's house and also a Jew from Zaleszczyki who was holding a bundle of belongings in his hand. Kibzoy was also there, but he did not have any advice for us. At the end, the farmer suggested that we should hide in the forest until Thursday evening. On Thursday, he would go to Tłuste to find out how much he should charge for hiding a Jew, and then he would tell us the price. If we could pay the price according to the going "rate" – he would make the effort and try to hide us. We did as he said and went to the forest. There, we divided ourselves into two "camps": my wife and I separately, and my brother-in-law and the Jew from Zaleszczyki separately. We came to an agreement that if the farmer did not come to us on Thursday evening, we would all meet in a certain location and make a decision together.

The farmer did not come to us on Thursday. We met in the designated location and decided to go to him in order to hear his decision. His son stood at the entrance to the farmer's house and blocked our way. Meanwhile, we heard a shout from my wife and my brother-in-law who were walking far behind us. The farmer's son ran to see the reason for the shout and we used the opportunity and entered the house. The farmer woke from his sleep and when he saw us he ordered us to leave his house at once. He did not want us for any price. You left your millions somewhere else, he said, and you came to me with empty hands. At the end he agreed to leave the Jew from Zaleszczyki in his home in exchange for the bundle of belongings in his hand, and ordered us to leave immediately. With great difficulties we got permission from his wife to stay in their home until dawn.

We left the house before sunrise and turned to our friend "Maxim", but he was unable to help us. I was ready to pay him 50 Zlotys to deliver a letter from me to the manager of the Kozia-Gora farm, and bring me his reply if we could come to the farm. At first "Maxim" agreed to do so, but changed his mind and returned the letter together with the payment. We did not have another choice but to walk to Kozia-Gora, a distance of six kilometers. When we got closer to the farm, my wife tied a scarf to her head in the manner of a peasant woman and planned to enter the farm that way. At the same time my brother-in-law and I hid in the field. A short time later, my wife returned and called us to get out of our hiding place. She met Yoshe Grill next to the well and he told her that an order had arrived earlier allowing the Jews to return to the farms. The Jews were also promised that nothing bad would happen to them.

We returned to the farm and approached the hut were we once lived. There, we met the pharmacist Vaks and his wife whose son was shot together with his fiancée. Also the Meler family from Zaleszczyki was there. Our belongings were no longer there and our places in the hut had been taken. We turned to the work manager and he ordered Shechter, the camp commander, to clear our former places in the hut. And so I returned to my former place, and at that moment I was the happiest man in the world.

The news that the surviving Jews were allowed to return to Kozia-Gora spread as fast as a lightning. A heavy rain fell on Saturday morning and the surviving Jews, who came out of their hiding places in the fields and in the forests, started to arrive. Among the arrivals was my sister Rachel Meiman, her husband and two children. They were on the Holovtshinza farm during the massacre but were able to jump out of a window and escape. They escaped to Tluste and hid in the home of a Christian neighbor. Also my sister-in-law Feige Hendel arrived without shoes on her feet and was covered only with a blanket that one of the farmers gave her. She also escaped from Holovtshinza and saved her life. She gave her two children to our Polish friend Ostropolski who hid them in his attic. The day after the massacre it was clear to him that the children's parents perished in Holovtshinza, so he kicked them out of his home. The oldest boy met one of the farmer's sons who told him to follow him. He joined him and the farmer's son gave him to a German who shot the boy and killed him. The younger boy, Shlomo Hendel, was hidden by a farmer in a corn field. The farmer fed him and in the evening brought him to his parents in Kozia-Gora.

The survivors arrived in Kozia-Gora in a horrible condition: neglected, lonely and desperate. At first the work manager did not agree to take all of them, and claimed that he could only take those who lived on the farm before the massacre. He also wanted to use this opportunity to get money for the right to stay on the farm. On Monday morning, a messenger arrived from Patti [Vathje] with an order that all Jews could stay on the farm and work there. To us, the survivors, this was very important news and aroused the hope in us that we would survive.

The order to allow the surviving Jews stay in the labor camps did not arrive by chance. In 1942 the management of the "Caoutchouc" plantations approached the Gestapo in Chortkov and asked to allow six thousand Jewish workers in the Tłuste district to work in the plantations. The Gestapo in Chortkov and later on in Lvov rejected this demand. The decision in this matter was transferred to General Frank in Krakow and he opposed it. In the end, the management approached Himmler directly, but his answer never arrived. Meanwhile, the murderers continued with their work. At first they "purified" the town and later also the farms. Only after the massacre of 17 Tamuz [20 July 1943] and only after a few hundred Jews remained in the whole area, a permit arrived from Himmler to keep six thousand Jews alive in the area. Patti, who brought the news from Chortkov, said with joy mixed in pain: Yes, the order arrived, but to our sorrow – too late.

Also after the permission to live on the agricultural farms was given, there were Jews who were afraid to leave their hiding places in the forests and return to the farms. The family of Manheim, who was the former owner of the Mishkov [Myszków] farm, also acted that way. The 15 family members hid in the forests for almost a year, from June 1943 until February 1944. In February they were attacked by a Ukrainian mob who killed all of them. Only one son, Moshe, was left. Later on he was transferred to the Soviet Union.

After it was ordered not to kill the surviving Jews, everyone calmed down and the work entered its regular course. Sixty Jews were registered in the Kozia-Gora camp with a number of children among them. The camp commander was Shechter from Zaleszczyki, but the work manager did not trust him. At five o'clock in the morning everyone had to be counted and, if someone did not show up, the manager came to the hut and hurried him with his whip. The hardest work was during harvest season. Twelve Jews studied and became harvest experts and the rest walked after them and stacked the sheaves. The work manager showed up also during working hours and urged the workers with his whip. He was a sadist and enjoyed our sufferings. Because of the hard work a number of Jews left Kozia-Gora and moved to the farm in Lisowce. There, the manager was Frank and the work was easier. Only 38 Jews remained in Kozia-Gora.

And so, we passed the end of the summer in hard labor. Before Yom Kippur I was planning to ask the manager to release us from work during our holy day. A few days before the holiday I told him that I wanted to talk to him. He probably understood what I wanted to talk to him about, and postponed the conversation to the next day. The next day he left the farm for three days so we would have no one to talk to... and on Yom Kippur we worked in the field as though it was a regular day, but we fasted. The manager returned on the same day. When he found out that we had fasted all day, he punished us and ordered us to work until half past ten at night. Only at eleven o'clock at night we were able to eat something.

During the fall we pulled sugar beets from the fields and this work was harder than the harvest work. We worked until eleven or twelve at night, many times in the rain and in the cold. In the meantime, rumors spread that the Kozia-Gora Jews would be forced to move to Chortkov. We knew very well the meaning of this matter. Again, panic erupted in the camp. The young people escaped to the forests or found work with the local farmers, but they were not always safe at the farmers' homes. There were a number of farmers who employed the Jews all summer long without pay, and at the end of the season they handed them to the police who executed them.

And this was the case with a Jew from Tluste by the name of Gavriel Braun. He worked for a farmer in the village of Korolyovka [Karolówka]. The police was informed about him and came to pick him up from his working place. He begged them to let him go. They promised to release him if he would tell them where other Jews were hiding. Braun was not able to stand the test and he informed on other Jews. One of them was Ester Reizenberg, daughter of Shmuel Zandberg from Zaleszczyki. She was also hiding in the home of one of the farmers with her four-year-old son. The police came and killed the mother, but by miracle the boy was saved. The farmer's wife, who hid the mother and child, carried the child in a sack on her shoulders to Kozia-Gora farm, and gave him to Mrs. Vaks who was Ester Reizenberg's sister. From her we also found out how their hiding place had been discovered. Both the boy and his aunt survived.

On November 1943, when the working season ended in Kozia-Gora and in the other farms, we were sent to work in Roshanovka. Because of the extreme cold weather we were housed in better structures that were called "Teshvorki." There, we were engaged in "indoor" work – removing kernels from the corncobs. Our food ration was very small and we were forced to steal potatoes in order to satisfy our hunger. In December, our situation worsened and typhus joined the hunger and the filth. The illness spread and turned into an epidemic. During the first period of the epidemic the police came and killed people who were sick with typhus. Dr. Krasutski's wife wanted to protect her sick son from the policemen. Before they arrived she laid next to her son and when they arrived she begged them to kill her in place of her son. The policemen killed both of them. A short time later, Patti gave an order that the policemen were not allowed to kill those who were sick with typhus without the permission of the farm managers. Only then the killing of the sick stopped for a short period of time.

The order that was given by Patti came after the mass slaughter by the Ukrainian police on Holovtshinza farm. On Wednesday, 9 Tevet (5 January 1944), three Ukrainian policemen came to Kozia-Gora and entered the farm manager's apartment. He welcomed them with food and drinks and they got very drunk. He also gave them hay for the horses. Before they left they told him that they wanted to "practice their shooting a little", but he did not let them do so. They left the farm and returned to Holovtshinza. There they attacked the Jews and shot and killed 28 of them. Among the dead was my sister's son Nisan Meiman, R' Yosel the slaughterer from Tluste, my brother-in-law David Hendel, Shpigel and others. Patti's order came after this massacre.

But also after the order was given, there was an event in Kozia-Gora when seven Jews were killed. In one of the last days of January, the farm manager traveled to Tłuste drunk and returned an hour later with a number of policemen. Immediately they opened fire towards the Jews. After they killed a number of them, they called two Jews to search the victims' pockets. At that time I was working in the field spreading manure, together with a group of eight people, and none of us wanted to do this "work". The messenger – the farm's blacksmith – advised us to go with him so we wouldn't anger the policemen who would come and shoot us. So, I went together with Berish Hessing's son. The policeman, Mroz, who excelled all the time with his cruelty, ordered us to search the pockets of the murdered, and give him all the valuables that we found there. Later he also ordered us to remove their clothes. The first victim was lying on top of a tall hay stack under the barn's roof. Hessing climbed to bring the body down and saw that the victim was his father, Berish Hessing. He started to cry bitterly, but Mroz aimed his gun at him, forced him to calm down and search his father's pockets. He found 3000 Zlotys and gave them to the murderers. Later, Mroz aimed the gun at me and asked: "What are you doing here old man?" I answered that I worked in the field. He shook his head and I realized that he wanted to stick a bullet into me. At the same moment the police commander came out of the manager's house. The commander called me and asked me who I was and from where did I come. I told him that I was Berel Glick from Tłuste. He knew my name and heard good things about me. He turned to Mroz and told him to leave me alone since "he was the most honest Jew in Tłuste." Later on, the work manager came to me and said with a satanic smile: "If not for the police commander you would have already been in the next world...."

As aforesaid, the murderers "visit" ended with seven fatalities. Among the dead were Berish Hessing, Yakov Neiman's wife, Mendel Metsger (the son of Shelom Metsger), Miller with his wife and his young daughter (from Zaleszczyki) and another casualty. The murderers left after they finished their work and the work manager left immediately after.

23. The attacks of local gangs

A few days after the mentioned event, rumors spread that Ukrainian gangs started to attack Jews on the nearby farms. The gang members attacked the Jews at night, robbed their money and their belongings and killed them. One night at eleven o'clock, the farm watchman knocked on the door of our hut and demanded that we open it. From the window I saw a number of gang members dressed in military uniform, and I had the feeling that this time we would not escape the death that was waiting for us. The thugs broke the door, ordered us to turn the light on in our room and stand around the table. Even a five-year-old boy, who was sleeping on the stove, was taken down and forced to stand next to the table. After that, the thugs informed us that they came to make a "collection" for the Polish army and that we needed to donate 4000 Zlotys. We thought that the gang leader looked familiar to us since he demanded that we put the money on the table without us looking at his face. Only two out of the fourteen people in the room had money to "contribute" – I gave 229 Zlotys and the pharmacist Vaks 200 Zlotys. The thugs left us with 10 Zlotys so we could buy bread, took the rest of the money and left. The thug who stood by the door shot at us, but miraculously no one was hurt. Before they left they warned us not to move from our places. We stood close to the table for half an hour until I had the courage to walk to the door and lock it.

After they visited our room they entered the second room. There, they were offered 50 Zlotys from each person in the room. In the same room they shot and killed a Jew from Buczacz by the name of Pohoriles and a woman from Chortkov. In the third room they killed the son of Berish Hessing. One shot hit Byosha Teiber and amputated one of his fingers. The work manager came to us after the hooligans left and asked in a cynical laugh: "So, you had visitors?" He sat with us for a short time, drank a glass of spirit and left.

The next night the watchman knocked again on our door and asked us to open it. He calmed us down and told us that the same thugs had attacked the work manager and his clerk. The clerk was injured in his leg, but the work manager was seriously wounded. He asked him to bring the pharmacist Vaks, maybe he would be able to help him. The pharmacist came back in the morning and said that it was necessary to amputate the clerk's leg. The work manager was wounded in sixty-six places in his body. Both of them were taken to the hospital and we never saw them again.

The management of the Kozia-Gora farm was transferred to the hands of Patti who was the manager of the farm in Tluste. We continued to work hard, first in Tluste and later on in Holovtshinza. At the end of January 1944, four workers were chosen from each farm and sent to cut trees in a forest that was located thirty kilometers from Tluste. The travel to work and back lasted six hours and we were only able to work two hours a day. My brother-in-law

Chaim Bronshtayn and I were the experts. Our duty was to mark the trees that were worthy of cutting. This work lasted until the end of February or the beginning of March 1944.

Two weeks before our work ended we saw unusual movement of German vehicles on our way to the forest. When we passed by the town of Ułaszkowce, where twelve Jewish survivors were still working, Yitschak Drohobitser went to see them and they told him that the Russians broke the front line and took over the cities of Podvolotchisk [Podwołoczyska], Zabrosh [Zbaraż], and Tarnopol. Also in the forest the head forester told us that something had happened on the battlefront. He urged us to finish our work and leave since the partisans were wandering around the forest.

For the next two weeks we continued to travel to work every day. When we came to work on Purim [9 March 1944], the head forester ordered us to return immediately because the situation on the battlefront was very bad. We ate (according to Patti's order we received bread and jam every day) and returned to Tłuste. Hilel Kenigsberg came towards us and informed us that we would no longer travel to work in the forest. Each one of us would return to his own place, and there we would have to prepare metal containers for the Germans' wagons so they would be ready for the road.

When I came to Kozia-Gora I met a farmer who knew me well. During our conversation he told me that the Ukrainian nationalists had consulted each other and decided to liquidate the last of the Jews before the arrival of the Soviet army. By doing so, they would kill all the witnesses to their loyal cooperation with the Germans. He advised me to find a hiding place as soon as possible.

To our sorrow, the message that the farmer gave me came true on the same day. On the next day, 10 March 1944, we were told by a farmer who came to the farm that the farmers in Holovtshinza had killed all the Jews, 48 of them, on the same night. Most of the Jews who lived in Kozia-Gora, including Vaks and his wife, escaped to Tłuste. Only ten Jews were left on Kozia-Gora farm. In a letter that was sent to me from Tłuste, Mrs. Vaks wrote me that my wife's sister Feiga Hendel and her two children survived the massacre in Holovtshinza. On the eve before the murderous attack, one of her Christian friends came to her and warned her not to sleep in the camp. She took her two children and her brother's son and went to the Christian cemetery, where they spent the whole night. The five members of Natan Shechter's family joined them. From all the Jews who were staying in Holovtshinza, only five remained alive, all of them were seriously wounded.

Immediately, delegates from all the farms started to come to Patti with one request: that he try to protect the farm workers from the Ukrainian rioters. Patti advised all of them to move to Tłuste where he would be able to protect them to the best of his ability, and ordered to clear three huts to house the arrivals. All survivors from the farms, from the forests and even Jews who were hidden by their Christian friends, started to gather in Tłuste. My wife, my brother-in-law and I remained in Kozia-Gora until Tuesday, 14 March 1944. On Tuesday a Christian friend came to us and advised us to leave the farm. We listened to his advice. On the same night the rioters attacked the farm and beat a number of Jews.

The German retreat was hasty and hurried. Also Patti received an order: pack everything and be ready to leave Tłuste. Patti ordered us to pack – horses, wagons, sheep, cattle, grain, machines and equipment. We, the few survivors, felt like we were placed between the hammer and the anvil, between the Ukrainians and the Germans who wanted our souls. Only the presence of Patti stopped them from executing their plot.

Salvation came from a place that we did not expect. A local German commanding unit arrived from the battlefront and took over the farm. Patti handed us to the supervision of the commander. He explained to the commander that the five hundred Jewish workers had served the Germans with loyalty during the three years of occupation, and now the "Ukrainian pigs" wanted to destroy them. He expressed his wish that the commander agree to take care of us and protect us.

Despite the rain and the mud that made it harder to approach the huts, the commander came to our huts at dusk with another German. They were shocked when they saw our condition. The commander gestured to us with his hand but no one wanted to endanger himself and walk towards him. In the end I came out with another Jew from the camp. His first question was: what do you eat after you are done with your work in the farm? I answered him that one thousand tons of potatoes were buried in pits on the farm, and if he would allow us to take only one kilogram of potatoes per person each day – he would find a way to revive our souls. The German answered and said: yes, but you can not survive only from that! Later on they left us and went on their way. The next morning the commander sent to our camp a butchered cow, a few sacks of corn flour and one ton of potatoes that we divided equally among us.

A few days passed, the Soviets arrived to Chortkov, and it was time for the local command unit to leave. A military unit of around eighty people arrived in its place. The commander probably informed them about the Ukrainians' intentions towards us since, close to his arrival, he posted a guard in our camp.

The crowdedness in the huts was unbearable and we lived in horrible conditions. In this desperate situation the pharmacist Vaks decided to commit suicide and swallowed poison pills. By chance a few Jews from Hungary, who had been released from a labor camp, happened to be in Tluste. There were a number of doctors among them. They tried to save Vaks' life but were unable to do so. He suffered all night from horrible pain until his death in the morning. He tried to convince me and my wife to do the same, but my wife did not want to listen to him, mostly because of her nephew who lived with us.

Early Thursday morning, 23 March 1944, a squadron of Ukrainian policemen passed by and entered our camp. Two of them came to us and demanded that in five minutes we should give them five liters of alcohol – if not, they would kill all of us. A great panic broke out in the camp and people tried to escape through the windows in order to save their lives. When the matter became known to the German commander, he came to the camp and ordered the Ukrainians to leave at once. They obeyed him and left. A short hour later a special messenger arrived to the German squadron with an order in his hand. They were ordered to leave the area immediately without taking their cargo. After the Germans departed only one German soldier was left with a machine-gun to guard the cargo. He did not let us walk outside and ordered us to stay in our huts.

Around three o'clock in the afternoon, a farmer came to the camp and told us that the town was completely empty. No one was walking in the streets, and it was possible to hear the sound of the approaching Russian tanks. About an hour later, the sound of the Russian tanks reached our ears. We looked outside and saw that the last German soldier had left and he was no longer there. We all left the camp and started to run towards town. The roads were full of Russian tanks and Russian soldiers. There was no end to our excitement and our happiness. We actually kissed and hugged every soldier who passed us. One of the Russian soldiers advised us not to walk in the streets because of the possibility of a German attack. I wanted to move to my home together with my family members, but the house was partly destroyed. My wife did not want to stay in a ruined house and wanted to return to the camp and sleep there. So we all returned to the camp and found fifty Jews there.

As we arrived at the camp a group of airplanes appeared in the sky, I was sure that they were Soviet airplanes. I stood quietly and counted them. There were 27 of them. Suddenly, I saw two large bombs falling from one of the planes. At the same moment the twenty-seven planes dove and bombed the camp. I threw myself on the ground and hid next to a garbage pile. A terrible fire burnt around me and I did not know where to go and what to do. A few minutes later it was quiet around me. I got up and saw a horrible sight. My brother-in-law Chaim Bronshtayn was laying not far from me, his body was split open and torn in half. My wife was killed next to the hut door and remained sitting there dead. The flames ran wild all over the camp and I was able to hear people crying for help from every direction. They were lying under the burning ruins without the ability to get themselves out of there. I stood shocked and lost and I did not know what to do. Eventually I recovered. At first I moved the bodies of my wife and my brother-in-law from the burning huts so they would not burn further. Suddenly, I heard a boy shouting from the other side of the hut. It was Motele' the three-year-old son of my sister-in-law Feiga Hendel. A pit had been created under the hut by one of the bombs and the boy crawled out of it. An eleven-year-old boy, Motel Melzer, the son of my brother-in-law Meir also survived. Both of them were wounded.

In the meantime Jews arrived from the town and started a rescue operation. I took the two wounded children on my shoulders and moved them fifty meters from the burning camp. Other wounded were also brought there and a hospital was created without doctors or medicines. We found a little alcohol and a few dry pieces of bread and tried to calm the wounded and ease their pain. One of the wounded, Motya Shevats, who became drunk from the alcohol, sang and cried all night.

A number of wounded died during the night, among them was the daughter of Shaul Drohobitser. More than forty Jews died in this last disaster, eighteen were burnt to death in the huts and the rest were killed.

I stayed with the wounded in the "hospital" until after the Sabbath. On Sunday morning I transferred the two children to my house and put them in the kitchen. My nephew Motel Meltzer was seriously wounded, but there was no reason to leave him in the "hospital" since there was no medical care there. Three days later two doctors who were residents of Tluste arrived: Dr. Milch and Dr. Weinloes. They started to take care of the wounded and through their persistence the Soviet authorities agreed to transfer the seriously wounded to the hospital in Chortkov. The boy Motel Melzer was also transferred.

The surviving Jews, around five hundred of them, recovered a little and settled in Tluste. The local population, Christians and Jews, emptied the grain warehouses and also took other items that the Germans left behind. The Soviet army did not interfere. Day after day, Jews who had hidden in different locations around town, started to arrive. Among them were the two daughters of my neighbor Leib Stein of blessed memory, one of the oldest and well-known families in Tluste. Also his son-in-law, Baruch Lublin arrived with his three children.

Early Friday morning, 31 March, Baruch Lublin walked by my window looking worried and confused. He told me that there was a chance that the Germans were coming back to "visit" us. A large platoon of sixty thousand men was trying to break the Soviet ring in the Kamieniec-Podolski area. If they succeed they might come back to Tluste, so we must escape towards Chortkov.

On Great Sabbath, 1 April 1944, there was a strong snow storm and it was extremely cold. At five in the morning I walked out of my home and saw how everyone was escaping on the road leading to Chortkov with their bundles on their shoulders and their babies in their arms. In this manner all the surviving Jews escaped from town. Only a handful stayed: me, the two orphans of my brother-in-law Hendel, my neighbor Fishel Pfeffer an old man around the age of seventy who was seriously wounded, and a woman from the area whose name was Genzler. Bluma Freindlich, the daughter of Leib Stern, asked the farmer who hid them before to hide them again. Mendel Hoisfeld, his wife and their child had also done the same. The farmer took them to his home, but later on murdered them.

And so a few were left in town, a handful of Jews that a boy can count. With great bravery we started the preparation for the holiday of Passover. We collected a few cooking pots from the vacant homes, brought potatoes and beets, prepared a barrel full of water and also brought firewood to the house. And so, we were ready to spend all the days of the holiday in our apartment without stepping out of the front door.

The bad weather continued during the Sabbath and Sunday. As a result, the Germans' advance toward Tluste was delayed. On Monday evening the weather improved and a number of Soviet tanks were posted near my home. They started to shoot at the Germans and the whole house shook from the power of the fire. We left the house and stood by the front door since we were afraid that the ceiling would fall on us.

The bombardment lasted for two hours, later on the shooting stopped and silence took over. We went to bed but we were not able to sleep. An hour later I heard a conversation in German: "The Russians were here..." and I knew that the Germans had arrived for the second time.

Friday, 7 April 1944, was Passover eve. I started a fire in the oven and made it kosher. We were ready to eat potatoes during the days of the holiday. Generally our situation was very bad. Every moment a German could kill us; we were not able to walk in the streets because the Ukrainians would murder us there. If the Germans were to stay for a long time, it was possible that we would run out of water. The commander assistant heard the children speaking Yiddish among themselves, and so he asked me of our origin. Even today I still owe him an answer...

And so we sat together with the Germans for a few days. Later on, the officer left and only the S.S. men remained. We waited anxiously for the moment that the Germans would be forced to leave town. I felt like needles were piercing my flesh when one of the officers told his friend: "Hans, it looks like we are going to stay here for a long time..." An hour later the same Hans came and informed his friend that they were leaving the next day because the Russians had crossed the river.

On Monday, 10 April, early in the morning, the S.S. men departed from my home and left town. Before they left they warned me to be careful since a special platoon might arrive and burn and destroy everything. The next day I dressed the boy Shlomele' like a peasant boy and sent him to bring a bucket of water. That way I was planning to receive information of what was happening in the streets. He returned and told me that the Germans were posting heavy cannons in town and three of them were pointed in the direction of the village of Lisowce. And, indeed, heavy shelling started.

At night I heard a strange noise. I looked through the window and saw that my neighbors' homes were on fire. Those were the homes of Wachstein and Yankel Schorr that stood only ten meters from my home. The Germans from the destruction platoon poured gasoline on the piles of wheat in the farmers' yards and torched them. The farmers twisted their hands shouting and crying. We did not know what to do. We were afraid to leave the house for fear that the murderers would hurt us and we were afraid to stay at home because the fire was spreading. In the end we stood by the front door and waited to see what would happen. To our luck the fire died around three o'clock in the morning. The German destruction platoon fulfilled its duty and left town.

On Wednesday and Thursday we saw a number of Germans walking around town. On Thursday another powerful gun battle took place and our house looked like it was going to crumble. Around four o'clock, the shelling stopped but the machine guns kept on firing until around eight in the evening. Another hour passed until the silence was broken and I heard the voices of Russian soldiers near my home.

And this is how we were liberated for the second time by the Soviet army on Thursday, 13 April 1944, at nine o'clock at night.

[Pages 121-131]

The Book of Lamentations of the town of Tłuste

by Yosef Schechter

Translated by Sara Mages

The war between Germany and Russia started on 22 June 1941. Eight days later, with the Russians' retreat from Eastern Galicia, the skies of our lives started to grow darker and we felt the winds of the approaching holocaust storm. Our Ukrainian neighbors walked with jubilant faces and waited impatiently for the arrival of their "liberators." They waited anxiously and hoped for their arrival for many months. On the last days, before the Russian retreat was completed, it was possible to hear the speeches of Ukrainian nationalists' leaders on Radio Kraków. They announced the establishment of an independent Ukrainian country in Eastern Galicia. Together with that, they called on the masses to get ready for a total destruction of the Jewish population. Even before the Soviets evacuated their armed forces during their hasty retreat, young Ukrainian villagers attacked their Jewish neighbors and murdered them with great cruelty, with axes, sickles and other tools that they had in their hands.

On 7 July 1941, the Magyar army, the army of the country of Hungary which was allied to Nazi Germany, arrived to our place. They went over the Carpathian Mountains, passed by the cities of Kołomyja and Horodenka, crossed the Dniester River and reached Tłuste on their way to the former Polish-Russian border. They did not behave righteously, and there were many incidents of robbery and beatings. They were the first to stable their horses in the synagogues, and the first to rip the Torah scrolls. Nevertheless, it was possible to continue to live under the shadow of their regime. In contrast to other towns in our area that lived under German rule from the beginning, we lived in "Paradise." These words apply only to the town itself, because the Ukrainians ruled limitlessly in the nearby villages, and murdered all the Jews who lived there to the last of them. Killed among others in the village of Swydowa [Swidowa] were: Eliezer Waltser and his family, and Fishel Rubinstein and his family. Perished, among others, in the village of Szypowce were: Shlomo Schwartz and his family, and Michael Metzger and his family. Also, many Jewish soldiers who did not have time to join the Russian army and walked back to their homes were beaten with great cruelty and murdered by the Ukrainians. Almost all of the Jews were murdered in the town of Lashkewitz [Ułaszkowce], among them many Jewish soldiers who were murdered on their way home.

In the beginning, the Ukrainian population did not treat us with hostility, but under the influence of propaganda and provocation bad winds started to blow in our direction. The Ukrainians also reorganized the military organization "Sich". Jews were taken to different manual jobs and were forced to supply workers to clean the streets and rebuild the train station that was badly damaged during one of the bombings. It was hard labor that was accompanied with torture and humiliation.

In the meantime, a difficult and responsible assignment was enforced on the town's Jews. The Hungarians expelled from their country around fifty thousand "foreign" Jews who were not able to prove their Hungarian citizenship. On their way these Jews passed through our town, and the town's Jews, who were also in great trouble, were given the task to care for their exiled brothers who arrived bare and penniless. Immediately, a temporary committee was established and took on itself the duty of caring for the exiled who passed through our town, and for those who were able to stay there. The members of the committee were: the director Pel [Fel], Dr. Krasutski, Berel Glick, Yisrael Yorist, Yeshaya Rosenthal and others.

On 1 September 1941, control of the town was transferred to the hands of the Germans, and immediately they started to lay down special laws against the Jews. These laws were published on posters that were printed in large letters and pasted in key locations in town. The gentiles gathered in large groups to read the posters in which the Jews were disgraced and humiliated. First of all, Jews from the age of twelve and up were forced to wear the "mark of disgrace," the symbol of their Judaism. The symbol was a white ribbon, 20 centimeters wide, and a large blue Star of David was printed on it. The ribbon had to be worn on the right arm over the elbow, so it was possible to see a Jew from a distance. Any Jew who did not wear the ribbon was shot to death. The Jews were not allowed to walk in the main streets or leave their neighborhood. The laws became more serious from day to day. At the beginning, Jews were allowed to buy food in the market an hour a day, and a short time later they were not allowed to go to the market square.

At that period of time the first "*Judenrat*" was assembled in town. The "Gestapo" men started to come to town every day, and when they arrived they walked from house to house and robbed them. At the time when the Gestapo men were in town, the whole town was in a state of fear and terror. We abandoned everything and escaped to the fields. On one of their visits, many Jews escaped to the cemetery. The Nazis noticed them and chased them with their vehicles. They caught Akiva Langholz and Shimshon Ofenheim from Berezdów (Yisrael Fiderer's father-in-law), beat them up with great cruelty and transferred them to Chortkov [Czortków]. Only after a lot of pleading and payment of a large ransom the two men were released from the hands of the Gestapo.

Based on a Gestapo command, the "*Judenrat*" conducted a census of all the Jewish population. At the end of the census, 170 Jews were chosen for transfer, on 15 November 1941, to one of the labor camps specially built for Jewish laborers. The camps were built in the villages of Kamionka and Borki-Wielkie near the cities of Skalat, and Podwołoczyska, and in the villages of Stupki and Hluboczek near Tarnopol. The camp in Kamionka was a death camp. In four weeks, half of the people who were sent there from our town died or were shot to death. The Ukrainian police guarded the workers on their way to work, and many of the workers were shot on the way to work.

The camp's managers were S.S. men. Each morning they inspected those who left for work, and those who looked sick had to stand on the side. Twenty to forty people were taken out in each "selection." They were taken out of the camp and forced to go into one of the pits that was always ready to receive its victims. When they reached the bottom of the pit they were shot to death and buried there.

The camp's workers were marked with a yellow patch, and each worker carried it on his chest and on his back. On the way to work they were forced to sing Jewish songs like "*Vetaher Libeinu*" or other Hassidic melodies. The work was very difficult. They repaired roads and quarried rocks. They left camp before sunrise, and walked eight kilometers to their place of work without food. Under these conditions people fell and died like flies. At night they slept on a bed of hard wooden boards, and they were not even given a little bit of straw to lie on. As long as the Jews lived in the cities, each of the workers had a relative or a friend who sent him a package to keep him alive. But after life went wrong in the cities, because of the frequent *"aktzyot,"* the shipment of these packages stopped and the food portion that they received in the camp was not enough to live on.

The first group of workers sent to the labor camp in November 1941 was a group of "volunteers." They were told that they were leaving for only three weeks, and later on another group of workers would be sent to replace them. In addition to that, they were threatened that if they did not come on their own free will, their families would be harmed and they might be killed. When the town's residents realized that the promise was not kept – that those who left for the labor camp were not replaced by other workers, that half of them found their death in the camp and the remaining workers were facing the same fate – there was no one who wanted to go to the labor camp. When one hundred and fifty people were called to work in the camp in February 1942 – no one reported. The Gestapo men showed up immediately and, with the help of the Ukrainian police, they started to search for people in their homes and in the cellars. With difficulty they were able to abduct sixty or seventy men. Among them were four members of the *"Judenrat"*: Krasutski, Shrentsel, Moshe Pfeffer and Yisrael Krampf. The *"Judenrat"* men were held captive in Chortkov until May. The first two were released in exchange for fifty other Jews who were sent to labor camps, the last two did not want to be released under those conditions, and were sent to labor camps together with many other Jews who were abducted from the whole area. The abductions to labor camps were held every two weeks, but the preparations were done in secret so the residents would not have the time to hide and to escape.

At the same time, we started to set up "bunkers," hiding places where we later hid during the *"aktzyot."* For many weeks I lay hidden in the "bunker" freezing, when it was extremely cold outside. In December 1941, the Germans issued an order to deliver to their hands all furs that were owned by Jews. Anyone who violated the order was likely to be shot. And indeed, there were a number of incidents when Jews were punished by death for this violation.

This situation lasted until the middle of the summer of 1942.

The "Wehrmacht" camps

During the first days of the Soviet regime in our area, the lands of the large estate owners were divided up among the farmers. Later on, in the years 1940-1941, "*Kolkhozes*" and "*Sovkhozes*" were established on sections of this land. When the reign passed to the hands of the Germans, the authorities received the management of these farms through a special administration unit that was called "*Liegenschaft*" in their language. Even with their negative attitude towards each Jew, there were a number of capable Jews who remained in their former positions and continued to fulfill an important duty in the management of the estates. There were a number Jews like that around Tluste: Yozek [Jozek] Steckel, the Kenigsberg brothers, Klinger, Katz and others.

In the spring of 1942, a change took place in the way the estates in Tluste, Jagielnica and Jeziorzany (Uziran) were managed. The management of these districts was taken out of the hands of the "*Liegenschaft*," and transferred to the hands of the "Wehrmacht". The reason for the administrative change was the "*Caoutchouc*" plant.

The first experiments of growing this plant and producing artificial rubber from it were done by the Russians. Apparently the Russians meant to grow it in the area around Tluste and in Eastern Galicia, whose soil was similar to the Ukrainian soil. The Germans found the "*Caoutchouc*" seeds and decided to continue with the experiments. Since the topic was the production of rubber, a material with military value, the whole matter was given to the hands of the "Wehrmacht." The official name of the factory was "G.G. Caoutchouc" and the administrative office was located in Jagielnica.

In April 1942, the "Wehrmacht" ordered the "*Judenrat*" to supply a few hundred female workers for the "*Caoutchouc*" plantations. Most of the working age men were already in the labor camps, so they decided to employ women on the new plantations. The registration took place on Passover, and was accompanied with fear and apprehension that stirred panic in the city. All the candidates had to report to a certain location in order to be examined by the labor office commissioner from Chortkov. However, at that time we already knew about the "*aktzyot*" that took place under the guise of such gatherings. Therefore, a special representative from the "*Judenrat*" was sent to Jagielnica to see how the "survey" would pass in that city. He returned and confirmed that everything passed peacefully. Nevertheless, not all the young women reported, from fear that the Germans would change their tactics. When the Germans came to arrange the survey, delegates of the "*Judenrat*" had to walk from home to home and hurry the young women to the survey's location. In the end they were not able to complete the "quota," and again it was necessary to pay a lot of money to appease the Germans' anger.

The work on the "*Caoutchouc*" plantations lasted all summer, and the young women left for work every day. Since there was a lot of work, the Germans were force to bring young women from the Tarnopol area, Brzeżany and other cities. The young women were housed in special camps that were built in the villages near the farms.

The preparations for the big "Aktzyot"

In the summer of 1942, after the liquidation of the Jews in most of the cities in Eastern Galicia was completed, the "Gestapo" headquarters started to liquidate the survivors in Tłuste and the surrounding area. As the first step, Jews were taken out of the work manager's control, and given to the exclusive control of the Gestapo. Already in March 1942, Jews, who survived the attacks of Ukrainian rioters in the villages, were transferred to our city. In July, all Jews who were unfit to work – old people, women and children - were exiled from Zaleszczyki and Chortkov. Most of them found refuge in our town and because of this the congestion grew. Tłuste's Jews did everything possible to care for the exiled. A community kitchen was established, and I also took part in its operation. Berel Glick and A. Shapira z"l also worked there. A very difficult kitchen duty fell into my hands, and I worked with great dedication from first light to a late hour of the evening. Not once I had to escape in the middle of my work, and find myself a place to hide, because of the abductions that took place in the middle of the day. The abductees were sent to labor camps, and only a few of them returned and survived.

One of those days remained carved in my memory forever. A few days earlier a group of German experts arrived in our town. They were engaged in welding railway tracks and defective rail cars. The "*Judenrat*" was forced to supply a large number of Jewish workers, including those who received their food in the community kitchen. The leader of the group was a German Nazi, who terrorized the Jewish workers and hit them with murderous blows. In addition, he demanded bribes from the "*Judenrat*," in money and valuables, and increased his demands from day to day. On the same day, 11 Elul [24 August 1942], the "*Judenrat*" was not able to fulfill his demands. The oppressor became very angry and informed the Gestapo in Chortkov by phone that the Jews did not supply the demanded number workers. The Gestapo people left immediately to "to impose order," and what is the nature of their "imposing order" – we already knew that from experience.

The oppressor demanded one hundred workers, something that was impossible to do since most of the young people were located in labor camps, and others worked in "*Judenrat*" jobs in the town. As usual, the few Jews who were in town and were able to work hid during the panic. And now, the "*Judenrat*" was forced to recruit the one hundred required workers and prove to the Gestapo that the Jews were already waiting and ready to go to work, and prevent severe punishment. In order to save the situation, all the "*Judenrat*" clerks, whose number was high, were drafted for work, and they also came to call on the kitchen workers. At that time, only B. Glick and I were in the kitchen. Every afternoon we gave a slice of bread and coffee to the town's children. At that time we were busy weighing the bread, 100 grams a slice. Suddenly a "*Judenrat*" man came, told me what was happening and demanded that I go with him to work. When I got closer to the train station I saw that the situation was very serious, but it was impossible to escape since we were surrounded from each side. The German sadist welcomed us with a whistle, and started with military foot drills. After that he gave us a speech and informed us that this matter would cost us dearly. Again, a military parade was performed, and afterwards we were forced to empty the rail car in five minutes and put the iron bars in a designated place. When we finished this work we were forced to return the iron bars to the rail cars, again and again a number of times. We worked very hard, and all that time the German oppressor stood with his whip in his hand hurrying us to finish the work. When he saw that we were doing as he asked, he gathered us for a second military parade and led us to a second location for a new test. Long and heavy railway tracks were stacked there. I can't estimate the length and the weight of each one of them. I remember well that around sixty men carried each one of them on their shoulders, and were overpowered by its weight. We were ordered to run and not to stop, and when one of us caved under the weight, he was severely beaten. And so we were forced to carry a large number of rails on our back for a long distance. After we were done with this work, we were given a new assignment that we definitely were not able to do. We were told to lift rail cars that were lying on their sides. We tried hard, our bodies were covered with sweat, we were badly beaten but we were not able to lift the rail cars. Later on we were led back to the first location, and again we were ordered to load and unload the iron bars a number of times, one after the other. In the end, all of us were ordered to enter to the empty rail car, and the German ran us in under atrocious blows. Then, one of the "*Judenrat*" members was allowed to approach us. He informed us that the "*Judenrat*" tried to bribe the German and calm him down, but it looked like the matter was lost since the Gestapo men were already on their way, and they were going to arrive at any moment....

It is impossible for me to describe our condition and our feelings. I bit my flesh with my teeth, and inside my heart I started to say farewell to my loved ones, to my wife and my only daughter, and also to my beloved mother who was sent a few days later, on 14 Elul, to the Belzec death camp together with a few thousands of Jews from our area. We were sure that we would be sent to one of the labor camps, where those who arrive never return. In the end we heard the rattle of approaching cars. We understood that our "guests" had arrived. Then the rail car was unlocked and we were taken out. Again, we had to stand in a military formation and again they counted us. For a large sum of ransom money they let us go, but not without a punishment. We were imprisoned under lock and key for three consecutive nights in the police station cellar after a day of work in the train station. The next day the cruel German received a good payment from the "*Judenrat*" and his attitude towards us improved.

As soon as we got out of this trouble, a new one arrived. On the same week, on Thursday 14 Elul, I was in the kitchen in the morning distributing breakfast to those who were leaving for work. B. Glick who worked with me did not come to work on that day due to an illness. As I finished serving the meals, my wife came frightened and full of fear, and told me that Gestapo people were in the "*Judenrat*" office. I left the cooks in the kitchen, and hurried to Glick, maybe I would be able to hear from him what was happening in town. He also knew about the arrival of the Gestapo people, but since he was a sworn optimist he did not pay too much attention the matter in order not to cause unnecessary panic. On the way home I realized that the matter was not simple. Indeed, the "*Judenrat*" people informed us that the Gestapo was demanding only two hundred additional female workers to work in the

"Wehrmacht" camps, but we knew from experience that we could not trust the words of the "*Judenrat,*" since at times they were only the Gestapo's tools and eased their work. So we left everything and hurried to hide.

It is a shame to tell what the "*Judenrat*" people have done on that day. The searches already started in Chortkov at 11 o'clock at night. They searched and dug all over the ghetto, took out the Jews whom they found and led them to a centralized location. The same thing was done in Jagielnica during the morning hours. Only a few Gestapo men came to our town – it is possible they were busy in other towns and did not have enough murderers – so they wanted help with their work. They demanded a certain "quota" of people to transfer to the death camps, and the "*Judenrat*" responded to them and agreed to supply 300 people. Among them was also my mother h"yd , who lost her eyesight during the war. And so she was led to the train station and pushed into a car together with 120 people who stood tightly to each other, packed like herrings. Among the three hundred people were seventy young women from the Kozia-Gora camp. They were beautiful young women, the best of the Jewish youth in the cities of Tarnopol and Jezierzany. While the "*Judenrat*" people were busy collecting Jews to complete the quota, the Gestapo men were free to travel to Kozia-Gora, stopped the work in the fields and led the young women to the train station. Even today my heart is aching when I remember the lovely young women who were led to the death camp. When the young women were led through the town's streets they were ordered to sing, and made their way towards their terrible fate singing "*Hatikvah.*" Another victim, who was killed in town on the same day, was Shlomo Teiber, the son of Pini [Pinchas] Teiber.

But this was only an introduction to the great "*aktzyot*". This "*aktzya*" took place in only three cities. In other places people only shook in fear and nothing bad happened to them. But we knew very well that it was only the beginning, and the great evil deed was before us and would come shortly.

The "*Aktzya*" in the autumn of 1942

During the days between the Jewish New Year and the Day of Atonement [mid-September], Gestapo men appeared in the "*Judenrat*" office and gave big "orders": a large number of suits, material for coats and a lot of leather items. After they gave their "order," they rushed to Zaleszczyki where they ordered the surviving Jews to vacate the city so it would become *"Judenrein"* – free of Jews. It was the first sign of the approaching *"aktzya."*

On Yom Kippur eve and on Yom Kippur day, a new kind of fear, panic and depression, prevailed in town. At first, the Jews from Zaleszczyki started to arrive in our town, the last place of refuge. This matter disturbed the life in the town and caused panic. In addition to that, the *"Judenrat"* put pressure on the town's residents in order to complete the Gestapo's "order". Each person was invited to the *"Judenrat"* office, and there he was told the amount of money that he had to pay as part of his donation, an amount that he was not able to raise. Those who were not able to fulfill the *"Judenrat"* demand were put in a jail that was located in the cellar. At the same time the *"Judenrat"* people, together with the Jewish police, went to that person's home to conduct a rigorous search in order to discover a cache of hidden money or valuables. In this search, they even dug in the ground or under the floor. On Yom Kippur [21 September 1942] the "guests" arrived and demanded money, watches, rings and other valuable items, and again the people of the Jewish police invaded the town in order to conduct searches and uncover treasures.

In addition to the Jews from Zaleszczyki, surviving Jews also arrived from the towns across the Dniester, such as Horodenka, where an *aktzya* took place the week before Rosh Hashanah. The few hundred surviving Jews arrived in our town via secret routes.

On the first day of Sukkot [25 September], we found out that terrible *"aktzyot"* were taking place in all the towns around us. This news came from towns in Borszczów district: Borszczów, Mielnica, Skala, Korolówka and Jezierzany, and also in the towns of Kopyczyńce, Probużna and Chorostków in Kopyczyńce district. On Simchat Torah [4 October 1942], an *aktzya* took place in Chortkov, and then we knew that on the next day, on *Isru Hag* of Sukkot, our turn would come.

During the week of Rosh Hashanah, I was busy preparing a hideout in the home of my next-door neighbor, together with other tenants of the same building. Immediately after we learnt about the *"aktzya"* in Chortkov, I transferred my family in secret to the hideout in my neighbor's home, and we did not leave it until the end of the *"aktzya."* On the termination of the holiday we stood on our guard all night. At midnight we sent all the people to the hideout, and only I and the home owner, Oizer Schweitzer, were left out of the bunker. We had an excellent look-out position, and we were able to see any movement and hear any noise on the road leading to Chortkov. When daylight came, we saw a caravan of cars arriving from the direction of Chortkov. We understood and we knew that the Gestapo murderers were coming to us.

Immediately we went down to the bunker, but we left the doors to the house unlocked in order to leave the impression that we had run away from the house. When we sat inside the pit we heard the sound of gunfire around us, and the sound of shattered doors and windows. We also heard the sound of those who were walking above us, and I was afraid that the murderers could hear the sound of our heartbeat, which struck in our chests from fear and tension.

The gunfire ceased before evening and one of us dared to leave the bunker. He came back with the news: "the matter is over" and then we all came out of the pit. The house was in a state of disarray, like after a "pogrom." The doors and the windows were broken, many items were looted and what was left was thrown all over the place.

I went to the street for a few minutes in order to take a quick look and see what happened there. In the street I saw the bodies of those who were shot to death. I walked to my home, locked the door and hurried back to my hideout. We found out that during the day around one thousand people were abducted and sent to the death camp in Belzec. Among them were a number of "*Judenrat*" people and the Jewish police (Krasutski, Krampf, M.Y. Lehrer, and others).

We spent the whole night in our hiding place, and only in the morning I went out to see what had happened to my brother and to the rest of my family members.

I ran across town to the home of Aharon Meiman, where my brother Zalman was hiding together with his family members. When I entered the house I realized that something had happened there. From one of the rooms I heard the sound of a baby crying. I recognized the voice of my brother's baby daughter. A few moments later my brother came out of his hideout, hugged me and with a voice full of tears told me that his wife had been taken together with those who were led to their death. For a full day everyone lay hiding in the bunker, but they did not take the baby with them for fear that she would reveal the location of their hiding place. The baby cried all the time, and the mother, whose heart was aching to the sound of her daughter crying, came out of hiding in order to feed her and quiet her. Before morning, at the same moment, the murderers came and took her. The people who were in the bunker heard the murderers ordering the mother to take the baby girl with her, but she refused to do so. Maybe she hoped that the girl would be rescued by the people who remained in the bunker.

Now I had a new worry: I also had to take care of my brother and his family. Besides the baby he also had a boy, Shlomele', a smart five-year-old boy who understood the tragic situation. Not once he turned my attention to the danger and the need to run and hide.

All through that day I ran around like a crazy man. It became clear that more than one hundred bodies were left lying in the town and in the fields around it, and it was necessary to take care of their burial. I went out to collect the bodies together with other people. The bodies that were located in the fields were completely naked because the gentiles removed their clothes and took off their shoes. In one of the pits we found a dead man that the dogs started to gather around. In one of the homes we found dead bodies in a bunker. I remember that one woman, the daughter of Pesach Melzer, was left sitting frozen on a chair with her hands raised over her head. We collected the dead and together with many other Jews we hurried to the cemetery.

The sight in the cemetery was terrifying and heart-rending. There were those whose faces were mutilated, others were lying and their abdomens were hacked to pieces. Among them also there were babies who had been strangled by their parents or their relatives so they wouldn't give up the location of their hideout. We buried all of them in a mass grave, men and women separately. There were also those who were buried in a special grave by their family members. Among them was also the Rebbitzin Sheindel, the Rabbi's mother. When the family's hiding place was discovered, the old Rebbitzin [the rabbi's wife] refused to go with everyone to the assembly area, and the murderers shot her and killed her on the spot.

After the "*Aktzya*" – the centralization of the survivors

On the same week that the "*aktzya*" took place in Tluste, similar "*aktzyot*" also took place in Buczacz and in Monasterzyska. All together, around twelve thousand Jews were taken out of the Chortkov district. Immediately after the "*aktzyot*" an order was given that all the district's Jews must move to one of three locations: the towns of Buczacz, Borszczów and Kopyczyńce; Chortkov was no longer a Jewish city. The few Jews who remained there after the two "*aktzyot*," and after the "removal" of the Jews who were unfit to work, gathered in a few buildings in a German labor camp where the Jews worked. In exchange for a large bribe, the Gestapo agreed to add a fourth location to the three locations listed above, the town of Tłuste. Naturally, the money needed for the bribe was collected from the townspeople.

Shortly, groups of Jews who had been evicted from the nearby towns started to arrive in our town. They came by cars and on foot and filled all the houses, twenty people or more in each house. People were forced to sleep in the cellars and in attics, trembling from the cold and suffocating from lack of air. The typhus epidemic spread in town and killed many day after day.

In the middle of November 1942, another "*aktzya*" took place in Buczacz. At first they started to whisper, and in the end they started to talk openly and with certainty that, by the beginning of January, the whole district would be "cleansed of ews" – "*Judenrein*" in the murderers' language. The "*Judenrat*" received an order to put an end to all the mutual aid organizations. The first to close was the community kitchen, and we were ordered to give all the "equipment" to the Gestapo. It was a sad and comical sight, when the "equipment" of few broken pots and a number of rusted knives and spoons was packed.

The members of the "*Judenrat*" and its leaders, headed by the members of the district "*Judenrat*," started to scatter and leave the cities so they wouldn't be there during the final liquidation. They received work in the "Wehrmacht" camps, and in the end received permission from the Gestapo to allow three hundred and fifty Jews to live and work there. The workers in those camps carried a special mark, the letter 'A' on their lapels. In the village of Swidowa, special huts were built for the lucky ones who received work there.

At the end of December, in the last week of 1942, the murderers invented a new form of extermination: "abductions" or "*lapanki*" in a foreign language. It was an independent "action" of the Ukrainian police, without the assistance of the Gestapo. All of a sudden they grabbed any person they met in the street. They imprisoned the abductees in the police station cellar, and later on transferred them to the prison in Chortkov. The abductions lasted until the end of December 1942 and during first days of January 1943.

My family and I hid during the days of the abductions, and none of us was abducted. But during one of the abductions I was informed that my brother Zalman and his son Shlomele' were among the abductees. Despite the danger, I got out of hiding and ran to the *"Judenrat"* office and asked them to try to release them. The *"Judenrat"* did try to release the detainees, but the intervention was not successful and they were sent immediately to Chortkov where they waited for their execution. But suddenly, for unknown reasons, they were released from prison. During my long stay in different cold hideouts I caught a cold, ran a high fever, and became ill with typhus.

The year 1943

On 13 February, before I was able to stand on my feet because of my illness, we received the news that an *"aktzya"* was taking place in Buczacz. I was in a state of great panic. First, I was not able to stand on my feet in order to get up and escape. Second, I was afraid that the healthy people wouldn't let me enter the hideout from fear that I would infect them with my illness, since proper disinfection was also not available. Without a choice, I was forced to stay at home and see what would happen to me. In the end we found out that the *"aktzya"* took place only in Buczacz, the location of the larger concentration of Jews in the district, around fifteen thousand people. So at first, the Nazis wanted to lower the number of Jews in this town, and arranged an *"aktzya,"* even during the winter season when the conditions were not easy for an "action" of that sort. The matter was not easy for them since most of the Jews had well-concealed "bunkers" where they hid from their pursuers.

Until the week of Passover [week of 20 April 1943] we were forced to flee and hide in the shelter a number of times, and each time we stayed there for a week or so. The pursuits and the oppression by the Germans and by the local population increased so much that it was impossible to leave the front door. The Gestapo people suddenly arrived in town, entered homes and shot the people or took them outside and shot them there. Once, they entered the home of Dr. Bernard Meltzer, took him and his family to Chortkov where they shot and killed them. Another time they walked directly to the home of the veterinarian Spiegelglass, entered his home and killed all of his family. After they left, the executioners came to the "*Judenrat*" with the following demand: "bury these dogs immediately." One day, they shot and killed forty Jews. Among them was Mendel' Hesing, an educated and talented young man and the leader of "*Betar*" in our town. The next day they came to the "*Judenrat*" and said laughing: "That was a stupid game..." Surely, they were used to killing thousands at a time, not just forty souls.

An interesting fact: a Pole with a Jewish face lived in one of the buildings where the Jews lived. They also shot and killed him. The next day they came and wrote a "report" about this sad event.

These were the small "*aktzyot*" of the beginning of 1943. As we learnt later, the final liquidation of our district's Jews was postponed by five months, from the beginning of 1943 to the beginning of the summer of the same year.

The great spring "*Aktzya*" 1943

Exactly a week before Passover we found out that a terrible "*aktzya*" was raging in Buczacz. Exactly on the eve of Passover we found out that a terrible slaughter started in Borszczów and continued on the next day. On the first day of Passover, when the matter was known in our town, people left their homes and fled to the fields and to the forests, and the town almost emptied of its residents. Many of the escapees were beaten and robbed in the fields by Ukrainian hooligans.

The matter of the Jews' flight to the fields and to the forests was not a secret. The Nazis decided to wait and postponed the "*aktzya*" in order to give the escapees time to return to their homes, so they could attack them unexpectedly later. And indeed, many of the Jews returned by 27 May, and only then the great "*aktzya*," in which almost all the surviving Jews were exterminated, took place in Tłuste.

Meanwhile, the management of the "Wehrmacht" factories received a permit from the Gestapo to employ one thousand five hundred Jews on the farms under their ownership in the villages: Swidowa, Roshanovka [Różanówka], Kozia-Gora, Ułaszkowce, Lisovtza [Lisowce], Mochovka [Muchawka], Talanivka, Milovtza [Milowce], Shipovtza [Szypowce] and Shershenovza [Szerszeniowce]. Labor camps were established on those farms and huts were built to house the workers. The Jews were afraid of these camps and did not agree to go them on their own free will. And then the abductions continued. The abductions usually took place at night, and we were forced to stay in our shelters day and night without leaving them at all.

We misled ourselves thinking that because of the need for workers, the Gestapo would postpone the liquidation until the end of the working season in the fields. The Gestapo men also misled us. They told the "*Judenrat*" that according to the instructions that they received from Kraków and from Berlin, they would not continue to plan any more "*aktzyot,*" And so, the situation continued until the week of *Lag Ba'omer*. In the same week we felt that a large "wedding" would take place soon. Again, many escaped to the fields and to the forests, and after they spent a few days in the outdoors they got tired and started to return to their homes. On Wednesday evening, 21 Iyar, we found out from the "*Judenrat*" that an "*aktzya*" would not take place on that night. They knew that an "*aktzya*" would take place, but they were positively sure that it would not take place on that night... After many inquiries and demands, the people calmed down and went to sleep, and even allowed themselves to undress. Also, the members of my family lay down to sleep, and I also joined them and went to bed.

At three o'clock in the morning my wife roused me from my sleep. She stood twisting her hands and said to me: "Take a look what is happening in the street." I looked and saw the murderers running around with guns in their hands. My wife grabbed our daughter in her arms and together with her sister ran from the house. I heard the last shouts of despair escaping from their mouth, and I knew that we were lost. In an instant, I got dressed and crossed through the attic to my neighbor's home. Many people were already there, twisting their hands and running around in despair like trapped mice. It was impossible to hide in that house. There were too many people there, and it was impossible for everyone to enter the concealed shelter. Also, during the last week surviving Jews were exiled from Buczacz to Tłuste.

Suddenly I saw a Jew removing the Jewish badge from his lapel and running outside. In an instant I did the same and ran after him. I heard the sound of gunfire outside. I saw an open house and entered it. I met a group of frightened people there, and found out that the homeowner had left the house and took the key to the cellar where the bunker was located. Meanwhile the sound of gun fire was getting closer and closer. I stood as though I was paralyzed. I lost my wife and my daughter, and I was in great danger. Any moment the murderers might come and take us.

In the end we found an axe, used it to take the padlock off the door, and managed to reach the well-concealed bunker. There were nine of us there. Immediately we heard how the murderers were searching the house and the cellar. The searches continued all day long. Each time, another group of murderers, who spoke German or Ukrainian among themselves, came. They pulled up the floors and demolished the walls in their search for a hideout. We sat in the shelter without making a sound. My cough was suffocating me, but I was afraid to cough. And so we sat in the airless bunker all of that day until evening.

Only in the morning we became aware how great the destruction was, and the magnitude of the terrible slaughter that took place in our town. Nearly three thousand Jews were shot to death and buried in three graves in the cemetery. I found out that also my wife, my daughter, my brother and his son were among the victims of the massacre. It is humanly impossible to describe the look of the town after this destruction. I doubt that we will ever see another horrible sight like that anywhere in the world. A few hundred dead bodies were still lying in the streets and it was necessary to bury them. The homes were open and all that was in them was taken out and robbed. For a few days we were busy burying the dead in the cemetery. Later on we started to work and made efforts to stop the blood that was flowing from the mass graves. We kept on raising the earth dam around them, but the blood kept on flowing over it and flooded the area. I remembered what I studied in my youth about the blood of the prophet Zechariah. His blood kept on flowing from his grave and it was impossible to stop it. At that time we assumed that it was only a legend, and here, we saw this horrible sight with both eyes. I stood with the shovel in my hand and scraped the earth in order to stop the blood flow, and in my heart I knew that this was the blood of my loved ones and my relatives, the blood of my wife and my only daughter. The blood of my brother and his son, the blood of my friends and my peers – and I was alive!... and, to add to all of that, our gentile neighbors – near and far – stood around us and saw how Jewish blood was flowing without a stoppage.

In the same week, seven days after the great "aktzya," an order arrived from the Gestapo that in a matter of hours all the surviving Jews must concentrate in a narrow section of town where the Jewish ghetto would be located. My home stood on that street. Fifteen buildings, maybe twenty, were allocated for the "ghetto," but there were around three thousand Jews in town.

I will never forget this sight, the sight of three thousand Jews holding their belongings in their hands, running to secure a place in the narrow "ghetto." My home also filled with their belongings and there was not an empty space. I remember that I cried at the sight of this horrible crowdedness, more than the time when I cried for the loss of my family. It was a bitter cry for the fate of my unfortunate nation. Again, I did not want to stay in town, and begged to be taken to work in one of the camps. The next day I moved to the labor camp in Lisovtza [Lisowce].

*

I arrived at the labor camp in Lisovtza on Friday, the first day of the month of Sivan, 4 June 1943. I arrived there at dusk, a short hour after the people returned from their work in the field. On the next day, Saturday morning, I left for work with them.

Early Sunday morning, the "work manager" came from Tłuste. Patti [Vathje], a German who raked a great fortune from our "Judenrat," but in exchange did all that he could to save Jews from the "aktzyot." At any rate, this is how we saw him. Also on that day, since he knew about the preparations for the "aktzya," he ordered to send the largest number of Jewish laborers to work in the fields so they wouldn't be in the "ghetto" during the "aktzya." He also appeared in our camp very early in the morning, around five before morning, gathered all the camp's laborers and lectured before them. He warned us that we must work with trust, and none of us should leave his place of work because we might get punished for doing so. A number of us asked for his permission to go to town and bring their belongings, and to that Patti answered that he might allow them to go at another time, but not today. He did not mention a word and a half about the possibility of an "aktzya," because it was the Gestapo's secret and he was not allowed to reveal it. He strictly forbade us to go to town on that day, but a number of people from the camp did not listen to him, went to town and were killed on the way.

After that we left for work. Around eleven o'clock we saw from a distance a number of vehicles full of Ukrainian policemen and Gestapo men heading towards town. Later on we found out that they were the same murderers who performed the "*aktzya*" in Borszczów. After they finished their work there they came to do their work of killing and murder in Tłuste.

In the afternoon hours, when it became known to us what was happening in town, we spread throughout the fields so they would not be able to see us. We started to consult each other about what to do, since we were afraid that they might also attack us. Some of us had families in town and worried about their fate. In the midst of things, a refugee arrived from the town – a young man from Horodenka by the name of Meir Eber, who had escaped during the "*aktzya*" and left his mother, and his mother-in-law, in town (he and his wife survived). From him we found out the full details of the "*aktzya*" and how the murderous attack had started on the same Sunday. Meanwhile it became darker and it was hard for us to decide what to do. In the end we decided to return to the camp. A short hour later we heard the sound of cars approaching the camp. Immediately all of us got up and escaped. I jumped over two barbed wire fences and hid under a pile of hay in a farmer's yard. I met Berel Hernes there and we agreed to go to town first thing in the morning to see what had happened there.

We arrived in town by secret routes and stole our way into the "ghetto". Again we saw the same horrible sight. The streets were full of bleeding dead bodies. After this destruction no one wanted to stay in town. Those who had the opportunity hurried back to the labor camps. Only around two hundred people, the elderly or those with small children who were not accepted in a labor camp, remained in town. They were housed in two buildings, and two days later they were ordered to move to Chortkov. They were murdered on the way before they were able to reach the city. On the same day also the last Jewish survivors were murdered in Chortkov. It was also the day that the last surviving Jews were murdered in Borszczów and Kopyczyńce.

We continued to work in the camp for two weeks and lived in fear all the time, but nothing happened to us. Once, while we were working in a field near Buczacz we heard the sound of gunfire. Gentiles who passed by told us that the Jews in the camp in Swidowa were being liquidated. It was the largest camp, and around six hundred Jews lived there. Again, panic broke out in our camp and we did not know how to act and what to do. Those, who still had a little money, left the camp and went to the forests around Uziran [Jezierzany]. On the same day that the Swidowa labor camp was liquidated, all the Jews were liquidated in the camps around the town of Chortkov.

Three days later, a great panic broke out among the Germans and the Ukrainian police, and they started to pack their belongings for the road. As we found out later, a large Russian partisan squadron tried to open a path towards the Soviet front. Germans in the small towns were afraid of a partisan attack, and hurried to escape to the larger cities where they were under the protection of the German army. Our joy was premature. A few days later the partisans were driven away, and the Germans and the Ukrainian police returned to their first place.

Eight days after the murder of the Jews in Swidowa, the Ukrainian police held a massacre in all the labor camps and killed around 80% of their residents, or maybe even more.

On Saturday night, 17 July 1943, I worked in the field, threshing. Suddenly I heard the sound of gunfire coming from the nearby forest. A mortal fear fell on me. I knew that they were hunting for Jews who were hiding in the forest. The Tluste Jews who were killed at that time were the three sons and daughters of Ratzie Dubester – Munie, Rachel and Rivka – and also the granddaughter of Ester Yorist. It is possible that Tsilya, daughter of Teme Pfeffer, was also killed there.

Early Monday morning, I was on guard duty together with Berel Hernes. In the morning, after people left for work, we went to bed. As we fell asleep we suddenly heard a noise. We got up and found out that on the same night the camps in Roshanovka [Różanówka] and Shershbovitz [Szerszeniowce] were attacked. I went outside and came across a Jew who had escaped from Shershbovitz. It was Mendel from Chortkov, son of Mrs. Hikand from her first husband. He said to me: "Don't ask questions, get up and run." I ran to the field where I found other people who had also left their work and escaped. I was together with a group of fifteen people. We hid in a wide wheat field that was surrounded with trees on both sides. We lay there all day, and when we did not hear the sound of gunfire, we sent a man to the camp to see what was happening there. The messenger came back and told us that most of the people had come back to camp, and the work "manager" gave an order to leave for the field at night and continue with the threshing. A few of us said that we should also return to the camp because we escaped from there without a slice of bread, and also all of our belongings were left there. I opposed it. If nothing happened – our belongings would remain there, and if something happened – it was better that we be far from the location of the incident.

Before morning, while it was still dark, we suddenly heard the sound of gunfire coming from all directions. It seemed like the gunfire was directed at us, and indeed the shooting was nearby. At that moment a murderous attack started in all the camps which were only one or two, or maybe three kilometers apart from each other. The shooting lasted all day long, and stopped only before evening. Only on the third day we dared to get out of the field. We lay under the hot sun during the day, and got wet from the dew during the night. One night a very heavy rain fell on us. We did not eat all that time, and we also did not have any water.

On the fourth day we stole our way into the village. There we learned who had been killed from Tluste: Pinchas Epstein and his wife Hinda Epstein, Kozia Gabe (Gabai, daughter of Mordechai Gabe), and a person by the name of Herman with his wife (her maiden name was Chana Warberg, granddaughter of Yosi Epstein). In the fields we met a number of Jews who had escaped from the farms, and they told us that the same terrible murderous attack also took place in all the camps, and in a number of them almost all the Jews were exterminated.

A great miracle happened in our place, in Lisovtza [Lisowce]. The work manager came in the middle of the "aktzya" and intervened in favor of his Jewish workers. He claimed that during the burning work season he could not give up his Jewish workers and he did not have any other workers to replace them, and so he was able to stop the "aktzya." It was the one and only incident of this kind in all of Poland. Thanks to him a large Jewish community, the largest in the whole area, was left in Lisovtza. It happened on 17 Tamuz 5703, 20 July 1943.

After the "aktzya," the managers of the "Wehrmacht" farms did not know if they were allowed to employ the surviving Jews or not. We wandered in the fields, days and nights, and we did not know what would happen to us. Every once in a while, a number of us went to the farm to learn what they thought about our future. Once, I entered the farm and found a number of our people standing looking worried and desperate. They told me that the farm manager had just told them that we had two hours to vacate the place. He did not want to employ us since we walked around worried and frightened, and fearing the next attack. Since he also did not want bloodshed in the area of his farm, it was better that we leave the place. Only two choices were left to us after his message: to give ourselves to the hands of the police, or to hide in the forests.

We already started to consult with each other where to turn and where to go for many hours. Then, the farm manager came together with Patti, the farm manager from Tluste, and informed us with great joy that they had received a promise from the Gestapo that an "*aktzya*" would not take place until the end of 1943, and we could return peacefully to work.

I don't know if a promise of that kind did come from the Gestapo, or if the work managers wanted to calm us down since they needed our work. At any rate, we accepted the news with great satisfaction since the labor camp was the only place where we were able to live legally. At that time Jews were not allowed to live in any residential areas, so we returned to work. We regarded the promise with great skepticism since we had heard many soothing promises in the past two years, and after each one of them there was a greater and crueler massacre than the one that preceded it. Therefore, we were afraid to sleep on the farm, and after a day of hard difficult work we went to sleep in the fields even without eating dinner. Early in the morning we had to return to the farm before the manager arrived to give the work orders, so he wouldn't find out that we had spent the night outside the camp. We were in great trouble since not everyone was able to return on time, and the manager threatened that he would not tolerate the matter and would inform the Gestapo or the police, and the results were known. We also suffered a lot from the Ukrainian population in the village. Groups of thugs walked around at night searching for hiding Jews, and each person that they found was badly beaten by them. A number of Ukrainian nationalists, under the leadership of the village clerk, Kutiz Mostovi, excelled in it. Each Jew who fell into their hands outside of the camp grounds was beaten until he bled. The summer passed in hard labor and torture. As long as the wheat was standing in the fields I slept between the pathways. After the harvest I hid between the sheaves or spent the night in the yard of one of the farmers.

Jewish "Partisans"

Already in May of 1943, at the time when the city residents were liquidated in Chortkov district, a number of young people from Buczacz left for the forests armed with weapons. I found out about this group of young people during my last visit to Tluste. I talked to one of them in my home, a young man from Horodenka, but I do not know his fate. When we stayed on the

Ułaszkowce farm, a large group of armed Jews was organized in the forests around Jezierzany and also in the area of Tsigan/Kala (northeast of Borszczów – *ed.*). From time to time messengers from these groups arrived to us and kept in regular contact with us. We helped them to acquire weapons and food, and served as a "supply base." At times, when their existence in the forest was in danger, they came to hide with us. These groups did not survive long because they were attacked and killed.

It should be noted that Ukrainian nationalist gangs took a greater part in the extermination of the Jews who hid in the forests, if they were armed or not, than the Germans. Generally, the extermination of Jewish survivors in the camps, in the fields and in the forests, was mostly done by the Ukrainian police. Their attitude towards Jews was worse than the attitude of the German S.S. men, who killed and murdered only after they were ordered to do so. The Ukrainians murdered under their own initiative and out of vengefulness, and they killed at every opportunity and every step of the way. They suddenly appeared in the middle of work, beat us, undressed us, and robbed any amount of money or valuables that they found. They shot and killed each Jew they met outside the camp area. So it was in all the camps, mostly in Holovtshintza [Hołowczyńce] where a day did not pass without victims.

I always tried to stay away from them, and I was successful most of the time. But once, I fell into their hands. It was a day before *Tisha BeAv* [Ninth of Av – 22 July 1943]. We were in camp eating lunch, and all of a sudden we found out that the people of the Ukrainian police were in the village. As usual, I grabbed all my possessions in my hands – my winter coat, a bundle of bread and my water cup – and left the hut in order to hide and disappear from sight. As I put my foot out of the hut, a number of murderers together with the police commander stopped me. They aimed their guns at me and ordered me to undress. I did as I was ordered, and stripped to my skin while the farmers stood and watched the show. One of the murderers stayed by my side, and the others scattered and entered the rest of the huts. At first, the policeman ordered me to take my clothes and toss them on the ground a number of times, one after the other. Later on he ordered me to take the clothes and put them in the hut. When we were in the hut, he ordered me to put the clothes on the floor and to stand against the wall with my back facing him. I thought that my last hour had arrived, but my luck played and I was "unscathed" – meaning that I only received a few good blows from the policeman, and he stole the rest of my money that I kept sewn inside my clothes. His friends acted the same way in the other huts. This was their daily routine.

We were worried about the approaching winter, when the working season would end and we would not be needed. The difficult winter conditions also frightened us, since we could not exist in the fields or in the forest in the mud and in the snow. In addition, our clothes were completely torn and we walked almost barefoot. A typhus epidemic broke out, and the gentiles, even the honest ones who sold us food for the full price, did not let us step on their threshold or wander around their village from fear that we would infect them. Now all of them tried to get rid of us. They sent a delegation to the farm manager and promised to supply him with enough workers if he agreed to exterminate the Jewish workers. Meanwhile, the death rate increased in the camp and we were forced to bury our dead in secret, so they wouldn't discover the extent of the epidemic. We took them to the field under the cover of night, dug a grave for them and concealed it. In a way, this situation was worse than the "aktzyot."

On 30 November 1943, the surviving Jewish laborers were liquidated in "aktzyot" that took place in a number of camps in the Chortkov district, a distance of 23 kilometers from our camp. We also found out that the camp in Kopitshinza [Kopyczyńce], where one hundred Jews worked, was liquidated. Again the fear of the "aktzya" fell on us. After midnight, at two o'clock in the morning, we left the camp in secret and wandered in the fields, in the extreme cold and in the blizzards. It is difficult to comprehend in our simple brain where we found the energy to endure all these sufferings. To work all day with very little food, to walk with rags wrapped around our feet, and to spend the whole night without a roof over our heads. We kept our clothes on and, because of the difficult winter conditions we were unable to wash properly. As a result, we were infested with lice that increased the spread of the typhus epidemic. With difficulties, we managed to reach the end of the month of December, the period of Christmas. We hoped that during the days of the holiday, the gentiles would be in a state of holiday spirit and forget us. But also in this matter our hopes proved false.

During the last week of December many Jews were killed in Holovshintza. The target was the extermination of those who were ill with typhus, but many healthy Jews were also murdered. Among them was Yosel Schilder the slaughterer from Tłuste. He was one of the healthy workers who were forced to dig the burial pit. After the work was done they were also murdered. The murderous Ukrainian police suddenly arrived at our camp on Saturday, 1 January 1944, at 12 noon. At that time we did not work. Luckily a few moments earlier I had left for one of the remote corners of the yard. The murderers shot and killed a number of Jews, among them: Yosel Zandberg [Sandberg] (who was healthy), Meltzer's wife Pesia, Sosia Weinstock the sister-in-law of the baker Leib Stein, Roize Tauber the mother of Shlomo Niame. After they finished their work, the murderers continued on their way to a second farm. The village council ordered us to bury the dead immediately. It was very cold outside, so we collected the dead, put them on a sled and took them to a location behind the forest. There, the gentiles gave us a corner to bury them in a place where they buried the corpses of their horses. Sandberg continued to have spasms along the way. After we dug the pit in the frozen ground, and the work lasted a very long hour, he still showed signs of life. We were desperate. The day got darker and the gentiles from the nearby villages started to gather around us, and we started to worry that they would attack us. In the end we lowered the bodies to the grave and returned grieving and hunched to our gloomy "home." At the same time there was light and happiness in the farmers' homes that we passed on our way – they were celebrating their holiday, the first day of the year 1944.

In the same week, there was a second attack on our camp. Also this time I was not in the camp during the attack. Half an hour earlier, I had left for work in a field that was far from the camp. This time the number murdered was higher than the number of those who were murdered in first attack. The murderers chased their victims and shot at them. Shot in this manner: Alter Grill, the two daughters of S.L. Schechter, and Elyakom Scheinholz, the son-in-law of Hirsh Blikstein, who escaped together with his ten-year-old son. The boy was able to escape and survived. The father was shot and killed.

It became known to us that the Ukrainian police commander did not want to leave one Jew alive. He did not want any witness to the actions of the Ukrainian population and the police, and a single Jew who would aspire to avenge the blood of his brothers. At that time it was clear and known that the Germans would be forced to retreat from the areas that they had captured. And indeed, a few weeks later the great German military retreat started. Russians who cooperated with the Germans and Ukrainian policemen, also escaped to Russia. Then, a new chapter of trouble and persecution by the escaping hooligans started. They were helped by local gentiles who pointed at us and informed them of our location. Not far from me, one of them cut down a Jew with his sword and killed him. I escaped as fast as I could and slipped into the forest. A second Jew who was caught by them while he was escaping was hung on a tree in the middle of the village. Fearing the rioters, we left the camp despite the bad weather and wandered in the fields like a lost flock.

Local Ukrainians also attacked Jews in the other camps and killed many of them. In Holovshintza, rioting gangs attacked on Purim eve [8 March 1944], and killed over fifty Jews with their axes. At the end of the matter, about six hundred Jews who were lost in the fields settled on the farm in Tłuste. There, under the protection of the "Wehrmacht" they felt secure from the Ukrainian rioters. Indeed, the Germans protected and guarded them. But, I was afraid to go to the camp. I found shelter with one of my gentile friends, and stayed there until the arrival of the Russians.

However, fate was cruel to us also after the Russians' arrival. Out of all the town's residents, only the Jews went out to welcome the Russian tanks who were the first to arrive. Every gentile sat in his own home. At that happy moment, when the few survivors stood around their liberators, neglected, hungry and covered with rags, with hearts full of happiness for their salvation, a group of thirty German airplanes suddenly appeared and started to bomb the camp. And again, one hundred Jews perished in this bombing.

During the first days after the Russians' arrival, Jews who hid in the homes of honest gentiles tried to settle in some of the ruined buildings. But eight days after the Russians' entry, the Soviet army was forced to retreat because of the pressure of a number of German regiments. They surrounded the area around Kamieniec-Podolski, and broke through the blockade. Again, the town was abandoned and given to the hands of the Germans for eleven days. This event happened during the holiday of Passover.

After Passover, when we found out that the Russians were back in Tłuste, a number of us tried to return home. I also returned to town for a few days, but the loneliness bothered me. I did not have a place to lay my head and food to support myself. Therefore I left town on 4 May, and planned to reach Chernowitz where my oldest brother and other family members once lived. When I arrived in Chernowitz, I arrived to a different world. Jews with beards and side-locks lived there. On the Sabbath they prayed in the synagogues and ate Halla and Sabbath pie as in the old days. I did not think that I would find a decent concentration of Jews just a short distance from the killing fields of Galicia. Also Romania did not pamper its Jews. Only fifteen thousand Jews from Bukovina remained in Chernowitz. But for us, the few survivors of Eastern Galicia who saw the total liquidation of their towns, it was a sensational and joyful experience, and we did not know how to thank our creator that we were rewarded to see that.

I spent around three weeks in Chernowitz. I found that none of my relatives had survived – they were all murdered in Transdnistria. Two days before the holiday of Shavuot, I joined a group of Jews from Bukovina, and we left on foot for the Bukovina Romanian border. When we arrived in the town of Mialni, in the district of Dorhoi, we heard that the Russians had liberated all of Romania from the Germans. We continued on our way in order to reach Bucharest. We traveled mostly on foot, without a penny in our pockets and dressed in rags like poor beggars. On Yom Kippur we arrived in Bucharest.

The "Joint" [American Jewish Joint Distribution Committee] was already active in Bucharest, and there was also a committee for Polish Jewish survivors. There I received 40,000 Pounds for clothes and additional 18,000 Pounds for food each month. When I heard that a boat was sailing to Israel, I tried to be included among its passengers. On 25 October 1944, I left Europe for Israel.

During my journey, I had sufficient time to think about all that we had experienced during the three years of Nazi regime. My heart was full of curses for the country that was saturated with our brothers' blood, for its residents who helped to the best of their ability with the work of slaughter and murder. Even the best of them were happy when they saw us being led to the slaughter, and they filled their homes with the property that they stole from our homes. I thought in my heart that we had to boycott these countries, they way we boycotted Spain after the expulsion. None of our brothers and sons would step on this cursed land, since most of its citizens took part in our destruction and did not allow the few survivors, who wandered for weeks and months in the fields and in the forests, rest. And with an evil eye they looked and searched for them in order to slaughter them. They chased us with raging revenge that human history never saw before. I knew that I did not have the power and the talent to express the atrocities that our town and all of the Polish Jewry experienced. I had only one request in my heart and in my mouth that I would live to see when God would avenge our revenge on all those who shed the blood of our brothers and the members of our nation like water.

The sailing was very difficult. We were taken to a ship which looked as though it was going to break up at any moment, and it was a miracle that all of us did not drown in the sea. After three days of difficult sailing we arrived at Istanbul. We were kept in the port for three days, and we were not allowed to go ashore. In the end, we climbed to the shore exactly by the train station and appropriate and organized rail cars were given to us for our journey to Israel. On the Sabbath, 4 November, we arrived in Israel.

[Pages 131-136]

The "Great *Aktzya*" and afterwards

by Shlomo Trembowelski

Translated by Sara Mages

I begin my story with the *aktzya* known as "The Thursday *aktzya*." Unlike the previous *aktzyot* and pogroms, this time the murderers gathered the town's Jews, men, women and children, and led them in groups to the local cemetery. There, they forced them to undress and put their clothes in neat piles. They stood them near the open pit which was designed to be a grave for a great number of people, and shot them to death. As it turned out later, more than three thousand Jews were murdered in this *aktzya*.

The day after the *aktzya,* a command was given to reduce the size of the "ghetto," and the few survivors had to concentrate within a few hours in two streets near the Russian [*ed. –* Ukrainian] Church. This command caused panic among the survivors who, among them, were only a few whole families. Everyone rushed to "grab" a place in one of the houses, to find a place to sleep. People carried with them all that was left in their hands from the *aktzyot* and previous lootings, especially their few remaining clothes. They hoped that they would be able to exchange them for a slice of bread as they had done in the past under mortal danger. This time, the farmers who came in masses with their wagons from the nearby villages weren't interested in "barter." They simply grabbed all that they could carry from the women and the frightened children. I remember that the Ukrainian town clerk tried to drive the farmers away with his stick, and didn't allow them to plunder and rob. But his efforts were fruitless. They loaded their wagons with all they could and transported the lootings to their villages.

I moved with my family to a half-ruined room from where everything had been taken and looted. In one of the corners, in the floor, was the entrance to the bunker that had been discovered. Its occupants were taken out and led, together with everyone, to the mass grave in the cemetery. We knew that also around us, around those who remained, the ring of extinction was tightening and the purpose of concentrating us in a narrow area was to make it easier for them to exterminate us. After all, the concentration in Tłuste included the remaining Jews from the whole area. Apart from the workers in the labor camp, the whole area was "*Judenrein,*" as it was named by the Germans.

We passed a night full of anxiety as we stood close to the window panes and listened to every whisper, to every knock on the door or window of one of the adjacent houses. Various thoughts run around in my head. Here I see before my eyes my sister-in law, Rivke Dachner, with her daughter whom her father, my brother, Meir, never saw because he was drafted to the Red Army and fell captive in the hands of the Germans. They killed him immediately, together with other Jewish prisoners. I see my sister-in law, my wife's sister Bashe, my brother, Avraham, who was captured in 1939 on the Polish front and later, after he escaped from Majdanek, he fell in the Warsaw uprising. I see my relatives, on my father's and my mother's sides, who were exiled from Uziran [Jezierzany] to Tłuste, and neighbors and friends who are no longer alive. I try to count them on my fingers, but the list is long, twice and three times larger than the number of my fingers. Each time I remember additional names, and again, I start to calculate the balance of the terrible bloodshed...

The sound of a person's footsteps, a cautious and silent step, reached my ears and distracted me. I can't see anything in the darkness and I go outside to "smell" what is going on. Morning twilight is approaching, and once again, the disturbing thought returns and is constantly pecking in the brain: Where to run? Where to hide? It became clear that the best way is to escape to the forest. But with whom can I flee? – With my sick and feeble wife and my infant? And this, without any means, without acquaintances and without a weapon! The feeling of a haunted animal that escapes from its pursuers and from the hunters who seek its soul, overcomes me. And, with that, the desire to live is getting stronger, not to die a despicable death... After all, we are confident that the enemy's defeat will eventually come!

I pass in my memory all my gentile acquaintance, those I had worked with, and I come to the conclusion that they might kill me for various reasons. First and foremost, out of greed. From the lust for Jewish property that is inherent in them and the desire to get rid of a Jew at the appropriate time. To my sorrow, these suspicions materialized at a large scale.

And now I remember Makowiecki's farm where I worked paving the stable after we were deported from Torskie (this is a story in itself). On this farm, which the Germans transferred to their disposal, I found several Jews who worked in all kinds of jobs, and I decided that I had no other choice but to reach it. First of all, to escape from here and to try to extend our life on earth, even a little. To do that, I needed to reach that farm by secret routes and meet the supervisor who oversaw the management of several farms around Tłuste. Later, labor camps for Jews were established on these farms, and that also in order to concentrate them and facilitate the work of extermination of the rioters.

So I reached the farm by indirect roads and by chance I met the supervisor as he was riding his horse. I approached him, took my hat off, and asked him if he could hire me to work on the farm. He didn't answer me immediately, measured me from head to toe, and in the end directed me to H. Kenigsberg who lived on the farm for some time with a number of Jews. Maybe he would be able find me a job on the farm. With that, he mentioned that I would have to "live" in the labor camp at Kozia Gora. Every day we had to come from there to work and return in the evening. It turns out that I didn't tell him a thing and a half about our child because I knew in advance about the fate of children in the camps... And now, I have to say that the camp in Tłuste was sort of a refuge for Jews who survived the *aktzyot* in Tłuste and other locations, and also for Jews from labor camps around Tłuste such as Lisovitz [Lisowce], Holovtshintza [Hołowczyńce], Swidowa, Roshanovka [Różanówka] and others which were liquidated by the Germans with the cooperation of the Ukrainian police.

I returned to Tłuste to bring my wife and my son to the farm. Again, the three of us reached it by indirect routes and in secret so the non-Jewish workers wouldn't notice the boy. Kenigsberg placed us in an abandoned and dilapidated house that once served as an apartment for one of the supervisors. We decided immediately that in the evening my wife would go to sleep at the camp in Kozia Gora and I would stay with the boy in the dilapidated house on the farm. We arranged a hiding place for our boy under the sleeping bench among old tools. The boy knew to enter his hiding place each time he heard a stranger's footsteps getting closer to the house. Kenigsberg helped me with this matter and every couple of hours we kept guard by the window to prevent a sudden attack. The only chance, in a case like that, was to have enough time to escape through a hole that we prepared in the fence. It was better for us to be shot during an escape than fall in the hands of the murderers.

At the same time, before the last *aktzya* in the ghetto, surviving family members were seen walking around, a father who lost his wife and his children, a couple without their children, and children without their parents. It's difficult to describe the magnitude of the distress of these children. Not once it was possible to see them crawling on all four in places where a little vegetation grew as they chewed grass like ducks. They envied those who died a "natural" death, from typhus and dysentery.

However, they weren't given a lot of time to die a natural death. One day, on a Sunday, I left for work early in the morning with another Jew, a refugee from Germany. We worked next to one of the barracks and had to build a stone foundation under the corners (the bricks that we used were brought to us from the ruins of *Beit Ha'Midrash*...). Suddenly, we heard the sound of gunfire from the direction of the ghetto. The shooting continued and we understood what was happening in the ghetto...

Without waiting long, I took my family and slipped out the farm yard. We mixed with the masses of gentiles who came out frightened from their churches and hurried to their homes. When we arrived at the sand hill of Yakend [Hikand] we were able to see a large movement in the cemetery's grounds, where a grave was prepared for the masses. On the way, we had the time to get a slice of bread and a bottle of water for our child from one of the gentiles. Our destination was the forest, and we were hoping to reach it at night, in the darkness. For the time being, we hid between the corn stalks which were quite low for that season. We hid there until the next day and kept the boy pressed against our bodies to protect him from the cold. The boy understood that we were hiding because it wasn't the first time that we hid with him.

We decided to postpone our departure to the forest and wait until morning in order to hear details of what had happened in the ghetto. That is why we approached the fields around Kozia-Gora. Indeed, we met Jews there who escaped, as we escaped, and also Jews who fled after the *aktzya*. We learned from them that this time the killers were able to concentrate and eliminate about three thousand souls. Gavriel Braun, who also escaped after the *aktzya*, told me how Yosef Schisler, a childhood friend from Uziran, perished together with his family. This Yosef Schisler invented a special kind of "bunker" and built similar bunkers for a number of Jews. He built a bunker like that also for himself and invited Gavriel Braun and his son to hide there. At the last moment, the bunker didn't look right to Yosef Schisler and he moved with his family to another bunker in the next building. The rioters found that bunker and killed everyone who hid there. The first bunker wasn't discovered and its inhabitants were saved from death... I learned from him that it was "quiet" on the farm and the murderers didn't arrive there at all.

Now, there were two options before us: to carry out our decision and hide in the forest, or to return to the farm which was saved this time from the rioters. It was safer to stay in the forest, but the difficulties that were waiting for us, especially since we took care of a small child, prevented us from following this road. Therefore, we decided, without a choice, to return to the farm even though we knew well the dangers that lay ahead for us there.

We returned in secret ways to the farm. The Jewish farm workers were convinced that the hand of the murderers had also reached us and were very puzzled when they saw us return safe and sound. They told us that a group of armed Germans came a short time after we left, ambushed the Jews who fled the way we fled, and also shot and killed several of them. They hid wherever they could, but in fact, it was relatively quiet on the farm.

The mentioned *aktzya,* was the last *aktzya* to be held in the ghetto. After the *aktzya* the murderers realized that there were still a number of Jews who managed to survive in various ways. Therefore, they stood and declared that these Jews were allowed to move to a number of farms and live there as farm workers, but the town itself had to remain "free of Jews." The permission to move to the farm was given only to healthy young men who were able to work. The elderly were ordered to "report" to the town of Chortkov [Czortków]. But, they didn't arrive there. The farmers who transported them to Chortkov told us that the Gestapo's murderers stopped them on the way, removed the Jews from the wagons, and led them somewhere...

Panic began when the order about the concentration of the surviving Jews in the farms was given. Each of them wanted to secure himself a place in a village where he had friends among the Christian population. Thus, the last Jews left the town tired and hungry, infested with lice and ill with typhus, weary and feeble, and gathered in the same "trap," in the labor camps that the Gestapo prepared for them. The farms that were chosen for this purpose were: Roshanovka, Holovtshintza, Swidowa, Lisovitz, Kozia-Gora, Milovtza and others. The farm in Tłuste wasn't included in the list of places that Jews were permitted to live in. The Jewish laborers were allowed to be and work there only during the hours of the day. Swidowa was considered a "permanent place," meaning, that it was a legal labor camp. Since it existed before the last order was given, Jews from Tluste and refugees from other towns concentrated there. I remember how Moshe Ampel parted from me before he left the farm in Tluste and went to Swidowa. "Shlomo", he said, "I am afraid that we won't ever see each other again... it's a pity that you decide to stay here and not move to a more secure location." He nodded to me with his head and left the farm with tears in his eyes. And, indeed, we never saw each other again. The camp in Swidowa was the first to be surrounded early one morning by the Germans, and all the Jews who were there were shot and buried in a mass grave. Only one person survived, Yeshaya Ampel, who wasn't hit and pulled himself out of the pit...

Things ran on the farm in Tluste as before. Kenigsberg and I continued to stand "on guard" by the window and concealed a break in the fence with extreme caution. One night, when I sat by the window, I saw unusual movement in the Ukrainian police headquarters which was located in Zelig Roth's house. I heard the rattle of motorcycles from that direction. A short time later, we heard the sound of gunfire coming from the direction of Roshanovka, Holovtshintza, and Kozia-Gora. At the first light, we saw Jews who were hiding in the yard. They, like me, endangered themselves and didn't go to sleep in Kozia-Gora.

We saw that there was no possibility to escape from the farm because *aktzyot* were held in all the villages around us. Therefore we made an effort to hide, each to the best of his ability... Luckily, this time the murderers didn't arrive to this farm. Later, refugees who were able to escape from Holowczynce, passed by the farm, but they were afraid to enter and continued with their flight. It was a mistake and they paid for it with their lives.

The murders in the villages continued until the afternoon. Tzvi Kimmelman z"l, from Lashkivitz [Ułaszkowce], survived by a miracle in Roshanovka camp. He hid in the bushes near the administration building. From his hiding place, through the leaves, he was able to see to a certain extent what was happening in the camp. According to him, a number of supervisors participated in the *aktzya* in Roshanovka camp. They were headed by the Polish farm manager who made efforts to find where Kimmelman was hiding without knowing that he was hiding very close to his house...

At the end of the *aktzya,* the German oppressor, Brauner, who conducted the murder, passed next his hiding place and said to the camp's supervisors who had helped him: "Jews will no longer be here on the farm, for every Jew that you'll be able to find and bring to the police, you'll get a thousand Zlotys and one kilogram of sugar or salt..."

A large number of Jews found their death in the *aktzyot* which took place in the labor camps, and many more died in the fields during their escape. The murderers loaded the victims' clothes and belongings on wagons and transported them to the central warehouse that was located in Berish Hessing's house in Tłuste. The farm managers received an order from the Gestapo not to allow any Jews to remain in the camp and the whole area was declared "free of Jews." The farm in Tłuste wasn't included in the list of "labor camps" and the Jews who were staying there were saved by miracle from a certain death. However, in the morning of the day after the killing we were informed that we must leave the farm because the whole area had to remain "free of Jews."

We sit in the same hut and none of us can get a word out of his mouth. An oppressive silence reigns in the room. I glance at our son who sleeps peacefully and ponder in my heart: how good for you, my child, that you don't know what awaits us! My wife and others are crying slowly... Where will we go? To whom? Could we leave this place in time? And here, the door opens and Mr. Reicher, the refugee from Germany, enters. He suggests that a number of us should approach the "work manager" and ask him to let us stay on the farm until evening... We went with him even though we knew in advance what the answer would be. And indeed, we received the predicted answer: he can't help us and we must do what we think...

So, we sat in the same hut until noon and were careful not to go outside, so that the supervisors who walked outside wouldn't notice us. We decided to sit there until evening, and if in the meantime they'll not come to "take" us, we would disappear into the darkness even though we didn't know where...

At noon, a Pole who was one of the farm's clerks entered and announced that the Gestapo allowed all the Jews who had survived yesterday's *aktzya* to return to their previous places... We received the news with apathy because we knew the meaning of it very well. Again, they plotted to assemble all the escaping Jews in one location to ease their work of murder.

Nevertheless, the Jews returned without a choice, even those who had managed to live in the forests for quite a long period of time. The "*Banderovtzim*" wandered in the forests, and each Jew that fell into their hands was murdered with great cruelty and severe torture. At times, they dressed like "partisans" to find the hiding places of the Jews in the forests, and the camps in the villages and on the farms filled again. Jewish craftsmen started to arrive to our farm in Tłuste. The "work manager" transferred them from other camps because he needed their work. With them came Mendel Zumerman from Ułaszkowce, who was a baker by profession. Thanks to this Zumerman we received, secretly, a little bread because there was no control on the amount of flour that he received and the amount of bread that he returned. Sometimes, also the Polish storekeeper helped us a lot and allowed us to "visit" the potatoes in the warehouse.

As mentioned before, most of the Jews who had escaped to the forest returned without a choice and settled in the camps with the Gestapo's "permission." Occasionally, the Ukrainian police visited each camp to "exterminate" the sick, usually those who were ill with typhus. The sick were taken to the yard, to the garbage pile next to the stable or next to the cowshed, and were shot and killed there. Jews who were found walking outside the camp were taken to the cemetery in Tłuste and shot and killed there. Later, they didn't "bother" to lead a few Jews to the cemetery and killed them in the shed next to Zelig Roth's house. In this manner the eldest daughter of Berel Holenberg was also murdered. Each time we heard the sound of gunfire coming from that direction, we knew that we had to get ready because they would call us to come, take the body and bring it to the cemetery for burial. In this way, I had the opportunity to bury Moshe Feder who was murdered while trying to escape from the Ukrainian police. A detective who knew him chased him to the camp. He hid under the wood shed, but the detective shot two bullets in his head and killed him. The Ukrainian policeman, Starovski, who was known to take part in each Jewish mass murder, grabbed me and ordered me to bury the dead man on the lakeshore across from the camp. I buried him there with the help of his younger brother.

In the summer of 1943, the hope that we would be librated started to spark in us. Russian partisans were seen in the area. The "work manager" and the rest of the Germans from the farms near Tłuste quickly left the area in great panic. However, several days later they returned to their places. This time, the rioters "eliminated" the camp in Kamionka near Skalat. My brother-in-law,

Fishel Scharf, and other young men managed to escape and reach Kopyczyńce, and there they were murdered by the Ukrainian police. Moshe, the son of the miller, and his son came to our camp and from them we learned what had happened there.

In those days I received an order to leave for Roshanovka to repair the feeders in the cowsheds. Yona Schechter was given to me as a helper. It was clear that the journey there and back was dangerous. We weren't allowed to be outside the camp and the "piece of paper" that was signed by the farm office didn't have any value in this case. For that reason, we walked on side roads to hide from those who could see us. In Roshanovka we found a number of exhausted Jews who were infested with lice and many of them were sick. Winter was getting closer and it was cold outside and frigid in the early morning hours.

Once, when we were busy with our work, we saw a young man, one of the camp's inmates, beating a young woman who was barefoot and dressed in rags. She cried and shouted and he continued to beat her. I approached him and asked him: "Why, and for what, are you beating her instead of helping her?" And to that he answered: "She doesn't want to work! And secondly - who are you and what is your name?" I begged before the young man to let her go, after all, she is barefoot and must be hungry. But he continued to beat her. For a moment, I forgot my position and who I was talking to. I stood and "treated" the young man with "the gift of the hand," as hard as I could. He was stunned – the matter came to him as a surprise. He didn't say a word and left the area. When he left, he turned to me and grumbled: "Oh well."

A second young man, probably his friend, saw the whole scene from a distance. He came to me and said: "Shlomo, you have done wrong! Starovski might show up at any moment and the young man wouldn't hesitate to inform on you... and then, you already know.... I want to do you a favor – the matter will cost you 1000 Zlotys and I will take care of it... I was tempted and told him that I'm ready to bring all that I could get tomorrow because I have nothing for myself. And if "he" doesn't agree – he can do whatever he pleases. And indeed, this is the way it was. When I came back to camp I told my friends what happened and they collected 500 Zlotys for me and also a pair of wooden shoes for the barefooted girl. In addition to that, we brought with us a little bread, cut it into slices and divided it among the sick in the barracks.

Among the sick was also the wife of Meir Wachstein. She lay among the other patients and her son was next to her. I also gave them two slices of bread. The boy swallowed his slice very quickly, before his sick mother was able to eat her share. Then he turned to his mother, took a large size of her portion and put in his mouth... I turned my eyes from this sight and tears choked my throat. I never saw them again, and I don't know what happened to them in the end.

In general, the camp's inmates were in a terrible state: hunger, sickness and, last but not least - lice. It was another blow in addition to all the blows. They swarmed by the millions and there wasn't a vacant place from them. As hard as people worked to clean themselves from them, they couldn't get rid of them. Each time they returned and reappeared as if they were under the skin, and woe to the person who surrendered and gave up the constant struggle! The cowsheds were also full of lice, but people still hid there from the cold. Every once in a while, Starovski and his men conducted searches and took the sick and the lice-infested Jews to the garbage pile, to their last road... I know of only one case when one of his victims was able to foil his plot, Beni Peffer, who recovered from typhus and was about to be shot. He managed to take the gun from the murderer's hand and escaped. He lived for some time, until he was murdered by a Ukrainian on the day of liberation.

We finished our work at Roshanovka camp and returned to the camp in Tłuste. At the same time the Ukrainian police conducted a "campaign" to eliminate those who were with ill with typhus in the camp. Thus, those who couldn't or didn't have the time to hide were shot. In this way Bertsi Stupp was murdered during his escape, and in this way they murdered young Krasutski and his mother who was trying to protect him with her body. Sheintshe [Scheindel] Margulies was murdered as she lay in bed. Her daughter, who was lying next to her, hid under her mother's body and wasn't hurt. Later, she was removed from under her mother's body as she was completely covered with her blood. Binyamin Henger's young son and several other Jews were also murdered at the same time.

From time to time, Jews who hid in the forests or those who could no longer hide at the homes of Christians came to our camp. Maybe they began to fear their "hosts" or maybe they no longer had the means to pay them. At the same time a father and his daughter came to our camp from the village of Slowodka [Slobódka] near Tłuste. Patti [Vathje] met them as they were wandering, hungry, tired and very neglected, in the fields near Roshanovka. He called them to come to the camp and handed them to the Ukrainian police. With an aching heart we watched as the police took them. When we saw that they were being led in the direction of Roshanovka we felt better... but on the next day we found out that Starovski had ordered them to run and then he shot and killed them. These cases of murder in the fields weren't uncommon and they took place every day.

In that period there was an increase in the number of Jews who were murdered by gangs of "Banderovtzim" who searched for Jews who hid in the forests or in bunkers. At the same time, I received word that my mother was murdered in a gentile's yard, a place where she hid together with several other Jews. Sometime later, the gentile farm workers returned and told that us they saw a pit next to the forest and a number of bodies were seen under the cover of snow. They pointed out the exact location of the pit. The thought that maybe my mother's body was also there immediately bothered me. I didn't think for long and approached my friends with a request that they agree to accompany me to the pit to bury the bodies. Of all of them, only young Stupp agreed to go with me. We somehow reached the camp in Holowczynce, and there two additional friends, Spiegel and Hirsh Schporen, volunteered to go with us. I remember that, while I wandered around the barracks in search of volunteers, I came across people who were lying in a state of dying.

We set off in the direction of the forest as we sank in the snow and in the mud, and we couldn't find the place. We walked around for several hours until we saw a large group of birds circling in the air near the forest. And, indeed, it was the place... Several corpses were lying in one of the trenches that remained from the days of the First World War. They were found beneath snow where they were torn and half-eaten. I couldn't identify my mother z"l by her face because it was half-eaten. I identified her by one of her fingers which became bent during a surgery and remained bent all the days of her life.

The second body was that of a woman by the name of Kenigsberg from Zaleszczyki. Also, this body was mostly eaten and her dentures lay in her abdominal cavity. The third body was that of a young woman. I think she was a member of the Kleiner family from the village of Miskov [Myszków]. One of the arms was eaten from this body. We recognized two other bodies: Rishe Shapira and her father-in-law. In the last body we saw a sign that a bullet hit his neck. We found no signs of gunshot in the rest of the bodies, and who knows in what kind of torture they found their death.

We dug a grave in great haste and buried the bodies. My friends hurried to go back, but I wasn't able to move from the place. My friends dragged me away as my lips whispered: *"Yitgadal veyitkadash..."* I wanted to cry, but the tears didn't respond to me. We left the horrible mass grave that we just dug with our heads lowered. We returned to the camp as darkness fell. My friends welcomed me without saying a word but with a spark of happiness in their eyes that we returned unharmed...

To our great joy, the withdrawal of the Germans from the Russian front began. Transports of wagons harnessed to horses flowed continuously in the direction of Uścieczko and Zaleszczyki. Transports of Russians and Ukrainians who cooperated with the Germans were accompanied a number of elderly German gendarmes. A platoon of Vlasov's men passed by the village of Lisovitz [Lisowce] and slaughtered the Jews in the camp. They hung the son of Mender Mahler on a tree. A number of seriously wounded arrived to our camp, including Berel Hernes. The *"Banderovtzim"* also used the opportunity, not only to murder Jews, but also to steal German property. One day, a number of young workers, men and women, were taken out of our camp to work in a field near the village of Holowczynce. A number of *"Banderovtzim"* attacked them, removed the leather strap from the threshing machine and, as they left, they shot into the group of young people who stood together in one place full of fear and panic. A number of young people were hit, and my sister-in-law, Breintshi, was hit and fell dead on the spot. Also the local farmers didn't sit idle. In Holowczynce, the local farmers used the opportunity and massacred the Jews who were there. Several wounded arrived to us the day after the slaughter and also a number of people who escaped safe and sound.

Among those who returned from the Russian front was also a detachment of Hungarian Jews. When they learned that there were several Jewish survivors in our camp, they came and brought all they could: food, medicine, candles and clothes. One of them took off his shirt and gave it to one of the camp residents. They also brought a doctor who took care of the wounded. They were also worried about their future and looked for ways to escape. We told them in which forest they could hide and stay until the arrival of the Russian army. Most of them have done so. They fell captive by the Russians and were later released.

The men in our camp began to prepare hiding places for times of trouble. I also tried to prepare a "bunker" for myself. When I worked in the cellar at the home of the farm manager, I used the opportunity and broke a hole in the cellar's wall. But I wasn't successful. After I dug for a meter-wide, I came across a second wall and was forced to stop. There were those who believed that during the German retreat the farmers would change their ways and give shelter to their Jewish friends for a short period of time, until liberation. Beni Pfeffer came to me and suggested that I should go with him to a "good-hearted" gentile who would agree to hide us. I agreed and went to inform my wife. Fortunately, my wife opposed the idea and we didn't go with him. Beni Pfeffer went and took his brother-in-law, Motel Goldschmidt, with him – and they didn't return. As it was told later, the "good-hearted" gentile told a Ukrainian policeman about their arrival. He came and shot them to death. In this manner the gentile assured himself that he wouldn't have to return the assets that Pfeffer entrusted in his hands.

This event actually happened on the day of liberation. At noon, several Ukrainian policemen arrived to the camp. They arrived in a wagon, on their escape from the approaching Russians. When they saw the Jews they demanded "vodka" from them, and even mentioned the amount that each of the barracks had to give them. I entered the hut and, without thinking much, we slipped away through the window and escaped in the direction of the sand hill of Yakend [Hikand]. There, we sat on the ground and burrowed into the sand. Light snow started to fall at night and we were happy with the natural "cover" given to us.

Suddenly we heard cannon shots, I got up and saw a tank standing on the road leading to Chortkov and shooting into town... I stood up and started to run to town as if I wasn't using my own strength... My wife wanted to stop me and called me with the last of her strength, but I didn't listen to her... I went down to the town and there I found a tank, a Russian tank with Russian soldiers, and the camp residents standing around the tank kissing it, kissing the cold steel... and the Russians were standing and laughing out of kindness. I approached one of the Russian soldiers, hugged him with all my strength and kissed him as tears flowed from my eyes... and the soldier wiped his face as he comforted me – "It's nothing, please calm down..."

I turned my head towards the camp and here was Yosef Frades running with his daughter to the Polish Church (his only son was killed by a Gestapo officer next to the bridge leading to the camp, when a gentile woman pointed out that he was a Jew). At that moment, German bombers appeared and everything turned dark around... I started to run towards the camp, through Meir Sterling's house which stood open without doors and windows, and jumped into a bunker that I found in one of the rooms. But I immediately got out of there. I was afraid that if the house would collapse no one would know the place of my burial... I left for the yard and found "shelter" in a wooden outhouse. But not long after, the structure collapsed and I felt kind of a burn on my left shoulder. I don't remember how long I lay under the collapsed building, but when I left the sky was brighter and the noise fell slightly silent. I started to run towards the camp, through the camp's yard to find my family. The camp was burning, all the barracks were burning, and also our shed was burning. Dead and wounded lay around and screams and moans were heard from all directions... I continue to run through the water, I don't want to run on the road because one of the "birds of prey" is still circling in the air... I reach the hut, which was once the residence of one of the farm workers, and to my surprise I find my family, Shmuel Fiderer, and a few others as they lie flat on the floor.

I look out the window and see that the planes are bombing the "village of Tłuste" and I feel in my soul a sense of relief: please let them taste the flavor a little, please let them suffer a little...

The bombing ended and it was quiet all around. I tore my dirty shirt and with my wife's help I bandaged my wounded arm. Meanwhile, dusk fell and we had to find a place to sleep as free people... We left for the road and met other survivors, some of them were whole and some were wounded who could still walk. We started to look for a more or less safe place to sleep, and here we were again near the cemetery... the gentile wanted to take us to his place, but he advised us that all of us should not sleep in one location because it is not "healthy" to appear in a large group... I took with me a group of people and together we went, in total darkness, in the direction of town. There, we entered the cellar in the home of Hersh Wolf Shechner and settled there for the night. There was a woman with us who had lost one of her arms in the bombing. She moaned all night, but she tried to suppress her moans so that her voice wouldn't be heard out of the cellar.

In the morning we went back to the camp and found a number of people who were looking for their missing relatives. They also didn't find them among the dead because they were burnt inside the barracks and not a trace was left of them. We found part of a body, and the sons of Shaul Drohobitzer [Drohobyczer] determined that it was the body of their father Shaul z"l. We helped them to lift their sister Rachel, who was critically wounded, but she passed away during the treatment. With the help of the Russians, and with the help of Dr. Karol Roth, we started to move the seriously injured to the hospital in Chortkov. After that we started to bury the dead.

Each and every one of the survivors looked for a place to settle in, some in a half-destroyed Jewish house and some in one of the farm buildings which remained standing. I "settled" at the home of Mendel Hoisfeld together with the homeowner who survived with his family. When the front was breached again by the Germans, Mendel Hoisfeld wanted to take me and my family to "his" gentile who had hid them all the time in the village, I didn't accept his offer and joined the retreating Russians. Mendel and his family, and several of his relatives (Leib Stein's young daughter, her daughter and a cousin named Kupperman) left to hide with the gentile. They went and never returned because this time "his" gentile didn't let them get away, or maybe it was the work of "his helpers" from among the people in the village. Who is wise and informed?

The matter of my escape with the Russians is a story in itself and has no connection to my memories about the "life" in the labor camp.

———

[Pages 137-142]

Tłuste and in Roshanovka

by Leah Drohobitzer

Translated by Sara Mages

In 1939, the Second World War already started to show its signs in our town. Poland was divided between Russia and Germany: its northern section, with half of the city of Warsaw, was captured by the Germans, but its southern section, and in it Eastern Galicia, was under the rule of Soviet Russia. Many refugees from the German-occupied territory came to our area and brought with them stories of horror and atrocities. These stories sounded horrible and unreal to such an extent, that we thought that they were the product of peoples' imagination, and no one believed in them.

In 1941, the Germans captured Galicia and the persecution of Jews began in this part of Poland. Some of the town's residents tried to escape with the retreating Russians, but many were forced to return because the roads were blocked by the Russian army and its vehicles. Our family, the Drohobitzer [Drohobyczer] family, was a big extended family with many sons and daughters, brides and bridegrooms, who were firmly established in the town, and it was difficult for them to leave the family and run. In addition, none of us estimated the enormity of the horror and the danger that was facing us. Only the eldest son and the second son, Yisrael and Avraham, tried to escape for their lives, but they weren't able to break through and were forced to return to the town.

My brother, Yisrael, who was married and father to a boy, lived with his family in the Post Office Street, in the building where the courthouse was located in before the war. That building was our property and a place of residence was allocated to my brother after his marriage. After the failed escape plan, my brother left his apartment and came to live in our house on Market Street. My second brother, Leib, who lived with his family at the home of his father-in-law in the small town of Mielnica, also came to Tłuste at the outbreak of the war and lived in a rented apartment at the house of one of our relatives. The third brother, Moshe, lived in Chortkov [Czortków] with his father-in-law. Four more children remained at home: Yitschak, Chana,

Avraham and me. Our brother, Yisrael, joined us with his family. My father's sister and her three children lived in our home, and also two refugee families from Hungary and Romania. All of us lived in a three-bedroom apartment. In addition, we weren't allowed to leave our front door, and those who disobeyed the order were likely to be shot.

*

With the arrival of the Germans, a Ukrainian "militia" was organized and, ever since, our lives were in their hands. The members of the militia were greedy and hungry for robbery and murder. Every once in a while, they generated riots in the town and in nearby villages. Every day they brought to town for burial the victims of their acts. Jews with broken heads, amputated hands or legs, or amputated tongues. The Ukrainian dignitaries tried to restrain the fury of the mob a little, but their impact was minimal. The Jews in town tried to defend themselves. At night, a number of families gathered together in one apartment, armed with any kind of "weapons": axes, shovels, sticks and such. At night, we sometimes heard the sound of gunfire from different corners of the town, and they increased the fear in the heart and prevented any possibility of rest.

Meanwhile, a "Judenrat" (Jewish council) was organized in the town, and became the mediator between the German authorities, the Ukrainian "militia" and the Jewish residents. It was a life or death mediation because, quite often, the "Judenrat" was ordered to hand over "ransom" money or valuables to the Germans or to the militia. In such cases, members of the Judenrat walked from door to door and quite often took, with blows and curses, the last item that the homeowner was able to exchange for a loaf of bread or a glass of milk for their babies, who were crying from hunger. The hunger in town increased from day to day because the farmers weren't allowed to sell or give any food items to the Jewish residents. In exchange for a loaf of bread or a cup of grits, I secretly knitted articles of clothing for Ukrainians who used the cotton thread that they robbed from the stock that the Russians left during their retreat.

From time to time, members of the Ukrainian militia "conducted inspection" at the Jewish homes and at the same time murdered them with the butt of their guns. During one of these visits they stood my little brother against the wall and, as a joke and a game, aimed their guns at him, and his face turned white as chalk. I dropped to their feet and pleaded before them to save his life. I asked them to take my life instead of his – and that softened their hearts. Usually, the Ukrainians didn't miss an opportunity to quench their thirst for Jewish blood, and did their work under the slogan: "to liberate Ukraine from the Jews." The song "we will shoot and slaughter until we expel them" never left their lips. Even the "good non-Jewish neighbors" followed every movement that the rioters made, and their eyes expressed happiness to our demise.

The campaign of pogroms and torture in our area started with a unique incident. In the nearby town of Chortkov, the Ukrainians opened the prison after the withdrawal of the Russians and found the bodies of many political prisoners. Most of them were Ukrainian nationalists who were arrested by the Russians for their sin of criticizing the Communist regime. It was noticeable that many of the prisoners had died after a difficult torture, and parts of their bodies were scattered in the prison cells. Since the Jews were known as supporters of the Communist regime, the torture campaign against the Jews began. A curfew was declared in the town and any person who left his front door bore responsibility. They enlisted men to bury the dead, and later, each one of them was beaten to death and buried together with the murdered. In this manner the first phase of the Jewish annihilation began in our area, and it was fully executed by the Ukrainian mobs.

The second phase was executed by the Germans, in a typical German order and according to a pre-arranged system. The declared direction was to "purify" the town from the sick and the old, and those who were unable to work. Each person who was captured – was shot immediately on the spot.

One day, a notice was published that all men who were fit to work would be sent to labor camps, where their lives would be protected. Actually, these "labor camps" were sort of concentration camps before the death march. However, since there wasn't any contact between those who were sent to the camps and their family members, nobody knew the nature of these camps. There were a number of sons in our family and it was difficult to decide which of them would be the "victim," who would report for transport to a labor camp. After a lot of consideration, the fate fell on my brother, Yitzchak, who wasn't married. There was a great cry in the town and many sons separated from their families without knowing their destiny. But, there were those who went willingly, with the hope that their lives would be protected and secured.

We didn't get any reports from the sons, and we only found out about their bitter fate from rumors that filtered in. Meanwhile, those who remained started to build an emergency shelter in case of an "aktzya." Under the cover of darkness, the men dug a pit under the house where it was possible to hide in time of need. They removed the earth and scattered it so the non-Jewish neighbors wouldn't notice it. At the same time, the women and children guarded the area against the possibility that a stranger would approach the house. A pit was also dug in our house and my father invested a lot of work, a lot of thought and great ingenuity. The pit opening was camouflaged with great skill, and even the sharpest eye wasn't able to notice it. In one of the "aktzyot," the Germans searched and searched, but they weren't able to find it. He has done this work after he recovered from typhus fever.

By the way, we were almost caught in that "aktzya." The lack of air caused my father to cough. The Germans intensified their search and started to pull the floor boards. But, a miracle happened. After they pulled a floor board in the corner, they found a treasure. They stopped their search and left. Fresh air entered through the crack in the floor and we could all breathe.

My mother, Rachel, was no longer alive in those days. She died a year after the outbreak of the war. She was a righteous woman and wasn't able to see the sufferings of others. Once, she gave her bed to others and slept on the cold floor during a difficult winter. Later, she fell ill with pneumonia and didn't recover from her illness. During her illness she kept on saying: "If I could only see my son Yitzchak who was sent to a labor camp one more time it would be easier for me to die." Her wish was granted. After many pleadings, great risks and bribes, we were able to bring her son back to her. Our food ration consisted of bread that we baked on our own. The flour, which I received as payment for the clothes that I knitted for gentile neighbors, was ground in a meat grinder. The hunger was so strong at home that, at times, father took one his sons' bread ration. Ultimately, he became swollen and was infected with a difficult intestinal disease. It was impossible to take care of him and he almost died. One day, he didn't show any signs of life so my brother Yitzchak and I tried to give him vinegar to drink. My brother opened his mouth, I poured the liquid into his mouth, and we brought him back to life. In this manner we continued with our miserable life. During the day, we searched for food to eat and at night we sought refuge in holes and cracks so the enemy's cruel hand wouldn't reach us.

On Rosh Hashanah, a year after the death of my mother z"l, rumors arrived about an upcoming "aktzya." On that day, I went with my sister Chana to visit our brother Leib. His apartment was in the town center and one of the windows overlooked the cemetery. I remember his last words in which he tried to prepare us mentally for the future: "Our mother isn't away from us, I look at her every day and I'm sure that we'll reunite soon." He was peaceful and accepted his verdict without anger. He used to say: "I imagine in my mind that I'm seventy - and after all - at seventy you die..." When there were frequent reports on the upcoming "aktzya," everyone began to flee for their lives, like birds fleeing before the arrival of a storm. Everyone searched for a place to hide, some in the fields out of town, and some with one of their gentile acquaintances in exchange for a gift of money or valuables. Our brother Leib suddenly came and asked to take Avraham, who was the joy of his parents, to his well-fortified and secure hideout. However, before he had the time to convince us to let Avraham go with him, we found out that the "aktzya" already started and entire families had left their homes and were hiding in holes and cracks. Leib returned immediately to his house to hide in his hiding place together with his family. We also started with the preparations: we brought Yisrael's wife, Chaya, and her baby to a gentile who lived out of town in exchange for a payment, and the rest of the family and the families who lived in our house entered the bunker which was prepared in advance in our house. Yitzchak locked the house from the outside to give the impression that we had left it, and hid in the neighbor's dog house.

A short time later, the son of one of the gentile neighbors discovered Yitzchak and handed him over to the Germans. On his way to the concentration area, he saw how they were leading Chaya, Yisrael's wife, together with her son Yosele. She begged before the policemen and her baby was crying as if he felt that his end was near. At the concentration area, he found out that our brother Leib and his family were led to their last road. At that moment he decided to try to stay alive at all costs. He got up and walked to one of the German guards and pretended that he was a member of the "Judenrat," who was helping the "militia" to bring Jews to the concentration area, and he had to go to fulfill his duty. Thus, he was able to leave the concentration area and reach our hiding place. He came in a state of fainting and we weren't able to get anything out of him. Only in the evening, after the "aktzya," we learned that Leib and his family and Yisrael's wife and her baby were sent to the death camp in Auschwitz. The boy, Yosele, was bright and beautiful, and even though he was only a few months old, he became silent when he was told: "the Germans are coming." Yisrael and his five-year-old daughter, Yehudit, stayed with us and ever since I was like a sister and mother to her. The girl became attached to me and we didn't separate from each other, even in the most difficult situations. I was already twenty-five years old, but the feeling of orphanhood was shared by both of us.

After the "aktzya" our life returned to its usual "course." Hunger continued to bother us and, from the lack of food, my brother, Avraham, the youngest child in the family, became ill with tuberculosis. We had some medicine left from the time that my mother was sick and I tried to cure him with it. When the "militia" came to search for a piece of meat, or a drop of milk which the Jews were forbidden to use, he gathered his energy and walked as if he was healthy, because the sick were sent to their death. Obtaining food was done under the threat of death. A woman went out to search for a drop of milk for her children – and was shot on the doorstep. Another woman was caught a short distance from her house – and she also found her death. In this way the extermination campaign was conducted in various methods.

Before the "perfect" and fastest way of delivery to the death camps was found, the Germans gathered their victims at the cemeteries and ordered them to dig their own graves. Those who volunteered to dig the graves were promised a "grace," to be first in line. In this way their sufferings would be shortened because they would not see the death of their family members. Those sentenced to death were forced to undress and stand in line. A plank was placed over the grave and five people were placed on it. After they were shot and fell into the pit, five others went up to the killing place. There were those who stood bravely before death, others cried or prayed. They were those who miraculously obtained a few drops of poison and took their lives before the hand of the Germans got them.

In most cases the Germans abused their victims and enjoyed the sight of the execution. They threw children into the pit alive to save bullets. There were many cases when adults have fallen into the pit when they were still alive. Not once I mentioned my mother whose ancestral merit stood for her and she didn't see any of this. She was awarded to die a natural death and was brought to a Jewish grave. Indeed, she also suffered a lot. I remember that evening when the Germans attacked us, threatened us with their drawn guns and demanded our money. Mother stood before them with her arms spread, as if she was trying to protect us and hide us. She always put herself in danger to protect others, and it seemed that she also tried to help us after her death. Once, a local peasant woman saw her in a dream. She asked her to bring food to her family who were hungry for bread. The peasant woman, who believed in the dream, fulfilled her wish and brought us food every once in a while.

Winter arrived. It was a very difficult winter and we remained without clothes and shoes. That winter, the "Judenrat" failed to supply what was imposed on it by the Germans, and our brother, Yisrael, paid for it with his life. He was sent from the "Judenrat" to the police station on the excuse that he had to bring with him a notebook, and there they stood him against the wall and shot him. The policemen wanted to replace him with another brother, but Yisrael insisted that they should kill him not his brother. A messenger was sent from the police station to bring Yitzchak, but when he arrived, they already carried Yisrael, as blood was dripping from his head. Such were things. And what was left to do in such a situation? Also the crying was meager in comparison to the horrors!

The calamities occurred in a particular order. An order had been issued that all the Jews who remained in town had to move to one quarter, to the street where the movie theater "Gwiazda" (The Star) was located. The aim was to concentrate all the survivors in order to facilitate the work of extermination. The surviving members of our family moved to the home of our cousin, Leitsi Teiber, together with a number of other families. Our brother, Moshe, joined us there. He had escaped on foot from the labor camp in Tarnopol and arrived to Tłuste. In the first days of the war he lived with his wife's parents in Chortkov. His wife and children were sent to Auschwitz and he was taken to the labor camp in Tarnopol. Moshe was a talented man and excelled in the game of chess, so he befriended the German camp commander. Once, out of "friendship," the commander offered to shoot him to death to shorten his sufferings. Moshe rejected his "kind" offer and decided to escape from the camp. He was fair-haired and did not look like a Jew. Thus, he was able to reach us.

Even before we could nourish our eyes with him, the ghetto was surrounded and a shower of gunfire rained down on us. Each of us escaped to a place where his legs carried him. Moshe escaped to the field, my younger sister Chana, my niece Yehudit and I entered an open pit. My father, together with my brother Yitzchak, hid in our neighbor's shelter. Inside the pit we found another family who was hiding there. We were all in fear, because the pit was known to the Germans as a refuge for Jews. We went down there with no choice, just to delude ourselves that we are somewhat protected. And indeed, a short time later a German arrived accompanied by members of the militia, our former neighbors. They ordered us to get out as their guns were pointed at us. For a moment a thought crossed my mind. Maybe it's better to be killed in the pit and be buried in there than getting out of it. I pulled my head out of the pit so the bullet would hit me in the temple and save me from unnecessary torture. My sister and my niece hid behind me. And here, our cousin, Perl, jumped out of the pit (she was there together with her daughters), knelt before our neighbor, the militia man, and offered him a ransom for our lives: a gold watch, a piece of fabric and fifteen dollars. The Ukrainian accepted her offer, took the ransom, allowed us to climb on the roof and even promised to protect us.

All that night we heard the sound of gunfire and the shouts of the victims. Suddenly, we heard a light noise from the edge of the roof. Those who were hiding inside the shelter heard us talking and called us to come down to them. The lack of air the bunker was unbearable, but we stayed there until dawn. The Germans left the town in the morning, and the militia, together with the Judenrat, collected the bodies of the victims for burial. My father went to look among the bodies for Moshe, who had disappeared, but he was only able to find his clothes and several pictures of his family. He wasn't able to find his body. Moshe wanted so much to live! Before the "aktzya" he pleaded before Yitzchak to go to the village with him and hide with one of the farmers because he had a few items of value in his pocket to pay him. Maybe, he had the feeling that he might be one of the first victims if he continued to stay in town.

After the "aktzya," the Germans announced that the town was free of Jews and we were ordered to move to a labor camp in the nearby village of Roshanovka [Różanówka]. While we were debating if we should respond to the order and move to Roshanovka, a farmer from the village of Borakovka [Burakówka], who was one of our acquaintances, came and offered to hide us if we transferred what was left of our property to his hands. The farmer was also the owner of a flour mill and supplied us with flour in times of emergency. The farmer's son was a member of the Ukrainian nationalist organization and had contacts with the militia. The place looked safe enough to us, but it wasn't advisable for all of us to go there together. In many cases, Ukrainians handed over Jews who were hiding in their homes to the hands of the police after they got their valuables. For that reason, it was safer to be in the labor camp. Therefore, we decided to separate into two groups: my brother Avraham, my sister Chana and my niece Yehudit would go together with our father to the labor camp, and my brother Yitzchak and I would go to the farmer. It was decided that in case of danger the rest of the family would come to hide at the farmer's house.

The labor camp in Roshanovka was built on the grounds of an agricultural farm, and the farm manager was a Jew who lived as a Christian with forged papers. The people in the camp were engaged in agricultural work in the fields. Yitzchak and I sat in the farmer's attic wondering about the fate of our family members in the labor camp and about our own fate. At times, people from the camp came to us under the cover of darkness, dragging their legs from hunger and looking like shadows. Through the hatch in the attic I was able to see nature in all its glory and blooming trees, but there was wilderness in my heart. A nursery school was in front of the house, and from my hiding place I was able to see the joy in the children's eyes. I heard them singing and thought in my heart: G-d Almighty! are they better than us that you favored them! Sometimes, they warned us when the Germans arrived in the village, and we were forced to jump to the garden and hide among the bushes.

Meanwhile, rumors started to arrive that the Germans were defeated in Stalingrad, and Russian partisans who had been seen in our area started to organize fighter groups against the Germans. From time to time, Avraham came to sit with us in the hideout, but he wasn't able to cope with the boredom and he returned to the camp with Yitzchak. One of the reasons for that was the fact that the location of our hiding place became known and we were forced to leave, and I was the only one who remained there. Avraham prepared a hiding place for me on the roof inside a pile of straw. For a long time I didn't receive any sign of life from the camp, so I asked the farmer's wife to find out what had happened to my family in Roshanovka camp. Through her I received a note that we might be liberated soon, and that Avraham was going to join a partisan squadron. Later, it became clear that it was a plot done by Ukrainian nationalists. They spread a rumor that it was possible to join the partisans in order to discover who among the Jews wanted to join them. The Jews didn't realize that it was a bluff, and when many among them volunteered – the Germans surrounded the camp and held a massacre. The matter took place at the height of the summer, the corn was ripe and stood tall, and many escaped from the camp and hid there. The Germans hunted the escapees. At first they found my little niece, Dushka (Yehudit) and then they found Avraham. Avraham tried to escape but the little one called him with a voice full of fear and he returned. Both were led to a pit, which was dug at the center of the farm, and the bodies of the dead were thrown into it. The gentiles, who witnessed the act of murderer, told me that Dushka asked to die first because she was no longer able to cope with the torture.

On the same night, I dreamt that I was descending into a dark grave and a snake was twisting tightly around my body. I woke up screaming, full of fear and horror. The following night, Yitzchak and Chana came, and it looked strange to me that they weren't talking about Yehudit and Avraham. When I asked for the reason, they lied to me and told me that both of them were hiding with a farmer. But after they broke into tears I discovered the whole truth. I wanted to take my own life, I detested my life and I was ready to give myself to the police. Yitzchak told me that our father survived, but gave himself to the police and asked them to kill him. We thought that everyone was murdered and we were the only survivors. Then, we found out that our father was taken in by a gentile woman who worked for us before the war. He fainted on the way to the police station and was lying in the mud. The peasant woman found him in this state and brought him to her house. Since then, he remained on her farm and secretly helped her with the farm work so the neighbors wouldn't notice him. The surviving Jews returned to the camp. The supervisor collected all of them with the claim that he needed laborers. Thus, the survivors found a home and a shelter for a few more days.

The camp residents lived in a long barrack, a stove stood in the center and bundles of straw lined the walls and served as beds. There was no water in the place, the straw swarmed with lice, and the filth and dirt became unbearable. The parasites killed many and the dying shouted in their last moments. When someone reached this stage, the people in the camp used to say: he's already watching the stars. The situation worsened with the arrival of winter. People were left naked and had nothing to cover themselves with. The chill penetrated the bones and froze the blood. Many became ill with typhus, and the hallucinations of those who were burning with fever became part of the nightly way of life in the barrack.

The healthy went to work on the farm every morning. Because of the emergency situation there wasn't enough time to thresh the wheat in the summer, and it was necessary to do the work in the winter. In the morning, people had to break their way through the snow which was about a meter deep. The work was done with primitive tools and everyone was exhausted. At times, people fainted during their work, and when it happened, the supervisor lashed them with his whip and brought them back to work. The threshing work was difficult and the barns were covered with thick snow. The sheaves froze and stuck to each other and it was difficult to separate them and feed them into the machine at the required speed. The supervisor used his whip and lashed those who had fallen behind.

Yitzchak also returned to the camp. My sister Chana and I stayed with the farmer in Borakovka and hid in his cellar. The cellar was dark and not a single ray of light entered it. There were a lot of mice there and they jumped on our heads as if we were dead. The air in the cellar was suffocating and smelt bad because we couldn't go outside to use the bathroom. Our existence on the farm was kept secret and we lived in fear all the time. Not once I wanted to end my life, but Chana begged me not to leave her alone. From time to time, the woman of the house came to us and told us horror stories, such as the story about a Polish farmer who hid Jews in exchange of a few kilograms of gold. After he received his payment he killed them. Maybe she also wanted to prepare us for a similar end. Since I suspected her I tried to influence her by contacting her religious feelings and reminded her that G-d rewards each person according to his deeds.

One day, the cellar door opened and a strange man came in and called us to follow him. Chana turned pale, fell to his feet and begged him to let her live.

We were sure that our last hour had arrived. The man calmed us down and told us that in the past he worked in our house. Our father and our brother, Yitzchak, were staying at his house, and he now came to take us and save us. He came from the village of Anilovka [Anielówka], and he was the son of the woman who took my father to her house. Later, Yitzchak arrived there and he was the one who sent him to get us. His cart stood outside of the village and, in order to reach it, we were forced to crawl on our knees through the fields so the neighbors wouldn't see us. From sitting for such a long time, our legs were almost paralyzed and we had difficulties standing on them.

How happy we were when we met again with our father and Yitzchak after we had lost hope that we would see them again. This farmer was willing to let us stay with him until the end of the harvest season. He was the head of the village and no one dared to open his mouth against him. Many in the village knew my father because they worked for him during the "good days" and remembered his good attitude towards them. Despite that, we nearly got caught by the police a number of times. Every day we heard about Jews who got caught in their hideout by the police and were shot on the spot. In the end, the police discovered that we were hiding in the village and we were forced to leave. Father and Yitzchak went directly to the camp and I stayed in the village with Chana. My sister had light hair and it was difficult to see in her face that she was Jewish. Once, the gentile woman came running and shouting at us: leave immediately, the Germans conducting a search, I don't want to die because of you. But it was too late to hide and a few meters from us a young Jewish man was discovered and shot. Chana jumped and climbed on the roof and I jumped after her. The gentile woman was nearly paralyzed from fear that they would find us in her house, but a miracle happened and the searchers didn't come to that house.

After a short period of living in fear, Chana also went to the camp and I was left alone. Once, I sneaked into the cowshed to spend the night there. Suddenly the door opened and a lamp blinded my eyes. I sat and waited for my sentence. The gentile left to consult with his friend and I followed him. It was better for me to be killed in the yard than be raped in the cowshed. I knelt down and pretended that I was an orphan girl who shepherded the farmer's cattle, but they didn't pay attention to my words because they knew who I was. They didn't have firearms with them but they beat me up until I fainted, and then left.

After recovering I also went to the camp. I was swollen, my bones were broken from the beating I received and all my limbs hurt. It was cold outside and the road was covered with snow. In this manner, I arrived to the camp in Roshanovka. It was difficult to get used to the special way of life in the camp, to the filth, hunger and all the rest. I suffered a lot until I "acclimated," until I learnt to purify my body, to steal white beets to revitalize my soul and be like all the inmates. In the camp were also "classes" of people with special privileges who slept in the manager's home – a brick house called "Zonzovka." The manager, a gentile with enormous dimensions, selected the most beautiful young women to satisfy his lust, and in exchange let them sleep at his home (fortunately, I wasn't gifted with beauty and remained in the barrack). The manager's assistants, from among the survivors of the "Judenrat," were also allowed to sleep in his home thanks to the money that they robbed from the unfortunate. Many of the camp's inmates slept in the cowshed, because it was warmer there and it was also possible to pull out a few grains of wheat from the animals' food ration.

Chana contracted typhus. Every day I forced her to go out to work so she wouldn't be a victim to the cruel decree of killing the sick. I had nothing to help her with. At night, I wrapped my arms around her to warm her up, and gave her white beet juice to drink. I was desperate and nothing looked right to me. And then, a rumor reached our ears that the militia was coming to visit the camp. On the same night, all the people from the hut escaped to the fields and I stayed with Chana to protect her. I was forced to calm her down and tell her that everyone went to sleep in the cowshed since it was warmer there. However, the visit wasn't held on that night but on another day. All the people in the barrack escaped for their lives, and I was the only one left. I was ready to end my life and end of all the sufferings. A woman from Horodenka, who didn't have sufficient time to escape, was shot next to me. I was forced to carry her out while her body was still warm. They didn't touch me, maybe they realized that I was ready to give up my life, therefore, they left me to continue to live in pain and agony.

The hour of fury passed and life continued as usual in the camp. Pesya Benimins was dying in a corner, I rubbed her body with snow but the dirt sucked her last drop of blood. I also gave the same service to her daughter Salya.

One night, while the camp's inmates slept, the farm's gentiles who guarded the camp set fire to our barrack. Their scheme was probably to blame us for insurrection or acts of sabotage, or maybe they just wanted to burn us with all the filth and dirt. As fate would have it, I woke up in time. I immediately alerted all the people in the barrack, who were sound asleep, and we began to extinguish the fire. The matter took place in the winter and a lot of snow was available for us to extinguish the fire. There were those who saw the burning of the barrack as the end for any hope and the loss of the last escape. I saw it as a sign from the heavens that the end of our sufferings had arrived. I had a feeling that something was going to change for the best, and the light of the fire would light up the darkness of our lives.

At the same time, the echoes of canon fire started to reach our ears and we understood that the Russians were advancing and getting closer in our direction. The Jewish inmates of Roshanovka camp scattered in every direction. A few hid in caves and others went to their gentile acquaintances. The surviving members of our family, my father, Yitschak, Chana and I, moved to the labor camp near Tłuste, around two kilometers from Roshanovka. The work manager, Patti [Vathje], was married to a Jewish woman who hid her origin. A German "Wehrmacht" military unit was also stationed in that camp. All the escapees from the other camps in the area arrived to that camp and lived there in horrible congestion, crowded and stressed.

One day we were told that the Russians were advancing and were a few kilometers away from the town. And indeed, we already heard the sound of cannon fire. The militia started to run wild and we got scared and panicked. We were sure that the Germans, together with the militia, would finish us before their retreat. Thus, we experienced two hours of tension and anticipation. The gunfire became stronger and closer, and the windows in the barrack shattered.

Two hours later the first sign arrived – the Russian vanguard. We burst out and just extended our arms not knowing what to say. We stood, still consumed by sadness that the dead weren't able to see the downfall of the Germans. Together with that, we had no desire to continue and live in such emptiness.

We returned to the camp and our first thought was: How to get a loaf of bread? Father suggested that he go together with Chana to one of the neighbors, to Hanyoshka, to ask for a loaf of bread. Chana was pleasant and was accepted by all our gentile neighbors and we assumed that they would not refuse her request. We didn't realize that the war was not over yet and bitter surprises were still waiting for us.

Yitzchak moved away from us because he ran to search for his fiancée, and left us in the camp. As we were standing and debating which one of us would go with father, my sister or me, German planes appeared and started to bomb the camp. I felt kind of a light rubbing and fell unconscious. When I recovered, I found myself lying under my father's body. The barrack was destroyed and buried underneath it and one of its sides went up in flames. First of all, I tried to get out from under my father's body and check his condition. I shook his body, but he was lifeless. Shrapnel hit his abdomen and his intestines spilled out. He saved me from death with his body. I was only wounded in several places. The air battle between the Germans and the Russians continued. Under a shower of bullets and fire I ran to search for Chana, calling her name. Suddenly, a horrible sight appeared before my eyes: torn bleeding shreds of human flesh. Among all these I found my sister. I shouted with all my strength: Chana! Chana! Her eyes opened for a moment, and she was still able to say the word "Help!" and closed her eyes. I pulled her out of the pile of debris with the hope that she was still alive. I didn't realize that I had touched Tuntsia Fasler's injured shoulder. She only said: "Don't hurt me" and immediately died. No one was around me, and there was only destruction and death around. With my last strength I pulled Chana to the nearest cellar. Yosef Schechter, a family friend, appeared from his hiding place and helped me.

In the cellar I found several people, including my brother Yitzchak. I started to take care of Chana's injuries. I ripped her shirt and rubbed her and she pulled my hair from pain. I saw in it a sign of life and there was no end to my happiness. I didn't realize that the main injury was on her back. We transferred her to the house that was vacated by the Germans' advance unit. All the wounded were concentrated there. She showed signs of life all that night, but at dawn the wound opened and blood gushed out of it. I shouted: Help me! The Russian army passed through the town, and we weren't able to find a doctor. Yitzchak took a chance and brought a Ukrainian doctor. The doctor gave her an injection and, to this day, the thought that maybe the injection was a lethal injection is still torturing me.

The house was full of dead and wounded, and the shouts reached the center of the heavens. Bertsi [Berl] Glick was sitting next to me taking care of a two-year-old boy, who was a member of his family, and his wife was lying dead next to him. Many of the dead were burnt and all of them were buried in a mass grave. We saw the suffering and the death of our beloved relatives in the last moments before the arrival of the liberation that we had longed for.

[Pages 142-146]

How I was saved from extermination

by A. Goldhaber

Translated by Sara Mages

When the war between Germany and Russia erupted on 21 June 1941, the Russians enlisted all the young people to the army. I was able to avoid the draft since no one was able to replace me at work. Immediately after the Russian army retreat, on 6 July 1941, Ukrainians started to attack the Jews who lived in the villages, and thousands of Jews were murdered and executed in different ways. In Swydova [Swidowa], a village near Tłuste, the Jews were murdered and their bodies were torn to shreds, and to this day no one knows where their bones were buried. In Ułaszkowce, fifteen Jews were found drowned in the Seret River and not a single Jew remained alive in the surrounding villages. Also, many young Jewish men who escaped from the Soviet army were murdered. The killer's hand reached them on their way home. There was also unrest in Tłuste. For four days nobody dared to leave his front door, and everyone hid in holes and cracks. Only thanks to the interference of the local priest everything passed in peace. And so we lived our lives in fear until August 1941.

On 3 August 1941, the police brought to town a large number of Hungarian Jews who were exiled from their homes and their towns. A terrible crowding situation was created in town – fifteen to twenty people were forced to live in a small room. Also, food items became more expensive, and the Christians did not want to sell us anything since the police also bothered them. But, despite all of that, the situation was not extremely bad since the Germans were not in town yet, and it was possible to get along with the Hungarian army.

On 1 September 1941, notices were posted in the town legalizing the Nuremberg laws in our place. And so were the words of the notice: each Jew must wear on his right arm a white armband with a blue "Star of David," Jews are not allowed to trade or buy from "Aryans," a Jew is not allowed to walk in the main street, a Jew is not allowed to be seen in the street after six o'clock in the evening, and so on and so on... A "Jewish council" ("*Judenrat*") was established, a Jewish police was organized and their duty was to supervise the fulfillment of the new regulations.

On 13 September, all the Hungarian Jews were collected and taken across the former Russian border, to Kamieniec Podolski. None of them returned from there, and so around forty thousand Jewish martyrs were murdered. Every once in a while, the Germans came to town. They beat the Jewish residents with murderous blows, sometimes with the help of the Ukrainian police. At first, all the Jewish property was confiscated. Searches were conducted in each Jewish home and every item of value was taken out of it: furniture, suits, clothes, and even underwear. On 25 November, the "*Judenrat*" received an order to supply 200 Jews to work in forced labor camps. I also received a note, in which I was ordered to report for a transport to a labor camp, but I hid in time because I knew that death was waiting for me there. I hid for three weeks with one of my Christian friends. At the same time the Jews were ordered to deliver all of their silver, gold, and furs to the authorities.

In November 1941, news started to arrive about the "*aktzyot*" that took place in the nearby towns. On 4 December the first "*aktzya*" took place in Horodenka, and more than two thousand Jews were taken to a forest near the Dniester River and shot there. On 18 November, the same thing happened in Zaleszczyki, and 1600 Jews were killed there. At the same time, it was relatively quiet in Tłuste. Indeed, there were a few isolated murders, but mass "*aktzyot*" did not take place in our town. The news about the "*aktzyot*" in the nearby towns increased the tension, and the Jews lived in constant fear. At the same time, everyone started to dig a "bunker" for himself, an underground burrow where they were planning to hide in time of danger.

On 10 March 1942, the abduction of Jews for a transport to labor camps resumed. At the same period of time, mass "*aktzyot*" occurred in other towns in our area: in Chortkov [Czortków], Berezdów and Buczacz, and for the second time in Horodenka. In April 1942, the surviving Jews from Zaleszczyki arrived to our town after their town became "*Judenrein*" – cleansed of Jews. The Germans allowed us to rest from April until September 1942. They came, every once in a while, to the "*Judenrat*" with unusual and different "orders", but an "*aktzya*" did not take place. But at the same period of time we had our own Gestapo men – the people of the "*Judenrat*" and the Jewish police, who started to collect taxes, conducted searches and took what the Germans left behind. At times, the Jewish police beat people up until they fainted and lost consciousness.

Since people were afraid to go to the labor camps, everyone started to search for a job. There were times that they not only gave up their wages, but also paid those who agreed to employ them. This provided the "*Judenrat*" with the opportunity to collect a large fortune in exchange for obtaining a work "permit" from the labor office. At that time, the economic situation in town was very bad. People walked around swollen from hunger, were satisfied with one potato meal a day and only dreamt about bread.

On 6 September 1942, a great panic suddenly broke out in the streets. From a window we saw Jews running and heard shouts and babies crying. We saw the police and the people of the "*Judischer Ordnungsdienst*" [Jewish police] abducting Jews in the street – the "*aktzya*" started! Immediately we went down to the "bunker" and hid. On the same day around five hundred Jews were abducted and sent somewhere by train. The official name that was given to this act was "transfer," but we already knew that the transferees were transported to their death.

On 5 October, two hundred Germans and policemen suddenly arrived, and a real "wedding" started. 150 Jews were shot to death in the town, and additional 1100 were sent by train. On that day, the first victim from our family fell. My stepmother did not want to hide in the "bunker" and was taken out of the house. When we came back home after the "*aktzya*," we found destruction and ruin there. Everything was looted and only the four walls remained. Also the walls and the floors were broken in many places, because they searched for "bunkers" and hideouts inside them. Many Jews were dragged out of their "bunkers" after the Jewish police discovered them there. Terrible sights occurred in the bunkers. Mothers suffocated their children with their own hands so they wouldn't give up the location of the hideouts with their cries and shouts.

The slaughter lasted until seven in the evening. The same thing occurred on the next day in Berezdów and in Uziran [Jezierzany]. After the "*aktzya*", the surviving Jews from those locations were transferred to our town. We thought that that they would leave us alone for a few days, but it was not so. Day after day they came to us drunk, and attacked the remaining Jews. Every day there were 15-20 victims. On 3 December 1942, 40 Jews were shot. These acts of murder continued until 15 December 1942. Jews were abducted again to labor camps in the five days between the fifteenth and twentieth of December. This time the matter was easier for them: Jews volunteered to go to the labor camps because they realized that there was no difference, here or there – they were not able to save their lives.

The Germans appeared only every once in a while because of the vast amount of snow and the intense cold outside, but on the other hand the typhus epidemic caused the death of many. No wonder, we lived in crowded conditions, twenty or more in a small room. There were only four towns in the entire Tarnopol region where Jews still lived: Berezdów – 3000 Jews, Buczacz – 5000, Kopyczyñce – 4000, Tłuste – 6000. Those who remained alive anticipated the fate of their dead brothers at any moment. The head of the Gestapo expressed himself once: if a Jew will be able remain alive after the first of January 1943 – I am willing to remove my hat in his presence. All of us waited for a miracle. We realized that there was no hope for a quick end of the war. Many tried to escape to Romania, but only a few were able to get there. Most of them were shot and murdered on the way.

The epidemic spread quickly in town, and there was not a home without a number of sick, three, four and even five sick people. Every day ten or fifteen people died, but no one was impressed by that. Almost everyone wanted to die, and it was better to die a natural death. And so the months of January and February passed. "*aktzyot*" were not held during that period of time because of the epidemic, but the Germans found themselves another way. Every day they abducted Jews from the streets, and anyone who left his front door was abducted and taken somewhere. In a period of six days, around five hundred people were abducted this way. The epidemic slowed down a little in March. According to the "*Judenrat*" around 1400 people died from the epidemic in a period of three months. Over four thousand Jews remained in town.

Again, in April 1943, it became known that new "*aktzyot*" had occurred in other towns. We also found out that an "*aktzya*" would take place in our town on 8 April. This time we did not see the benefit of hiding in the bunkers, therefore we started to escape to the forests. I also escaped together with my father and brother to a forest that was eight kilometers away from town. The Ukrainian police found out that only a small number of Jews remained in town, and they informed it by telephone to the Gestapo. April 8 passed in peace without any events. We stayed in the forest for three days, and when we realized that it was quiet in town we started to return to our homes, one after the other. We were sure that the matter would take place, but we did not know when. On 1 May, the "*Judenrat*" received an order to supply one thousand physically fit people to work in the labor camps on the farms. The work itself did not deter us, and we were only worried that it was a new hidden trick to entrap us. Therefore no one went to register. Then, the "*Judenrat*" enlisted the help of the Ukrainian police, and started to abduct every person they met. These abductions continued day and night. By 20 May, around one thousand Jews had been abducted that way. Around three thousand, three hundred Jews remained in town.

On 25 May 1943, a train with twenty empty cars arrived in town. We were sure that they were meant for us, and again we escaped and scattered in the forests. May 26 passed in peace and, on first light, 27 May, at three o'clock in before morning, four hundred Germans and Ukrainian policemen arrived and started a horrible massacre. Three hundred Jews who tried to escape were shot and killed in the town's streets. Two thousand people were collected and brought to a large plot of land in town, and fifty people were selected to dig pits in the cemetery. Later on the people were led to the cemetery in groups of one hundred. There they undressed them, shot them, and laid the bodies one on top of the other. They threw the children alive into the pit. The Christians who witnessed the sight told us how people went to their death with complete apathy. There were many who lost their mind and started to sing out of madness. When the angels of destruction finished their work, they left town saying: we are not done yet, we will return to this place. For three days the blood of the murdered boiled like in a cauldron, spouted and sizzled like a boiling geyser.

We returned to town the day after the "*aktzya.*" Not a living soul was seen in the streets apart from those who were busy collecting the corpses. Around one thousand Jews remained in town. On 1 June 1943, all the remaining Jews were force to move to two streets. No one was allowed to go outside the "Jewish quarter," and Christians were not allowed to enter it. Again, hunger started to bother us, but not for a long time.

Daily "*aktzyot*" took place at the same time in three nearby towns. In four days the whole area became "*Judenrein.*" They started to search for the surviving Jews who escaped to the forests, and cut them with their bayonets. Every day we were worried that the liquidation campaign would also reach us.

It was impossible to escape to the forest because the police guarded the Jewish quarter. We lost all hope, sat and waited to die. Again, each one of us tried to get a job on one of the agricultural farms, although it was only a kind of "injection", an "extension of time", for a few more weeks. All the young people scattered, and only the old and children were left. Parents left their children and sons left their parents because there wasn't another choice. Everyone thought about himself. I was also confused and desperate, because I was forced to leave my father alone. I asked the "*Judenrat*" to let him go with us, but to no avail.

On Saturday, 5 June, we felt that the ground was burning under our feet, that we only had a few seconds to save our lives. I walked like a mad man, and consulted with my father what to do. He said to me and to my brother: go, you are still young and I have already lived most of my life. May G-d help you! Nevertheless, I decided to stay, so we would go through it together! And we stayed....

On Sunday 6 June, at ten before noon, I went to the "*Judenrat*," maybe they would agree to let my father go with us. And suddenly – gunfire....and Jews were running from every direction... we went out, and here we were surrounded by Germans and policemen. The matter began suddenly. It was impossible to run back home. My brother and I started to run to the fields, and the bullets whistled around our heads. Not once we came across the bleeding corpses of those who had been shot to death. In the end we were able to break the circle of death, ran a distance of four kilometers, reached the edge of town and hid in a field. We clearly heard the sound of gunfire and shouts from the town. We heard each burst of machinegun fire, and also the hand grenades that were thrown into the bunkers. A shiver passed through my heart with each shot – again a number of Jews found their death... I was not able to sit down, are we going to find anyone alive when we return to town?

The shooting lasted until the late hour of the night. Before morning, I turned to go back to town without paying attention to the danger. I saw a horrible sight on the way. People were lying in puddles of blood... and it was impossible to recognize their faces for the amount of dumdum bullets that hit them. A number of them were in agony and asked for a merciful killing. I arrived in town and with a shaking heart entered my home. A dead person was lying next to the bed in the first room, and there was no one in the next room. I ran out to the street and asked the "*Judenrat*" people if they saw my father. But none of them saw or knew. I started to search among the dead bodies in the street, but I was not able to find him. I climbed to the attic and saw the sight that I was afraid of... my father was lying dead. He was facing the ground and there was a bullet hole in his back. My eyes darkened and I became dizzy. My legs became heavy and didn't obey me. I left to find my brother, but when we returned we were not able to find our father's body because it had been removed from there.

On the same day around nine hundred Jews perished, and only an isolated few who were able to escape survived. The one hundred remaining Jews were forced to go to Chortkov on the same day, and were murdered on the way. And so Tłuste became *"Judenrein"* – purified of Jews. My brother and I turned to the farm in Lisovtza [Lisowce], and remained there.

But they also did not allow us to live in peace in the labor camps. On 23 June 1943, the Swydova [Swidowa] camp was surrounded, and five hundred Jews were shot and killed there. No one was able to escape. A great panic broke out in our hut to the sound of this news. People started to scatter because they realized that the camp did not provide any security. I was confused – where could I go without a small coin in my pocket? If we fled to the forest – we would die there from starvation. But in fact there was no different in the matter, also here and also there death was waiting for us. My brother did not want to go to the forest, and I did not try to talk him into it because I did not know what was better. Therefore, I got up and went alone despite the fact that the roads were dangerous.

When I passed by the Wierzbowa forest I entered the home of a Christian woman and asked her for a little water. I saw that she felt sorry for me and participated in my sorrow, so I stood and described my situation to her.

She advised me to remain in the forest and said that she was willing to feed me. And so I wandered alone in the forest for about three weeks. On 18 July, I heard the sound of gunfire. I was sure that the shooting was coming from one of the camps. And surely, I was not wrong. Two hundred Jews were shot in the Shipovtza [Szypowce] camp and in Szerszeniowce. Only a small group of the camp's residents were able to escape. On the next day the same thing happened in the rest of the camps. I asked the woman to go to the camp in Lisovtza and find out what happened to my brother, but she was afraid to go.

After the camps were liquidated, they started to encircle the forests, so it was no longer safe to hide there. I dug myself a pit in the forest, two meters long, one meter wide and eighty centimeters deep. I was not able to stand in it, and I was forced to lie down all the time. The surviving Jews who escaped from the camps that were liquidated lived in two camps: around one hundred people in the Lisovtza camp and around eighty in the Ułaszkowce camp.

At that time, we started to see Russian partisans in the forests. A difficult winter started; the Germans came to search the forest very often, and many Jews were discovered. Also, the road to the home of the Christian woman who gave me my food was dangerous, but I did not have a choice and to my luck I was not caught. And so I remained alive until the day of liberation in March 1944.

Segments from the forest diary......

Wednesday, 25 August 1943, I did not close my eyes all night. My whole body is wounded and bruised. This is the third month that I've not changed my shirt. Today I received a newspaper and found out that the British captured Sicily. It is cold in the forest, winter is approaching – and I am naked and barefoot. I can't ask anything from the Christian woman. She is very poor and she is sharing her last piece of bread without any payment.

Thursday, 26 August 1943. It is unpleasant to go and ask for food. This is the third month that I receive my food without the ability of payment. The woman brought me one of her brother's shirts, and also made it possible for me to wash.

Friday, 27 August 1943. On my way to the woman's house I met a group of partisans. They did not hurt me; only told me to hide properly because liberation will arrive soon. I wanted to join them, but they did not agree.

Sunday, 29 August 1943. I can't sleep at night because I ponder day and night. I suffer from headaches and dizziness, my heart is beating very hard and my nerves are very tense.

Tuesday, 31 August 1943. Two Jews who were found hiding in a Christian home in Ułaszkowce were shot.

Friday, 2 September 1943. In the morning I heard the sound of gunfire in a forest not far from me. It is possible that the forest was surrounded at night. I am afraid to leave and go to the woman's house, but I am forced to go because I was left without a drop of water. She told me that the Germans found five Jews in the forest and shot them to death. I hear the news with apathy... it is all the same for me....

Saturday, 4 September 1943. On the way I met a young Jewish man from Zaleszczyki who wants to escape to Romania. He gave me 2000 Zlotys so the woman will change them in town for dollars. I received the money from him, but I never saw the young man again.

Tuesday, 7 September 1943. A young Jewish man was shot not far from my hideout. According to the woman's description it was the young man who gave me his money. Now I decided to bring my brother Reuven to me.

Wednesday, 8 September 1943. I sent a letter with the woman to my brother in Lisovtza, and told him that the woman would come to take him next week. I also received an answer from him.

Friday, 19 September 1943. A group of thugs attacked me when I walked in the forest at night. They beat me, wounded me, and robbed all of my money. Now I am desperate. I was hoping to be together with my brother and again I was left without money.

Tuesday, 13 September 1943. I obtained a new fresh newspaper. Historical events are happening in high speed. Italy surrounded, and the Russians already reached the Dnieper River. Are we going to be rewarded to reach the day of liberation?

Saturday, 17 September 1943. Again we can see partisans in the area, Ukrainian partisans not Russians. To us, the Jews who live in the forest, they are not less dangerous than the Germans.

Wednesday, 28 September 1943. Again, it is not safe to stay in the forest. 50 Jews were shot in the Uziran [Jezierzany] forest, and 250 Jews in the Skalat forest. I don't have a choice, I must stay here.

Saturday, 1 October 1943. It is impossible to stay in the forest, and the cold is unbearable. Life in the camp is difficult, and desperate people report to the police station and ask to be shot. Many take their own lives, and if salvation will not arrive soon, also the last few surviving Jews will be lost.

Thursday, 13 October 1943. Many Germans are walking in the forest searching for Jews to complete the "quota". The sound of gunfire is being heard all day, and many Christians hand over the Jews who hide in their homes.

Saturday, 15 October 1943. Again, eight more Jews were found in the forest and shot. Only nine Jews were left hiding in this forest.

Wednesday, 19 October 1943. Three Jews were found and shot in the Teklówka forest, around one kilometer from here.

Friday, 21 October 1943. 36 Jews, who were found hiding in the villages, were shot in Tłuste.

The noose is getting tighter from moment to moment. Are we, the survivors, are we going to be able to hold on?

Tuesday, 1 November 1943. News arrived that the situation in the battlefront is for the better. The front is closer, around 200 kilometers from here. Salvation is approaching, but are we going to be alive then? The echo of canon fire is being heard from a distance, and German airplanes are flying around in the air. Who will give me a few more weeks of life? It is very cold in the forest, but it is not the worst. The worst is yet to come. When the snow will fall, we will be lost, our footsteps in the snow will lead them directly to our den. But we hope that salvation will arrive before the arrival of the snow.

Sunday, 13 November 1943. Until today I lay without food, and now the snow is melting. The Germans started to search the forests with great detail, and every day new victims fall. The Soviets captured Kiev, and they are getting closer. Typhus started to kill again, and those who are not shot to death – die from the epidemic.

Friday, 18 November 1943. This is the third day that I lay sick. My legs are swollen from hunger. I can't walk a step, and I can't walk to eat. Food did not reach my mouth all day yesterday, but I don't want to die from starvation. In spite of that, today I will gather the rest of my strength and go.

Wednesday, 1 December 1943. Reuven came to me this morning. All the camps are being liquidated and the Jews who remain alive separate and go in different directions. Apparently their intention is to kill the last Jewish survivor.

Monday, 5 December 1943. It is snowing all day, but I don't have any choice, I must go outside and walk. May G-d help us...

Tuesday, 27 December 1943. We are fasting for the second day because we are unable to go outside. I lay pondering, how can a man overcome all of that? To lie in a dark pit when the body is diseased and full of wounds and the pain is unbearable. The hunger and the cold bother us, and in addition to all of that – the fear. In spite of that, we are alive... we live with the power of hope, and maybe we will be able to survive if the matter will not last too long. Meanwhile, the end of December arrived – and salvation is not visible on the horizon....

Saturday, 31 December 1943. Again, eight new victims: six in Holovtshintza [Hołowczyńce], and two in Tłuste.

Saturday, 21 January 1944. It is eight days that I lie with a forty-degree fever. A disease attached itself to me, "a blow" to my side, and I suffer from terrible pains. I can't lie down or sit, and I revive my soul with a little bit of snow...

Wednesday, 15 March 1944. I did not write during the past few weeks because there was nothing new. Every day was the same – hunger, fear and terror. The Christians tell us that the Soviets are getting closer, and we should expect them to arrive in a week. It is simply difficult for me to believe it...

Monday, 20 March 1944. The sound of gunfire is explicit and obvious. Is it truly possible that we were chosen to survive out of three and a half million Polish Jews?

Tuesday, 21 March 1944. The gunfire is increasing, there is a large movement of airplanes, Germans and Russians all mixed up. The heart is beating hard from happiness and hope... here is the salvation that we are waiting for the past three years, and millions of Jews were not rewarded to see it...

Wednesday, 21 March 1944. I hear the sound of footsteps. I thought to myself – here comes our end... but it was the Christian woman who came to give us the news that we can come out: the Soviets arrived. So we came out of the darkness of the pit to the air of the free world.

Caption next to the photo: R' Aharon Goldhaber, one of the best teachers in town. He knew how to throw bitterness at his students and sweetened their studies. He was rewarded that his offspring live in Israel.

[The same in Yiddish]

———

[Pages 147-149]

In the Labor Camp in Kamionka

by Eliyaho Albin

Translated by Sara Mages

In 1939, when war broke out between Germany and Poland, panic spread among the Jewish residents who feared that the Ukrainian population would hold pogroms against the Jews. A general mobilization was announced, and people walked confused and helpless because they didn't know what tomorrow would bring. However, this situation didn't last long. The Poles withdrew within seventeen days and the Russians took control of Eastern Galicia under the agreement between Russia and Germany. The Jewish population calmed down a little, but with that, there were concerns about the future. It was not known how the war would end and to whose hands the region that we lived in would fall.

The concerns were confirmed. The bitter hour arrived when the war broke out between Russia and Germany. The fear of attacks by Ukrainians became very real and, indeed, such attacks took place in the villages around Tluste and almost caused the total extermination of the Jews in these villages. However, nothing happened in Tluste and this time we only paid with fear. The German radio announced with great satisfaction that the Ukrainians murdered over sixty thousand Jews in Galicia, especially in the villages. And indeed, this was true. Jews were brutally murdered with work tools and cut to pieces with knives held in the hands of their Ukrainian neighbors.

Our fate slightly improved in the first period because our area was occupied by the Hungarian army who behaved more or less humanely. For a bribe they even helped us to bring the Jews who were murdered in the villages to a Jewish grave. This relative calm lasted three months, and then the regime changed and transferred to the hands of the men of the German S.S. A "Judenrat" (Jewish council) was immediately assembled and, before long, one hundred and fifty people were sent from Tluste to a labor camp. Each person who was recruited to work received a draft order in which he was ordered to report on a certain date to the district office in Chortkov [Czortków]. No one dared to evade. All the recruits, myself included, reported on time to the office in Chortkov, and from there we were taken to the labor camp in Kamionka.

The concentration place of the recruits was the large square in the yard of the Chortkov Rabbi. There, we met young people from all the cities in the area and also a number of old people. People were organized by cities, and the men of the S.S., who were holding lists in their hands, called the name of each recruit. They announced that we should be ready to leave immediately for the road, each with a backpack on his shoulders. And indeed, the journey to the train station began immediately. At the beginning of the march we realized that it wasn't just a departure for work, and that we would return home at the end of six weeks as was promised to us by the Judenrat. From the moment the S.S. men took over control of us, they started to beat us with rubber clubs for every small delay during the march. Most of the blows fell on the elderly because they didn't have the energy to walk at the required pace. In this manner we marched to the train station and saw with a trembling heart how people were beaten at no fault of their own.

Freight cars already stood ready for us at the train station. We were ordered to enter quickly into the cars and, again, those who weren't able to carry out the order at the required speed were beaten. There were also big dogs that helped the oppressors to scare us into the cars, so each of us felt himself happy when he was deep inside the cars. It was so crowded in the cars that it was impossible to sit and we had to stand all the way. In this way we traveled until the day turned dark. Suddenly the train stopped, the door to the car opened, and two S.S men broke into it and started to hit us without mercy. Naturally, those who stood by the door received all the beatings. By chance I stood at the other end of the car. After that, an order was given that all items of value – money, watches, soap and even food – had to be given to the men of the S.S. who stood on the side. Those who stood nearby gave all they had in their possession and the others also gave something. Then, the S.S. left us with additional blows. They continued to do so in all the cars, and when the act of robbery ended the cars were locked and the journey resumed. We didn't know where we were going, but based on the stops along the way we realized that they were taking us in the direction of Tarnopol. We traveled until the late hour of the night. People got very tired standing so tightly, but there was no other choice. In addition, it was bitterly cold and snow was falling outside, something quite unusual for that time of the year, 15 November.

At three o'clock in the morning the train stopped next to one of the stations, but it didn't approach the station. The doors opened and the men of the S.S. welcomed us with blows and shouts: get out immediately and run down. We ran downhill accompanied by blows and scolding of the S.S. and the Ukrainian policemen, and chased by police dogs.

The road downhill was covered with snow and it was difficult to walk on it. Each person who slipped and fell was beaten to death by the S.S. and the Ukrainian policemen who stood along the road, a distance of about one hundred meters from each other. When we got down, a new gang of S.S. thugs welcomed us with a shower of blows with their rubber clubs. They ordered us to line up in rows of four and marched us to the camp. In this manner we marched, beaten, wounded and groaning from pain, a distance of four kilometers to the notorious Kamionka labor camp.

Two S.S. men, and two Ukrainian policemen, stood at the entrance to the camp and counted us with blows. The leadership of the camp was in Jewish hands. The commander was, Mr. Kalts, a German Jew with a good personality. His deputy was one by the name of Yisraelik who had the merciful quality of a Jewish man. They took us to the barracks where we had to sleep. There were already people in the barracks. They had arrived before us from the district of Tarnopol. Fear fell on us when we saw people walking with bandaged faces. Most of them were wounded in the head and face. We asked the meaning of it, and it was explained to us that this was not a camp for a six-weeks stay, but a death camp from which no one comes out alive. They beat here incessantly: they count and beat on the way to work, and count and beat on the way back from work, and not mentioning the time at work. Yisraelik took us to our beds – four wooden beds, one on top of the other, and each for two people. We lay down to sleep, but none of us was able to fall asleep from the excitement and the concern for our future.

*

At five o'clock in the morning they already chased us out for the roll call. S.S. officers arrived at seven and started to check, according to the lists, if everyone was there. In any case, it was impossible to escape from there because the camp was surrounded by an electric barbed wire fence. The matter took until eleven, and at the end of the roll call they ordered us to hand over any sum of money or a watch in our possession under the threat of death by shooting. Apparently, no one dared to defy the order and handed all that was left in his hands, either local currency or foreign currency. All that lasted until two in the afternoon. After that, we were ordered to get a haircut and be ready to go to work after roll call on the next day. In this way our first day in the camp has passed. It was extremely cold outside and a lot of snow fell. It was also very cold inside the barracks. Eight iron stoves stood in each barrack, but they stood there only as a decoration so the representatives of the Red Cross would see them when they inspected the working conditions in the camp. A delegation of the Red Cross came to visit the camp twice while I was there, but none of us dared to approach them and tell them about our sufferings, about the beatings and the meager ration of food which wasn't enough to sustain a man. They clearly saw our condition, but they also didn't dare to ask questions.

Our second day of our stay in the camp arrived. Two "Ordnungsdienst" (Jewish policemen), who were under Yisraelik's command, entered the barrack at four in morning. They woke us up with shouts and whistles and ordered us to go and get our "breakfast." There was one kitchen for one thousand five hundred people. By the time that we, the new people, arrived to the kitchen to receive our cup of coffee, there was already a very long line and not enough coffee for all of us. At six, we had to appear at the location of the roll call. The camp commander and his helpers were already there and they ordered us to line up with shouts and scolding, so much so that terror has fallen on us.

At eight, the men of the S.S. arrived to take us to work. They divided us into different types of jobs, and each of them was difficult and hard. I was sent to work in the quarry, a distance of ten kilometers from the camp. The quarry was inside a forest, and non-Jewish workers also worked there, but they worked under humane conditions and also received wages and food. We, the Jews, didn't get anything all day long, apart from blows. There were also other jobs, such as pulling railway tracks and wooden railway sleepers for paving. Some worked in road construction. They were forced to sit in one place and chop rocks, and many of them caught a cold. Others delivered rocks in wheelbarrows. They were exhausted from the hard work and lack of sufficient food. I decided that it was better for me to work hard than take a chance of catching a cold in lighter work, and somehow I managed to hold on. There were those who weren't able to hold on and died from starvation.

Two members of the Ukrainian police led us to work, and during work we were guarded by the men of the S.S. and Ukrainian policemen. In addition, big dogs guarded the area so none of us would be able to escape. Every day we were brought back to camp tired and exhausted, weary and wounded. There were those who didn't have the strength to walk and then we took them between two of us so the killers wouldn't notice it. Two S.S. men and two Ukrainian policemen stood at the entrance to the camp and counted those who entered, again accompanied by severe beating. After we returned to the camp we had to go to the kitchen and receive a cup of soup for dinner. The soup was prepared from beans and grits and included a little meat. However, this meat was from horse carcasses, and those who ate it immediately came down with diarrhea. Eventually, a typhus epidemic broke out among the camp's workers and the weak weren't able to recover from it. The sick were taken to the corridors and many died there of hunger and torture. The bread ration was distributed at ten in the evening, a loaf of bread for twenty people. Each of us was forced to be satisfied with eighty grams of bread a day. From day to day, the number of workers was reduced under these horrible conditions. After a short time, only half the people who were brought to the camp remained, and every once in a while new people were brought to the camp to replace them. There were many who ransomed themselves with large sums of money and with the intervention of the Judenrat. Liberation from the camp cost from eight to ten thousand Zehuvim per person, and there were those who handed their last coins to free their father or brother from the death camp. Once, the Judenrat announced that for one month it was possible to release people from the camp dirt cheap, for only one thousand Zehuvim. At that time the money was already gone from the pockets of many, but those who had the means handed the money to the Judenrat. In the end, all this money was lost because no one was liberated. From time to time the Judenrat found different excuses to take money from Jewish residents and use it to save their own friends.

*

Not many who survived the camp in Kamionka are still alive. Here, in Israel, there are a few people from Tłuste who witnessed everything that happened in this camp, but I doubt that there is a man who has the strength to tell and describe everything that he saw and experienced there. Every hour and every day, they had enough material for an entire book. Is it possible to imagine that a brother could beat his brother to death to please the oppressors? But the fact is that a "nice young man," Yisraelik, has done that. During roll call he hit more than the S.S. men. This roll call usually took place once a month, on Sunday at eight o'clock in the morning. Not once it happened that one of us wasn't able to stand and collapsed. If the S.S. men didn't notice it – Yisraelik noticed it, and then the poor man received his punishment. I will never forget the horrible sight that I have seen in one of these roll calls. A young man from Probużna, about 16 years old, collapsed and fell. One of the S.S. men attacked him and beat him with his rubber club until he lay helpless. The heart shrank at the sight of the young man who was writhing in pain and moaning in a heart-rending voice. We saw these sights more than once. At times people died on the spot, and then the murderers set their dogs on them and ordered them to drag the people from the place.

Jews who helped the Nazis were also punished – none of them remained alive. A few managed to escape from Kamionka camp, others were ransomed with money paid by their relatives, the rest were exterminated by the Nazis and the camp was set on fire.

[Pages 149-150 - Hebrew]

How I survived the Great *Aktzya*

by Tzvi Koch

Translated by Sara Mages

In 1939, when the Russians invaded our area, the property of the large merchants was confiscated at once. I was also one of the large merchants and my property was also confiscated. These merchants were not allowed to get any work and from time to time new taxes were enforced on them. After many attempts, by using contacts and with a payment of large sum of money, I was able to "purify" my name and remove it from the large merchants list. With that, also the name of my family was purified and we became "honest people".

In 1941, Tłuste was captured by the Germans. At that time I lived in the village of Nirkow [Nyrków], a distance of twelve kilometers from town. On the first night of the Germans' rule, Ukrainian murderers attacked us and robbed all that we had in our possession. My family and I jumped half-naked through the windows and escaped to Tłuste. There, I lived in the home of Yisrael Yorist.

A number of decrees were published during the first days of the German rule in Tłuste. The Jews were not allowed to be outside their homes after five o'clock in the evening, and every Jew had to wear on his sleeve a white armband with a blue Star of David. Around that time also the first "Judenrat" was established. Some time later, the Germans demanded a certain number of Jews for transport to labor camps. They promised that they would stay in the labor camps for only three weeks, and later on they would be replaced by others. The "Judenrat" prepared a list of the town's Jews and selected from it the people who would be sent to the labor camps. Those who were selected did not object since they trusted the Germans' promise. In fact, none of them returned. Those who wanted to take a family member out of the labor camp approached the "Judenrat" and, after a negotiation for the amount of ransom money, the "Judenrat" determined who would be released. The first camps were Kamionka near Lvov and in Borki-Wielkie.

The Germans continued to demand that the "Judenrat" deliver people for the labor camps, but they were not able to find people who were willing to go on their own accord. The "Judenrat" was forced to grab people from the streets and to conduct searches in order to fulfill the Gestapo's quota. After the quota was filled, those who hid were able to come out of their hiding places, but they were required to pay ransom money to the "Judenrat" fund. I was also one of those who was not caught. I was forced by the "Judenrat" to pay ransom, and indeed I paid.

The money that was collected by the "Judenrat" in place of going to a labor camp, or for the return of those who were sent to a camp, was used to fulfill the Nazis' and the Gestapo demands. The demands were many and the requirements were large. Every now and then, they demanded leather, cash in dollars, and the "Judenrat" was forced to fulfill all of their demands. For that purpose the "Judenrat" extorted money from any possible source. In one of the searches for additional Jews for a labor camp I was in bed, ill with typhus, so they were not able to send me to work. After the quota was filled and the mission ended, the "Judenrat" people appeared in my home to search for my two brothers who were hiding there. They asked me where my brothers were, and when I told them that I didn't know, they forced me to get out of bed, despite the fact that I was sick, and locked me in the "Judenrat" prison. There, I found a number of rich Jews who were also locked up. It was clear that they had arrested us in order to extort money from us.

In general, I was at odds with the "Judenrat". There were two reasons for that: first, because I was rich and it was possible to demand money from me, more than was possible to demand from other residents. Second, because I had connections with people of the Ukrainian police due to the bribes that I paid them. Not once I was able to release Jews and save them from all kind of trouble not by the way of the "Judenrat"; and the matter angered them. Once I was able to save Minisia Tepper [Mina Tepper], daughter of Pinchas Teiber [Teiwer], from the hands of a Ukrainian policeman. He was beating her, wanting to arrest her for her "sin" of baking bread, a matter that was forbidden for Jews and carried a death sentence. The second time I was able to release Yisrael Yorist. He had been arrested by the Ukrainian police under an order given by the "Judenrat" for refusing to give his furniture to the Gestapo. Then, they ordered to arrest me in his place. I was arrested. My rescue acts hurt the "Judenrat" income and they agreed to release me only if I paid the losses that I had caused them.

After the first step, the abduction of Jews for transport to labor camps, the "aktzyot" started. That is, the murder of Jews by the Germans with the cooperation of the Ukrainian police. After each "aktzya" the number of Jews in town diminished. As their number decreased those who were left were crowded together in one neighborhood. After the great "aktzya", which took place on a Thursday, when more than two thousand Jews were murdered, the Gestapo ordered the few Jews who were left to concentrate in one narrow street where a "ghetto" was established for them. Later, some of them were sent to labor camps that were established in the town's environs, in the villages of Roshanovka [Różanówka], Lisowtza [Lisowce], Podsniatinka and Swydova [Swidowa]. The surviving Jews believed and hoped that those who were sent to labor camps would survive, and those who remained in the ghetto would be liquidated sooner or later. But it was not easy to be included among those who were sent to a labor camp. Only the physically fit young people were sent there and also those who bought the right and paid money to the "Judenrat", or by "favoritism." In fact, most of the Jews who were left were relatively young, since the old people were already killed in one of the "aktzyot". We need to mention, that there were not any children in the labor camps because it was forbidden to keep children there. A few children arrived with their parents and were kept in secret and hidden under mortal danger. Any child that was found in the camp was executed immediately.

One of the "aktzyot" that I remember well was the Sunday "aktzya". Usually they did not execute an "aktzya" on a Sunday, because of the "sanctity of the day." This time, the Nazis tried to perform an "aktzya" in the nearby town of Borszczów, and for some reason they were not successful. For that reason they suddenly appeared in Tłuste and started to shoot every Jew who came across them. In previous "aktzyot" we always knew in advance that something was going to happen and many found a place to hide. This time the matter came as a surprise and we did not have the time to run and hide.

I was saved from the great "aktzya" by a miracle. Before morning, Gestapo men and Ukrainian policemen surrounded the town and opened fire. They called the Jews to come quickly out of their homes and started to search each house for hidden Jews with the help of the "Jewish police". They brought them to the collection point which, this time, was located in a large field near Yorist's home. My mother of blessed memory, my brother David and I hid in a bunker in Yorist's home. We had just enough time to enter it before the arrival of the murderers. Two days before the "aktzya" I told my brother David that we should leave town and go to the village of Nirkow [Nyrków] or to Podtsuhor near Nirkow, where I had prepared two bunkers with two Poles. I learned from

Dr. Averman, the leader of the Judenrat, that the ground was burning under our feet, but Dr. Averman and my brother claimed that it was possible to delay the matter.

When the shooting started we went down to Yorist's bunker. A short time later, the murderers discovered the bunker, opened the upper lid and shouted: "Jews come out!" I came out of the bunker and the others followed me, apart from my mother and two young women who stayed inside the bunker. S.S. men, Ukrainian policemen and one Jew waited for us on top. We were led to the gathering location where many Jews, who were brought there before us, were already waiting. Everyone sat on the ground with their arms raised above their heads. The Germans placed two big wooden crates nearby, and the Jews were ordered to throw inside them all the money and valuables in their possession before they sat on the ground. While I sat with my brother, I suddenly saw Dr. Averman walking by with a German officer. I called him by his name: Dr. Averman! He noticed me and said something to the German officer. Then I heard the officer calling me by my name: "Herman Koch!" I left the circle and at the same time I shouted towards my brother: "David Koch!", as though they were also calling him. He was afraid to get up from his place because he could have been shot for doing so by the armed guards. I shouted towards him: "Come quickly, you have nothing to lose!" He listened to my voice and came out of the circle. And so, about thirty people were taken out of the circle thanks to the intervention of Dr. Averman and other members of the "Judenrat" who were able, here and there, to influence the "aktzya" organizers to give up a number of people that they recommended.

The Jews who were taken out of the circle were ordered by the Germans to collect the dead bodies that were scattered in different streets in town. Those were the bodies of Jews who were killed during their escape. For that we were given a cart harnessed to a pair of horses and driven by a Ukrainian farmer. The Jews who remained in the collection area were led in groups of one hundred to the cemetery and shot to death.

This is how I survived this "aktzya" and stayed alive. After everything ended, I went together with a Ukrainian policeman, who was one of my acquaintances, to search for my mother in Yorist's bunker. I found her there and went to call my brother. When I came back with my brother I found that, in the meantime, Ukrainian rioters had entered the bunker, stabbed my mother and beat her with murderous blows. Despite that, she survived and was rewarded to immigrate to Israel with us.

It is worth mentioning two "episodes" from this "aktzya". During the "aktzya" a number of Jews hid on the roof of Moshe Wasser's home near the gathering point. The matter became known to the murderers. They climbed on the roof and threw the unfortunate from the roof to the road. They crashed before my eyes and the eyes of all the people who sat there. The second incident: among those who sat in the collection area was Tluste resident Simcha Gelber or, as he was called, Simcha the "Kleizmer". Simcha approached the person in charge and asked him to let him live since he could still work and be useful. In addition, he also told him that he was a musician. To that the German answered him: "Go and bring your violin!" Simcha went to his home accompanied by a policeman and brought his violin. The German ordered him to play before the Jews who were sitting and waiting for their death. But that also did not help Simcha. He was sent to the cemetery in the last group. He probably found his death there since I have not seen him anymore.

I left Tluste after this "aktzya". First I went to the labor camp in Roshanovka, and from there I went to hide in the bunkers that I prepared for myself in Nirkow and Podtsuhor. I lived there until March 1944 when the Russians arrived and liberated our area. In 1945 I arrived in Israel.

———

[Pages 151-152]

The Great *Aktzya* of May 1943

by Bella Shoham

Translated by Sara Mages

It happened on one of the last days of month of May, the month of spring. The trees wore a green blanket, the sun sent her warm rays to the world, and the birds sang and flirted with joy: Spring had arrived! Spring, the messenger of rejuvenation which brings the joy of life to all living creatures. But that spring brought the Jews of Tłuste, as it did to all the Jews in the area, the blackest news, the news of death and destruction. The final extermination was approaching – "the final Jewish liquidation" as the German oppressors called it. The tension among the Jews of the town – whose number of residents was increased by a few thousand since the area's Jews moved there – increased from hour to hour. For many months they suffered from hunger and humiliation, congestion and filth. They were always subjected to pillage and plunder. But now, their existence was in danger, their chance of continuing to live on this earth was shaken.

Twilight, Wednesday 26 May, Jews were walking like shadows in the back streets, like prisoners waiting for the execution of their sentence. Bitter and shocking rumors arrived from the nearby towns, from Chortkov [Czortków], Buchach [Buczacz], and Borshov [Borszczów]. Liquidation "aktzyot" were held in all those towns according to an accurate plan, the terrible plan of the murderers of the Jewish nation. Everyone felt and knew that Tłuste's turn had just arrived. In a few days, or maybe in a number of hours, the calamity would reach them. Everyone walked depressed, without a spark of hope in their vacant eyes. How could they expect a miracle? Why would the great miracle, for which Jews in all the surrounding towns waited in vain, happen in Tłuste?

A rumor spread in town: tonight they would abduct girls for transport to a labor-camp. My mother decided immediately that I should not stay at home. I must go to the Christian family B., who lived in Naharonika [ed. – apparently a reference to Nahiryanka / Nagórzanka, near Jagielnica], and sleep there. Thanks to my mother, who was Mrs. B.'s school friend, I was welcomed at their home. I spent many days in their home – I worked on the farm, helped their son with his homework, I stitched and embroidered. I did all that I could in order to please them, in order to receive a slice of bread for me and for the members of my family who suffered from hunger and shortage. I arrived with my mother to the home of the B. family, but I did not dare to enter. I was afraid that maybe this time they would refuse to take me in. And what would I do then? Where would I turn and to whom would I go? My mother entered before me in order to receive their approval. A few moments passed and my mother came out of the house. An expression of satisfaction was spread over her worried face. "Get in my daughter – she said – they are taking you in willingly, but please don't come back in the morning until I come to get you." My mother kissed me as the tears choked her throat, and hurried to return home. The hour of six before evening was getting closer. After that hour, a Jew was not allowed to be seen in the streets.

With a heavy heart, I climbed in my bed fully dressed. The feeling of fear and anxiety gained control over me. I repeated the evening prayer that I had started to recite since the arrival of the bad days: G-d please let me see the morning light and please leave me in the bosom of my family! Woe G-d! Why, why all this torture, and for how long are we going to suffer?

I woke up at two o'clock at night to the sound of frequent gunfire that landed like hail. I understood everything... Mrs. B. approached my bed and whispered with a sad voice: "aktzya, listen, aktzya in town... Get dressed quickly and climb to the attic above the cowshed." I was trembling as though I had fever and answered her: "I will not go, I will run home to my parents, and if we are sentenced to die – we will die together".

Mrs. B. was against this thought. In spite of my wish, she walked me to the cowshed and climbed with me to the attic. A Jewish boy, around the age of ten, was lying there pale and trembling from fear. I recognized the boy, he was from Horodenka. His parents perished in the "aktzya" and he was left alone. He had arrived on foot to Tłuste, found shelter with the B. family and shepherded her cows. Mrs. B. covered both of us with sheaves of straw and returned home. The shooting continued nonstop like in a battlefield. We heard the shouts and the orders of the killers, the screams of the murdered and the crying of children. Nearby we heard a Jew calling "Shema Yisrale" and falling to the ground. The moments crawled slowly and the brain was full of thoughts, fear and terror. The pain and sufferings turned my body and my soul into one big bleeding wound. Is it possible that they just kill and murder nonstop! And you, G-d, where are you? Why do you look, observe and keep quiet? The shooting lasted and lasted... and during that time my brain emptied from any thoughts, I froze, I did not feel anything, I did not think about anything. I only lay and waited.

In the afternoon, Mrs. B. climbed to us and with tears in her eyes she begged before us: "Save yourselves and me! The murderers are going from house to house searching for Jews in hiding, if they will find you in my home – we will all be lost together. Please, leave my house and save my soul and your souls together." Both of us went down to the cowshed, me and the boy. I took my coat off, the one that had an armband with a blue Star of David stitched to its sleeve. Mrs. B. tied a colorful headscarf to my head and an apron to my waist. I took a shovel and threw it on my shoulder and so I left the cowshed completely indifferent to those who would see me. The boy came after me with the shepherd stick in his hand, and used it to take the cows out of the cowshed. At the same time three images appeared at the gate and scared us to death: a Gestapo man and two Ukrainian policemen who came to search the house. They measured us from top to bottom with a penetrating suspicious look. The boy became very pale and turned towards the field as though he wanted to escape. I stopped him and with a forced laugh I said to him in Ukrainian: "Why are you so frightened, you little stupid, they might suspect that you are a Jew! Say hello to the policemen and go do your work! My words probably convinced the angels of death that we were not Jewish. One of the two policemen turned to us and said with kindness: "Come on, for devil's sake, get going!"

We turned towards the field and went away. We were shocked and we did not believe what we saw. Is it possible? Were we truly saved from the hands of the murderers? Again, the will to live, to exist, awakened in me. The apathy and the paralysis that took over me when I lay idle in the attic passed and were no longer there. I did not know if it was the will to live, or maybe the fear of death. I only knew that we needed to hide as soon as possible, and disappear from the eyes of the murderers.

With quick steps we crossed the garden and got closer to the wheat fields. The stalks were tall and full, the wheat harvest season was getting closer, but the blood harvest was at its height and continued non-stop and without a limit. We entered between the stalks, the boy left his cows and I threw away the shovel. The two of us started to crawl on our fours inside the standing wheat. We crawled for a few hundred meters until we moved away from the village. The shooting continued without a break and did not stop for a moment. We ran out of energy and our bodies trembled from anxiety and fear. The boy breathed heavily and, every once in a while, wet his lips with his tongue. His face was pale and he was completely wet from sweat and covered with dirt. He lay next to me holding my hand, as though I had the power to protect him from trouble. The memory of my family members rose to my heart. They remained in town, inside the frenzy, the shooting and murder, and who knows if they were still alive. I broke in a bitter cry, and the boy put his hand on my mouth so the sound of my cry wouldn't be heard. I restrained myself and repressed my feelings, but the tears choked my throat. In my imagination I saw my father and my mother, my brother and sister, my aunts and their children and those who were dear to me, and I did not know if I would be able to see them again!

A short time later, the sound of repetitive voices and gunfire reached our ears. And again, silence, voices and gunfire. After strenuous listening I realized that the voices were counting in German from one to ten. After each counting we heard a spatter of gunfire. At the beginning, I did not understand what was happening. At the end, I raised my head and saw that our legs had carried us to a field near the cemetery. From our hiding place I was able to hear and see how the executioners carried out their murderous plot. People were sent to the burial pit in groups of ten, fathers with sons, mothers with babies in their arms, and those wild beasts, the scum of the human race, shot and enjoyed this devils' game. Who knows who is entering the pit now? Maybe my parents with my sister and my brother? But what is the difference, they are all my brothers! The heart was aching so much.... And this hell continued for hours upon hours, until it seemed that it would never end....

Evening fell, darkness covered the face of the earth, and the shooting continued. Only at around nine o'clock the shooting stopped and silence and stillness prevailed. Over and done with. Everything became silent. Everyone was dead. I had the feeling that I was also dead, although I was breathing and was able to move. We continued to lie in the standing wheat. An hour later I heard a whispering voice calling my name from a distance. At first we got scared, but later on we started to walk in the direction of the voice. It was the voice of Mrs. B. who came to look for us in the standing wheat. After quarter of an hour we met her and she informed us that the "aktzya" had ended and it was possible to return home. I wanted very much to hurry and run to my home to see if anyone remained alive, but Mrs. B. did not let me do so. "There is an order," she said, "forbidding to go out into the streets and it also applies to Poles and Ukrainians." She also told me that around three thousand Jews died in the "aktzya."

Mrs. B. took us again to the cowshed and brought us food. We asked for a lot of water because our throats were parched from thirst. We tasted a little of the food, climbed to the attic and lay down, but I was not able to fall asleep. I did not close my eyes all night. It is difficult to describe my mental state during that night. The bitter tormenting thoughts did not let go: three thousand Jews were killed today in Tluste, three thousand Jews in one day, on Thursday – the day of the reading of the Torah! And G-d saw all of that and kept silent. And what about my family, is anyone of them still alive? Will I be able to see them again? And if all of them perished with the others – why did I remain alive? What for, and for whom? In a few more hours I would know the whole truth. Terrible fear attacked me from the worry of discovering the truth. It was better that the night not end, so it wouldn't be necessary to go to town and see what happened there.

At six o'clock in the morning I departed from the B. family. I thanked them from the bottom of my heart for everything they had done for me and turned to go to town. I knew what was waiting for me in town, and I was prepared to see the horrible sights. Despite that, I was shocked and I did not believe what my eyes saw. The whole road was strewn with the bodies of murdered Jews. Fear and horror fell on me in the presence of this sight. Wherever I turned I saw only blood, blood and crushed skulls. Here lay the body of a four-year-old girl, and there, among the weeds, the body of an old Jewish man. Where would I escape to from this hell? I continued to walk and came across a body of a family member, my cousin who came to town from the village only a few days earlier. What should I do? I started to run like a maniac, but where to? Where is our home and who is still there?

Suddenly I heard a voice calling my name and immediately after that a choked cry "My daughter, my daughter, you are alive! Is it really you or a dream that my eyes see?" It was my mother. She saw me and ran towards me. This time they remained alive, all the family members, indeed, they remained alive – but only for ten more days…

[Page 153]

What I went through during the German occupation

by Yisrael Gertner

Translated by Sara Mages

Even before the Germans entered our area, the Ukrainians rose and killed many Jews in a number of places: Svidovh [Swidowa], Lashkovitz [Ulaszkówce], and Czopowicze [Szypowce]. 15-20 people were killed in the Metzger's flour mill. The Magyars [Hungarians] arrived in our town first, although the rule was in German hands. At the same time, the Magyars expelled around thirty thousand Jews from their country, claiming that they did not have passports. Some of those Jews arrived in Tłuste, and remained in town. A short time later, the Ukrainians complained that the Hungarian soldiers were looting their vegetable gardens in order to give the vegetables to the Hungarian Jews. Then, an order was given to expel all the Jews who arrived from Hungary. Most of them were expelled as far as Kamieniec Podolski, which was over the Russian border, and were shot to death there. Only a few of them did not obey the order and remained in our town.

Later on, the abduction of Jews for transport to the notorious Kamionka labor camp started. Around three hundred Jews were sent from our town, among them were a few members of our family: myself, my brother's son Manie Gertner, may the Lord revenge his blood, and my sister's son Natan Sperber (who now lives in Israel). There, the real hell started. I was there for only 9 weeks, and during that time I was included three times in the list of those who were selected for execution. Two weeks after our arrival I was placed in a group of forty men, and seven men from that group were chosen for execution. Among them was also Rochtsi Gertner's son-in-law. After nine weeks my nephew, Shimshon Gertner of blessed memory, was able to release me with a ransom payment of 250 Dollars.

Afterword, the "aktzyot" chapter started. To our great regret, the "Judenrat" expelled three hundred Jews, and seventy young women were taken out of the Kozia-Gora farm where they worked as laborers. All of them were sent in freight cars to the Belzec death camp. In the second "aktzya" the Germans abducted around one thousand people. Among them were: Tłuste's rabbi, R' Shmuel-Aba Chodorov, and his family, my brother's son, Shimshon Gertner,with his wife and child, and also my brother-in-law and my aunt. They were also taken by train to an "unknown destination". They also did not know their destination. There were more Jews waiting in the train stations along the way, and when they got closer to Rawa-Ruska they met a number of Jews who worked near the railroad. They shouted to them: "Jews, escape for your lives, because they are taking you to the ovens!" They were transported in cattle cars with their windows blocked with barbed wire. My nephew Shimshon cut the wire, and as the train was moving he threw his wife out first, and he and his brother-in-law jumped after her. The Germans who guarded the "transport" shot after them, but they did not hit them. The train continued on its way, people fell at a distance of about two kilometers from each other, and they met later on. My nephew left my aunt and his boy inside the car. After they met, the three of them arrived to Rawa-Ruska. Jews still lived there, and they helped them with money and with arrangements. A German company sent a delivery truck to Zaleszczyki, and the three were sent in this truck as laborers. The driver brought them to their homes and received a carpet as a payment. Leib Drohobitzer [Drohobycer] was also in the same car, but when Shimshon offered to help him to jump out of the car, Drohobitser told him that he did not want to take part in it because it was better for him to "rid himself of the matter once and for all".

Shimshon's wife was in her fifth month of pregnancy when she jumped from the train, and four months later she gave birth to a baby girl. When the girl reached the age of eight months the great "aktzya" took place in Tłuste, and everyone perished in it. Ten days later the last "aktzya" took place, and then my wife, my daughter, and all the remaining family members perished. Later on, an order arrived that Tłuste should remain "Judenfrei" and all the surviving Jews were ordered to move to Chortkov [Czortków]. Immediately after their arrival they were taken to the cemetery and shot there. We did not travel to Chortkov, but turned to the labor camp on Milovtza [Milowce] farm. There were forty of us there. Twice we were attacked by the Gestapo men, and only twenty out of the forty were left. Later the "Banderovtzim" [Bandera's gang members] started to bother us. A member of the "Banderovtzim" gang secretly advised me that I should not sleep in the camp or on the farm, but change my location every night. After that those thugs attacked us. They strangled Shmuel's brother-in-law and his son with ropes, and also killed a teenager from Buczacz. Eight days later the farm in Tłuste was liberated.

My sister's son, Natan Sperber, tells about the liquidation of the Kamionka labor camp in these words:

He worked with three hundred men in a quarry and in the forests near Kamionka. They called this place "Kamionka 1". When the partisans started to get closer, a German accompanied by five Ukrainian policemen came with a machine gun and took everyone to the village. Some of the Jews started to escape, and the Ukrainians started to shoot after them. The first to be shot was Yeshayho Mazer, and others were shot after him. My sister's son was able to escape. Since he knew where I was, he walked a distance of around one hundred kilometers at night until he reached our camp. My brother's son Manie also escaped, but we found out that he was caught in Skalat and shot there.

Among those who were killed in our town was also the veterinarian Spiegelglass, with his wife and daughter. One day, a number of Gestapo men arrived from Chortkov and asked for the location of his apartment. They approached his apartment, murdered the whole family, left their bodies in the apartment and took off.

[Page 154]

The testimony of a doctor

by Dr. Baruch Milch

Translated by Sara Mages

From testimony against the Gestapo men, Paul Thomanek and Kurt Koellner.

In 1935 I was certified as a physician in Prague. I lived with my family in Podhajce, in the district of Tarnopol, until the outbreak of the war in 1939. At the beginning of 1940, after the Russians captured Podhajce, I was transferred under the order of the authorities to Tluste and worked there as a physician until the outbreak of the war between Germany and Russia in June of 1941.

At the beginning of July 1941, German troops also occupied Tluste, and for about half a year after the occupation I also served as a municipal doctor in Tluste because there wasn't a Christian doctor in the town. At the end of 1941 I saw, for the first time, the Gestapo man, Thomanek, at the Ukrainian police station. He was there accompanied by two other S.S. men, Koellner and a third man whose name I don't know. They asked me, as the municipal doctor, if the two–week–old baby that was found dead under a cross was Jewish or Christian, and the reason for his death. I couldn't express an opinion whether the boy was Jewish or a Christian because he wasn't circumcised, but I was able to determine the time of death and his age. I don't know what the end of this matter was.

During the occupation, there were 500 to 600 Jewish families in Tluste. After that, all the Jews from nearby cities such as Zaleszczyki, Buczacz, Jagielnica and Horodenka, were deported and brought to Tluste Ghetto. The ghetto was reduced, more and more in terms of area, until five thousand Jews lived in a very narrow area.

There was only a Ukrainian police. About twice a week the men of the Gestapo came to the "Judenrat" from Chortkov [Czortków]. They always came in a truck, which was covered with a black canvas, and accompanied by a small passenger car. The arrival of the black car always aroused fear and panic. Paul Thomanek, Kurt Koellner, Peckmann and Brauner were known as the most awful among the men of the Gestapo.

In July 1941, the Germans already assembled a "Judenrat." The men of the S.S. came to the "Judenrat" to impose and collect the "contributions," meaning the silver and gold quotas that we were forced to give them. After that, came the "fur operation" in which we had to give all the furs and the materials for sewing furs. It was followed by demands to provide workers for labor camps, at first in Kamionka and Globocak [Hluboczek], and after that for the establishment of a labor camp near Tłuste for planting orchards for the production of Caoutchouc, for the rubber industry in the labor camps in Lisowice [Lisowce] and Rozanowka [Różanówka].

Hundreds of people were dragged to the labor camps by the Ukrainian police. The Gestapo man, Koellner, was the person in charge of Jewish matters in the Gestapo office in Chortkov. The S.S. man, Thomanek, was the director of the camps in Chortkov and the surrounding area. Later, came a period of "transfer operation" which was directed by Thomanek and Koellner. Approximately at the end of 1941, or at the beginning of 1942, eighty young Jews were required to come to the train station in Tłuste. When the quota wasn't met, young people were taken out of the nearby houses to complete the required number. They were brought to the train station and loaded for Belecz.

In March, or April 1942, I was brought to the labor camp in Kamionka together with about eighty other Jews. There, I hid the fact that I was a doctor and worked for almost a year in the quarry. Two to three thousand Jews from the District of Tarnopol worked at the labor camp in Kamionka.

At the beginning of 1942, I witnessed how Thomanek shot and killed Spiegelglass, Tłuste's veterinarian, together with his wife and daughter. Spiegelglass lived outside the Jewish quarter, out of the city. I lived together with my family in a room which was located a distance of two houses from his apartment. One day, between the hour of seven and eight in the morning, a passenger car arrived. Thomanek and a Ukrainian policeman named Schab got out of it. A second Gestapo man remained in the car. Thomanek approached the house and knocked on Spiegelglass' window. Spiegelglass came out and I was able to hear Thomanek's question: what is your name? After I heard his answer, Thomanek shot and killed him from a distance of approximately one meter. I was at a distance of 10–12 meters.

Spiegelglass fell dead on the spot and then, Thomanek entered the apartment. I heard the sound of additional shots and later found out that Spiegelglass' wife and his eleven–year–old daughter were shot to death. After that, Thomanek and the Ukrainian policeman left the area in the car. Half an hour later a cart arrived from the "Judenrat" to remove the bodies. His wife and his daughter were still in their nightgowns. I saw that with my own eyes.

It's possible that the reason for the "special operation" was due to the fact that a Ukrainian veterinarian arrived in Tluste a short time before the murder. However, the Christian population and the agricultural farms preferred to use the service of Spiegelglass.

I was also a witness to a second crime in which Thomanek and Koellner took part. Once, on a Friday, Thomanek and Koellner arrived together with four or five S.S. men from Chortkov to Tluste in the well–known black truck and in a passenger car, and demanded from the "Judenrat" to immediately provide them with a large number of young workers to load the wheat that accumulated on the agricultural farms in the area. Since there were only a few who were willing to do so (at the sound of Thomanek's name many escaped for their lives and hid in fear), the Gestapo men, together with Koellner, entered the houses that stood near the "Judenrat" building and took out of them twelve young Jews. They brought them to the "Judenrat" yard, and there they were shot to death by Thomanek and Koellner. I was then in a nearby house, at the home of a Ukrainian family by the name of Sush, who received medical treatment from me, and I saw everything through the window. From among the murdered I knew two sisters by the name of Kurzer, and a young man by the name of Hessing.

Later, the men of the S.S. entered the nearby houses, to the place of residence of the Spitzer and Stupp families that I visited before noon on the same day because there were several people there who were seriously ill with typhus. They also shot a number of sick people there. Later, all of them were found shot to death. They were also shot by Thomanek and Koellner.

From July 1943 to February–March 1944, I was at the Lisowice camp while my family remained in Tluste. In the summer of 1943, in one of the aktzyot, about three thousand Jews were collected at the local cemetery and shot to death next to the pit, which was dug as a grave for the masses of victims. My mother–in–law and my sister–in–law also perished then.

Some of the detainees in the Lisowice camp were sent and transferred to Silesia. I was released in Glaubitz by the Russians in February of 1945.

As I've been told, the members of my family were killed in the following ways: The great aktzya of the summer of 1943 started at three o'clock in the morning and continued until five in the afternoon. My family was hiding with a farmer at the edge of the city. My son was three years old then. A Ukrainian cook hurried to a nearby restaurant where Thomanek and Koellner were eating, and told them that my family was hiding with a farmer nearby. Even though it happened after the aktzya ended in the cemetery, the S.S. men also took my family there. My wife and my mother–in–law were shot and killed and my little son was thrown alive into the pit after them.

———

[Page 155 - Hebrew]

Memories from the Holocaust era

by Chaya Rosenblatt

Translated by Sara Mages

Mordechai and Yota Rosenblatt had three sons: Yeshaya, Tzvi (Hersh) and Kalman. Yeshaya lived in Grodek near Zaleszczyki and was murdered there by the Ukrainian worker, Pilka, who hid him for a short period of time after he escaped from Berezdów Ghetto.

Tzvi was sent by the "Judenrat" to the labor camp in Kamionka and died there a few months later. His wife, Leah, was captured by the Ukrainian police in Rozanowka [Różanówka] and was murdered about six weeks before liberation.

Kalman Rosenblatt, who was wealthy, was arrested by the Russians. He sat for several weeks in Chortkov's prison, until he was released from there for a fee of ten thousand dollars. When the Germans arrived, the family hid for two days in a forest near Ułaszkowce, and later returned to Tłuste. In 1941, during the Hungarian regime, the Hungarian police came to rob his property and only left after they received a large sum of money from him. The family suffered a lot also from the Jewish police. From time to time they came to search for hidden money, and during these searches uprooted doors, windows and floors.

For a certain period of time, they worked on the Keshnzshina [Ksiezyna] farm near Slone [Słone]. There, they were helped a lot by a gentile named, Doshak, who guided and advised them where it was possible to hide. In the winter of 1942, they returned to their home, but in January of 1943 they were expelled from their home by a Ukrainian policeman and moved to live at the home of Ahron Baumister. In the spring, they moved to Holovtshintzh [Hołowcyńce] where they lived in the labor camp and worked in the fields. They felt themselves lucky because they weren't sent to the camp in Kamionka. In this manner, they managed to survive the "aktzyot" that were held in Tłuste at that time. During the "aktzyot" they escaped to the forests and later retuned and continued to work. Chaya, Kalman's wife, worked for individual farmers and for her work she received a meager meal that she shared with her husband.

In the summer of 1943 (May or June), an "aktzya" was held in Holovtshintzh, but Kalman Rosenblatt and his wife managed to escape and hide in the woods. After the "aktzya" they returned to Holovtshintzh. In November 1943 (27 Kislev 5704), the Gestapo man, Brauner, came to the farm and shot and killed many Jews. Among them was also Kalman Rosenblatt.

In January 1944, a typhus epidemic broke out in Rozanowka, the place where Chaya Rosenblatt hid. There was no water in the camp. They used snow for drinking and ate beets. All the camp's inmates used the one wooden comb that they had in their possession. There was only one needle in the camp and the Jews used it to patch up their "clothes" which turned into rags.

Rozya Horovitz from Zaleszczyki, the twenty–one–year old daughter of Shemaria Horovitz, was taken to Chortkov [Czortków] together with nearly two thousand Jews. There, they were going to be executed, but they were kept alive for about a week because the ground was frozen and it was impossible to dig a grave for them. She said that after they were starved for a week they were given a sack of bran, and those who were able to snatch – snatched. They used snow for drinking water and, when she was thirsty and wasn't able to get a little water, she injured her finger and quenched her thirst with the blood that she sucked from her finger.

Rozya Lang, daughter of Shabtai Lang, had a little beautiful daughter. The wife of the director of Holovtshintza [Hołowczyńce] farm adopted her as a daughter and all the children envied her. However, on the day that the "aktzya" was being held in Holovtshintzh, the woman handed her "daughter" to the hands of the Gestapo. The Jews of Holovtshintzh were buried next to the cowsheds, together with the carcasses of dead dogs and cattle.

The veterinarian, Spiegelglass, was murdered together with his wife and nine–year–old daughter, Zoshia, at his home. The girl wiggled and rolled around the room until she covered all the furniture with her blood.

Mrs. Mann took care of her little granddaughter whose parents were killed in the "aktzya" in Tłuste. One day, Chaya Rosenblatt found the girl's red dress flapping on one of the fences. It became known to her that Mrs. Mann was shot and the girl had been smashed into a stone because the murderers didn't want to waste a bullet on a Jewish child. Both were buried in Holovtshintzh.

On Yom Kippur 1943, the Jews collected 500 Zloty and gave it to the "zhontse" [gendarme/ military policeman] to let them pray.

———

[Page 156 - Hebrew] [Page 215-230 - Yididsh]

A night of horror – one of many

by Dov Pfeffer

Translated by Sara Mages

I would like to describe a night of horror that I, my wife Sabina, and my daughter Paula, went through a short time before liberation. We were at the labor camp in Chipowtza [Szypowce], where only a few of the camp's workers remained after the "aktzyot" that were held there. We started to feel that there was a change in the situation and the Russian front was getting closer to us. Each one of us started to search for a place to hide with renewed enthusiasm, out of hope that the bad days wouldn't last long. My wife and my daughter were hidden by a farmer inside a small pile of straw that he prepared for that purpose. One day, at dusk, the farmer approached us and demanded that we should leave his place at once. According to his words, the "Banderovtzim" [Bandera's gang] discovered that we were hiding at his place. Our cries for help and our tears didn't help us, and we were forced to leave for the road in very bad weather.

At the same time, my brother, his son and also my father, Fischel, were in Chipowtza camp. My brother worked there as a blacksmith. His wife Dora, and his son Ascher, were staying with him. We didn't know that my brother and the rest of the workers had left the camp and moved to the labor camp in Tłuste. Therefore, we headed for Chipowtza farm which wasn't far from where we hid in the farmer's house. To our amazement, no one was on the farm. A large pile of straw stood there, so we decided to climb to the top of the pile and hide there. On top of the pile we found a "bunker" which was probably prepared by one of the camp's workers. The bunker was narrow and the three of us were only able to stand there. A few hours later we suddenly heard the sound of coughing. We knew that Antoni Shevetshuk [Szevchuk], the farmer who hid us, suffered from asthma, so we assumed that he came to call us to come back out of remorse that he threw us out of his house. I thought of going out to him, but I didn't do so. Another half an hour passed and we heard the sound of several people talking. It was a group of "gangsters" who came to explore and find us. We heard them talking, saying that only Jews can hide in this place. After that they started to dig in the pile of straw. They were so close to us that we were able to hear the sound of their breathing. Of course, we were terrified, but fortunately they didn't find our hiding place even though they returned twice to the same location and continued in their search. It was truly a miracle from the heavens...

In the early hours of the morning, long before dawn, we left our hideout and went to the home of Antoni Shevetshuk. Shevetshuk's wife came out to the sound of the dog barking and, when she saw us, she was amazed that we were still alive. She asked us what we wanted, and we asked her to lead us though the forest to the camp in Tluste. She agreed to our request and we left for the road. She already knew that my brother was shot and killed two days earlier so maybe this was the reason why she wanted to keep us away from her house. However, she did not tell us anything about it. When we arrived to the camp in Tluste, we found my father, my brother's wife and her son there. Only then I learned about the tragedy that happened to my brother. A short time later we were liberated from the German murderers. They didn't have the time to liquidate the camp in Tluste, even though they probably had a plan to do so.

An interesting incident happened in our town, Tluste, during the Nazi regime. A large section of the synagogue was destroyed. The police issued an order to demolish the whole building. However, the order wasn't carried out because nobody wanted to do the job. A few days later they found a Christian carpenter who agreed to do the job, and the "Judenrat" was forced to provide a Jewish boy to help him. And here, as the carpenter was busy sawing the roof beams, a beam fell on him and killed him on the spot. His Jewish helper wasn't injured at all. In this manner the carpenter got his punishment from the heavens for "volunteering" to destroy the building of the synagogue.

———

[Page 226 - Yiddish]

My road of pain and wandering

by Rokhl (Rose) Rubinstein-Tenenbaum

Translated by Yael Chaver

On June 21, 1941, Hitler's accursed gang set foot on the soil of our town. The Jewish population was immediately greatly panicked. The Germans' first deed was to take away Jewish men, supposedly for work; but they never returned from that "work." At first, we consoled ourselves with the thought that the German nation was too good, too noble, to persecute innocent, helpless people in this way. But, unfortunately, we soon realized the awful truth: that these nice, tactful Germans had, over the past twenty years, become murderers and bloodsuckers. This is how my husband, Shloyme-Mayer, my children, and I, fell into their hands. My husband was soon ripped out of our arms, but he will never be ripped out of our hearts.

A Judenrat was created in our town; its mission was to help the German bandits. The Germans demanded gold, silver, and jewelry; and the Judenrat had to supply them. Judenrat members protected their own families and friends, and therefore had to press the others even more strongly. Next, the Germans started to demand that the Judenrat supply them with Jews: today, young people able to work; tomorrow, the elderly; and the next day, small children. The Judenrat had to comply. Children were wrenched from the arms of their helpless mothers and tossed into a wagon. They were taken to their deaths this way, but half of them were dead before they ever reached the designated spot.

I witnessed children being torn from the arms of their mothers. They were preparing to snatch my two children away. I heard one German tell the other, "Why are you waiting?" But God himself gave me strength. I twisted away and started running with my children through fields, swamps, and mud patches, until we fell into a heap of straw. We burrowed into that straw, and lay there for three days and three nights, famished and weak, without a crumb of bread or a sip of water. Afterwards, I took my children on the arduous way to my mother's house, in Tluste. My mother was beside herself with joy. She had already mourned and wept over us – she was sure we had already been murdered.

But the joy was short-lived. Soon the terror began again, along with endless fleeing and wandering.

[Page 227 Yiddish]

The first 'action' in Zaleszczyki took place on November 14, 1941. They issued an order that all Jews able to work go and clean up the barracks; but those who went never returned. On that occasion women and children were allowed to stay at home. In this way, the German murderers decreed a time for everyone. News of this soon arrived in Tluste and gave rise to terrible dread among the Jews.

Then, a decree was issued forcing all Jews to move into the "ghetto," the cramped side alleys of the town. Jews were forbidden to walk on the main street, from Czortkow to Zaleszczyki. One day I scampered through that street and suddenly heard someone shouting behind me. I immediately realized that I had run into trouble and had been caught for a heinous "crime." I stopped, and started to apologize, stammering. I was beaten and whipped, but miraculously emerged alive. The policeman had heard sudden loud yelling from somewhere and let me go. I came home to my children, more dead than alive. Thus we lived in constant terror, which increased day by day.

One Friday, the SS men came into town, started in on the liquor, and got completely drunk, singing songs about the "cursed Jews." That day, they killed 40 people. They later said it had been "only a joke." They continued to play such "jokes" on us from time to time.

*****

On Yom Kippur Eve of 1942 [20 September], I was in Skalat. My brother, Yankev Rubinstein, was in the Borki-Wielki extermination camp nearby, where many of our young people from Tluste were murdered. I helped my brother escape from the camp, but did not have the joy of seeing him come home alive. After much roaming through fields and forests, he was caught between Jasłowiec and Tluste. I was told that he had a revolver and died a heroic death. He was thirty years old.

As soon as they noticed that my brother had escaped from Borki-Wielki, I was arrested in Skalat. I was supposed to be sent to Borki-Wielki after Yom

Kippur, to be shot by the camp commandant. I spent the eve of Yom Kippur in the jail of the "Judischer Ordnungsdienst" [Jewish police]; the time for Kol Nidre was approaching. An elderly woman brought me some food to eat before the fast, but my throat was choked. I sat, lost in thought and deeply depressed – I would soon have to leave the sunlit world and go into the dark grave, leave my beloved children and never see them again. I began to shudder and shiver all over. In the midst of all this, I heard the old woman sigh, and say, "Don't despair, God is our father." That lifted some of my dark thoughts. I drank some water she gave me and wished her a good year; she then left.

After Kol Nidre, the mood in the room of the Jewish Police was better, even a bit happy: people exchanged good wishes for another year of life... The commander of the Jewish Ghetto Police, Dr. Brif, came in to see me, extended his hand, and expressed a wish that I would see my children again. I was strongly affected by this wish and almost wept but, when I realized where I was, the tears stuck in my throat.

People started to leave the room. I had to return to my dark, barred cell for the night. For a long time, I tossed on the cold cement floor, until my tired eyes closed. Then I was enveloped by a sweet dream: I saw my beloved children near me. They cuddled with me, and the smallest said, "Mama, never leave us again..." The oldest said, "Mama, I want to go ahead of you!" My heart was torn to bits. I knew I had to part with them forever. I woke up, wet with tears and sweat, and had to face the horrible truth: my terrible, desperate situation.

Yom Kippur Day started. Everyone was rushing to synagogue to beseech God with the same wish: not to fall into the hands of the murderers. I was sitting in jail, guarded by one of the Jewish police. The guard changed every two hours. My guard accompanied me to synagogue for the "Yizkor" memorial prayer, so that I could pray for the souls of my dead. When I entered the synagogue, all eyes turned toward me. I realized that everyone considered me lost. I could not scream or cry, but only look ahead with a frozen gaze.

I was returned to my cell after "Yizkor." The hours passed quickly; the day was almost over. Suddenly, there was a commotion among the police force. A fellow sufferer was brought in, a woman whose husband had escaped from the camp. She was carrying a small child, and they were both wailing. They started to take her to an interrogation, and in the meantime I used this opportunity to go into the next room.

[Page 228 Yiddish]

No one noticed that I had gone. I went over to the window, opened it quietly, and jumped out. I fell into a cellar, but did not lose consciousness. Getting up quickly, I ran. I soon saw a haystack, ran and burrowed in. I lay there until late that night. After I crept out, I started wandering around through the fields and forests until I was able to come home, and my beautiful dream came true: I embraced my children. In this way, thanks to God's miracles, I escaped death.

Reuniting with my children and mother was a great joy. But the joy didn't last long. Soon, we heard of more 'actions' coming, and talk of exterminating the Jews. Once again, we began fleeing like mice into holes.

On Simkhes-Toyre of 1942 [3 October], my two children and I were in Jagielnica, not knowing where we could shelter. I met the wife of the Zalyszczyn Rabbi, who agreed to take me and the two children into their hiding place (my eldest, Yehuda-Aryeh, was 9, and the younger, Yitzchok, was 4).

The Jagielnica 'action' was on Monday, the day after Simkhes-Toyre. The previous night, right after the end of the holiday, we lowered ourselves on ropes down into a cellar that was well-concealed. We lay there until noon, hoping that the 'action' would soon be over and that we would be able to remain hidden. Suddenly we heard the murderers banging and running around, overhead. The dogs of the military unit sensed that there were Jews in the cellar below, and they started looking for our hiding place. It wasn't long before they discovered us and started yelling "Out!" As each person came out, he was "honored" with a few blows to the head, shoulders, wherever they could reach. We were then stood in rows of four and taken to an assembly place.

The large square was already full of thousands of people who had been rounded up. Everyone was ordered to sit with upraised arms. At exactly 2 p.m., we were commanded to get up and prepare for transport. We were all herded into freight cars. Soon, the train started rolling to Belzec, where the gas chambers and crematoria awaited us.

The cars were terribly crowded; the air was stifling. Some of the people couldn't endure it and died at the beginning of the trip. All of us who were living envied the dead. Everyone's eyes were dulled, as though we were insane. Some recited vidui or screamed "Shma yisroel!" We all knew we were going to our deaths.

Suddenly, everyone started shoving towards the car door. Like a heavenly angel, a chance to save ourselves appeared. A board had been pried loose on the side of the car and people scrambled to jump off the rushing train. My two children and I also jumped out. The murderers started shooting at us. My older son was hit by a bullet and started bleeding. He fell and lost consciousness. I ran to him and bound up his wound. I revived him with my tears. The poor child was very weak. I brought him some water from the river, and pulled up a carrot from the field, to keep him alive. We were lucky to escape the clutches of the murderers, but we were exhausted and famished, naked and barefoot under the free skies.

When we got back to my mother's house, her joy was indescribable. People in Tluste thought that we were no longer alive. Home was very precious to us, after our long tribulations. My son's wound was in very bad shape. The bullet had been a dum-dum [expanding bullet], and the injury site was infected and oozing. I called Dr. Meltzer, good man that he was. May it be to his merit: he did what he could, and God did the rest.

The Jewish population faced a miserable winter. Thousands of Jews came to Tluste from the surrounding towns, which were now "Judenfrei" [free of Jews]. A typhus epidemic started to spread in the crowded and impoverished conditions. Hundreds of people died. But everyone preferred death by disease to death by bullets. I heard Golda Shpitzer scream at the dead person, during a funeral, "Oy, I envy you..." It was a very harsh winter, with hard frosts and deep snows. More than once, we had to sleep outdoors, to save ourselves.

Passover was coming up. We baked matzah, but did not get to eat it. The day before Passover [20 April], a panic broke out, and the entire Jewish population ran out into the villages, fields, and forests, to save themselves. But that was useless.

[Page 229 Yiddish]

The murderers discovered that the Jews had left the town, and never came. Only several weeks later did they attack the town unexpectedly. It was on

Thursday, the 22d day of Iyar, in 1943 [27 May 1943]. That is the date of our annual memorial at the Tluste association of New York.

I will never forget that day, because that is when I lost the dearest thing a person can have in the world –my mother. She went, like all the others, to her martyrdom as a Jew. Her last words to me were "May God keep you and your children!" It seems that her last wish has come true: my children and I remained alive.

It was shortly after dawn when the murderers charged in. They took up positions at all four corners of town and watched all the streets and paths. The beasts of prey started to collect their victims and took them to the assembly place, in a vacant lot near the church. They herded together everyone they found, and then took them to the cemetery in groups of one hundred. Three pits had already been dug, and planks laid across them. People were shot in groups of ten and dumped into the pit.

My children and I lay in a pit the whole day, together with others. It was as if we were buried alive. We were suffocating, drenched in a deathly sweat, and were sure we would never emerge. The day was endless, and the bullets thundered ever more strongly. There were more murderers, too. Ukrainian bandits had come to help, and they kept rushing around to find more victims. Only when the sun had gone down and it grew dark outside did the terrifying shooting stop. We waited for the right moment and crawled out of the dark pit, one by one.

Ten days later, there was another 'action' in the town. My children and I were then in Rozanowka [Różanówka]. We lay in the fields, but we heard the sounds of shooting even there. Among those killed then were my uncle, Mordkhe Rubinstein and his entire family. Only one son survived, Avrom Rubinstein. After that 'action,' Tluste was 'Judenrein' [purified of Jews]. Anyone left alive couldn't show their face in town. Luckily for us, there were work camps in the nearby villages: Rozanowka, Swidowa, Muchowka, Hołowczynce, Kozia-Gora, and others. It was possible to work there temporarily, as long as you weren't shot or became too weak.

I was lucky to have had Rozanowka, the village where I was born and grew up. It is only two kilometers from Tluste, and I would often walk along the pleasant road to town. I made my first friend there, Feyge Shpitzer (Yitkhok Shpitzer's daughter), who later married David Wasser. Tluste was a small town. Living conditions were difficult, but people were happy and there was much warmth and sincerity. The young people had a good upbringing, and it was fun to spend time with them. No one ever thought there could be such a catastrophe.

My children and I were in a work camp in Rozanowka. Children were not allowed in the camp, and I had to keep them outside. I spent the day and the night in two different places. That was also a piece of luck. One fine day in Tammuz [ca. July 1943], they attacked the camp and killed more than 60 Jews. That day, I was with my children in a field, and that saved us.

After those attacks, and attacks on other camps, a major panic broke out. We were afraid that the work camps would also be made "Judenrein," sparing no one. God sent us an angel, called Pati [Vathje]. He was the chief commandant of all the camps in the villages, and did not let the last few Jews be murdered. He claimed that he needed them for work; besides, their time would come. So, the camps continued to exist.

We endured a terribly harsh winter, without food, clothes, or shoes. We ourselves can hardly believe today that we were able to endure such conditions. Gradually, we began to hear that salvation was approaching, but we were afraid we would not live to see it. But God willed it, and we lived to see Hitler's downfall.

Only a handful of Jews had the good fortune to live to see liberation. In the last few months, many Jews were murdered by the followers of Stepan Bandera and other Ukrainian gangs. Soviet army forces arrived only on March 23 and saved the few Jews who remained alive.

———

From the days of the Holocaust

by Lucia Teiber

Translated by Sara Mages

Our town was captured by the German army few days after the war between Germany and Russia broke out. The fascist Hungarian army arrived first and the Germans arrived later. A few days later, the Germans imposed their atrocious decrees on the Jews, such as the obligation to mark their nationality by a white armband with a Star of David, various limitations, beatings and acts of murder. Terrible rumors started to arrive about the horrible acts that took place in other cities, and we had the feeling that, sooner or later, incidents of that sort might also happen in our place.

On one of the cold grey autumn days, we learned that the Germans were planning to organize an "aktzya" in our town. A panic broke out and everyone started to search for a place to hide. Also our small family, my parents, my younger brother and I, found a place to hide in one of the barns of a Polish family. However, before dawn the owner of the barn demanded that we should leave the place. To our sorrow we didn't go far. A Ukrainian policeman stopped us and ordered us to come with him. I was a young girl, only around thirteen, but I always had the feeling that in cases like that it's better to try to escape. I separated myself from my parents and escaped. Apparently, the policeman wanted to shoot me because I heard my father pleading with him not to do so. Later, he tried to run after me, but changed his mind and returned. Maybe he was afraid that by doing so the rest of the family would also escape.

I never saw my parents and my brother again. Since then, I was orphaned from my father and my mother and remained alone and lonely. I decided to fight with all my strength to stay alive. One day, I learned that a Jew by the name Glantsberg [ed. Ginsberg] was searching for people to work on an agricultural farm. I managed to join those who left for work and was very happy that they agreed that I join them even though I was still a young girl. There were twenty people in the group. We traveled in a wagon to the village of Rosochacz [ed. near Ułaszkowce] and started to work on the farm. A short time later the number of workers reached seventy. The farm manager was a German whose name I can no longer remember. He was a good and honest man and protected us from the Gestapo. The residents of the village of

Rosochacz were known to be cruel evil–hearted people, but they didn't dare to hurt us because of the manager's good attitude towards to us. The living conditions weren't very bad, and we were also not short of food. We received our food from the local farmers in exchange for the clothes that we brought from home.

One day, it was at the end of the summer, when we were busy with the threshing, the German's wife suddenly appeared in the field, riding on her white horse and holding a rubber whip in her hand. She surveyed the Jewish workers with a murderous glance, swore at them and lashed every Jew who came across her way. It was a bad omen, and I realized that we were in great trouble. And indeed, the Gestapo arrived a short time later. They surprised us early in the morning and a great panic broke out among the Jews. There was no way out because the Germans surrounded us from all directions. Luckily, I managed to escape again and came to the house were we lived. There, I climbed to the stove's smoke chimney, the wide smoke chimney that was found in each farm house in the area. There were already two men inside it – Gedalya Teiber and a young Romanian whose name I can no longer remember. (Gedalya Teiber found his death later, after he survived this attack). The Germans looked everywhere to find Jews in hiding, they even looked inside the dark chimney with flashlights, but luckily they didn't notice us.

The Germans gathered and took with them most of the Jewish workers. Only a few remained on the farm. We weren't able to stay for a long time in this place because we learned that the Ukrainian population was finishing the German's work and murdering the Jewish survivors with great cruelty. Without a choice, we started to wander from village to village. Meanwhile, I learned that about one hundred and fifty workers remained in the camp in Tłuste. I decided to join them and started to walk towards the town. It was during the period in which the end of the German regime was getting closer, and the roads were full of German soldiers who escaped from the Red Army. I arrived in Tłuste when the Soviet advance party arrived in the town and the remaining Jews welcomed them with great joy. However, the happiness didn't last long. Suddenly a group of German planes appeared in the town's sky and attacked the camp with bombs and machine–guns. A large number of people were killed in this attack and only a few survived – and I was among them. A miracle happened to me. The barrack where I was staying wasn't hit at all.

———

[Page 157 - Hebrew]

What I went through during the German occupation

by Zalman Wachstein

Translated by Sara Mages

After the Germans entered Tłuste I stayed a few more weeks at home. Later, I was taken to the camp in Kamionka together with 110 townspeople. There were about eight hundred people from the neighboring towns in the camp. The conditions were very bad. Twenty to thirty people died there every day from starvation, from the beatings and the shooting of the murderers. In their place, the Germans brought other Jewish workers. In this manner, a very long period of time had passed until I returned safe and sound from this hell.

New troubles began at home. "Aktzyot" and various persecutions were carried out. During the "aktzyot" I hid with my family in a bunker that I dug for myself. The murderers searched for Jews, but they were not able to find us because the bunker was well hidden. At the beginning of 1943, the murderers issued an order that all the remaining Jews must leave Tłuste and move to Chortkov [Czortków] Ghetto. I knew that it was only a ruse and a plot on their side, and that they were planning to kill us there. I took my child and we hid for several weeks in the fields and in the forests. In the end, it was impossible to remain in the fields because the gentiles chased us everywhere. Therefore, I was forced to move to the farm in Trabnis [Trawneh] where ninety Jews lived and worked. They also accepted me to work, but I was afraid to sleep on the farm since I knew the murderers' tactics. For that reason, I took my son every night to sleep in the fields. And indeed, my fear was not in vain. One night, while I slept in the field, I heard the sound of gunfire coming from the farm. I understood that an "aktzya" was taking place there. At the same moment I saw people running around me, people like me who slept outside the camp. Sixty people were killed in the camp, and at the same time we survived from death.

The survivors wandered in the fields and in the forests. Twelve members of our group were caught by the Ukrainian police and murdered. Again, we could no longer hold on. First, because they chased us incessantly and second, it was in the winter of 1943 and the rain, snow and cold bothered us a lot. For that reason we scattered in different directions. I went with my child to the village of Kopyczyńce where I had an acquaintance among the residents. We lived there until we were liberated by the Russians. Surely, in our place of hiding we did not lack problems and hardships.

———

[Page 158 - Hebrew]

An eleven–year–old girl who fought for her life

by Sonia Margules–Alterman

Translated by Sara Mages

The year is 1943. The retreating Red Army is leaving our town. Darkness envelops us and heavy clouds hover above our heads. The Nazi army captures Galicia and opens the oppression of the Jews and acts of horrible massacres. Death lurks everywhere and rail cars transfer our loved ones by the thousands to the gas chambers and the crematoriums of Belzec and Majdanek.

I was only eleven in those days. We still live in our home but for the most part we hide in dark bunkers, without light and without food. Rumors spread that we have to leave our home and move to a "ghetto," and indeed, the rumor is verified. My mother is also leaving her home with everyone and moves to the "ghetto" with her five children and a load of only five kilograms. It was the last stop. The survivors crowded there on Thursday evening, twenty four hours before the commencement of the Sabbath. Three days later, the gates to the ghetto were locked. No one could enter and leave. We felt that our last hour had come, that a terrible slaughter was about to happen, and there was no savior. Only God knows who will survive this destruction.

With dawn, a day of misery and horrors awoke for the surviving Jews in Tluste. My mother left the ghetto in secret as she was carrying my three–year–old baby sister in her arms to get a little food for her starving children. In the meantime, the angels of death appeared and broke into the ghetto. They arrived dressed as "students" so the Jews wouldn't recognize them and try to escape from their hands. Suddenly, the terrible "aktzya" began. Shivers pass in my bones when I remember those horrible moments. Each person hurried to save his life – and I was small then, poor and helpless. In the ghetto we lived in a small farm house which stood on the ghetto's border. I jumped through a small window and rolled downhill. I crossed the railway tracks and continued to run without turning my head. Many people ran around but only a few of them managed to reach safety because the Germans rained gun fire on us to make sure that none of the condemned to death would be able to escape. I ran with all my strength until sunset. I didn't eat all day, I didn't drink a drop of water and my lips burnt from dryness. In the evening I found myself in a thick forest alone and lonely and shaking from fear. In the end I was overpowered by exhaustion, and fell asleep.

When I woke from my sleep and opened my eyes, I saw Fischel Langholz's two children next to me. The three of us were happy that we were not alone. A short time later, Russian partisans emerged from the thick forest with bayoneted rifles. We were frightened when we saw them, but they calmed us down and said that they didn't have any intention to hurt us, on the contrary, they knew our bitter fate and felt sorry for us. They promised to bring us a little food to revive our souls. And indeed, they returned a short time later and brought us bread and water. They offered Langholz's older son to join them, they said that he would be able to help them, but he didn't want to be separated from us. The partisans left as they came and disappeared as if the earth swallowed them.

At sunrise, we turned towards the town and started to get lost in the forest. On the way we met a number of nuns who were traveling in a cart. They warned us not to return to the town because the Germans were still walking around, searching for Jews who managed to escape. Nevertheless, we returned to the town.

The road was strewn with the dead and wounded. The wounded shouted for help, but no one came to their aid. The streets were washed with blood and the town was completely empty. We learned that the few survivors were sent to a labor camp out of the town. Among them was also my beloved mother, my eldest sister, my two brothers and my three-year-old baby sister. My mother was sure that I was also killed and began to sit "Shiv'ah" for me. She fainted when she suddenly saw me in the camp. When she recovered, she didn't believe her eyes and said that it was only a false vision since I was no longer among the living.

All of us worked in the camp, also me, the little girl. I worked together with the adults. We suffered a lot in the camp, from hunger and from the beatings that were given to us by our supervisors. After a year full of sufferings and hardship we snuck out of the camp at night and returned to the town, to the labor camp in the farm in Tłuste. My brother, Hersh, found his death there only a couple of weeks before liberation. A few days later, my mother was shot to death as she lay in bed.

We went through terrible years that would never be erased from our memory. We'll remember what Amalek, of the twentieth century, has done to us and keep in our hearts the memory of our loved ones who were killed by the Nazi murderers. We'll remember those who weren't awarded, like us, to live in the liberated State of Israel.

May their souls be bound in the bond of everlasting life.

———

[Page - 159 Hebrew] [Page 236 - Yididsh]

The liquidation of the Jewish community in the village of Tzapowitz [Szypowce]

by Yeshaya Rosen

Translated by Sara Mages

Immediately after the outbreak of the war between Germany and Russia a great joy was felt among the Ukrainian residents. They talked openly that when Germans arrived they would be able to take revenge on the Jews, attack them and rob their property. After the withdrawal of the Russian army, prior to the Germans' arrival, gangs of rioters were organized in the villages. They intended to descend on Tłuste and start with acts of murder and robbery. However, there were also those who delayed them and advised them to wait and see how things will turn out. Meanwhile, Hungarian army troops, allies of the Germans, arrived. They didn't hurt the Jews and also prevented attacks by the Ukrainians. This matter didn't please the Ukrainians. They falsely accused the Jews that they collaborated with the few communists who remained in the German occupied area, that they attacked peaceful villages, killed the poor farmers and burned their homes. This libel was circulated by their emissaries in the villages, who turned to the Ukrainian population with a call: "Brothers, hurry to get organized so that you can eliminate your Jewish neighbors before they destroy you."

This news arrived to our village in the afternoon and caused great panic among the Jewish residents. At that time, I was at the home of Yisrael–Meir Landman z"l. A Hungarian officer, who spoke German, was also there. He calmed us down and said: "You, the Jews, don't be afraid from the rioters. Our duty is to keep the order and we'll protect you." To the sound of this good news I hurried to go home, to tell the members of my family what I've heard from the officer. Our house was around half a kilometer away from the Landman's house. Farmers, among them many that I had known, ran through the streets as they were carrying axes and pitchforks in their hands. All of them were shouting: "Come brothers to avenge the Jews who crucified Jesus, and now they are rising to kill us." When I saw that, I panicked, ran to Liebush Langholz' house, and hid there.

At the sight of the riot, members of the Hungarian Army came out and started to shoot in the air to stop the rioters. Together with that, the officers negotiated with the rioters and it was agreed to gather the Jews in the council building to investigate if there was any truth in the Ukrainians' claim. Members of the Ukrainian "militia," and "volunteers" from among the Ukrainians were sent to collect the Jews and bring them to the council building. We didn't know about this agreement, and when I saw armed "militia" members getting closer to Langholz' house, a thought crossed my mind that they were coming to kill us. I hurried and hid behind a crate that stood in the corner. From there, I heard how the Ukrainians drove out the family with rudeness and urged them to go to the council building according to the order that they have been given by the Hungarian commanders. A short time after the family left, one of the neighbors entered the home, opened the closet door and took out clothing and various items, as much as she was able to carry.

I lay panicked in my hiding place and didn't dare to get out of there until evening. When darkness fell, I jumped out the back window, reached the yard of a Polish farmer and hid inside a large stack of straw. I spent a horrible night there full of fear and worries. I didn't know if anyone from my family and from the remaining Jews in the village were still alive, or if all of them were murdered under severe torture. In addition, it was a stormy night and a heavy rain fell. Only in the morning I found out from the farmer that all the Jews survived death thanks to the interference of the priest and the decisive action of the Hungarian army. In addition to that, it became known to me that on the same night a number of Jews were killed in the village of Koshlovitz. Members of the Metzger and Schwartz families hid inside Metzger's flour mill. At night, the Ukrainians broke the doors, entered and killed all of them with great cruelty. Only one soul was saved from the massacre – Bona, daughter of Yisrael–Avraham Heler z"l, who was engaged to Leibus, son of Michael Metzger. Later, she was murdered in the great "aktzya" in Tluste.

I was shocked by this news, I wanted to see my family, but I was afraid to walk in the village in the middle of the day. Only before evening I returned home and found my mother crying, not knowing the fate of my father Yechiel and my brother Shmuel (he survived the Holocaust and lives in Russia). Later, we found out that both of them escaped to the fields, and from there they walked to Tluste at night. During our absence, the gentiles took all the personal belongings from our home, but when we came back they started to return some of it.

We remained in the village for three or four months, and then came the order that all the Jews in the villages would be exiled to Tluste and their property would be confiscated. We arrived to the town naked and destitute, with only a belief that very soon our enemies will suffer a defeat and we would be saved. But this hope proved to be false. The war continued and masses of Jews, who were deported from Hungary, arrived to Tluste. The overcrowding grew from day to day, we were forbidden to trade with the farmers, and many died from starvation and diseases.

A short time later, the Germans stated to oppress us and terrorize our lives. They established a "Judenrat," whose duty was to extort money and valuables from the Jews and force them to go to labor camps. One day I was also caught by two Jewish policemen who "drafted" workers to the labor camp in Kamionka. I started to plan my escape from their hands. And indeed, I was able to evade them when they took us to the street and ordered us to stand in rows. I escaped from the town and wandered in the fields until I found work on one of the farms in the area. There, I received the news about the transport of Tluste's Jews to the death camps. The heart ached to the sound of this bitter news and I didn't believe that I would be able to hide and survive. Despite all of this, I didn't lose hope and tried to hold on any way I could.

In 1943, the Germans, with the cooperation of the Ukrainian police, started to hold "aktzyot" in Tluste and the surrounding area to eliminate all the Jews in the region. The surviving Jews were placed in a "ghetto." After the "ghetto" was liquidated they declared and announced that whoever dared to hide and save a Jew would be severely punished and his property would be confiscated. The farm owner, with whom I found work and shelter, also panicked and sent me away from his home. I found, together with my brother, Shmuel, refuge at the labor camp in Rozanowka [RÃ³Å¼anÃ³wka] which was under the authority of the "Wehrmacht." There were about three hundred Jews there, the survivors of the ghettos of Zaleszczyki and Tluste. One day, when we were in the fields, we heard the sound of gunfire coming from the direction of the village of Swydova [Swidowa]. We learned that all the surviving Jews were murdered in that labor camp. Immediately, all the workers escaped and scattered in the fields and in the forest. My brother Shmuel and I didn't return to the camp and hid in the fields and in the forests. We only came out once a week to ask the farmers for food. A few days later, it became known to us that the Germans and the Ukrainians also liquidated the camp in Rozanowka. We continued to hide in the fields and eventually dug a pit in the ground and hid there for nine whole months, until the entire area was liberated by the Red Army.

———

[Page 160 - Hebrew]

The Jews of the village of Hinkovtza

by Sara Kimelmann

Translated by Sara Mages

The village of Hinkovtza [Hińkowce] was a distance of seven kilometers from the town of Tłuste. About fifteen Jewish families, who made their living from small trade and agriculture, lived there. They were simple Jews, honest and kindhearted, and were very attached to the village of their birth where they lived for many generations. The relationship between them and their Ukrainian and Polish neighbors was generally good, and this matter helped them and saved them from a lot of suffering during the first period of the German occupation.

The Jews in the village were closely tied to their Jewish brothers in Tłuste. They traveled to the rabbi in Tłuste to ask their questions in matters of kashrut and the like. They paid their taxes to the community of Tłuste and every year, before the holiday of Passover, they sent their contributions to "Maot Chitin." In 1941, when Hungarian Jews were exiled from their homes and wandered across Eastern Galicia to Ukraine, towards their tragic end, several exiled families found refuge in Hinkovtza. The Jews housed them in their homes and protected them from persecution by the village authorities by paying ransom for their souls. In March 1942, the Jews of Hinkovtza were forced to leave the village and move to the ghetto in Tłuste.

I would never forget the beloved woman from the town of Tłuste who took our family in her home. She gave us a room and sheltered us. Her home was like the gate to the town and many Jewish refugees from Horodenka and other cities, who managed to escape from the areas that became "Judenrein," found a warm meal and a word of encouragement at her home. Refugees from the area, the first victims of hunger and persecution, were in Tłuste. They were the first to be sent to labor camps, which were established in Kamionka and Borkie, and none of them managed to get out of there alive. Some found their death from hunger or from the typhus epidemic that raged in the town. Most perished in the various aktzyot, which were held in the town, and on the farm in Holovshintza [Hołowczyńce], to which they fled and where they were imprisoned in a "labor camp."

May this article be a memorial for the martyrs of the village of Hinkovtza, who found their death during the years of the Holocaust, and their bodies are scattered in mass graves in Tłuste and in camps in the area.

———

In Lashkewitz and in Tłuste

by Tzila Kimelmann–Hanin

Translated by Sara Mages

Immediately after the withdrawal of the Russians in July 1941, even before the Germans entered, a pogrom against the Jews took place in Lashkewitz [Ułaszkowce]. It was held as though in retaliation for the murder of Ukrainian prisoners in Chortkov's prison by the Soviets before their withdrawal. After the pogrom, many families in our town received threatening letters from local Ukrainians in which they were ordered to leave town, or they would face a bitter end. Many took their belongings and moved to Tłuste, Chortkov [Czortków], or other locations. Our family also left town and we moved to Tłuste. We earned our living working in the nearby villages where labor camps were built for the Jews. The general manager of those camps was a German by the name of Patti [Vathje], whose attitude towards the Jews was quite fair. Patti tried a number of times to protect his Jewish workers from the different "aktzyot", but his success was very small. In the end, most of the workers in those camps were exterminated one way or another.

Just after our arrival in Tłuste, my father worked in Rozshanovka [Różanówka] camp. I worked in Kozia–Gora camp and we lived in Tłuste. My older brother, Shalom, was taken to the labor camp in Borki–Wielke, and perished there in 1943. On a winter day, at the beginning of 1943, my mother went to one of the farms to bring a little food for her family – and never returned. She was probably murdered on her way. After the death of my mother, the three of us, my father, my small brother and I, moved to Rozshanovka camp and worked there until we were liberated in March 1944. A number of "aktzyot" took place there, but we were able survive unharmed.

In the last days before liberation, the surviving Jews gathered on the farm in Tłuste. Many were killed or wounded in the German bombing which took place just before the Russians arrived in Tłuste. After liberation, my father enlisted in the Soviet army and returned from there in 1946. We met in Poland and from there all of us emigrated to Israel.

———

[Page 231 - Yiddish]

Memories and Experiences

by Shmuel Fiderer (Ben-Moshe)

Translated by Yael Chaver

Soon after the Germans took our town in 1941, a local young man came to me and showed me a letter from his uncle in Krakow, for whom he worked before the war broke out. The young man was able to flee after the first bombs fell and came home safely to Tłuste. He was furious as he showed me the letter, saying, "You read it, and tell me what you think about the writer and the letter."

The text of the letter was as follows: "My dear nephew! As far as I know, you still have too much clothing, not counting the underwear and clothes you left with me when you fled. In my opinion, you will no longer need these clothes. Think about selling them as soon as possible, because you will need the money urgently. Keep only one suit, and work-clothes as well. Make efforts to find work for yourself and your nearest relatives, as soon as possible. Regrettably, I cannot send you your belongings, as I have exchanged them for food."

When I had finished reading, the young man asked me, "Well, what do you think of such a letter?"

At that time, we knew nothing about the deeds of the Germans, because ever since September 17, 1939, we had been under Soviet rule. But I knew the young man's uncle was smart and an experienced, energetic merchant. I thought about the letter and starting reading "between the lines." I realized that this was a letter of warning, to let us know that we were facing a period of hunger and want, and possibly other dangers as well (about which he did not dare to write). I therefore advised the young man to obey his uncle, because the letter was a wink and an allusion to the difficulties awaiting us under German rule. The young man did not agree with me and left in anger.

At that time, the area – between Kolomiya and Husiatyn – had not yet been occupied by the Germans themselves, but by their allies: the Hungarians (Magyars). Soon after entering Tłuste, the Hungarian army placed an order with me for some signboards and guidebooks. They paid me with Hungarian cigarettes, which were in demand at the time and could be exchanged for the best foodstuffs. After I read the letter, I started seeking work for myself in earnest. I realized that it would be better to work far away from the town. I found work with a friend of mine, a Ukrainian academic named Kautsch. He was the manager of the Kushilovtse [Koszylowce] and Popovtse [Popowce] estates. I took Mutsye Schwartz with me, and we both left for Popovtse and worked there for several weeks. When we had finished work, Kautsch sent us each 50 kg of flour and 150 kg of potatoes. It was a fortune at the time, because food was already scarce and hard to obtain in town.

When we returned to Tłuste, the Hungarians were no longer there. As soon as I got back, I was told that a Gestapo guy named Zocher was in charge. He organized all the properties in the Tłuste area into one real estate group. He demanded that the Judenrat send him all the artisans in town for work. Mutsye Schwartz and I also started to work for Zocher.

Zocher was considered a sadist in Tłuste. He was very strict about work and would often beat the Jewish workers for the slightest thing. He was especially dangerous when he caught someone not working. He would then administer a merciless beating. I believe he was also mentally ill: he was a kleptomaniac and often "stole" from his office workers the writing implements he had given them. He was very pleased with me and with Mutsye Schwartz, and we never heard a bad word from him. He even saved me from going to the labor camp in Kamionka, when the Judenrat wanted to exile me there.

At that time, the Judenrat had to send the first contingent of workers to Kamionka and Glubochek [Hluboczek]; I was also on that list. When Zocher found out, he called me in and told me to inform the Judenrat that he, Zocher, had forbidden me to go; he ordered that I be taken off the list. At that time, the Judenrat did not yet understand the limits that the Germans set to its power. They replied that they were not taking his demand into account, and that I would have to follow the Judenrat's orders and go to the camp. When I reported this to Zocher, he said once again, "But you will not go; let them go themselves..."

[Page 232]

In the early evening, after work, he called in Iska Vaysglas [Izka Weisglas], handed him a document, and ordered him to go with me to the Judenrat, read the contents out to them, and then hand me the documents. The document plainly read, "The Jew Samuel Fiderer is busy with the real estate of Tluste and should not be ordered to do anything else." The Judenrat then agreed to remove me from the list. In this way, Zocher saved me from certain death. It turned out that almost all those who were sent to the Kamionka labor camp were tortured there and murdered. Only a few people were able to ransom their way out, for great sums of money. In the end, the Germans saturated the entire camp with gasoline and set fire to it, to erase all traces of their crimes. The Commandant of the camp was an SS officer named Thomanek, who also took part in the "actions" in the surrounding towns. In Tluste alone, he himself shot more than 2400 Jews, the whole time swilling vodka and gorging himself on cake, meat, and other delicacies. He also liquidated the Swidowa labor camp.

Zocher stayed in Tluste for a short time. He was replaced by an SS officer named Stoll, who came from Holland. Stoll settled in Torskie, a town between Tluste and Zaleszczyki, and brought in all the Jewish artisans from Tluste, including myself and Mutsye Schwartz. It was in Torskie that I received my only blow from a German. While Stoll was away, his deputy tasked Schwartz and me with quantities of work that were physically impossible to carry out. When I heard what he demanded of us, I burst out, "Impossible!" Fleischer gave me a stinging slap and said, "For us Germans there is no such thing as impossible," and left the building. When Stoll found out, he had a sharp exchange with his representative about the attitude towards the laborers in general, but I had to suffer the slap.

We stayed in Torskie until the Wehrmacht took over the so-called real estate. The "commander" of real estate in the Tluste area was a German named Pati [Vathje]. He ordered me to leave Torskie and come to work for him. I took Mutsye Schwartz with me. When we came to Tluste, we were sent to work for the General Directorate in Jagielnica. The first director there was an SS officer named Kuehne, of whom everyone was terrified. He would even beat the German soldiers with a whip. Once we arrived in Jagielnica, we announced ourselves at the General Directorate office. A company leader took us to a small two-room house and ordered us to make eighteen signs in white script on a black background. "That will surely take you several days,' he said, "so you will sleep here and receive food." With that, he went away and left us alone.

Jewish children were working in the garden around the house, supervised by SS men and Ukrainian policemen. Terrified, Mutsye Schwartz asked me, "Well, what do you plan to do?" I told him that we needed to finish the job as quickly as possible and get out of there.

We had brought quick-drying paint with us, and immediately went to work. We finished the entire job in a few hours. Schwartz asked me, "What do we do now?" "I'm going to tell General Director Kuehne," I said. The frightened Schwartz grabbed me by the jacket and begged me not to go, because Kuehne would kill us... I paid him no attention and went to the office to announce that we had finished our work.

Three "Frauleins" were sitting in the office and smoking cigarettes. One of them asked me, "What do you want, Jew?" "I came to inform the Herr General Director that we have finished our job," I said. Kuehne was in the other room and heard my answer through the half-open door. He immediately came in and asked, "What did you say?" I answered boldly, "The signs are already finished, Herr General Director." "All?" he asked again. "All!" I answered. "Did the inspector see them?" (The inspector was the company leader, under whom the Jewish girls worked.) "No," I said. "Then go and call the inspector, I'll be there soon." I went to call the inspector. In the meantime, Kuehne put on his belt with the revolver; he took his whip and brought his constant companion, the terrifying dog, and we all went in to examine the work.

The two Germans inspected the signs carefully, looking for any defects, but found nothing. It was very clear that they were satisfied with the work. "What do you want from me now?" Kuehne addressed me now in a friendly manner.

[Page 233]

I answered that we would like to return to Tłuste, if possible. In an irritated tone, Kuehne said, "Wow! I sent a car to Tłuste just five minutes ago! It's too bad that I didn't send you with it." I then asked if he would arrange for us to go home in a horse-drawn cart. "You will have that soon," he said, and immediately ordered a cart to be ready for us, along with two separate passes, and sent us back to Tłuste in style.

* * *

Six months after they arrived, in the spring of 1942, the Germans took over the management of Polish and Jewish properties, which had been "nationalized" before the Soviet takeover. They planted a tropical crop called koksagiz, whose roots contain a moisture that can be used to manufacture synthetic rubber. The Germans tried this crop in various places, but it succeeded only in our area, around Tluste. Because rubber was important for military purposes, the management of the entire enterprise was handed over to the German Wehrmacht. The office was in Jagielnica.

Management of all the properties in Tluste and the close surroundings was held by a high-ranking SS officer named Pati [Vathje]. His rank was Oberleiter. The plantation managers would order most of their workers from the Judenrat for all their jobs, including field labor. The workers were concentrated in special labor camps. Thanks to that fact, and largely also thanks to the decent leadership of our Oberleiter Pati, a certain number of Jews in the Tluste labor camps were saved and survived the general extermination of the Jews of Poland.

At the end of summer 1943, all Jews capable of work were assembled in labor camps, by Gestapo order. Afterwards, they finished off all the Jews in town, rendering it Judenrein. The Judenrat was also dissolved at that time.

By then, my wife and I had already been working a long time at the Szypowce estate. My job was to mark the newborn lambs, so I was working outside the camp. In the middle of the field, far enough from the farmyard, the Germans built a large stable, where they brought many of the sheep taken from the Russian kolkhozes.

Work went on without incident until December 1943. One Friday, when I came back from work, I met several townspeople who had ridden in from the surrounding camps. They had terrible news: they had heard that the camps around Tluste would also be made Judenrein, and the Gestapo had ordered that Jews should no longer work on the estates. They said that work in the Tluste camp had been stopped since yesterday, and the Gestapo had ordered that the Jews in the camps be liquidated as soon as possible. They asked me to go to Tluste and find out whether all of this was really true. I told them that I would go to Tluste first thing in the morning. I couldn't go there at night, because there was a good chance that I would not be let in.

As long as the Tluste Judenrat existed, its members were in touch with the German administration. When the Judenrat was disbanded and its members hid in bunkers, there were several people who could still approach the Oberleiter. The first was Hillel Kenigsberg, who was the economic adviser of the Tłuste camp. The second was his wife, Manya Kenigsberg, who worked in Pati's kitchen. Third was Yosef Frades, who was barber to the Germans and the Ukrainian police until the end. I was the fourth. I was working at Szypowce, and the Polish property manager, Poplarski, received an order from the Oberleiter to provide me with horses, to travel whenever I needed to, even if they needed to be taken off plowing. This was how I got horses the next morning to go to Tłuste. I took along a few chickens, some eggs, and a big lump of butter for the Oberleiter, and started off for Tłuste.

The Tłuste camp consisted of wooden barracks; Hillel Kenigsberg and Sholyme Trembovelski [Shlomo Trembowelski] were the only ones who lived in a brick house, formerly the residence of the guards. My meetings with Hillel and Yosef were always sincere, but this time Kenigsberg did not greet me so warmly. I found him lying on his bed, fully dressed, his face red with agitation. His wife was also in the house, as she was no longer allowed to work in Pati's kitchen.

[Page 234]

I greeted them, but neither answered. I went on, to the room of Shloyme Trembovelski, where I found only Yosef Frades. Trembovelski was no longer there.

Frades, too, did not respond to my greeting. He sat, hunched over and frozen, staring straight ahead. When I came into the room I noticed that his shoes were wet, and realized that he had just come from a journey. I immediately asked him where he had been. He answered, angrily, "What do you want of me, Fiderer?" "I want to know where you were," I answered stubbornly. Frades lowered his gaze and answered quietly, "I've come from the Ukrainian police."

"What did the Ukrainian police tell you?" "And do you believe what they say?" he burst out. "Yes," I answered with certainty. "Everything the Ukrainian police commander told me was always right." Frades then recounted: The commandant had told him, confidentially, that they had received written word from the Gestapo announcing that the entire Tłuste region had been classified by the German authorities as Judenrein. From now on, the Ukrainians could do whatever they wanted to the Jews; Jewish lives and deaths were in Ukrainian hands. The Ukrainians wanted the Germans to finish us off as quickly as possible. But the commandant added, angrily, "What do they think, the niemakes (Germans)? They murdered all the Jews, and now they want us to kill all the remaining Jews, which they will then photograph to show that it was the Ukrainians who killed the Jews! No, we will not harm you. Please tell Shmuel Fiderer, and also tell him that I will visit him in Szypowce and will tell him everything myself."

"Well, do you believe that, Fiderer?" "Yes," I answered, encouraged. "I certainly believe it all!" This conversation was followed by a pained silence. I finally broke it, asking, "Why doesn't either of you go to Pati?" Frades looked at me as though I were insane. "In that case," I went on, "I will go to him myself!" I turned away and left the room. I calculated that, in any case, I had nothing to lose by going to Pati.

When I came into the kitchen and gave Miss Janka (Pati's friend) the little food that I had brought, I noticed that Mrs. Kenigsberg was now also in the kitchen. As soon as Mrs. Kenigsberg heard that I intended to go to see Pati, she had gotten out of bed and gone into the kitchen, to hear the coming conversation between myself and Pati.

I had myself announced to Pati. Whenever he heard I was there, he would call me into his office and ask for all the details about the farm and the dairy at Szypowce. This time he did not call me in, but rather let me wait. After a while he came into the kitchen, greeted me with a smile, and said, "The only one who remembers me is Fiderer. Thank you for that." He started quizzing me about the farm. When he had finished he started to leave. I asked him, "Herr Oberleiter, will we Jews be sleeping peacefully in 24 hours' time?" I had asked him this question once before, prior to an "action," when he told me to get out of town. That time, he answered. "You will not be sleeping peacefully!" I later understood very well what he had meant. I used the same question now, because I did not know how else to ask him. Pati turned back to me and answered, "I give you my word of honor as an officer: you will be able to sleep peacefully for three, or even four months."

As soon as he said that, Mrs. Kenigsberg left the kitchen to tell her husband the good news. I wasn't satisfied with that answer, and asked him further, "If so, why don't you let the Jews work in the fields?" "You're right," he answered, "go and tell Kenigsberg that all the Jews should start working again this afternoon." With that, he parted from me and went away. When I came to see Kenigsberg, wanting to announce the good news, he became very annoyed, and said in Polish," You idiot, you! Why did you ask only about the next 24 hours?" I responded cynically, "They say that in the course of 24 hours either the nobleman or his dog might die [ed. The ending to a well-known Yiddish anecdote according to which a Jew is given five years to teach the local nobleman's dog how to read, and tells his worried wife that either the nobleman or the dog might die in that space of time – in other words, anything might happen over time]. But I can tell you why I asked about the next 24 hours.

[Page 235]

"Many of the Jews in the camps have prepared bunkers and hiding places at the properties of peasants. They will need a minimum of 24 hours to gather food and clothing, and to disappear into the bunkers." For me, this was irrelevant. I had not prepared any bunker, because I distrusted the Polish and Ukrainian population. My trust did not increase after the commander of the Ukrainian police came to me in Szypowce and told me what I had already heard from Yosef Frades. He assured me once again that the Ukrainian police would not harm Jews. He told me only that we should be very wary of the SS units before their retreat; the Red Army would arrive in a matter of days or several months at the most. I reported Pati's words to Kenigsberg, saying that all the Jews should resume work. We parted in a cheerful mood.

I left Tluste and went to the surrounding camps, to report on my conversation with the Oberleiter and his promise: we could work peacefully in the camps for three, even four months. That was in December 1943. His promise indeed came true, as we were liberated by the Red Army on March 23 [1944]. Exactly four months passed between his promise and our liberation.

———

[Page 235 - Yiddish]

Various Memories

by Eliyahu Albin

Translated by Yael Chaver

The Judenrat always knew in advance when an "action" would take place, or when Jews would be grabbed for work in a camp. They did not know the precise day it would happen, but they knew the approximate times. In fact, they let their friends and acquaintances know, as well as people who would pay for the information. When the SS were rounding up Jews for the camp, or during an 'action,' members of the Judenrat and the "Ordnungsdienst" (the Jewish police) went with them. For a large sum of money, or the right connections, you could be exempted from the labor camp.

My older brother paid the Kamionka camp leader to free me, thanks to the help of the Judenrat in Podwoloczyska. The Tluste Judenrat demanded a great deal of money from my brother. My brother Sheftel risked his life, removed the blue-white patch, and went to Kamionka as an "Aryan." He found a connection to the camp commander, Paul Thomanek, and bargained for my release in return for 5000 złoty. However, the Tluste Judenrat did not like this. The head of the Judenrat went to Thomanek in the camp and told him that he could demand three times that amount, 15,000 złoty. Otherwise, I would remain in the camp... There was no choice but to gather that money over eight days and send it through the Judenrat in Podwoloczyska.

On Christmas Eve there was an opportunity: the high-ranking SS officers went to Germany, and the camp was run by ordinary SS men. They wanted to earn some money, so the Judenrat made an agreement with them to free some Jews in return for a payment of 500 złoty per Jew. Each family with a member in the camp – a father or a son – sold their last possessions to ransom them for 500 złoty. At that time, there were about 140 Tluste Jews in the labor camp. The Judenrat took all the money from the families but did not free anyone; they divided the money among themselves, reasoning that all the Jews would be murdered in any case, and there was no point in returning them to Tluste. The money enabled the Judenrat members to hide.

The story of the Judenrat's hiding place is true. Berl Holenberg, a Jew from Tłuste, was once seeking a hiding place for himself. He got as far as the hill where the Judenrat members were hiding. Holenberg was a native of the area and was well known there. He had escaped from the camp during an "action" and wanted to hide in the hill. A kind of tunnel extended for more than a kilometer into the hill. Holenberg stayed there, in pitch dark. The peasant who brought the Judenrat members food once a week (at 2 a.m. on the night between Saturday and Sunday) found Holenberg sitting alone. He suggested to the Judenrat that they take him in and he would feed the additional person. They would not agree, saying, "No, we don't want a witness afterwards." They suggested that the peasant dig another tunnel for Holenberg, far from their own hideout, and bring him food there.

[Page 236]

The peasant had no choice but to do so. He dug a tunnel for Holenberg, who stayed there for eight months. During the cold winter months, his feet froze. The Judenrat members were sure that Holenberg would not be able to survive under such harsh conditions.

I know this from their actions towards me and my brother. We were hiding with the brother-in-law of the goy (non-Jew) who hid them and supplied them with food. When they found out, they asked the non-Jew to come and discuss something important. The non-Jew went with his brother-in-law on Saturday night. They [the Judenrat members] welcomed him cordially, had a drink with him, and the non-Jew told them that he was also hiding two zhydkes. To make a long story short, they gave him [the brother-in-law] 500 dollars to get rid of us. On Tuesday, our "landlord" came home to his mother, very agitated, and told her that he had enough money and did not need the two brothers any more. His old mother gave him a piece of her mind and told him that she would not do this, that she had been hiding the two Jews for ten months, and she would go on hiding them for a while and would save them. We heard this from the mother of our "landlord." He himself continued to be angry at us. We eventually had to threaten him: if we were denounced, we would denounce the Judenrat members. From then on, we were very wary of him. We had two revolvers, which we kept loaded. In addition, we never let the peasant come close and spoke to him only from a distance.

This situation went on for six weeks, until the Russians arrived. After our liberation I met Berl Holenberg. He told me what had happened to him, and I told him about my experiences. I also told him that I had known about him but could not help.

———

[Page 237 - Yiddish]

The Jews in Hinkevitz [Hińkowce]

by Sarah Kimmelman

Translated by Yael Chaver

In the village of Hinkevitz, approximately seven kilometers from Tłuste, there were about fifteen Jewish families who made their living by small trade and farming. They were simple, honest Jews, and were deeply connected to the village; they had good relations with their Polish and Ukrainian neighbors. The good relations even continued shortly after the German invasion.

At the same time, they had strong connections to the Jews of Tłuste. They would travel to Tłuste for the rabbi's decision on religious matters, and they contributed to the annual Passover food fund. In 1941, when the Hungarian Jews were driven into Ukraine (sic), a few families stayed in Hinkevitz. The Jews of Hinkevitz took them in and often paid bribes to protect them from persecution. Eventually, all the Jews – strangers and locals alike – were forced into the Tłuste ghetto, in March 1942.

I will never forget the dear Jewish woman from Tłuste, who took in our family, gave us a room, and cared for us. Her house was at the entrance to the town, and many fleeing Jews, from Horodenka and other towns in the area, received a warm meal and encouragement from her. The incoming Jews were the first casualties of hunger and persecution in Tłuste. They were the first to be sent to the labor camps at Kamionka and Borki, from which few returned alive. Some died of hunger and typhus, but most were murdered in the various "actions" in Tłuste and the Holowczynce labor camp.

Let my few words be a memorial to the martyrs of Hinkevitz, whose bones are scattered in the mass graves in Tłuste and the camps around it.

———

The End of the Swidowa Jews

by Rokhl (Rose) Rubinstein-Tenenbaum

Translated by Yael Chaver

In Swidowa [Świdowa], a village near Tłuste, the local peasants published and carried out the terrible decree against the few Jewish families of the village, early in the Nazi occupation. One Thursday evening, Ukrainian bands attacked the Jews, who were not prepared and had gone to bed peacefully. The bandits used their farm tools – scythes, rakes, and spades—and murdered all the Jews in the village in this grisly fashion.

The martyrs were buried outside the village. News of the Swidowa pogrom made a terrible impression in Tłuste. One of my uncles, Fishel Rubinstein, lived in Swidowa with his two daughters, two sons-in-law, and one grandson. They were all tragically murdered that night. There also lived in the village a very observant Jew, a true righteous man (tzaddik), Leyzer Waltzer. People said afterwards that when he was attacked he said, "Everything is from God," and submitted to his tragic fate.

———

[Page 238 - Yiddish]

Mama

Chaim Fiderer

Translated by Yael Chaver

In commemoration of my murdered mother Ratse Fiderer-Margulies, may she rest in peace; she was in Vienna, and deported to Theresienstadt on August 27, 1942 – and then probably, like all the others, to Auschwitz...

I don't know your birth date,
I don't know your death date;
I know only that I lost you forever,
I know you were martyred by the Germans.

I know you were driven from your home,
Tormented and tortured in the Nazi hell;
An 80-year-old woman, you were chosen,
Along with others, to burn in the gas oven...

Though you did not miss a single fast day,
Always believed the Holy Creator
Would protect you from trouble, from hardships,
You shared the fate of millions.

I say *kaddish* for you year after year,
You live in my imagination, as though I see you now;
Your motherly love – like a prophecy
Ordering me to flee from the beast's jaws...

I fled aimlessly, wandering
Over lands and seas, until I found rest,
And you? You were caught by the murderous gangs –
And I suffer and grieve every day, every hour.

לזכר עולם
לקדושי קהילת טלוסטה
שהושמדו על ידי הנאצים
והאוקראינים בשנים תש"ב תש"ג
בגיטו ובמחנות עבודה
שבסביבה
ארגון יוצאי טלוסטה והסביבה בישראל

Memorial plaque for the martyrs of Tluste in the "Holocaust Cellar," Jerusalem*

Translation of plaque from Hebrew:

In eternal memory of the martyrs of
the Tluste community
Destroyed by the Nazis
and Ukrainians in 1942-1943
In the ghetto and in work camps
Of the surrounding countryside.
[signed]
Organization of Tluste Survivors in
Israel

* **Editor's note:** Israel's first Holocaust museum, established in 1948, on Mount Zion near the traditional site of King David's tomb. The better-known, larger, Yad Vashem was founded in 1953.

Survivors' Testimonies

[Pages 161-163]

The sequence of events during the war

by Hillel Kenigsberg

Translated by Sara Mages

On 6 July 1941, the last Soviet troops left town after they blew up the train station, the grain and straw warehouses next to it, and also the trains which stood at the terminal. Later, when the Germans arrived in town, they forced the Jews to clear the rubble. The town was also slightly damaged by the fire which took hold of the buildings near the train station.

On Sunday, 7 July 1941, the local Ukrainian authorities immediately organized. The day passed quietly, but the pogroms against the Jews in the surrounding area, which were organized by the Ukrainians, began at night. The town of Ulaskovtzh [Ułaszkowce] opened it. Every year, on 7 July, a festive gathering and a large annual fair, with the participation of farmers from the entire area, was held in Ulaskovtzh. Masses of peasants, who were inflamed by the inciting speeches of the Ukrainian priest and the local school teacher, came out of the church and started to attack the local Jews and also the monastery, which the Russians had turned into an almshouse for old men and contained a number of Jews. The attack in Ulaskovtzh served as a signal to the Ukrainians in all towns and villages in the surrounding area. The refugees from these places came to Tłuste and aroused panic in the town. We feared that that the murders would also spread to Tłuste, but thanks to the calming speeches of the Ukrainian priest Izbulskie [ed. Anton Navolskyy], the Ukrainian bank manager Bablokov [Badluk], and the lawyer Androshinov [Andrszczyn], nothing had happened in our town.

Two days later, the advance guard of the Hungarian army arrived and took control of the town. The attitude of the Hungarians towards the Jews was quite good. The Germans were already in the nearby city of Chortkov [CzortkÃ³w] and terrible things took place there. They forced the Jews to dig out the bodies from the graves in the prison yard and bury them again. Several Jews were killed in this operation.

A Jewish council, which was composed of the intelligentsia circles and wealthy residents, was organized in Tłuste. It was assigned to negotiate with the Ukrainian and the Hungarian authorities on any matters related to the Jews. At the end of July, camps after camps of Jews, who were expelled from Hungary, started to arrive. Some of them remained in the towns across the Dniester River, but most of them were expelled farther east, toward Kamieniec–Podolski. In the first days of August, Hungarian drivers arrived from Kamieniec and told us that, in a single day, about thirty thousand local Jews and also refugees who arrived from Hungary were shot and killed there.

The first Germans arrived in town in the first half of August. They housed their offices in Zaleszczyki, organized a "Judenrat" in Tłuste and appointed a Ukrainian police force. First and foremost, they ordered the "Judenrat" to supply them leather coats, boots and woolens. The "Judenrat" organized a Jewish police force, enforced taxes on the Jewish population, and drafted Jews to work. In late August, an order was issued that each Jew must wear an armband on his arm (it was a moderate attitude in comparison to Chortkov. At the beginning, about three hundred people, from among the intelligentsia, were taken out and shot near the city.) A short time later, an order was issued that all Jews who lived in the villages and in the suburbs must move to town. In October, it became known in town that in Zaleszczyki the Germans took some of the Jews, selected those who were fit to work, and the rest, about 600 Jews, were shot to death.

On Yom Kippur, the Jews of Zaleszczyki were expelled to nearby towns and only two hundred Jews were allowed to remain in the town. More and more refugees arrived to our town from nearby towns, and the density increased from day to day. Jewish homes were marked with a Star of David. At the same time, they also started to draft people for the Kamionka labor camp and the "Judenrat" was forced to supply a certain quota of Jewish workers. In our town, as in other locations, the rich were able to redeem themselves by paying ransom.

*

In September, a notice appeared that all Jewish farmers must report to the agricultural office in Chortkov. There were seven or eight Jewish farmers in our town, but we weren't able to report in Chortkov because it was forbidden to leave the town. Therefore, we reported to the municipal office which was managed by Ukrainians who directed us to the "Judenrat." The "Judenrat" ordered us again to report to work at the German agricultural building. In the end, they only kept the four farmers that they have chosen, and I was one of them. The commander was a Gestapo man by the name of Zocher, and the whole town feared him. He was the director of "Liegenschaft" [real estate]. At that time, the Germans took over the agricultural farms which had been "nationalized" by the Russians, and began to demand that the "Judenrat" supply them work forces for these farms. They also recruited the former farm managers to help the Aryan managers who were appointed by them.

In February 1942, the management of "Liegenschaft" was transferred to the hands of the "Wehrmacht," who turned to the "Judenrat" and demanded about ten thousand workers for the agricultural farms. With that, they turned to the Gestapo in Chortkov with the demand not to hurt the farm workers during the "aktzyot." The Gestapo refused to ensure that. The matter was transferred to the management in Lvov and from there to Himmler himself. The answer to this matter was late to come, and in the meantime the Gestapo men acted as they saw fit, meaning, without "favoritism" towards the workers on the agricultural farms.

In the month of March 1942, the "Liegenschaft" management left Tluste, but two members of the administration, I and my sister's son, were left in place. The manager of the department was a very decent German agronomist.

In May, a new manager, a reservist by the name of Patti [Vathje], arrived. He was also very decent and over time helped the Jews of Tluste a lot.

In July 1942, the men of the Gestapo arrived in town and demanded to hand over to them 10% of the town's people, among those who "had become a burden" on the "Judenrat." About two hundred people, old and feeble, were turned over then. To complete the "quota", the Gestapo brought 75 young women who worked at the Kozia–Gora farm near Tluste. All of them were taken to the train station and sent "in an unknown direction."

The second "aktzya" took place on 5 October, 1942. In this "aktzya" the Germans collected, with the help of the Ukrainian militia, about one thousand of the town's residents. They put them in train cars and transported them to Belzec death camp. All the Jewish residents left their homes, hid in bunkers or fled the town. The Germans removed all the property from the abandoned houses and the rest was looted by the local population.

After the second "aktzya," the situation of those who remained worsened. The town was filled with refugees from towns in Stanislaw district. The extermination of the Jews ended in those towns and they were declared "cleansed of Jews" (Judenrein). In Tłuste, as in other towns in the area, the Germans started to organize "labor camps." Only Jews who managed to receive the letter "W" were accepted there. This matter involved lot of work and many difficulties. At the same time, a typhus epidemic broke out, and about fifteen people died from it every day. In addition to that, there was always fear of an "aktzya." According to a rumor, the entire district of Tarnopol had to turn "Judenrein" by the end of 1942 and, according to the Gestapo's timetable, Tłuste was the last in line.

In the last days of December 1942, the Ukrainian militia started to grab Jews on the town's streets and send them to Chortkov and there they were interned in the Gestapo's prison. The abductions lasted for several days, until the beginning of January 1943. A number of abductees were released after payment of large ransom and the others were held in prison for a long period of time. All of a sudden, the Gestapo leadership informed the district Jewish council in Chortkov that the Jewish detainees would be released and the council should find absorption places for them. It seemed that the winter conditions prevented them from conducting "aktzyot" on a large scale, and a relative calm prevailed during the winter months.

The fear of "aktzyot" started again after the cold days had passed. People were afraid to sleep in their homes and started to stream to labor camps as if they were a place of refuge. In May, news arrived about the "aktzyot" that were conducted in nearby towns, and people started to worry that Tłuste's turn would come soon. A certain date was even stated – some said that the "aktzya" would take place in the morning of May 25. Only a few people remained in town, most of the residents fled to the fields and to the forests. Only those who had a secure hideout remained in the town, and the elderly and the sick were forced to stay.

And here, the day passed and nothing happened. People started to believe that it was a false panic and most of them returned to their homes. Later, members of the "Judenrat" confirmed that an "aktzya" was planned for 25

May. Two "Volksdeutsche" informed the Gestapo headquarters in Chortkov that the Jews escaped from their homes and for that reason they postponed the execution of the judgment to 27 May.

On Thursday, 27 May, at five o'clock in the morning, we suddenly heard the sound of gunfire coming from all directions. About six hundred Germans surrounded the town and all the roads were blocked. The Germans gathered about three thousand Jews in the market square and led them in groups of 100–200 to the cemetery. There, they were shot and buried in a mass grave that was dug by seventy young Jewish men. After the three thousand were shot and buried, the Germans also killed the young men who dug the grave and sorted out the victims' clothes. Only one boy, aged eleven, managed to escape the shower of bullets and survived the war. The murder was conducted by a person named, Tumanek [Thomanek], who killed 600 Jews with his own hands. Apart from the three thousand who were killed in the cemetery, about eight hundred Jews were killed in the town's streets when they tried to escape from the hands of the murderers. On the day after the "aktzya," the Jewish militia collected the bodies and brought them to the cemetery for burial.

The Jews who were on the farms and in the labor camps weren't hurt in the great "aktzya." They also didn't hurt the members of the "Judenrat" and the Jewish militia. More than one thousand Jews gathered in the town with the hope that they would be left alone for several months. But also this hope was dashed. About a week after the great "aktzya" came the final liquidation of the remaining Jews in the town.

It happened on Sunday, 6 June 1943. Patti, the manager of the agricultural farms, knew what was going to happen and warned the workers not to dare to go to the town. On the same day he also tried to gather as many workers as possible from among the town's residents. At 11 o'clock in the morning, a group of Gestapo men arrived in the town, locked the ghetto, which at that time was reduced to only two streets, and started to hunt the surviving Jews who were inside it. The Jews who were caught were taken to the cemetery and shot and killed there by Tumanek, the "aktzya" commander. It should be noted, that it was the one and only time that an "aktzya" was held on a Sunday, on the Christians' day of rest.

Eighty Jews remained in the town after this "aktzya." They were sent to Chortkov under the order of the Germans, and there they were eliminated.

Several members of the "Judenrat" and the Jewish police managed to cross the Romanian border with the help of one of the Ukrainian leaders. Some of the town's wealthy men also joined them. A Ukrainian guide transported them across the border, and there he turned them over to the Romanian police. They were brought back to Zaleszczyki after they were robbed of everything in their possession and handed over to the Germans. On the same day, all of them were shot and killed.

After the liquidation of the Jewish population in Tluste the town was declared "free of Jews." Several hundred Jews remained in the labor camps on the agricultural farms and lived under very difficult conditions. Only twenty-three Jews remained under Patti's protection on the farm in Tluste. At the same time, detachments of partisans began to appear in the forests around the town. Sometimes, the partisans attacked the farms to get the supplies they needed, but they didn't hurt the Jews. On the contrary, they encouraged them with words and promised that their bad situation would not last for many days. However, they refused to let the Jews join their companies. They justified their refusal with the fact that they also suffered from shortage of weapons and supplies.

The Germans probably suspected that there was contact between the partisans and the Jews, and it may be that these concerns prompted them to eliminate the Jews in the labor camps despite the severe shortage of workers. On 15 July 1943, an "aktzya" was conducted at all the labor camps. Only a few managed to escape to the forests to save their lives. The wicked didn't touch the farm in Tluste since it wasn't an official labor camp. Theoretically, the farm workers had to live in the Kozia–Gora camp, but Patti disobeyed the order and allowed them to stay in the farm.

All the labor camps were eliminated after the "aktzya" in the camps, and the Jews weren't allowed to stay there. The camp managers denied access to each Jew who tried to return to the camp or to the farm. Also Patti ordered the Jews to leave the farm, but when he saw their distress he agreed to keep them.

Every Friday the farm managers gathered in Jagielnica. On the Friday of that week, Patti returned from the meeting around three o'clock in the afternoon, and before he entered his home, he approached the Jewish workers and said: "the matter that we've been waiting for finally arrived, but unfortunately too late. Permission came from Himmler to employ about six thousand Jewish workers in the labor camps." He informed us that from now on the labor camps could exist legally and the Jews would be able to return and work there. The Jews who escaped to the forests and lived there under very difficult conditions started to return to the camps, but also here their situation was very difficult because they constantly feared attacks. In addition, they were always hungry because the food ration was poor and inadequate. The conditions on the farm in Tluste were relatively better. Patti and the other managers and supervisors treated us well. We worked in the vegetable garden and ate stolen potatoes that we "pinched" from the fields. Most of the workers weren't from Tluste. They were refugees from the nearby towns who arrived to Tluste and miraculously survived.

When autumn arrived and after it winter, a typhus epidemic spread among the camp's inhabitants. In addition to that, we also suffered a lot from lice infestation. Again, the Ukrainian police found a reason to destroy the Jews to exterminate the disease. At that time, murderous attacks by the "Banderovtzim" began in the camp and each attack cost dozens of victims. The police used the opportunity of Patti's absence from the farm in Tluste, and killed five people. A woman was lying on one of the beds with her little daughter. Both were sick. The policeman shot the woman and killed her, but he didn't notice the girl and she remained alive. After the police left, the girl jumped up and came to our hut and her nightgown was soaked with her mother's blood. The girl – her name is Margalit (Margulis) – survived. A seventeen–year old boy, who looked very sick after recovering from typhus, was also killed in this manner. His mother refused to step aside despite the policemen's warnings, and then the policemen also shot her. She was Lutka Krasotzka [Lotti Krasutski] and her son Norbert.

From the beginning of 1944, refugees who collaborated with the Germans began to arrive to the Tluste area from Russia. Among them were many members of Ukrainian police companies, who murdered every Jew who came their way. In February, a regiment of ten thousand Cossacks from the Don region, who joined the Germans in their retreat, passed by. They also caused many deaths among the Jews. In Lisovtza [Lisowce], they disremembered many Jews with their swords, and dozens of Jews were injured by them. At that time, the Ukrainian policemen weren't allowed to enter the labor camps, but every Jew who was caught outside the camp boundaries was brutally murdered by them.

On 16 March 1944, the German headquarters evacuated the farm in Tluste and took all the farm equipment. The local headquarters (the labor headquarters) was left in place. We didn't suffer from the Germans (who belonged to the regular army and not to the Gestapo), and they even tried to help us a little. In contrast, the Ukrainian policemen threatened that they would have time to finish us off at the last moment.

Liberation day, 23 March 1944, arrived. A company of Ukrainian policemen passed in the early morning hours. They began to rage and demanded vodka from the Jews as they were threatening with the pistols in their hands. The German company commander accepted the Jews' request and came to drive the policemen away. A few hours later, the last German company got the order to retreat, and left the farm and the town. Close to three o'clock, the first Soviet tanks arrived and the surviving Jews came towards their liberators with open arms and crying from happiness. However, their happiness didn't last long. A squadron of German planes suddenly appeared over the camp, dropped several bombs on the barracks, and even shot those who gathered in the camp's yard. About seventy people from among the survivors perished in this bombing and many were wounded.

Ten days later, a German regiment which was surrounded by the Soviets around Kamieniec managed to break the blockade and advanced towards Tluste. The Soviet army advised the few surviving Jews to join them in their retreat to Chortkov. All the Jews, apart from twenty sick and wounded, joined the Soviet army. In each town they were joined by the local survivors and, when they arrived in Skalat, their number reached to about a thousand people.

The migration, in the footsteps of the Soviet army, lasted about four weeks. Later, the front line moved away from our region and the Jews began to disperse, each to his own place. However, a short time later the vast majority left the country, which was saturated with the blood of their relatives and compatriots, and moved to the city of Chernovtsy [Chernowitz] where a relatively large group of about ten thousand Jewish survivors remained.

———

[Pages 164-167]

The farm in Tłuste during the war

by Maria Kenigsberg

Translated by Sara Mages

The Germans entered our town on 6 July 1941. For three days the town and surrounding area were without a specific rule. During these few days the Ukrainians attacked the Jews who lived in the surrounding villages and murdered them with great cruelty. In town, two Ukrainian leaders, the priest and the lawyer, influenced the masses of Ukrainians not to hurt the Jews. Under the influence of their words, the Ukrainian militia detained the Ukrainian rioters who arrived from the villages and did not let them enter the town. Zumerman and his wife, who lived in one of the villages, survived but their three children were murdered by the rioters.

After three days, a Hungarian military regiment arrived in our town. The Ukrainian mayor, who expected the Germans to arrive, built a triumphal arch decorated with a Ukrainian and a German flag, but the matter was not right in the eyes of the Hungarian commander. He called the mayor, slapped his face and ordered him to remove the two flags.

The attitude of the Hungarians towards the Jews was relatively good. Surely, they drafted many Jews for forced labor, but in a peaceful humanitarian way. There was one ruffian among them who abused Jews, and because of him a number of Jews drowned while building a bridge over the Dniester River.

Two weeks after the arrival of the Hungarians, the first Jewish exiles arrived in our town from Hungary. Apparently they were Jews with Polish citizenship. Nicely dressed, they were transported in vehicles and brought many valuables with them. Some of them were allowed to remain in our town, and the rest were transported farther, to the area of Kamieniec Podolski. Many Jews served in the Hungarian army, some of them as drivers, and they helped a number of Jews to return to their homes, to Budapest. A few weeks later, we found out from the Hungarian drivers, who returned from Kamieniec Podolski, that the Germans held an "aktzya" there, and shot and killed around twenty thousand Jews from Romania and Poland who escaped together with the

Soviet army and stopped in Kamieniec. One woman from Kamieniec was able to move to the Soviet sector and reach Moscow. There, she told on the radio about the Germans' acts of terror against the Jewish refugees.

A few weeks later, at the end of the summer, the first Germans arrived. I walked in the street and saw them humiliating a Jewish girl. This was their "premiere" act. After that, a German by the name of Zocher arrived and received the management of the farm in Tłuste. He was a bad man who beat Jews. He came to the "Judenrat" and ordered different items and furniture for his apartment. In addition, he requested a number of Jews who were knowledgeable in agriculture. My husband and my brother were among those who signed up. He employed them in different jobs in the farm. They worked very hard and Zocher stood over them with a gun in his hand hurrying them up. He himself lived like a king and held magnificent parties. The "farmers" worked for him during the winter months.

At the beginning of 1943, the Germans started to confiscate the Jews' furs. The furs belonging to my brother–in–law and my husband were also confiscated. At the same period of time I started to come frequently to Zocher's apartment on the farm. My former cook, Modra Monka [Mudra Munk], worked as a cook in his home, and she asked me to come and help her serve since she was not an expert in this manner. Once, during a party, I came across Zocher. He stood in the company of a Nazi by the name of Stoll, who was going to take over the management of the farm. According to my armband he realized that I was Jewish and shouted at me: "What are you doing here?" I answered him that I came to help the cook with the preparations for the party. He did not believe my words, but when he saw how well I worked, he softened and let me stay until the end of the party. At the end, nothing was changed in the management of the farm. Zocher remained in his post and since then I was allowed to come to his home with his knowledge and permission.

Sometime later, Zocher was transferred to Berezdów, and an agronomist by the name of Hanf took his place. Together with him came a new manager by the name of Patti [Vathje]. My husband stayed to work as Patti's helper, but I lived in our home, which was kind of a villa, together with a family from Hungary. It was a woman by the name of Kato whose husband returned to Hungary with the Hungarian army drivers. They did not have the time to transfer her, and she lived in our home together with her husband's parents.

A few of my closest relatives lived in Horodenka: my father, my oldest sister with her daughter, and also my brother with his wife and two children. After the great "aktzya" of December 1941, in which a few thousand Jews were murdered there, my niece Leila [Lilka] arrived in Tłuste and moved into our home. Under her initiative we started to build a "bunker" in our home, in case an "aktzya" would take place in Tłuste. On 15 August 1942 my husband's nephew arrived from the farm with a special message. Lauterbach, one of the German farm managers, sent him together with my son to bring me to the farm since the Germans were planning to hold an "aktzya" in town. We all went to the farm, and there they hid the whole family in the attic of the department agronomist's home, and in the attic of Lauterbach's home. My child and I remained in Lauterbach's apartment. In order to engage me in any kind of work in his home, he tore a shirt and gave it to me to repair.

On that day, the first "aktzya" took place in Tłuste. According the "quota", the "Judenrat" was demanded to hand 350 people, mostly old people, to the hands of the Gestapo. The old people were ordered to take brooms with them, so it would look like they were being taken to a place of work. In addition, the Germans took seventy young women from the farm in Kozia–Gora. All of them were taken to the train station and sent to a death camp, probably to Belzec. On the same day my sister, Leila's mother, arrived in Tłuste from Horodenka. She arrived at the time that the old people were collected and taken to the train station. She had enough time to hide in a corn field near our house, and waited until we returned home.

On 5 October 1942, a second "aktzya" took place and around two thousand men and women were killed. Patti told us in advance about the "aktzya" and we informed other Jews. Patti told us that those who would work on the farm on that day would not get hurt. Many of the workers asked him to let their family members stay on the farms, and he agreed in a number of cases. In spite of that, members of the Ukrainian police arrived to the farm, together with the Germans, and took a number of Jews who were hiding in the workshops.

Approximately at the same time, the last "aktzya" took place in Horodenka, and the last surviving Jews were liquidated in the city. My father and my oldest brother also got caught, and were locked up for three days in a warehouse without food and water. Later, they were led to the rail cars and sent to Belzec. My father, Henryk Spiegel, was seventy–two years old at the time. Despite his advanced age he spoke to the hearts of his brothers to fate, who were younger then him, and asked them to open the door and jump out. They hesitated to do so, so he pushed his way to the door and jumped out. Many jumped after him. Also my brother was able to jump out of another car, but he did not meet with my father despite the fact that both of them jumped near Stanisławów. My father arrived in Stanisławów, and from there he left on foot to Horodenka. On the way he was caught and taken to the Ukrainian police station. There, he was given to the hands of a Ukrainian policeman who was ordered to bring him to the police station in Horodenka. To his luck, the policeman was a former worker on my brother's farm; he knew my father and released him on the way. In Horodenka, which was already "Judenrein", he met my sister–in–law and her children, and all of them reached us in Tłuste. My brother Max [Markus] Spiegel arrived after them.

Patti advised my husband to move his family to the farm. So we moved to live on the farm where an apartment was allocated for us together with the Ukrainian supervisors. They treated us with fairness, and somehow it was possible to live on the farm. At last, Patti received management of the farm in Tłuste, and the management of two other farms. A German by the name of Frank was appointed manager of the other farm. He was related to the Governor General of Poland and was a very honest man. He treated the Jews with fondness and never sat at the table without his Jewish helper, Katz, father of my friend Erna. After we moved to live on the farm I started to work as a cook in Patti's kitchen. A young man, Bercio Lublin, worked with me. He dealt with the ironing and took care of all the household matters.

And so we lived in relative calm until the end of May 1943. Rumors started to circulate during the last days of the month of May about an upcoming "aktzya". According to rumors, the "aktzya" was going to take place in the morning of 25 May. Most of the town's Jews escaped to the fields and the forests. When this rumor proved to be false, most of them returned back to town. Only the very few, who were very cautious, did not return. At first light, Thursday 27 May, at 3.30 before morning, the sound of gunfire was heard from all directions. The "aktzya" had started. The farm was full of Jews at that time. During the months of reprieve the Ukrainian supervisors moved to live in town, and Jews came to live in their place. A panic broke when the shooting started, and everyone was running around looking for a place to hide. I saw many Jews running out of the farm and falling from the policemen's bullets. I entered Patti's room – he stood undressed, pale as dead. This time he also did not know in advance that an "aktzya" would take place. Meanwhile, five Gestapo men arrived to inform Patti about the "aktzya." They brought a truck with them and loaded it with a large number of shovels from the farm's yard. They also ordered lunch for fifteen Gestapo officers. The commanders of the "aktzya" were young handsome men. A number of them were not able to eat, and one of them sat shaking all over. They probably got encouragement injections before the "aktzya." The Jews who worked on the farm belonged to the W" group, and they were not harmed in that "aktzya,"; but outside of the farm boundaries the lives of the Jews were not protected. The teacher, Albin, worked in the farm's office. He wanted to reach the farmyard and was killed right by the gate. From the farmyard we were able to see what was happening in town. Jews were taken from their homes and congregated in the market square. At two o'clock in the afternoon they started to lead them in groups to the cemetery. The pharmacist Falber walked together with his wife, his young daughter, and his father–in–law, Pel, the manager of the Jewish bank in town. The Germans wanted to keep Falber alive, but he refused to separate from his family. In most cases people walked quietly without shouting or weeping.

And the moment upon which they started to eliminate the Jews who were brought to the cemetery arrived. At the same time four Gestapo men sat down to eat lunch at Patti's apartment. Suddenly I heard the voice of my young son, Edzio, calling me from his hiding place in the attic. I climbed up to him and started to calm him down, but he was not able to relax. "I am afraid" he said, "I see from the window how they shoot the Jews." Meanwhile also Patti came in with teary eyes. From the window we were able to see the cemetery and a meadow next to it. The Gestapo men stood around it laughing and ridiculing. The victims were ordered to undress before they were executed. They climbed in groups of five on the board that was laid across the burial pit. One of the Germans stood on the side and gave the order to shoot. They left the beautiful girls until the end. Among them also was the daughter of Falber, the pharmacist. Before they eliminated them they undressed them, took their pictures and after that they shot them.

The Ukrainian policeman Shrab [Schab] and the Gestapo man, Tumanek [Thomanek], stood out with their great brutality during the "aktzya". Tumanek, who originated from Silesia, was the commander of all the camps in the area where Jews resided. He was a fat man, and had the look and the face of a pig. There was not a day when he did not kill at least two Jews. In this "aktzya" he set aside one thousand Jews, and killed them with his own hands.

The Germans wore gloves during the execution and, after they were done, they removed them and threw them into the burial pit. Close to four thousand people were murdered in that "aktzya."

A short time after the "aktzya", Tumanek arrived to the farm accompanied by a number of Gestapo officers. At the same time my husband was at the apartment of one of the Polish farm workers. One of the officers entered the apartment and when he saw my husband he asked him: "What are you doing here, Jew!" My husband explained to him that he was helping to manage the farm. Meanwhile Tumanek entered and confirmed it, but he aggressively demanded that he take him to his wife who was also staying on the farm. At that time, I was hiding in the attic with my son, with Mrs. Averman (she had been caught with all the Jews, released and arrived at the farm), and with the teenage boy Bercio who worked in the kitchen.

Meanwhile Patti returned from his evening walk, and Tumanek left the farm. I was in great danger because according to the rules the worker's wives were not allowed to stay on the farm with their husbands. They had to live in a special camp that was established in Chipowtza [Szypowce].

The few Jews, who were caught and brought back to Tłuste after the "aktzya," were packed in a narrow street that constituted a closed "ghetto." Some of these Jews were transferred to the farms as workers under a special permit that was given by the "Judenrat."

Around two weeks after the "aktzya," on Saturday, Patti told my husband that he urgently needed a large number of workers for the next day, Sunday. He needed to enlist them immediately, out of the town's Jews, and they must be on the farm by seven o'clock in the morning. My husband asked him: "What about the workers who have wives?" To that Patti said: "Let them come with their wives." My husband ordered as many Jews as possible from the "Judenrat" office, but only eighty people arrived. Also not all the workers' wives arrived. An "aktzya," in which all the remaining Jews in town were killed, took place on the same Sunday. Only the few who were able to hide in secure bunkers survived. It was on 6 June 1943. Patti tried to engage all the Jews who were ordered to work in all kind of jobs in locations far from the farm. He himself arrived early in the morning, rode his horse from farm to farm, and tried to employ each Jew that he met on his way.

After this "aktzya" I moved to the camp in Chipowtza [Szypowce] and left my son with my husband on the farm in Tłuste. Patti advised us that I should try to obtain "Aryan papers" so that I could travel to Hungary and live there as non–Jew. I rejected the idea because I did not want to save only my own life. There were a number of rich Jews in the Chipowtza camp, and also the wives of "Judenrat" members. I was there alone with my brother–in–law, my husband's brother. My husband wrote me that I should try to save my life any way I could, but I did not stay in that camp for a long period of time. Despite the ban, my husband brought me back to the farm. Patti knew about my arrival and ordered to employ me in the kitchen. My husband had sent the boy to one of the managers on the Kozia–Gora farm. In his opinion the boy was safer there than with him on the farm. When I returned to the farm also the boy was brought back.

A few days after my return to the farm, on the night of 15 July 1943, a number of vehicles and carts arrived at the police station which was located near the farm. We woke up and saw a large number of Germans and Ukrainian policemen. We heard the orders that were given: you travel to Holovtshintzh [Hołowcyńce], and you to Kozia–Gora. We understood that something serious was going to happen on those farms. We also saw vehicles full of policemen traveling on the road leading to the Lisowtza [Lisowce] farm that Frank managed. A short time later we heard the sound of gunfire, and we started to search for a place to hide. We were sure that they would also come to us. I wore my coat, sat in the house and waited for their arrival. I was desperate and accepted my fate. Two people who escaped from Holovtshintzh hid in a ditch not far from the farm. The Ukrainian policemen Dubitshenko [Dubiczenko] walked by the ditch and when he saw a Jewish woman hiding there, he said: "I did not see anything, but hide well so somebody else will not see you." He was a good man. He pretended to search for Jews in the roads, but in fact he warned them to hide, and when he came across a bunker he tried to conceal it better.

The murderers did not arrive to our farm. My husband hid in the warehouse, and also the rest of the Jews hid wherever they could. I was angry at my husband for not bringing me to his hideout, but it became clear to me that he had asked one of the Poles to bring me to him, but the Pole did not say a thing and a half to me about that. When I sat and waited, the Ukrainian police commander, Kushliak [Koszulak], and a German policeman by the name of Hubert, who was a good and decent man, entered. They walked around the house, met a number of Jews, but they did not hurt them. On the contrary, they tried to calm me down and ease my fears.

After the "aktzya" we found out that the murderers were not able to perform their plot in the Lisowce. The manager Frank stood before them and announced that if they destroyed his Jewish workers he would desert the farm and abandon it. A number of Jews, who were trying to escape, were murdered there, but those who remained at work survived thanks to Frank's interference. In contrast, a total liquidation took place in Holovtshintzh and at Rozanowka [Różanówka]. At Rozanowka, two Jews tried to defend themselves with weapons and were shot by policemen. They were killed immediately in the place. Patti, who arrived at Rozanowka during the "aktzya," wanted to intervene in favor of the Jews, but he was not successful because the Germans were very angry.

After the "aktzya" an order arrived from the Gestapo not to accept Jews to work on the farms. Patti informed us about the order, and added that he did not know how to advise us. We were desperate because living around the farm area meant liquidation by the police. In this desperate situation we started to think that suicide was the only solution for our distress. With the help of a German farm worker we sent a letter to my husband's relative who owned a pharmacy in Chortkov [Czortków], and asked her to send us enough poison. But she refused to do so (later she committed suicide after the liquidation of the Chortkov ghetto). The farm was divided into two camps – those who supported suicide and those who opposed it. Those who supported suicide asked Trembovelsky to build a chimney in their apartment so they would be able to poison themselves with the fumes. But he refused to come to their help. "I will fight to my last drop of blood" he answered. And indeed, he survived together with his wife and his sons. Our six year old boy, who heard all the conversations about suicide, started to question us in the matter. When he found out that it meant going to sleep and not waking up, he started to cry and shout: "I don't want to die, I want to live!"

In the end Patti agreed to allow all of us to stay on the farm against the orders that he had been given. "Surely your lives are not safe here" he said, "but they are not safer anywhere outside of the farm." Two days later my husband came with a smile on his face, gathered all the Jewish workers, and told them about a surprising change that had taken place. Patti invited him and showed him a letter that arrived from Himmler permitting to employ six thousand Jewish workers. "To my great sorrow the letter arrived too late," said Patti. And so the surviving Jews were allowed to stay on the farms. Patti informed all of the farms in the area and, again, all the Jews who were wandering and hiding in the forests gathered there. After all, it was the most comfortable and the safest way to exist.

Again, we entered to a period of relative calm that lasted for two or three months. At the beginning of the autumn a new trouble jumped on us – typhus. With the spread of typhus in the area, the Ukrainian police started to eliminate the sick. Already at the beginning of autumn we receive the news that the police had killed thirty Jews on Trawna farm near the town of Borszczów, following a typhus epidemic that had broken out there. There were a few cases in our camp, but the people tried to walk for as long as they had the energy to do so, and not to fall into bed. And indeed, there were those who were able to recover from their illness by walking. The illness did not skip our family; my husband, our little son and I, became ill. Luckily my sister Chava [Eva] was on the farm with us and took care of us.

One day, in the afternoon, we heard that Jews were running around the yard. It turned out that it was the Ukrainian sanitary police. We were able to bribe them and they left. It was around 11 before noon. In the afternoon the door suddenly opened and six Ukrainian policemen led by their commander entered our room. My son Edzio and I lay in bed. Young Krasutski, who had just recovered from his illness, got out of his bed and stood next to my bed. Also my husband and my sister were in the room. The commander turned to my husband and asked: "Do you know how to run?" We knew the meaning of this question. My husband got up and answered: "If it is required, we will run...." They asked about the child's illness and my sister answered that he was sick with the whooping cough. After that they entered the next room we immediately heard the sound of gunfire. We also heard the sound of gunfire coming from outside. The policemen returned to our room, ordered Krasutski to leave the room, and killed him behind our window. They killed Mrs. Margulies in the next room, but the girl who lay next to her was able to hide from the policemen and was not killed. Krasutski's mother ran after her son, and when he dropped dead – she fell on his face. The policeman Mróz ordered her to leave, but she answered: "after you killed my son you can also kill me," so they also killed her. Bercio Lublin was already walking after recovering from typhus; when he saw the policemen he started to run, but he was shot and killed. After they executed all these murders, they searched the bodies and robbed every item of value. They took a diamond bracelet from Mrs. Krasutski. Before they left they ordered the Jews to bury the dead. Patti was not in the farm on that day, he only came on the next day.

At the beginning of 1944, a new period of riots started, and the "Banderovtzim" started to run wild in the area. Again the Jews were the first, although they also attacked the Poles and even the Germans. According to Patti's request, 25 soldiers were sent to the farm to protect it from the "Banderovtzim" attacks. Once they attacked Lisowce, and Patti sent ten soldiers to protect the place. During this period the Germans protected us from the Ukrainian rioters.

The "Banderovtzim" attacks increased and, at the beginning of March 1944, they held a massacre in Holovtshintzh. The murdered were buried in the camp, and the wounded were brought to the farm in Tłuste. Slowly, slowly the farm became the last place of refuge for the Jewish survivors in the whole area.

One day, two senior "Wehrmacht" officers arrived on the farm. When the Jews saw them they became frightened and started to flee. My husband began to talk to them, and they asked to see the Jews who lived on the farm. My husband also feared them and advised them not to enter the hut where the wounded were lying. Despite his warning, they entered, looked at the wounded and showed great concern for their poor condition. They were also interested to know what they were given to eat. In the end, a unit of 36 soldiers arrived in the camp and their commander received the duty of "camp commander." These soldiers had an excellent amount of supplies and demanded people for work. And so, fifty Jews were fed by thirty six soldiers. The squadron commander supplied wheat and corn to feed the Jews on the farm, whose number at the time was around four hundred.

*

Meanwhile the front got closer and closer, and one day Patti started to pack his belongings. The Jews were very worried because Patti had protected them in the most difficult situations. Also during the last days we needed his help when Vlasov's men arrived together with the retreating German army, and the Cossacks came for a visit from the Don region.

Before he left, on 15 March 1944, Patti approached the German commander and asked him to take care of us. The commander treated me with kindness and asked me to continue to manage his home the way I did during Patti's days. He expressed the hope that he would be able to protect us until the arrival of the Soviets, because the local headquarters was the last to leave the area during a retreat. And indeed, there were a number of occasions when the Germans saved us from the hands of different rioters who came to the area during the last days of the Germans retreat.

The day the Soviet army arrived was a day of happiness, but it turned into another day of tragedy. The Germans bombed the farm just before the arrival of the Russian advance army. Eighty Jews out, of the four hundred survivors, were killed in this bombing.

On 1 April the Soviet army was forced to retreat. We joined them and arrived in Skalat. A warehouse full of Jewish clothes was discovered there and we were given the opportunity to change our clothes. From Skalat we went on foot to Zaleszczyki, and from there we crossed the Romanian border. A Jewish officer in the Soviet army transferred us with his car to Chernowitz. It seemed to us that we had arrived in another world, totally different from the one that we had lived in during the last years.

———

[Pages 168-169]

In Tluste and in Rozanowka camp

by Klara Shatil

Translated by Sara Mages

A. The great "*aktzya*" in Tluste

Around two months before the great "aktzya," starting on 27 May 1943, rumors circulated in town that the Germans were planning to hold an "aktzya" there. The Jews gained experience from the previous "aktzyot" and started to search for a place to hide. They started to build bunkers inside their homes, in the cellars and under the roofs. The hideouts were mostly between double walls and in tunnels. Many Jews prepared a refuge for themselves at the homes of their Ukrainian neighbors or in one of the nearby forests.

My sister and I joined a number of friends, who had a secure place in the nearby forest, and were in good relations with the forester. We spent seven days in the forest, and when nothing happened in Tluste we returned home. In town, we took turns guarding at night in order to sense the approaching danger and give ourselves enough time to hide in the bunker. Such nightly rotations existed in almost all the buildings and stopped when people got tired of it.

On 27 May 1943, at 4 before morning, the first shots were heard. When we woke up we realized that the ghetto was completely surrounded by the Gestapo and the Ukrainian police, but we had enough time to go down to the cellar and hide in the bunker. During the day we heard the sounds of steps and banging in the cellar, but the policemen were not able to find our bunker. We sat there all day and also the following night. At night we realized that the danger was over. My fiancé decided to climb up to the apartment and bring a little food and clothes. One of the women, a mother to a small child, joined him. It is possible to assume that when they turned the light in the room they caught the attention of a Ukrainian policeman who was wandering in the empty homes in order to loot them. He caught my fiancé and the woman on the cellar steps and demanded that they give him all their silver and gold. I heard the sound of a shot and, after that, the voice of my wounded fiancÃ©, Mordechai Warmbrand, who begged before the policeman and promised to give him everything that he had. "Give!" The policeman shouted, and took all the gold from his hands. After that we heard another shot. They were the last victims of the great "aktzya." Fate wanted the first and last victims of the "aktzya" be the residents of our building. The first was the homeowner, Mrs. Krampf, who did not have enough time to go down to the bunker and was shot by her front door.

B. In Rozanowka camp

In the villages near Tłuste there were labor camps in which the Germans settled Jewish laborers to work in the "Caoutchouc" plantations. One of the camps was located near Rozanowka [Różanówka] village. The work was difficult and exhausting, and the food ration that was given to us once a day was very small. The work day lasted from sunrise to sunset.

After the last "aktzya," on 6 June 1943, Tłuste was declared "Judenrein" – free of Jews. The few survivors were forced to turn to one of the labor camps where it was possible to live legally. My sister and I moved to the camp in the village of Rozanowka which was located around two kilometers from Tłuste. In addition to the difficulties, which were caused from the hard work and the small food ration, we suffered a lot from the Ukrainian supervisors and managers. They treated us with great cruelty and took the food that was given to us by the Germans. We were forced to sell our last items of clothing and exchange them for a little food.

One day, at the end of July or at the beginning of August 1943, around 4 o'clock in the morning, we suddenly heard the rattle of cars. Immediately we felt that a tragedy was going to happen and we escaped with our lives to the nearby fields. We lay in our hideout all day. The shooting lasted all day and never stopped. Later, we found out that around eighty camp residents were killed on that day. They were buried in a mass grave in the camp grounds.

After darkness my sister and I came out of our hideout, but we did not know where to go and to whom to turn. Suddenly we saw two young Ukrainian men who ordered us to follow them. They probably wanted to rob all that we had in our hands and maybe also to kill us. They demanded money, gold and watches from us, but we had nothing to give them. On the way an older farmer joined us. Immediately he started to scold them for frightening us and took us to his home. He fed us and allowed us to sleep in his barn. At night the two young men returned. They demanded money and valuables from us, but when they realized that we had nothing of value, they took our shoes and our coats.

In the morning we left for the road in order to return to the camp and, to our joy, we met on the way a number of Jewish workers from the camp. The survivors reported for the daily morning line up in the camp's yard, as though nothing had happened. Simply there was no other choice. My sister and I also returned to the camp. Around eighty people remained there.

Summer passed, autumn came, and with it came the rain and the chill. The rain leaked into the hut and soaked us to our bones. The food ration improved a little. We collected potatoes in the fields, and we were able to cook or roast them on the fire. One night, the field kitchen, where the workers' soup was cooked, was stolen; and since then we no longer received our small ration of thin soup. After we collected the potatoes, we worked in the farm's storerooms and ate corn kernels that we stole from there. Those who were caught by the storekeeper suffered a bitter fate.

With the arrival of winter our lives became more difficult. Our clothes and shoes were torn, and we went to work with rags wrapped around our feet. In addition to the hardship that was brought to us by the cold and the hunger, a typhus epidemic spread among the camp's workers. Many of the sick died from the lack of medical care. We buried the dead at night so the local residents and the German authorities would not sense it, since there was a danger that they would liquidate the whole camp. Also a serious lice plague spread around the camp, and there were cases of people who were tortured to death by this plague. The typhus epidemic provided the Ukrainian police with an excuse to come to the camp and shoot whomever they wanted, the sick and the healthy. Later they stopped shooting people, only looked at us, nodded their heads, and decided that we were not even worth a bullet – one way or another death would come and finish all of us.

We did not have clear knowledge about the situation of the war, but news filtered through that the Germans were retreating. We feared that during the chaos of the retreat we would fall victim to the Ukrainians' cruelty. And indeed, it was not an empty fear. One night the rioters attacked the camp in

Holovtshintzh [Hołowcyńce] and murdered 40 Jews with great cruelty, with axes and knives. The residents of our camp started to make plans for the day of trouble. Some arranged for a place to hide with the local farmers, and the rest, without any other choice, waited for their fate.

At the beginning of March 1944, the Germans' great retreat began. The few Jewish survivors left their camps, gathered on the farm in Tluste, and waited there for the arrival of the Soviet army. During those days, happiness and sadness were mixed together: happiness for the forthcoming liberation, and grief for our love ones who were not rewarded to live and reach the day of liberation.

On 23 March the first Soviet tanks appeared in Tluste. But, during the first moments of happiness, German bombers arrived, bombed the camp, and killed many of the last survivors.

[Pages 169-171 - Hebrew]

The story of the cave in Hinkovtza

by Klara Spector

Translated by Sara Mages

After Tłuste was captured by the Russians, all the estate owners in the area were forced to leave their homes and their property, and move somewhere else. One of the estates was owned by a Jew named Merdinger. When Merdinger was forced to leave his estate, with his wife and his two children, they moved to the home of his friend Oskar (Yehoshua) Schechner in Tłuste.

About a year later, the Russians retreated and the town was captured by the Germans. Some time later, the Germans started to liquidate the town's Jews. Three families, Merdinger, Schechner and Spector built themselves a well–concealed bunker in Schechner's home that was large enough to accommodate thirty people. They hid there during the first two "Aktzyot," but the danger that the "bunker" would be discovered was great. Then the three families discovered a possibility of rescue from a place that they did not expect at all.

A horse groom named Linkiewicz worked on the Merdinger estate in Hinkovtza [Hińkowce]. He was a fool and a drunk, and had a very bad name in the whole area. He did not have any friends and no one wanted to associate with him or be in his company. Everyone knew that he was bad and feared him. His wife was drafted to work by the Germans and sent to Germany. A young educated good–looking woman ran his household, and he also lived with her. He had two children – a seventeen–year–old boy and an eight–year–old girl [actually, fifteen–year–old – ed.]. His house stood at the edge of the village, far from the rest of the homes and near a big sand hill. The hill was narrow and was about a half–kilometer long. The sand was of good quality and was used in the manufacture of glass or porcelain. In the years before the war, the sand was mined and sent to glass factories. As a result of the mining, a "maze" of dark corridors and nooks was created in the middle of the mountain, and a man could wander and lose his way there.

One day, during the Nazi occupation, Linkiewicz came to Merdinger with this offer: he would be willing to conceal him and hide him so well that "even the devil would not be able to discover him". Merdinger knew the man and knew his character; and for that reason he was not willing to listen to him and to accept his offer. But his friend Schechner spoke to his heart and was able to convince him that a man of that kind could be trusted, because he was known as a drunk and a fool, and no one would suspect that he was hiding Jews. At the end of the matter they came to an agreement, and a letter of agreement was written. In it, Merdinger and Schechner promised to support Linkiewicz and his family all the days of their lives. And more than that – Merdinger promised to give him half of the value of the Hinkovtza [Hińkowce] estate. In addition – all the property that Merdinger and Schechner would take to their hideout would be transferred to Linkevitz at the end of the war. The property owners promised to leave their shelter dressed in the same clothes that they entered it.

After the agreement was signed, Linkiewicz started with the preparations. Gradually he transferred to the hiding place household items, kitchenware and bedding; and, after everything was prepared, he started to transfer the people, one by one or two together, out of fear of an evil–eye. And so he transferred and hid twelve people.

Klara Spector (the sister of Yehoshua Schechner) and her husband Mordechai Spector, the Hebrew teacher, were not included in this group. Merdinger was afraid to increase the number of people and he refused to include them. After the two families left for their hideout, Spector and his wife were afraid to stay in town and the two of them moved to Rozanowka [Różanówka]. Spector worked there in the field and Klara worked as a cook. Later on, they moved from Rozanowka to Holovtshintzh [Hołowcyńce] where a Jewish labor camp was still in existence.

A Christian woman lived in Holovtshintzh, and she knew very well Yehoshua Schechner, who had been rewarded to hide together with the Merdinger family. This woman was also in touch with Linkiewicz. With the help of this woman, Klara transferred a pleading letter to her brother, asking him to seek permission from Merdinger to let his sister and her husband hide with them. Linkiewicz' mistress brought the answer to this letter and informed them that Merdinger did not agree to add two people, only one – Klara. When Klara informed her husband that she would not agree to leave him and go alone to the shelter, he broke into tears and begged her to go alone so both of them would not be lost. But if she would move to the shelter, maybe she would be able to influence them to let him join. As a result, she called off her objection and Linkiewicz' mistress delivered a peasant woman outfit to her. Dressed in this costume, and with a sack on her shoulder, she walked from Holovtshintzh to Hinkovtza. Linkiewicz' mistress led the way and she walked some distance from her. It was harvest season and the presence of a strange woman carrying a sack on her shoulder did not arouse any special attention.

In this manner she walked the whole way and no one stopped her. Two weeks after the arrival of Klara Spector, Merdinger agreed to add her husband Mordechai Spector. He was transferred at the bottom of a wagon loaded with sheaves The two of them had to agree that they would be satisfied with the food ration that their relatives would set aside for them – Schechner, his son, and Schechner's sister, Hinda, who was also not included in the first group. Merdinger was afraid that he might not have enough food...

The woman from Holovtshintzh who had negotiated the Spectors' matter was also involved in this "conspiracy" and Oskar Schechner fully trusted her. Her duty was to organize the supplies, meaning obtaining enough food for fourteen people in hiding and for the four members of the Linkiewicz family. She bought and brought large quantities of food and while doing so she had to make sure that no one was suspecting her and following her. She did not know where we were hiding because this matter was also concealed from her.

Linkiewicz' mistress baked bread and cooked for everyone, and Linkiewicz himself brought the food in buckets at two o'clock in the morning. His seventeen–year–old son walked after him with a bucket of water in his hand. The bucket was heavy and the teenage boy was skinny. In the light of the lamp, Klara Spector saw that the boy was sweating and breathing heavily. Linkiewicz camouflaged the entrance to the cave with rocks which were covered with sand. Each time he came he had to clear the entrance to the cave with a hoe, and the cave dwellers also helped to clear the entrance from the inside. Because of all these difficulties he came only once a day, during night hours. Each time he heard a suspicious sound, he hurried to hide behind one of the bushes. Because of that, the people in hiding also had to change their daily routine – they slept during the day and were awake during the night. They slept from six in the morning until six in the evening, and from seven in the evening to the morning they ate, talked, quarreled and sometimes they even sang....

Also the prayers were said in accordance to the law and custom. They knew when Rosh Hashanah and Yom Kippur occurred, and fasted on that day. They also had prayer books – Linkiewicz brought them the same way he brought their clothes and belongings. The cave where they lived was narrow and long. Linkiewicz built wide benches along the walls and they were used as beds and a place to sit. As they sat on the soft bedding, the women were busy knitting or darning socks and singing at the same time, and the men joined them. They sang in Russian or in Yiddish – and so the time passed.

The women lived in peace, but they did not prevent themselves from the pleasure of gossiping about each other. On the other hand, the men interrupted each other and were angry for every small or big issue. Once, Merdinger attacked Schechner and wanted to kill him, despite the fact that he was his best friend. Despite all the friendship that he felt towards him, he guarded the distribution of the food very carefully. He insisted that Klara and her husband Mordechai be fed only from their relatives' rations – those of her brother, his son Gabriel and her sister Hinda, the way it was agreed.....

Oskar Schechner wrote a diary. He sat and wrote in the light of a candle – Linkiewicz also supplied candles. During the first days, he also brought us newspapers every Thursday. But later on he stopped bringing them since people started to suspect him and wondered – since when Linkiewicz had become a member of the newspaper readers?

The temperature in the cave was the same in the summer and in the winter. There was no shortage of air and that influenced the health of the people. During all the days of their stay in the cave none of them became sick, not even the children. But there was never enough food, and Linkiewicz' wife had done all that she could and cooked buckets full of food. They always cared to leave a supply of food for times of trouble – maybe Linkiewicz would get drunk and would not come, or maybe he would be afraid to come because of the evil eye...

There was always a shortage of water. The single bucket that Linkiewicz' son brought was used for drinking, washing dishes and at times for a small bath. One day Gabriel, Schechner's son, grew tired of sitting and doing nothing, and he went for a walk in the long corridors. An hour later he returned from his tour and told with a great enthusiasm that he had found water – a small pool of water covered with scum – but none of us believed his story. A few days later one of the children fainted and there was not a drop of water in the bucket to revive him. Then they remembered the water pool that Gabriel had found, and they asked him to lead the way to the pool. And indeed, they found the pool. The water filtered into it in a secret way. It dropped from the walls and was collected in the pool. When spring arrived and the snow and ice melted, the stream of water increased. Two barrels were brought and they always stood full of clear water that was even good for drinking. Since then we did not know a shortage of water, and Linkiewicz' son stopped to accompany his father in his nightly trips.

A short time later, Linkiewicz' son became ill with typhus. The cave dwellers had a new worry. They were afraid that if the son died, Linkiewicz would desert them from sorrow and trouble, and wouldn't bring them their food ration. Therefore they gave him a large sum of money to call a doctor to heal his son. And indeed, the son recovered and when he came for the first time after his illness, everyone hugged and kissed him....

During Christmas they felt that the food ration that was brought to them was smaller than usual. They did not dare to ask Linkiewicz for the reason in order not to hurt him. In the end, Merdinger, who had provided his income for many years, approached him and asked him the reason in the most delicate way. The response that he received froze the blood in our veins. Linkiewicz told him that one night when he approached the cave he had heard a light sound coming from one of the hills. He put down his buckets and went to see the source of the sound. And there, in one of the caves, he discovered a Jewish family from Hinkovtza. The father came out at night to ask one of his farmers' friends for food. At first, they gave him some, but lately they had refused. The family was starving and he asked him for a little food. He was not able to refuse them – and that was the reason for the shortage of food....

Everyone was deeply moved by the sound of his story. Everyone knew that family. They gave Linkiewicz additional money so he would be able to supply food for that family, but the matter did not last long. The village children discovered the Jews in that cave and brought the Germans to it. The Germans did not dare to enter the cave, so they brought bundles of straw and started a fire at the entrance to the cave, in order to suffocate the Jews or force them to come out. To the family's fortune, there were many openings to the cave, and they were able to escape though one of them.

Before Christmas they gave Linkiewicz a lot of money so he would be able to prepare a lot of food for the holiday. On holiday eve, after midnight, Linkiewicz came, as he did each night, but this time he did not come alone. He brought his mistress with him and she carried a bucket full of food. They also brought two baskets full of cakes, beer and brandy. They came to the cave to sit with us and celebrate the holiday eve with us.

Linkiewicz' "wife" was warmly welcomed by us. Most of the cave residents did not know her or had not seen her before, but they knew that they owed her a lot for her kind heart. The "table" was set immediately and everyone sat down to eat and drink and enjoy himself. The party lasted for many hours. Linkiewicz' "wife" received many expensive gifts: a gold bracelet from Klara Spector, a gold coin from Yehoshua Schechner, and a ring from his sister Hinda. Mrs. Merdinger gave her an expensive fur. The woman also told us that two days before the holiday she had visited a priest in Zaleszczyki and confided in him that she was hiding and feeding fourteen Jewish souls. She also gave him money to pray for their well being. The priest told her to take a good care of the Jews... and if G-d willing, they might convert and enter the Christian faith....

Then Yehoshua Schechner got up and announced that it would never happen. They entered the cave as Jews and they would leave it as Jews. Mrs. Linkiewicz, who knew Yehoshua Schechner and liked him, said: "and I thought that you would be the first one!" "You are completely wrong," he answered her, "I was born a Jew and I will die a Jew!" The woman laughed, she was a wise woman and she was not angry about his words to her.

Everyone was surprised that she had the courage to reveal to a priest the secret of hiding Jews, but she calmed them down and told them that the priest had been hiding Zaleszczyki's Rabbi in his home, disguised as a priest. The Rabbi was an enlightened man and, when guests arrived to the priest's home, he sat with them as though he was one of them.

Yasyo the cat also walked between our legs and jumped on the knees of one of us. It was the fifteenth soul in the cave. Linkevitz brought it to the cave to chase the mice that bothered the people's rest.

*

At the end of March 1944, Linkiewicz brought the news that the Germans had started to retreat. We did not have any newspapers and therefore we were forced to rely on the news that Linkiewicz brought us. But he guarded his mouth and did not say much.

One night Linkiewicz came with his wife, and this time they brought a lot of food. When she saw us wondering and marveling, she asked us not to ask anything, just "eat and enjoy yourselves." Everyone understood from her words and her behavior that something had happened....

When they finished eating Linkiewicz' wife said calmly: "Thank G–d, you are free!"

Everyone started to kiss her from happiness and appreciation. They sang and kissed each other. At that time the Russians were already in the village. Everyone wanted to get out of the cave immediately, but Linkiewicz' wife did not allow them all to leave. According to her advice only half of the people left, and the second half left on the second day.

And this is how Klara Spector was saved from death, she and her husband with her. According to the agreement with Linkiewicz, she left her hideout wearing the same shabby dress that she arrived in. Daylight blinded her after living for a long period of time in permanent darkness. First, they went to Tluste but they were not able to find their home. It had been destroyed by the local farmers, just as the rest of the Jewish–owned houses had been destroyed in town. Somehow they found shelter in a shabby hut and lived there.

The Spector couple decided not to stay in the ruins of Tluste, but to move west together with the Russian army. On their way to the city of Tarnopol they stopped in Kopitshintza [Kopyczyńce] where Linkiewicz found them. He told them about a tragedy that had happened to his family as the result of the rescue mission that he was involved in. During his absence, the "Banderovtzim" came to his home and murdered his son. They pulled his eyes out and threw him in the well – since he had supplied drinking water from it to the Jews. His wife hid under a bed in a neighbor's house, but she was discovered and shot to death.

From Tarnopol, the Spector couple continued to follow the Russians to the city of Risha. On 10 May they arrived to the city of Čechy in Czechoslovakia. From there they moved to the British sector in the city of Linz. Mordechai

Spector was arrested there for entering with forged documents and, after he was released from prison, he found it right to change his name and his surname. The name that he chose for himself was Avraham Guttmann.

In 1949 the couple arrived in Israel. Spector–Guttmann found work as a cultural lecturer in Holon, but he passed away eight months after his arrival in the country.

———

[Pages 172-173 - Hebrew]

The testimony of a native of Buchach

by Yitzchak Schwartz

Translated by Sara Mages

The third "aktzya" was held in Buchach [Buczacz] in February 1943, and the fourth "aktzya" was held in April 1943. At the beginning of May 1943, the Germans announced that the town must be "Judenrein." Therefore all Jews who remained alive had to move to Tłuste, Kopyczyńce or Chortkov [Czortków]. Our family moved to Tłuste. On the day of our arrival Jews were abducted for work in labor camps on farms near the town. Two days later the great "aktzya" was held in Tłuste. In the house where we were was an attic hideout, inside a smoke chimney. Thirty building residents gathered there, including my two sisters. My parents and I didn't have the time to enter that hideout but, at the last moment, just before the murderers broke into the building, we went down to the cellar and covered the entrance with a down comforter. In the end, the murderers discovered the hideout in the attic and took all the people out of it, but they didn't find us. One thousand six hundred people found their death in that "aktzya." At first, they gathered all the people in the square next to the church and from there they led them to the cemetery in groups of one hundred people. The Ukrainian policeman, Schab, asked the Germans to let him shoot the Jews and his request was granted. And so, he killed hundreds of Jews with his own hands. The two big pits in which the murdered were buried were covered with soil, but the blood flowed out of them non–stop. Then, a delegation of municipal engineers visited the place and, according to their instructions, the pits were covered with an additional layer of soil and a layer of lime was placed on top of it.

On Sunday, 6 June 1943, people were abducted in the town for work at the Kozia–Gora farm. I was also abducted for work, but in the afternoon I managed to escape from there with another boy. When we arrived close to the train station we saw a large number of Germans and Ukrainian policemen traveling and getting closer to the town. Before long, shots were heard from the town. It was the first time that the Germans held an "aktzya" on a Sunday, the day of rest. The town was completely surrounded by Germans and policemen. About fifteen people were able to break through the blockade and escape from the town. The policeman who stood on guard shot at us, but I wasn't hit. On the way, we met many farmers who hurried to the town to participate in the looting. One farmer recognized that we were Jews and wanted to bring us back to the town. Meanwhile, other farmers arrived and we started to beg them to let us go. They demanded money from us in exchange. I had 100 Zehovim with me and my friend had 150 Zehovim, but the farmers demanded more. In the end, they let us go. We ran to Czerwonogrod forest, a distance of 14 kilometers from Tluste, and stayed there for a day and a night. The local farmers found out that many Jews were hiding in the forest and came to the forest armed with axes to rob and kill the escapees. I heard the shouts of the Jews who fell in the hands of the farmers, and each one of us escaped for his life. I ran barefoot into nettle bushes and was burnt all over my body. In the end, I reached the other side of the forest, but during my escape I separated from my friend and never saw him again. On the other side of the forest I met seven Jews. In the afternoon of the next day we returned to the town. To my great joy, I found my parents were alive. They were able to hide in the cellar, in the same place where they survived the first "aktzya."

After these frequent "aktzyot," everyone understood that the Germans intended to completely eliminate all the Jews. The only way to stay alive, even for a short time until the end of the harvest season, was given to those who were able to join one of the labor camps on the farms around the town. Our family decided to join a group of 40 Jews who hired seven wagons and tried to reach the "experts" labor camp in the town of Buczacz. Half way, in one of the villages, we encountered a German "punishment delegation." They came to punish the farmers for the murder of two Gestapo men who were found dead in the village. According to rumor, they were going to kill every tenth farmer in the village. When we saw the Germans, we escaped to the nearby forest. Eleven people from our group were shot and killed by the Germans and the rest were forced to walk to Buczacz. After we deserted the wagons their owners returned to Tluste and took with them all of our belongings.

Before we entered Buczacz my father and another Jew were sent to the town to learn what was happening there. They entered a locksmith named Haber, whose apartment was on the outskirts of town, to hear from him what was happening in the "experts" camp. He wondered why Jews were coming from Tluste to Buczacz when, at the same time, the experts escaped from Buczacz to Tluste. He said that according to a rumor the Germans were planning to liquidate the experts' camp in two or three days. Again, we returned to Tluste with a number of people from the group. There, it became known to us that on the same day (12 June 1943), all the Jews were taken from Tluste and sent to Chortkov, and the town was declared "Judenrein."

We decided to return to Buczacz for the second time. When we arrived to the experts' camp everyone was packing his belongings to move to the labor camp in Swydova [Swidowa]. We didn't have another choice and joined them. The conditions in the camp in Swydova were very difficult. The work was difficult and the supervisors abused us every step that we made. The food ration was very small and the farmers weren't allowed to sell us food. On 23 June 1943, at 2 o'clock at night, the camp was surrounded by the farmers and by the policemen, who started an "aktzya.". Seven Jews committed suicide by swallowing poison. Many tried to hide inside the pits. Those pits were used to store potatoes in the winter, but in the summer they were empty and full of garbage. Our family also entered one of the pits together with other Jews, but the murderers took them out and led them to the gathering location where the Jews were waiting to be shot. My mother hid me at the bottom of the pit and covered me well with leaves and garbage. The murderers searched the garbage with their daggers to discover the Jews who were hiding there but, to my luck, they didn't find me.

After the "aktzya" I met a Jew who managed to escape from the gathering area and learnt from him a few details about the execution of the "aktzya." He told me that before the "aktzya," a number of Gestapo men arrived with suitcases to collect the Jews' money, but the Jews opted to rip up the paper money so it wouldn't fall into German hands. For that they received severe beatings from the Gestapo. From my hiding place I heard the sound of the cantor praying "El Male Rachamim" [G–d is Full of Mercy]. Some Jews said a "Viddui" [confession] and a young woman started to sing "L'Internationale" and other songs. Later, I found out that this young woman lost her mind during her stay in the camp. In Swydova camp was a member of the "Bund" movement from Tłumacz, a strong daring young man. His friend tried to encourage him to rebel, but he wasn't moved and didn't move. It was inadvisable to resist, he said, when there was no chance to win. The matter could only bring us difficult torture. Before the execution they were forced to undress, and a weapon was found in this man's clothes and in the clothes of another Jew. The Nazis separated them from the other Jews, tortured them with great cruelty and, in the end, hung them from a tree. The "aktzya" lasted all day, and the farmers kept on bringing additional Jews that they found in different hideouts.

*

The night after the "aktzya," I came out of my hiding place and escaped. For three days I wandered in the villages and in the forests and met five Jews who also managed to survive the "aktzyot" in other camps in the area. We decided to turn to the farm in the village of Mochabka [Muchawka] because it seemed to us that the farmers in that village were calmer and more decent. Within two weeks, about thirty Jews were absorbed on the same farm. Two weeks later the Ukrainian police came and killed all of them. I survived thanks to the fact that I was in Swydova on that day. One hundred Jews from Chortkov, who belonged to the "experts" group, were brought to Swydova camp which was emptied from its inhabitants. I remained in Swydova and worked in each job in the fields. For a short period of time I also worked in the vodka distillery.

For six months, from July to December 1943, the number of Jews in Swydova camp decreased, and only 20 out of the 100 experts who were brought there remained. Many escaped to the forests and fell in the hands of the "Banderovtzim" and many died in the typhus epidemic that raged in the camp. A number of us dug a bunker in the forest and hid in it. Fifteen people, myself included, found an abandoned house in the forest and moved there. A week later, I went to a nearby village to search for work. On the same day the farmers attacked the residents of the house and killed all of them. I was saved only due to the fact that I wasn't there at that time.

I walked from farm to farm to look for work, and only on the third farm the manager agreed to give me a job. Fourteen young men and women worked there almost legally. Ten days later, the manager warned us of an approaching attack. We didn't go to bed that night, but we entered the hayloft and hid inside a pile of straw. At midnight the "Banderovtzim" came and took three pairs of horses, nine pigs and grain from the farm. Before they left they asked the farm watchman if there were any Jews there, and he pointed to the hayloft. They took us out of the hayloft and started to demand money and jewelry from us while shooting in the air to frighten us. We had nothing in our hands to give them, and they were planning to carry out their threats and shot us. At the last moment, a group of Germans arrived from the village of

Chipowtza [Szypowce] and started to shoot at the "Banderovtzim." A battle broke between them and we managed to escape during the commotion.

After we were saved from this attack, we turned to another farm where a German unit was situated. Since we were safer there from an attack by the "Banderovtzim," we worked on that farm the entire month of February 1944. We found out that the Ukrainians were plotting to kill all the Jews to the last of them, so they wouldn't testify about their crimes during the Nazi occupation. We stopped sleeping in the barrack and scattered among the farmers' yards. I slept in the hut together with an elderly man and his sick son. One night, I left the barrack around eleven and went to sleep in the barn. On the same night the "Banderovtzim" attacked the barrack and killed a sick boy. His father escaped in the direction of the barn where I was hiding, but a bullet hit him near the barn and he fell. For a long hour, I heard his cries before he died. On the same night all the Jews who were sleeping in the farmers' yards were murdered, around twenty–five of them. Only three were able to escape for their lives.

We escaped to the farm in Lisovtza [Lisowce] where around fifty Jews gathered. During the Germans' retreat, a unit of Vlasov's men came to the area. They attacked the few Jews and murdered eleven of them in various cruel ways. The remaining Jews escaped to the farm in Tłuste where the German "manager," Patti [Vathje], protected the surviving Jews from Ukrainian rioters. Around three hundred Jews who survived until the arrival of the Soviet army gathered there. More than a hundred of them were killed during the Germans' air attack on the farm a short time before the entrance of the Soviet army.

———

[Pages 174-175 - Hebrew]

With Russian partisans

by Shmuel Eisen

Translated by Sara Mages

A.

I was born in Tłuste in 1932. My father was Meir Eisen and my mother's name was Feiga from the Asing [Hessing] family. My father had a shoe store. I studied at the primary school and managed to finish the fourth grade by the outbreak of the war. When the Soviets entered they put me back in the fourth grade. My father had to liquidate his shoe store and he became a manager in the shoemakers "union" in our town. Our situation was relatively good. There were various rumors about the Germans' atrocities in the occupied territory, but no one wanted to believe them. For that reason no one thought of escaping when the war between Soviet Russia and Germany broke out.

There were several thousand Jews in Tłuste, but their number increased during the war. Jews came to our town from the entire area. The first Jews came from Hungary. They were deported from there and brought to us together with the Hungarian army. Most of them were wealthy Jews who brought with them some of their assets. Many were robbed later on by the Ukrainians. There were also those who tried to return to Hungary, but they were chased to the Dniester River and drowned.

In Tłuste we went through three "aktzyot." During the first "aktzya" our family hid in a field. My father and my mother were still alive and I also had two brothers: Yakov, who was born in 1935 and survived the Holocaust, and a little brother who was born during the war. In the first "aktzya," about three hundred Jews were sent "somewhere." In the second "aktzya" about one hundred people were shot in the place and one thousand people were sent by train to Belzec. Among them were also my mother and my little brother. I don't know from where people knew that "people were burnt with electricity in Belzec." The third "aktzya" in Tłuste was carried out by the Gestapo. About three thousand five hundred people were murdered then. They were brought to the cemetery, forced to get on a board that was laid across the burial pit, and the men of the Gestapo shot and killed them. The members of the Jewish militia were forced to help the Germans, and they were the ones who told us later how the masses of Jews were murdered. They were also forced to go down the pits and move the bodies closer together. There have been cases in which the Germans threw live children into the pit. Two girls managed to escape from the pit and returned to town, but they were like crazy and didn't say anything. The victims' clothes were placed in special warehouses and later shipped to Germany.

The few Jews who remained after this "aktzya," several hundred in total, were sent to work on a farm that was about two kilometers from Tluste. My father also went there together with me and my brother. We lived in barracks and worked on difficult labor. There were no policemen on the farm, and no one watched over us. However, there was a Ukrainian police force in the village and in the town, and every Jew they met outside the farm was immediately killed on the spot. The farm manager was a Pole. He didn't bother us, but every day we had to give him fifty Zlotys for each Jew who was on the farm. That amount was paid for the food that was given to us, but in reality we were only given some bread and soup. The rest we were forced to buy from the farmers in the village. Not everyone had money, but the wealthy among us helped the poor and paid their fees to the farm manager.

We lived on that farm for six weeks. After six weeks, rumors began to spread that an "aktzya" would be held very soon. We placed guards around the camp to warn us ahead of time. I stood on guard on the night that the police came. It was a beautiful summer night and the sound of frogs croaking was coming from a nearby lake. The air was warm and I forgot the duty that was given to me and started to think pleasant thoughts. Suddenly I heard the sound of singing and immediately realized that it wasn't the voice of the village farmers. It was the sound of the Ukrainian policemen. I started to shout loudly to wake everyone up, but I was too late because the policemen were riding their horses, and a few minutes later they were inside the farm. People jumped undressed from the windows and started to run wherever their legs carried them. The policemen shot at them from automatic rifles and machineguns and, with the help of their horses, they gathered the people in one place. I don't know how many people were able to escape but probably not many of them because I saw many bodies on the next day. My father my brother and I started to run towards the fields. My father was hit and fell, and only my brother and I were able to run and hide. It was around three o'clock in the morning.

We were able to sneak into the town, to a Polish friend by the name of Hrabowiecki. He was an old religious Pole and he hid us in his attic all day and night.

We returned to the farm early the next morning. We didn't have any money, only a gold watch, as our father kept all our money. We found our father lying dead in the field together with the rest of the murdered. He was naked as the day he was born and everything was taken from him. The farm manager allowed us to bury our father and gave us shovels. My brother and I buried him naked because we didn't have any clothes to dress him with. I remember his burial place well, and I will always be able to find it.

After we buried our father, we went to the forest. We didn't have any money, but many Poles lived in that village and everyone knew us and treated us well. They were afraid to hide us in their homes but never refused to give us food. We slept in the forest and at night, when it was quiet in the village, I left my little brother and went to bring bread. Every day I went to another farmer and in this manner they fed us for many months.

B.

We learnt from the locals that gangs, dressed in Soviet uniforms, were located in Czerwonogrod forest, a distance of fifteen kilometers. They were searching for Germans and took revenge on them. They also looted the Ukrainians in the villages and took everything they could carry. We knew that they were Soviet partisans and I wanted very much to reach them. We weren't able to remain in the forest for much longer because of the approaching winter. Therefore, we started to move in that direction and the farmers showed me the way to find them.

When we arrived at the partisans' camp, I left my brother behind and approached the camp. One of the soldiers shouted towards me: Stop! Who is coming? I raised my hands and told him that I was a Jew who escaped from the "aktzya." The soldier approached me and asked me who came with me. Then he asked one of his friends to go with me and bring my brother. My brother was a young boy, around the age of eight. They advised me to take my brother to a residential area and place him with a reliable person, and then I would be able to return and join their squadron. We agreed that when I came back I would introduce myself with the password "Hersh the Jew." I returned with my brother to Tłuste and went to Ignatz Vishnievski [Wyszyński]. I gave him the gold watch that I had in my hand and told him the location where our family buried their valuables. I promised to give him everything if he would hide my brother until the end of the war. He promised to do so and fulfilled his promise. At the end of the war we dug out the treasure from its hiding place, and gave him everything. Indeed, we were poor and empty and had nothing in our hands, but he kept his promise and I also wanted to keep mine.

I left my brother in Vishnievski's hands and returned to the forest. The partisans gave me a uniform and everything else that I needed. It was a large group. I don't know how many people were there, but there were many infantries and cavalries, and even tanks and cannons. There was also a unit with trained dogs, and each soldier in that unit had a wolf dog. The dogs were able to tell from the footprints if a stranger was in the area. In that case they didn't bark, but pulled the soldier's pants to the location where the stranger was. The camp was surrounded with dugouts and there were also underground bunkers.

I stayed with the partisans for a full year. Day after day they trained me to ride and shoot. I had to hold the reins in my mouth so my hands would be free to load the automatic rifle. It was difficult to learn this art, but I was able to overcome all the difficulties until I was one of them. They took me everywhere. We came to the villages at night and sometimes during the day. At night, only the infantries and the horsemen went, and during the day they were escorted by tanks. We went without any fear when we learnt that the Ukrainian police was present in a village. We went and caught them, and later hung them on the trees in the forest. The Germans never approached the forests.

Once, we came across Germans who came to the village of Nyrkov [Nyrkêw] to collect the quota of wheat from the farmers. Our vanguard squadron informed us immediately that the Germans were in the village. Silently we surrounded the village and killed many of them. It was a real battle. I also rode my horse and shot at the Germans with the automatic rifle that I held in my hand. They weren't policemen, but men of the "Wehrmacht." A few officers were able to escape, many were shot and killed and about one hundred and fifty fell captive. We didn't hurt them. We only took their uniforms and gave them civilian clothes with a special prisoner stamp. They worked for us all the time and their condition was good. They received the same food that we got, and nobody bothered them. We always had plenty of food. We ate meat everyday and always had brandy in several big barrels. I didn't drink, but washed my body with brandy.

At times, Soviets airplanes arrived and supplied us with weapons, ammunition and canned goods. At times they also brought orders and instructions. When we heard the buzzing of the airplanes at night, we immediately knew if it was one of ours. Then, we shot a colored rocket to indicate the location of our camp.

When the front got closer to our area, we received an order to inform the Germans that if they looted and sabotaged during their retreat, they would receive the same treatment when we would arrive to a German territory. The matter didn't help much because the Germans always looted. When we found out that the Soviets entered Tłuste, we came out to welcome them. I was the youngest partisan so I was given the red flag and rode in front between two officers. I also had partisan documents but I had to return them together with my weapon. When I separated from them, they were ready to let me stay in the army, but I didn't want to continue to live the life of a warrior. I also could not ignore my brother whom I had left with Mr. Vishnievski, and I also did not want to leave him alone for an additional period of time.

We are now in Krakow together with a Jew from Romania who took care of us and helped us. I want to travel to Israel and work there, and if it will be necessary, to fight – at least I will know what I am fighting for.

———

[Page 175 - Hebrew]

A resident of Zalishchyky [Zaleszczyki] and Tłuste

by Berta Doller

Translated by Sara Mages

Our family escaped to the forest before the first "aktzya." We returned after the "aktzya" and since then we didn't know rest. German cars appeared from time to time and took dozens of Jews with them. We knew they didn't take them to work, but for abuse and extermination.

My mother also perished in the great "aktzya." My mother hid in a "bunker" in our house, but this house was chosen as a station for the collection of the property of those executed. At first, a German entered, conducted a search and took a woman and her child from the hiding place. With that the search had to end. But the policeman, Schab, wasn't satisfied with that. He claimed that many more Jews were hiding in that house. After an additional search he took my mother and three others out of the hiding place. A Ukrainian, one of our acquaintances, told us that my mother begged for her life, cried and begged to let her live, taking into account her young children, but the murderer didn't let her go and dragged her to the concentration place of those being led to the slaughter.

During the next "aktzya" I was in the labor camp near Tłuste together with my father; my sister remained in Tłuste.

The "aktzya" was held on 6 June 1943, and after this date the town had to remain "Judenrein." My sister escaped together with an eight–year–old boy, who was our relative, and other Jews in the direction of the village of Rozanowka [Różanówka]. Schab and his policemen friends shot after them with a machine–gun. Many fell on the way including the boy whom she led. My sister was in shock for several days; later she came to the farm and stayed with us.

My father contracted typhus and my sister contracted it from him. The policeman, Dobianko [Dubiczenko], arrived together with the commander of the Ukrainian police, took out a number of patients from the adjacent barrack, and shot them. I managed to hide my sister under the bed, but I wasn't able to take my father out his bed. Dobianko ordered me to take my father out. I refused to do so. Then, Dobianko took my father out and aimed his gun at him several times, but each time I managed to dissuade him from shooting my father. The last time I grabbed the gun from his hand and promised him three thousand Zlotys if he would let my father go. Dobianko and Schab agreed to take the money from a farmer who was keeping it for us. Out of fear, my father lost his ability to talk, and it didn't return to him until his death. He passed away a few days later. On the same day the murderers killed 51 Jews. On the next day they also came to take me, but I managed to hide together with my sister in a pile of straw.

After the death of my father I escaped with my sister from Rozanowka to Tłuste. There were no Germans in the villages, but our lives were threatened by Ukrainians who attacked and killed Jews with knives and other slaughtering tools. I saw how Berel Eringer was mortally wounded in his abdomen and suffered from severe pain. The Jews asked the Ukrainian militia to shoot him and end his suffering, but their answer to that was: "it's a waste of bullets." He died after several hours of difficult torture.

We worked on the farm in Tłuste until March 1944, until liberation. A few hours before the arrival of the Soviets, Schab came with several members of the Ukrainian militia and demanded the Jews to give them four liters of brandy within fifteen minutes. Otherwise, they would murder them all. We approached the commander of the German company, which camped in the area, and asked for his help. He drove the policemen away and saved our lives. The Soviet advance force arrived to the area in the afternoon.

The Soviets were forced to retreat ten days after their arrival. I escaped with my sister and all the surviving Jews to Chortkov [Czortków] and from there to Kopachintsy [Kopyczyńce], and Podvolotchisk [Podwołoczyska]. We ate the little food that was given to us by the Soviets and the rest we obtained from the farmers.

In May 1944, our area was finally liberated from the German occupation, and then we returned to Tłuste.

———

[Page 176 - Hebrew]

In Tłuste and in Lisowtza

by Moshe Schulman

Translated by Sara Mages

The Germans arrived in our town at the beginning of July 1941. The Gestapo headquarters was located in Chortkov [Czortków] and from there they came to us to establish a "Judenrat." At first, the "Judenrat" included the bank manager, Yakov Pel, Akiva Langholz, Leon Krasutski, Yisrael Krampf, and others. They were given the duty to collect all the valuables from the Jews and hand them to the Germans, and they also had to supply Jewish workers for various jobs. They remained in their duty for only a short period of time. When they realized that they were forced to send their brothers to death, they gave up this "honor" and resigned. Others came in their place and fulfilled the Gestapo and the Ukrainian police orders without remorse. In October 1941, they abducted my son, Yoel [Joel], and sent him to the labor–camp in Kamionka. He was released from there only thanks to his young age, but suffered a lot before his release. At work, the Jews were beaten with murderous blows and a number of them were also murdered.

My son and I somehow managed to find agricultural work. We weren't used to this work, but we managed to hold on. Bad days arrived when the abductions and the "aktzyot" began. The first "aktzya" was held in July 1942. By order of the Gestapo, the "Judenrat" collected about three hundred old and crippled Jews who were transferred "somewhere" by train. Before the war there were about two thousand five hundred Jews in our town. During the war their number increased to about eight thousand because the remaining Jews from the towns in the area escaped to our town or were sent by the Gestapo to Tłuste, to the last ghetto that remained in the entire area. There were also a few hundred Jews from Hungary in our town who were deported from there and remained in Tłuste.

The great "aktzya," in which most of the Jews of Tłuste and the entire area perished, was held in the month of May 1943. Gestapo men and Ukrainian policemen suddenly attacked the town and removed people from their homes to the execution site. Many were shot and killed in their homes. The work of murder was easy for them because the Jews lived in a small area, in a few streets. There was an excellent bunker in my building. Thirty people hid there and survived. More than three thousand Jews were killed in that "aktzya."

A few days later, on 6 June 1943, the last "aktzya" was held in the town. The Germans killed close to one thousand five hundred Jews, almost to the last one left in the town. After that Tłuste was declared "Judenrein." The very few who survived were given the opportunity to move to the farm in Lisowtza [Lisowce] and work there in agriculture. I also went there with my wife and three sons. They took my oldest son on the way and only by miracle I managed to save him. The farm manager was a German named, Bamberger [Bodenburg – ed.]. He treated us with relative decency, as long as he needed workers, and didn't let the Ukrainian police to hurt us. The worst among the Ukrainian policemen was Schab. He was very active in all the "aktzyot" and the Germans, Pavel [Pal] and Bruner [Brauner], worked with him. It should be noted that many Poles were also murdered by Schab, among them was a priest named Skadzinski [Szkodziński].

[Page 177 - Hebrew]

In Lvov and in Tłuste

by Rachel Landmann

Translated by Sara Mages

When the Germans entered Tłuste I was in Lvov [Lwów] together with my husband, my daughter and my nephew. We stayed in Lvov for nine weeks and suffered a lot there. We were strangers in this city and hunger bothered us. We also didn't take clothes and underwear with us and we were dirty. The Germans and the Ukrainians grabbed people in the streets, beat them and abused them. Once, they caught four thousand Jews, lay them on the ground and rode on their backs with bicycles. My nephew was taken to Janowska camp and came back three days later all wounded. He told us that he was saved from death thanks only to the fact that he was fluent in the Ukrainian language. At the end of nine weeks we decided to return home, to Tłuste. The journey lasted two weeks because we walked only at night for fear of danger.

A new disaster descended on us in Tłuste: our house was bombed and destroyed during the arrival of the Germans and we remained homeless. Troubles started a short time later - the murders and the "aktzyot." In the first "aktzya" they asked only to "transfer" the elderly and the maimed, but about eighty young women who worked at the Kozia-Gora farm during the harvest season were taken together with them. And now, the second "aktzya" was held. We prepared a "bunker" in the cellar, but at the last minute I changed my mind and convinced my husband to go and hide with a Polish farmer, Mazor, who knew us. The farmer chased us from his house at two in the morning. We had to flee to the field and there we hid in the potato bushes. We lay there for two days despite the fact that the "aktzya" lasted only one day. We didn't know that the danger was over and it was possible to go back home. We found our apartment empty. Everything was looted from it. The suffering was terrible. We didn't have water, not in the house and not in the yard. We had to draw water from the well in the town center, but Jews weren't allowed to draw water from that well since it was in the "Arian" section of the town. Therefore, we were forced to steal water. Those, who were caught "stealing" water, were badly beaten or murdered. Furs and all items of value were taken from us, and those who were caught hiding them didn't come alive from the hands of the murderers.

Meanwhile, it became known to us that a third "aktzya" was going to take place. My sister, her husband and her two daughters lived with us at that time. We went to the street to see if it was possible to cross. Suddenly, we came across two Ukrainian policemen, Schab and Dobianko [Dubiczenko], who walked accompanied by two huge dogs. Schab wanted to stop us, but Dobianko told him to let us go because very soon all the Jews would be caught together and there was no need to take care of individuals... They were only satisfied that they set their huge dogs on us. The dog tore my sister's coat and bit her until she bled. We fled to the fields. We hid in the field and in the forest for two days in pouring rain, and when we returned two days later we didn't resemble a human being. We found out that it was quiet in the city and the "aktzya" was held on the night that we returned home. As planned, we had to go down to the hideout in the cellar, but we hid in the attic. On that night thirty people were taken out of the cellar but our hiding place was not discovered. My brother-in-law didn't have the time to reach us and fell victim during the "aktzya.'

Jews were being abused not only during the "aktzya," but also during "quiet" times. Once, a young woman from Buczacz left to get a little milk from one of the farmers and Schab shot and killed her for this horrible "crime." On the same day, a young woman from Horodenka left to buy potatoes and she was also shot by Schab. When he came to a Jewish home, Schab introduced himself: "I am Schab, the Jews' murderer."

The last "aktzya" arrived - the liquidation "aktzya." This time we also managed to hide in the field. The Jews who remained alive after the last "aktzya" were sent to labor camps. However, they took young people who were fit to work. They didn't want to accept me because of my age (I was close to the age of fifty). For two weeks we, me, my husband and my daughter, wandered lost in the forests. Later, we entered the camp and each time the manager was due to arrive we fled again to the field. A typhus epidemic broke out in the camp. My husband also became ill and then the Ukrainian police came and shot him to death. This was also my sister's fate. When someone didn't show up to work, the Ukrainian police came on the following day and killed him. The police found part of a radio in Yisrael Hirschbein's possession and for this crime Schab arrested him and his daughter. The members of the Judenrat asked Schab to hand the two prisoners to the Germans, but Schab answered that he himself would decide their judgment. He took them to the cemetery. On the way he tortured the young woman and then he killed both of them. The young woman was critically wounded and suffered for a whole day until she died.

During the last period of the German regime I was with my little daughter at the camp in Lisowice [Lisowce]. Vlasov's men came to our area at that time and helped the Ukrainians and the Germans to eliminate the Jews. One of them caught me and my daughter. I managed to escape from his hands and take my daughter. Next, he attacked a beautiful young woman and severely injured her neck. The woman suffered from terrible pain for a whole day until she died.

I escaped from the camp in Lisowice to the farm in Tluste. Also there we suffered a lot from the hands of the Ukrainians and from Vlasov's men. Finally, the Soviet army arrived and liberated us from the Germans. There was no end to our happiness. Half an hour after the arrival of the Soviets a group of German bombers arrived and bombed the farm. The bombing was very heavy and all the buildings caught on fire. I was sure that this time I wouldn't be able to save myself and my daughter. By miracle I arrived to a home of a Pole and hid in his cellar. My daughter was only slightly wounded. A week later, the Germans returned and again we had to escape with the Soviet army. We arrived half naked and barefoot to Podvolitchisk [Podwołoczyska] and stopped there. At that time we only lived from the Soviets' handouts, and for a long time we lived in poverty and suffered hunger and cold.

[Page 178 - Hebrew]

In Tłuste and in Holovtshintzh

by Moshe Spiegel

Translated by Sara Mages

After the great "aktzya" in Tłuste on 28 May 1943 [27 May 1943 – ed.], in which around three thousand five hundred Jews were murdered, I moved with my family to the camp in Holovtshintzh [Hołowcyńce]. At that time, every Jew from Tłuste and the nearby towns, tried to find a place in one of the camps. Around three thousand surviving Jews, who hid during the "aktzya" in different locations in the town and the vicinity, were forced to move and crowd together in one street. I did not want to remain in a "ghetto," and therefore I was one of the first to reach Holovtshintzh together with my family that included: my father Henrik Spiegel, my son, my sister and her daughter, and also my brother's two young sons. There were three big huts in the camp that were designed to accommodate 600 people, but 1100 people who arrived in the camp crowded in them, among them were children, women and the elderly.

The camp manager was an evil–hearted Pole, who did not neglect an opportunity to abuse the Jews and extort money from the wealthy. There was a group of rich Jews in the camp who were not forced to go to work and were allowed to cook their own meals. The farmers' wives sold them food from their farms, and the camp management turned an eye on that.

On Sunday, 6 June, while we worked in the sugar–beet field, we suddenly saw four cars full of German soldiers traveling on the road leading to Tłuste. A quarter of an hour later we started to hear the sound of gun fire coming from the town. A great panic was aroused among the workers, and we started to run towards the nearest forest in order to hide there. On the way we met a number of Jews who had also escaped from the town to the forest. The Germans shot after the escapees and many of them were hit and fell. The "aktzya" lasted from 11 in the morning to 6 in the evening, and around one thousand eight hundred people were killed.

A few days later a few hundred people moved back to town. According to a Gestapo order they were sent to Chortkov [Czortków], but they were killed by their escorts before they arrived there. We found out about this matter from the few Jews who were able to escape and also from the carters who transported the Jews to Chortkov.

We lived in Holovtshintzh camp in constant tension and fear, and we did not know what the next day would bring. In the middle of July 1943, I worked in the field together with 200 camp workers. A Polish farmer, who brought grain to the flour mill, passed by and when he saw us he turned and said: "why are you standing and working here?" There is an "aktzya" in Swidowa. At the sound of his words the workers scattered and started to run to the forest. Meanwhile the Ukrainian residents raided the deserted camp and looted what was left of our belongings. Also, the Jews in the other camps started to flee to the forest when they heard about the "aktzya" in Swidowa. There was always a direct contact between the camps, and messages and warnings were transferred from camp to camp by Polish "runners" who were hired and paid for that purpose.

We wandered in the forest on that day and on the following day, and later on we returned to the camp. They were also those who remained in the forest for a full week. We found out that all the Jews were liquidated in Swidowa. One of them was able to escape completely naked from a burial pit. One of the farmers gave him something to wear and he arrived in our camp and stayed with us. The panic and the fear from the "aktzya" became stronger in the camp. We walked hopelessly and we did not have the patience to continue with our work.

On 14 July we found out by chance, that the Germans and the Ukrainian militia suddenly attacked the camp in Tshrshnovtza [Szerszeniowce] and murdered close to two hundred Jews. We begged before the two non–Jewish workers, the storekeeper and the bookkeeper, to travel to Tshrshnovtza and bring us clear information of what happened there. The storekeeper traveled there and when he returned he told us that the information was correct. Again, panic spread in the camp. We placed guards around the camp and went to sleep. At night a Ukrainian friend came to warn me that the Germans had arrived in the village. They were sitting in the local council house and getting drunk. I awoke the camp residents and informed them about the situation. There were those who believed me, but those who were always the first to run did not pay attention to my warnings and went back to sleep. I took my father and my son and ran out of the camp. I also informed my sister and the rest of my family members. It was around 3.30 before morning. We moved around four hundred meters away from the camp, hid in the standing wheat, and waited for things to come. A short time later we heard the sound of gunfire so we got up and started to run. The camp was completely surrounded. Only one place was open and a few people managed to escape from there, but they were attacked by the local farmers who beat them and robbed their money.

We sat in our hiding place, together with eleven other people, all day until the late hour of the evening. I lost my father on the way and he disappeared. I was not able to sit calmly in my place because I was worried about my family members. I returned with my son to the village, met a peasant woman and asked her if she knew something about their fate. From her I heard the bitter news that over two hundred people had been murdered including my father and my sister's two sons. The three of them were hiding in a field among the stalks, but a Ukrainian discovered their hiding place and notified the murderers. By chance it was a gentile who at one time worked for the brother of my brother–in–law, Hillel [Hillary] Kenigsberg. My sister escaped to the village and there the Ukrainians felt sorry for her and saved her. My sister's daughter, Leila, a young beautiful woman, removed the armband from her sleeve and left the camp. A Ukrainian policeman came towards her and ordered her to join a group of people who stood waiting for their execution. She refused to go and told him: "if you want you can kill me right here, but I am not going there." The policeman aimed his gun at her. She closed her eyes and waited for the shot. A few seconds passed and the shot did not arrive. Leila opened her eyes and saw that the policeman was smiling at her saying: "I feel sorry for you, hurry and hide". She was frozen and was not able to move from her place. The policeman pushed her lightly to a nearby corn field, and from there she escaped to the same gentile who had warned me of the danger on the same night.

On the day after the "aktzya" we did not know where to turn, and we wandered lost in the fields and in the forests. We tried to return to the farm, but we found out that the evil– hearted farm manager Yaramitsh was full of anger at the Jews, and did not want them to stay on his farm.

I turned to the storekeeper, Yanek Zavarskei, and he gave me a little bread and fat. I took my son to the nearest cemetery and climbed to the mortuary's attic. I thought that nobody was there, but the place was full of Jews and we were not able to find a place to sleep. We sat there until morning. Around six o'clock I saw a gentile traveling in a cart delivering milk to Tłuste. Without thinking much I climbed on the cart with my son and traveled to the camp in Tłuste. My oldest sister Eva was there with our sister Manya [Maria] Kenigsberg. I consulted with Manya what to do, and she told me that she could not give me any advice. According to a rumor, they were also planning to liquidate the farm in Tłuste. We were totally desperate. Suddenly my brother–in–law came and brought the news that an order had arrived from Himmler to leave six thousand Jews alive to work in the agricultural farms. Patti [Vathje] brought this message and added: "to our great sorrow the order arrived too late!"

After we received the news about Himmler's order, Patti instructed my brother–in–law Kenigsberg to collect all the Jews who were scattered all over, and to reestablish the labor camps. I hurried to the camp in Holovtshintzh. Patti arrived after me and ordered Yaramitsh to bring the Jews back to the huts and to reestablish the camp. Again, two hundred Jews gathered there (two hundred were killed and two hundred were hiding in different locations). Among the two hundred, there were twenty young children, orphaned from their fathers and mothers. There weren't any rich Jews among the survivors. Most of them had been killed because they had relied on their "immunity status" and did not escape. Yaramitsh was not happy with us since he was no longer able to extort money from us. The Ukrainian police came to the camp every day, and we were forced to collect money in order to bribe them and prevent further tragedy. It was clear to them that we were not able to give them the large sums of money that they were used to receiving. Diseases spread among the camp's residents because of the shortage and the hunger. My son also got sick. I knew that he was sick with typhus, but I told everyone that he was sick with rheumatic fever. The storekeeper Zavarskei helped me a lot. Each time the Ukrainian police arrived he tried to keep them away and appease them. Eventually my son recovered without any medicine.

After the reestablishment of the camp we worked in peace and without interference for five weeks. After that an epidemic broke out in the camp, and again our lives were in danger because of the illness and also because of the Ukrainian police visits. Yaramitsh raged with anger and demanded workers, but most of his workers were sick. The Ukrainian police came together with the German oppressor, Brauner. Yaramitsh met them and complained that the Jews did not want to go out to work. The first result was – one Jew among the sick was murdered. He was a Jew from Zaleszczyki. When he saw the policemen he tried to escape to the nearby river. The murderers' bullets reached him by the river bank. Four Jewish men from the camp brought his body back for burial.

———

[Page 179 - Hebrew]

A native of Horodenka who survived in Tłuste

by Runia Bermann

Translated by Sara Mages

The first "aktzya," in our town, Horodenka, was held in December 1941, and about two thousand five hundred residents perished in it. Several people who weren't shot to death managed to get out of the pit of death in the darkness of the night and returned to town. Among the survivors were also the slaughterer's wife and one of my relatives.

The second "aktzya" was held on Rosh Hashanah 1942 (in the month of September). The vast majority of Jews from the town and from the neighboring towns were gathered under the guise of "registration to work" and detained for several days in the farm buildings near the train station. Later, they were transferred to the death camp at Belzec. My father was also among them. A short time after that our town was declared "free of Jews" (Judenrein). A few Jews managed to cross the border to Romania. Some of the surviving Jews moved to Kołomyja and some to Tłuste across the Dniester River. Our family also escaped to Tłuste.

On 27 May 1943, the great "aktzya," in which three thousand five hundred Jews were murdered, was held in Tłuste. Among them were also my mother and my sister. I was wounded in my shoulder and remained alone and lonely. Another "aktzya" was held ten days later and about one thousand Jews perished in it.

A month after the great "aktzya," on 27 June 1943, a labor camp which absorbed the surviving Jews from the town and the neighboring towns was established in Tłuste. There were only two young people under the age of seventeen there: myself and a ten–year–old girl. The Jewish militia wanted to remove me from the camp, but I adapted slowly to the work and remained there. In this way we spent the summer in the camp and a harsh winter arrived. We suffered a lot from the cold and the filth, from hunger and shortage. There were about six hundred Jews in the camp. The Nazis and the

Ukrainian rioters didn't come to the camp and "aktzyot" weren't held there. In March 1943 [ed. 1944], the Soviet army liberated us from the Germans. My ambition is to arrive, as fast as possible, to our country to join the work force that builds our homeland so that we could strengthen it and avenge the blood of our parents, brothers and sisters.

———

[Page 180 Hebrew]

The *minyan* in my town, the town of Tluste

by Shimshon Meltzer

Translated by Sara Mages

Each and every morning I hear the sound of a *shofar* coming from *"Ohel Meir,"*
and I know that Elul arrived – and the heart is excited and pounding,
and Elul–of–childhood awaken in my soul and awaken a vanished world
and my eyes are closed and my face is silent and the brain hallucinating and dreaming.

And it came, the dream, with a lot of color and sound, a lot of details and matters,
and shows me everything explicit and clear, without any doubt and hesitation,
and I have this thought: is it true, this year, is it true that a *minyan* wouldn't be there,
not even a single one, not a *minyan* in the holidays in my town, in my town, the town of Tluste?

And a kind of childhood idea rises in my heart, a kind of idea from the world of fabrication
(yet, all of us, when we were little, we all believed it!)
that in the darkness of the night the dead come, wrapped in shrouds, *tallitot*,
in masses they rise from their grave, and come together to the House of God ...

And in a whisper, audible only to them, the cantor whispers,
and in a murmur, in deep secret, they answer dressed in *tallitot*,
and terrible and majestic is the nightly scene... and if so – and if so, probably
this year, this year there's also a *minyan* in my town– and what a great *minyan*! – of the dead...

And a thought comes to my mind, that the *minyan* shouldn't only be at night,
also during the day, also in the middle of the day, and it would be a spoken *minyan* of the dead!
After all, there isn't a single Jewish child alive who would see and be afraid,
There isn't a single Jewish woman alive who would abort her fetus from fear.

But it is difficult to determine the proper location for that *minyan*:
all the synagogues in town were destroyed and the conqueror leveled them to the ground.
Only the Great *"Shul"*, the little temple, only a small remnant survived,
they did not have the time to smash all its stones, they were not able to burn them all...

And I am rebuilding the temple, restoring its thick walls –
they rise before me with all their ornamental paintings, with all the blue marble,
tall windows are torn in the walls, candles are burning,
and in the middle stands the table, and Eliyahu bench by the pulpit...

And the ceiling rises on the walls...I most certainly remember it!
it was spread like a big sky, stars and clouds in its blue,

and pictures around...because here in Tluste (yes "here" Woe, Alas to me!)
there were not four pillars, as it was customary to support the big ceiling.

The ceiling was built at the time in Chortkov and they worked diligently in the *Kloiz*'s yard to decorate it,
and the old man said that he doesn't want Jachinim–Boazim
to hide from him the view of the Ark when he peeks from his room –
and they brought great builders from Vienna and have done daring deeds!

And they made scaffolding there, one on top of the other, a kind of suspension bridge in the roof,
and leaned the beams on it, the heavy ceiling was hung –
and when the *Admor* stood on the threshold, on the Sabbath and more on a holiday,
and saw the sea of heads in the *Kloiz* and encircled the congregation with his eyes...

And the same builders also hung the ceiling in the town of Tluste,
and the same artists also painted it the same way –
if my eyes are blurry and my face is fallen, my soul is looking–looking
and sees every painting, decoration and ornament, big and small alike.

How do I specify, how can I describe and tell about them all? like
the tiger and the eagle, the deer, the lion, each animal in its nature, in its habitat,
the zodiac year and the flags of the tribes, each one is embedded in its place,
and the symbols of the holidays with their articles of service, each of the right size.

In the east the beautiful Ark, decorated in a combination of sawn wood
above it, on the second floor – the tablets, on the third floor – the crowns,
and up above – a colorful window, its lights – a glorious fusion
and a Star of David enclosed in a circle, divides its area into pieces.

And pigeons float up there, above the raised Ark
from moment to moment a pigeon flutters – to the women's section in the west;
or a swallow crossing the air like an arrow from window to window
almost touching the roaring lion or the big wing eagle...

In the west the doors are wide open, the heavy oak doors,
on three steps we will climb to the vestibule, it is cold, dim and big;
it's cool from its cold stone floor, dim because it has no window.
There, we studied the *Humash* from Dudi Pfeffer, there we stayed six weekdays...

And we will install stairs in the main entrance, because young and old would come,
and we will install an incline to the women's section, so a baby girl would be able to climb...
there will be no benches, there will be no pillars – people will crowd together,
and because of the overcrowding, the burden on the public, they will hurry up to finish the prayers...

[Page 181]

The dead must have a shortened prayer, without a tasteless saying.

And perhaps now they have also changed the wording as a sort of renewed order of prayer,
a kind of shortened order of the regular prayers with the addition of a question mark,
an exclamation mark and wonder and demand, for example: "*Yitgadal Veyitkadash*?!"

*

Chaim Schwarzbart will rise first from his grave and go to arouse the ghosts...
a Jew from a good family, kind–hearted and honest, with a profession – the maker of tsitsiyot;
Only at the end of days when the need for *tsitsiyot* declined miraculously in the market,
he started to help Michel the *Shamash* and came to be his partner.

He would take the big–big lantern, light the candle in it and go,
drag his feet from mound to mound, in paths covered with thorny plants –
He must remember, as before, the names, the details, when and how,
how they were put to death and led to burial in mass graves.

He will not knock with a hammer, and will not knock with a stick ... with sweet–sweet singing,
he will awake them in his melancholy–melancholy voice, in a crying–bagging song,
as he did on the night of *Selichot* in childhood, in a childhood that is all sweet,
as he stood behind the dark window and sweetly sang:

Please wake up, because every night your soul rises up
to give account of your activities to the creator of light and morning.
Wake up, wake up, for the work of the Creator,
wake up, wake up, for the work of the Creator!

Yet, in his honest way he also wouldn't forget those scattered around,
not in the cemetery – in the villages, in the forests, buried alone or together;
for example, Asher Kurzer, my teacher who taught me the Book of Proverbs in the melody of a preacher,
and with him my rabbi, R' Pinchas Lapiner, who taught me the *Gemara* in a glance...

The clear reasonable sayings of King Solomon – didn't attract my heart,
the rich moral, that he collected wisdom as women, did not please the lad,
but what wisdom did I earn from everything at his home, from extreme poverty,
from the few blessings and the many crafts of a teacher, cantor and *mohel*...

HaRav Pinchas Lapiner, preacher in the holy community of Tluste, who taught me the *Gemara* in a hurry –
May his memory be blessed! Woe, how I loved him and how he captured my heart!
He skipped the negotiations, skipped from page to page,
and taught me delightful legends – and I loved his skipping!

In life they were far in nature, even though both taught me

only one tractate – poverty, one according to the plain meaning, the second according to homiletical interpretation.
But together, one day, they were shot in the nape at the hand of the same soldier,
and both were buried where they fell, in the heart of the town, in a plot of land...

He will go to bring our rabbi, HaRav Shmuel–Aba Chodorov, from afar,
from the fields of Belzec, him and the whole congregation that was sent from the town –
and there's doubt, great doubt, that even the dead, that distance for him is like a laugh
and sees and hears everything, will discover their grave and recognize their ashes...

But our rabbi would probably amass from his ashes and form a little flesh and tendons,
and will stand ready on the mound to welcome Chaim the *Shamash*...
he's still a young man, the position was imposed on him, and he has been told to teach and judge –
he inherited the rabbinate from his great father, who was burnt in bad illness in fear.

And our teacher and rabbi sat and studied, studied like a boy in the *Cheder*
from "Zalman the *Melamed*" the great scholar, who wandered to us from afar;
and for every difficult thing he was asked – he was not lazy, he stood
and travelled to Zalishchyky to ask the great rabbi, R' "Leibli *Dayan*."

The tender soul distanced himself from controversy, from every authority in town,
was meticulous to precede with "good morning," and enquired to the homeowner's health.
He entered into conversation with each boy in the *Kloiz*, as an equal with the young –
a true story, I greeted him in the street and he answered innocently, and I was bareheaded!

And I regret that we were jokers, mimicking the ridiculous speech
that he gave on the third of May in honor of the birthday of the Marshal of Poland,
he couldn't deliver a speech in a meeting and a public sermon on a holiday,
but he knew how to preach condolences on a day of destruction, and to lead the community...

He highly respected his righteous mother, the tall and dignified.
She was like a remnant from days passed, and bore with dignity the rabbi's house,
When they came to take everyone to Belzec she stood majestically on the doorstep
and said: I will not go! If to die, I will die here! – and she died there on the doorstep.

Surely her son would miss her, this is her closest son,
and he would go quickly towards her with his innocent eyes, his small red beard,
and tell her, as a grandson among the grandchildren: "Good morning to you, my mother, good morning!" –
and so he would wake up and awaken the congregation in Belzec to go to Tluste...

Baruch–Izik Vitashka, is the community leader in our town for dozens of years,

the *Shamash* would have to search for him in the torture camp in Janowska in Lvov;
He escaped to his son, to his daughter, and all of them, including the small grandchildren,
must have been taken to the famous camp and were tortured and sent and never returned.

From a large wealthy family, highborn, scholar and a *maskil* –in secret.
But he was known to our people, I also knew him, the story:
At the beginning, when he came to our town – son–in–law to Shimshon Klein! Esther's husband! –
he kept in secret, in a small special dresser, "Pesukim" with "commentary"...

[Page 182]

And here, that morning, when they thought Esther was lost
when she had difficulties giving birth to Donya – this is the third day and more! –
Shimshon Klein walked in the apartment and searched, and checked every suspicious corner,
and finally he finds the hidden dresser and the books of that "trouble maker!"

And immediately he opens a window – on a cold winter day – to the big yard,
and tosses the volumes to the pure snow and shouts: "You killed her!"...
and suddenly a rising scream emerges from the woman's room
and in a few moments, "*Mazel Tov*," there's a daughter! and she's beautiful, like no other!

And indeed, she was beautiful, and it is possible that for the sake of the good–looking earthly daughter
he left her, the "fairy," and stayed away from *Haskalah* and hearsay books.
With all that, after many years, still in my days, in secret he "read" with pleasure,
and he read my first poems in "*Hasolel*" booklets and said I understand...

Meir Klein, his property partner and brother–in–law, is the most important in town.
He will come from Chorostkov, there he hid and there he died was buried.
He fled in fear of the Red Army which exiled the rich –
He didn't want to be exiled again in faraway frozen Siberia.

He was there during that war, "bailed" together with Vitashka,
and returned lower than a hyssop... but their assets have returned – and also their glory.
Although they had to pay a lot of taxes to the kingdom, a lot of property tax,
they were considered "landlords," behaved with authority and announced their nature.

And both in the east of the *Kloiz*, in the south wing, in the north wing...
And to Meir, it was customary to wait with the prayer, on the Sabbath and weekdays...
Not one of the troops got angry and complained about this practice,
If a person hurried to his home, to his children, and if he just wants to eat!

And in particular they resented his habit to come late on weekdays, a considerable delay,
and go before prayer to *Tarfik* and read the "*Kvila*" first...
But reading the newspaper was a major and important necessity for him
the matters of parcelling, agrarian reform, what tax the authority imposes?

He was a member of "*Agudat Yisrael*," and read a Polish newspaper,
but a Zionist... he was a Zionist, the kind of "Zionist in the heart"...
"If only I could" he told me, the boy, quietly without making a sound,
to uproot our estates from here, from Poland, and carry them to *Eretz–Avot*!

And Saklovska, Lituvtza, are masters, think, and we are "landlords?"
Not mastery, only slavery! Taxes and taxes and taxes! Like a press and a wringer!
Seemingly – masters, actually – slaves whose ears were offered by the door.
The fields, the forests – not to sell, not to divide – only the bread remained.

"Only the bread"... in the end he also did not have a loaf of bread,
In Chorostkov he died of starvation, the richest man in the community
And since he has nothing and no longer a possessor of property at all,
this time they will no longer wait – he will surely hurry up and come to the prayer...

Yankel Shpitzer was always in a hurry to prayer, came early and entered.
He's *Baaal–Musaf* of the *Kloiz*, and with all the claims that his opponents claimed,
he had a blessed version and clear dictation, and since then
he rose – in the women's section, more women found the page.

He received from Hersh–Kopel himself! not a scholar, but knows the meaning of the words.
He placed the verses correctly, and emphasized what needed to be emphasized;
and all loud and strong, his clear speech filled the entire *Kloiz*,
and the voice, penetrated the women's ears – and his face is blazing–blazing ...

Therefore, really, they gossiped behind his back, and whispered with laughter...
especially Hershel Meyer wanted to find him unfit, as a result of that act,
witnesses saw him kissing his sister–in–law, his guest from faraway place.
And there were many questions–answers... on that subject... but the voice covered it all!

I still see him standing wrapped in a *Tallit*, in the *Musaf* of an ordinary Sabbath,
a step away from the lectern and walking step by step –
they also gossiped about that: what is this freedom with the cantor?
But when his voice and his wording sing in my ears – my heart trembles in me...

And so he will also be *Baal–Musaf* now, for the dead, in the whispered prayer,
although the big voice is not needed – but the wording would be counted.
And this time there is no reason to think if he would remember the women's section.
Surely he would pray as a God–fearing man, with distress and a broken heart – – –

Antshel Pfeffer, the "*Shulfter*" would not object... he would agree to the matter, of course!
From the horse dealers, head and shoulders above the crowd,
With his honesty and the force of his words he won and was elected *Gabbai*,
but he knew the limit of his knowledge, and was careful in the honor of a scholar.

Was the eldest brother, the cattle traders, and they were honored with his honor.
They helped and contributed for the repair of the damaged House of Prayer –
In his days the doors were stabilized and the Holy Ark's fence has been restored.
In his days the silver–tray, the "*Yad*," and the also crowns were repaired.

How great when he stood on the Sabbath and holiday to the cantor's left,
Handing out *aliyot*, dignified and inferior, from Cohen to *Haftarah*,
and watching from his height, looking around – and Alas to the rebellious son,
who allowed himself to speak aloud during the reading of the Torah!

[Page 183]

And strange, but now it seems me that only he, he alone is the man who was
suitable and worthy for the honorary post of first–*Gabbai* in the "*Shul*"...
Antshel Pfeffer – he too became a legend to me,
he would never thunder his voice, and he would never frighten with "be quite"!...

Leizer Walzer, is *Baal–HaMusaf* of the Devishnitz *Kleizel*, will tackle *Shacharit*.
In his life he was delicate and frail and all of him not from this world,
his pigeon eyes staring into the distance, to a district and in the end
his sanctified death surely helped him to get closer to paradise...

His stature is low, wrapped in an adorned prayer shawl.
From the time he approached the lectern and stood – and stood like a pillar and didn't move,
he did not move his small decorated head, his small elegant stature,
only his voice flows like a flute and comes out sweet and intense!

He lived in Swidowa and merged the study of the Torah with his tavern,
and before Passover he set his Kosher wine business in the town of Tluste.
The gentiles themselves, the good neighbors, decided to kill,
and one day they killed "their" Jews with sharp pitchforks, with shovels.

And they threw all of them to the horses' graves... at the beginning, in the first days!
Later, when a wagon loaded with coffins for the dead arrived from Tluste,
to collect the martyrs for proper burial – they raised their pitchforks at them
and said: those who touch them – would be murdered with the same pitchforks and shovels!

With all that, he will know the time... there wouldn't be any objections on his side!
He will come and he will lead his small congregation in a quick step from Swidowa ...

and also his son Yedil – the sharp and pleasant to hear – will help him with the prayer.
He was always close to his father and did not remove his hand from his.

Moshe Willner, is known – the *Mincha* is his, on weekday, on holiday and the Sabbath,
a right of claim of many years, and for that no one ever complained.
Even now, before evening, on the sorrow of Sabbath evening, I will hear "*Ata Echad*"
in his voice that it is pouring into my heart with the redness of the burning west...

He had one more right of claim: the auction at *Simchat Torah.*
He was a loyal shopkeeper in the store at his home, his speech moderate and dignified.
When he sold the "*Maftir*" for the whole year, and all kinds of "merchandise,"
he raised the price and overcharged just like a trader in Lod...

What a thrill he provoked in this negotiation, very tense!
But he also knew the limit, and sometimes he was quick to stop:
And the "third time" – at the beginning of the negotiation, he hurried and finished abruptly,
when he knew that the buyer is not allowed to add and give any more...

Adorned with lineage, son of a rabbi and son–in–law of one of the geniuses in Poland,
was not sharp minded but worshiped God with all his heart.
He who is blind as the servant of the place! he claimed: they cannot destroy,
they spread panic for nothing, there will be salvation! salvation will come!

And even at the time when he was led to the *Sammelplatz*, to the thousands
he shouted with another: "*Hashem* is the God! "*Hashem* is the God"!
And the Nazi whips with his whip, and the blood dripping, drops–drops,
and the Nazi continues to slap, and both of them continue to shout and receive more flogging...

Yankel Scherl will be the *shofar* blower; he blew in the "*Shul*" in the last years.
He would also be a reader; he knows how to read, and according to grammar!
To be truthful, he was a Zionist, and vague, and had all kinds of "ideas,"
But he was also a God–fearing man, and did not have much doubt.

I still remember how he stood and read in the women's section in the Chortkover *Kloiz*
on *Simchat Torah*, during the special *minyan* for the young generation.
Only there they pledged for "*Keren Hakayemet*" – what a daring act! –
instead of saying "*El Male*" to the *Admor*, they said it to Zev–Binyamin–Theodor.

Known as Doctor Herzl... slowly, and with a lot of importance, he explained the matters,
and read the blessings in the ears of each young boy called to the Torah
as if it was the first, and if he has never read these verses dozens of times,
He was engaged in all matters of the world, in life, reading and prayer.

He was attached to his small shop and was satisfied with the spiritual center and Hebrew.
He raised his son to life in Zion, fattening him with the Torah like a bull.

But it seems to me that when he stood waiting by his leather shop door –
he did not wait for a gentile to come, he only waited for a poor man riding a donkey...

A beautiful soul who supported himself all of his life, and was not involved with the community.
Maybe because of that he was rewarded to die of typhus, alone, in isolation.
And he was led in a cart that collected the dead for burial each morning,
and it is possible that during those days they still dug a grave for each person...

HaRav Shemshili Heller, from a lineage of holy angels, geniuses, righteous,
also this time will ascend as a Levi, like in the *minyan* of the working youth.
He was angry at those who postponed the end, damaged the activity of the young,
and associate everything to Messiah, and find refuge in the shadow of the kingdom.

He himself could have done righteousness, but became a small grocer...
He stopped saying the Tehillim alone and entered a hot argument:
"And if so, if the Messiah will come, there's no need to welcome the bridegroom?
There's no need to prepare, no need to do, just to postpone the end of days!"

[Page 184]

He loved to bring amazing interpretations that spoke of redemption,
and clearly articulated the name of our country, didn't swallow, as is customary.
On Isru Chag, the day after Simchat Torah, he left in a full train
from the second *aktzya*, and maybe they hastened his end and he arrived suffocated...

*

Each morning and morning I hear the sound of the *shofar* coming from "*Ohel Meir*"
and I know that Elul arrived – and my heart is beating from excitement,
and Elul of the town of Tluste awaken in my soul, awakening the world of the dead,
and my eyes are closed, my face is silent, and the brain is hallucinating and dreaming.

And I combine the *minyan* in my town, in my dead faraway town,
and like a not elected *Gabbai*, the last, I will take care of each detail and matter.
And assign roles to the characters, who have survived in my soul,
and nothing would be missing in the congregation of ghosts, in my imaginary vision, in the *minyan*.

Who will approach the lectern each day – for *Shacharit*, *Musaf* and *Mincha*.
Who among the men will be called to the Torah?
and even before the Psalms – who will approach and say the blessings,
who is fit to pray *Ma'ariv*, and who among them will say *Kol Nidrei*...

I calculate the number of people, the number of those who would come to the prayer:
The first *aktzya*, 14 Elul 5702 – three hundred were deported
(at the beginning they didn't understand the meaning of the matter).

The first, who were sent to Belzec by train, would be the first to come to the *minyan*.

And the second *aktzya*, around nine hundred the day after Simchat Torah 5703,
the townspeople and residents of places nearby.
They were also sent by train to Belzec (and this time the terror was known).
They were the second to be sent from Tluste, they would be the second to return.

And in the third *aktzya*, 24 Adar in the year 5703 to the creation,
about three thousand men, women, children and pregnant women were killed.
They were rounded up in an empty lot in the town center and were chased with clubs,
downhill, on the bridge, and again downhill, and on the mountain, up to the cemetery.

In the cemetery they found a dug up grave waiting for them,
sixty Jewish men dug it with their weak hands,
a long–long deep ditch, the width and the height of a man.
Above this grave a kind of wooden bridge was extended from edge to edge.

And they undressed them and kicked them to that bridge in a line,
and killed them with a bullet for seven, six in a row,
and they fell to the pit from the bridge and were buried warm,
and the hand that laid them separated children and women from the men.

And in the fourth *aktzya*, on 3 Nisan in the same year, the
big pit was added, a burial pit for one thousand human souls.
There was no one there to separate women from men and children,
and the one who was shot and the one who fell alive – suffocated drowning in blood.

Added to them are victims of the camps, Rozanowka, Holowczynza and others.
Added to them those who died of typhus, hunger and those who froze in a lone bunker.
Added to them, those murdered in hideouts by a gentile with an ax and a stick.
Added to them are those killed in the bombings before Passover 5704 – – –

All will come wrapped in *tallitot*, even with borrowed *tallitot*,
all will arrive wrapped in shrouds, even if they're borrowed shrouds.
Is it possible that they will come the way they walked to their death? the bodies which fell
into the pit – can come out of the pit? naked bodies soaked in blood!...

So I ponder all day, and at night my soul cannot rest –
they come to the prayer... the great crowd...and the rabbi...and each who has a role...
they pass, and I hear their whisper... and there is no end to the procession...
but, I don't dare to open my eyes, I am afraid to look – – –

To distract, I finish and arrange the order of the prayer:
Yosel Schilder, the ritual slaughterer, a fine young man with a golden mouth, will
pray *Neila!*
Chaim Schwartzbart, he's Chaim the *Shamash*, is walking around close to the *Neila*,

And after him Viktor the gentile, to fix the dripping candles...

Many, many lighted candles...how can it be possible that they wouldn't drip?
After all they must drip! must mix with the tears of the dead...
But, in any event, here is Viktor the gentile, he's also walking here...
He's crushing the straw with his heavy boot...and loading the shovels on his shoulder...

And I know why his boots are so heavy and so wet,
why he's carrying the tools on his shoulder... after all – he is the keeper of the graves.
And in the third *aktzya* they submerged those shot one on each other, many many,
and the blood, still warm, is oozing and bursting and spilling around and to the side...

He's walking, this Viktor, this cemetery gentile, the innocent with compassionate heart,
digging every day, fencing the blood around so it wouldn't spill –
and the blood is flowing beneath them like a powerful spring, bubbling–bubbling blood,
like a mighty caldron that meal is cooked in it, and it is bubbling and boiling– – –

Shortly before sunrise I wake up, my eyes wide open and my face is tearful,
like in a dream, the imaginary fabricated *minyan* of the dead is flying away and disappears
Only the blood that is boiling in the mighty caldron is bubbling bubbles and bubbles,
Only the boiling blood isn't disappearing and openly looks into the eyes – – –

[Page 239 - Hebrew] [Page 266 - Yiddish]

Personalities and Figures

Personalities and Figures

Translated by Sara Mages

Rabbis

Important rabbis, great in Torah and piety, who were also the sons and great–grandchildren of great and holy, served as rabbis in Tluste almost throughout the period of its existence.

The community of Tluste was among the young communities in Eastern Galicia, and it can be assumed that it existed for only three hundred years (5500, by the abbreviated era, is probably the date engraved on the headstone of Sara, mother of Baal Shem Tov zt"l). It seems that for several generations the small community didn't have its own rabbi, or a presiding judge, and was subjected to the district court judge in Chortkov. A Hassidic story tells that, when Baal Shem Tov was still a teacher's helper in Tluste, he dared to rule on the matter of an abandoned wife, and when it became known to R' Hershel', the district rabbi in Chortkov [Czortków], he was outraged and hurried to Tluste to scold Baal Shem Tov for his act.

The first, from among the rabbis of Tluste that we know details about, was R' Dov–Bertsi Shapira, son of R' Meir zt"l from Shepetovka, and grandson of R' Pinchas from Korets. He was the brother–in–law of the Admor, R' Chaim of Kosov, and under his influence he was elected to be a rabbi in Tluste. The tohel" (shtiebel), in which R' Bertsi and his son, R' Shimon, were buried, is located in the cemetery in Tluste. R' Alter Shapira, son of R' Shimon who was the presiding judge of the holy community of Vikno, wrote his family's genealogy book. HaRav, R' Yehoshua– Heschel, grandson of the rabbi from Nizhyn zt"l, and grandson of the Admor, R' Chaim of Kosov on the side of his Rebbetzin wife, served as a rabbi after the passing of R' Bertsi,

In 5654 (1894), after the passing of R' Yehoshua–Heschel, R' Pinchas Chodorov was appointed rabbi of our town. He was the son of the rabbi, R' David from Ros–Banila [Banyliv], grandson of the Admorim, R' Pinchas of Korets and R' Chaim of Kosov, and son–in–law of R' Katzenelenbogen. R' Pinchas Chodorov was one of the greatest rabbis of his generation. He perished in the cholera epidemic during the First World War, in the year 5675 (1915).

The last Rabbi of Tluste was R' Shmuel–Aba Chodorov hy"d, son of R' Pinchas. He perished, together with his family, during the Holocaust. In the aktzya, which was carried out on Yisro Chag of the holiday of Succoth 5702 [October 1941], all of them were sent to Belzec extermination camp. The Rebbetzin, Mrs. Sheindele Chodorov, widow of R' Pinchas, refused to go to the assembly point and was shot at her doorstep.

Community leaders

As was customary in most Jewish communities, there was also a fierce war in Tluste between the various Hasidic camps for the control of the community council. At the beginning of this century the power was in the hands of the Vizhnitz Hasidim and at the head of the community stood R' Chaim Nagler. Later, the Chortkov Hasidim won the election, which took place close to the First World War, and R' Baruch–Izik Vitashka was appointed head of the community. After the First World War his brother–in–law, R' Meir Kleiner, son of R' Shimshon Klein, was appointed head of the community. The members of the community council were: Akiva Langholz, Shmarya Epstein, Shmuel Meltzer, Yakov Pel [Fel], Berel Glik and others.

R' Baruch–Izik Vitashka came to Tluste as the son–in–law of the master, the estates owner R' Shimshon Klein. He came from a respected family, was an educated Jew and a "maskil" in secret. Later, he left the "Haskalah" [Jewish Enlightenment] because of an event that took place (when his wife had difficulties giving birth). He was a member of "Agudat Israel" together with his brother–in–law and his partner, Meir Kleiner.

Akiva Langholz was the son of R' Chaim Langholz, one of the richest men in town. R' Chaim belonged to the Vizhnitz Hasidic sect and was a loyal friend of the rabbis – R' Yehoshua Heshel and R' Pinchas Chodorov. Together with that he was an educated Jew who knew how to speak in German and Polish with the "Polish landowners" with whom he had trade relations. His son, Akiva Langholz, was considered to be half assimilated. The ruling language in his house was Polish and his four sons hardly knew how to speak in Yiddish. His eldest son, Dr. Leon Langholz, was a scholar and a researcher of the Polish language. His second son, Izyo, addressed the Germans with a rebukeful speech before his death and died on the sanctification of God's name.

R' Shmaya Epstein was the Gabai at the Vizhnitz Kloiz. His father, R' Yosef Epstein, was one of the important Vizhnitz Hasidim in Tluste and great God-fearing. He prayed with great enthusiasm and was especially enthusiastic with the recitation of "Shirat HaYam – Az Yashir Moshe" [Song of the Sea, also known as the Song of Moses].

Cantors and prayer readers

For a long period there were special cantors in our town. During the High Holidays the town's rabbi, and several God-fearing Jews who knew how to sing, led the prayers. Professional cantors settled in our town only in the last period and they, of course, needed another livelihood to supplement their income.

The first cantor in town was R' Alter Wasser. His father, Yehoshua Wasser, was a cantor at the court of the Admor, R' David–Moshe, in Chortkov. Apart from his work as a cantor he also engaged in useful drawing and painted oriental pictures, embroidery patterns, and so forth. After he left Tluste the cantor, R' Yitzchak Wolfsburg, who was also a scribe, settled in the town. After the First World War, R' Antshel Kremer [Anczel Krämer], was elected as the town's cantor.

It is worth mentioning here the many prayer readers in town, who led the prayers on the Sabbath, festivals and High-Holidays, and acquired a crowd of admirers for their pleasant prayers and we should mention them in accordance with the synagogues where they prayed.

In Beit Ha'Midrashe – R' Yakov Schor, the slaughterer R' Feibush [Feybush] Zomer [Sommer], and R' Ovadia Fenster.

In the Chortkov Hasidim "Kloyz"– R' Hirsh–Kopel Rosenkratz, R' Motye Spitzer, and after him his son R' Yakov Spitzer, and R' Moshe Katz.

[Page 240]

In the Vizhnitz Hasidim "Kliezel" – R' Chaim Nagler, R' Shlomo Shy"v [ritual slaughterer] (Schechter), R' Eliezer Valtzer, and R' Yosef Schilder – the last ritual slaughterer in town who perished during the Holocaust.

In the Kopyczynce Hasidim "Kloyz"– R' Feibush Holenberg.

Slaughterers

As in each city and town the slaughterers were God–fearing educated Jews who were accepted by the public. Usually, there were two slaughterers in a town, and since the job was generally given as "right of possession," from father to son or from a father–in–law to his son–in–law, a sort of two "dynasties" of slaughterers were created in the course of time.

One of the eldest slaughterers in Tluste was R' Eliezer Leiber who was called by all "Leiber shochet." He originated from Skala, from the Schtuk family. In his old age he emigrated to Eretz–Yisrael and settled in Zefat. In his place he left his son–in–law, R' Mendel Shochet, who was a great scholar (his name is mentioned in the Book of Questions and Answers of Rabbi Schwadron from Brzezany). After the death of R' Mendel Shochet, R' Shlomo Shochet (R' Shlomo Schechter) was accepted in his place. All these slaughterers were Vizhnitz Hasidim and the representatives of the Vizhnitz "Kollel" in our town. After the death of R' Shlomo his son–in–law, R' Yitzchak Glantzer, was appointed in his place. He was one of the students of the Genius Rabbi of Trzebinia who was a follower of the Rebbe of Chortkov. He was a virtuous young man, but little Tluste was too small for him. He sat for only one year in our town and later was accepted as a slaughterer in Podgorza near Kraków.

R' Neta Shochet, who was a scholar and a "Cabbalist," served the community as a ritual slaughterer together with Eliezer Leiber. After him, his son, R' Feibush [Feybush] (his wife came from the well–known Nagler family in Tluste), inherited his place. R' Yisrael Schnitzer, son–in–law of R' Feibush, served after them. Later, he transferred the "right of possession" to his son–in–law. The last slaughterers in Tłuste were: R' Yosef Schilder hy"d, and R' Shalom Lam hy"d. Both perished in the Holocaust.

Melamedim and teachers

At the beginning of this century there were two melamedim [teachers in a Heder] for small children in our town: Matiya Gertner (Matiya Katsh) and Aba Melamed. Other melamedim taught Chumash with Rashi up to the study of the Gemara: Kehet Melamed, Naftali Melamed, Birech Melamed, and Mordechai Melamed. Those who taught the Gemara were: R' Velvel Melamed and R' Shmuel Neuman. A teacher of a special kind was R' Shenor Rosenbaum [Rozenboim] who was a Zionist and member of the Haskalah movement. His daughter, Miriam, was the kindergarten teacher in the Hebrew nursery school before the First World War.

Hasidim, the practical men in town, weren't satisfied with the local melamedim and brought melamedim, great in the Torah and piety, from the outside for their sons. Such were R' Zalman Melamed (Kelman), R' Mendie {Mendel} Melamed from Budzanów, R' Binyamin from Uziran [Jezierzany] and R' Yitzchak'l from Yagel'nitsa [Jagielnica].

A teacher for a few was the preacher, R' Pinchas Lapiner, who wasn't a resident of our town. He was called the "the preacher" because he preached twice or three times a year. His livelihood was always insufficient. He used to skip the negotiation in the Gemara and move from Aggada to Aggada [rabbinic literature] to the joy of his students.

In the days of the First World War, approximately in 1916, R' Aharon Goldhaber settled in our town. He served as an excellent melamed and approached the level of a teacher. He was the son–in–law of R' Yedel Shochet from Horodenka. Most of our townspeople who leave in Israel and know Hebrew – were his students.

The study of the Hebrew language was established in the town before the First World War. The first teacher was Mr. Tashlitzki and after him Mr. Zilberhaber. The teacher, Mordechai Spector, settled in the town after the First World War. He and his wife Klara (Nonzia) were saved from the clutches of the murderers and emigrated to Israel after the Holocaust. However, Mordechai

Spector died shortly after their arrival to the country. There was another Hebrew teacher in our town, Mr. Yosef Lechter, husband of Rachel Zoibel. For a short period of time a Russian refugee named Meydman (now in Israel), served as a Hebrew teacher. Before him was a teacher named Pigur, also a refugee from Russia who mostly taught the young adults.

Up to the First World War, a general school for Jewish children, which was founded by Baron Hirsch, was established in the town. The principal of the school was Yakov Pel who also managed the loan fund next to the school. The school was closed after the war but the loan fund continued its activities with the help of the American Jewish Joint Distribution Committee. He also managed the registration of newborns and the registration of the deceased.

Scholars

There were several high-ranking scholars in town and those, who knew how to pass judgment when the rabbi was absent from the town, were: R' Zalman Kelman who was a teacher, R' Yankel Schor and R' Hershel Meir. To them we should add: R' Yisrael Glik, father of, Dov-Bertsi Glik, who settled in Tluste in the last years before the Second World War and conducted the daily page studies. He was a fine blend of a significant God-fearing scholar and a well-educated man with progressive and tolerant views. The man who led the daily page studies in our city was R' Efraim Blecher, son-in-law of R' Shmarya Epstein. He was also the organizer of "Agudat Yisrael" in our town.

Zionist activists

The first Zionists in our town were Ben-Zion Libman, Aba Gutsman, Yisrael Schechner, Mordechai Mozer, Mager, Luvdig Steckel, and Yakov Schrel. Aba Gutsman was a dignified man that a Herzl beard adorned his face. He immigrated to Israel, lived and died in Haifa.

After the First World War the young Zionists: Avraham Stupp, Mosher Pfeffer, Isador Herman, Mendel Schechter and Yehoshua Sternlib, went into action. Over the years Dr. Avraham Stupp became a wellknown Zionist leader.

In the years between the two wars, chapters of all the Zionist parties and Zionist youth movements, which existed in the Diaspora, were established in our town: Hashomer, Hitachdut, Gordonia, General Federation of Zionist Youth, Revisionist Zionist Movement, Beitar, Hehalutz, Hehalutz Hatzair and Mizrahi.

[Page 241]

"Keren Hakayemet L'Israel" committee in Tłuste 5693–1932/3

Members of these associations were also active fundraisers for the national funds (*Keren Hakayemet L'Israel* and *Keren Hayesod*), "*Ezra*" – the aid fund for the *Halutzim*, and "*Tel–Chai.*" The leaders of these organizations (by alphabetical order) were: Moti Eidelsberg, Meshulam Eiger, Leon Brandes, Berl Hernes, Yosef Lechter, Shmuel Fiderer, Bernhard Pfeffer, Beno Pfeffer, Shmuel Primes, Zechariah Kreizler, Baruch Kritzer, Eliezer Kremer, Yeshayahu

Rosenthal, Mager, Karol Roth, Herman Steinig, Meir Sternlieb, and Dudel Schechner. R' Ahron Goldhaber was the leader of "*Mizrahi*" in town.

One of the young activists, whose leadership was discovered mostly in Israel, was Yosef son of Yitzchak Shechner z"l. He emigrated in the first years after the San Remo resolution together with his young wife. He was the first emigrant from our town after the First World War. He was one of the first *Halutzim* who paved the roads in Israel and later became a locomotive driver on the Haifa–Zemach line. Later, he settled in Tel–Aviv and worked for "*Solel Boneh.*" He was elected chairman of the "Tluste Immigrant Society" when it was established in 1952, and served in this position until 1962, when he suddenly died at the age of 65.

Writers and scientists

In the last generation Tluste provided one researcher, one poet and a Zionist leader. All three are well known and all three became famous after they had left their homeland. This is not the place to evaluate their scientific, literary and public activity, and we will have to be satisfied with some personal details that determine their connection to the community of Tluste.

Dr. Dov–Ber (Bernhard) Wachstein was born in Tluste in 1868 to his parents, Moshe and Sara Wachstein. In his youth he studied in *Beit Ha'Midrashe* and saw his future there. His sister–in–law, Malcha Wachstein, wife of R' Shmuel Wachstein, volunteered to teach him to read and write in Yiddish. He finished high school in the city of Radowce in Bucovina and later moved to Vienna. With the help of Rabbi Gideman, the rabbi of the community of Vienna, he was accepted to the university. Rabbi Gideman also recommended him before the city's rich as a teacher to their sons. When he taught at the home of Weiss, one of the wealthiest members of the community of Vienna and its dignitaries, Weiss' daughter fell in love with the young man from our town and eventually they got married. Later, Dr. Bernhard Wachstein became famous as an important researcher of Jewish history in Western Europe.

At the request of the Tluste Organization in Israel, the Jewish community of Vienna sent us the following evaluation of Dr. Bernhard Wachstein (signed by V. Krel and Dr. Feldsberg):

Vienna, 21 July 1965

In reply to your letter from 23 June 1965, in which you asked for the details we know about the personality of the former community librarian, Dr. Bernhard Wachstein, we are honored to inform you:

Dr. Bernhard Wachstein was born in Tluste in 1868. After completing his studies in the Talmud, philosophy, history, and bibliography he settled in Vienna and, as a librarian at the well-known Jewish library of the community of Vienna, he reached an important position in the world of science. His research mainly related to the history of the Austrian Jewry, especially the deciphering of inscriptions on tombstones in ancient cemeteries. These inscriptions also served as a foundation for his research. According to the instructions of the historical committee of the community, which was established to research the history of the Viennese Jewry, Dr. Bernhard Wachstein wrote his essay "The inscriptions of the old Jewish cemetery in Vienna" (the old Jewish cemetery is located in the ninth district, in Rossau Street near the first Jewish hospital in Vienna. Later, a Jewish nursing home was built at the same location). In 1917, this essay was published in two volumes. A second essay: "Hebrew epitaphs on headstones" was published in 1907. He also published a collection of "Jewish private letters from 1619." In 1916, he wrote the book," Hebrew tombstones from the XIII–XV century in Vienna and surroundings." In addition, he published a collection of documents from the ancient community of Eisenstaedt named, "Certificates and documents on the history of the Jews in Eisenstadt." Finally, he also collected in the book, "The epitaphs of the old Jewish cemetery in Eisenstadt," which was published in 1922. In 1929, he contributed a great amount of material to the book "The history of the Jews in Moravia."

[Page 242]

He wrote his greatest work in three volumes during the years 1922–1930. The name of the essay: "To the bibliography of the memory and mourning lectures in the Hebrew literature."

Dr. Bernhard Wachstein was extremely humble. He opted to stand in the shade but his essays, especially his great knowledge, shone like stars in the classic period of the Jewish community of Vienna.

Dr. Bernhard Wachstein, who held the title "government advisor," frequently lectured at the Jewish Theological Institute in seminars and various cultural events at the Jewish community of Vienna. Thanks to his extensive knowledge he always managed to captivate his listeners because he was able to tell unknown events in the history of the Jews of Vienna.

Dr. Bernhard Wachstein died on 15 January 1935 and was buried with great honor at the central Jewish cemetery, entrance 4, section 3, row 4, number 9. The saying "May the memory of the righteous be of a blessing," which is often said in a memorial service, was realized by Dr. Bernhard Wachstein, thanks for his many activities in the service of the Jewish community of Vienna.

It is our honor to contribute our part to the memorial book in which the memory of the Jewish community of Vienna will also be mentioned.

*

Shimshon Meltzer was born in Tluste in 1909 to his parents, Shmuel and Sara Meltzer. In his youth he received traditional Hebrew education. At the age of sixteen he moved to Lvov and studied at the teachers' seminar. Among his teachers were also: Dr. Avraham Stupp and Leon Langholz from our town. At the end of 1933, he emigrated to Israel with his wife. Since 1936 he was a member of the editorial staff of "< i>Davar" and later became the editor of "Davar Leyeadim" and "Atidut." He became famous mostly for his pleasant playful poems which were published in several books. Some of his poems are dedicated to his town, Tluste, and his life there. He deserves the nickname "Tluste's poet." A number of his poems are brought in the Yizkor Book that is before us.

*

Dr. Avraham Stupp was born in Tluste in 1897. His father, Dr. Moshe Stupp, who was a scholar and God–fearing Jew, was one of the important Chortkov Hasidim in town. In his youth, his son received a traditional and religious education. He finished high school in Lvov, studied history at the University of Lvov and received a doctorate degree in philosophy. Later, he became a history teacher at the Jewish–Polish teachers" seminar in Lvov. In Lvov he became involved with the Zionist movement and became the secretary of the central Zionist council in Lvov. In 1924, he established the youth Zionist movement "Achva," and became chairman of the general "Halutz" council in Poland. He served as a delegate to the last ten Zionist Congresses and was a member of the administration of the World Alliance of General Zionists. For dozens of years, since 1935, he has been a member of the Zionist General Council, and for several years he was also a member of the presidium of the Zionist General Council

In 1939 he emigrated to Israel and settled in Tel–Aviv. In Israel, he was the general manager of the Housing Council, and continued with his Zionist activities as a member of the General Zionist Council in Israel. During the years, 1951–1955, he was a member of the second Knesset.

Doctors and Lawyers

In recent generations, Tluste has been blessed with good and dedicated doctors, most of whom were good Jews and loyal Zionists.

The first in this line is Dr. Yeger. He later left Tluste and moved to Lvov to continue his medical work there. His son, the engineer Moshe Zayad (Marzel Yeger), lives in Israel and works for the municipality of Haifa.

After the First World War, in 1922, Dr. Gershon Kanapas, a native of Horodenka, settled in Tluste. He excelled in his Zionist activity and his great devotion to the town's residents which was revealed, in all its might, during the typhus epidemic that swept Tluste in1925. Dr. Gershon Kanapas spent days and nights trying to save the victims of the plague until he also fell ill. To the dismay of the townspeople, all the doctors" efforts to save his life didn't help.

The brother–in–law of Dr. Kanapas z"l, Yehuda Anosh, who lives in Kvutzat Shiller, is telling:

Dr. Gustav (Gershon, son of Yehoshua) Kanapas was born in Horodenka and was the son of Dr. Oskar Kanapas and his wife, Salomea, from the Shlieber–Kurtzer family. His mother was the daughter of Dr. Gustav Kurtzer who was also a resident of Horodenka in his last years. Gustav studied at the gymnasium in Lvov and was one of the outstanding students. He was in danger of being expelled from school when it became known that he belonged to a clandestine Zionist organization named *"Koach."* He completed his university studies at the College of Medicine in Vienna where his older sister, Yula, also studied. After the First World War, during which he served in the

Austrian army as a medical officer with the rank of lieutenant, he married his girlfriend, Shoshana Shpitbart from Chortkov, who, in the meantime, changed her medical studies to a musical career (as a pianist). In 1922 the couple settled in Tłuste and in a short time Dr. Gershon Kanapas earned the affection and the respect of all the town's residents.

[Page 243]

In the winter of 1925, a typhus epidemic broke out in Eastern Galicia and caused many casualties. Dr. Kanapas invested tremendous efforts into his medical work that far outweighed his physical abilities (during the war he was stricken with a heart ailment due to a long and exhausting march). He not only provided medical assistance, but also provided material assistance to his poor patients in addition to the free medical help. He also paid for the medicines at the pharmacy (after his death his father paid his remaining debt to the pharmacy).

The struggle to conquer the epidemic took revenge on the young doctor. He contracted the typhus from one of his rural patients and the disease overwhelmed him despite all the efforts of the doctors, who were not local (such as Dr. Manowarda from Zalishchyky [Zaleszczyki]), and despite the superhuman efforts of his parents and his Zionist friends from the town. Half an hour before his death he received a telegram stating that his wife had given birth to a boy. He just had time to say: "I don't have the energy to rejoice"...

It should be noted, out of appreciation, that a number of residents neglected their families and dedicated all their time and efforts to help the revered doctor. The death of a doctor, and a beloved friend, brought heavy mourning to the town. People said: "Since the death of HaRav, R' Pinchas Chodorov, there wasn't such a large funeral in the town.

The circumcision ceremony was held in Chortkov in the presence of the deceased's sister and her husband, and in the presence of several doctors. The child was named Gershon (Gustav) after his late father. Sometime later, the child was transferred to Horodenka, to his grandparents' home, where they cared for him during all the years of his childhood. The widow continued to study music and eventually became the principal of a music school in Tarnopol. When the Second World War broke out, the child was deported, together with his grandmother, to Russia. At the age of fifteen he returned from Russia to Eastern Galicia to search for his mother. And indeed, he found her in Tarnopol and joined her. Both were murdered there at the hands of Hitler's soldiers. The child's grandmother, Mrs. Salomea Kurtzer, survived the war in Russia and at the end of the war came to Israel, to her daughter and son–in–law.

*

In the years prior to the Holocaust there were several Jewish doctors in town. Dr. Shmuel Albin, son–in–law of Yakov Steckel, lived in town until the 1930s. Dr. Albin was one of the first doctors in town and was also an active Zionist. The doctors who were in town during the Holocaust: Dr. Mansberg (lived in Tłuste since 1922), Dr. Grünberg, Dr. Baruch Milch (from Podhajce) and Dr. Bernhard Meltzer. Dr. Meltzer was a native of Tłuste, the son of David Bronstein and Zvia from the Meltzer family. His wife, Rivka, was the daughter of R' Berel Kuttner. They, and their two daughters, were murdered in a forest near Chortkov according to the "efforts" of the Ukrainian doctor, Smetzyczyn.

Also the veterinarian doctors were Jewish: Dr, Shpritzer before the First World War, and in the last period, Dr. Spiegelglass, who was murdered, together with his family, in a Gestapo "special operation." The pharmacy was also in the hands of a Jew named Emil Titinger. During the Russian and the German occupation there was another Jewish pharmacist, Dalek Falber, son–in–law of Yakov Pel.

*

All the lawyers in town were Jewish. Prior to the First World War the lawyer, Dr. Emil Bleicher, was known in the town. His office was at the home of R' Natan Hikand, and R' Natan was his clerk. Among the first lawyers in town was also Dr. Katzner who, for a certain period of time, was chairmen of the General Zionist Council. There were other lawyers in town: Dr. Safir, Dr. Seiden, Mager, Karol Roth (chairman of the Revisionist Zionist Alliance), Dr. Szmuc, and for a short period of time – the lawyer Mandstein. There was a Jewish judge at the court house named Presler (his wife survived in Russia and emigrated to Israel in 1965).

Bankers and estate owners

Some of the town's Jews were engaged in providing of loans with interest, but only one of them, Berel Kuttner, has reached the level of a "banker."

Greater was the number of Jews who were estate owners or lessees of estates. The prominent among them were: R' Meir Kleiner and R' Baruch–Izik Vitashka owners of the estates in Lisowce and Teklovka [Teklówka], and R' Duvid Merdinger who owned the Worwolince estate, Sigmund Weissglass owned the estate in Shersheniovtse [Szerszeniowce], R' Avraham Pohorles owned the Hinkowce estate.

Several estates in the Tłuste area were the property of the Buber family from Lvov, father of Professor Mordechai–Martin Buber, and were leased to Jewish tenants: the estates of Rozanowka [Rozanówka] and Holowczynce were leased to Yakov Steckel and Kehat Koenigsberg [Kenigsberg], and the estate in Podsniatinka [Podsniatynka] was leased to Osias (Yehoshua) Steckel. In his youth, Martin Buber came sometimes to spend his vacation on one of these estates.

Merchants and craftsmen

Most of the townspeople were engaged in trade. Most were small storekeepers or medium–sized merchants. Only a few have risen to the level of large merchants and reached affluence and richness. Many were pious Torah scholars. During the last period, many leaned to Zionism and their sons were active in the Zionist social unions in the youth movements and the *Halutz* movement.

Some of the town's residents engaged in various crafts and served not only the Jewish population, but also the Christian population. As in other cities in Galicia, there was also an association of craftsman in our town named "*Yad Harutzim*" which dealt in various forms of help to needy members.

*

We have tried to describe and mention a number of the most prominent figures in our town and to complete the description in the book. There is, of course, no possibility of bringing up the entire life that has been wiped off the face of the earth with cruelty that has no brother and example in the history of humanity. These descriptions will serve, just like the entire book, a memorial to the town and its people whose loving memory is so precious to each of us.

———

[Pages 244-248]

Seeing Tłuste from afar

by Dov Sedan

Translated by Sara Mages

A.

Whenever I remember my homeland in the Diaspora, my travels and my wanderings around the towns of Galicia rise before me, and I see the image and the portrait of each community the way it was drawn to me in the days when I stayed there. I'm troubled for each community that I skipped, usually out of necessity, and mostly if it was close by or exactly in the middle of my way. One of the communities that I yearned to be in, and I was not there – is the town that is called Toist or Tlist in the Jewish language and, in the mouth of the gentiles, Toyst, if they were Cossacks, Tłuste – if they were Poles. The origin of the name is probably from the word fat, referring to the fatness of her soil, or referring to the fatness of her owners. The matter of the different pronunciation of the names by the gentiles was explained to me in my first year of high school in the town of my birth. Our geography teacher, Mr. Kostinovitch, who was an enthusiastic Russian, worked very hard to light our eyes in the doctrine of the map of Eastern Galicia, and repeated the names with us, and repeated them again, out of the assumption of a first–rate educator that those common to the Cossacks were the principle ones, and those common to the Poles were tasteless to him. If my memory doesn't fail me, his lesson was the first to inform me of the existence of that town, since I did not have the opportunity to hear about her before that, despite the fact that I heard about closer and farther towns from her. More than that, since my childhood I was told that many of the surnames of the families in our town derived from the names of towns and cities, and I tried to guess their origin by changing them around. It did not occur to me that this was also the case with the name of the Tauster family who lived in our town. A year did not pass since the teacher's lesson, and I was given the opportunity to hear about this town from a young man, Nachman was his name, who wandered together with his whole community, the community of Dzvinatz Gorni, to our town. I already told at length about this young man in my book "The Circle of Youth," and now I will bring it in a condensed form: That town was captured by Russian troops and was sentenced to exile, and the location of the exile, Siberia. But when they passed through our town, the members of our town got up and liberated them from their captors. Once they liberated them, they housed them in "Beit Ha'Midrash" which was named after R' Zelig, the son of R' Bezalel. And we, the town's boys, were regular visitors there. We saw that all the members of the town were sad, but he, Nachman, was happy. And what was he happy about! He vowed to be in every place that Baal Ha'Shem Tov was. He had already visited a few places, and now he was rewarded to be in Brody, and he took the trouble to see all the corners that Baal Ha'Shem Tov appeared in, according to the tradition of our townspeople. So I became his guide, and in our many walks, which I already told about in that book, I heard his stories about Tluste, Kosov and Kitev, and he drew these towns before me, and it was as though the life story of Baal Ha'Shem Tov was weaved in them. Subsequently, when I read stories about Baal Ha'Shem Tov, mostly about the way they were connected to that area and breathing its air. I started with Buber, Reuven Pahan, and S.Y Agnon, by way of Ber Horovitz and Michael Braouer, as far as Stanislav Vintsnz, Yeshaya Tiber and others. That whole area stood before me, settlement after settlement, with their landscapes, the way that young man, who had left in the footsteps of his teacher, drew them before me, and I did not know if he was rewarded to finish what he had started, meaning, if he was able after he disappeared from our town to follow the wandering line from Ostora to Zholutsk. Two years have passed since I met that young man, and the group of towns rose again before my eyes, including the town of Tluste. Also, this time, from the words of a teacher, R' Meir Balaban, who researched the history of the Jews in Poland. He was my religion teacher in Lwów's High School where I studied. He served as a rabbi in the Austrian army and lived in occupied Poland. During his vacation he came to visit us and honored us with his words. Most of them were about the Hassidut and its causes and even about Okop, the town of his birth, and the nearby town of Tluste where he grew up. Together with his words he amused us with the interpretation of the name Okop. Some explained that the name originated from the word payment, redemption, as it was a stop where prisoners, who fell captive in the hands of the Tatars or the Cossacks, were released. And there are those who interpreted it from the word Okopi, meaning rampart. Supposedly, it was the location of the three holly ramparts that the Polish poet, Krashinske, placed in his show, "An ungodly comedy," as Christianity's last defense post. After he brought the two different meanings of the name before us, he smiled and said: and the common side is not before us, but it is a popular saying, and he ended: you heard children, popular.

Apparently, the three incidents were meant to bring me to Tłuste when I left to wander around the towns of Galicia. And, indeed, a number of times I almost fulfilled my wish, and here I was in Mikolintza [Mikolince], and I was in Chorostkov [Chorostków], and I was in Trembowla, and I was in Chorostkov and I was in Kopychintse [Kopyczyńce], and it is not necessary to say that I was a number of times in Chortkov [Czortków], and in Buczacz, and I said and I added, and I said in my heart: now, now I am also going to Tłuste. And I did not go, and surely I had a reason to visit her – I also left in the footsteps of a great man, my landsman Rabbi Nachman Krochmal. I was planning to hunt for shreds of rumors about him, and I investigated him in my town, the town that he abandoned at a young age. Yosef Klosner and Shimon Ravidovitz brought some of it in their books. I was in Zlotshev and I climbed on top of the hill where the same thinker walked, and I was in Tarnopol where he is resting in peace, and in Lwów I even talked to his grandson, the son of his daughter, Mrs. Rieza who was called Rozilia. He is Henryk Biegeleisen who is a great researcher in the books of Poland, and a small researcher of his grandfather's writings. According to him, it was only through the reading of Yehuda Leib Landa's dissertation about Nachman Kohen Krochmal's philosophy, and the articles of Meir (Max) Visberg, and Yermia Frenkel. According to what I saw, strange things were published in the name of this elder, and I need to bring up that, in the midst of our conversations, he asked me: who was equal to his grandfather from among the Polish philosophers? I answered him: Ziskovskei, because both of them took the trouble, one in the modification of a trio and the other in the modification of a quad, and each person to the history of his nation. The same grandson put on an innocent face and said: and I was more modest, and I thought, like all the experts, about Trantovske. He wanted to say, that I, the youngster, saw his grandfather as a lamp, and he, his old grandson, sees him as a candlestick. And here I said in my heart, maybe there were traditions in Tłuste that were based on Rabbi Nachman Kohen Krochmal's son–in–law, he is Wilhelm Biegeleisen, father of the literature researcher, who was a doctor there by the name of Fizikus. Fizikus was the friend of Heinrich Franzos, the district doctor in the nearby city of Chortkov, and he was called Kreiz–Fizikus. His son was the famous author, Karl Emil Franzos, who described the town where he grew up in his stories (he calls it Barnow), and also the towns around it, including the town of Tłuste.

Certainly, it is possible to reflect about the fate of the two area doctors' sons. One of them, the son of doctor Franzos from Chortkov, was attracted to the German culture, literature and language. After he specialized in classic psychology he searched for a career in it, and it would have been open before him if he also added to his composition (a reasonable translation of Vergilius ecology from Theocritus language, meaning in the dialect of my generation) a certificate of conversion from Judaism. But he, whose measure of knowledge in the history of his nation and its literature was the size of a sesame seed, saw it on himself to follow his father's words who told him: you were born a Jew and you must stand for your Judaism, because it is possible that this is what the Lord wants, and because your brothers to faith, who are treated badly by the law, need good and educated people to do them right and protect them. And so he went and studied law against his will, and ended up being an author. The first thing that he wrote, after he and the Christian girl, with whom he fell in love, swore to each other in secret that she would stand for her belief and he would stand for his belief, did not stand to her oath, was an extensive description of life in the ghetto. His work was evaluated differently by the disputing rabbinical religious authorities. The judgment that is closer to me is the judgment that the leader of the Zionists in Galicia, A. Stand, gave when he talked about the deplorable way our image was drawn in the European literature, and the fact that damage that it brought was greater than the benefit, since their blindness was greater than their clear vision. While the other, the son of the doctor from Tłuste, was attracted to the Polish culture, literature and language, and when he specialized in it, he became one of its important researchers. Surely, they would have given him a higher cathedra if he had added a certificate of conversion from Judaism to his essay, but he did not add it, despite the fact that his knowledge of Jewish history and its literature was smaller than a sesame seed. Out of necessity he held the position of a high school Polish literature teacher in the Ukrainian high school in Lwów. He was loved by his students and loved them in return. He was also a close friend and a companion to Ivan Franko, the great Ukrainian author of that generation, and we still remember their last meeting. When Biegeleisen came to visit his dead friend, he found him in his bed covered with an old torn sheet, and his naked body, with blue marks, and his waxen face were visible through the hole. The friend went to his class and told his student about their poet: he was as poor as your nation, go, go, so you will remember the face of this great man to the end of your days. The question, did he feel around him the rustle of the poor and needy nation of his ancestors, is a question. The end of the answer is hidden in the fact, that when he reached an old age he became a teacher in the town's Jewish high school, which was established after the pogroms against its Jews. We said: the end of the answer, because in addition to what I wrote about him, others, who wrote in our language about their meeting with him (Yisrael Viglo, Shelomo Landekotsh–Rechev) said that the old man, even if he wanted to, was not able to catch up with what he was late for, since his sons had already converted and their name was not Biegeleisen, but Zleoinskei, or something like that. According to rumor, one of them, or one of his sons, wandered with the Polish refugees to Tel–Aviv, and was a teacher in one of its high schools. I heard the rumor from Yitschak Lamdan, but I did not want to believe in it, since it is difficult to think: that the great grandson of Rabbi Nachman Krochmal was a convert from Lwów. Why do we need to think such a very difficult thought: the great grandson of Rabbi Nachman Krochmal was a convert in Tel- Aviv? Anyhow, in the words of that poet: this is also the moral of God and there is a lesson in it.

B.

Let's us move from the shadows, the shadows of the vicissitude generation, and see the light of the sincere generation. I said: the vicissitude generation despite the fact that it was also the struggling generations, that also, like the ones before them, realized that they needed to break the fence that their ancestors built around themselves with their rules and traditions. And they leave their towns, put Beit Ha'Midrash aside, and go to the cities and to the universities. But now, they choose what they want to study, and the spirit of their studies connects them deep in their hearts to their nation. One of them was Berel from Tłuste, who is called Bernhard Wachstein; and whoever wants to know more information about him can kindly go to the comprehensive monograph of Meir Balaban that was printed at the beginning of Wachstein's book, which was published in 1938 by Yivo [Institute for Jewish Research] in Vilna–, of which Balaban was one of its honorable members. I've already talked about Bernhard Wachstein in the pages of "Davar", on the occasion of his seventieth birthday, and now I will allow to myself to repeat it and add additional text about my teacher and rabbi, the proprietor of the monograph: at the beginning of his evaluation he brings the chain of fighters and rebels who preceded that wise man, and placed Shimon Bernfeld in the lead. But even this prominent figure is not exceedingly typical, since we know a lot of details from his autobiography, starting from what he published in the memorial book of "Beit Asif" and ending with what he published in "Reshumot" [the official journal of Israel], that his war against the Haskalah lacked the war between father and his son, since his own father, R' Moshe, was a Maskil and a member of the Haskalah movement [the Jewish Enlightenment movement]. I hope to publish two of his documents that were kept in my hands – his diary booklet from Lwów, and also his speeches in the Hebrew club in Stanisławów. It is easy to understand why Henryk Biegeleisen was linked to this chain – since we saw that he did not come from a Yeshiva or from Beit Midrash, and not only that he did not experience what they experienced, it is possible that he did not reach his height from reading a prayer from the Sidur, so how could we include him among the fence breakers when his father already found it broken, since his famous father–in–law opened it widely before the Haskalah. Back to the matters of the others who are included as members of the chain – there is something out of the ordinary also in them, and we need to treat them according to the skipping words of the owner of the monograph. Surely, this kind of writing fit Wilhelm Feldman, who started as an antagonist (or in his words: a little Jew), later in the future he was the lead researcher of Polish literature, and at the end, when he was at death's door, as a convert from Judaism. This kind of writing is also suitable for those who remained in the system, like Shemuel Wolf Guttmann, the son of the bartender from a suburb of Lwów, who ended as its enlightened Rabbi, and also, Yehusua Tahon, who ended as an enlightened Rabbi in Krakow and the captain of Galicia and Poland Zionists.

However, we can't even classify Mordechai Ehrenpreis and Tzvi–Peretz Hayot as fence breakers, because the father of the first who was a publisher and bookseller and the father of the latter who was an eminent scholar, already took a different stand on the bridge that connected tradition and Haskalah, and the passage to the bridge that connected tradition to modernism was not that far. But it is not so with Dov–Ber Wachstein that the definition of breaking and leaping fits him, although it is a different leap and a different break than the one that the Maskilim generation knew – a break out of the traditional Jewish existence, the way it was crystallized in a typical

Hassidic town, and a leap into a modern Jewish existence, where the collective historical awareness and its knowledge is the great foundation that unites the old traditions to the new, as one new unit. It is giving us more than we need to see, Wachstein as a young brother to the Jewish historians before him, and we need to see him as the big brother to the Jewish historians of his days and days to follow, mostly the historians that his homeland provided, who came out of the modern Jewish movement and went to her. We are talking about Meir Balaban, Moshe Schorr, Yitschak Shifer, Mordechai Vishnitser, Emanuel Ringlblum, Filip Fridman of blessed memory and Avraham Yakov Braver, Natan Michael, Gelber and Refaell Mahaler, may they live.

It's a pity that the mentioned monograph about Wachstein dealt in short about his life, and did not extend it the way it extended the details of his work. From the few details, we hear that Wachstein came as an older Yeshiva student, bound with troubles behind him and before him, to the secondary school in Bradovitz Bukovina (Galician students were attracted to it because of its German character and its proximity – later also Berel Luker from Kutin studied there, maybe because of its German character and its distance, and eventually Avraham Shvadron, who is Sharot, a native of Zlotshov also studied there). Later on, he went to Vienna where he studied at the university and in a rabbinical Yeshiva. His main interest was in philosophy and history. It is possible that he dreamt about a cathedra in philosophy but, when he was on the crossroad, two events decided his fate – the first event was the position that was given to him in the library of the Jewish community of Vienna, and the second event was his marriage to his student Maria Weiss, whose rich father was the owner of a distillery. Free from worries of earning an income, he sat in his beautiful office in his handsome villa and worked with great dedication that did not cease until his death. He continued to progress in his job – first as a small clerk, later on as a deputy, and at the end as a director. His work revived the institution, widened it and organized it well. These are the main subjects of his research: bibliography, epigraphy (mostly epigraphs on tombstones), genealogy, translation of letters, community registries and such, biographies of great Torah scholars, eulogies and the like, the library catalog, and above all a treasured volume of "Minchat Shelomo" (a gift from the benefactor Sali Cohen) with its five indexes. And the same applies to his index of eulogies and to the important book that he published together with Yisrael Tablicht and Alexander Krixtitbipoler, about the Jewish publicists in Vienna. The book provides a reliable detailed bibliography of all the Hebrew periodicals that were published there. In Wachstein's share fell: "Bikkure Ha-Ittim", "Kerem Hemed", "The new Bikkure Ha–Ittim", "Meged Geresh Yerahim", "Avnei Neizer", "Ozar Neá͵¥mad", "Bikkurim", "Kohav Itschak" , and the rest were divided between his friends to work on. It is an important reference book, and a researcher of the Haskalah literature in central and eastern Europe can't do his work without it. His greatest work was in epigraphy – the tombstones of the old cemetery in Vienna. Theoretically, the main part was the inscription on the stones, the explanation of the text and its language, but attached to that was an abundance of explanations and the like, that provided the history of the community and details of hundreds of issues and conflicts. The same applies to his book "Stones of fire", about the cemetery in the historical community of Eisenstadt, and again: theoretically the headstones and, in reality, the history of Burgenland's Jews on all sides and aspects. In the matter of texts – here is the collection of letters from 1619, most of them in Yiddish and a few in Hebrew, which were written on the same day in Prague, Friday before noon, and were designated to Vienna but never arrived at their destination. The messenger was caught on his way (and it was a secret way between the two cities, since the connection between the cities was forbidden due to the stench, meaning the epidemic). The letters were taken and were not opened until they were discovered hundreds of years later, when two wise men troubled themselves with them, Alfred Landa, on the linguistic aspect, and Wachstein, on the historical aspect, and a whole new world was discovered. And it also worth mentioning the publication of letters from later generations, the letters of Velvale Zebrazer (Binyamin Zev Ahronkrantz) to his brothers and his friend Moshe Ornstein, and Ozer Rohatinger (a comedian and one of the first members of "Hovevei Zion" in Lwów) and such. And to the matters of ledgers and archive documents – mostly a book of documents and scripts connected to the history of Eisenstadt's Jews and the seven communities. It is full of issues that split into different directions until it is possible to use it for full essays and, indeed, we already found those who were helped by it. And yet, he did not slow down, he wrote tens of small works, and the equal part in all of his activities: he is not only bringing documents and explanations, allegedly he does not edit the material only compile it, but the person who looks at his order and the energy that was invested to collect it, knows that there is a creation before him, and he feels that the researcher took on himself to bring the full life picture out of the frozen remnants, out of the dryness, but the one who lends a listening ear not only hears the rustle of the life of the investigated material, but also the sound of the researcher's soul who sunk himself into the research. It is pity that, until now, no one came to drink from these wells of life, which looked dry, buried under a layer of sand–parchments and dust, and when he will peel their skin he will hear the sound of a vibrating warm heart.

C.

We prolonged a little in the way of life and the activities of our history and literature researcher that Tłuste provided. We saw him exploring the history of community after community, and we hid this question under our tongue: and he did not see to investigate the history of his birthplace? And the answer for this question is clear and unclear. It is not necessary to say, that he, he is the proper address to investigate his own town and know her history, and we found historians from Galicia who wrote books – each person about the history of his own town – Balaban about Lwów, Moshe Schorr about Pshemishl [Przemyśl], Natan Michel Gleber about Brody, Raphael Mahler about Sanz [Tsanz], and so on. But, in this respect, Wachstein is not among them, and we can only talk about two small subjects of study, a direct one, that Balaban is mentioning, and it is his research about the tombstone of Baal Ha'Shem Tov's mother in Tłuste, and an indirect one, that Balaban is not mentioning, and it includes two works. One, a small collection of jokes that was published in German (1929), and the other, a small collection of Yiddish proverbs by the name: "The study of the life work of Ignaz Bernstein" which was published in Yiddish (1936).

In the matter of the first subject, which is directly connected to Tłuste, he brings in his article (Menora, Vienna 1925, booklet 2) the inscription on the tombstone: "Taf Kuf/ by the abbreviated era/on this mound/ this stone is a witness/ Sara B.A. his mother/of Ysr. B. Shem/ died on the day/.../..." In his usual way he initiates a large scale research, and explains that the date Taf Kuf (1740) contradicts the legend that Baal Ha'Shem Tov was an orphan in his childhood, since in that year he was around the age of forty. He interprets the initials B.A. to daughter of Adel, out of the assumption that Baal Ha'Shem Tov's daughter was born close to the death of her grandmother, and was named after her. This assumption does not fit Baal Ha'Shem Tov's biography, which does not mention that a daughter was born to him during his wisdom years. We need to add Balaban's objection that traditionally the Hassidim wrote the mother's name in small notes, but not in the body of a tombstone wording where traditionally the father's name is written. Therefore, he inclines to read: daughter of Aharon, or daughter of Avraham and such, but he agrees with Wachstein's evaluation that the abbreviation Ysr. for Yisrael, is not common, and also the abbreviation B. Shem, for Baal Shem, is also uncommon. Although Wachstein dwells on the question of who wrote the wording and when it was written, he does not come to a conclusion or maybe he does not want to express it, perhaps because of his obsession with the holy tradition of his town. But Balaban, who sees himself exempt from that, assumes that the whole tombstone is apocryphal, and it is possible that it was written many years after the death of Baal Ha'Shem Tov. He even compares it to the imaginary archive of Baal Ha'Shem Tov's letters, whose forgery is recognized from the contents. And, to my opinion, he had the desire to compare similar things and did not distinguish between an act of innocence and an act of deceit, and one way or the other, a small exaggeration.

To the matter of the last subject that links indirectly with Tluste – it is possible to assume that when he came to collect jokes and proverbs, he was helped with what he personally heard, meaning what he heard during the days of his childhood and his youth, and in his jokes he even mentions names of places around his town. It is fitting that the members of his town, the elderly whose memory kept the tradition of their town, and their sons, who received it from their hands, should read these small researches.

D.

We have to admit that, in the matter of the history of Tluste, we did not gain a lot of wealth from her researcher son, but what her researcher son did not do, her poet son did in days to come, and he is Shimshon Meltzer. I did not hear about him in the days that I longed to visit Tluste and, for some reasons, I skipped her and skipped her again. To justify myself, I need to say that I lacked the last push to do so – in those days there was not an active chapter of the "Hehalutz" in that town and, in my duty as the leader and administrator of the central office, I visited all the chapters wandering from town to town by train, by cart and even by foot.

It is true that I wondered a little about it, since all the towns around her, mostly Chortkov [Czortków] and Buczacz, were buzzing with the sound of the Halutz movement, and she, Tłuste herself, had a close relation to the Halutz youth movement. When the leader of Galicia's Zionists – Dr. Gershon Ziffer – returned before the First World War from his journey to Eretz–Yisrael, he brought two ideas with him. The first was the building of a Hebrew high school in Jerusalem, and the second was the establishment of a youth movement in the spirit of the "Hashomer" movement in Eretz–Yisrael. And indeed, a chapter of "Hashomer" was immediately established in Galicia, which started as a scout movement in the formula of General Baden–Powell, and continued after it was incorporated with a related movement (the independent Jewish education association of "Zeirei Zion"), as the well known "Hashomer HaZair" movement. The first two chapters of "Hashomer" organization were located in Lwów and in Tłuste. In her first pictures, you find the town's natives: Marzel Yeger, he is Moshe Zayad, who works in the municipality of Haifa, and he is also the son of that town's doctor who later left for Lwów. And you can also find there Ludvig Stekel who went to Dobromil and became a pharmacist in Tel–Aviv. Just as I left Galicia and went to Warsaw to work on the editorial board of "Haatid" I received a letter from Tłuste and, in it, a question from a teenage boy by the name of Shimshon Meltzer, asking about the possibility to study in Bezalel Art School in Jerusalem, and for the school's address. I answered him from the pages of the weekly magazine, and I think that this was the first time that his name was published in public. I remember that I read his words with excitement, since three years earlier I was also planning to emigrate to our country. I was invited by Boris Schatz to practice, as much as I was able in my view and the view of others, the art of letters and labels, drawings and decorations, and I did not respond to the invitation since I turned to another direction – the renewal of the Halutz movement in our region. At any rate, I remember the name of Shimshon Meltzer, as someone with a talent for painting who wanted to practice it, until I received, many years later, a poem signed by him that was published in "Hasolel", whose editor was my landsman, Yakov Netaneli– Rotman. I thought: are there two Shimshon Meltzers, one a painter and another a poet (since there was also a Shimshon Meltzer in Chortkov who nowadays is a member of Kibbutz Hameshulash, which was founded by Yisrael Cohen, so I wondered and said: there are three of them) since it did not come to my mind at that time that the two talents wrestled each other – from the refusal of Mordechai Tzvi to Asher Barash – and, in the end, poetry won. Although they force our visitors to treat them the way Gottfried Keller, who also knew the same struggle within him, was treated by his visitors. And they will find how the unique quality of painting is rolled up inside the unique quality of poetry and story telling.

What I was not able to know, in the way I was Shimshon Meltzer's patron in a small matter on the pages of "Haatid" in Warsaw, that I would be his patron in a larger matter on the pages of "Davar" in Tel–Aviv, since, as the editor of the literature section, I published his first poem "Mother" in "Davar" and, later, most of his songs and poems. Subsequently, he became one of "Davar's" employees and editors. His poem "Mother" was the first poem that he published in our country, and my memory whispered to me that I saw an earlier poem of his in the "Orha" collection, and from that it became clear to me that the writer was living in our country. I looked for him and I found out from Nahman Bergman, who knew the poet as a teacher in his birthplace Horodenka (after the departure of the previous teacher S.I. Pigles who is Penueli), that indeed it was him. I asked him to invite him to my home and some days later we conducted a long conversation of a thousand canvases and, it is not necessary to say that, since then and until now, the conversations grew to a value of tens of thousands of canvases.

I didn't know what my young friend would be able to learn from me, but if he were to add to his heap of love also a grain of my love to our childhood's district, let us say that I received my payment, since I learned a lot from him and he is the one who raised Tluste before my eyes, his reader, in a way that I live there the way he lived there, and my sin for skipping her – was fully reformed. I already talked about it at length in my collections of articles in the book "Between judgment and reckoning," and now I can say in brief to each person who asks about the illustration of Tluste in his poems, that he is asking to distinguish between those who lived with God and those who live below: where I can find you, and where I can't find you.

E.

The townspeople, who survived and found salvation, have done a nice thing when they created a memorial to their place of origin and wrote all that was kept in their hearts, and in their memory, on the pages of a book, and invited a graceful man, my childhood friend, Gabriel Lindenberg, to be their man of action. And if I am allowed to give them, the natives of the town, a word of advice, I will say that they should remember the basic rule, that those who start a good deed must finish it, and in the same way that they awakened the history of their town, maybe they should write about its immigrant sons, mostly about those who immigrated with the pious men of olden days and instilled in us the love of our country...

———

[Page 248]

The author of "The Dybbuk" under our roof

by Shimshon Meltzer

Translated by Sara Mages

At an early hour of a freezing, snowy winter night, a sleigh stopped in front of our house and the bell on the horse's neck silenced. Father went out to see who had arrived and returned with a tall Russian officer with a small pointed beard. It turned out that the officer, who was dressed in a long military coat, was a Jew, a representative of the Russian committee for the aid of the Jews of Galicia who had suffered from the war. He asked to hold a committee meeting that evening, and the young man who brought the guest to our home left immediately to gather the members of the committee. The "great room," which we didn't use that winter because we had nothing to heat it with, was heated in honor of the guest, and a number of homeowners gathered there for a meeting. The meeting itself, as it was found out later, was short because there was nothing to discuss. The aid committee had no money and its representative was able to help with only one thing: there were leftovers of clothing and bedding at the committee's warehouse in Kolomyia. The committee was given an order for the storekeeper to issue them to Tłuste's needy. In spite of that, they sat in the great room until the late hour of the night. Why? Because the guest wanted to hear stories and tales about Ba'al Shem Tov and other Tzadikim. Among the participants was R' Avraham Mentschel, the elderly father of R' Mendel Mentschel, and he told wonderful stories, one after the other, and the guest sat and wrote in his small notebook.

After midnight, the question of accommodation arose and R' Avraham Mentschel insisted that the guest go with him to sleep at his son's home so he could tell him more stories about the Tzadikim and their wonders, and the guest left with him. Father z"l was offended and disappointed because there was plenty of room to sleep in our home, and there was no need to move the guest in the middle of the cold night. He also suspected that the elderly R' Avraham Mentschel would finally agree to accept the guest's offer of a payment for his tales– And it appeared that this fear was justified, because the guest finished his notes about our town, Tłuste, in these words: "If one gives, take take" – (see the chapter from "The destruction of Galicia" which is brought in this section, in Yiddish).

The next morning, the guest came to say farewell to my father. This time the conversation took place in the "front room" and I was present. The guest looked around, as if he was trying to memorize the appearance of a Jewish room in Galicia, the home of, so to speak, a "wealthy Jew." A small "painting" in a thin frame was hanging on the wall and my name was written inside a decoration of flowers. The guest asked, "Who wrote these beautiful letters?" and father said: "My youngest son, the one in front of you." Then, he turned to me and asked: "Young boy, do you study at the Heder and what are you studying?" I told him, and he asked: "Could you say a sentence from Rashi?" I told him word for word, he patted my cheek and said: "What a fine boy, a good boy," and I wondered about this "Russian officer" who spoke Yiddish and asked about the weekly Torah portion–

A few years later, the play "The Dybbuk" became famous throughout the Jewish world, and the book, "The Destruction of Galicia," also arrived in our town. In it was a description of S. Ansky's visit to our town, and I knew that a "real author" had stayed in our home, and a "real author" had patted my cheek and had told me: what a fine boy, a good boy–

The note that Ansky gave father z"l, instructing the storekeeper in Kolomyia to give the leftover clothing to Tluste's poor, was kept by my father as a souvenir. It was signed by S. Rappoport, and father must have felt that this "officer" was an important man and it was fitting to keep his signature. The handwriting was large and clear, like a child's handwriting, and I especially remember the shape of the letter Tet in this handwriting: The letter Tet should turn upwards and to the right, like an unfinished Shin, but the letter Tet in Ansky's handwriting looked as if it couldn't make up its mind, it turned upwards with a turn to the left.

A few years later, when my time came to emigrate to Israel, father gave me that note and told me: "I am making you a messenger of a mitzvah, take this note and give it for safekeeping to the most important collection of signatures in Jerusalem. There is a possibility that we can preserve it here, and there is a possibility that we will not be able to. In Jerusalem it will certainly be preserved."

A few days after my arrival in Israel, I gave the note with the signature of S. Rappoport, who is S. Ansky, to Dr. Schwadron's signature collection and it must be kept there to this day.

[Pages 249-260]

My Teachers

by Shimshon Meltzer

I had around ten teachers in our town, the town of Tluste, and from each one of them I learned something. All of them were honest G–d fearing pious Jews, versed in the Torah and distinguished scholars. They did not perform their work, the work of the Lord, by fraud. All of them tried hard to teach the Torah to their students and to give them something from themselves. But what they had for themselves and how much of it they were able to pass to their students – in that they were very different from each other. And this is the reason why only some of these teachers remained carved in memory. Even this list is short and slowly fading, but the memory of others is hidden in my heart. I remember them, their teachings, their customs and habits, with love. I even remember with fondness their small–talk, and my soul is beating in me when I bring their names on this page.

*

My first teacher was called Moti Kutsh,
his old house was hunched and leaning to fall,
I was brought to him on a gloomy autumn day
to start the Aleph–Bet with sound and song.

And it happened when I approached the rabbi with my *Sidur*
to read A–Ba–Ga, Da–Ha–Va in a whining voice,
the writing looked elegantly decorated to me
and each letter looked defined and pleasant to me.

Everything looked glowing and full of light to me,
like the colors of a rainbow extending to the
heavens on a rainy sunny day......
because I discovered the *Sidur* through a tear.

I was around the age of four and a half when I was brought to the home of "Moti Kutsh." I probably studied with him for two "periods," the winter–period and the summer–period, until the eruption of the First World War. My first "period" with R' Moti Kutsh was rewarded with a wide and detailed description in my book "Aleph" and, to be truthful, I must admit and inform that all that I described in that book I really remembered from the "*Heder*" of R' Moti Kutsh. I was too young when I started to study in his "*Heder*" and I can't remember all the details, the order of studies, the recess and the games. Most of the information in "Aleph" is from a later observation in the "*Heder*" of R' Dudi Pfeffer, who was in fact the most "important" teacher in our town with whom I was not rewarded to study, "by miracle," because of the war and the escape from the town that lasted for almost three years. His class was in the "vestibule" of the great synagogue. A wide and big room, its floor was paved with stones and it did not have any windows. Air and light streamed through small windows under the ceiling and through the entrance door when it was opened for a few minutes. There were many students, around forty in number, and they were divided into a number of "classes" according to age and their degree of knowledge. Each class sat next to its table and "repeated" in a chorus what the rabbi ordered to "repeat" in a great confusion of voices. I was around the age of fifteen when I stood in the same hall, looked at that "*Heder*" and everything that was happening there with a "critical eye," in order to describe it in a "written essay" for my Hebrew teacher, Mr. Mordechai Spector. Even today, I keep this work in a notebook and I wonder about the measure of ugliness and wickedness that I invested in that description. It was full of darkness and gloom, and there wasn't even one spark of light in it. I don't know who was "responsible" for this hostile "vision": my Hebrew teacher, who tried with all his might to open my eyes, and the eyes that were opened – were opened to see that, or maybe it was the writings of Mendele Mocher Sforim that I read continuously when I was sick for a full month. The continuous non–stop reading provided me with the full treasure of Mendele's vocabulary, and it is possible that it directed my eyes to see everything through Mendele's eyes... and the sight, as I said, was darkest from dark. My ancestral merits probably stood for me when I came to describe my first "period" in the "*Heder*" in my book "Aleph." The "sights" that I saw "behind my tears" were illuminated by the light of mercy, love and kindness.

In the "*Heder*" of R' Moti Kutsh I learned to read and to pray. When the war erupted, and I was around five and a half, I was already familiar with the *Sidur* and the proof for that: when we escaped from Tluste to Horodenka we stopped in Uścieczko by the Dniester River. The bridge was already burnt and the ferries that were promised by the military had not yet arrived. There was a nice forest near the river. The Jews wrapped themselves with their prayer shawls and the young men adorned themselves with their *Tefillin* and stood to pray *Shacharit* [morning prayers] in the forest. At the same time, I held my *Sidur* in my hand and knew how to follow the congregation and the cantor.

The meaning of the name Kutsh is not completely clear to me, and, when I asked my landsmen, they were not able to give me a clear answer. It is possible that the word Kutsh is a distortion of the word Kortsh, meaning, root, trunk or dwarf, and the rabbi was called by that name because he was short. And, if so, his name was close and similar to the name of a teacher greater than him, and he is Yanush Korchak. The meaning of his name is simple: Kutsh – carriage, and it might be based on a story about a trip that he took, or maybe one of his family members took, in a carriage of powerful lords...

*

Clearer and safer is the name of my second rabbi with whom I studied in the town of Zaleszczyki. We arrived there via an indirect route, through Horodenka. We stayed there for a year and a half during the days of escape and exile, and out of fear of the Cossacks.

The rabbi was called Teshapki Melamed by all and, as we know, Teshapka means a hat in Polish and Ruthenian. And here we need the saying of our Sabra sons: why was he named Teshapki?

Why – hat? But, it is possible to assume that also this title was probably based on a real event or on an event that could have happened, such as when the rabbi entered a government office and the Austrian clerk, a Pole who hated Jews, berated him because he did not act quickly to remove his hat.

He was an easy going person and I can't remember if he ever scolded me or another boy. There were around twenty of us. I see all of us sitting next to a long table laid with the best for the feast of *Lag Ba'omer*. At that time, Tluste was in the Russian zone and was wiped dry from everything good but Zaleszczyki, which was in the Austrian zone, was blessed with the best. The abundance was also present in our *"Heder"* – figs, dates and different kinds of candy. Two of my cousins studied with me at Teshapki, and were partners to the same feast. My first cousins: Michael Meltzer who now lives in Haifa, and Mordechai Sternkar who now lives in Beit–Shearim.

When the front got closer to the Dniester, we were forced to escape from Zaleszczyki to Czerniowce [Chernowitz] on the first day of the holiday of Shavuot. I ran to my rabbi's house to collect the three pilgrimages *"Mahzor"* that I left there. I was very sad for the *"Akdamot Milin"* [a religious poem]. Such a beautiful great poem and the first that I learned by heart. I was not rewarded to read it in the synagogue on that day. Exactly at the time that *"Akdamot Milin"* was read in the Dripaltikyt Street synagogues in Czerniowce, we entered the same street together with other escaping refugees sitting on top of farmers" wagons. The wagons were loaded with our belongings, women and children sat on top of the bundles and the men walked behind them...

Additional pain was caused to me by the special lovely poem *"Yeziv Pitgam"* [Aramaic hymn in praise of the Torah] that I also knew by heart, but without fully understanding it. Now this short song is totally "wasted" on me. Will my father have the time and the will to open the *Mahzor*, to test me and listen to me reciting the entire poem by heart?

This short poem was "special" in my eyes since all of its lines ended with the same rhyme: "Rin", and the repeated endings sound like rin–rin–rin–rin, which were lined one under the other at the end of the page. In my eyes, they looked like water dripping from the edge of the roof, one drop after the other, like a string of beads. They sounded in my ears: rin–rin–rin, meaning: tif–tif–tif, drip, drip, drip... you the reader, don't wonder that the string of beads sounded and looked that way to me, the child. This vision and sound already had a base and a root in R' Motie Kutsh's *Heder*. When we started to study *Parasht Vayikra* from the *Chumash*, our group read it and translated it to Yiddish in a loud voice: *"Ben–Bakar"* [a calf] – *"A Yengel Rint"* meaning: a dripping boy. This was closer and clearer to us than the correct translation: *"Ben–Bakar"* – *"A Younger rind"*. The word *"Rind"* was not common in our language, and we did not assume that the words *"Rinder Fleisch"* (beef) that our mothers said was somehow connected to *"Ben–Bakar"* – *"A Yengel Rint"*...

Teshapki Melamed's *Heder* was located in his apartment at the end of the road "on top of the mountain". Many years later, when I was a grown boy and traveled from Tluste to Kołomyja, I turned to Zaleszczyki to show my companion the few places in the city that were connected to my childhood memories. Only the Dniester remained mighty and impressive the way it was, but the rest of the places had changed their look and size. The big buildings of my childhood became smaller in my adolescence and now looked smaller and shorter. Long distances shrank to a few steps, the "tall mountain", where Teshapki's house stood was a slope. I found only one small closed alleyway. The rabbi's house did not stand on "top of the mountain" but at the end of that alleyway that indeed rise up on a hill.

The rabbi was no longer alive, but the great experience was alive in me with the same strength that existed in me during that "time" in that "*Heder.*"

One day I returned to the *Heder* after a lunch break and, behold, a group of Jews dressed in *kapotes* [caftans] with beards and side locks were struggling with a saw and a hammer, nailing unpolished white boards together, and building a kind of long box. A few of my friends from the *Heder* stood around them in a half-circle, and one of them whispered to me: "they are making a coffin for a dead person... the old man in that house died...."

Not too many minutes passed and the dead man was taken out. His bent body was wrapped in shiny shrouds, and he was placed inside the coffin. I escaped like a shooting arrow, ran back home shocked and terrified, but I did not have enough energy to run inside the house. Breathing and exhaling I ran into the tobacco store that was owned by our best neighbor, R' Yedel Kutner. He was a wise Jew who liked me and talked to me a lot, and his jokes and candy were always waiting for me. What happened? Why are you so pale? He asked me and pressed my head into his chest. I was only able to emit one word – "I saw". "What did you see?" – he asked. "A dead person" – I answered, and started to cry. "Ha! the old man next to your *Heder*?" – "yes, yes", "and because of that you cry? My little fool! He was a very old man, a hundred years old or maybe more, and he died a righteous death!"

A "Righteous death?" What is it? His words did not explain much and I continued to cry. I did not cry for the old man. I saw him many times sitting on a bench next to the house, warming in the sun and "chewing". "What is he always chewing?" I asked my friends. "He is chewing nothing and he does not have any teeth". But he was alive, alive, and now I saw him dead. They placed him in that coffin, and they put two unpolished boards on top of it, and they took a hammer and nails to seal him inside. With nails...

And so, I discovered death for the first time, and the childish heart cried from fear and knew why he was crying and why he was afraid. He probably knew that in a year or two deaths will appear in his family, his brother – far away, and his mother – very close. "I was nine years old, still a child, and death – doubled –looked straight deep into my eyes".

*

The days of war and "exile" in Horodenka, Zaleszczyki, Chernovitz, and Sasów skipped me to the *Heder* of R' Dudi Pfeffer, which was crowded and very noisy. So I moved to the *Heder* of another teacher, who was the opposite of R' Dudi: thin and delicate, feeble and quiet. I don't remember his name, but I remember him and his wife the Rebbitzin: a white scarf was always tied to her head, the ends of her loop snuck out from under her delicate chin like two little wings, and her beautiful small face was made out of very thin wrinkles, like an apple that ripened late in the autumn. The rabbi's face was also shriveled and wrinkled, and his very thin voice sounded like his wife's voice. His wife's face was clean without the signature of a beard, but the rabbi also lacked a beard, not even one hair! Not that he shaved it, G–d forbid! but because he never grew a beard! So the children swore and testified, and said that because he did not have a beard he also did not have children.

I don't understand the connection between a missing beard and the lack of children. But I feel sorry for this small couple, who lived in peace and loved each other like a pair of doves. It showed when the Rebbitzin brought the rabbi his daily lunch in a clean basket. She waited until he was done with his meal and took the empty dishes back home with her in the same basket....

His *Heder* was in the Tradesmen Synagogue which was also located in the great synagogue. The entrance was through R' Dudi Pfeffer's *Heder*. There were few students there and the studies were conducted in tranquility and calmness. The students bragged that their rabbi never hit them and they never heard a word of scolding from his mouth. On the contrary, the students of R' Dudi Pfeffer claimed that their rabbi talked in a woman's voice, his face was a woman's face, he did not have a beard, never had one and would never have one... and my luck played for me, and I was not brought to that rabbi, but to the *Heder* of R' Ahron the Melamed.

*

R' Ahron Goldhaber was not a native of Tluste, Horodenka or any other town. He came to our town after the war and immediately earned the name of a good outstanding teacher. His "*Heder*" was located in the big house of the

Mani Gertner family, near "Gvitzsa" hall in old Targovitza. The big room also served as a synagogue on the Sabbath (since most of the synagogues in town were destroyed). There were three classes there. The largest class had four or five grown up boys and they only studied Job for two hours in the afternoon. The melody of Job's complaint is still ringing in my ears which were always open to receive everything enticing. R' Ahron read it with affection, as though he was listing his own complaints to the ears of his older students. The melody came from the bottom of his heart, and entered my guts and my kidneys despite the fact I understood very little of the contents. I greatly doubt that a small portion of that lamentation and joy, argument and flurry of emotions, are still echoing in the ears and the hearts of his five older students... Three of them are still alive and live in three different faraway lands. They were too old, too experienced in the fearful events of the war to be able to comprehend the talk of Job that was mixed in R' Ahron Melamed's crying soul...

The young class was also small, five or six boys. Besides the *Chumash* with *Rashi* we also studied Yehoshua. But I did not stay in that class for many days. There was an older boy in that class, in the small class, probably two years older than me, but his brain was weak. The rabbi told me to "repeat" the chapter that we studied in Yehoshua until he understood it. I "repeated" it with him once, twice and three times, but he was not able to understand it. On the next day, when R' Ahron came to test us on this chapter, that poor boy stuttered and did not know the meaning of the words. When my turn came to read and explain, I looked at the rabbi and without looking at the book I said one verse and translation only by heart, since I had memorized it from the repeated reading with that boy. R' Ahron heard a number of verses to the end of the chapter, thought for a moment, and said to me: you are not good. I looked at him with wonder and I was ready to start crying. I was sure that he was not going to let me be a "repeater" to that boy, but R' Ahron repeated and said: you are not good for this class, move to that table.

And so I moved to the middle class, the big class. Around twenty students sat next to the long table, and matters were brighter and happier there. In "*Pasuk*" [a sentence in the bible] we studied the Book of Isaiah (at that time I was not able to tell the difference between Isaiah and Joshua, but years later I decided to correct the distortion). In the Torah: at first I studied *Parasht Vayechi* with all the "details" about my second "self," about "the brothers

Shimon and Levi" and the proof that only they, Shimon and Levi, plotted together to kill the whole city of Shechem and sell their brother Yosef... all these matters were lofty, exalted and royal. Yosef was second to be king. His two sons – great heroes. Yehudah – strong and mighty and the father of future kings: "The kingship will always be in the tribe of Yehudah" ...and the "family members" were also pleasant and friendly, they also liked Yosef, as it says: "He was an assistant to the sons of his father's wives, Bilhah and Zilpah"... we are forced to say against our will that: "the brothers Shimon and Levi" were of the same opinion... but for the sake of the truth – the childish heart hated them. On the contrary, the two brothers were heroes, carried weapons and knew how to frighten a town full of gentiles – it was a pleasant and lovely thought and I wished I had two brothers like them!

On the Sabbath I'm tested. I know all of *Parasht Vayechi* with *Rashi*, all the way to the end. And I know the verses by heart – twice as much: in *Rashi's* short and condensed language, the holy language, and also in my rabbi's Hebrew version with the special melody. And the childhood voice is ringing like a bell and blows like a flute, and fills all of our "front room" .....

R' Ahron liked me, and also his tall wife with the delicate face, the Rebbitzin, showed me great affection. There are two girls in the house and now a boy was born. Tomorrow he will be circumcised and R' Ahron is calling me to help him with a matter of holiness: the foundation beam of the old house where the *Heder* is located, a beam that is protruding from the wall and crumbling from old age and rot. He is taking a piece of broken rotted wood and crumbling it slowly, slowly to a fine powder. Later, he sifts it with a thin sieve – and the brown–red "flour" will be thrown on the circumcision tomorrow to stop the blood... and the baby, thank G–d, will grow up and become a boy, and the boy will become a teen, and the teen will become a young man. And he stood before all the horrors of the war and he is now in Israel, and he is, Avraham Goldhaber, May he live.

How good it would have been if they had allowed me to study with R' Ahron for three–four periods, but the Kingdom of Poland thought and found out that R' Ahron was needed to enforce its military power and drafted him to one of its forces. R' Ahron Goldhaber was his name, but he did not have gold and he did not have money to redeem himself from the army, and the best *Heder* in town was scattered among other teachers. How did the family earn a living? At that time, I was too young to be interested in this matter and investigate it.

*

Probably at the same time the lot fell on me to become one of R' Asher Kurtzer's students. Before the war he was a teacher in Baron Hirsh School. After the war he lived in a building next to the former school. That building was fully occupied with those who returned to town from their "exile" and found that their homes had burned down. R' Asher Kurtzer had a number of occupations. He became a cantor, a *Mohel*, and a teacher, but all of them did not provide an income to his family and did not drive the poverty away from his home.

R' Asher was not a "*Melamed*" [a *Heder* teacher] but a "Teacher". He had few students and taught in his home, a one-room apartment. From all that I learned from him I remember only The Book of Proverbs. I remember that he did not explain the meaning, wisdom and moral of the verses. He translated them in "Germanit" Yiddish (probably using a book of "commentary" that he owned) and, to our ears, his translation was something that needed a translation and an explanation, therefore:

> The clear reasonable words of Solomon – did not attract my heart,
> the rich moral from which he collected wisdom like women, did not
> please the lad,
> but what wisdom did I earn in his home, from extreme poverty,
> from the few blessings and the many crafts of a teacher, cantor and a
> Mohel....

"From extreme poverty" – G–d forbid that you think that it is a figure of speech, out of the need to find a rhyming word for Solomon. The poverty in that home was elevated and lofty; it was an elegant aristocratic poverty. The speech in that house was pleasant and noble. On Thursday, market day, the woman and the man calculated what they needed for the Sabbath. This is missing and that is missing, but probably only an accidental shortage, a temporary shortage... and indeed, it was only "temporary". After a few years the two boys grew up and helped to provide the family, if not with abundance, with honor.

*

R' Ahron Goldhaber was taken to the army in the middle of the summer and the students scattered among the different teachers until the end of that period. After the holidays, R' Shimon Gabai from Estisheski was brought to Tluste. He was an outstanding *Gemara* teacher. The "*Pasuk*" was pushed to a corner, and even the *Chumash* with *Rashi* were pushed to Thursday afternoon and Friday morning. All the days of the week were dedicated to a page in the *Gemara*.

I don't know what moved R' Shimon to choose "*Masechet Ktovot*" and start with the second chapter.

We were children of war, and the matter of a woman claiming her marriage contract after she became a widow, or divorced her husband, did not stimulate the souls of 18 teenage boys who sat around the table in the "Vizshnizer Kloiz" (the synagogue of the Vizhnitz Hassidim). Surely, in a week, three or four students (myself included) had a command of the *Gemara* page and in the negotiation that was strange to us (it was winter outside, the bells rang on the horses' necks and snow fell and covered the town with a white scarf). There were a few sweet words and, ever since, their good taste remained in our language: the woman who was widowed is simply a woman who became a widow, a veil is the scarf that a bride wears, and the "mouth that forbids is the one that permits", a great basic rule that always stands for me in the time of need. And, above all, the "*Migu!*" [a Talmudic claim – why do I need to lie] a concept that your tired young brain can't understand and learn the meaning of, but after you earned it for yourself – it is yours forever and you treat it like a treasure.

R' Shimon was required to prepare a test for the Sabbath, not only for the three or four "good heads," but also for all the students. The poor man worked hard – and all for nothing! Every Thursday, with great sadness and devoted pain, he repeated in a red weak face: you study and study and study, and when you arrive at the end of the matter – there is no one at home! (pointing his thumb up).

Of course, the word "children" was directed at those who did not know and not at the three or four who knew. But, R' Shimon was not comforted with the few "good heads," and every week he felt sorry again for the failure of his intermediate students. What else could he have done for those students?!

The boy Munya Gabai brought him to destruction. Munya was the rabbi's brother's son, an orchard tenant who lived out of town on the road to Zaleszczyki. Munya was a wild lad and his brain in front of a *Gemara* page was like an empty bottle that was very well plugged. It was opened like a pigeon coop and all kind of "ideas" and inventions flew out of it. He entertained the other boys with them and distracted them from their studies. In winter, the rabbi left the "Vizshnizer Kloiz" with a big checked woolen scarf wrapped around his head and his back, exactly like the scarf that women wrap with (and he was the only man that I saw wrapped in such a scarf), and under the scarf it was possible to see his bent back. I knew that, because of the chill outside, the rabbi was leaning and wrapped in that way, but I could not put my feeling aside that the troubles that Munya brought on him bent his back......

A few years later, after Munya drowned in the water reservoir near the mill on the road to Swidowa, he was taken by a cart to the home of Dr. Albin, as though he was able to revive the dead. In my heart I was sure that it was a punishment from the heavens for the grief that he caused his uncle, R' Shimon Gabai, but I felt that the punishment was too severe...

R' Shimon had another relative who studied in our *Heder* and his name was Vali (Avraham), the son of Mordechai Gabai. Vali was one of the three or four good students, not with the power of his quick understanding, but with the power of his great dedication. He was a tender good teenage boy. He was also a partner to the great grief that his rabbi and uncle R' Shimon suffered, from the pranks of his cousin Munya. In order to compensate for that – he studied with great dedication. A few years later, when we grew up and the town's youth started to think about their future and broke their way into the "big world" and for education – he remained the only student to sit in *Beit Ha'Midrash*, and he studied the Torah with the dedication of a real diligent *Yeshiva* student, the way it was done in the old days. His father and all the members of the town expected greatness from him. In secret they also told wonder stories about the charitable deeds that he performed with the daily meals that they brought him in Beit Ha'Midrash, and the pocket money that his father gave him.

He was a year younger than me, and his "comprehension" was slower than mine, but in the two or three years after his Bar Mitzvah, at the time that I was busy in different works and read a lot of secular books that I found in the Zionist library and in the Hebrew School – he sat from early morning to the late hour of the night and studied, and studied, and studied – the *Gemara*. During those three years he became a real diligent Torah scholar, and I, what did I achieve – I filled my belly with Shmuel Leib Gordon, the "Hebrew version" of Kerensky, and all kinds of books that were not "religious books." I knew that his way was better than mine, but I did not have the power to change my mind. My road led me to Lwów [Lemberg], but he remained in Tluste, in *Beit Ha'Midrash*, studying diligently on his own. And his road was only a few hundred steps, in the morning from his father's house, across the bridge to *Beit Ha'Midrash*, that the rich woman, Mrs. Rivka Braksmayer, built, and at night he returned the same way. For that he crossed twice a day and he did not know any other way.

But he was destined to travel once all the way to Lwów on his last journey. And in spite of the fact that his father's home was close to Tluste's cemetery – it was forecast that his tender and graceful body would be buried in the Yanovski cemetery – ten full years before the place became a death camp and a burial ground for the Jews of Lwów and the extended area.

Even he, the good, innocent and honest, like his cousin Munya who drowned, was taken to Dr. Albin – to his clinic in Lwów for an appendectomy. The matter became known to me in the evening and when I hurried to that clinic the next morning – I already found him lying dead on a high bed. Blood was flowing slowly from the oilcloth, dripping from the bed to the floor and accumulating in a small puddle. He arrived to Lwów too late and died during surgery or shortly after it.

He was around eighteen when he died. If he had died in Tluste, probably the whole town would have come to accompany him, and the town's wise students would have given him a great eulogy. Now that he died in Lwów his funeral was arranged in haste. The funeral left the Jewish hospital in Rapaport Street and the coffin was not carried on the shoulders, but transported on a *Hevrat Kadisha* cart – no one eulogized him or cried for him, no one walked after his coffin besides the members of *Hevrat Kadisha* and a few poor people who accompanied them for the *mitzvah* and for the hand out. My arm was inside the arm of his unfortunate father, R' Mordechai Gabai, and we walked heavily after the cart, along Rapaport Street, and the father was not shouting and was not mourning, but he whispered all the time: "Shimsheli, you are the only one who knows who I am leading to lay inside the grave," and I only shook my head and I was not able to say even one word, since my tears choked my throat.

*

On Passover eve, R' Shimon Gabai returned to his town of Uścieczko and never returned to us. Maybe he missed his family members, or maybe he longed to see his tiny little town that resided by the mighty Dniester. And maybe he did not long for the Dniester that rolled its great waters with a broad royal serenity, but maybe for the little tributary, the Dzhuryn, that rushed with a great noise to the Dniester? since this Dzhuryn passed not far from his home. Once, about seven years after I was his student, I found him standing on the small wooden bridge above the yellowish tributary looking at its stormy water after a summer rain that fell on that day. "Shalom Rabbi!" – I shouted from a distance, he greeted me, immediately recognized me and called me by my name, but he did not shake my hand, probably not to embarrass the young woman who walked with me since he was not able to shake her hand. But the rabbi did not abstain from looking at her, at this young woman, and asked if she was my "bride." In order not to confuse the answer I simply answered "yes." The young woman blushed and I think that R' Shimon's face came alive. At the same time, I thought that he was not an "idler," and perhaps in his youth he read Schiller's poems and Goethe and Heine, and the proof of the matter: when he was kind to us during class, he kept on promising us that if we would be good children and also study hard in the next week, he would pay for the favor with a favor and teach us German grammar. He never reached the point to keep this promise, and we also did not crave that he would keep it – these terms looked strange and magical to us, and were above our understanding, but we were sure that he was able to keep his promise if he was able to do so. Now I said in my heart. Is it possible that he knows German grammar without knowing a little German literature or poetry?

*

For the summer period, R' Shimon Gabai, son of Muni Gabai, came in his place. They resembled each other in their height and in the same shiny red face, but while the father's face was adorned with a beard and his head with side locks – the son's face was smooth and it looked like it was covered with oil. I don't know if the son removed the hairs of his beard with some kind of a "potion" that the Jewish religious laws allow to use, or if he was shaving it with a real razor. The second possibility was probably closer to the truth. If not – from where did all the frequent injuries come to his face? And if so, how did the *Heder* boys' fathers ignore it? since all of them were pious and most of them were Chortkov or Vizhnitz Hassidim.

The "*Heder*" was no longer in the "Vizhnitzer Kleizel" but at the home of Mrs. Leah Stupp, in a room that she leased cheaply for that purpose since her son, Muny, was also one of the students. Heaven Forbid! Leah Stupp was not a widow. The head of family, R' Izik–Leib Stupp, was a Vizhnitzer Hassid, a scholar and a cantor with a stylish pleasant voice. But since Mrs. Leah was wise and knowledgeable, she was not only a housewife but also the active soul in the fabric shop in her front room and in her egg business on market day – the whole family was named after her.

The main difference between R' Shimon Gabai and his son, Muni Gabai, was only in the fact that the father was called by all "Shimon Melamed," but his son was called from the beginning and also during all that "period," "Muni the Teacher." And what did Muni the teacher teach us? Maybe he came to keep his father's promise and really teach us German grammar with all the six tenses in it? Or maybe he would start teaching us the books of the prophets according to their order, from first to last, with *Rashi*, with *Mezurut* and with the commentary of Rabbi Meir Leibush ben Yehiel Mikhal? Heaven Forbid! It did not come into his mind. He was not brought to Tluste even for that! His father, R' Shimon the Melamed, taught us about a woman who became a widow and she was demanding her marriage contract, but the son Muni the teacher, taught us the matter of bringing a divorce across the ocean, and the need to declare who wrote it and who signed it! If Muni the teacher had pointed to us on a certain map of Eretz–Yisrael (one of those was already available at that time in our town, published by *Amkroyt et Freynd* in Przemysl, since the days were after the Balfour and the San Remo declarations!), they would have lit our eyes saying: here is the land of Binyamin and the city of Rekem, and here is the city of Acre (still there today), and here is the city of Ashkelon. R' Yehudah spoke about these cities in the *Mishnah*: "From Rekem to the East, and Rekem is like the East; from Ashkelon to the South, and Ashkelon is like the South; from Acre to the North, and Acre is like the North" – unmistakably the matters would have been clearer in *Masechet Gitin* [a tractate of the Talmud devoted to the validity of the divorce document and how it may be written and delivered]. But Muni the teacher did not show us any kind of a map, did not bother to explain why R' Yehudah was setting boundaries only in the east, south and the north, but not in the west. He only bothered himself with a question of the witnesses, who signed it – i.e. to effectuate it, and the witnesses who handed it over. We were not attracted to this problem, and I think – also the heart of the teacher was not attracted to it. His heart was attracted to something else

In the same summer, Ms. Miriam Rosenbaum visited our town. She was the daughter of R' Shenor Rosenbaum who is "Shenor Melamed." Only my friends and I knew of his good name, but we were not rewarded to see his face and study the Torah from his mouth. This Miriam was well educated and spoke Hebrew in the days before the World War. She even founded a Jewish Zionist society in our town for women who studied Hebrew and Jewish history. Now, she came from afar (from America!) to visit her town, Tluste, and she was staying at the home of Leah Stupp, the home where our *Heder* was located. Besides the fact the Miriam was perfect, she was also a beautiful woman. And the soul of Muni the teacher longed to talk to her! He was not able leave his students, approach her directly and start a conversation out the fear of what the students and their parents would say! He did not dare to talk to her or take her for a walk in the streets or out of town, from the fear of what people would say! So he sent her small letters, small folded notes, and he used me as his messenger to deliver them. And I would leave the room and walk to the other room, hand the small letter and wait for a written answer. And at the same time, I enjoyed the glowing face of that Miriam. And at the same time Muni the teacher apologized to me and said while his red face was getting redder: All his intention with these letters was to revive his knowledge in the wisdom of Gabelsberger's Stenography since these little notes were written in Stenography letters and good things come in small packages...

Miriam is reading and smiling, replying what she was replying, also in Gabelsberger's Stenography, and telling me that she likes me. Is it not something! Miriam the scholar, who knows how to speak Hebrew! But she is not the only one who likes me. Also the girls my age and the girls who are older than me by a year or two, who come to Mrs. Leah Stupp's store to buy a piece of white fabric and print a nice sample for a Sabbath tablecloth – they also like me! For what reason? Because, all the nice samples are drawn in advance. You copy them from a paper that is pierced with tiny little holes by spreading blue powder on it and spraying some kind of a liquid to set the color so it will not be erased. But, it is not the same for monograms – those you have to draw for the name of each girl! And I'm the one who knows – the one who knows everything and knows from where! Muni the teacher turns an eye on the fact that I disappear for hours from the study table. He probably trusts my good "grasp." And I stand and draw a monogram, a great letter for the name of the girl, curly and intertwined with her surname. To complete the art work I decorate them with leaves and blossoms, and the girls stand around me and look at my work with wonder, and one of them, Feigale' the beautiful (the wife of Zechariah Krizler, Canada), is bending over me and actually leaning on my back. Her golden braid is gliding on the left side of my neck and her hot breath is patting the right side of my neck, and under my hand the blossoms are blooming for the completion of her monogram...

The monograms and the golden braids of the beautiful Jewish girls sweetened my summer days, and the teacher Muni did not scold me – and for that I remember him well!

*

From this sublime we fell, myself and a number of my 'Muni the teacher' school friends, to the ownership of a "distinguished *Gemara* Melamed" from Budzanów. Without a doubt, he was a modest, G–d fearing Jew and a Torah scholar. But even a great scholar – May he forgive me up there in heaven! – was not a helpful teacher. Besides his moral lectures I can't remember any of his teachings. The *Heder* was located in the big *Beit Ha'Midrash*, and the studies were in the *Beitzah* Tractate. The Melamed from Budzanów (May G–d forgive me! I can't even remember his name) was a strange creature, and a number of tales that the world was telling about lazy Melamedim, were told about him. I will repeat and tell here one of them the way it remained in my memory:

Once upon a time, during the intermediate days of Passover, the Budzanówni Melamed from the town of Budzanów, left on the road leading to the village of Verbuvitch [Verbovczy] to converse the words of the Torah with R' Yisrael Glick. On the way he got tired (one of his legs was shorter than the other and he limped a lot). So he sat on the edge of a field to rest a little. Suddenly he felt sleepy and said to himself: the day is still long, I will nap a little and continue on my way. He took off his shoe with a sole that was the way of all other soles, and took off his other shoe with a sole that was eight times thicker since this leg was shorter. He stood the two shoes one after the other, the way they walk and said in his heart: when I will wake up from my sleep the shoes will show me the way and tell me to what side I need to turn in order to continue on the road leading to Verbuvitch. A prankster passed by, saw the two shoes and the order in which they were standing, and figured out the intentions of the Budzanówni. What did he do? He took the two shoes and changed their direction, standing them in the direction of Budzanów. When the Budzanówni woke up, he immediately looked at his shoes and knew in what direction he needed to walk. He put his shoes on and left. An hour later he returned to Budzanów. What "A great wonder," he said to himself, "this Verbuvitch became larger! Verbuvitch is a small village but her buildings are the buildings of a real city.". Very quickly his amazement grew bigger. "This street," he said to himself, "looks exactly like my street in Budzanów, and this house looks exactly like my house." He stood before his window and looked inside and saw his wife sitting by the table, a holiday scarf on her head and wire glasses on her nose, and she was reading what she was reading, since on a holiday she was not able to patch or knit, but he was still afraid to enter his home in case the woman was not his wife, only looked like his wife, or, G–d forbid!, it was the work of a witchcraft. He gathered his courage and shouted through the open window "show me the Ketubah!" Only after he saw the Ketubah that was written and signed legally – he calmed down and returned to his home and to his wife.

*

It became colder after the holidays and, by Hanukah, the river and the area around it were completely frozen. The brave students came out of all the *Heder*s to slide on the ice and only I and my friends, the Budzanówni students, were missing from there. How is it possible? We started to sneak out from the dry and weary studies of the "distinguished *Gemara* Melamed," who was not able to revive the matters that he taught us and make them interesting. He also started to lecture us about our morals, and the mouth that was stuttering and swallowing his words during an explanation, was the same mouth that emphasized his preaching in a pleasant and slow voice. He stabbed them in our flesh with the same pleasure that a cobbler pulls out small nails between his lips and nails them into the sole with direct blows. The regular version of the reproof was like a repeated song: If you don't want to study the Torah, what will become of you? You will not able to be a woodcutter or a water drawer, because you are not strong enough for that, you can't be a rabbi or a judge, a butcher or a Melamed – because you don't want to study the Torah. The only thing that is left for you is to be a tailor or a cobbler – is that proper and fit for your father, whatever his name is, for his son to be a cobbler or a tailor?"

When my turn came to hear this song of reproof, which was said in a pleasant voice and the great pleasure of someone who invented a convincing argument for the purpose of studying the Gemara, I already had a convincing answer ready in my mouth.

Rabbi – I answered politely – Is there a reason why all the Jewish children should be rabbis and judges, slaughterers or Melamedim? Surely, also cobblers are needed in the world! Never mind me, I buy ready made shoes from the factory, but rabbi, you can't live without a cobbler! Without cobblers in the world, who will make you a shoe with a sole that is eight times thicker than the other?

I was sure that the rabbi would be strict with me for mentioning his deformity, but I was wrong. He smiled with pleasure and said: "Shemsheli,' you are a wise lad, but you don't want to study. If you wanted to study, you would study and you would be able to reach the real knowledge." And he did not know that I actually wanted to study, but his teaching was dim, unclear and boring, and it did not enter the heart and not even the ear.

Once he came to *Beit Ha'Midrash* and his entire head, side locks and beard, his eyebrows and mustache, were covered with fine feathers, exactly like the snow that fall outside in the morning. The only thing that was protruding from the sea of hair and feathers was his round flat nose. Probably, in the same night, the pillow under his head came undone. Shemsheli', his said to me in a laughing voice (G–d knows why he always had the happy face of someone who enjoyed life)" bring me a small mirror from your home. You know that, according to the Jewish code of laws, a Jewish man is not allowed to look at himself in a small mirror, but when there are feathers in his hair, he is allowed to look in a small mirror," and again, a smile of satisfaction. I brought him a small round mirror that its diameter was the diameter of an egg. The rabbi brought the small mirror to his eyes, to his nose, to his side locks, and for a long hour looked at the image that was reflected from the small mirror, and he was not satisfied. Probably he was amazed from the great wonder, that a man can see himself in a mirror, and maybe he was so pleased from his beauty. At the end he gave me the small mirror back and smiled a smile of great satisfaction for deceiving *Shulchan Aruch*, R. Yosef Karo, and the "Ramah" [Rabbi Moses Isserles] all together and enjoyed what was strictly forbidden for him to do ....

"You are a good lad," he suddenly said to me, "When you reach the age of Bar Mitzvah I will tell you the secret of how to create a person. Not in the explicit way and not like the Golem that the Maharal of Prague [Moreinu ha–Rav Loew] created, but a real person."

The rabbi probably wanted to buy my heart, but his words with the added spark in his eyes did not scare me for some reason, and my heart left him and never returned.

*

I came home and told my father: I don't want to study with the Budzanówni. Father said: next period you will study with another Melamed. I said to father: this is not what I meant. I want to transfer to another Melamed right now! Father wandered: in the middle of the period? And to whom do you want to transfer? I said: I want to return to Ahron Goldhaber! Father became difficult: and you left him two years ago! I answered father: I did not leave him. He left town and went to the army, now that he has returned and a few of my former friends study with him, I want to go back to him. Father answered: and to study one page of *Gemara* a week? I added to his answer: but to also study the *Homesh* with *Rashi*, *Pasuk* and writing!

Father, of blessed memory, agreed. I was the youngest child, was orphaned from my mother and he liked me a lot. It was a courageous thing for him to do. To take a "sharp minded child" (this name was given to me) from the hands of a "distinguished *Gemara* Melamed" (the name that was given to the Budzanówni), and bring him back to a Melamed who taught him two years before. And what will they say about it in the Chortkov Kloiz? and it is possible to assume that it will cause a great financial loss since the Budzanówni was hired by the parents for a full period with a promise of tuition and food. And without a doubt, my father stood by his obligation in addition to the tuition that he paid R' Ahron.

*

This time, the *Heder* of R' Ahron was in his new apartment. Twenty–six boys sat on both sides of the long table, a bench on this side and a bench on the other side, from the end of this wall to the end of the other wall. Only a narrow passageway was left at the end of the table. R' Aaron stood behind the outside bench, one of his legs was standing on the bench in between two boys and a book was placed on the knee of that leg. And he read to us from that book as though he was reading it for the first time and the words were illuminated and happy! In the morning R' Ahron read and explained with a good mind and good taste, and in the afternoon we studied "Yeshaya" – the way it was done two years ago! But how different it tasted now and how different it felt. Two years ago I was the youngest in the group, the youngest among the older boys, number twelve or thirteen in the order of students, and now I'm the third, the second, and if you want to say – the first!

What is the "order of students" Only those who were R' Ahron's students know this secret! I already told that R' Ahron stood behind the outside bench that faced into the room, his leg on the bench and the book on the knee of the same leg, and so he stood and read each *Mishnah*, or each verse in the *Gemara*, or a whole chapter from the book of Yeshaya, and when he finished he asked: "Who say first?" – And the explanation of "say" is: to repeat and say everything, word by word, one from the source and one – a combination of translation, explanation and interpretation, nothing was missing! If a volunteer was found – he is the "first in the order", if a volunteer was not found – R' Ahron decided who will "say" first and who will "say" second, who will "say" third, and so on until the last one, all the twenty–six students, so each Mishnah, each verse, and each chapter were "said" twenty-six times. And by doing so, the students' order of importance was decided, and everything that was studied sunk well in the brain and was carved very deep in the heart and was never wiped off.

I don't remember the names of all the students, but I remember the first five: Dudel Shechner who lives in Costa Rica, his cousin Butzi Shechner whose fate I don't know, Moshe Wachstein–Ami, the nephew of Dr. Bernhard Wachstein, who is now older and a farmer in Beit–Shearim, and his next door neighbor in Beit–Shearim, Kalman–Mordechai Sternklar, who is my relative and my partner to the sad period of exile in Lwów. Each time I visit Beit-Shearim – we spin memories from R' Ahron's *Heder*, and I entertain Moshe Wachstein with a truthful imitation of half a verse from Yeshaya, the way he said it in the evening of the same summer day in the same *Heder* in the new apartment. He was a tall skinny boy, his voice was also high, thin and shirking, and in this voice, that was elevated and extended high above, he blazed the words, like the high pitch of a metal flute, and said them with a lot of emotion. And I will swe-e-e-p it with the be-s-o-o-m of destruction, said the Lord of host....

On Thursday, in the afternoon, we studied *Humash* with *Rashi*. Each one of us read a verse and when the last word was still between his lips – his friend who was sitting next to him started the next verse, and so the reading was going around in high speed along the table from here and from there, continuously and without a break, and Alas to the boy who did not pay attention, and did not follow the reading, and his friend who sat next him already read in his place.

On Friday, after all the Torah portion of that week was fixed in our hearts, R' Ahron taught us some writings (it is a wonder how all the first Melamedim neglected to teach us writing, except for Muni, who from time to time taught us a few lines in Yiddish and German in large Gothic letters). We were not able to buy note books in the market, but we made them from blank empty pages that we found between the "*Ektim*," the documents from the Austrian courthouse and other government offices, which were cleared from the cupboards and were used mostly for paper bags in the stores. Many families, adults and children, were busy making them, but empty pages were kept for writing and the notebooks were made out of them. Those notebooks were not lined, and R' Ahron had a small ruler and a small pencil, and with them he lined row after row in such a speed that the eye was not able to catch what his hand was doing. And before we turned here or there – twenty–six notebooks were lined with straight lines, in equal distance from each other, as though they came from under the hand of a magician. R' Ahron wrote a line at the beginning of the page, a line for each one of us, and we copied this line twenty times until two lined pages were full. At times we wrote in the holy language, at times we wrote in Yiddish, and at times both of them together – and the two languages served as one, with love and peace, and we almost didn't feel that we had two different languages before us.

Until the end of that winter period and another summer period, I was rewarded with good explanations and the system of R' Ahron Goldhaber. For the next winter period most of his "older" students left. I was also forced to leave and return to a "distinguished *Gemara* Melamed" and this time I became the student of R' Feybush the slaughterer.

*

Many years ago, R' Feybush, the slaughterer, was probably a handsome wise student without a stain on his clothes since he was the Chortkov

Hassidism slaughterer, and they were known to be strict with their clothes and their appearance. But in my days he was already an old man. The hair on his head and his beard was white or yellow and his mustache was yellow – from the tobacco and from the tobacconist.

In my time, R' Feybush did not slaughter animals, but people brought him chickens a number of times a day. And, while he was teaching seven or eight students around the square table in his only room, he used to say to the first maiden who came: "sit on the bench and wait until another poultry will arrive and I will reply to you," What is the "poor" word here? – I wondered in my heart, here is going to his death a white roster, a duck or a goose, some of its red hot blood will be poured into the trough that was made for that purpose, and some on the snow next to the house (if we are talking about geese that are not plucked, only something was taken from under their wings and thrown on the snow outside). And our rabbi says "reply"!

When the rabbi finally goes to "reply," we take a break and go outside. The home of R' Feybush was very close to the river and the frozen reed marsh and the days were glorious winter days!

Across from R' Feibush's home, on top of a hill, is the workshop of R' Yedel Stupp the carpenter. And there, the saw is sawing boards, cutting corners and joints at the end, and the sculpting tool is sinking deep into the soft white board, and the sawdust is flying in the air, and the resin on top of the boards emits a good aroma and mixed with the smell of the boiling carpenter glue and the smell of the snow outside... Despite the chill – the window is open, Yedel the carpenter and his apprentice are always happy, and they don't chase me away from the window. On the contrary! Yedel loves to talk and he is always in a good mood. Not only that he lets me look at his work and ask him different questions, but he himself starts the conversation and explains the secrets of his work and the "thought" in it! And when I continue and ask a new question on the basis of what he already explained to me, he praises my good understanding and concludes his impression on me: "instead of Torah there is wisdom there"

*

What Torah and what wisdom did I buy from R' Feybush the slaughterer? I swear that I don't remember! I don't even remember the name of the *Masecha* that we studied. From that whole winter with Feybush the slaughterer nothing remains with me apart from a good understanding in carpentry that I purchased from R' Yedel Stupp through observation and conversation, and apart from one small "picture" in my poem "Snow":

> A goose that was slaughtered untied his legs
> freed himself from his slaughterer and escaped;
> He ran without making a sound or waving a wing
> and his blood spilled on the snow.
>
> And so ran the goose with the slaughtered neck
> to the white faraway world... –
> and from the long slaughtered neck
> coral after coral are rolling

*

In that winter, comfort and salvation came to me from another source. There was a second slaughterer in our town, R' Shlomo Schechter. Before the war, when there was still a fierce opposition between the Chortkov Hassidim and the Vizhnitzer Hassidim, he was the slaughterer of the Vizhnitzer Hassidim. But during the days of peace, a separation of that sort was unknown. R' Shlomo had three sons: Mendel, Yosel and Zalman. I always remember Mendel walking in the street with a book tucked under his arm (Herzl diaries or Zshtlovski's writings) and he was walking and arguing with friends about the current matters of the world: The Balfour declaration, the mandate on Eretz–Yisrael that was given to mighty England, and opposed to both of them – what is the value of Territorialism?! It is possible that thanks to the never ending arguments in the matters of Zionism, he immigrated to Israel on time, did not reject hard work, and now he and his family live in Tel–Aviv, a nice established family. A couple of years later, the middle brother Yosef, became my best friend even though he was a number of years older then me. Both of us remember with love those summer days when we laid on a large pile of good smelling hay, "swallowing" many chapters from the first book of prophets – to complete what I lacked from my studies with R' Ahron who skipped me from Yehoshua to Yeshaya. Also my friend Yosef saved his soul from the holocaust and arrived to Israel. From him I learned the details and the dates for my poem "The Minyan in my town, the town of Tluste." He and his wife live in Kiryat–Shalom. The youngest son, Zalman of blessed memory, was my age and for a time my friend in the "*Heder.*" He was a good smart lad, but he was not a quick learner and his soul did not want to study the Torah. R' Shlomo was sorry about that, and wanted to teach him more than he studied in the *Heder*. In order to add desire to his studies – he searched and found a friend for him, and I was that friend, and that's how I became the student of R' Shlomo the slaughterer, not in order to pay tuition but to serve as a companion to his son. And so, I became a member of R' Shlomo's family and a friend to his middle son, Yosef, the pleasant and nice.

And how different was R' Shlomo the slaughterer, who taught me in the afternoon, than R' Feybush where I studied before noon! R' Shlomo was always dressed clean, and his beard, in which the first silver strings started to intertwine, was always well kept. When he checked the ritual slaughterer's knife, running it over his special fingernail, I realized how good looking his hands were, how delicate his fingers were and how beautiful his other fingernails were! He always spoke with kindness, he never raised his voice, even during class, and his explanations were done with good taste and kindness.

Also R' Shlomo stopped his teaching and left the room to butcher a chicken in a special chamber across the hallway near his apartment, but he always returned clean without a stain or a spot. His butcher knives frightened me, mostly the big ones. All of them were placed in their special cases, in a special corner between the wall and the oven. G–d almighty! How many times I saw this tender and gentle Jew, who did not even hurt a fly on the wall, swinging a big butcher knife and with a quick move, slaughter a big cow!

R' Shlomo was a lot younger than R' Feybush and slaughtered all the animals. Once, after the termination of the Sabbath during the intermediate days of Passover, I followed R' Shlomo together with my school friend Zalman to the municipal slaughter house across the bridge on the road leading to Chortkov. A large cow was lying on the floor with its back and front legs tied together and two young men were holding its large horns. R' Shlomo took out his large slaughterer knife, looked at it for a moment, lowered himself to the cow and grabbed the skin on her neck with his left hand. When I was ready to watch him bringing the big knife down – a large cut opened in the cow's neck and its hot blood spilled from the stone floor to the drain. My eyes darkened, my head was spinning and I was ready to fall. With weak knees I walked back home and for many years, after that year, I did not taste the taste of meat...... I did not even go to the home of R' Shlomo, mostly out of fear of his many slaughterer knives. The small ones and the big ones, between the wall and the oven ——

*

And this is the place to mention another Melamed whom I studied with as an only student. Although I am not sure of the order of time, I remember that I studied with him during the summer period. And I'm not sure if it was the summer that followed the winter that I studied with the slaughterers R' Shlomo and R' Feybush.

This Melamed was the preacher R' Pinchas Lapiner who was not a native of our town. He came from a distant place, maybe from Lita, and for some reasons chose to live in our town Tluste. According to my opinion in those days, he deserved to serve as a preacher in a larger community or, at least, travel around the communities in the preachers' tradition. But, he sat permanently in our town and preached only two or three times a year. He preached: on Shabbat *Hagadol* [the Shabbat before Passover] (as we know our Rabbi, R' Shmuel Chodorov of blessed memory, was not a great preacher), during Shabbat Teshuva [the Shabbat before Yom Kippur] and maybe two or three times more during the year. On those Shabbat eves, hand written notices were posted in all the synagogues and in *Beit–Ha'Midrash*. They were the size of half a note book page and glued with a little glue. They announced: G–d willing, on the Sabbath, at three o'clock, the preacher Pinchas Lapiner will preach in *Beit–Ha'Midrash* and the listeners will be delighted. And indeed, the listeners were delighted. The preacher Pinchas Lapiner was knowledgeable in *Nevi'im and Ketuvim*, and *Misrash Aggadah*, and as a great expert he was able to thread twenty or thirty verses with one common word, to question from this verse to this verse, from that verse to that verse, all in one big pile of questions. And all the verses connected to each other and strung together like a string of pearls. He ended with: "And a redeemer will come to Zion", kissed the *Parocheth* [the curtain of the Holy Ark], removed his *Talith* and folded it like an artist who created a beautiful work. When he was done organizing his equipment, he descended from the steps in front of the Holy Ark. And once again, he was "idle" for the next six months, until the next sermon. Only G–d knows from where he was earning his living and supporting his little modest wife and their lovely and sweet daughter, whose beauty, even the great poverty was not able to cover.

I was given to this R' Pinchas to study two hours a day and I went to him willingly and happy. Supposedly, he was teaching me the *Gemara*, but we skipped the difficult negotiation and passed from *Aggadta* to *Aggadta* [legend]. We both felt that we were cheating, but what could we have done? Everything depends on the heart, both of us were attracted to the words of the legends, and not only that we skipped from page to page and from chapter to chapter, we did not stay in one tractate [of the Talmud]. From *Sanhedrin* we moved to *Gittin*, but Heaven forbid! not to the matter of bringing a divorce from a country across the ocean. From page 55 column 2 to the bottom of column 1 on page 58, we read all the legends about the destruction that rumbled the heart – the days were probably close to *Tisha B'Av* – from Kamtza and Bar-Kamtza to the story of a man who fancied his rabbi's wife, an act that cannot be removed from the heart and will never leave it! And from there we skipped to the chapter that dealt with the hiring of workers in *Baba Metzia*, because there are also a lot of legends there. At the end we painlessly passed – Woe to the shame! – to read *Ain Yakov* exactly the way "simple Jews" read it in *Beit Ha'Midrash* or in the tradesmen's synagogue. "There is nothing bad in it," R' Pinchas consulting me, "they are also the legends of the Torah, and if they don't sharpen the brain they warm the heart." And R' Pinchas was rubbing palm to palm, as though it was winter outside and he needed to warm them.

All that I told here about this rabbi, I told out of love and appreciation. He was one of the few Melamedim whose teachings still live in me. He was modest and humble in his life, walked in the shade and on side roads. And when he walked on a side road, a German soldier shot him in the neck and killed him on the spot. I built a stanza for him in my poem "The Minyan in my town," let us copy it here:

> R' Pinchas Lapiner, the preacher of the holy community of Tluste,
> taught me the *Gemara* in a hurry –
> May his memory be blessed; Woe how much I loved him and how he
> captured my heart!
> He skipped the negotiations, jumped from page to page,
> and taught me joyful legends – and I loved his skipping.

The death of R' Pinchas Lapiner is told in the poem mentioned above. When and how did his gentle wife and beautiful daughter die? – The one who knows his nation's troubles is the one who knows!

*

I told about nine Melamedim with whom I studied, but in reality there are ten stories, since I studied twice with R' Ahron Goldhaber and told about him twice. And between the ten I swallowed the stories of two Melamedim with whom I did not, but I knew them and their *Heder* very well. I did not want to skip them just because I was not one of their students. If I did not study with them, many children in our town studied with them, and it is possible that many of them are still alive and live around the world, including in Israel.

According to the review of our Tluste, I must add and tell here about two more teachers that I studied with as an only student. Not as a boy, but as a lad of fifteen and sixteen, out or my own free will, conviction and desire. But according to the age and time, they do not belong to the chapter of my childhood teachers.

One of the two was R' Yisrael Glick of blessed memory, our "relative by marriage." The father of my brother–in–law, Dov Glick May he live long and happily, who sold his home and all of his belongings in the village of Verbovitch [Verbovczy] in order to emigrate to Israel. But on his way to emigrate he settled in our town of Tluste, to "wait a little" for his son, my brother–in–law, who was also planning to emigrate to Israel and take me, the teenager, with him. In the period of one summer and one winter I came to the home of my in–law, R' Yisrael Glick, who lived out of town near the "Hikand Mountain" and studied two or three hours with him. In the summer we studied in the shade of a rose bush that grew in the garden next to the house. And in winter we studied in the only room of the small apartment. And the father of my brother–in–law was sick and lay in bed, and I read for him in a sad quite tune.

The father of my brother–in–law, R' Yisrael Glick, recovered from his illness and, when spring arrived, his nobility arrived because the study of the "daily page" was introduced and he became the teacher and rabbi of the whole town:

> My in–law Serueli' Glick, hurries each morning to the Chortkov Kloiz,
> every day he reads a page from the tractate with humility and a
> modest soft voice,
> and a father, a son, and a grandson are sitting around him listening to
> his voice.

A Torah that was placed in a corner is dozing off,
and it seems that it will be forgotten soon, and it seems that it will
disappear soon.
Suddenly it started to wake up, breathing with great force.

He opened the gate to the Torah and led his students step by step;
He straightened each curve in the road and untied each tangle and
complication,
everything without a sound and uproar, only with satisfaction and
carful consideration.

But he was not rewarded to emigrate to Israel. The way his beautiful
teachings entered the heart of his listeners below, they probably entered the
hearts of his listeners above, and for that reason he was probably called to the
next world. His many students in the Chortkov Kloiz were orphaned and I
mourned him alone, the only student that he taught at home.

And the second teacher was the Hebrew teacher Mr. Mordechai Spector,
who also came to our town from afar, and established a private Hebrew
school. I, the "private" student, studied: Nevi'im, Ketuvim, grammar and
"writing" – to write and to correct, to copy and again to correct and copy,
Jewish history and world events, and everything that was available at that
time in the Hebrew study books. At first I studied with him in secret and paid
my tuition from the money that I earned drawing signs for the shops (most of
the signs in town were my handy work) and in 1933, before I emigrated to
Israel, the big sign that was placed in front of the home R' Hershil Meir, with a
branched–antlered deer in the middle [Hersh – deer]. Later on, when winter
came and the sign work stopped (the paint didn't dry, and in any case, the
signs outside were covered with snow!) and I did not have the money to pay – I
told my "secret" to my father of blessed memory. Out of the goodness of his
heart he agreed to pay for my tuition in the name of "to give for a good
cause"... since the Hebrew teacher was considered to be a secular man, and
who–knows–what–he–was–teaching– there (and indeed we sat and studied the
holy scriptures with an uncovered head, spitefully, as though with a covered
head our studies were not "modern and scientific" enough).

I studied with the two teachers at the same time, the same summer and
the same winter. I clearly saw the difference between them and the
contradiction between them. This one was not like that one. This one wanted

me to loath all the old, to open my eyes and see the ugliness in it, to awaken in me the desire for the new. And that one wanted me to love all the best and beautiful in the old, to open my eyes so I could see all the splendor in it, to explain to me that you can't build the new on the destruction of the old, only on the base of the old one.

And the equal side between them – both of them aimed their studies to the future, to the future of the young man who was ready to spread his wings and fly out of the nest. And both of them wanted to prepare him for the road: this one is teaching him all that he needs for the high school that he is longing to join, and that one is teaching him all that he needs in order to separate the essence from the subordinate, between the straw and the grain, and G–d forbids! that the young man will turn his back on it all.

The words that I wrote here are abstract, they only hint. But the words in my poem "In the shade of a rose bush" provide a better explanation and a better picture, and the man who said it in a song does not return and say it in an ordinary speech. Therefore, the one who wants to know this small and pleasant story, can kindly turn to that poem in my book "Scattered light".

*

When my first small collection of my poems: "In seven strings" was published just before the break of the war, by the "*Davar*" publications, Tel-Aviv 5699, I was still able to send a few copies of the book to Tluste, one to my teacher Mordechai Spector and one to Rabbi R' Ahron Goldhaber. The teacher Spector probably did not have the time to answer me, if he did, I would have remembered it and his letter would have been kept with me. The Melamed, Rabbi R' Ahron Goldhaber answered me immediately, I still have his letter written in his golden language and this is what it says:

"With G–d's Blessings: a day that was blessed twice in the order of days (5699).

May the mountains bring peace and blessing to you my student author, our teacher and rabbi Shimshon May his light shine.

Thank you very much for the gift that you sent me from the fruit of the land, decorated with seven beloved strings like a sapphire and a diamond. And thank you that you remembered and the minister of forgetfulness did not rule you. I read from your book and I wondered how you turned in such a short time into a hero and became so successful, because this book can really raise the soul. My beloved, these poems are very lofty and I see a happy future for you, since a man with a spirit will rise higher. I wish you a lot of success in the land of our patriarchs and may your name be known around the world. My beloved! Despite the fact that I learned very little from this book and I lack the knowledge, I do feel the importance of your book. I bless you with the same blessing of the tree. May it be the wish that your offspring will be like you.

Don't make fun at the style of my letter which is written in the language of a stutterer, because you know that I belong to the old generation and you can't bring the old from the new. Surely you will add to your first book and I ask you to send me a book each time. And with that I finish my letter, live in peace, a quite and fresh life, bless your family and friends in my name. Your friend, Ahron Goldhaber."

I was not able to fulfill R' Ahron's request and send him additional books. A year later, in 5700 [1940], when my poem "Meir the musician became a commissar" was published in a small book, "Tluste my tiny little town," I was already cut off, far and distant, as though I was on a different moon, as though it never existed and was only a fable and a fantasy.

*

Now I am giving the letter that R' Ahron Goldhaber of blessed memory wrote me to the hands of the editor of this book. I ask him to create a plate and publish it the way it is – to be in front of the readers of this book. Probably a few of them, the students of R' Ahron, will recognize their Rabbi's handwriting. This is the handwriting in which he wrote the upper row in their lined notebook, this is the handwriting from which they learn to write in Yiddish and Hebrew – and if they look in their own letters, maybe they will recognize the Rabbi's letters in them.

The intermediate days of the holiday of Succoth, 5676 [September 1915]

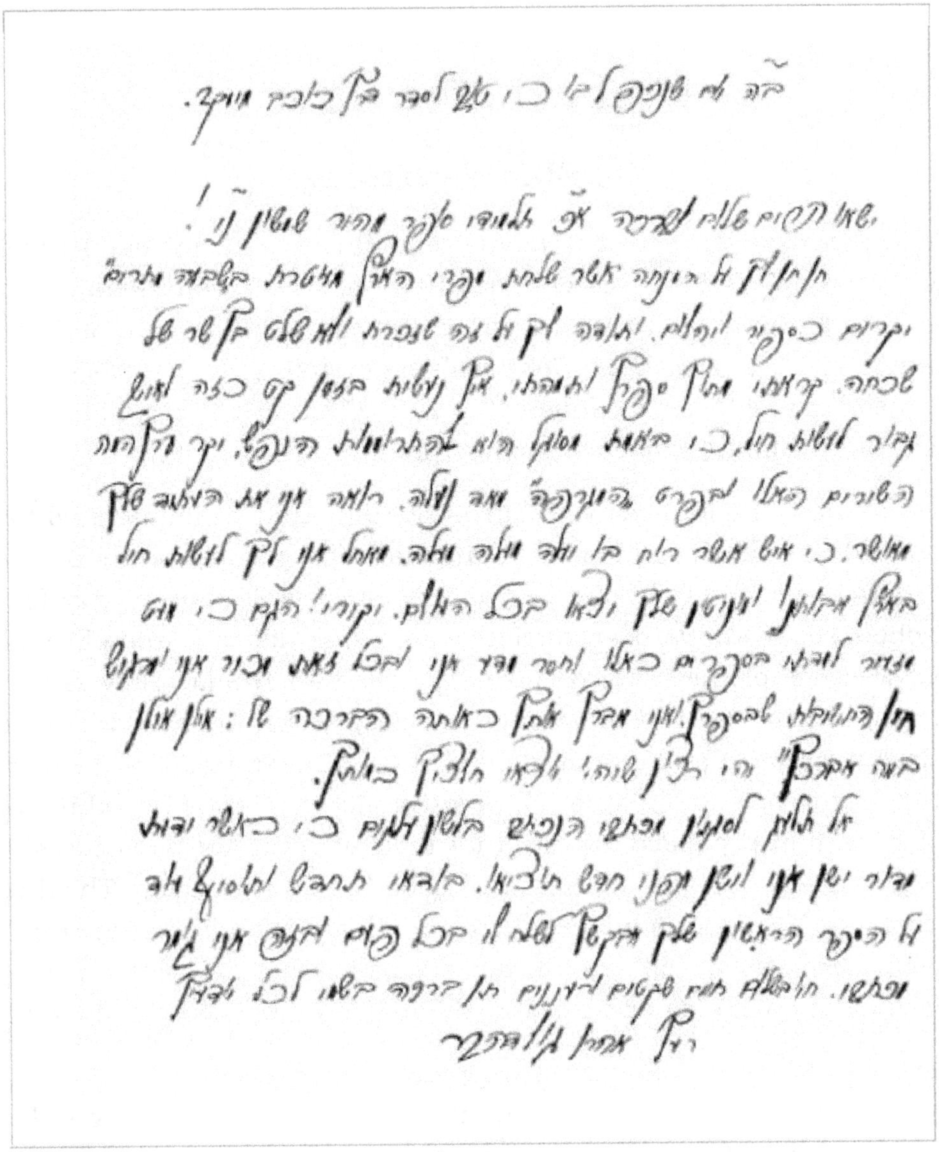

The handwritten letter is translated above

[Pages 261-263]

Michael Mesing z"l

by Shlomo Mesing

Michael, son of Menachem (Mendel) and Shoshanna (Sasia) Mesing, was born in Tluste in 1908. In his childhood he received a traditional education. He was among the first to join the youth movement "*Gordonia*" and was also the organizer of the branch of "*Gordonia*" in our town. He was also one of the active members of "*Keren Kayemet leYisrael*" in Tluste, and among the organizers of the first "*Halutzim*" training program in our area.

In 1929, immediately after the riots of 5689 (1929), he immigrated to Israel together with the first company of "*Gordonia.*" The group's first stop in Israel was Hadera. After a stay of one year in Hadera, the Jewish Agency for Israel approached the group with an offer to move to Hulda and rebuild its ruins. Michael was one of the first volunteers to move to Hulda. They faced many difficulties, mostly the lack of water, but despite the many difficulties they didn't lose their spirit and continued their work to restore the place with vigor and stubbornness. Cheerful and full of joy of life, they approached the digging of the first well in the place, hoping that their work would be successful. But their hope was dashed and all their hard labor came to nothing. The drill hit a rock and the diggers' happiness ended. However, also after this great disappointment, the members of the *Kvutza* [communal settlement] didn't abandon the soil of Hulda and continued to cultivate it with all their strength.

There was no end to Michael's happiness when he was finally rewarded, after great efforts, to bring his parents to Israel and to Hulda. But his happiness didn't last long. In 1935, in the month of Sivan 5695, a typhus epidemic broke out in Hulda. Many members fell ill, and three of them, among them Michael, perished in the epidemic.

Michael was one of the best *Halutzim* who gave their lives for the building of the country.

May his soul be bound in the bond of life of the renewed nation!

From members words about Michael

Pinchas Lubianko (Lavon): "The terrible death plucked three victims"– said the news item. Your mute faces chase me nonstop. I see you day and night, and the question, which cannot be answered, erupts nonstop: For what, and why? I see you as healthy young men, I see Michael, our Michale", the serious and devoted, in heart and soul, to the *Kvutza.* For ten years he lived the life of the movement and was one of its first builders. He carried the load of the *Kvutza* almost from the beginning of its establishment, suffered from unemployment, hunger and malaria in Hadera and was among the first who went to Hulda to lay the foundations for its development. Only a few months ago he brought his parents to the *Kvutza.* The father was surprised to see the order of life in the *Kvutza,* and there was no limit to his amazement when he saw his son, the "farmer," and he himself held to any work in order to "earn" his bread. Also the mother participated in the young womens' work and was influenced by the new way of life. She believed that together with her son, Michael, she would be able to build a peaceful and secure future for herself.

...and what can I say to you, my beloved, in far and near Hulda? Can we also overcome this blow? That faith must win over despair? That life, creation and war demand victims? Our entire *"Gordonia"* family united with the *Kvutza* in Hulda with its pain and great tragedy.

You don't need these meaningless and banal words of comfort. You know very well that you are not alone and lonely. You feel deep inside the will of those who left, and the duty of life – for life.

My beloved brothers, honor to the memory of the dead, honor to your suffering and stubbornness.

(From the article "On the way" written in Polish and published in the movement's journal).

Zalman: When I arrived to the *Kvutza* I already found him there. I did not know him from abroad the way I did not know the rest of the members. But Michael stood out among everyone as a handsome young man with black hair, black shiny eyes, and a smile on his face. He mostly excelled in his will to help the new member, the "green," whether with advice or whether with an act. Even though he came to Israel only a few weeks before me, he was like a veteran in everything. He was aware of everything that was happening in the *Kvutza*, actively participated in all of its affairs and also in the affairs of the entire movement. Also, the affairs in Hadera, and the community of workers within it, were not foreign to him.

When it was decided to leave for Hulda and rebuild its ruins, Michael was given the duty to guard the place. Michael did not know Arabic and not even the Arabs' customs and started to study Arabic in his characteristic diligence. He sat for hours next to the Arabs' well and listened to the conversations of those who came to draw water. By doing so, he learnt to speak like one of them and they respected and appreciated him for that. Despite the fact that he stood on guard, day and night, he did not neglect the matters of the *Kvutza*, and was one of its active members. Also, in the most difficult situation he knew how to defuse the tension with a proverb or by telling a joke – and the matter became easier on the heart.

It is impossible to describe his happiness when he was able to bring his parents to Israel, but the happiness did not last long. He also became ill with typhus during the epidemic in Hulda. He was taken to the hospital and never returned from there. Even today, twenty–five years after his death, his image is standing before my eyes.

May his memory be blessed!

(From a booklet in memory of the typhus epidemic victims in Hulda)

Frida Sidrer. I knew Michael Mesing z"l when we were members of the movement abroad, and even before I knew him – I've heard about him. I knew that Michael is a friend that you can count on because his dedication to the matters of the movement was "well known." If you're going to organize a "summer colony" in the district – you had to turn to Michael, and if a pioneer training group was in trouble and needed immediate help – he was the one to address. He was active in the movement as he was waiting to fulfill his aspiration – to immigrate to Israel.

And the desired day arrived. His face beamed from happiness because he was granted to join "*Gordonia* A" group when we were still in Hadera. I remember his enthusiasm as though it was today, how he waited for his first day of work in Israel, the stubbornness with which he strived to acclimatize to the country, as if he knew that time was short and he needed to meet the requirements... Michael reached the height of his activities after he moved with some of our friends to Hulda, a place where our fate connected, and connected to the place with bonds of love. We did not imagine, then, that the place that he loved so much would be so cruel to him...

One of the most responsible duties in Hulda of those days, as a secluded Jewish settlement within an Arab territory, was the guard duty. The duty was given to Michael and he fulfilled it with dedication. He learnt to speak Arabic and dedicated himself to create a "neighborly" relationship with the Arabs. Over the years he fulfilled a number of duties in the *Kvutza*. He was always aware of the problems, feared each failure and was happy with each accomplishment.

Michael was friendly and full of life. He was always the first to sing, dance, and hike to study the area. He loved to help his fellow man, was sensitive to injustice and was always willing to help.

Michael reached the height of his happiness and satisfaction when he brought his parents to Israel. He brought them to Hulda, to his home, and cared for them as a dedicated and loyal son. Our life was difficult at that time and we lacked the basic necessities, but Michael tried to encourage his parents and explained to them that this was only the beginning.

But fate wanted differently. Because of malnutrition and contaminated drinking water, our members contracted typhus. Twice we experience the epidemic without a loss, but the third epidemic killed three of our members, and Michael Mesing z"l was one of them.

The earth of Hulda, which he loved so much, covered him. He wanted to work it and redeem it from its barrenness.

A typhus clinic was built in Hulda in memory of the typhus victims. Each time we enter the clinic our eyes meet his picture. His warm eyes, his optimism and warm heart were captured in that picture, but these eyes closed too early, for eternity. May his memory be blessed!

(From a memorial booklet)

Arye Navon: The twenty–five years that have passed did not remove the great shock of the summer of 1935 from our hearts. It was such a difficult blow that only a few of us believed in those days that the Kibbutz would be able to recover, to overcome and continue to exist for us and for our children, and it is worth to return and bring out a few memories from that miserable year.

It was a period of "prosperity" in Israel, and the stream of pioneers increased. The mandate authorities allocated 62,000 immigration permits – the largest number in all the years of the British rule in Israel. The construction work in the cities reached a new height, and new subdivisions appeared almost overnight. Agriculture developed in giant steps with the realization of the "Arlosoroff Project" (the development of the lands in Masada and Sha'ar HaGolan in Emek–Hayarden, and the expansion of the settlements in Emek–Zevulon and Emek–Hefer). The whole country was full of excitement and satisfaction from the progress.

Also in Hulda, whose members knew many hardships, the signs of recovery started to appear. We were busy working in permanent jobs in the "*Yachin*" orchards and in our orchard. A young "supplement" arrived, and provided, together with the members of Migdal, a serious core to the Kibbutz. Two outside contracts – the Lod airport and the water line to Jerusalem were nearly completed, and all of our members were back at home. The atmosphere in the kibbutz was jubilant, and we lived in the formula of those days – work during the day and song and dance in the evenings and at night. We were young and our families lived safely in the European countries... and we waited for the authorization to settle in Hulda permanently. Every once in a while we heard surveys of our progress, and the names Herzfeld, Hekster, Kaplan, Weitz – the directors of the settlement department of "The Jewish Agency for Israel" – were like road signs on the road for a permanent settlement that we so longed for.

The Kibbutz was surrounded by friends who were happy with our progress and came to celebrate the Sabbath and the holidays with us.

And suddenly, on the holiday of Shavuot 5695, we discovered that the water that we were drinking from the Arabs' well was contaminated (as it was determined later by a committee of experts who inspected it). Many of our members became ill with typhus. More than forty members were taken to the hospitals in Jerusalem and Tel–Aviv, but the first victims fell at home – before we felt the enormity of the tragedy, three of our members died in a period of two weeks – Meir Rosner, Michael Mesing and Yitzchak Lerer. Hadassa Bletman was buried after them and Litvak, a Zionist from Lvov, died in Tel-Aviv. He befriended us on the boat and came to visit us for the holiday. He became ill and did not recover from his illness.

The work in the Kibbutz stopped. Out of eighty members, more than forty laid in various hospitals, some of them in serious condition. The healthy members were busy traveling and visiting their sick friends. This situation lasted until after Rosh Hashanah, until all the members recovered from their illness and returned to the kibbutz.

In the yearly meeting, which took place on Tishrei 5696, the first evaluation of the tragedy that hit our kibbutz was done. The will to live and build, the memory of our beloved victims and the responsibility that was cast on those who survived, energized us and strengthen our lines. It gave us the will to continue with the building of the Kibbutz, the first "*Gordonia*" kibbutz in Israel. Also the international "*Gordonia*" movement and the different organizations in Israel encouraged us during those difficult days. That summer was the melting pot for our social unity and loyalty to the movement, and increased the feeling of destiny that we took on ourselves.

*

When we return in our memory to those days, tears pour from our eyes and the images of our love ones, who were taken from us, appear before our eyes.

Michael Mesing, the veteran among the typhus victims, reached the height of his aspiration and was rewarded to fulfill the dream of his youth. He lived for six years in a kibbutz in Israel, and was able to bring his parents to him. He was twenty–seven at the time of his death.

The pioneers of Israel, who were taken at the prime of their lives and at the beginning of their dreams, rest in the shade of Herzl Forest.

May their memory be blessed! (From the memorial booklet)

During his short life in Israel, Michael corresponded with his friends abroad, mostly with Shimshon Meltzer who kept many of Mesing's letters from that period. Below is the first letter that was sent from Hulda to Lvov in May 1931:

My dear Shimshon!

I was surprised to receive your last letter, but, together with that, I also felt that I received it as a reward for your six months of silence. I would have written you during that time, but I did not know your exact address.

First I have to give you the order of events to this day. As you know, we received Hulda for a period of five years, to work the land, the forest and the olive grove that exist here. A unit of ten people was assembled from our four groups in Israel. Five people from our group, I included. I'm here for more than four months, and I'm satisfied with Hulda and its people.

First of all – we came to rebuild Hulda. Could you have a greater satisfaction than rebuilding the ruins? Hulda is located within an area of Arab villages, a point in the middle of the sea, and we have the historical duty to not only hold on, but also to create a friendly relationship with our neighbors despite the past as the Arabic proverb say – what happened – passed, and we need to behave here according to this proverb. In order to live with the Arabs we need to know their philosophy, and create our relationship with them according to it. The Arabs treat us as old friends and they are very sorry for the "happiness" – the riots – and now they promise us a long– lasting friendship. They say that their hands were not in all of that, but the hands of the "distant" Arabs, but who is a fool to believe them.

Hulda is an incredibly beautiful place and resides by the valley that is called "Emek–Ayalon" in the bible, and if you want or don't want, you must remember the command that Yehoshua gave: "The sun, stand still on Gibeon! And the moon in the valley of Ayalon!", and the moon is really beautiful here. I already know how to recognize its shape in other locations because I am a watchman in Hulda, and the moon is always walking with me in the yard.

There is a big forest in Hulda – "Herzl Forest" – 600 Dunam with long double avenues of pine, cypress and palm trees. There are two very narrow avenues, and each one has a different name. One is the "Love Avenue" – a double row of Jerusalem pines. There is shade in this avenue, and as it is written: the couple that strolls here – is guaranteed to have privacy. This avenue leads from the big house – Herzl house – along the forest to the valley – "Emek Ayalon". The second avenue starts by the entry to the yard and leads along the olive plantation to the grave of Efraim Zitsik – and it is called, no more and no less, the "Desperation Avenue." When the planned road will be paved along this avenue, its name will be changed.

And around the house – forest, forest, and again forest. All kind of trees – cypress, palm, pine and locust, and not far from the home, among the oldest trees, we built a swing that reminds me of the swing in your yard in Tluste.

I ask you that you will answer me in time, and write me all that is happening around you. Write me all of that in details in your next letter.

For now, be blessed. Yours Michael

In Hulda's forest (1934)
Standing right to left: **Michael Mesing, a member of the *Kvutza*, and Shimshon Meltzer**

[Page 264]

A story of blowing the *shofar*

by Mordechai Tabori (Teiber)

Translated by Sara Mages

One day, in the period after the First World War, several young men, refugees from Russia, appeared in our town on their way across the seas. Sometime later, they managed to arrange their affairs and left our town. Only one of them remained and found his livelihood in hard labor, the work of a porter.

One day I entered the "kleizel" of the Vishnitzer Hasidim and found the young man lying on a bench, writhing in pain. I immediately went home and told my mother, may she rest in peace. Without thinking much, my mother put the Turkish scarf on her head, wrapped herself in a long shawl and headed to the Kloiz. I followed her, holding a few pears in my hands and a bottle of raspberry juice to revive the spirit of the patient. On the way, we bought an additional bottle of soda water and so we entered and came to the sick young man.

My mother asked him about his pain, and he replied with great difficulty and with all his strength. I helped my mother to lift him and we gave him a drink to revive his soul. After he calmed down a little we called Dr. Albin, who gave him a sedative injection and informed us that we must transfer him immediately to a hospital for an operation. My mother approached the community council and did not rest until the young man was transferred by cart to the hospital in Zalishchyky [Zaleszczyki] because there was no hospital in our town.

Several weeks passed and the young man returned to Tluste. He had recovered from his illness and was about to travel to America. Before his departure he came to see us and thank us for our help. We also received a letter of thanks from him from America.

On Rosh Hashanah, after that act, I prayed in the Great Synagogue. And here it happened, after the cantor repeated the "Shmone Esre" prayer, the "Baal Tokea" [the shofar blower] couldn't produce the sounds of the shofar.

Others, from among the worshipers tried with their strength and ability, and didn't succeed. I, the boy, went over to "Baal Musaf" and asked him to let me try, and, in his distress, he agreed to that. And here, surprisingly, my blows were very successful – and so we overcame the delay caused to the cantor and the worshipers.

The next day, on Tzom Gedalya, at the time of Mincha prayer, R' Eliezer Waltser z"l came with his son to the Heder where I studied and asked me to join the "minyan" for an early Mincha prayer so he could say "Kadish" and return to his home in Swidowa before it turned dark. His son got into a conversation with me and asked about the details of the blowing of the shofar that he had heard from people. In addition, he asked if I had dipped in the "mikveh," the way pious Jews do before blowing a shofar. I kept quiet because I did not have an answer. R' Eliezer Waltser asked me: "And if you did not dip in the "mikveh," did you do a good deed that gave you the right to be "Baal Tokea" on Rosh Hashanah?" I pondered and pondered, and at the end I told him: "Once, a critically ill young man lay on the bench that you are sitting on and my mother and I saved his life," and I told him the details of that story. Then he said to me: "It's possible that this good deed is equal to dipping in the "mikveh," and maybe, it is more than equal, and it allowed you to overcome the delay of "Sammael" [Satan] during the blowing of the shofar."

———

The refugees from Jarosław in Tłuste

by Yisrael–Isar Yakter

Translated by Sara Mages

Jarosław, 1939. In September, Hitler's soldiers captured our peaceful town, and it did not occur to us then that in a few months we would be "Jarosław's refugees" in the town of Tłuste. By a difficult route, desperate and foreign, without a friend or acquaintance, we arrived in Tłuste at the end of that year. The townspeople lived their special life, but we met Jews who welcomed us warmly. The town was in the Russian–occupied area, and we saw our successes of crossing from the German–occupied area to the Russian area, as a great and important achievement, because the Jews still lived a normal life there. Our father z"l, a learned God–fearing Jew and a Blez's Hassid, found people to his liking in Tłuste, and told us about the wise and God–fearing Jews that he had met. He befriended the rabbi of Tłuste, R' Shmuel–Aba Chodorov, hy"d, the slaughterers Shalom and R' Mordechai, hy"d, Yakov Spitzer, R' Mendel Bliman. R' Meir Klein, R' Baruch–Itsha Vitashka, and R' Moshe Vilner – all beloved Jews who were murdered on the sanctification of God's name, hy"d, He also befriended R' Bertsi Glik [Berl Gluck], may he live a long life, who now resides in Israel. We will always remember and recall for the best those innocent and honest Jews whom we met in the town of Tłuste.

In this manner we lived peacefully in the hope that before long everything would return to normal, and our status would be like an episode in our lives. However, this period was like paradise in comparison to the tragic period which began with the invasion of the Germans to the area where we found refuge. The Hungarians, the Germans' allies, arrived first and even though we did not know then the level of the Germans' cruelty, we were happy that our town fell in the hands of the Hungarians. Hungarian Jews, dressed in long "kapotot" and wide hats in the style of Hungarian Hasidim, arrived after the Hungarian army. But our joy was dashed shortly after, when local rule was given to the hands of the murderous Ukrainian police. Before long, special Nazi decrees against Jews came into effect and completely erased the distinction between the refugees and the veteran residents of the town. Again, there was no value to property, to a house and to ancestral merit.everyone became destitute and unworthy like those refugees.

In the days of distress, in the struggle for existence which continued day by day and hour by hour, Tłuste's Jews did not hesitate to come to the help of their troubled brothers. When the Hungarian Jews arrived in Tłuste, the townspeople came immediately to their aid and handed them their last piece of bread, and we need to speak with admiration and respect about the actions of these people.

It should be noted that the Jews of Tłuste did not lose their humanity even in desperate situations. I remember that, during the distribution of flour to the needy, many residents gave up their share so they would not benefit from charity. They opted to go hungry, to sell their last shirt, so they wouldn't need the gift of flesh and blood.

In this manner life continued in the ghetto until the great "aktzya" of 22 Iyar 5703 [27 May 1943], in which our beloved father, R' Mordechai, son of R' Tzvi Yakter z"l, perished. I will never forget his last words, when he already knew that his fate was sealed and he stood on the verge of extinction: "Children," he said "this is a judgment from the heavens, and we need to accept it with love. I only want to ask you one thing: if one of you can save his life – don't think about each other." After he gave his last will, he walked towards his fate with sanctity and purity, wrapped in his tallit and crowned in his tefillin. Our brothers, Yosef–Arye, Menashe–Aharon, and David, and our sisters, Freida–Roisa and Beshe, also perished in the great "aktzya." Almost an entire Jewish family was destroyed in one day.

These, to our deep sorrow, are the bitter memories that were left to us, to me and my sister, Leibe, from the town of Tłuste. There we weaved, together with our love ones, our future dream and hoped to survive and see the day of liberation, but, to our great sorrow, we left our family in a mass grave together with Tłuste's Jews, and only a few of us were able to survive.

———

[Page 265]

The hospitality of Tłuste's people

by Dr. A. Drokes

Translated by Sara Mages

With the permission of the former residents of Tłuste, who are busy publishing a memorial book for the members of their town who perished in the Holocaust, I will light a candle in memory of Sara and Pinchas Epshtein [Epstein] z"l, by posting my memories about my meeting with them, which took place a few days after the beginning of the Second World War.

On Rosh Hashanah eve I arrived with my wife and our two young children, and my wife's parents (the Lieberman family) to Tłuste's town center. We asked the Jews, who surrounded our car, to bring us to a hotel where we would be able to stay during the days of the holiday. And here, a couple, a man and his wife, approached us and invited us to their home. Their approach was so gentle that we accepted the invitation. They were, Sara and Pinchas Epshtein, parents of Tzvi and Klara Epshtein, who now live in Israel. We were greatly surprised that our hosts gave their own bedroom and beds to my wife's parents, and went to sleep on the floor in the next room. As far as I remember, the children, Tzvi and Klara, went to sleep at a neighbor's house.

The Epshtein family fed us and our Christian driver during the two days of the holiday and a few days after the holiday, and refused to hear about a payment. Since then, we befriended this family, and our friendship with the couple's children continues today here in Israel.

The parents of Tzvi and Klara Epshtein were kind, and Tłuste's Jews should be proud of them. Every year my wife and I mention this event to our children as a testimony of the love of the Jewish nation that would never end in our hearts.

———

The devotion of a Tłuste doctor

by Rachel Landman

Translated by Sara Mages

There's no day that I don't remember the wonderful image and precious soul of Dr. Baruch Milkh [Milch], and his dedicated work to save people from death. Every day, and every night, he walked around to offer help to people who were ill with dangerous diseases, such as typhus, without paying attention to the danger of contracting the diseases and the danger that he faced from the Nazi predators. Thanks to the medical help that he gave to his patients many of them survived a certain death, and I am among them.

I want to wish Dr. Milch a long life and that he continues his medical work for the benefit of everyone who needs the help of his blessed hands.

[Page 266]

Types and Figures

[Page 278]

The dying pains of Jewish Tłuste

by Dr. Baruch Milch

Translated by Sara Mages

I'm not a native of Tłuste. I spent my childhood and my adolescent years in Podhajce, but during the Holocaust I lived and worked in Tłuste, where I lost the members of my family who were brutally murdered together with the townspeople and the residents of the surrounding area. As a doctor, I had access to places that were forbidden to the rest of the Jewish residents, and had the terrible "right" to see the horrors up close. A number of these terrifying experiences are included in my testimony against the Gestapo men, Thomanek and Koellner, and were printed in this book ("A doctor's testimony"), and I would like to add a few more events that I was an eyewitness to.

As we know, Tłuste and the entire area were captured first by the Hungarian army and, only later, rule was transferred to the hands of the Germans. At the same period, thousands of Jews were deported from Hungary where they and their ancestors had lived for many years, under the claim that they were not Hungarian citizens. According to the Germans' deceit methods, these Jews were given the option to rebuild their homes in the Russian-occupied zone and take the places of Russians who died in the war or had left their homes and fled with the Russian army. Several thousand Hungarian Jews also arrived to Tłuste and the surrounding area. In Tłuste, the "Judenrat" took care of them and their needs, but in the villages these Jews were abandoned to the "mercy" of Ukrainian farmers who stole their belongings and killed them without mercy.

One day, I traveled in a cart to Rozanowka [Różanówka] to visit a patient, an important gentile among the residents of the village. When I arrived to the village, I saw a horrible sight that shocked all the fibers of my soul because we weren't accustomed yet to sights of horror that later became part of the daily routine under the Nazi rule. About two hundred Hungarian Jews, with their belongings, crowded in the square in the center of the village as they were surrounded by farmers armed with various tools. Some were also armed with rifles. All of them were ready to "fight" the helpless Jews, to attack them and destroy them. They were standing and waiting for the arrival of the Ukrainian police or the men of the Gestapo, who were to arrive from a nearby town. There were already a number of dead Hungarian Jews who were murdered before the arrival of the police. The farmers claimed that the Jews came to the village to capture it and take their homes. And indeed, there was a measure of truth in the claim: the Jews were brought to the village during harvest time, at the time when the farmers were busy in the fields, and when they saw their empty homes – they assumed that these were the homes that were promised them. When the gentiles returned for their noon meal and discovered the "invaders," they were ready to kill them.

I took advantage of my position as a well–known doctor in the area to quiet the spirits. At first, I quickly visited the important patient and placed him in my cart to transfer him to Tłuste's hospital. When I arrived to the village center I stopped and put my cart with the patient between the two camps and explained to the farmers that the "invasion" was a result of a misunderstanding. I asked to temporarily bury the murdered Jews in the place and promised, in the name of the "Judenrat," to transfer them in the next few days to the cemetery in Tłuste. The Jewish refugees walked behind me to Tłuste. I travelled ahead with the patient and dozens of Jews, men, women, and children walked behind me until we arrived in Tłuste.

Over time, the sights of murder and atrocities became part of our daily life. In the capacity of my work, I've seen shocking sights. I saw people die in the "aktzyot," in starvation and epidemics. I visited homes in which patients, who were sick with typhus, inflammation of the brain and pneumonia, lay on the floor in every room. Some patients behaved like people who lost their mind, but all of this pales in comparison to the horrifying sight that I've seen after the second "aktzya," the day after Simchat Torah 5701(1942) – (ed. actually Simchat Torah 5703: 4 October 1942). I entered a patient room in the temporary hospital that we established near the Great Synagogue, and was shocked when I saw that all the beds were flooded with blood. All the patients that we, the four Jewish doctors, had treated with so much dedication lay murdered in their beds. Each was shot in his head.

I was a witness to the death of the last community in Eastern Galicia, or maybe, in all of the Jewish communities in Poland, where a few hundred Jews miraculously survived. It is hard to describe what the survivors felt when they met for the first time in the ruins of Tluste. There was not a shred of joy in this meeting. On each of us lay a heavy load of horrible and bitter memories. None of us got used to the cruel thought that we survived and all our loved ones perished. The atmosphere was tense. Some of the Jewish homes and all the synagogues were completely destroyed, and the rest of the buildings stood without windows or doors, empty and emptied. Christians, or a number of survivors who gathered from the entire area, lived in some of them.

I also went to the cemetery. The guard, a gentile named Victor, was still protecting the headstones as if they were his private property and almost all of them remained intact. The four mass graves sunk about half a meter below ground. I remembered the horrifying sight that I saw in that place two days after the "aktzya." Now, it was quiet there, it was perfectly clean and deadly silent …

I also visited my apartment and former clinic which stood empty, but I hurried to escape from them. I thought I heard the voice of my little boy shouting: "Father, where have you been all this time?" and the sound of my wife calling: "How did you survive from the hands of the murderers?"

To this day I do not know how it happened. I don't understand how I, and all the survivors, remained alive after the brutal mass slaughter. I would never understand from where we derive the energy to start a new life after all that happened to us.

And if we succeed in reaching a land of safety and re–establish a home and a family – we will remember and not forget, because there would never be a penance to our brothers' spilled blood!

[Pages 279-287]

List of Martyrs from Tovste, Ukraine

Transliterated by Gladys Paulin

Edited by Yocheved Klausner

יזכור עם ישראל

את בניו ובנותיו, קדושי קהילת טלוסטה והסביבה, אנשים נשים וטף, שנהרגו
ונשחטו ושנחנקו ושנשרפו על־ידי הצוררים הנאצים בימי המלחמה והשואה
בשנים ה'ת"ש — ה'תש"ד ליצירה. תהא נשמתם צרורה בצרור חיי האומה.

The Nation of Israel will Remember

Its sons and daughters, martyrs of Tluste and its environs, men, women and children, who were murdered, slaughtered and incinerated by the evil Nazis during the war and Holocaust years in the years 5700 to 5705 [1939-1945]. May their souls be entwined for eternity in the life of the nation.

א Alef	ב Bet	ג Gimmel	ד Dalet	ה Hey	ו Vav	ז Zayin	ח Chet	ט Tet	י Yod	כ Kaf
ל Lamed	מ Mem	נ Nun	ס Samech	ע Ayin	פ Peh	צ Tzadik	ק Kof	ר Resh	ש Shin	ת Tav

Family name(s)	First name(s)	Maiden name	Sex	Marital status	Father's name	Mother's name	Name of spouse	Additional family members	Remarks	Page

א Alef

Family name(s)	First name(s)	Maiden name	Sex	Marital status	Father's name	Mother's name	Name of spouse	Additional family members	Remarks	Page
EUGENSTEIN	Aizi, Aizik		M							279
AUERBACHH	Yekel		M	Married					son-in-law of Lea STUPP	279
AUERBACHH		STUPP	F	Married		Lea	Yakov (Yankel)			279
ETLINGER	Rachel, Rochele		F							279
ETLINGER	Wolf		M	Married						279
ETLINGER			F	Married			Wolf			279
ETLINGER	Aizik		M					his family		279
ETLINGER	Moshe		M	Married						279
ETLINGER			F	Married			Moshe			279
EIDELSBERG	Motie		M	Married			Gitel			279
EIDELSBERG	Gitel	HARTMAN	F	Married			Motye			279
EIDELSBERG	Hillel		M		Motye	Gitel				279
EIDELSBERG	Pesach		M		Motye	Gitel				279
EIDELSBERG	Lusi		F		Motye	Gitel				279
EIDELSBERG	Chana		F							279
EIDELSBERG	Etel		F			Chana				279
EIDELSBERG	Yosl		M			Chana				279
EISEN	Meir		M	Married			Feige			279
EISEN	Feige	HESSING	F	Married			Meir			279
EINHORN	Hersch		M	Married			Maltze			279
EINHORN	Maltzie	ROTCHEN STREICH	F	Married			Hersh			279
EINHORN	Herman		M	Married						279
EINHORN			F	Married			Herman			279

EINHORN	Lanek		M		Herman				279
EINHORN	Moshe		M	Married			Matzie		279
EINHORN	Matche	MAIMON	F	Married	Anron- Aron?		Moshe		279
EINHORN	Peretz		M	Married			Malka		279
EINHORN	Malka	SHECHTER	F	Married			Peretz		279
EINHORN	Hersch		M					brother of Peretz EINHORN	279
EISS	Meir		M	Married			Rachel		279
EISS	Rachel	WILNER	F	Married			Meir		279
EISS	Munie		M	Married	Meir				279
EISS			F	Married			Munie		279
EISS	Chaim		M	Married					279
EISS			F	Married			Chaim		279
ALBIN	Ruven		M	Married			Chaia Reize		279
ALBIN	Chaia Reizie		F	Married			Ruven	Rosa	279
ALBIN	Sheftel		M		Ruven	Chaia Reize			279
ALBIN	Sheindel Danya		F		Ruven	Chaia Reize			279
ALBERGER	David		M	Married			Pesia		279
ALBERGER	Pesie		F	Married			David		279
ALBERGER	Beni		M		David	Pesia			279
ALBIN	Dr. Shmuel		M	Married			Carola		279
ALBIN	Karola	SHTEKEL	F	Married			Shmuel		279
ALBIN	Hinke		F		Shmuel	Carola			279
ALBERGER	Yosef		M					son-in-law of Benjamin LUBLIN	279
ALBERGER	Munie		M		Yosef				279
ALTSCHULER	Avraham		M	Married					279

Family name(s)	First name(s)	Maiden name	Sex	Marital status	Father's name	Mother's name	Name of spouse	Additional family members	Remarks	Page
ALTSCHULER			F	Married			Avraham			279
ALTSCHULER	Bizie		M	Married						279
ALTSCHULER			F	Married			Bisye			279
AMPEL	Moshe		M	Married			Feige			279
AMPEL	Feige	PFEFFER	F	Married			Moshe			279
AMPEL	Gusta	NUSSBOIM	F	Married			Yeshayahu			279
EPSTEIN	Rachel	BRECHER	F				Shmaye			279
EPSTEIN	Pinchas		M	Married	Shmaye	Rachel	Sara			279
EPSTEIN	Sara	ROSENZWEIG	F	Married	Natan		Pinchas			279
ERINGER	Berel		M	Married			Chaitze			279
ERINGER	Chaitze		F	Married			Berel			279

ב Bet

Family name(s)	First name(s)	Maiden name	Sex	Marital status	Father's name	Mother's name	Name of spouse	Additional family members	Remarks	Page
BADLER	Yeshaia Moshe		M							279
BLIMAN	Mendel		M	Married			Breina			279
BLIMAN	Breina		F	Married			Mendel			279
BLIMAN	Toibe		F		Mendel	Breina				279
BLIMAN	Nisan		M		Mendel	Breina				279
BLIMAN	Kopel		M		Mendel	Breina				279
BLIMAN	Moshe		M		Mendel	Breina				279
BLEICHER	Dr. Emil		M	Married						279
BLEICHER			F	Married			Emil			279
BILER	Hodye		F	Married			Zalman			279
BILER	Hinde		F		Zalman	Hodye				279
BILER	Sara		F		Zalman	Hodye				279

BILER	Basha		F		Zalman	Hodye			279
BIRGER	Eli		M	Married			Ratse	3 children	279
BIRGER	Ratze	STUPP	F	Married	Shmuel			3 children	279
BLAUSTEIN	Munie		M	Married			Fridzye		279
BLAUSTEIN	Friedze	SPITZER	F	Married	Hersh		Munie		279
BLAUSTEIN	Lunye		M		Munie	Fridye			279
BLECHER	Hinda	EPSTEIN	F		Shmaye				279
BLECHER	Elimelech		M			Hinda			279
BESNER	Chaim Leib		M	Married				children	279
BESNER			F	Married			Chaim Leib	children	279
BESNER	Yeshaya Leib		M					his family	279
BESNER			F					?	279
BESNER			F					husband	daughter of number 84	279
BLUM	Chaia		F						279
BLUM	Perl		F					his family	279
BLUMENFELD	Chaim		M	Married			Ester	1 child	279
BLUMENFELD	Esther	BRUKNER	F	Married	Mendel		Chaim	1 child	279
BLIKSHTEIN	Alter		M					his family	279
BLIKSHTEIN	Sala		F		Hersh				279
BERMAN	Gavriel		M					his family	279
BERNSTEIN	Hersh		M	Married			Frieda		279
BERNSTEIN	Frieda		F	Married			Hersh		279
BRAUN	Gavriel		M	Married			Chana		279
BRAUN	Chana		F	Married			Gavriel		279
BRAUN	Mania		F		Gavriel	Chana			279
BRAUN	Peppi		F		Aizik				279
BRANDES	Leon		M	Married			Genia	children	279

BRANDES	Genia	KAMERLIN G	F	Married			Leon	children		279
BROIDA	Avraham		M	Married						279
BROIDA			F	Married			Avraha m			279
BROINER	Avraham		M	Married			Loti			279
BROINER	Lotti	KREISLER	F	Married			Avraha m			279
BROINER			M		Avraham	Loti				279
BROINSTEIN	Gusta+G1 31		F			Tzivia				279
BROINSTEIN	Chaim		M	Married			Shifra			279
BROINSTEIN	Shifra	MELTZER	F	Married			Chaim			279
BROINSTEIN	David		M		Chaim	Shifra				279
BROINSTEIN	Moshe		M		Chaim	Shifra				279
BRUKNER	Mendel		M							279
BRECHER	David		M	Married				his family	daughters, sons-in-law and grandchildren	279
BRECHER			F	Married			David	her family	daughters, sons-in-law and grandchildren	279
BRECHER	Aharon		M		David			his family		279
BRECHER	Yakov		M	Married						279
BRECHER		LUBLIN	F	Married	Benjamin		Yakov			279
BRECHER	Sale		M		Yakov					279
BRECHER	Mania		M		Yakov					279
BRECHNER	Israel		M	Married			Ita			279
BRECHNER	Ita	TEIBER	F	Married			Israel			279
BRECHNER	Mania		M		Israel	Ita				279
BRECHNER	Rozie		F		Israel	Ita				279
BRECHNER	Yosef		M		Israel	Ita				279
BRECHNER	David		M		Israel	Ita				279

ג Gimmel

Family name(s)	First name(s)	Maiden name	Sex	Marital status	Father's name	Mother's name	Name of spouse	Additional family members	Remarks	Page
GOTFRIED	Shmuel		M		Yitzhak					280
GOTFRIED	Sara, Surke	SILVER	F	Married		Rachel Lea	Moshe			280
GOTTESFELD	Meir		M	Married			Loti		son-in-law of Ratze DUBESTER	280
GOTTESFELD	Loti	DUBESTER	F	Married		Ratse	Yitzhak Meir			280
GOTTESMAN	Elia		M	Married			Ita			280
GOTTESMAN	Ita	STUPP	F	Married			Elya			280
GOTTESMAN			F	Married			Zisha			280
GOLDHABER	Aharon		M	Married			Beiltsche			280
GOLDHABER	Beiltche		F	Married			Aharon			280
GOLDHABER	Nachman		M		Aharon	Beiltsche				280
GOLDSTEIN	Mundek		M							280
GOLDSTEIN			F						mother of Mundik GOLDSTEIN	280
GOLDSCHMID	Tzipa		F							280
GOLDSCHMID	Motel		M			Tzipa				280
GOLDSCHMID	Munie		M			Tzipa				280
GABAI	Berel		M	Married			Malka			280
GABAI	Malka		F	Married			Berel			280
GABAI			F		Berel	Malka		children		280
GABAI	Hilel		M	Married			Chava	1 child		280
GABAI	Chava		F	Married			Hilel	1 child		280
GABAI	Mordechai		M					his family		280

GABAI	Shaya		M	Married			2 children			280
GABAI			F	Married		Shaya	2 children			280
GEIGER	Yehuda		M	Married		Hinda				280
GEIGER	Hinde	DANKNER	F	Married	Moshe Israel	Yehuda				280
GLASER	Chune		M	Married						280
GLASER			F	Married		Chone				280
GLASER	Avraham		M				his family			280
GLASER	Naftali		M	Married				beadle		280
GLASER			F	Married		Naftali		dentist		280
GLASER	Yakov		M		Naftali					280
GLASER	Chune Elkana		M		Naftali					280
	Shifra	GLASER	F	Married	Naftali		husband			280
GLASER	Shmuel		M	Married		Frumtsche	children			280
GLASER	Frumtze	MEIMAN	F	Married	Aharon	Shmuel	children			280
GLANTSBERG	Davidtze		M	Married						280
GLANTSBERG			F	Married		Davidtsche				280
GLANTSBERG	Shimon		M							280
GLIK	Malka	MELTZER	F	Married	Shmuel	Berel				280
GETER	Davidye		M	Married		Tcharne	2 children			280
GETER	Tsharna		F	Married		Dudye	2 children			280
GELBER	Avraham		M							280
GELBER	Yehuda		M		Avraham					280
GELBER	Moshe		M		Avraham					280
GELBER			F		Avraham					280
GELBER			F		Avraham					280
GELBAND	Berel		M	Married		Malka Gitel				280

GELBAND	Malka Gitel		F	Married			Berel			280
GELBER	Naftali		M	Married				children		280
GELBER			F	Married			Naftali	children		280
GELLER	Shmuel		M						son-in-law of Shalom VACHSTEIN	280
GELLER	Sheva		F					3 children		280
GERTNER	Ben Zion		M		Hersch			his family		280
GERTNER	Toibe		F	Married			Motye		wife of Motye the teacher	280
GERTNER	Chaia		F		Motye	Tovah				280
GERTNER	Wolf		M	Married						280
GERTNER			F	Married			Wolf			280
GERTNER	Zalman		M	Married			Perl			280
GERTNER	Perl		F	Married			Zalman			280
GERTNER	Israel		M							280
	Reizie	GERTNER	F	Married				husband	sister of Israel GERTNER	280
GERTNER	Israel		M	Married				children	from the town of Tluste	280
GERTNER			F	Married			Israel	children	from the town of Tluste	280
GERTNER	Yakov		M	Married						280
GERTNER			F	Married			Yakov			280
GERTNER	Natan		M		Yakov					280
GERTNER	Toibe		F		Yakov					280
GERTNER	Mechl		M							280
GERTNER	Manie		M		Mechl					280
GERTNER	Gedalia		M		Mechl					280
GERTNER	Natan		M		Mechl					280
GERTNER	Moshe		M	Married			Orne			280
GERTNER	Arna	PLATZKER	F	Married	Yitzhak		Moshe			280
GERTNER	Zeev		M		Moshe	Orne				280

GERTNER	Natan		M	Married		Chantze		children	from town of Tluste	280
GERTNER			F	Married			Natan	children	from town of Tluste	280
GERTNER	Sabina	FENSTER	F	Married			Shmuel			280
GERTNER	Blima		F		Shmuel	Sabina				280
GERTNER	Shmuel		M	Married	Ben Zion	Chava Chaia	Rivka	3 children		280
GERTNER	Rivka		F	Married			Shmuel	3 children		280
GERTNER	Shimshon		M	Married			Frieda			280
GERTNER	Frieda		F	Married			Shimsh on			280
GERTNER	Yosef		M		Simshon	Freide				280
GERTNER	Blima		F		Simshon	Freide				280
GERTNER	Shmuel		M	Married			Hodye			280
GERTNER	Hoda		F	Married			Shmuel			280
GERTNER	Gedalia		M		Shmuel	Hodye				280
GERTNER	Hersh		M		Shmuel	Hodye				280
GERTNER	Yitzhak		M	Married	Shmuel		Tzipa			280
GERTNER	Tzipa	HESSING	F	Married			Yitzhak			280
GERTNER	Manie		M		Yitzhak	Tzipa				280
GERTNER	Mosie		F		Yitzhak	Tzipa				280
GERTNER	Mintze		F		Yitzhak	Tzipa				280
GERTNER	Natan		M	Married	Shmuel			children		280
GERTNER			F	Married			Natan	children		280
GERTNER	Aharon		M	Married	Shmuel			children		280
GERTNER		EINHORN	F	Married			Aharon	children		280
GERTNER	Breina		F	Married			Israel			280
GERTNER	Chaia		F	Married			Ben-Zion			280
GERTNER	Rachel	HALPERN	F							280
GRABSTEIN	Itzik		M	Married			Fruma	1 child	grandson	280

Family name(s)	First name(s)	Maiden name	Sex	Marital status	Father's name	Mother's name	Name of spouse	Additional family members	Remarks	Page
GRABSTEIN	Fruma		F	Married			Itzik	1 child	grandson	280
GRABSTEIN	Moshe Leizer		M	Married						280
GRABSTEIN			F	Married			Moshe Leizer			280
GRAU	Benyamin		M							280
GRAU	Osie		M		Benjamin					280
GRILL	Alter		M		Yosi					280
GRINBERG	Dr.		M					children		280
GRINBERG	Samtzie		M	Married			Chana			280
GRINBERG	Chana		F	Married			Samtzie			280
GRINBERG	Shmuel		M		Samtze	Chana				280
GRINBERG			F		Samtze	Chana				280

ד Dalet

Family name(s)	First name(s)	Maiden name	Sex	Marital status	Father's name	Mother's name	Name of spouse	Additional family members	Remarks	Page
DACHNER	Berel		M	Married			Breina			280
DACHNER	Breina		F	Married			Berel			280
DACHNER	Tsharna		F		Berel	Breina				280
DACHNER	Gavriel		M	Married						280
DACHNER			F	Married			Gavriel			280
	Sosia	DACHNER	F	Married	Gavriel			husband		280
	Toive	DACHNER	F	Married	Gavriel			husband		280
DALER	Moshe		M	Married			Klara			280
DAOLER	Clara		F	Married			Moshe			280
DANKNER	Efraim		M	Married			Tcharne	children		280
DANKNER	Tcharne		F	Married			Efraim	children		280
DANKNER	Wawe		M	Married						280

	Zeev							
DANKNER			F	Married			Welvel Zeev	280
DANKNER	Mendel		M	Married				280
DANKNER			F	Married			Mendel	280
DANKER	Shabtai		M	Married	Moshe Israel		children	280
DANKER			F	Married			Shabtai children	280
DUBESTER	Ratzie		F					280
DUBESTER	Munie		M		Ratse			280
DUBESTER	Rachel		F		Ratse			280
DUBESTER	Rivka		F		Ratze			280
DROHOBITSER	Shaul		M	Married			Rachel	280
DROHOBITSER	Rachel	SCHECHTER	F	Married			Shaul	280
DROHOBITSER	Chana		F		Shaul	Rachel		280
DROHOBITSER	Avraham		M		Shaul	Rachel		280
DROHOBITSER	Israel		M	Married			Chaia	280
DROHOBITSER	Chaia	KASSIRER	F	Married			Israel	280
DROHOBITSER	Yehuda		F		Israel	Chaia		280
DROHOBITSER	Wolf		M		Israel	Chaia		280
DROHOBITSER	Arye Leib		M	Married			Genia	280
DROHOBITSER	Genia	FISCHLER	F	Married			Arye Leib	280
DROHOBITSER	Mordechai		M		Arye Leib	Genia		280
DROHOBITSER	Moshe		M	Married			Hela	280
DROHOBITSER	Hela	BUCHNER	F	Married			Moshe	280

R

| DROHOBITSER | Gershon | | M | | Moshe | Hela | | | | 280 |

ה Hey

Family name(s)	First name(s)	Maiden name	Sex	Marital status	Father's name	Mother's name	Name of spouse	Additional family members	Remarks	Page
HOCHMAN	Shaul		M	Married			Pulya			280
HOCHMAN	Folie		F	Married			Shaul			280
HOCHMAN	Dara		M		Shaul	Pulya				280
HOCHMAN	Meir		M		Shaul	Pulya				280
HOCHMAN	Mutzik		M		Shaul	Pulya				280
HALBERSTAM	Yekutiel		M	Married						280
HALBERSTAM			F	Married			Yekutiel			280
HALBERSTAM	Mariasie		F							280
HALBERSTAM	Yechiel		M			Maryasha				280
HALENBERG	Israel		M						father of Berel HOLENBERG	280
HALENBERG	Tantzie		F	Married			Berel			280
HALENBERG			F		Berel	Tantze				280
HALENBERG	Dalye		M		Berel	Tantze				280
HALENBERG	Nisan		M	Married			Dvora			280
HALENBERG	Dvora	LANG	F	Married			Nisan			280
HALENBERG	Feivish		M	Married						280
HALENBERG			F	Married			Feibish			280
HALPERN	Chaim		M	Married			Tovah	children		281
HALPERN	Tovah		F	Married			Chaim	children		281
HALPERN	Muntzie		F							281
HALPERN	Pesia		F							281
HOLZ	Mendel		M	Married			Rachel	children		281

HOLZ	Rachel		F	Married			Mendel	children	281
HOLZMAN	Moshe		M	Married			Mindye	children	281
HOLZMAN	Mindie	MARGOLIES	F	Married	Yosi		Moshe	children	281
HOROWITZ	Avrahamtzi		M	Married			Dvora		281
HOROWITZ	Dvora		F	Married			Avramtze		281
HOROWITZ	Aharon		M	Married			Eidl		281
HOROWITZ	Eidl		F	Married			Aharon		281
HOROWITZ			F		Aharon	Eidl			281
HOROWITZ	Yakov		M	Married			Sala		281
HOROWITZ	Sala		F	Married			Yakov		281
HOROWITZ			F		Yakov	Sala			281
HOROWITZ			F		Yakov	Sala			281
HOROWITZ	Yitzhak		M	Married					281
HOROWITZ			F	Married			Yitzhak		281
HOROWITZ			M		Yitzhak				281
HOROWITZ			M		Yitzhak				281
HOROWITZ	Meir		M	Married				3 children	281
HOROWITZ			F	Married			Meir	3 children	281
HOROWITZ	Etye	BOIMEISTER	F	Married	Aharon			2 children	281
HOROWITZ			M	Married			Etye	2 children	281
HARNIK	Aharon		M	Married				children	281
HARNIK			F	Married			Aharon	children	281
HARNIK	Tzipa		F	Married			Hersh		281
HOISFELD	Sosia		F						281
HOISFELD	Mendel		M	Married			Pesia		281
HOISFELD	Pesia		F	Married			Mendel		281
HOISFELD	Izia		M		Mendel	Pesia			281

HOISFELD	Pesia		F					sister of Aba HOISFELD	281
HOISFELD	Babe		F					sister of Aba HOISFELD	281
HIKAND	Herman		M				his family		281
HIRSCHBEIN	Beile		F						281
HIRSCHBEIN	Henzl		F						281
HIRSCHBEIN	Chaim		M						281
HIRSCHBEIN	Chaia		F						281
HIRSCHBEIN	Israel		M	Married		Malka	children		281
HIRSCHBEIN	Malka		F	Married		Israel	children		281
HIRSCHBEIN	Israel		M				his family		281
HELD	Chaim Hersh		M	Married			children		281
HELD		BILER	F	Married		Chaim Hersh	children		281
HELLER	Avraham		M	Married		Liba		another relative of the Loshkivitzer Rebbetzin	281
HELLER	Lieba	DRIMER	F	Married		Avraham			281
HELLER	Hersh		M		Avraham	Liba			281
HELLER			F		Avraham	Liba			281
HELLER			F		Avraham	Liba			281
EINHORN			M				children	son-in-law of Avraham HELLER	281
HELLER	Shimshon		M	Married		Toibe			281
HELLER	Tovah		F	Married		Shimshon			281
HELLER	Yakov		M		Shimshon	Toibe			281
HELLER	Israel		M		Shimshon	Toibe			281
HELLER	Rochtzie Rachel		F		Shimshon	Toibe			281
HELLER	Anale		F						281

HELLER	Babele		F			Anele			281
HELFGOT	Itzi		M	Married		Breina			281
HELFGOT	Breina		F	Married		Itzi			281
HELFGOT	Chaim		M	Married					281
HELFGOT			F	Married		Chaim			281
HELFGOT	Shabtai		M	Married					281
HELFGOT			F	Married		Shabtai			281
HELPER	Avraham		M	Married		Tzirl			281
HELPER	Tzirl		F	Married		Avraham			281
HELPER	Menachem		M		Avraham	Tzirl			281
HELPER	Chaia		F		Avraham	Tzirl			281
HELPER	Pesia		F		Avraham	Tzirl			281
HENDEL	David		M	Married		Feige Rachel			281
HENDEL	Rachel	MELTZER	F	Married	Shmuel	David			281
HENDEL			M		David	Feige Rachel			281
HESING	Basha	REINISCH	F						281
HESING	Hentzie		F			Basha			281
HESING	Berish		M	Married		Rivtze	children		281
HESING	Rivtze		F	Married		Berish	children		281
HESING	Gavriel		M						281
HESING	David		M	Married	Gavriel				281
HESING		KATZ	F	Married		David			281
HESING	Chaim		M		Israel				281
HESING	Rivka		F						281
HESING	Chaim		M			Rivka			281
HESING	Gavriel		M			Rivka			281
HESING	Chaim		M		Moshe Leibele		his family		281

HESING	Chaike		F		Chaim Aizik					281
HESING	Malye		F	Married			Israel Leib			281
HESING	Mintze		F							281
HESING	Sonia		M			Mintsche				281
HESING	Beni		M			Mintsche				281
HESING	Tzipa		F		Chaim Aizik			his family		281
HESING	Shlomo		M	Married						281
HESING			F	Married			Shlomo			281
HESING	Mendele		M	Shlomo						281
HESING	Ozie		M	Shlomo						281
HESING	Shimon		M	Married				children	the water carrier	281
HESING			F	Married			Shimon	children		281
HERTMAN	Shmuel		M	Married	Motel		Mistzie			281
HERTMAN	Mistzie		F	Married			Shmuel			281
HERTMAN	Leibish		M	Shmuel	Mistsche					281
HERTMAN	Rachel		F	Shmuel	Mistsche					281
HERTMAN	Avraham		M	Motel						281
HERTMAN	Yona		M	Married	Motel		Liba			281
HERTMAN	Liba	EISS	F	Married			Yona			281
HERTMAN	Feige		F	Motel						281
HERTMAN	Pesia		F	Motel						281
HERTMAN	Berel		M	Married	Tsvi		Chava			281
HERTMAN	Chava		F	Married			Berel			281
HERTMAN	Berel		M	Married	Yona					281
HERTMAN			F	Married			Berel			281
HERTMAN			M	Berel						281
HERTMAN			M	Berel						281
HERTMAN	Golda		F							281

HERTMAN	Hillel		M				Golda				281
HERTMAN	Basha, Batia		F				Golda				281
HERTMAN	Friedshe		F				Golda				281
HERTMAN	Chasia		F								281
HERTMAN	Yona		M	Married	Moshe Yakov		Roize				281
HERTMAN		SHIFRIN	F	Married			Yona				281
HERTMAN	Matche		F		Yona	Roize					281
HERTMAN	Shmuel		M		Yona	Roize					281
HERTMAN	Leib		M	Married	Moshe Yankel		Gitzie	2 children			281
HERTMAN	Gitzie		F	Married			Leib	2 children			281
HERTMAN	Malka		F								281
HERTMAN	Shmuel		M	Married		Malka		1 child			281
HERTMAN			F	Married			Shmuel	1 child			281
HERTMAN	Mendel		M	Married				3 children			281
HERTMAN			F	Married			Mendel	3 children			281
HERTMAN	Frumtze		F	Married			Natan				281
HERTMAN	Frume		F					2 children	daughter-in-law of Leibish HERTMAN		281
HERTMAN	Sara		M	Married				2 children			281
HERTMAN			F	Married			Sheva	2 children			281
HERMAN	Isidor		M								281
HERMAN	Bune Baruch		M	Married			Chana				281
HERMAN	Chana	WARNBERG	F	Married			Bunie Baruch				281
HERNES	Zalman		M	Married			Feige				281
HERNES	Feige	MELTZER	F	Married			Zalman				281
HERNES	Matzie		M		Zalman	Feige					281
HERNES	Tzvia		F		Zalman	Feige					281
HERNES	Yoel		M	Married			Tzipa				281

Family name(s)	First name(s)	Maiden name	Sex	Marital status	Father's name	Mother's name	Name of spouse	Additional family members	Remarks	Page
HERNES	Tzipa		F	Married			Yoel			281
HERSCHER	Avraham		M	Married			Mania			281
HERSCHER	Munie		F	Married			Avraham			281
HERSCHER			M		Avraham	Manye				281

ך Vav

Family name(s)	First name(s)	Maiden name	Sex	Marital status	Father's name	Mother's name	Name of spouse	Additional family members	Remarks	Page
WACHSSTEIN	Avraham		M	Married			Basha			281
WACHSSTEIN	Basha	GOLDHIRSCH	F	Married			Avraham			281
WACHSSTEIN	Yitzhak		M	Married			Sara	2 children		281
WACHSSTEIN	Sara	EIDELSBERG	F	Married			Yitzhak	2 children		281
WACHSSTEIN	Miriam Lea		F	Married			Shalom			281
WACHSSTEIN	Meir		M	Married	Shalom	Lea	Sara			281
WACHSSTEIN	Sara		F	Married			Meir			281
WACHSSTEIN	Moshe		M		Meir	Sara				281
WACHSSTEIN	Sala		F		Meir	Sara				281
WACHSSTEIN	Malka		F	Married			Yeshaya			281
WACHSSTEIN	Rachel		F		Yeshaya	Malka				281
WOLFBERG	Chaia	SHER	F		Yakov					281
WASSER	David		M	Married			Feige			281
WASSER	Feige	SPITZER	F	Married			David			281
WASSER	Yosel		M		David	Feige				281
WASSER	Yeshaya Leib		M	Married			Yeti			281
WASSER	Yeti		F	Married			Yeshaya Leib			281
WASSER	Shmuel		M		Yeshaya Leib	Yeti				281

WASSER	Sali		F		Yeshaya Leib	Yeti		281
WASSER	Moshe		M	Married		Tcharne		281
WASSER	Tcharne		F	Married		Moshe		281
WASSERMAN	Mordechai		M	Married			children	281
WASSERMAN			F	Married		Mordechai	children	281
WARENBERG	Tipora	EPSTEIN	F		Yosef			282
WARENBRAND	Michael		M	Married		Sonye		282
WARENBRAND	Sonya		F	Married		Michael		282
VITASHKA	Baruch Itzi		M	Married		Ester		282
VITASHKA	Esta		F	Married		Baruch Itzi		282
WIDBERG	Aharon		M			parents		282
WEINGARTEN	Shmuel		M			his family		282
WEINTRAUB	Leibish		M	Married		Dobe	children	282
WEINTRAUB	Dove		F	Married		Leibish	children	282
WEINLES	Rachel		F					282
WEINLES	Klara		F		Rachel			282
WEINLES	Chava		F	Married			wife of Dr. VILNER	282
WEINLES	Elias		M		Chava			282
WEINRAUB	Azriel		M					282
WEINRAUB			M		Azriel			282
WEINSTEIN	Eliezer		M	Married				282
WEINSTEIN			F	Married		Eliezer		282
WEINSTEIN	Munie		F		Eliezer			282
WEINSTEIN	Moshe		M		Eliezer			282
WEINSTEIN	David		M		Eliezer			282
WEINSTEIN	Sosia		F				Mother of Mendel WEINSTOK	282

Surname	Given	Maiden	Sex	Status	Father	Mother	Spouse	Other	Notes	Page
WEINSCHEL	Meir		M	Married			Bracha			282
WEINSCHEL	Bracha	METZ	F	Married			Meir			282
WEINSCHEL	Yosef Shmuel		M		Meir	Brucha				282
VEINSCHEL	Moshe		M		Nachum					282
WEISBROT	Yeshaya		M	Married			Sara			282
WEISBROT	Sara		F	Married			Yeshaya			282
WEISBROT	Shimshon		M		Yeshaya	Sara				282
WEISBROT	Frieda		F		Yeshaya	Sara				282
WEISBROT	Chaim		M		Yeshaya	Sara				282
WEISGLAS	Izka		M			Aneta				282
WEISGLAS	Aneta		F					Mother of Izka WEISSGLASS		282
WEISLANDER	Frieda		F							282
WEISLANDER	Chaitze		F	Married	Friede					282
WEISLANDER			M	Married			Chaitze			282
WEISLANDER			M		Chaitze					282
WEISLANDER	Zlate		F				his family			282
WILLBACH	Shalom		M					Dentist		282
WILLBACH			M					dentist. Brother of Shalom WILBACH		282
VILNER	Miriam		F							282
VILNER	Hersh		M		Miriam					282
VILNER	Esther		F		Miriam					282
VILNER	Tutzie Naftali		M	Married	Miriam	Bronia	children			282
VILNER	Breina	KLEINREICH	F	Married			Tutzie Naftali	children		282
VILNER	Moshe		M	Married			Ester			282
VILNER	Esther		F	Married			Moshe			282
VILNER	Fruma		F		Moshe	Ester				282

Family name(s)	First name(s)	Maiden name	Sex	Marital status	Father's name	Mother's name	Name of spouse	Additional family members	Remarks	Page
VILNER	Naftali		M	Married	Moshe			children		282
VILNER			F	Married			Naftali	children		282
VINKLER	Michael		M	Married			Chaia			282
VINKLER	Chaia	ROSENBLAT	F	Married			Michael			282
VINKLER	Azriel		M		Michael	Chaia				282
VINKLER	Note		M		Michael	Chaia				282
VINKLER	Yankel		M		Michael	Chaia				282
WENKERT	Yitzhak		M							282
WENKERT			M		Yitzhak					282
WENKERT			F		Yitzhak					282
WENKERT			F		Yitzhak					282
WECHSLER	Moshe		M	Married			Sara Rivka			282
WECHSLER	Sara Rivka		F	Married			Moshe			282
WECHSLER	Tzipa		F						sister of Moshe WECHSLER	282
WECHSLER	Babale		F		Tzipa			children		282
WECHSLER			M	Married			wife		refugees from Germany	282

ז Zayin

Family name(s)	First name(s)	Maiden name	Sex	Marital status	Father's name	Mother's name	Name of spouse	Additional family members	Remarks	Page
SALZMAN	Mintze		F							282
SALZMAN	Malka		F							282
SALZMAN	Feige		F							282
SOMMER	Rachel		F		Feibish				Daughter of Feibish the slaughterer (Shochet)	282
SANDBERG	Yosel		M	Married			Malka Tzirl			282
SANDBERG	Malka Tzirl		F	Married			Yosl			282

Family name(s)	First name(s)	Maiden name	Sex	Marital status	Father's name	Mother's name	Name of spouse	Additional family members	Remarks	Page
SANDBERG	Motie		M		Yosel	Malka Tzirl				282
SANDBERG	Leibish		M					his family		282
SANDBERG	Shmuel		M							282
SANDBERG	Rachel		F						Sister of Shmuel SIEBENBERG	282
SEIDEN	Dr. Shmuel		M							282
SILBERSTEIN	Avraham		M	Married				children		282
SILBERSTEIN			F	Married		Avraham		children		282
SILBERSTEIN	Erich		M					children		282
SILBERSTEIN	Yitzhak		M							282
SILBERSTEIN	Maltze		F							282
SILBERSTEIN	Rachel		F			Maltze				282
SILBERSTEIN	Tsvetel	GLANZBERG	F							282
SILBERSTEIN	Rachel		F							282

ח Chet

Family name(s)	First name(s)	Maiden name	Sex	Marital status	Father's name	Mother's name	Name of spouse	Additional family members	Remarks	Page
CHODOROV	Sheindel		F				Pinchas			282
CHODOROV	Rav Shmuel Aba		M	Married			Sosia			282
CHODOROV	Sosia		F	Married			Shmuel Aba			282
CHODOROV	Pinchas		M		Shmuel Aba	Sosia				282
CHODOROV	Blima		F		Shmuel Aba	Sosia				282
CHODOROV	Rivka		F		Shmuel Aba	Sosia				282

ט Tet

Family name(s)	First name(s)	Maiden name	Sex	Marital status	Father's name	Mother's name	Name of spouse	Additional family members	Remarks	Page
TABAK	Shifra	FIDERER	F		David					282
TAUBER	Shlomo Niome		M							282
TAUBER	Moshe		M		Shlomo Niame					282
TAUBER	Roize		F		Shlomo Niame					282
TEIBER	Avraham		M	Married			Keile			282
TEIBER	Keile		F	Married			Avraham		Kayle MALIES	282
TEIBER	Sosia		F	Married			Yosi			282
TEIBER	Sheindel		F		Yosi	Sosia				282
TEIBER	Ben-Zion		M		Yosi	Sosia				282
TEIBER	Seide		M		Yosi	Sosia				282
TEIBER	Hersh		M		Yosi	Sosia				282
TEIBER	Shmuel		M	Married	Avraham					282
TEIBER			F	Married			Shmuel			282
TEIBER	Ben-Zion		M	Married			Teme			282
TEIBER	Teme		F	Married			Ben-Zion			282
TEIBER	Rachel		F		Ben-Zion	Teme				282
TEIBER	Gitel		F		Ben-Zion	Teme				282
TEIBER	Misia		M		Ben-Zion	Teme				282
TEIBER	Israel		M		Ben-Zion	Teme				282
TEIBER	Berel		M			Chava				282
TEIBER	Hersh Tsvi		M	Married						282
TEIBER			F	Married			Hersh Tsvi			282
TEIBER	Matzie		F		Hersh Tsvi					282
TEIBER	Hersh		M	Married	Gedalia		Feige			282

Surname	Given name		Sex					Page
TEIBER	Feige		F	Married			Hersh Tsvi	282
TEIBER	Ben-Zion		M		Hersh	Feige		282
TEIBER	Shmuel		M	Married	Gedalia		children	282
TEIBER			F	Married			Shmuel children	282
TEIBER	Feige		F	Married			Pinchas	282
TEIBER	Shmuel		M	Married	Pinchas		Pesia	282
TEIBER	Pesia	SCHPAREN	F	Married			Shmuel	282
TEIBER	Moshe		M	Married	Pinchas		Tzipa	282
TEIBER	Tzipe		F	Married			Moshe	282
TEIBER			F		Moshe	Tzipa		282
TEIBER			F		Moshe	Tzipa		282
TEIBER			F		Moshe	Tzipa		282
TEIBER	Shlomo		M	Married	Pinchas		Breintsche	first victim in Tluste	282
TEIBER	Breintzie		F	Married			Shlomo	282
TEIBER			F		Shlomo	Breintze		282
TITINGER	Emil		M	Married				282
TITINGER			F	Married			Emil	282
TITINGER	Ludwig		M		Emil			282
TITINGER	Fridzia Frederich		M		Emil			282
TISCHLER	Muntzie		M					282
TEPER	Herz		M		Zeide		Shimshon	282
TEPER	Shmuel		M	Married	Zeide	Etel children		282
TEPER	Etel		F	Married			Shmuel children	282
TREMBOVELSKY	Avraham Efraim		M					282
TREMBOVELSKY	Meir Leib		M	Married			Rivtze	282
TREMBOVELSKY	Rivtze	DACHNER	F	Married			Meir Leib	282

Family name(s)	First name(s)	Maiden name	Sex	Marital status	Father's name	Mother's name	Name of spouse	Additional family members	Remarks	Page
TREMBOVELS KY			F		Meir Leib		Rivtze			282
TREMBOVELS KY	Rachel	LIEBMAN	F							282
TREMBOVLER	Iza		M		Chaim			his family		282

ל Yod

Family name(s)	First name(s)	Maiden name	Sex	Marital status	Father's name	Mother's name	Name of spouse	Additional family members	Remarks	Page
YONISHEVSKY	Kalman		M	Married			Dvora			282
YONISHEVSKY	Dvora		F	Married			Kalman			282
YAKTER	Mordechai		M						Yaroslav	282
YAKTER	Frieda Roiza		F						Yaroslav	282
YAKTER	Yosef Arye		M						Yaroslav	282
YAKTER	Menashe Aharon		M						Yaroslav	282
YAKTER	Neshe		M						Yaroslav	282
YAKTER	David		M						Yaroslav	282
YAKTER	Israel		M	Married			Eti	children		282
YAKTER	Eti	DUBESTER	F	Married			Israel	children		282

כ Kaf

Family name(s)	First name(s)	Maiden name	Sex	Marital status	Father's name	Mother's name	Name of spouse	Additional family members	Remarks	Page
KATZ	Israel		M	Married			Yente			282
KATZ	Yente		F	Married			Israel			282
KATZ	Moshe		M	Married						282
KATZ			F	Married			Moshe			282
KATZ	Chanale		F		Moshe					282
KATZ	Mendel		M	Married			Reize			282
KATZ	Reizie	ZEINWEL	F	Married		Rivka				282

Family name(s)	First name(s)	Maiden name	Sex	Marital status	Father's name	Mother's name	Name of spouse	Additional family members	Remarks	Page
KATZ	Fishel		M	Married			Rivtze	2 children	tailor	282
KATZ	Rivtze		F	Married			Fishel	2 children		282
COHEN	Rivtze		F						mother of Eli-Mendel COHEN	282

ל Lamed

Family name(s)	First name(s)	Maiden name	Sex	Marital status	Father's name	Mother's name	Name of spouse	Additional family members	Remarks	Page
LAM	Shalom		M	Married					"shochet" [ritual slaughterer]	283
LAM			F	Married			Shalom	children		283
LANG	Avraham		M					children		283
LANG	Shmuel		M	Married	Avraham					283
LANG			F	Married			Shmuel			283
LANG	Berish		M	Married			Chaitze			283
LANG	Chaitze		F	Married			Berish			283
LANG	Leitche Lea		F		Berish	Chaitze				283
LANG	Rochtze Rachel		F		Berish	Chaitze				283
LANG	Gavriel		M	Married	Berish	Chaitze	Sara	2 children		283
LANG	Sara		F	Married			Gavriel	2 children		283
LANG	David		M	Married	Berish	Chaitze	Gitel			283
LANG	Gitel	SCHPAREN	F	Married			David			283
LANG			M		David	Gitel				283
LANG			F		David	Gitel				283
LANG	Welvel		M	Married	Itche		Eti			283
LANG	Eti		F	Married			Velvel			283
LANG	Toibe		F		Welvel	Eti				283
LANG	Ben-Zion		M		Welvel					283
LANG	Chaim		M	Married			Chaitze			283

LANG	Chaitze		F	Married			Chaim			283
LANG	Berel		M		Chaim	Chaitze				283
LANG	Chana		F		Chaim	Chaitze				283
LANG	Chana		F						the milkmaid	283
LANG			F			Chana				283
LANG	Yosef		M				1 child			283
LANG	Motye		M				children			283
LANG	Moshe		M	Married			Maltzie	children	son-in-law of Yakov STERNLIEB	283
LANG	Maltze	STERNLIEB	F	Married	Yakov		Moshe	children		283
LANG	Shabtai		M	Married			Pesia			283
LANG	Pesia		F	Married						283
LANG	Roza		F	Married	Shabtai	Pesia	1 child			283
LANG			M	Married		Rosa	1 child			283
LANG	Shmuel		M							283
LANG	Shlomo		M							283
LANG	Chana Yte		F		Shlomo					283
LANG	Vitie		F		Shlomo					283
LANG	Miriam Gitel		F		Shlomo					283
LANG	Chaim		M							283
LANG	Machle		F							283
LANG	Zlate		F							283
LANGHOLZ	Efraim Froiki		M							283
LANGHOLZ	Leibish		M	Married			Rachel	3 children		283
LANGHOLZ	Rachel		F	Married			Leibish	3 children		283
LANGHOLZ	Malka		F			Elka				283
LANGHOLZ	Elka		F							283
LANGHOLZ	Akiva		M							283

LANGHOLZ	Lunia		M		Akiva				283
LANGHOLZ	Izia		M		Akiva				283
LANGHOLZ	Sheva Sheive		F						283
LANGHOLZ			M			Sheva Sheiva			283
LANGSNER	Moshe		M	Married		Leitsche (Lea)			283
LANGSNER	Leitche		F	Married		Moshe			283
LANDMAN	Yehoshua		M					son-in-law of Shlomo LIEBMAN	283
LAPINER	Pinchas		M				his family	preacher	283
LUBLIN	Tcharne		F						283
LUBLIN	Avraham		M						283
LUBLIN	Bintze		F						283
LUBLIN	Benyamin		M	Married		Toibe			283
LUBLIN	Toibe		F	Married		Benjamin			283
LUBLIN	Hersh		M		Benjamin				283
LUBLIN	Yosef		M		Benjamin				283
LIEBMAN	Hersh		M				his family		283
LIEBMAN	Hentze	TALLER	F	Married		Ortzie			283
		LIEBMAN	F	Married			husband and 2 children		283
LIEBMAN	Chana Mirka		F						283
LIEBMAN	Chaim Hersh		M				his family		283
LIEBMAN	Munie		M	Married			1 child		283
LIEBMAN			F	Married		Munie	1 child		283
LIEBMAN	Mantzie		F		Shmuel	Etye			283
LECHTER	Yosef		M	Married		Rachel			283
LECHTER	Rachel		F	Married		Yosef			283

Family name(s)	First name(s)	Maiden name	Sex	Marital status	Father's name	Mother's name	Name of spouse	Additional family members	Remarks	Page
LECHTER	Gitzie		F		Yosef	Rachel				283
LETZ	Sigmund		M	Married			Eti	children		283
LETZ	Eti		F	Married			Sigmund	children		283
LETZ			F						mother of Sigmund LETZ	283

מ Mem

Family name(s)	First name(s)	Maiden name	Sex	Marital status	Father's name	Mother's name	Name of spouse	Additional family members	Remarks	Page
MAHLER	Feibish		M	Married						283
MAHLER			F	Married			Feivish			283
MAHLER	Leibish		M		Leibish					283
MASER	Yeshaya		M							283
MAYBERGER	Etia Sima		F					his family		283
MAYER	Itche		M			Dvora				283
MAYER	Chaim Aizik		M							283
MAYER	Risye		F	Married			Hershel			283
MAYER	Shlomo Israel		M	Married			Rozie		maiden name of wife of Rubinshtein	283
MALTER	Michael		M	Married			Zlata	children		283
MALTER	Zlate		F	Married			Michel	children		283
MAN	Munie		M							283
MANDSTEIN	Dr.		M							283
MANSBERG	Dr. Shmuel		M							283
MEISELMAN	Avraham		M	Married			Golde			283
MEISELMAN	Golda	STOP	F	Married			Avraham			283
MEISELMAN	Roza		F		Avraham	Golde				283
MEIMANN	Aharon		M	Married			Roize			283
MEIMANN	Roize		F	Married			Aharon			283

MEIMANN	Kopel		M		Aharon	Roize				283
MEIMANN	Perl		F		Aharon	Roize				283
MEIMANN	Nisan		M	Married	Aharon	Roize		children		283
MEIMANN			F	Married			Nisan	children		283
MEIMANN	Artzie		M	Married			Sosia			283
MEIMANN	Sosia		F	Married			Ahrtzie			283
MEIMANN	Eidl		M	Married			Rachel			283
MEIMANN	Rachel	GLIK	F	Married			Yidel			283
MEIMANN	Nisan		M		Yidel	Rachel				283
MEIMANN	Perl		F		Yidel	Rachel				283
MEIMANN	Mendel		M	Married						283
MEIMANN			F	Married			Mendel			283
MEIMANN	Leibtzi		M	Married						283
MEIMANN			F	Married			Leibtzie			283
MEIMANN	Shalom		M	Married	Nisan		Dvora			283
MEIMANN	Dvora		F	Married	Chaim		Shalom			283
MEIMANN	Chaim		M		Shalom	Dvora				283
MEIMANN	Nisan		M		Shalom	Dvora				283
MEIMANN	Hersh		M		Shalom	Dvora				283
MEIMANN	Natan		M	Married	Nisan		Feige	1 child		283
MEIMANN	Feige		F	Married			Natan	1 child		283
MILCH	Pepa		F	Married					wife of Dr. MILCH	283
MILCH	Eliash		M			Pepa				283
MELER	Aharon		M	Married			Rachel	children		283
MELER	Rachel	NAGLER	F	Married	Yosef Leibish		Aharon	children		283
MELER	Moshe		M	Married			Dara			283
MELER	Dara	MELTZER	F	Married	Peisie		Moshe			283
MELTZER	Dr. Bernard		M	Married			Regina			283

MELTZER	Regina	KUTNER	F	Married			Bernard			283
MELTZER	Hodye Hodel		F		Bernard	Regina				283
MELTZER	Tzila		F		Bernard	Regina				283
MELTZER	Feige		F	Married			Meir			283
MELTZER	Sara		F		Meir	Feige				283
MELTZER	David		M		Meir	Feige				283
MELTZER	Peisye Pesach		M	Married			Bobtsche			283
MELTZER	Babtche		F	Married			Peisye Pesach			283
MELTZER	Leibl		M	Married	Peisie	Bobtze		children		283
MELTZER			F	Married			Leibl	children		283
MELTZER	Shlomo		M	Married				children		283
MELTZER			F	Married			Shlomo	children		283
MENSCHEL	Henye		F							283
MENSCHEL			F						mother of Henye MENSCHEL	283
MESSING	David		M		Leibish					283
METZGER	Asher		M		Aharon Shalom					283
METZGER	Mendel		M	Married	Aharon Shalom		Perl			283
METZGER	Perl		F	Married			Mendel			283
METZGER	Rivka		F		Mendel	Perl				283
METZGER	Chaim Moshe		M							283
METZGER	Ozie		M		Chaim Moshe					283
METZGER	Shmaya		M	Married						283
METZGER			F	Married			Shmaia			283
METZGER			F	Married	Shmaye			1 child		283
METZGER	Ruven		M	Married				1 child	son-in-law of Shmaye METZGER	283

Family name(s)	First name(s)	Maiden name	Sex	Marital status	Father's name	Mother's name	Name of spouse	Additional family members	Remarks	Page
MARGOLIES	Eliezer Leizer		M						blacksmith	283
MARGOLIES			F		Eliezer Leizer					283
MARGOLIES			F		Eliezer Leizer					283
LANGER			M						son-in-law of Eliezer Leizer MARGOLIES	283
MARGOLIES	Leib		M	Married			Sheindel			283
MARGOLIES	Sheindel		F	Married			Leib			283
MARGOLIES	Hersh		M		Leib	Sheindel				283
MARGOLIES	Lutche Lucia		F		Leib	Sheindel				283

] Nun

Family name(s)	First name(s)	Maiden name	Sex	Marital status	Father's name	Mother's name	Name of spouse	Additional family members	Remarks	Page
NAGLER	Chaim		M	Married			Breintsche			284
NAGLER	Breintze		F	Married			Chaim			284
NAGLER	Zishe		M		Chaim	Breintze				284
NAGLER	Ita		F						granddaughter of Yona HERTMAN	284
NAGLER	Sender		M		Yosef Leibish			his family		284
NAGLER	Lipa		M		Yosef Leibish			his family		284
NADLER	Roize		F						mother of Sonia and Yitzhak COHEN	284
NADLER	Zlota		F	Married			Sonye		name of Sonia COHEN's husband	284
NADLER	Moshe		M	Married				2 children		284
NADLER			F	Married			Moshe	2 children		284
NEUFELD	Antchel		M	Married			Gusta	2 children		284
NEUFELD	Gusta		F	Married			Antchel	2 children		284

NEUFELD	Zishe		M	Married			Gitel		284
NEUFELD	Gitel	TEIBER	F	Married			Zishe		284
NEUFELD	Herman		M		Zishe	Gitel			284
NEUFELD	Mina Mitzka		F		Zishe	Gitel			284
NEUFELD	Pepi		F		Zishe				284
NEUFELD	Shamai		M	Married			Henye		284
NEUFELD	Henya		F	Married			Shamai		284
NEURINGER	Klara	LUBLIN	F		Gershon		2 children		284
NUSSBOIM	Simche		M	Married					284
NUSSBOIM			F	Married			Simcha		284
NUSSBOIM			M		Simche				284
NEUMAN	Meir		M						284
NEUMAN	Yakov		M	Married	Meir		Leitsche		284
MEUMAN	Leitzie		F	Married			Yakov		284
NIRENBERG	David		M	Married			Elisheva		284
NIRENBERG	Elisheva		F	Married			David		284
NIRENBERG	Munie		M		David	Elisheva			284
NIRENBERG	Shmuel		M		David	Elisheva			284
NIRENBERG	Antchel		M	Married	David		Chana		284
NIRENBERG	Chana	HERTMAN	F	Married			Antchel		284
NIRENBERG	Natan Karpel		M	Married			Sosia	son-in-law of Tzvi EPSTEIN	284
NIRENBERG	Masie		F	Married			Natan Karpel		284
NIRENBERG	Moshe		M		Natan Karpel				284
NIRENBERG	Ester		F		Natan Karpel				284
NIRENBERG	Reize		F	Married				sister of Israel GERTNER	284
NIRENBERG			M	Married			Reize		284

ס Samech

Family name(s)	First name(s)	Maiden name	Sex	Marital status	Father's name	Mother's name	Name of spouse	Additional family members	Remarks	Page
SALPETER	Aharon		M	Married			Chaia			284
SALPETER	Chaia	FINK	F	Married	Marim		Aharon			284
SALPETER	Tzipora		F		Aharon	Chaia				284
SALPETER	Avraham		M		Aharon	Chaia				284
SALPETER	Moshe		M		Aharon	Chaia				284
SALPETER	Yakov		M		Aharon	Chaia				284
SALPETER	Sara		F		Aharon	Chaia				284
SAS	Chaim		M	Married			Elke			284
SAS	Elka	BODLER	F	Married	Moshe		Chaim			284
SEGAL	Shlomo		M	Married				children		284
SEGAL			F	Married			Shlomo	children		284
SEGAL	Hersh		M		Shlomo					284
STOP	Yidel		M	Married			Chana			284
STOP	Chana		F	Married			Eidl			284
STOP	Julius		M	Married	Shmuel		Guste	children		284
STOP	Gusta	LITVAK	F	Married			Yulius	children		284
STOP	Mendel		M	Married			Maltsche			284
STOP	Maltze		F	Married			Mendel			284
STOP	Meir		M		Mendel	Maltsche				284
STOP	Wolf		M		Mendel	Maltsche				284
STOP	Itze		M	Married	Mendel			1 child		284
STOP			F	Married			Itzi	1 child		284
STOP	Gitel		F						lady baker	284
STOP	Yehuda		M			Gitel				284
STOP	Munie		M			Gitel				284

Family name(s)	First name(s)	Maiden name	Sex	Marital status	Father's name	Mother's name	Name of spouse	Additional family members	Remarks	Page
STOP	Chaia		F				Gitel			284
STOP	Liba		F				Gitel			284
STOP	Simche		M	Married				children	the klezmer (musicians)	284
STOP			F	Married			Simcha	children		284
STOP	Yehuda Yidel		M	Married				children	wagon driver	284
STOP			F	Married			YehudaYidel	children		284
STOP	Gavriel		M	Married	Yehuda			children		284
STOP			F	Married			Gavriel	children		284
STOP	Mendel		M		Yehuda			his family		284
STOP	Shmarye		M	Married						284
STOP			F	Married			Shmaria			284
STOP	Antchel		M		Shmarye					284
STOP	Leib		M		Shmarye					284
STOP	Leib		M							284
STOP	Bertzi		M		Leib					284
STOP	Moshe		M		Leib					284
STOP	Lea		F							284
STOP	Munie		M							284
STOP	Feige		F	Married						284
STOP			M	Married			Feige			284

פ Peh

Family name(s)	First name(s)	Maiden name	Sex	Marital status	Father's name	Mother's name	Name of spouse	Additional family members	Remarks	Page
VOGEL	Israel		M	Married			Tzila			284
VOGEL	Tzila		F	Married			Israel			284
VOGEL	Shmuel		M		Israel	Tzila				284
VOGEL	Saltche		F		Israel	Tzila				284

POHORILES	Leibish		M	Married				children		284
POHORILES			F	Married			Leibish	children		284
POHORILES	Israel		M		Leibish					284
POHORILES	Shabtai		M	Married				children		284
POHORILES		MEZGER	F	Married			Shabtai	children		284
POHRER	Natan Hersh		M	Married			Faye			284
POHRER	Faye		F	Married			Natan Hersh			284
POTASCHNIK	Yosef		M	Married			Gitel	children		284
POTASCHNIK	Gitel	BRECHER	F	Married	David		Yosef	children		284
FALBER	Dala		M	Married			Lusia			284
FALBER	Lusya	FELL	F	Married	Yakov		Dala			284
FALBER	Litka		F		Dala	Lusie				284
VOLKENFLIK	Moshe		M					his family	photographer	284
FASLER	Note		M	Married			Sara			284
FASLER	Sara		F	Married			Note			284
FASLER	Tantzie		F		Note	Sara				284
FASLER	Izia		M		Note	Sara				284
FASLER	Fishel		M		Note	Sara				284
FASLER	Simcha		M	Married				children		284
FASLER			F	Married			Simche	children		284
PAPIEL	Shimon		M	Married			Tzipa	children		284
PAPIEL	Tzipa	TEIBER	F	Married			Shimon	children		284
FURMAN	Yosef		M						son-in-law of Rezie NADLER	284
FURMAN	Sara		F		Yosef					284
FURMAN	Breina		F		Yosef					284
FURMAN	Tzesia		F		Yosef					284
FURMAN	Shmarye		M		Yosef					284
FIDERER	Aharon		M	Married			Roza			284

FIDERER	Raza		F	Married			Aharon			284
FIDERER	Chaim Munie		M	Married	Mendel					284
FIDERER			F	Married			Chaim Munie			284
FIDERER	Israel		M	Married	David		Hendil			284
FIDERER	Hendel		F	Married			Israel			284
FIDERER	Rozja		F		Israel	Hendil				284
FIDERER	David		M		Israel	Hendil				284
FIDERER		REINISCH	F				Moshe			284
FIDERER	Yehuda		M		Moshe	Freide				284
	Feige Breintze		F							284
PINTENSTEIN			M	Married			Etel	1 child		284
PINTENSTEIN	Etel		F	Married				1 child		284
PINSKER	Leib		M					his family		284
FINK	Eliezer		M	Married			Feige			284
FINK	Feige	HERTMAN	F	Married			Eliezer			284
FINK			M		Eliezer	Feige				284
FINK	Marim		M	Married			Frume			284
FINK	Frume		F	Married			Marim			284
FINK	Ben-Zion		M	Married	Marim	Frume	Etke	2 children		284
FINK	Etka		F	Married			Ben-Zion	2 children		284
FINKELMAN	Eliezer		M	Married				children	the candlestick maker	284
FINKELMAN			F	Married			Eliezer	children		284
FINKELMAN	Leibish		M	Married			Tovah			284
FINKELMAN	Toibe		F	Married			Leibish			284
FINKELMAN	Zlate		F		Leibish					284
FINKELMAN	Zeinvel		M	Married	Leibish			children		284
FINKELMAN			F	Married			Zeinwel	children		284
FINKELMAN	Eliahu		M	Married			Hentshe			284

FINKELMAN	Hentze		F	Married	Yehuda		Elihu		284
PIPER	Dudie		M	Married			Tziporah	teacher	284
PIPER	Tziporah		F	Married			Davidye		284
PIPER	Malka		F		Dudie	Tziporah			284
FISCHBACH	Roize		F		Arye				284
FISCHBACH	Yona		M	Married			Shoshana		284
FISCHBACH	Shoshana		F	Married			Yona		284
FISCHBACH	Mania		F		Yona	Shoshana			284
FISCHBACH	Klara		F		Yona	Shoshana			284
FISCHBACH	Shlomo		M	Married					284
FISCHBACH			F	Married			Shlomo		284
FISCHBACH	Yona		M	Married			Chaitze		284
FISCHBACH	Chaitze		F	Married			Yona		284
FISCHBACH	Zeev		M		Yona	Chaitze			284
FISCHBACH	Yitzhak		M		Yona	Chaitze			284
FISCHBACH	Libe		F		Yona	Chaitze			284
FISCHBACH	Rivka		F					granddaughter of Yona FISCHBACH	284
PLOTSKER	Aizik		M	Married			Perl		284
PLOTSKER	Perl		F	Married			Itzik		284
PLOTSKER	Shlomo		M		Itzik	Perl		his family	284
PLESER	Mordechai		M	Married			Folie	children	"shochet" [ritual slaughterer]	284
PLESER	Folie		F	Married			Mordechai	children	284
FEDER	Moshe		M	Married			Tzirl	1 child	284
FEDER	Tzirl	SHECHNER	F	Married			Moshe	1 child	284
FEDER	Yentze Yakov		M					his family	284
FEDER	Nisan		M	Married				children	284
FEDER			F	Married			Nisan	children	284

FELD	Tzipe	SHECHNER	F	Married	Moshe		Yakov			285
FELSENSTEIN	Motye		M	Married			Miriam			285
FELSENSTEIN	Miriam		F	Married			Motye			285
FELSENSTEIN	Ester		F		Motye	Miriam				285
FELSENSTEIN	Surtzie		F		Motye	Miriam				285
FENSTER	Ovadiah		M	Married			Chentze			285
FENSTER	Chintze		F	Married			Ovadiah			285
FENSTER	Mintze		F		Ovadiah	Chintsche				285
FENSTER	Sala		F		Ovadiah	Chintsche				285
FELDMAUS	Moshe		M	Married			Dinah			285
FELDMAUS	Dina		F	Married			Moshe			285
PFEFFER	Antchel		M	Married			Chava			285
PFEFFER	Chava		F	Married			Antchel			285
PFEFFER	Yosef		M		Antchel	Chava				285
PFEFFER	Israel		M		Antchel	Chava				285
PFEFFER	Shulke		M	Married	Antchel	Chava	Neche	children		285
PFEFFER	Neche		F	Married			Shaulke	children		285
PFEFFER	Teme		F							285
PFEFFER	Tsilya		F			Teme				285
PFEFFER	Moshe		M	Married		Teme	Clara			285
PFEFFER	Klara		F	Married			Moshe			285
PFEFFER	Mendel		M		Moshe	Klara				285
PFEFFER	Yakov		M	Married			Malka			285
PFEFFER	Malka		F	Married			Yakov			285
PFEFFER	Feivish Yidel		M	Married	Yakov		Leitze Lea			285
PFEFFER	Leitche Lea		F	Married			Feivish Yidel			285
PFEFFER	Leitche		F	Married	Yakov			1 child		285
PFEFFER			M	Married			Leitze	2 children		285

PFEFFER	Leitche Lea	F	Married		Fishel			285
PFEFFER	Bene	M		Fishel				285
PFEFFER	Moshe	M	Married			children	brother-in-law of Berish HESING	285
PFEFFER		F	Married		Moshe	children		285
PFEFFER	Israel	M	Married			children	brother of Moshe, brother-in-law of Natan MEIMAN	285
PFEFFER		F	Married		Israel	children		285
PERLMUTTER	Este Miriam	F				children	daughters	285
PERLMUTTER	Hilel	M		Ester Miriam		his family		285
PERLMUTTER	Israel	M		Ester Miriam		his family		285
PERLMUTTER	David	M		Ester Miriam				285
PERLMUTTER	Yosef	M	Married	Ester Miriam		1 child		285
PERLMUTTER		F	Married		Yosef	1 child		285
PERLMUTTER	Chaia	F		David				285
PERLMUTTER	Chana	F		Shalom				285
PERLMUTTER	Hersh	M		Chaim				285
FERSTER	Nachman	M	Married	Shlomo	Perl			285
FERSTER	Perl	F	Married		Nachman			285
FERSTER	Rachel	F		Nachman Perl				285
FERSTER	Shimshon	M	Married	Nachman Perl	Rachel			285
FERSTER	Rachel	F	Married		Shimshon			285
PFAU	Adelca	M	Married		Eti			285
PFAU	Eti	F	Married		Adelka			285
PFAU	Nusye	M		Adelka Eti				285
PFAU	Klara	F						285
PFAU	Adela	F						285

PFAU	Munie		M	Married				1 child	285
PFAU		LIEBMAN	F	Married			Munie	1 child	285
PFAU	Genia		F						285
PFAU	Frieda		F						285
PFEIFERMACHER	Kalman		M	Married			Lea		285
PFEIFERMACHER	Lea		F	Married			Kalman		285
PFEIFERMACHER	Yosef		M		Kalman	Lea			285
PFEIFERMACHER	Rachel		F		Kalman	Lea			285
PFEIFERMACHER	Israel		M		Kalman	Lea			285
PFEIFERMACHER	Izia		M		Kalman	Lea			285
PFEIFERMACHER	Dara		M		Kalman	Lea			285
FRADES	Yosef		M						285
FRADES	Moshe		M		Yosef				285
FRADES			F		Yosef				285
FREUNDLICH	Blima	STEIN	F		Leib				285
FREUNDLICH	Golda		F			Blime			285
FRIEDMAN	Yakov		M	Married			Etye	rope maker	285
FRIEDMAN	Etye		F	Married			Yakov		285
FRIEDMAN	Artzie		F		Yakov	Etye			285
FRIEDMAN	Sosia		F		Yakov	Etye			285
FRIEDMAN	Chava		F		Yakov	Etye			285
FRIEDMAN	Mendel		M	Married			Malka		285
FRIEDMAN	Malka	MELTZER	F	Married	Pesach		Mendel		285
PRIMUS	Shlomo		M	Married					285
PRIMUS			F	Married			Shlomo		285
PRIMUS	Chinye		F		Shlomo				285
PRESSLER	Yakov		M					judge	285
PRESCHEL	Moshe		M	Married	Herzl		Sheindel		285
PRESCHEL	Sheindel		F	Married			Moshe		285

PRESCHEL	Herzl		M		Moshe	Sheindel				285
PRESCHEL	Tziporah		F		Moshe	Sheindel				285
PRESCHEL	Etel		F		Moshe	Sheindel				285

צ Tzadik

Family name(s)	First name(s)	Maiden name	Sex	Marital status	Father's name	Mother's name	Name of spouse	Additional family members	Remarks	Page
TSUMER								family	parents, 2 sons and 2 daughters	285
SEIGER	Mendel		M	Married			Frumtze			285
SEIGER	Frumtze		F	Married			Mendel			285
SEIGER	Tenie		F		Mendel	Frumtsche				285

ק Kof

Family name(s)	First name(s)	Maiden name	Sex	Marital status	Father's name	Mother's name	Name of spouse	Additional family members	Remarks	Page
KAHAN	Reize		F					father-in-law and family		285
KOTLER	Eliezer		M						the blacksmith	285
KOTLER	Aharon		M	Married						285
KOTLER			F	Married			Aharon			285
KOTLER	Shmuel		M		Aharon					285
KOTLER	Tzvi		M		Aharon					285
KOTLER	Malka		F							285
KOTLER			F			Malka				285
KOCH	Yitzhak Menachem		M							285
KALENBERG	Mendel		M	Married			Gusta			285

KALENBERG	Gusta		F	Married			Mendel		285
KALENBERG	Batia		F		Mendel	Guste			285
KALENBERG	Elimelech		M	Married			Rachel		285
KALENBERG	Rachel		F	Married			Elimelech		285
KALENBERG	Beni		M		Elimelech	Rachel			285
KALENBERG	Batia		F		Elimelech	Rachel			285
KALENBERG	Tuvye		M	Married					285
KALENBERG			F	Married			Tevel Tuvye		285
KATSNER	Dr. Isidor		M	Married					285
KATSNER			F	Married			Isidor		285
KOBERT	Natan		M						285
KOBERT			F		Natan				285
KOBERT			F		Natan				285
KOBERT			M		Natan				285
KUPPERMAN	Yakov		M	Married			Henye Gitel		285
KUPPERMAN	Henye Gitel		F	Married					285
KUPPERMAN	Hersh		M		Yakov	Gitel			285
KUPPERMAN			F		Yakov	Gitel			285
KUPPERMAN	Motye		M		Yakov			his family	285
KURTSER	Asher		M	Married			Sara		285
KURTSER	Sara		F	Married			Asher		285
KURTSER	Dania		F		Asher	Sara			285
KURTSER	Ester		F		Asher	Sara			285
KURTSER	Mania		F		Asher	Sara			285
KIMMELMMAN	Gavriel		M	Married			Otzie		285
KIMMELMMAN	Aitsche	SHECHNER	F	Married			Gavriel		285
KIMMELMMAN	Rivka		F		Gavriel	Otzie			285

KIMMELMMAN	Arye		M		Gavriel	Otzie				285
KIMMELMMAN	Yakov		M	Married			Nechama			285
KIMMELMMAN	Nachman		F	Married			Yakov			285
KIMMELMMAN	Rivka		F		Yakov	Nechama				285
KIMMELMMAN	Yakov		M	Married			Gitzie	4 children	teacher	285
KIMMELMMAN	Gitzie		F	Married			Yakov	4 children		285
KIMMELMMAN	Israel		M				children			285
KLEIN	Aizik		M	Married					tailor	285
KLEIN			F	Married			Aizik			285
KLEIN	Yeti	KUTNER	F				2 children			285
KLEIN	Kalman		M		Yeti					285
KLEINER	Meir		M	Married			Chana			285
KLEINER	Chana		F	Married			Meir			285
KLEINER	Pesach		M	Married	Meir	Chana				285
KLEINER			F	Married			Pesach			285
KLEINER			F		Pesach					285
KLEINER			F		Pesach					285
KLEINER	Mutzik		M		Meir	Chana		his family		285
KLEINER	Hersh		M		Eliezer					285
KLEINER	Yosef		M		Eliezer					285
KLINGER			M	Married				wife	the governor [or mayor] of Rozsanovka	285
KNISHBACH			M	Married			Sala	1 child		285
KNISHBACH	Sala	GLIKSTEIN	F	Married	Hersh			1 child		285
KELMAN	Zalman		M	Married			Frume		teacher	285
KELMAN	Fruma		F	Married			Zalman			285
KELMAN	Gitel		F						Brushhke's daughter-in-law	285
KELMAN	Munie		M	Married			Gitel	3 children		285
KELMAN	Rachel		F	Married			Munie	3 children		285

Family name(s)	First name(s)	Maiden name	Sex	Marital status	Father's name	Mother's name	Name of spouse	Additional family members	Remarks	Page
KELMAN	Mendel		M				Gitel	his family	tailor	285
KELMAN	Mordechai		M				Gitel		tinsmith	285
KELMAN	Hersh		M				Gitel			285
KOENIGSBERG	Avraham		M	Married						285
KOENIGSBERG			F	Married			Avraham			285
KOENIGSBERG	Kehat		M							285
KOENIGSBERG	Martzel		M		Kehat					285
KRAMPF	Yosef		M	Married						285
KRAMPF			F	Married			Yosef			285
KRAMPF	Israel		M	Married						286
KRAMPF			F	Married			Israel			286
KRAMPF	Yona		M		Israel					286
KRASOTSKY	Dr. Leon		M	Married			Loti			286
KRASOTSKY	Lotti		F	Married			Leon			286
KRASOTSKY	Norbert		M		Leon	Loti				286
KREISLER	Chaia Blima		F							286
KRITSER	Yehoshua		M	Married			Dvora			286
KRITSER	Dvora		F	Married			Yehoshua			286
KRITSER	Manya		F		Yehoshua	Dvora				286
KREMER	Tsvi		M		Eliezer					286
KREMER	Yosef		M		Eliezer					286

ר Resh

Family name(s)	First name(s)	Maiden name	Sex	Marital status	Father's name	Mother's name	Name of spouse	Additional family members	Remarks	Page
ROSEN	Shimon		M	Married			Rivtze			286
ROSEN	Rivtze		F	Married			Shimon			286
ROSEN	Yitzhak		M		Shimon	Rivtze				286

ROSENBOIM	Shlomo		M				mother	286
ROSENBOIM	Beni		M				brother of Shlomo ROSENBOIM	286
ROSENBOIM	Maltze		F				sister of Shlomo ROSENBOIM	286
	Henya	ROSENBOIM	F	Married			husband	sister of Shlomo ROSENBOIM	286
ROSENBLATT	Minye		F					286
ROSENBLATT	Hersh		M	Married		Minye	Breine	286
ROSENBLATT	Breina		F	Married		Hersh		286
ROSENBLATT	Aharon		M		Hersh	Breine		286
ROSENBLATT	Aka		M		Hersh	Breine		286
ROSENBLATT	Kalman		M	Married	Motyr	Eite		286
ROSENBLATT	Yte		F	Married		Kalman		286
ROSENBLATT	Yeshaya		M		Motye		his family	286
ROSENBLATT	Moshe		M	Married		Frieda		286
ROSENBLATT	Frieda		F	Married		Moshe		286
	Breina	ROSENBLAT	F	Married		Yitzhak		286
	Yitzhak		M	Married		Breine		286
ROSENBLATT	Menashe		M	Married	Moshe	Freida		286
ROSENBLATT			F	Married		Menashe		286
ROSENBLATT	Kalman		M	Married		Sabina		286
ROSENBLATT	Sabina	ALBIN	F	Married		Kalman		286
ROSENHOCH	Chaia		F	Married		Chaim		286
ROSENHOCH	Shlime		F		Chaim	Chaia		286
ROSENHOCH	Izia		M		Chaim	Chaia		286
MERSEL	Hinde		F				bride of Izia ROSENHOCH	286
ROSENTHAL	Yehshaya		M	Married		Rachel		286
ROSENTHAL	Rachel	HERNES	F	Married		Yeshaya		286
ROSENTHAL	Hersh		M		Yeshaya	Rachel		286

ROSENTHAL	Lusia	F		Yeshaya	Rachel				286
ROSENTHAL	Shalom	M		Yeshaya	Rachel				286
ROSENTHAL	Mendel	M	Married			Golde		painter	286
ROSENTHAL	Golde	F	Married			Mendel			286
ROSENTHAL	Wolf	M		Mendel	Golde				286
ROSENTHAL	David	M		Mendel	Golde				286
ROHT	Selig	M							286
ROHT	Hersh	M		Selig					286
ROTENSTREICH	Sheindl	F							286
ROTENSTREICH	Sali	M							286
ROTENSTREICH	Michael	M							286
RATSES	Chaim Shaul	M				his family			286
RUBINSTEIN	Yitzhak	M	Married			Ester			286
RUBINSTEIN	Ester	F	Married			Yitzhak			286
RUBINSTEIN	Yakov	M		Yitzhak					286
RUBINSTEIN	Mordechai	M	Married			Sheintze			286
RUBINSTEIN	Sheintze	F	Married			Mordechai			286
RUBINSTEIN	Shmuel	M		Mordechai	Sheintsche				286
RUBINSTEIN	Chava	F		Mordechai	Sheintsche				286
RUBINSTEIN	Yosef	M		Mordechai	Sheintsche				286
RUDI	Yechiel	M	Married				children	teacher. Kashilevitz	286
RUDI		F	Married			Yechiel	children		286
RUDI	Hersh	M		Yechiel					286
REINISCH	Eli	M							286
REINISCH	Hersh	M	Married	Eli					286
REINISCH		F	Married			Hersh			286
REINISCH	Yehuda	M	Married	Eli		Eti	children		286
REINISCH	Eti	F	Married			Yehuda	children		286

Family name(s)	First name(s)		Sex	Marital status	Father's name	Mother's name	Name of spouse	Additional family members	Remarks	Page
REINISCH	Babtze		F							286
REINISCH	Chaim		M			Babtzie				286
REINISCH	Sonia		F			Babtzie				286
REINISCH	Yeshaya Leib		M	Married	Shevach					286
REINISCH			F	Married			Yeshaya Leib			286
REINISCH	Genia		F		Yeshaya Leib					286
REINISCH	Matzie		F		Yeshaya Leib					286
REINISCH	Nusye		F		Yeshaya Leib					286
REINISCH	Meir		M	Married			Chava			286
REINISCH	Chava		F	Married			Meir			286
REINISCH	Munie		M		Meir					286
REINISCH	Shmuel		M		Meir	Chava				286
REINISCH	Mintze		F		Meir	Chava				286
REINISCH	Moshe		M			Chava			the bookbinder	286
REISS	Rachel		F					mother and brothers		286
RINGEL	Hersh		M							286
RINGEL	Natan		M					his family		286
RINGEL	Pinchas		M					parents		286
RINGEL			F		Pinchas					286

ש Shin

Family name(s)	First name(s)	Maiden name	Sex	Marital status	Father's name	Mother's name	Name of spouse	Additional family members	Remarks	Page
SCHATSBERG	Berel		M	Married				children		286
SCHATSBERG			F	Married			Berel	children		286

SCHATSBERG	Chaia		F						286
SCHATSBERG	Golde		F						286
SCHATSBERG	Benjamin		M			Chaia			286
SCHOR	Chaike		F			Chaia			286
SCHOR			F						286
SCHOR	Fishel		M	Married		Chaike	Gitel		286
SCHOR	Gitel		F	Married			Fishel		286
SCHOR			F		Fishel				286
SCHOR			F		Fishel	Gitel			286
SCHOR			F		Fishel	Gitel			286
SCHOR	Tcharne		F	Married		Gitel	Yakov		286
SCHOR	Sprintze Yente		F					son-in-law	286
SCHOR			F			Shifaitse Yente			286
SCHOR			F			Shifaitse Yente			286
SCHWARTZ	Asher		M	Married			Gitzie		286
SCHWARTZ	Gitze		F	Married			Asher		286
SCHWARTZ	Aharon		M		Asher	Gitsche			286
SCHWARTZ	Rita		F		Asher	Gitsche			286
SCHWARTZ	Mordechai		M					son-in-law of Blume SELTZER	286
SCHWARTZ			F					mother of Mutzik SCHWARTZ	286
SCHWARTZBART	Chaim		M	Married				beadle	286
SCHWARTZBART			F	Married			Chaim		286
SCHWEITZER	Meir David		M	Married					286
SCHWEITZER	Sime	FIDERER	F	Married					286
SCHWEITZER	Rosye		F		Meir David	Sime			286
SCHWEITZER	Moshe		M		Meir	Sime			286

Surname	Given Name	Other Name	Sex	Status	Father	Mother	Spouse	Children	Notes	Page
					David					
SCHWEITZER	Oizer		M	Married			Zisl	1 child		286
SCHWEITZER	Zisl		F	Married			Ozer	1 child		286
SCHUCHNER	Note		M					parents		286
SCHULMAN	Yona		M	Married				children	"shochet" [ritual slaughterer]	286
SCHULMAN			F	Married			Yona	children		286
SCHULMAN	Yechiel		M	Married						286
SCHULMAN			F	Married			Yechiel			286
SCHULMAN	Eli		M		Yechiel					286
SCHULMAN	Avraham		M		Yechiel					286
SCHULMAN	Hersh		M	Married	Yechiel		Gitzie			286
SCHULMAN	Gitze		F	Married			Hersh			286
SCHULMAN	Aharon		M		Hersh	Gitsche				286
SCHULMAN	Avraham		M		Hersh	Gitsche				286
STEIN	Leib		M							286
STEINBACK	Toibe		F						the niece of Bonie HERMANN	286
STECKEL	Yehoshua Osias		M	Married			Pesia			286
STECKEL	Pesia	KRASOTSKY	F	Married			Yehoshua Osias			286
STECKEL	Joseph		M		Yehoshua Osyas	Pesia				286
STECKEL	Yakov		M	Married						286
STECKEL			F	Married			Yakov			286
STERNBERG	Baruch		M	Married			Rivtze	children		286
STERNBERG	Rivtze		F	Married			Baruch	children		286
STERNBERG	Dvora Dvortze	WACHSHTEIN	F							286
STERNLIEB	Dvora		F		Yakov					286
STERNLIEB	Itzi		M			Dvora				286

STERNLIEB	Reize	F			Dvora			286
STERNLIEB	Neche	F	Married	Yakov		2 children		286
STERNLIEB		M	Married		Neche	2 children		286
STERNLIEB	Reizl	F	Married		Selig			286
STERNLIEB	Israel Leib	M	Married	Selig	Maltshe			286
STERNLIEB	Maltze	F	Married		Israel Leib			286
STERNLIEB		F		Israel Leib	Maltshe			286
STERNKLAR	Zalman	M	Married		Malka			286
STERNKLAR	Malka	F	Married		Zalman			286
STRASBERG	Babtze	F						286
STRASBERG	Sara	F						286
SCHEINHOLS	Mendel	M	Married		Otzie Breine			286
SCHEINHOLS	Otzie Breine	F	Married		Mendel			286
SCHEINHOLS	Zisl	F		Mendel	Otzie Breine			286
SCHEINHOLS	Eliakim	M	Married		Perl	children		286
SCHEINHOLS	Perl	F	Married	Hersh	Elyakim	children		286
SCHILDER	Aharon	M	Married		Feige	1 child		286
SCHILDER	Feige	F	Married		Aharon	1 child		286
SCHILDER	Yosef	M	Married		Tzipa		slaughterer	286
SCHILDER	Tzipa	F	Married		Yosef			286
SCHILDER	Zishe	M		Yosef	Tzipa			286
SCHILDER	Moshe	M		Avraham				286
SCHILDER	Yosef Chaim	M		Avraham				286
SCHILDER	Gitel	F		Avraham				286
SCHMUTS	Dr. Yakov	M	Married					286
SCHMUTS		F	Married		Yakov			286
SCHMUTS		F		Yakov				286

SCHMELTZER	Ben-Zion		M	Married			Etye			286
SCHMELTZER	Etye		F	Married			Ben-Zion			286
SCHMELTZER	Mordechai		M		Ben-Zion	Etye				286
SCHMELTZER	Berel		M		Ben-Zion	Etye				286
SCHMELTZER	Yoel		M		Ben-Zion	Etye				286
SCHMELTZER	Moshe		M		Ben-Zion	Etye				286
SCHMELTZER	Shlime		F		Ben-Zion	Etye				286
SCHMELTZER	Breina		F							286
SCHMELTZER	Klara		F			Breine				286
SCHNEIDER	Yosel		M		Yankel				name of father is Yankel MILACH	287
SCHNEIDER			F		Yankel				name of father is Yankel MILACH, sister of Yosel	287
SCHNEIDER			F		Yankel				name of father is Yankel MILACH, sister of Yosel	287
SCHNITSER	Israel		M	Married			Sheindel		"shochet" [ritual slaughterer]	287
SCHNITSER	Sheindel		F	Married	Feivish		Israel		name of father is Feibish Shochet [the slaughterer]	287
SCHAECHTER	Arthur		M	Married			Beile Lea			287
SCHAECHTER	Beile Lea	STERNLIEB	F	Married	Yosef		Artur			287
SCHAECHTER			F		Artur	Beile Lea				287
SCHAECHTER	Benjamin		M	Married			Mirke		"shochet" [ritual slaughterer]	287
SCHAECHTER	Mirke		F	Married			Benjamin			287
SCHAECHTER	Mantze		F		Benjamin	Mirke				287
SCHAECHTER	Chaia		F		Benjamin	Mirke				287
SCHAECHTER	Golde	WACHSHTEIN	F	Married			Yosef			287
SCHAECHTER	Gizia		F		Yosef	Golde				287
SCHAECHTER	Yosef		M	Married			Mechle	3 children	son-in-law of Moshe Israel LANG	287

Surname	Given name	Other surname	Sex	Status	Father	Mother	Spouse		Notes	Page
SCHAECHTER	Machle	LANG	F	Married			Moshe Israel	Yosef	3 children	287
SCHAECHTER	Yeshaya Leib		M	Married			Ester			287
SCHAECHTER	Ester		F	Married			Yeshaya			287
SCHAECHTER	Salke		F		Yeshaya Leib	Ester				287
SCHAECHTER	Ida		F		Yeshaya Leib	Ester				287
SCHAECHTER	David		M		Yeshaya Leib	Ester				287
SCHAECHTER	Tzipora		F	Married			Shlomo Hersh		name of husband is Shlomo Hersh Shochet [the slaughterer]	287
SCHAECHTER	Zalman		M	Married	Shlomo Hersh		Rachel			287
SCHAECHTER	Rachel		F	Married			Zalman			287
SCHAECHTER	Reize		F		Zalman	Rachel				287
SCHECHNER	Hersh Wolf		M	Married			Leitsche			287
SCHECHNER	Litze		F	Married			Hersh Wolf			287
SCHECHNER	Avraham		M		Hersh Wolf	Leitsche	his family	his family		287
SCHECHNER	Avraham		M	Married			Mintze	children		287
SCHECHNER	Mintze	FISCHBACH	F	Married			Avraham	children		287
SCHECHNER	Avraham		M	Married	Antchel		Yetka			287
SCHECHNER	Yetke		F	Married			Avraham			287
SCHECHNER	Dasie		F		Avraham	Yetka				287
SCHECHNER	Antchel		M		Avraham	Yetka				287
SCHECHNER	Isser		M	Married			Sara			287
SCHECHNER	Sara	STEINIG	F	Married			Isser			287
STEINIG	Herman		M		Isser				surname of the father, SCHACHNER	287
SCHECHNER	Eliezer		M			mother				287
SCHECHNER	Berl		M	Married			Lea			287

SCHECHNER	Lea	KIMELMAN	F	Married	Arye		Berel		287
SCHECHNER	Mintze		F		Berel	Lea			287
SCHECHNER	Rivka		F		Berel	Lea			287
SCHECHNER	Eliezer		M		Berel	Lea			287
SCHECHNER	Zisl		F	Married			Kalman		287
SCHECHNER	Chana		M						287
SCHECHNER	Yosef		M	Married			Sara		287
SCHECHNER	Sara		F	Married			Yosef		287
SCHECHNER	Shmuel		M		Yosef	Sara			287
SCHECHNER	Beni		M		Yosef	Sara			287
SCHECHNER	Yitzhak		M	Married	Pinye		Ester Gitel		287
SCHECHNER	Ester Gitel		F	Married			Yitzhak		287
SCHECHNER	Yakov		M	Married			Rachel		287
SCHECHNER	Rachel		F	Married			Yakov		287
SCHECHNER	Beile		F		Yakov	Ester Gitel			287
SCHECHNER	Israel		M	Married			Sheindel		287
SCHECHNER	Sheindel		F	Married			Israel		287
SCHECHNER			M		Israel	Sheindel			287
SCHECHNER	Meir		M	Married			Tzila		287
SCHECHNER	Tzila		F	Married			Meir		287
SCHECHNER	Moshe		M	Married			Menye		287
SCHECHNER	Menye		F	Married			Moshe		287
SCHECHNER	Rivka		F		Moshe	Menye			287
SCHECHNER	Natan		M	Married	Moshe	Menye	Zlata		287
SCHECHNER	Zlata		F	Married			Natan		287
SCHECHNER	Yosel		M		Natan	Slate			287
SCHECHNER	Moshe		M	Married			Frume		287
SCHECHNER	Frume	HERTMAN	F	Married			Moshe		287

SCHECHNER	Yonye		F		Moshe	Frume			287
SCHECHNER	Ruchhtze		F		Moshe	Frume			287
SCHECHNER	Reize		F						287
SCHECHNER	Wave		M			Reize			287
SCHECHNER	Aharon		M			Reize			287
SCHECHNER	Bracha		F			Reize			287
SCHECHNER	Tzvia		F			Reize			287
SCHECHNER	Pepi		F			Reize			287
SCHECHNER	Shmuel Aizik		M	Married			Frume		287
SCHECHNER	Frume		F	Married			Shmuel Itzik		287
ADLER	Frieda	SCHECHNER	F						287
ADLER			F			Frida			287
SCHECHNER	Herzl		M		Shmuel Itzik	Frume		his family	287
SCHERL	Yakov		M	Married			Tzipe		287
SCHERL	Tzipa		F	Married			Yakov		287
SCHERL	Pinhas		M	Married	Yakov	Tzipe		1 child	287
SCHERL			F	Married			Pinchas	1 child	287
	Mina	SCHERL	F	Married	Yakov	Tzipe		husband	287
SPATSINER	Chaim		M	Married			Tcharne	children	287
SPATSINER	Tcharne		F	Married			Chaim	children	287
SPAREN	Avraham		M	Married			Sprintze		287
SPAREN	Sprintze		F	Married					287
SPAREN	Chaim Munie		M		Avraham	Sprintze		his family	287
SPAREN	Zishe		M	Married	Avraham	Sprintze			287
SPAREN			F	Married			Zishe		287
SPAREN			M		Sishe				287
SPAREN			F		Sishe				287

Surname	Name	Sex	Status	Father	Mother	Spouse	Notes	Page
SPAREN	Hersh	M	Married	Avraham	Sprintze		children	287
SPAREN		F	Married			Hersh	children	287
SPAREN	Note	M	Married	Avraham	Sprintze		children	287
SPAREN		F	Married			Note	children	287
SPAREN	Siama	M	Married				2 children	287
SPAREN		F	Married			Sioma	2 children	287
SPAREN	Dudie	M	Married			Chana		287
SPAREN	Chana	F	Married			Dudie		287
SPAREN	Shmuel	M		Dudie	Chana			287
SPAREN	Hersh	M	Married	Shlomo		Feige	children	287
SPAREN	Feige	F	Married			Hersh	children	287
SPAREN	Reiza	F						287
SPAREN	Moshe	M			Reize			287
SPAREN	Friedze	F						287
SPAREN	Yocheved	F	Married			Shmuel		287
SPAREN	Lucia	F		Shmuel	Yocheved			287
SPAREN	Yonye	F		Shmuel	Yocheved			287
SPAREN	Tcharne	F		Shmuel	Yocheved			287
SPAREN	Natan	M		Shmuel	Yocheved			287
SPAREN	Hersh	M		Shmuel	Yocheved			287
SPIEGELGLASS	Dr. Mark	M	Married					287
SPIEGELGLASS		F	Married			Mark		287
SPIEGELGLASS		F		Mark				287
SPITZER	Hersh	M	Married			Dvora		287
SPITZER	Dvora	F	Married			Hersh		287
SPITZER	Yakov	M	Married			Golde		287
SPITZER	Golde	F	Married			Yakov		287
SPITZER	Hersh	M		Yakov	Golde			287
SPITZER	Avraham	M		Yakov	Golde			287

SPITZER	Miriam		F	Married			Yitzhak		287
SPITZER	Kopel		M	Married			Rachel		287
SPITZER	Rachel		F	Married			Kopel		287
SPITZER	Moshe		M		Kopel	Rachel			287
SPITZER	Peptze		F		Kopel	Rachel			287
SHAPIRA	Chaitze		F						287
SHAPIRA	Liba		F			Chaitze			287
SHAPIRA	Israel		M	Married			Breintsche	children	287
SHAPIRA	Breintze		F	Married			Israel	children	287
SHAPIRA	Pesia	NEUFELD	F		Shamai				287
SHAPIRA	Kalman		M			Pesia			287
SHAPIRA	Chanoch		M			Pesia			287
SHAPIRA	Risye Risyele		F						287
SPERBER	Chaim		M	Married			Henye		287
SPERBER	Henye		F	Married			Chaim		287
SPERBER	Miriam		F		Chaim	Henye			287
SPERBER	Motzie		F		Chaim	Henye			287
SPERBER	Shmuel		M		Chaim	Henye			287

[Pages 287-289]

List of Martyrs from Surrounding Villages

Transliterated by Gladys Paulin

Edited by Yocheved Klausner

Family name(s)	First name(s)	Maiden name	Sex	Marital status	Father's name	Mother's name	Name of spouse	Place of residence	Additional family members	Remarks	Page
ALBIN	Reizie		F					Ustechko			287
ALBIN	David		M			Reize		Ustechko			287
	Sheva	ALBIN	F	Married		Reize	Shmuel	Ustechko			287
	Shmuel		M	Married			Sheva	Ustechko			287
BRECHNER	Mechel		M					Ustechko	children	daughters	287
BRECHNER			M		Michel			Ustechko			287
GUTMAN	Shmerl		M	Married			Feige Rachel	Ustechko			287
GUTMAN	Feige Rachel	MILNER	F	Married			Shmerl	Ustechko			287
GUTMAN	Zlata		F		Shmuel	Feige Rachel		Ustechko			287
GINSBURG	Wolf		M	Married				Ustechko	2 children		287
GINSBURG			F	Married			Wolf	Ustechko	2 children		287
WALLACH	Berel		M	Married			Ester	Ustechko			287
WALLACH	Ester	MILNER	F	Married			Berel	Ustechko			287
WALLACH	Moshe		M					Ustechko			287
WALLACH	Chaia		F					Ustechko			287
SUESSMAN	Moshe		M					Ustechko			287
SUESSMAN	Kalman		F					Ustechko			287
KATZ	Zlata Eige	HELFER	F					Ustechko			287

NADLER	Eliezer		M	Married			Tzipora	Ustechko			287
NADLER	Tzipora		F	Married			Eliezer	Ustechko			287
NADLER	Chana		F		Eliezer	Tziporah		Ustechko			287
SENDER			M					Ustechko	his family	the fisherman, given name Sender	287
KOCH	Rachel		F					Ustechko			287
KOCH	Ester		F			Rachel		Ustechko			287
KOCH	Chaitze Klara		F			Rachel		Ustechko			287
KOCH	Yom-Tov		M			Rachel		Ustechko			287
KOCH	Motel		M			Rachel		Ustechko			287
FELDMAN	Zelig		M					Ugrin'kovtsy			287
FELDMAN	Danya		F					Ugrin'kovtsy			287
FELDMAN	Rosa		F					Ugrin'kovtsy			287
FELDMAN	Gedalia		M					Ugrin'kovtsy			287
FELDMAN	Munie		M					Ugrin'kovtsy			288
FELDMAN	Miriam		F					Ugrin'kovtsy			288
WACHSTEIN	Avraham		M	Married			Basha	Antonovka			288
WACHSTEIN	Bashe	GOLDHIRSCH	F	Married			Avraham	Antonovka			288
WACHSTEIN	Hersh		M	Married			Dvoshe Dvora	Antonovka			288
WACHSTEIN	Dvoshe Dvora		F	Married			Hersh	Antonovka			288
WACHSTEIN	Yakov		M		Hersh	Dvoshe Dvora		Antonovka			288
WACHSTEIN	Ruchtze Rachel		F		Hersh	Dvoshe Dvora		Antonovka			288
WACHSTEIN	Lea		F		Hersh	Dvoshe Dvora		Antonovka			288
WARENBRAND	Michel		M					Antonovka		son-in-law of Avraham	288

Surname	First name	Alt surname	Sex	Status	Father	Mother	Spouse	Place	Children		Page
										WACHSTEIN	
WARENBRAND	Etye		F		Michael			Antonovka			288
WARENBRAND	Sonia		F		Michael			Antonovka			288
WECHSLER	Welwel		M	Married			Breina	Antonovka			288
WECHSLER	Breina	WACHSHTEIN	F	Married	Avraham	Dvoshe Dvora	Welvel	Antonovka			288
WECHSLER	Yakov		M		Welvel	Breine		Antonovka			288
WECHSLER	Ester		F		Welvel	Breine		Antonovka			288
SKALKA	Beile	WACHSHTEIN	F					Antonovka			288
SKALKA	Kova Yakov		M			Beile		Antonovka			288
SKALKA	Eliahu		M			Beile		Antonovka			288
TZIRLING	Avraham		M	Married			Rachel	Antonovka	children		288
TZIRLING	Rachel	WACHSHTEIN	F	Married			Avraham	Antonovka	children		288
EISNER	Pinie		M	Married			Eti	Burakuvka			288
EISNER	Eti		F	Married			Pinye	Burakuvka			288
EISNER			F		Pinye	Eti		Burakuvka			288
EISNER			F		Pinye	Eti		Burakuvka			288
ACHSELROD	Moshe		M	Married				Burakuvka			288
ACHSELROD			F	Married			Moshe	Burakuvka			288
ACHSELROD			F		Moshe			Burakuvka			288
ACHSELROD			F		Moshe			Burakuvka			288
ACHSELROD			F					Burakuvka			288
BILER	Israel		M	Married			Minde	Burakuvka	1 child		288
BILER	Minde		F	Married			Israel	Burakuvka	1 child		288
BERGMAN	Pesia		F					Burakuvka			288
BERGMAN	Buntzi		F			Pesia		Burakuvka			288
BERGMAN	Raza		F	Married				Burakuvka	1 child		288
BERGMAN			M	Married			Rosa	Burakuvka	1 child		288
DEMBLING	Henia		F	Married				Burakuvka			288

DEMBLING			M	Married			Henia	Burakuvka				288
DEMBLING	Tcharne		F			Henye		Burakuvka				288
DEMBLING	Chaitze		F			Henye		Burakuvka				288
SINGER	David		M	Married				Burakuvka	5 children	tailor		288
SINGER			F	Married			David	Burakuvka	5 children			288
ECKSTEIN			M	Married				Burakuvka	children	son-in-law of Shlomo SHPAREN		288
ECKSTEIN			F	Married	Shlomo			Burakuvka	children			288
FISCHHOF	Mirke		F					Burakuvka				288
FISCHHOF	Israel		M	Married		Mirke	Frieda	Burakuvka				288
FISCHHOF	Freida		F	Married		Israel		Burakuvka				288
FISCHHOF	Zunie		M		Israel	Frieda		Burakuvka				288
PREMINGER	Hilel		M					Borokhiv				288
LEHRER	Note		M	Married				Drogichuvka				288
LEHRER			F	Married			Note	Drogichuvka				288
LEHRER			M		Note			Drogichuvka				288
LEHRER			M		Note			Drogichuvka				288
LEHRER			F		Note			Drogichuvka				288
LEHRER			F		Note			Drogichuvka				288
ELBERGER	Yakov		M					Gin'kovtse				288
ELBERGER	Frume		F					Gin'kovtse				288
BRUKNER	Israel		M	Married			Sime	Gin'kovtse				288
BRUKNER	Sime		F	Married			Israel	Gin'kovtse				288
BRUKNER	Mendel		M		Israel	Sime		Gin'kovtse				288
BRUKNER	Beile		F		Meir			Gin'kovtse				288
HALPERN	Rachel		F					Gin'kovtse				288
PINSKER	Frume		F					Gin'kovtse				288
PINSKER			F					Gin'kovtse		mother of Frume		288

Surname	Given name		Sex	Status	Father	Mother	Spouse	Place	Notes	PINSKER	Page
PINSKER	Hilel		M	Married			Etka	Gin'kovtse	1 child		288
PINSKER	Etka		F	Married			Hilel	Gin'kovtse	1 child		288
ROSMARIN	Yeshaya		M	Married			Etl	Gin'kovtse			288
ROSMARIN	Etel		F	Married			Yeshayahu	Gin'kovtse			288
ROSMARIN	Malka		F		Yeshayahu	Etl		Gin'kovtse			288
BERGENFELD	Shlomo		M	Married			Chaia	Vorgulintsy			288
BERGENFELD	Chaia		F	Married			Shlomo	Vorgulintsy			288
BERGENFELD	Bracha		F		Shlomo	Chaia		Vorgulintsy			288
BERGENFELD	Israel Zechariah		M		Shlomo	Chaia		Vorgulintsy			288
GOLDHIRSCH	Ester		F					Vorgulintsy	children		288
GOLDHIRSCH	Moshe		M	Married				Vorgulintsy			288
GOLDHIRSCH			F	Married			Moshe	Vorgulintsy			288
FEDER								Vorgulintsy			288
FELDMAUS	Shlomo		M	Married			Breina	Vorgulintsy	3 children		288
FELDMAUS	Breina		F	Married			Shlomo	Vorgulintsy	3 children		288
AUERBACH			M					Chervonograd	his family		288
BADLER	Meir		M					Chervonograd	his family		288
RIM	Zeide		M	Married			Frida	Latach	children		288
RIM	Frida		F	Married			Zeide	Latach	children		288
GRAS	Meir		M	Married				Lisivtsy			288
GRAS			F	Married			Meir	Lisivtsy			288
GRAS			M		Meir			Lisivtsy			288
GRAS	Chaim		M	Married	Meir			Lisivtsy	children		288
GRAS			F	Married			Chaim	Lisivtsy	children		288
HERMAN	Simcha		M	Married			Sheintsche	Lisivtsy			288
HERMAN	Sheintze		F	Married			Simcha	Lisivtsy			288
HERMAN	Beiltze		F		Simcha	Sheintsche		Lisivtsy			288

Surname	First Name	Other Name	Sex	Status	Father	Mother	Spouse	Town	Relation	Note	Page
GELBAND	Hersh		M	Married			Beile	Mukhavka	his family		288
GELBAND	Beile	YURMAN	F	Married			Hersh	Mukhavka	her family		288
YURMAN	Yitzhak		M	Married			Gitel	Mukhavka			288
YURMAN	Gitel		F	Married			Yitzhak	Mukhavka			288
REGENBOIGEN	Chaim		M	Married			Miriam	Mukhavka			288
REGENBOIGEN	Miriam		F	Married			Chaim	Mukhavka			288
REGENBOIGEN	Gitze		F		Chaim	Miriam		Mukhavka			288
REGENBOIGEN	Yosef		M		Chaim	Miriam		Mukhavka			288
ROTHOLZ	Hersh		M	Married			Henya	Mukhavka	his family		288
ROTHOLZ	Henye		F	Married			Hersh	Mukhavka	her family		288
GELBAND	Berel		M	Married			Mali	Meshkov			288
GELBAND	Moli	PFEFFER	F	Married			Berel	Meshkov		sister of Antchel PFEFFER	288
HELFER	Avraham		M	Married				Meshkov	children		288
HELFER			F	Married			Avraham	Meshkov	children		288
SILBERSTEIN	Avraham		M	Married				Meshkov	children		288
SILBERSTEIN			F	Married			Avraham	Meshkov	children		288
SILBERSTEIN	Arye		M					Meshkov	children		288
EISENBERG	Moshe		M					Naguzhanka	his family		288
GUTMAN	Lea		F					Nyrkov			288
GUTMAN	Rosa		F					Nyrkov			288
HERTMAN	Moshe		M					Nyrkov	his family		288
TAUBER	Moshe		M					Nyrkov	his family		288
ROSENBLAT	Hersh		M	Married				Nyrkov	children		288
ROSENBLAT			F	Married			Hersh	Nyrkov	children		288
ALBIN	Yoel		M	Married			Etye	Sadki			288
ALBIN	Etie	HOLZBERG	F	Married		Perl	Yoel	Sadki			288
ALBIN	Mendel		M		Yoel	Etye		Sadki			288

ALBIN	Rivka		F		Yoel	Etye		Sadki			288
ALBIN	Herman		M		Yoel	Etye		Sadki			288
ALBIN	Saratze		F		Yoel	Etye		Sadki			288
HOLZBERG	Perl		F					Sadki			288
MILLER	Michel		M	Married			Henya	Sadki			288
MILLER	Henye		F	Married			Michel	Sadki			288
MILLER	Chava		F		Michael	Henye		Sadki			288
SCHRAUBER	Israel		M					Sadki			288
SCHRAUBER	Yosef		M					Sadki			288
HOFFMAN	Shmuel		M	Married			Tcharne	Svidova			289
HOFFMAN	Tchnarne		F	Married			Shmuel	Svidova			289
HOFFMAN	Max		M		Shmuel			Svidova			289
HOFFMAN	Genia		F		Shmuel			Svidova			289
WALZER	Eliezer		M	Married			Sara	Svidova			289
WALZER	Sara		F	Married			Eliezer	Svidova			289
WALZER	Yidel		M		Eliezer	Sara		Svidova			289
WALZER	Muntze		F		Eliezer	Sara		Svidova			289
WALZER	Miriam		F		Eliezer	Sara		Svidova			289
MASER	Yeshayahu		M					Svidova			289
MEIMAN	Leibtzi		M	Married				Svidova			289
MEIMAN			F	Married			Leibtsche	Svidova			289
MEIMAN	Mendel		M	Married				Svidova			289
MEIMAN			F	Married			Mendel	Svidova			289
PERLMUTER	Meir		M	Married			Ester	Svidova			289
PERLMUTER	Ester		F	Married			Meir	Svidova			289
PERLMUTER	Shmuel		M	Married	Meir			Svidova	children		289
PERLMUTER			F	Married			Shmuel	Svidova	children		289
PERLMUTER	Yidel		M	Married	Meir			Svidova	children		289

PERLMUTER			F	Married			Eidl	Svidova	children		289
RUBINSTEIN	Fishel		M					Svidova			289
		RUBINSTEIN	F		Fishel			Svidova	husband		289
		RUBINSTEIN	F		Fishel			Svidova	husband		289
GENSER			F					Sloboda		sisters	289
DEMBLING	Hersh		M	Married			Chana	Sloboda	3 children		289
DEMBLING	Chana		F	Married			Hersh	Sloboda	3 children		289
DEMBLING	Melech Godel		M					Sloboda			289
PRIMUS	Benyamin		M	Married			Rivka	Sloboda	4 children		289
PRIMUS	Rivka		F	Married			Benjamin	Sloboda	4 children		289
KRIGESFELD	Moshe		M	Married			Sara	Sloboda	3 children		289
KRIEGSFELD	Sara	SHARF	F	Married	David Mordechai		Moshe	Sloboda	3 children		289
SCHARF	David Mordechai		M					Sloboda			289
SCHARF	Fishel Yehuda		M		David Mordechai			Sloboda			289
SCHARF	Meir Yitzhak		M		David Mordechai			Sloboda			289
SCHARF	Bashe Batia		F		David Mordechai			Sloboda			289
SCHARF	Breintze		F		David Mordechai			Sloboda			289
SCHREIFLER	Meir		M	Married				Sloboda	3 children		289
SCHREIFLER			F	Married			Meir	Sloboda	3 children		289
SCHREIFLER	Karp		M					Sloboda	his family		289
GERTNER	Zeide		M					Popovtse			289
DEMBLING	Welvel		M	Married			Frieda	Popovtse			289
DEMBLING	Frieda		F	Married			Welvel	Popovtse			289
DEMBLING	Fani		F		Welvel	Frieda		Popovtse			289

FENSTER	Zeide		M					Popovtse			289
FENSTER	Miriam		F					Popovtse			289
FENSTER	Sabina		F					Popovtse			289
FENSTER			F			Sabina		Popovtse			289
TZITRIN			F					Naguzhanka	3 children	daughters	289
BIRNBAUM	Moshe		M	Married			Ester	Tsapovka			289
BIRNBAUM	Ester		F	Married			Moshe	Tsapovka			289
BIRNBAUM	Chaim		M		Moshe	Ester		Tsapovka			289
BIRNBAUM			F		Moshe	Ester		Tsapovka			289
BIRNBAUM			F		Moshe	Ester		Tsapovka			289
GUTMAN	Yakov		M					Tsapovka	his family		289
GUTMAN	Berel		M	Married				Tsapovka	2 children		289
GUTMAN			F	Married			Berel	Tsapovka	2 children		289
WEISSTAHL	Yosef		M					Tsapovka			289
WEISSTAHL	Tzirl		F					Tsapovka		sister of Yosef WEISSTAHL	289
WEISSTAHL			F					Tsapovka		mother of Yosef and Tzirl WEISSTAHL	289
LANGHOLZ	Leibish		M	Married			Rivka	Tsapovka			289
LANGHOLZ	Rivka		F	Married			Leibish	Tsapovka			289
LANDWEBER	Meir		M	Married			Eti	Tsapovka	children		289
LANDWEBER	Eti	ROSEN	F	Married	Yechiel		Meir	Tsapovka	children		289
LANDMAN	Israel Meir		M	Married			Ester	Tsapovka			289
LANDMAN	Esther		F	Married			Israel Meir	Tsapovka			289
LANDMAN	Tsvi		M	Married	Israel Meir	Ester		Tsapovka	1 child		289
LANDMAN			F	Married			Tsvi	Tsapovka	1 child		289
LANDMAN	Malka		F					Tsapovka			289
LANDMAN	Rivka		F			Malka		Tsapovka			289

LANDMAN	Shmuel		M				Malka		Tsapovka			289
LANDMAN	Chaia		F				Malka		Tsapovka			289
MEZGER	Michael		M	Married				Rachel	Tsapovka			289
MEZGER	Rachel		F	Married				Michel	Tsapovka			289
MEZGER	Leibish		M		Michel	Rachel			Tsapovka			289
MEZGER	Pope		M		Michel	Rachel			Tsapovka			289
ROSEN	Yechiel		M	Married	Moshe			Chana	Tsapovka			289
ROSEN	Chana		F	Married				Yechiel	Tsapovka			289
ROSEN	Rachel		F		Yechiel	Chana			Tsapovka			289
ROSENHOCH	Leibish		M	Married					Tsapovka	children		289
ROSENHOCH			F	Married				Leibish	Tsapovka	children		289
SPERBER	Gedaliahu		M						Tsapovka			289
SPERBER	Welvel		M						Tsapovka			289
SPERBER	Frida		F						Tsapovka			289
SPERBER	Fantze		F						Tsapovka			289
BILER	Nachman		M						Koshylovtse		butcher	289
BILER	Natan		M		Nachman				Koshylovtse			289
HELD	Israel Avraham		M	Married				Malka	Koshylovtse			289
HELD	Malka		F	Married				Israel	Koshylovtse			289
HELD	Bune		F		Israel Avraham	Malka	Avraham		Koshylovtse			289
HIBSCHER	Eliezer		M						Koshylovtse			289
HIBSCHER	Moshe		M						Koshylovtse	his family		289
WAGSCHALL	Elimelech		M						Koshylovtse		?	289
VILNER	Zelig		M	Married				Chaia Sara	Koshylovtse			289
VILNER	Chaia Sara		F	Married				Selig	Koshylovtse			289
VILNER		MILLER	F	Married	Zeide	Sara	Moshe		Koshylovtse			289
VILNER	Zeide		M	Married				Sara	Koshylovtse			289

Surname	Given name		Sex	Status	Father	Mother	Spouse	Place			Page
VILNER	Sara		F	Married			Zeide	Koshylovtse			289
MARCUS	Leizer		M	Married			Elsa	Koshylovtse			289
MARCUS	Elza		F	Married			Leizer	Koshylovtse			289
MARCUS	Raza		F		Leizer	Elsa		Koshylovtse			289
MARCUS	Yosef		M		Leizer	Elsa		Koshylovtse			289
	Moshe Meir		M	Married				Koshylovtse	his wife and 6 daughters	"shochet" [ritual slaughterer]	289
SCHWARTZ	Shlomo		M	Married			Rachel	Koshylovtse			289
SCHWARTZ	Rachel		F	Married			Shlomo	Koshylovtse			289
SCHWARTZ	Hermine		F		Shlomo	Rachel		Koshylovtse			289
GINSBERG	Wolf		M					Ruzhanuvka	his family		289
GINSBERG			F					Ruzhanuvka		mother of Wolf GINSBERG	289
GINSBERG	Yosef		M	Married			Manye	Shutromintsy			289
GINSBERG	Mania		F	Married			Yosef	Shutromintsy			289
GINSBERG	Chaim		M		Yosef	Manye		Shutromintsy			289
GINSBERG	Tzvi		M		Yosef	Manye		Shutromintsy			289
GINSBERG	Herman		M		Yosef	Manye		Shutromintsy			289
HAMLER	Meir		M					Shutromintsy			289
HAMLER	Lea		F					Shutromintsy			289
BLANK	Gedaliahu		M					Shersheniovtse	his family		289
BLUMENFELD	Yosel		M					Shersheniovtse	his family		289
BRIMER	Yentze		M	Married				Shersheniovtse			289
BRIMER			F	Married			Yentsche	Shersheniovtse			289
BRIMER	Mania		F		Yentzie			Shersheniovtse			289
GLASER	Berel		M					Shersheniovtse	his family		289
HERTMAN	Berel		M					Novy Oleksinets			289
WALDMAN	Iza		M	Married			Sala	Shersheniovtse			289

WALDMAN	Sala	BLANK	F	Married			Iza	Shersheniovtse			289
WALDMAN	Yosef		M		Iza	Sale		Shersheniovtse			289
WALDMAN	Hersh		M	Married			Sosia	Shersheniovtse			289
WALDMAN	Sasya		F	Married			Hersh	Shersheniovtse			289
WALDMAN	Shabtai		M		Hersh	Sosia		Shersheniovtse			289
WALDMAN	Sara		F		Hersh	Sosia		Shersheniovtse			289
WALDMAN	Masha		F		Hersh	Sosia		Shersheniovtse			289
WALDMAN	Yosef		M		Hersh	Sosia		Shersheniovtse			289
WALDMAN	Iza		M	Married	Hersh	Sosia		Shersheniovtse	1 child		289
WALDMAN			F	Married			Iza	Shersheniovtse	1 child		289
WALDMAN	Leib		M	Married			Rosa	Shersheniovtse	1 child		289
WALDMAN			F	Married			Leib	Shersheniovtse	1 child		289
WALDMAN	Loti	GOTFRIED	F					Shersheniovtse		Tarsky	289
WALDMAN	Berel		M			Lati		Shersheniovtse			289
WALDMAN	Shimshele Shimshon		M			Lati		Shersheniovtse			289
WALDMAN	Mordechai		M			Lati		Shersheniovtse			289
WALDMAN	Meir Aizik		M	Married			Chantze Chana	Shersheniovtse			289
WALDMAN	Chantze Chana		F	Married			Meir Aizik	Shersheniovtse			289
WALDMAN	Miriam		F				Yosef	Shersheniovtse			289
WALDMAN	Shifra	PREMINGER	F	Married			Chanina	Shersheniovtse			289
WALDMAN	Henya		F	Married			Eliezer	Shersheniovtse			289
SCHWARTZBACH	Motye		M					Shersheniovtse	his family		289

INDEX

Please Note: Names appearing on pages 538 – 549 are not included in this index

Epilogue

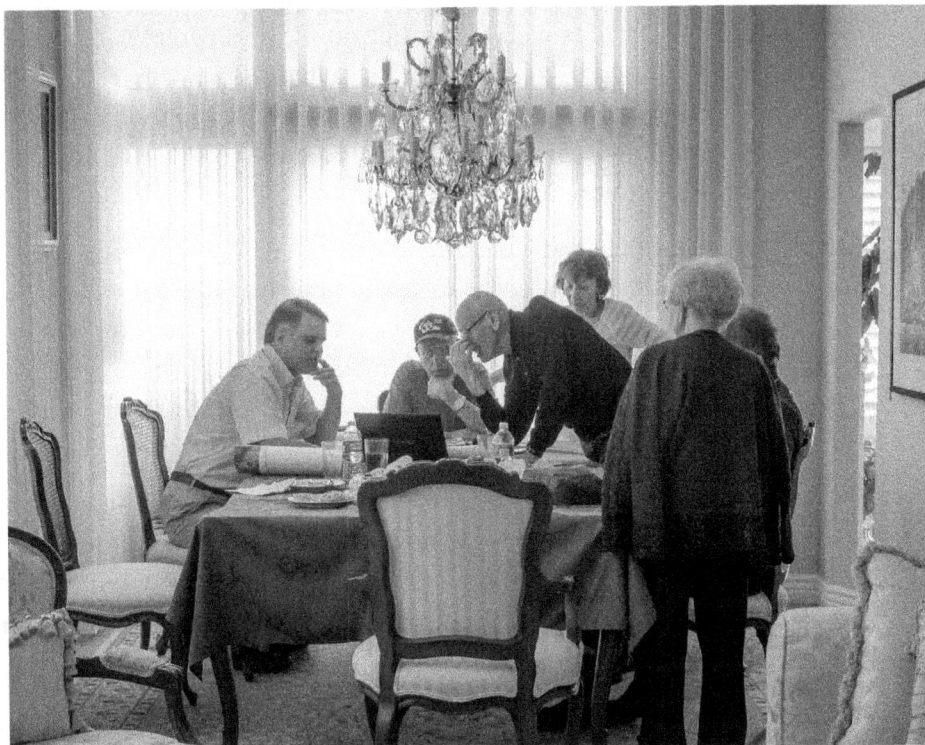

Douglas Hykle interviewing Tluste survivors Sam and Ike Langholz in Pasadena, 2014, in the presence of family members. Photo by Elon Schoenholz.

The *Sefer Tluste* was originally published in Tel Aviv in 1965, with contributions in Hebrew and Yiddish from over fifty authors, commemorating the town of their birth. The content describes the rich history and life of Tluste in more peaceful times, as well as the tragic destruction of the town's once-vibrant Jewish population. As such, the *Sefer Tluste* is an invaluable resource for learning about the town's distant and more recent past, until the end of the Second World War. The original volume includes copies of numerous photographs that appear nowhere else.

That said, it is important to appreciate that the contributors to the *Sefer Tluste* are only a fraction of the Holocaust survivors known to have been associated with the town and surrounding areas during the Nazi occupation, from 1941 to 1944. While the volume gives an impressive overview, from their perspectives, of what transpired in Tluste during that period, their collective account is by no means comprehensive.

Additional information can be gleaned from a variety of sources, including the following:

- More than 100 oral history interviews have been made by Tluste survivors, most of them conducted by the USC Shoah Foundation (sfi.usc.edu/vha) in the 1990s. Others can be found in collections held by

Yad Vashem (yadvashem.org), Yale University's Fortunoff Video Archive (fortunoff.library.yale.edu), the United States Holocaust Memorial Museum (ushmm.org), as well as smaller public and private archives. The interviews have been conducted mostly in English, Hebrew, Polish, Spanish and Russian; many also include written transcripts. The websites of the main repositories give details of where these interviews may be viewed; some of them are also available online.

- Separately, since 2008, I have conducted several dozen interviews with Tluste survivors living in Israel and North America. Typical of these is a series of interviews made over several years with Sam and Ike Langholz – brothers who generously shared with me their childhood experiences in Tluste. In many ways, they exemplify so many survivors who arrived in foreign lands with almost nothing, prospered through perseverance and hard work, and gave rise to wonderful extended families.

- The Jewish Historical Institute in Warsaw (jhi.pl/en) houses, additionally, an important hardcopy collection of several dozen written testimonials from Tluste survivors. Only a few of these overlap the accounts given in the *Sefer Tluste*.

- The testimony of survivors from Tluste given at German war crimes trials from the late 1950s to early 1970s is another extraordinarily rich source of information, not to mention the detailed accounts of perpetrators and other trial witnesses. Much of this original testimony is accessible in federal and state archives in Germany, and copies have been shared with institutions such as USHMM and Yad Vashem. Yad Vashem also maintains considerable documentation submitted by survivors in support of nominations for "Righteous among the Nations".

- Finally, there are at least a dozen full-length memoirs and diaries of survivors with a substantial connection to Tluste, notable among them: *Can Heaven be Void* (Baruch Milch), *Death of the Jewish Era* (Yehoshua Schechner), and *Father's Will* (Bella Shoham).

The *Sefer Tluste* was never intended to contain complete information on the victims and survivors of the atrocities in and around Tluste. Fortunately, other sources help to compensate for this deficit. These include Yad Vashem's Central Database of Shoah Victims' Names (available online); records of victims/survivors maintained by the International Tracing Service (ITS) in Bad Arolsen, Germany (also viewable at Yad Vashem and USHMM); as well as separate lists compiled by other institutions and private individuals.

Perhaps the greatest limitation of the *Sefer Tluste*, for over a half-century, was that the content was inaccessible to people who could not read Hebrew or Yiddish. In 2006, I gave a presentation about Tluste to a small gathering at the annual International Conference on Jewish Genealogy (IAJGS), held that year in

New York. In closing, I remarked: "Wouldn't it be great if these important testimonials could be translated into English, to make them more accessible!" Thankfully, Sara Mages took up the challenge, and voluntarily began translating the Hebrew texts into English. As I was already familiar with so many of the names of people and places mentioned in the *Sefer Tluste*, I offered to proofread and edit the English texts.

With the approval of the Young Tluster Society, arranged by Renee Steinig, the completed translations were gradually posted on the JewishGen.org website, as part of the major Yizkor Book project masterfully coordinated by Lance Ackerfeld.

Work on the Hebrew-to-English translations continued, on-and-off, for over a decade until late 2017, when Sara and I thought we were done. Just then, Lance suggested translating the Yiddish texts as well, together with several poems by Tluste's famous poet, Shimson Meltzer. This additional work—undertaken by Yael Chaver and Dave Horowitz-Larochette—proved to be very worthwhile, greatly enriching the volume.

The English translation of the entire *Sefer Tluste* memorial book was thus completed in mid-2018, and made available via a dedicated page on the JewishGen.org website. Hopefully, the print version will introduce the *Sefer Tluste* to a new readership, in a traditional format that will be appreciated for decades to come.

Douglas Hykle
www.tovste.info

www.ingramcontent.com/pod-product-compliance
Lightning Source LLC
Chambersburg PA
CBHW061833260326
41914CB00005B/978